Eve & Adam

Eve & Adam

JEWISH, CHRISTIAN, AND MUSLIM
READINGS ON GENESIS AND GENDER

EDITED BY

*Kristen E. Kvam, Linda S. Schearing
and Valarie H. Ziegler*

*Indiana
University
Press*

BLOOMINGTON AND INDIANAPOLIS

This book is a publication of

Indiana University Press
601 North Morton Street
Bloomington, IN 47404-3797 USA

http://iupress.indiana.edu

Telephone orders 800-842-6796
Fax orders 812-855-7931
Orders by e-mail iuporder@indiana.edu

Library of Congress Cataloging-in-Publication Data

Eve and Adam : Jewish, Christian, and Muslim readings on Genesis and
gender / edited by Kristen E. Kvam, Linda S. Schearing, and Valarie H. Ziegler.
p.   cm.
Includes bibliographical references and index.
ISBN 0-253-33490-X (cl. : alk. paper) — ISBN 0-253-21271-5 (pa. : alk. paper)
1. Bible. O.T. Genesis I-V—Commentaries. 2. Bible. O.T.
Genesis I-V—Criticism, interpretation, etc.—History. 3. Bible.
O.T. Genesis I-V—Criticism, interpretation, etc., Jewish. 4. Bible. O.T.
Genesis I-V—Islamic interpretations. 5. Bible. O.T. Genesis I-V—Feminist
criticism. 6. Eve (Biblical figure) 7. Adam (Biblical figure) 8. Feminism—
Religious aspects—Judaism. 9. Feminism—Religious aspects—Christianity.
10. Feminism—Religious aspects—Islam. I. Kvam, Kristen E. II. Schearing,
Linda S. III. Ziegler, Valarie H., date.
BS1235.3.E87 1999
222'.1106'09—dc21   98-39873

3   4   5   04   03

IN HONOR
AND IN MEMORY
OF THE BONDS OF
SISTERHOOD

CONTENTS

JEWISH PHILOSOPHERS AND HISTORIANS 64

CHAPTER THREE

Rabbinic Interpretations (200–600s CE)   *69*

INTRODUCTION 69

MIDRASH AND TALMUD 77

TARGUMS 100

CHAPTER FOUR

Early Christian Interpretations (50–450 CE)   *108*

INTRODUCTION 108

NEW TESTAMENT 116

CHAPTER FIVE

Medieval Readings: Muslim, Jewish, and Christian (600–1500 CE)   156

CHRISTIANITY 225

CHAPTER SIX

Interpretations from the Protestant Reformation (1517–1700 CE)   249

INTRODUCTION 249

FIVE REFORMATION THINKERS 261

CHAPTER SEVEN

Social Applications in the United States (1800s CE)   305

INTRODUCTION 305

ANTEBELLUM DEBATES ON HOUSEHOLD HIERARCHIES: PROSLAVERY AND ANTISLAVERY VIEWS 323

CHAPTER EIGHT

Twentieth-Century Readings: The Debates Continue 371

INTRODUCTION 371

Appendix 483
THE PREADAMITE THEORY AND THE CHRISTIAN IDENTITY MOVEMENT: RACE, HIERARCHY, AND GENESIS 1–3 AT THE TURN OF THE MILLENNIUM

INTRODUCTION 483

ACKNOWLEDGMENTS AND PERMISSIONS

We are grateful to the people who have helped bring this anthology into be-ing. The project started with—and has continued to be nurtured by—our students; we thank them for their concern for Genesis and gender. We also owe a debt of gratitude to the Indiana University Press staff (past and pres-ent)—to Bob Sloan, for grasping the underlying vision of the work; to Cindy Ballard, for answering the many questions that arose along the way, to Jeff Ankrom, for his suggestions about the organization of the material and for his assistance with questions of Arabic; and to Melanie Richter-Bernburg, for her courage in joining the project in midstream.

Many people have contributed to this volume. There were those who re-sponded to our requests for essays: Jouette Bassler, Judith Plaskow, Ann Holmes Redding, and Phyllis Trible. There were colleagues within our schools whose input we valued: from Saint Paul School of Theology, Warren Carter, Young Ho Chun, Emilie Townes, Grant White, Logan Wright, and Margaret Kohl; from Luther College, Judy Boese; from Gonzaga Univer-sity, Robert Kugler, Gail Jennings, Maria Spies, and Cecilia LaGasa; from DePauw University, Bob Bottoms, Bernie Batto, Bill Harman, Kathryn Millis, Roni McMains, and Paul Watt. Other colleagues provided support and encouragement. We were also greatly assisted by our library staffs, faculty support staffs, and student assistants. Scholars outside our immediate institu-tions also contributed to this project: Greg Carey, Bob Detweiler and the Dana Foundation, Elizabeth Clark, Cheryl Cornish, Betty Deberg, Margaret Farley, Carol Shersten LaHurd, Jane McAuliffe, Eric Mount, Otto Hermann Pesch, Barbara Rossing, Letty Russell, Ellen Umansky, and Amanda Berry Wylie. To each of them—as well as to the numerous friends who have talked honestly and passionately with us about the issues in this book—we offer our gratitude for their help and encouragement.

As for our professional societies, we would like to thank the sections of the American Academy of Religion and the Society of Biblical Literature that allowed us to present portions of the book in their sessions. Thanks also to the audiences who listened to and commented on segments of our work in progress.

We are especially indebted to Emory University for bringing us together initially as graduate students and then as collaborators on this project by en-couraging Linda to teach a course on Genesis and by supporting Kris and Valarie in their request to co-teach a course on Genesis and gender. We are also grateful to the sisters of the Graduate Divisions of Religion's Women Scholars. Recalling our experiences in this group, we dedicate this book in honor—and in memory—of what the Grimké sisters termed "the bonds of sisterhood."

And finally, a deeply felt thanks goes to the members of our respective families for their patience and inspiration over the six years it took to put this project together: to Valarie's spouse, Bill Nunn; to Linda's spouse, Angel Fitzpatrick, and to her children, Brittany, Sean, and Ariel; to Kris's spouse, Jeff Clayton, and to her children, Ellen and Joshua, as well as to her parents Doris and Adolph Kvam. This book could not have been written without their support and understanding. Thanks!

Every reasonable effort has been made to trace ownership of copyright materials. The publisher would welcome any information that would enable us to correct any copyright references in future printings.

CHAPTER 4

The Gospel According to Thomas, from *The Gnostic Scriptures*, by Bentley Layton (New York: Doubleday & Company). Used with permission.

The Gospel According to Philip, from *The Gnostic Scriptures*, by Bentley Layton (New York: Doubleday & Company). Used with permission.

The Acts of Paul and Thecla, reproduced from *Maenads, Martyrs, Matrons, Monastics* by Ross Kraemer, copyright © 1988 Fortress Press. Used by permission of Augsburg Fortress.

Jean M. Higgins, "Anastasius Sinaita and the Superiority of Women," from the CRITICAL NOTES of the *Journal of Biblical Literature* 97 (2) (1978): 254. Used with permission.

Origen, "Homilies on Genesis: 1 and 6," from *Origen: Homilies on Genesis and Exodus*, translated by Ronald E. Heine (Washington, D.C.: Catholic University of America Press, 1982). Used with permission.

Ambrose, "Paradise," from *Saint Ambrose: Hexameron, Paradise, and Cain and Abel*, translated by John J. Savage (Washington, D.C.: Catholic University of America Press, 1961). Used with permission.

John Chrysostom, "Homilies on Genesis," from *Saint John Chrysostom: Homilies on Genesis, 1–17*, translated by Robert C. Hill (Washington, D.C.: Catholic University of America Press, 1985), and from *Saint John Chrysostom: Homilies on Genesis, 18–45*, translated by Robert C. Hill (Washington, D.C.: Catholic University of America Press, 1990). Used with permission.

Augustine, "The Literal Meaning of Genesis," reprinted from *Saint Augustine: The Literal Meaning of Genesis*, vols. I and II, translated by John Hammond Taylor. © 1982 by Rev. Johannes Quasten, Rev. Walter J. Burghardt, S. J., Thomas Comerford Lawler (Mahwah, N.J.: Paulist Press). Used with permission.

CHAPTER 5

The Meaning of the Glorious Koran, translated by Mohammed Marmaduke Pickthall (New York and Scarborough, Ontario: New American Library/a Mentor Book, no date).

Al-Tabari, *Commentary on the Qur'an*, vol. 1, translated by John Cooper (London: Hakim Investment Holdings [M.E.] Ltd.).

Al-Kisa'i, *The Tales of the Prophets of al-Kisa'i*, excerpted with permission of Simon and Schuster Macmillan from the Twayne Publisher's book, *The Tales of the Prophets of al-Kisa'i*, translated from the Arabic by W. M. Thackston, Jr. © 1973 by G. K. Hall and Company.

Ibn al-Arabi, *The Bezels of Wisdom*, reprinted from *Ibn Al' Arabi: The Bezels of Wisdom*, translated by R. W. J. Austin. © 1980 by The Missionary Society of St. Paul the Apostle in the State of New York (Mahwah, N.J.: Paulist Press). Used by permission of Paulist Press.

Alphabet of Ben Sira, translated by Eli Yassif, "Pseudo Ben Sira, The Text, Its Literary Character and Status in the History of the Hebrew Story in the

Middle Ages" 2 vols. [in Hebrew], Ph.D. diss., Hebrew University, 1977, pp. 64-65, as cited in Joseph Dan, "Samuel, Lilith and the Concept of Evil in Early Kabbalah," *Association for Jewish Studies Review* 5 (1980): 21.

The Chronicles of Jerahmeel, translated by M. Gaster (London: Royal Asiatic Society, 1899).

The Fathers According to Rabbi Nathan, translated by Judah Goldin (New Haven: Yale University Press, 1955). Used with permission.

The Fathers According to Rabbi Nathan (ARNB), as cited in *A Rabbinic Anthology*, edited by Claude G. Montefiore and H. Loewe (New York: Schocken Books, 1974), p. 507. Used with permission.

Pirke de Rabbi Eliezer, translated by Gerald Friedlander (Brooklyn: Sepher-Hermon Press, 1965). Used with permission.

Rashi's Commentary: Genesis in *Pentateuch with Targum Onkelos, Haphtaroth and Prayers for Sabbath and Rashi's Commentary: Genesis*, translated by Morris Rosenbaum and Abraham M. Silbermann (London: Shapiro, Vallentine & Co., 1946). Used with permission.

The Commentary of Nahmanides on Genesis Chapters 1–6, translated by Jacob Newman (Leiden: E. J. Brill, 1960). Used with permission.

Moses Maimonides, *The Guide for the Perplexed*, translated by M. Friedländer, 2nd ed. (New York: Dover, 1956). Used with permission.

Isaac Kohen, *Treatise on the Left Emanation*, from *The Early Kabbalah*, edited by Joseph Dan, translated by Ronald C. Kiener (New York: Paulist Press, 1986). Used with permission.

The Zohar, vol. 1, translated by Harry Sperling and Maurice Simon (London and Brooklyn: The Soncino Press Ltd., 1973). Used with permission.

Christine de Pizan, "Letter of the God of Love," from *Poems of Cupid, God of Love*, edited by Thelma S. Fenster and Mary Carpenter Erler (Leiden and New York: E. J. Brill, 1990). Used with permission.

Heinrich Kramer and James Sprenger, *The Malleus Maleficarum*, translated and with an introduction by the Reverend Montague Summers (New York: Dover Publications, Inc., 1971). Used with permission.

CHAPTER 6

Balthasar Hubmaier, *Freedom of the Will*, from *Balthasar Hubmaier: Theologian of Anabaptism*, translated by H. Wayne Pipkin and John H. Yoder (Scottsdale, Pa.: Herald Press, 1989). Used with permission.

Martin Luther, *Lectures on Genesis*, from *Lectures on Genesis, Chapters 1–5*, translated by George V. Schick (St. Louis: Concordia Publishing House, 1958). Used with permission.

Margaret Fell, *Women's Speaking: Justified, Proved, and Allowed of by the Scriptures* (London: Pythia Press).

John Milton, *Paradise Lost*, in H. C. Beeching, *The Poetic Works of John Milton* (Oxford: Clarendon Press, 1900).

CHAPTER 7

Fred A. Ross, *Slavery Ordained of God* (Philadelphia: J. B. Lippincott & Co., 1857).

Samuel B. How, *Slaveholding Not Sinful*, 2nd ed. (New Brunswick: John Terhune, 1856).

Josiah Priest, *Bible Defence of Slavery: or the Origin, History, and Fortunes of the Negro Race*, with W. S. Brown, *A Plan of National Colonization*, 6th ed. (Louisville: J. F. Brennan for Willis A. Bush, Gallatin, Tenn., 1851).

Rev. Charles Elliott, *Sinfulness of American Slavery*, edited by Rev. B. F. Tefft, vol. 1 of 2 (Cincinnati: L. Swormstedt and J. H. Power, 1851).

Sarah Grimké, *Letters on the Equality of the Sexes and the Condition of Woman* (Boston: Isaac Knapp, 1838).

"Comments on Genesis" and "Comments on Timothy," from *The Woman's Bible*, edited by Elizabeth Cady Stanton (Salem, N.H.: Ayer Company Publishers, Inc., 1895, 1898). Used with permission.

Frederick Evans, *Autobiography of a Shaker, and Revelation of the Apocalypse* (American News Company, 1864).

Frederick Evans, *Compendium of Origin, History, Principle, Rules and Regulations, Government, and Doctrines of the United Society of Believers in Christ's Second Appearing*, 4th ed., issued in New Lebanon, N.Y., by the Shakers, 1867.

Paulina Bates, *The Divine Book of Holy and Eternal Wisdom, Revealing the Word of God*, vol. 1. Published by the Shakers at Canterbury, N.H., 1849.

John Humphrey Noyes, *History of American Socialisms* (Philadelphia: J. B. Lippincott & Co., 1870).

Mary Baker Eddy, *Science and Health with Key to the Scriptures*, from *Science and Health* (Boston: The First Church of Christ Scientist, c. 1875). Used with permission.

CHAPTER 8

Susan T. Foh, "The Head of the Woman Is the Man," reprinted from *Women in Ministry: Four Views*, edited by Bonnidell Clouse and Robert G. Clouse. © 1989 by Bonnidell Clouse and Robert G. Clouse. Used by permission of InterVarsity Press, P.O. Box 1400, Downers Grove, IL 60515.

The Authorized Daily Prayer Book, edited by Joseph H. Hertz (New York: Bloch, 1945, revised 1975). Used with permission.

Samuel H. Dresner, "Homosexuality and the Order of Creation," reprinted from *Judaism* 40 (3) (Summer 1991). © 1991 American Jewish Council. Used with permission.

Sayyid Abu al-A'la Mawdudi, *Towards Understanding the Qur'an*, vols. 1 and 2, translated and edited by Zafar Ishaq Ansari (Leicester: Islamic Foundation, 1942, 1972). Used with permission.

Sun Ai Lee Park, untitled poem from *The Bible through Asian Eyes*, edited by Masao Takenaka and Ron O'Grady (Auckland: Pace Consultants, 1991). Used with permission.

Judith Plaskow, "The Coming of Lilith: Toward a Feminist Theology," from *Womanspirit Rising*, edited by Carol P. Christ and Judith Plaskow. © 1979 by Carol P. Christ and Judith Plaskow (New York: HarperCollins Publishers, 1979). Used with permission.

Phyllis Trible, "Eve and Adam: Genesis 2-3 Reread," from *Andover Newton Quarterly* 13 (March 1973). By permission of Andover Newton Theological School. Used with permission.

Riffat Hassan, "The Issue of Woman-Man Equality in the Islamic Tradition," from *Women's and Men's Liberation*, edited by L. Grob, R. Hassan, and H. Gordon (Westport, Conn.: Greenwood Press, 1991). The reprinting of this abridgement by permission of Greenwood Publishing Group, Inc. All rights reserved.

Nancy Datan, "Forbidden Fruits and Sorrow," from *The Journal of Pastoral Counseling* 21 (1986). Reprinted by permission of Dean Rodeheaver and *The Journal of Pastoral Counseling* (New Rochelle, N.Y.: Department of Pastoral and Family Counseling, Iona College).

APPENDIX

A Minister, "Nachesh: What Is It? Or an Answer to the Question, 'Who and What Is the Negro?' Drawn from Revelation" (Augusta, Ga.: Jas. L. Gow, 1896), pp. 1-46, in *The Biblical and "Scientific" Defense of Slavery: Religion and "The Negro Problem,"* Part 2, vol. 6, edited by John David Smith (New York: Garland, 1993), pp. 1-46.

Prospero, *"Caliban." A Sequel to "Ariel"* (New York, 1868), pp. 1-32, in *The "Ariel" Controversy: Religion and "The Negro Problem,"* Part 1, vol. 5, edited by John David Smith (New York: Garland, 1993), pp. 191-222.

Wesley A. Swift, *God, Man, Nations & the Races* (Hayden Lake, Ida.: Aryan Nations, n.d.).

Richard Butler, "Who, What, Why, When, Where: Aryan Nations" (Hayden Lake, Ida.: Aryan Nations, n.d.).

Richard Butler, "The Aryan Warrior" (Hayden Lake, Ida.: Aryan Nations, n.d.).

Eve & Adam

General Introduction

Observers of American popular culture may recognize Genesis 1-3 as a text hotly defended by scientific creationists who want the "biblical account of creation" to be taught alongside evolutionary theories in the public schools. Long before Genesis 1-3 sparked debates about the teaching of science, however, interpreters were turning to—and arguing about—other foundational issues raised by the text. For centuries, the biblical account of creation has prompted readers to propose very different notions about what it means to be a man or to be a woman.

We discovered some of the historical uses of Genesis 1-3 independently from one another. Kris, a theologian, was writing a dissertation on Martin Luther's view of women. Her broader study of scriptural interpretation and gender provided impetus for looking at the Qur'an and its use in shaping Muslim understandings of women. Linda, a biblical scholar, was teaching a class in Genesis. And Valarie, a specialist in American religious history, was examining the role that scripture and women's ordination played in the 1987 removal of a Southern Baptist Church from the Shelby County Baptist Association in Memphis. As we shared our research with each other, we discovered that all of us were focusing on ways in which interpreters used the story of the first woman and man to justify the subordination of women to men or to argue for gender equality. The more we learned, the more we realized that Genesis 1-3 has for centuries been a pivotal text for defining the nature of maleness and femaleness.

In this book, we examine Genesis 1-3 and the ways that interpreters have used this text to define and enforce gender roles. We watch for instances in which interpreters have used Genesis 1–3 to confirm cultural presuppositions about gender roles and identity. We also note cases in which readers have found in Genesis understandings that moved them to challenge social norms.

In editing this volume, we have assumed that gender is a social construction and that communities of faith use sacred texts to give cosmological grounding to their notions of social order. As sociologist Peter Berger noted in his classic study, *The Sacred Canopy*, "Every human society is an enterprise of world-building. . . . Institutions, roles, and identities exist as objectively real phenomena in the social world, though they and this world are at the same time nothing but human productions." Religion plays a crucial role in the formation of human identities. It purports to describe a sacred cosmos and to locate individuals within that cosmos. When religions function powerfully, individuals and their cultures find themselves and their worldview defined by religious beliefs and practices. Berger celebrated "the unique power of religion to 'locate' human phenomena within a cosmic frame of reference," pointing to religion's role in relating "humanly defined reality to ultimate, universal and sacred reality."[1]

In legitimating social institutions by "bestowing upon them an ultimately valid ontological status," Berger argued, religion bestowed upon social institutions and roles—such as gender roles—an aura of permanence and inevitability. Indeed, he concluded, the same impulse that prompted human beings to generate society also prompted them to en-gender religion, "with the relations between the two products always being a dialectical one."[2]

In this volume we are not so much interested in working out the sociological theory of how sacred texts come to form cultures and to be formed by them. Rather, we wish to presume the dialectic between text and culture and to present interpretations of Eve and Adam as a case study of that interaction.

It is a fascinating story. Jewish and Christian communities have repeatedly called upon the Bible's accounts of creation to prescribe patterns of social order and to posit the "nature" of maleness and femaleness. Scriptural depictions of Eve and Adam also have had significant ramifications for Islamic understandings of gender even though the scriptural basis of Islam is the Qur'an—not the Bible.[3] Although the Qur'an never mentions the name "Eve" or its Arabic counterpart "Hawwa'," it does refer to "Adam and his mate."[4] Such references have provided Muslims with a scriptural orientation for their discussions of the "nature" of maleness and femaleness. Later commentators on the Qur'an identified Adam's mate as Eve even though the Qur'an itself did not.

THREE FAITHS, THREE THEOLOGICAL TRADITIONS

Although Jewish, Christian, and Muslim traditions used the story of the first woman and man to understand gender relations, each did so out of its own distinctive tradition. Differences in canon, doctrine, and hermeneutical approaches to the scripture shaped how each tradition read the story and understood its theological significance.

For example, many of the Jewish interpretations contained in this anthology display the remarkable freedom of expression and diversity of opinion characteristic of "midrash." In midrashic treatments of scripture, the reader is free (even encouraged) to ask questions of the text, either of what the text says or of what it leaves unsaid. Thus, while Genesis 3 is silent as to why the serpent spoke to Eve or why Eve gave the fruit to Adam, midrashic treatments raised these questions and then often went beyond the text to look for answers. These answers became part of an ongoing conversation within Judaism concerning the text's meaning and were preserved as an important guide for future readers. Whether the conversation centered on legal (*halakic*) or nonlegal (*aggadic*) matters, the result was a compilation of opinions considered authoritative for both the text's interpretation and the structuring of Jewish communal and family life.

Rabbinic treatments of Genesis 1-3 also reflect a willingness to hold conflicting interpretations in tension without needing to arrive at a "correct" reading. Talmudic as well as midrashic compilations, for example, preserve a variety of viewpoints concerning the meaning and significance of Genesis 1-3. For example, when it came to discerning from which body part God created Eve, a debate raged among rabbis as to whether Eve was created from Adam's rib, tail, face, or side. All these opinions are preserved and given equal standing in talmudic and midrashic literature. This is possible, as Gerald Burnes so aptly notes, because "there is no conflict in authority in this conflict of interpretations . . . it is the whole dialogue which is authoritative. . . . This means that there is neither occasion nor cause to determine the authority or correctness of this or that isolated interpretation."[5] For contemporary non-Jewish readers, this tolerance of diverse opinions will no doubt be confusing, even a bit disturbing. To other readers, more open to the polyvalent nature of all literature, such freedom may be welcome and may open new interpretive vistas.

Finally, readers would do well to remember that Eve plays a different role in Jewish theological reflection than she does in other traditions. The Jewish Eve, for example, is remarkably free from the doctrinal baggage that accompanies the Christian Eve. While Christian doctrine developed concepts of "sin" and a "Fall" based on Eve's disobedience, the corresponding rabbinical tradition of Israel's "pollution" after Eden was never, to any degree, central to Jewish thought. Moreover, since Judaism was not organized around orthodox doctrines or creedal statements, Eve's story could not play the foundational theological role in Jewish thought that it did for later Christian readers. What Eve's story could and did do, however, was to become the rationale for various Jewish practices and instructions.[6] Indeed, as Leila Bronner observes, the story of Eve became "a catechism of do's and don't's" for Jewish women.[7]

Christians also have pondered silences and tensions in Eve and Adam's story, but their readings have been shaped by their distinctive scriptural canon with its two "testaments." Canonical considerations have encouraged

Christian interpreters to assume not only that the two creation accounts in Genesis 1-3 spoke with a single voice, but also that these accounts were in harmony with New Testament descriptions of Eve and her daughters. Christians read the Genesis narratives through the lens of the New Testament, presuming that the entire Christian canon created a "biblical world." Until the advent of modern historical criticism (and, for most Christians, even after it), Christian interpreters saw nothing anachronistic about claiming that New Testament writers and their Hebrew Bible counterparts had the same understandings of Adam and Eve in mind. A task for much of Christian exegesis became formulating proposals for how one could hold together the varying tensions and disjunctions that occurred between and among texts.

The descriptions of Eve in 1 Timothy 2:12-15 have played a fundamental role in shaping Christian understandings of God's will for gender relations in this "biblical world." One of only two New Testament texts that refer to Eve by name, this passage argues that women must not exercise authority over men both because Eve was last in creation and because she was first in disobedience.[8] This rendering of Eve's story has encouraged the majority of Christian interpreters to subsume the creation account narrated in Genesis 1 into the creation account in Genesis 2. Thus Christians typically have concluded that God created woman after man to be his subordinate. That the woman was first to disobey God was proof of her derivative status, as well as of the dangers of allowing woman autonomy to run their own lives.

Another distinctive factor in Christian interpretations has been Christianity's development of a doctrine of "the Fall." For Christians, the opening chapters of Genesis depict a wondrously good creation in which human beings lived harmoniously with God and one another in a state of innocence and peace. When the first human couple ate the forbidden fruit, Christians have argued, they plunged humanity into sin and strife. This narrative of a good creation, followed by a devastating Fall, to be resolved by a cosmic reconciliation in Christ, has been crucial to Christian theology.

Adam and Eve as the first man and woman hold formative roles in this drama. Christians proclaimed that when Adam, the "type of the one who was to come," (Rom. 5:14, New Revised Standard Version [NRSV]) sinned, the entire creation was subject to decay, futility, and the reign of death. Christians announced a new creation made possible by the second Adam—Christ—in whom "all will be made alive" (1 Cor. 15:22, NRSV).

Typology was also pivotal to Christian discussions of Eve. Jesus was the second Adam who righted the sins of the first man. Who, then, might serve as the "second Eve," to right the sins of Adam's mate? Typically, Christians turned to Mary, the mother of Jesus, as their model for true womanhood. They found in her the virtues that Eve lacked—Mary was obedient, humble, and virginal. Because Mary submitted to God, she was the means through which salvation entered in the world, just as Eve, in her disobedience, was the instrument of the Fall.[9] Christians, in assuming that the first woman inaugurated the corruption of the entire creation, could not be theologically neutral about Eve or her daughters. Eve's role in the Christian drama of creation/ Fall/redemption was critical; and Christian theologians were suspicious that Eve's daughters carried the stain of her presumption.

An important factor in understanding Muslim readings of the first man and woman is that, unlike the Bible's account in Genesis 1-3, the Qur'an does not contain a single sustained narrative concerning the creation of human-kind and its subsequent disobedience. Instead, references to various facets of the primeval story are scattered across the span of the Qur'an's "surahs" or chapters. Moreover, not all references are in complete accord with each other. For example, the Qur'an offers several accounts of the first act of disobedience. Q.7:19-24 presents Adam and his mate as equally responsible for straying from God's command, while Q.20:120-21 underscores Adam's culpability. Differences such as these—and decisions about how to handle them—allow for varying conclusions about what the Qur'an reveals concerning the charac-teristics and activities of women and men.

Further, the Qur'an is silent on many details of the Adam and Eve story that are important to Jewish and Christian interpretations. For instance, the Qur'an never mentions either how or when Eve was created. It never speaks of a rib nor does it ever say that Eve was inferior to Adam. Yet other sources of Islamic theology—particularly the *hadith* (authoritative reports concerning the actions and sayings of Muhammad and his companions as transmitted by subsequent generations) and the *tafsir* (Qur'anic commentaries)—incorporate details not found in the Qur'an itself.

These nonscriptural materials offer glimpses of the intricate and complex relations of Islam to its monotheistic "siblings."[10] Western scholars have de-scribed Islam as "borrowing" themes and stories from Judaism and Christian-ity. The traditional Islamic understanding of the Qur'an as the "uncreated Word of God" cautions against speaking about extra-Islamic influences on the Qur'an itself. Yet the familiarity of Muslims with such non-Qur'anic no-tions as Eve's creation from a rib and her particular culpability for disobedi-ence indicates that Islam's interactions with Jewish and Christian understand-ings of Eve have influenced Muslim understandings of the first woman.

Since Jews, Christians, and Muslims approach the story of the first woman/Eve and first man/Adam from diverse scriptural, theological, and hermeneutical positions, it is not surprising that the story has spawned highly diverse interpretations. In addition, interpreters from all three faiths have ap-pealed to the story to provide legitimation for an incredible array of social customs. In many ways the text has functioned as a mirror—reflecting inter-preters' presuppositions about gender roles and social order. When we read commentary on Genesis 1-3, we learn as much about the interpreter as we do about the text itself. In spite of this diversity in interpretation and application, the readings of Adam and Eve often fall within two broad categories—those that assume that the story prescribes a hierarchical relationship between the sexes and those that posit an egalitarian one. It is to those two worldviews that we now turn.

TWO COMPETING WORLDVIEWS:
HIERARCHICAL AND EGALITARIAN

Readers who examine Genesis 1-3 closely will notice that the text gives two different descriptions of humanity's creation. In the first account, Genesis 1:1-2:4a, God created humanity after creating the earth and all other living things. The text appears to specify the simultaneous creation of male and female, noting that "God created humankind in his own image . . . male and female he created them" (Gen. 1:27, NRSV). The second account, Genesis 2:4b-3:24, offers a different chronology of creation. There, God formed man from the dust as the first of all creatures. After creating the rest of the animals and finding that none were suitable partners for the man, God caused a deep sleep to fall upon the man. God then took from the man a rib and fashioned from it the first woman, who was, as the man immediately recognized, "bone of my bones and flesh of my flesh" (Gen. 2:23, NRSV).

Throughout the history of interpretation, commentators have disagreed both on how to decipher the meaning of each individual story as well as on how to relate these two stories to one another. Debates have arisen over virtually every detail of the text. Significant discussions have focused on issues such as: does a simultaneous creation of male and female imply social equality between men and women? Does the creation of man before woman in the second account imply man's superiority to woman, or does woman's later creation indicate that God saved the best for last? What does it mean to say in Genesis 1 that male and female were created in the divine image? Do they share that image equally? Did the author of Genesis 2 intend to subjugate Eve to Adam by noting that God formed Eve from Adam's rib? Genesis 2:18 calls the woman the man's "helper." Does this term imply subordination?

Genesis 3, the story of the temptation, has given rise to an equal number of debates. Questions of significance have included: why did the serpent approach Eve, not Adam? Are women more likely to fall prey to deception than men? What is the relationship of sin to sexuality? In what sense was Eve a temptress? What exactly was Adam's sin? In verse 16 God informed Eve: "I will greatly increase your pangs in childbearing . . . yet your desire shall be for your husband, and he shall rule over you" (NRSV). Was God predicting the destructive behaviors set in motion by human sin, or was God prescribing punishment for sin? Similarly, when God decreed to Adam in verse 17, "cursed is the ground because of you. . . . By the sweat of your face you shall eat bread" (NRSV), was God condemning Adam to toil as punishment for sin, or was God predicting the results of Adam's sin? Was the subordination of women to men a result of sin, or was it part of God's original plan for creation?

Christian answers to this array of questions have tended to conform to two different models of interpretation. The dominant reading has found in

Genesis 1-3 a hierarchical creation, with woman subordinate to man. This reading has typically seen the second creation account as authoritative, either ignoring the first account, using only portions of it, or harmonizing the two under the assumption that the second account was a more detailed version of the creation of humanity. This latter interpretation has frequently argued that woman's subordination to man was part of God's original intention for the creation and not simply a result of sin. Christian commentators have been particularly prone to argue that Genesis 1-3 revealed God's intention eternally to subordinate women to men. Thus, Genesis 1-3 has functioned, more often than not, as a text that emphasized the parallels between God and men, while blaming women for introducing sin into the world and consigning them to the less glorious task of being man's "helper."

Though the hierarchical model has been the majority Christian view, it has always been challenged by a parallel tradition that saw Genesis 1-3 advocating gender egalitarianism. Given the patriarchy that has marked Western history, it comes as no surprise that the egalitarian reading has been a minority voice. Yet Genesis has consistently given rise to readings that have seen the original creation as one that established equality between men and women. Gender hierarchies emerging since Eden, this view has insisted, were signs that the creator's will was being thwarted rather than obeyed. At times the hierarchical reading has been so dominant that it virtually muted the egalitarian model, pushing it to the edges, where it surfaced as modest claims that the entire responsibility for human suffering should not be attributed to Eve.[11] In other instances, the egalitarian model has been more visible, arguing that women were created in the divine image to labor as equals with men in serving God.

Like Christian exegetes, Jewish readers of Genesis 1-3 also arrived at hierarchical and egalitarian readings. Unlike Christian approaches, many Jewish interpreters focused on specific biblical verses rather than whole chapters. In the case of midrashic and talmudic materials, for example, this means that instead of producing a sustained argument linked to either Genesis 1 or 2, the rabbis commented on individual elements within these chapters. In addition, such treatments reflected a remarkable tolerance for the coexistence of both hierarchical and egalitarian readings. Thus one talmudic sage, noting the sequence of punishments in Genesis 3 (serpent, woman, man), argued that, "Where it is a case of doing honour we begin at the most distinguished, but where it is a case of censuring we begin at the least important" (*Taanith* 15b). Another talmudic sage suggested that man was created last "so that he may be reminded that the gnats preceded him in the order of creation" (*Sanhedrin* 38a). In the first instance, last (in censuring) is the most elevated position, men being more important than either women or snakes. In the second, humankind's position in the order of creation (last) is interpreted as a cause for humility, not pride. So is last best or least, and what does this imply for gender relations?

Another example of midrashic and talmudic tolerance for diverse viewpoints is found in comments concerning the origin of death. While the speaker in *Genesis Rabbah* 17.8 suggested that women (i.e., Eve) "brought death into the world," *Deuteronomy Rabbah* 9.8 reported that God told Moses that Moses' own death was due to "the sin of the first man who brought death into the world." To further complicate the issue, when the righteous men complained to Adam in *Numbers Rabbah* 19.18 that he "brought mortality" on them, Adam replied that "I have only one sin to my account, while in your case, there is not a single man among you who has not at least four sins" implying that, to some degree, the men were responsible for their own mortality. Thus, a consideration of only those comments that are pejorative to Eve in talmudic and midrashic materials gives a skewed picture of the rabbinic Eve. It is an image that does not do justice to the more egalitarian vision of gender relations offered by other commentators.

Hierarchical and egalitarian models of interpretation also operate within Islamic understandings of gender and gender relations. In Islam, however, each exegetical model does not have a corresponding creation account in scripture that would make scriptural endorsement akin to the ways some Christian interpreters align Genesis 1 with gender equality and Genesis 2–3 with gender hierarchy. The multiple times the Qur'an speaks of humanity's original creation as well as the many ways it depicts humanity's initial disobedience complicate efforts to align each exegetical model with scriptural accounts of Adam and Eve.

The Qur'an never states that God created the first woman as either inferior or subordinate to the first man. The Qur'an, however, contains passages that portray a gender hierarchy even though these texts do not ground this gradation in Eve and Adam's relationship. Hierarchical views instead are often lodged within broader descriptions of women's relations to men. For example, amid a discussion of women who are divorced, Q.2:228 maintains: "Women have such honorable rights as obligations, but their men have a degree above them."[12] Similarly, Q.4:34 states, "Men are in charge of women, because Allah hath made the one of them to excel the other, and because they spend their property (for the support of women)."[13]

A hierarchical understanding of gender relations can find support in Islam's scripture by appealing to these texts. Indeed, such texts can provide the lens through which one looks at the relationship between Eve and Adam. When the relationship of the first couple is interpreted in the light of depictions of gender hierarchy, these texts offer Muslims scriptural support for seeing subordination as God's original intention for women and dominance as God's initial design for men.

On the other hand, the Qur'anic portrayals of the first woman can provide the lens so that Eve's relation to Adam sheds light on the Qur'an's more general statements about women. Then the absence of Qur'anic ascriptions of inferiority and submission to Eve becomes the basis for seeing gender equality as the will of God for all the descendants of Eve and Adam. The equality of the first couple thereby mitigates the force of Qur'anic passages that endorse gender hierarchies. As the Muslim selections in our final chapter demonstrate, decisions about how to correlate the Qur'anic portrayals of the first woman with other Qur'anic depictions of women shape the interpretive dynamics at work in debates about the proper role of women within contemporary Islam.

We invite the reader to observe the interplay between the two models of exegesis in the readings we have collected for this anthology. You will find here refinements of each position that, on first glance, will seem improbable; you will also find considerable repetition as generation after generation reiterates the principal points of the hierarchical position. We invite you to consider these readings carefully, remembering that interpretations of sacred texts have a concrete payoff: they provide cosmological grounding for the larger social order—or for doubts about it.

RELIGION, SOCIETY, AND SACRED TEXTS: THE PAYOFF

We do well to begin our consideration of the relationship between sacred texts and social order with a note of caution. As Elaine Pagels, in a study of Gnostic readings of Genesis 1-3 has cautioned, we must always remember that "symbolism is not sociology."[14] By this she meant that biblical interpretations do not have necessary social applications. It is reductionistic, for example, to assume that readers who notice women judges in the Hebrew Bible or who find in the New Testament a positive depiction of the mother of Jesus will invariably conclude that women are men's political or social equals. Similarly, we cannot conclude that readers who view Genesis 1-3 as critical of women will inevitably mistreat women in their own cultures. The dialectic between the social construction of religion and of society is a complicated process. We would do well not to oversimplify it.

Carol Christ has sounded a similar note in her assertion that "symbols have a richer significance than any explications of their meaning can give."[15] With Clifford Geertz she has defined religion as "a system of symbols which act to produce powerful, pervasive, and longlasting moods and motivations." Though for Christ it is reductionistic to conclude that a religious symbol has only a single meaning, she does insist that religious symbol systems create "moods" that themselves become "motivations" that translate "into social and political reality." In the case of Genesis 1-3, which in her reading provides symbol systems that legitimate male domination of women, Christ argues that the text cannot fail to create moods and motivations that "keep women in a state of psychological dependence on men and male authority, while at the same [time] legitimating the political and social authority of fathers and sons in the institutions of society."[16]

Advocates of an egalitarian reading might disagree. Nevertheless, we are interested, in this volume, in exploring connections between interpretation and social applications. We assume the presuppositions that readers bring to a text help shape their reading of it; we also know that texts can challenge and even reconfigure interpreters' presuppositions. Readings of Genesis 1-3 are important not simply because they provide an interesting case study in the history of interpretation. Rather, the history of interpretation of Genesis 1-3 is important because the text has so often provided proponents of hierarchical and egalitarian social orders justification for their positions.

The history of the United States is replete with such instances. As Carol Karlsen has observed, Eve functioned for Puritan interpreters as the arche-typal witch. Because Eve had refused to submit to male authority, she pro-vided a model for the New England woman who likewise threatened to topple the hierarchical social order constructed by Puritan men. Such women were seen, literally, as "the devil in the shape of a woman"—they were malevolent, demonic powers that society must quell.[17]

Apologists for African American slavery in the antebellum period were quick to use Genesis 1-3 in their defense. If enforced labor and gender hierar-chy were the result of Eve's sin, it required little imagination to argue that the hierarchies of master and slave were also logical developments of sin. Writers such as George Fitzhugh extended the argument to contend that capitalism, by pitting citizens against one another in the competition for economic suc-cess, threatened to starve the masses of people. Concluding that free society creates enmity among people and that "slavery and Christianity bring about a lasting peace," Fitzhugh suggested that a wider extension of slavery, com-mitting to bondage not only African Americans but also European Americans innately unsuited for economic success, was the appropriate solution.[18]

Clearly the creation account in Genesis has been of critical significance for U.S. cultural understandings of gender and social order. Dramatic as the examples of witchcraft and slavery are, numerous other readings of Genesis 1-3 equally relevant to the social sphere have also occurred in the history of interpretation. Some celebrate the equality of men and women. Some hy-pothesize that God is feminine as well as masculine. Others find in Genesis a statement of male superiority as well as a blueprint for hierarchical political systems.

SOME METHODOLOGICAL CONSIDERATIONS

In the chapters ahead we offer a suggestive—rather than an exhaustive—his-tory of interpretation of Eve and Adam. We are convinced that this story deeply influences contemporary culture and its institutions. We have sought to demonstrate that influence in two ways. First, in chapters 1 through 6, we consider classic discussions of gender roles prompted by this story in the three faith traditions that trace their lineage back to the primeval couple. Second, in chapters 7 and 8, we consider recent discussions of the story as applied not only to gender roles but also to such topics as slavery, race, sexual orientation, and doctrine of God.

Chapter 1 presents textual selections from Genesis 1-5 with a commentary highlighting gender issues. Chapter 2 offers postbiblical Jewish interpretations that emerge in the period from 200 BCE to 200 CE. Chapter 3 traces the variety of interpretive options present in midrashic, talmudic, and targumic traditions of 200 CE to 600 CE. Chapter 4 then backtracks to cover Christian readings found in the New Testament, extracanonical sources, and the writings of early church leaders. Chapter 5 examines medieval Jewish and Christian readings, as well as introducing classical interpretations offered by a third faith community that arose in this period: Islam.

From the breadth of Chapter 5, we narrow the focus in chapters 6 and 7 to selected Christian writers. Chapter 6 completes our consideration of premodern Christianity by examining readings from the Protestant Reformation in Europe. Chapter 7 examines applications of Eve and Adam's story to highly contested issues in the United States in the nineteenth century: slavery, women's rights, free love, and the genders of God. Chapter 8 continues this examination of the story's social applications into the twentieth century. It widens the purview, however, by once again presenting Jewish, Christian, and Muslim readings. And finally our appendix revisits the issue of Genesis 1-3, race, and hierarchy that we examined in chapter 7 by examining white supremacist voices from the nineteenth and twentieth centuries.

In selecting materials for inclusion in these eight chapters, we made decisions concerning the work's scope and arrangement. That we chose to present an anthology rather than an analytical narrative, for example, is the result both of our interest in primary sources and our desire to provide readers with easy access to them. That our anthology is selective rather than exhaustive is due to our attempt to cover 2500 years of interpretation in a single volume.

Yet in making these selections we realize that there was a trade-off. Texts and their writers are, after all, a part of a larger sociocultural context. It is a context that anthologizing tends to deemphasize by presenting materials excerpted from their sources and unmediated by extended scholarly comment. In an attempt partially to overcome this we have furnished each chapter with an introduction as well as providing mini-introductions to most writings. Yet we do not claim to give our readers thorough background information on each period's history. Readers seeking such information would do well to consult the sources mentioned in the endnotes.

Another thorny methodological issue is how to arrange selections from different faith traditions. Should we attempt an integrated approach by showing the connections among the three traditions? Such an approach, while recognizing points of commonality and literary connection, runs the risk of blurring the boundaries that delineate traditions. Yet treating the three traditions separately could imply that there was no interaction between them. Ultimately, we decided to arrange the bulk of the material by traditions. We wanted first to give our readers a sense of interpretive developments within

Judaism, Christianity, and Islam. But in chapter 8, we categorized our readings by themes rather than by faith communities, hoping that our readers would see not only the distinctiveness of each tradition's consideration of Eve and Adam but also the commonalities as well.

A few remarks on translation decisions are in order. First, we decided to retain the precise wording of the English translations of texts selected. Readers, however should be aware that translators often use the term "man" to render words that could have a more gender-inclusive sense in their original languages. When readers want to know a particular author's usage, they should consult the text in its original language. Second, while we frequently standardized scriptural, talmudic, and midrashic citations within the selections, no such attempt was made to standardize transliterated words. For readers unfamiliar with Hebrew, Greek, and Arabic, such terms were kept to a minimum (without affecting the sense of the text). When retained, they were transliterated for easier reading.

Another decision we made involved the editorial footnotes or endnotes accompanying some of the texts we selected. To simplify our anthology, we are not reproducing many of these notes. We urge readers who desire further information to consult the sources we cite.

We invite readers to consider the range of interpretations our selections set forth, and to continue to ask the intriguing hermeneutical and sociological questions that they raise for our consideration: why has the hierarchical reading been more attractive to interpreters? What factors might prompt interpreters to argue for the egalitarian model? What difference does it make if the larger social order is grounded in religious notions of hierarchy or equality? How might authority in cultural institutions such as the family, the community of worship, the workplace, and the government function differently in the two understandings of creation? Are there ramifications for understandings of race, the environment, and international relations? To what extent have religious notions conformed to prior cultural assumptions of social order? Under what conditions have religious notions challenged those cultural assumptions? What extratextual factors have influenced interpreters of biblical texts?

We wish you good reading.

NOTES TO GENERAL INTRODUCTION

1. Peter Berger, *The Sacred Canopy* (Garden City, N.Y.: Anchor Books, 1967), pp. 3, 13, 25, 33-36.

2. Berger, *The Sacred Canopy*, pp. 33-39, 47.

3. According to Muslim understanding, Islam, as a religious institution, came into being when God called Muhammad to prophethood by revealing the Qur'an to him. Muslims understand these revelations to be in continuity with the revelations

God had made through earlier prophets. Islam sees Muhammad as the final prophet—the so-called "Seal of the Prophets"—because the revelations he received from 610 CE to 632 CE both correct and complete the revelations that other "people of the book" received through the succession of prophets that began with Adam.

4. The use of "mate" to translate the Arabic *zaujah* (for a woman) follows the suggestion of Riffat Hassan in "Made from Adam's Rib: The Woman's Creation Question," *Al Mushir* 27 (Autumn 1985): 126-27. English translations of the Qur'an usually render the word as "wife."

5. Gerald L. Burnes, "Midrash and Allegory: The Beginnings of Scriptural Interpretation," in Robert Alter and Frank Kermode, editors, *The Literary Guide to the Bible* (Cambridge: Harvard University Press, 1987), p. 632.

6. Paul Morris notes that themes from Genesis 1-3 are woven into the fabric of contemporary Jewish life in a variety of ways:

> The fourth of the seven blessings of the marriage ceremony recalls that God "gladdened" the first couple's wedding (*Prayer Book*, p. 771). A wife lights the Sabbath candles as a task enjoined on her as an antidote to the "curse of Eve" (*Gen. R.* 17.8). The laws governing the relationship between husbands and wives are likewise designed to overcome the same curse (Gen 3.16; *b. Pes.* 72b). As Adam was born and judged on Rosh-Ha-Shanah (New Year), so every Jew is judged on that day. (Paul Morris, "Exiled from Eden: Jewish Interpretations of Genesis," in Paul Morris and Deborah Sawyer, editors, *A Walk in the Garden: Biblical, Iconographical and Literary Images of Eden* [Sheffield: JSOT Press, 1992], p. 118)

7. Leila Leah Bronner, *From Eve to Esther: Rabbinic Reconstructions of Biblical Women* (Louisville: Westminster John Knox Press, 1994), p. 22.

8. 2 Corinthians 11:3 is the other New Testament passage that refers to Eve by name. For an interesting discussion of how Paul uses Eve's name in a non-gender-specific way to signify both male and female Christians, see Elisabeth Schussler Fiorenza's *In Memory of Her: A Feminist Theological Reconstruction of Christian Origins* (New York: Crossroad Publishing Company, 1987), pp. 234-35, 265-70.

9. Christians have widely debated the levels of responsibility Eve and Adam had for the Fall. For some, Eve deserved most of the blame because the Fall happened when she disobeyed God's command. For others, Eve simply initiates the Fall; it takes Adam as "head" of the human race to complete the Fall.

10. This complex and sensitive matter cannot be discussed in detail here. It is important to note the long history of charges that Muslims have "misread" the Bible and the judgmental approach that marked much of modern Western scholarship on this topic. For a discussion of differences in the approaches of Qur'anic exegetes and Biblical scholars, see Jane Dammen McAuliffe, *Qur'anic Christians: An Analysis of Classical and Modern Exegesis* (Cambridge: Cambridge University Press, 1991), pp. 28-31.

11. It is worth noting that passages in the Qur'an that refer to the primeval couple never blame the first woman for introducing sin into the world. Unlike New Testament readings of Genesis 1-3, Qur'anic commentary either blames both the man and the woman for disobeying God, or blames the man alone (Surah 20:115-22).

12. Surah 2:228 as translated by A. J. Arberry in *The Koran Interpreted* (New York: Macmillan Publishing Company, 1955), vol. 1, p. 60.

13. Surah 4:34 as translated by Mohammed Marmaduke Pickthall in *The Meaning of the Glorious Koran* (New York and Scarborough, Ontario: New American Library, n.d.), p. 83.

14. Elaine Pagels, "Pursuing the Spiritual Eve," in Karen L. King, editor, *Images of the Feminine in Gnosticism* (Philadelphia: Fortress Press, 1988), p. 188.

15. Carol Christ, "Why Women Need the Goddess," in Carol P. Christ and Judith Plaskow, editors, *Womanspirit Rising: A Feminist Reader in Religion* (San Fran-

cisco: Harper & Row, 1979), pp. 274, 279. The quotation from Clifford Geertz was originally published in his "Religion as a Cultural System," in William L. Lessa and Evon V. Vogt, editors, *Reader in Comparative Religion*, 2nd ed. (New York: Harper & Row, 1972), p. 206.

16. Christ, "Why Women Need the Goddess," p. 275.

17. Carol F. Karlsen, *The Devil in the Shape of a Woman* (New York: Vintage Books, 1987), pp. 177-81.

18. George Fitzhugh, *Sociology for the South, or The Failure of Free Society* (Richmond, Va.: A. Morris, 1854), pp. 29-33, 85-87, 212, 225.

CHAPTER ONE

Hebrew Bible Accounts

INTRODUCTION

> For two millennia now the Judeo-Christian tradition has placed man a little
> lower than the angels and woman a little higher than the demons.[1]

No other text has affected women in the Western world as much as that found
in the opening chapters of Genesis. The biblical story of the first man and
woman became for many readers a blueprint for relationships between all men
and women. Yet in spite of the wide-ranging influence of Genesis 1-3, there is
surprisingly little agreement among readers concerning what these chapters
actually say about such relationships. Do they present a message of subordination or one of mutuality? Or do they contain two messages in tension with
one another? As you will see from the scholars surveyed in this introduction
(and from those whose writings are included in this book's last chapter) contemporary opinion ranges widely on what Genesis 1-3 says about men and
women.

The Story/ies of Creation

Genesis 1:1-2:4a contains a story of creation. In six days, the heavens, the
earth, and all living creatures are created from a watery chaos. Following
the animals' creation on the sixth day, Elohim (God) creates humankind in

Elohim's own image. The first man and woman are created simultaneously and jointly receive Elohim's command to be fruitful, to multiply, and to subdue and have dominion over the earth. Their creation, Elohim remarks, is "very good." On the seventh day, Elohim rests.

In Genesis 2:4b, however, the creative process begins again, this time with an arid wasteland devoid of life. The missing prerequisites for life—water and someone to till the soil—are provided by Yahweh Elohim (LORD God), and thus human and plant life appear. After an unspecified period of time the story unfolds to reveal a garden to inhabit, creatures to name and befriend, productive work to do, and a specific prohibition to obey. Yet all is not complete. Putting the human creature to sleep, Yahweh Elohim removes a body part and fashions it into a second creature. The chapter closes with a man and woman who are naked and happily unashamed of it. But it is the chapter, not the story, that ends on this idyllic note.

In chapter 3 we meet a new character—the wily serpent. The dialogue between this smooth-talking snake and the woman concludes with both woman and man sampling the forbidden fruit. Fear, shame, and some strategically placed foliage immediately follow. When confronted by Yahweh Elohim, both man and woman place the blame for their actions elsewhere: the man blames the deity and the woman, and the woman blames the snake. Ultimately all three characters—snake, woman, and man—receive punishments from Yahweh Elohim. The story concludes with the woman being named, the couple being clothed, and the man and woman being expelled from the garden. Their expulsion is finalized by sword-wielding cherubim who now guard its entrance.

In 1711, one reader commented upon the discrepancies within Genesis 1-2. On the basis of style, theology, content, and divine names, the German pastor H. B. Witter suggested that Genesis 1-3 contained not one, but two creation stories. By the end of the nineteenth century, after much challenge and refinement, the suggestion that sources lay behind Genesis 1-3 had blossomed into a full-blown hypothesis concerning the authorship of the Pentateuch. Called the Four Source or JEDP theory, it suggested that the Torah/Pentateuch was composed of four documents: J (Yahwist, 10th c. BCE), E (Elohist, 8th c. BCE), D (Deuteronomy, 7th c. BCE), and P (Priestly, 6th-5th c. BCE). According to this theory, Genesis 1-3 contained a doublet, that is, two accounts of the same event. Genesis 2:4b-3:24 was from the Yahwist source and dated c. 900s BCE (during the reigns of David or Solomon), while Genesis 1:1-2:4a came from a much later period (the exile or postexilic period, c. 500s-400s BCE) and reflected the concerns of its priestly writers.

Recent challenges concerning the dating, provenance, and existence of J, E, D, and P have called into question much of the Documentary Hypothesis. Literary critics, for example, argue that doublets, a traditional criteria for the existence of sources, have a literary function and represent artistic crafting. Others suggest that the attempt to get behind the text to hypothetical sources is futile and should be abandoned in favor of analyzing the text itself.

Genesis 1–3: Contradictory Visions of Gender

Many who read the accounts in Genesis 1–3 conclude that within these chapters lie two stories with two different messages concerning gender. They disagree, however, as to what these messages are and how they relate to one another.

Anne Gardner,[2] for example, describes Genesis 2–3 as "strongly sexist"[3] with Genesis 1 functioning as its corrective. Drawing on Ancient Near Eastern creation accounts, she argues that stories similar to Genesis 2–3 contain male culprits, not female ones. By making woman the villain, the Yahwist significantly changed the story pattern commonly found in the surrounding cultures. This was done, Gardner argues, to turn the story into a polemic against goddess worship.[4] Since P (Gen. 1:1–2:4a) did not perceive goddess worship as a threat, P "deliberately took issue with Genesis 2:4b–3" by stressing the "simultaneous creation of male and female (Gen. 1:27)."[5] Thus P could declare that humankind's creation was "very good" (Gen. 1:31) and, as Gardner emphasizes, "that included the woman!"[6]

Whereas Gardner views P as a corrective to J, other scholars suggest that J corrects P. According to Phyllis Bird,[7] for example, P's image of woman in Genesis 1 is not as egalitarian as scholars like Gardner assume.[8] P is not, as some might hope, an "equal-rights theologian."[9] While the P account addresses sexuality in its biological aspects, it is the J account that emphasizes the psychosocial aspects of sexual relationships:

> Genesis 2–3 supplements the anthropology of Genesis 1, but also "corrects" and challenges it by maintaining that the meaning of human sexual distinction cannot be limited to a biological definition of origin or function. Sexuality is a social endowment essential to community and to personal fulfillment, but as such it is also subject to perversion and abuse. Genesis 2–3 opens the way for a consideration of sex and sexuality in history.[10]

Thus for Bird, Genesis 2 contains an ideal image of gender relations—an image that becomes perverted in Genesis 3. Genesis 1, however, is neither for nor against women's equality.[11]

Not all scholars believe that the differences between Genesis 1 and 2–3 represent an effort to correct. Literary critic Robert Alter,[12] for example, agrees that the two accounts are essentially contradictory (the first being egalitarian and the second hierarchical), but this is because the subject matter itself is contradictory and "essentially resistant to consistent linear formulation."[13] The tension between stories is not an accident of compositional merging, but the product of intentional artistic crafting. This literary tension mirrors the "bewildering complex reality" of human relationships.[14]

Genesis 1–3: A Unified Vision of Women

The above positions of Gardner, Bird, and Alter all assume that Genesis 1–3 contains different, even contradictory, visions of woman. Other scholars, however, disagree with this conclusion and insist that these chapters present a unified image. The contours of this image, however, remain controversial. In her earlier writings, for example, Phyllis Bird suggested that P and J were of like minds when it came to women:

> While the two creation accounts of Genesis differ markedly in language, style, date and traditions employed, their basic statements about woman are essentially the same: woman is, along with man, the direct and intentional creation of God and the crown of his creation. Man and woman were made for each other.[15]

Azalea Reisenberger[16] reaches the same conclusion as Bird albeit by a different route. Reisenberger, informed by the rabbinic tradition of Adam as hermaphrodite, suggests that woman came from the side (not the rib) of the 'adam. She views the separation of woman and man in Genesis 2:23 as analogous to humankind's simultaneous creation described in Genesis 1:27. For Reisenberger, Genesis 2 recapitulates Genesis 1, with both maintaining "the equality of the sexes."[17]

While Bird and Reisenberger conclude that Genesis 1-3 envisions mutuality and egalitarianism as the goal of gender relations, others would argue that subordination and hierarchy are the essential vision of Genesis 1-3.

Raymond C. Ortlund, for example, argues that Genesis 1-3 presents a unified vision of male "headship" as well as "male-female equality."[18] After admitting that neither expression ("headship" or "equality") is found in Genesis 1, Ortlund suggests that God's use of the term "man" in Genesis 1:27 ("God created *man* in his image") "whispers male headship, which Moses will bring forward boldly in chapter two."[19] For Ortlund, male headship and male-female equality are not mutually exclusive. "Headship," Ortlund insists, is not "domination." That is, men are divinely appointed leaders and protectors of women but they are not given a license to be tyrants or wife abusers. Ortlund can affirm that men and women are equal (both are made in the image of God) because he locates this "equality" in the realm of the spirit rather than the structures of society and family. Thus while Ortlund argues that Genesis 1-3 contains a unified vision of gender relations that allows men "headship" while also affirming equality, his vision is, in reality, one of a "benevolent" hierarchy.

Beyond Genesis 3

Another issue, perhaps not as prominent as discussions of Genesis 1-3's internal consistency, but nevertheless important, is how one should understand Genesis 1-3 in relation to Genesis 4-5. For many readers, Eve's story concludes with her expulsion from the garden. Even scholarly treatments of Eve often conclude at the end of chapter 3. Literary critic Mieke Bal,[20] for example, views the woman's naming in Genesis 3:20 as the final element in

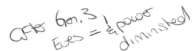

her characterization.[21] Scholars like Mary Phil Korsak[22] and Ilana Pardes,[23] however, stress the importance of Genesis 4-5. Korsak likens Eve's account to a symphony, with the third movement in Genesis 4 and the finale in Genesis 5.[24] Thus Genesis 1-3 is part, but not all, of the first woman/Eve's story.

According to Pardes, Genesis 1-3 contains a challenge to, and reaffirmation of, patriarchy that is echoed in Genesis 4-5. For Pardes, the maternal naming speech in Genesis 4:1-2 signals Eve's literary emergence as Adam's equal.[25] Eve's strength and power are diminished, however, by the end of chapter 4, and by chapter 5 have vanished completely.[26] Thus just as some see in Genesis 3 the distortion of the egalitarian vision of Genesis 2, so Pardes sees in 4:25-5:3 the diminishment of the egalitarian vision of 4:1-2.

Genesis 1–3 and Ancient Israel

As we have seen thus far, there is tremendous diversity of contemporary opinion concerning what Genesis 1-3 (and 4-5) actually say about women. This makes it difficult to speculate on how these texts might have informed their ancient readers. Was Eve's story used to subordinate Israelite women or to provide them with an image of equality? It would be helpful if we could analyze how biblical writers understood the significance of Eve's actions in the Garden. But it is precisely at this point that we run into a curious problem. There is no mention or allusion to the first woman/Eve in the Hebrew Scriptures beyond Genesis 5. Given the prominence of Adam and Eve in early Jewish and Christian literature this is quite astonishing. As Carol Meyers observes,

> Her [Eve's] story is so well known that it is somewhat surprising to find that in the rest of the Hebrew Bible, the story of Eden is not a prominent theme. Neither are the actions of Adam and Eve ever cited as examples of disobedience and punishment, although the long story of Israel's recurrent rejection of God's word and will provides plentiful opportunity for drawing such analogies.[27]

This silence does not stop Meyers from using the story to reconstruct gender roles in ancient Israel. Supplementing Genesis 2-3 with insights from the social sciences, Meyers concludes that Genesis 2-3 is a wisdom tale. Its purpose was "to enhance the acceptance by both females and males of the often harsh realities of highland life and to provide ideological sanction for large families and for intense physical toil in subsistence activities."[28]

Meyers is aware that using Genesis 2-3 for women's history is somewhat perilous. She admits that,

> Even though there is a general assumption that the Bible is an accurate reflection of at least some aspects of Israelite society, and although this assumption may be valid at many levels, when it comes to gender it must

be carefully examined. Theologians and feminists alike need to be cautious in drawing conclusions about Israelite women from biblical texts not only because an overlay of interpretation may occlude the text but because the texts themselves may not have a one-to-one correspondence with reality.[29]

Yet in spite of this, Meyers declares that:

> Not only does Eve represent Israelite women, she is also a product of the way of life of women in that world. The social realities of everyday life provided the raw materials from which the biblical narrator forged the now famous tale. The artful crafting of that simple yet powerful narrative is inextricably linked to the life experience of the Hebrew author. . . . It also constitutes the audience, the social group to be addressed by and moved in some way to respond to the multifarious messages of the story.[30]

The extent to which biblical ideology can be equated with ancient reality remains a thorny issue in biblical studies in general and in gender studies in particular. For example, in what chronological period should we seek the "daily reality" behind Genesis 2-3? Meyers assumes that the reality behind Genesis 2-3 is that of rural, premonarchic Israel.[31] Yet proponents of the late dating of Genesis 2-3 place this material in the exile (or even later). While this fact would not exclude an earlier date for a preliterary form of the story, the fact that the rest of the Hebrew Scriptures do not mention Eve might indicate that they do not know her.

It is uncertain how far we can get behind Genesis 2-3 to Eve's real-life counterparts. In the more than two thousand years since its writing, however, Genesis 1-5 has had a profound effect on its readers. While the extent to which Eve's story influenced the women of the writer's own society is uncertain, the degree to which it shaped her daughters' lives in the centuries that followed is legendary.

Background to the Selections

The biblical selections in this chapter are from the New Revised Standard Version. Following each selection we have provided a verse-keyed commentary that identifies translation, syntactical, and interpretive issues that touch upon gender. In writing this commentary we kept two criteria in mind. First of all, our comments are limited to only those items that concern gender. Other issues, no matter how tantalizing and worthy of comment, were passed over. Those readers who would like to explore these aspects of the text are advised to use a good commentary on Genesis as a study guide. Second, our purpose in providing a commentary was not to give readers the "correct" way of reading a verse, but simply to familiarize readers with Adam and Eve's story and to alert them to issues evoked by its content. Chapters 2-8 of this book will explore how succeeding generations of readers struggled to deal with many of the issues highlighted in our commentary.

NOTES TO CHAPTER I, INTRODUCTION

1. Adrien Janis Bledstein, "The Genesis of Humans: The Garden of Eden Revisited," *Judaism* 26 (1977): 187.

2. Anne Gardner, "Genesis 2:4b-3: A Mythological Paradigm of Sexual Equality or of the Religious History of Pre-Exilic Israel?" *Scottish Journal of Theology* 43 (1990): 1-18.

3. Gardner, "Genesis," p. 15.

4. Gardner, "Genesis," pp. 14-17.

5. Gardner, "Genesis," p. 17.

6. Gardner, "Genesis," p. 18.

7. Phyllis A. Bird, " 'Male and Female He Created Them': Gen 1:27b in the Context of the Priestly Account of Creation," *Harvard Theological Review* 74 (1981): 129-59.

8. Bird, "Male and Female," p. 155.

9. Bird, "Male and Female," p. 156.

10. Bird, "Male and Female," pp. 158-59.

11. Bird, "Male and Female," p. 157.

12. Robert Alter, *The Art of Biblical Narrative* (New York: Basic Books, 1981).

13. Alter, *The Art*, p. 145.

14. Alter, *The Art*, p. 147.

15. Phyllis A. Bird, "Images of Women in the Old Testament," in Rosemary Radford Ruether, editor, *Religion and Sexism: Images of Women in the Jewish and Christian Traditions* (New York: Simon & Schuster, 1974), pp. 41-88.

16. Azila Talit Reisenberger, "The Creation of Adam as Hermaphrodite—and Its Implications for Feminist Theology," *Judaism* 42 (1993): 447-52.

17. Reisenberger, "The Creation of Adam," pp. 451-52.

18. Raymond C. Ortlund, Jr., "Male-Female Equality and Male Headship: Genesis 1-3," in John Piper and Wayne Grudem, editors, *Recovering Biblical Manhood and Womanhood: A Response to Evangelical Feminism* (Wheaton, Ill.: Crossway Books, 1991), pp. 95-112.

19. Ortlund, "Male-Female Equality," p. 98.

20. Mieke Bal, "Sexuality, Sin and Sorrow: The Emergence of the Female Character (A Reading of Genesis 1-3)," *Poetics Today* 6 (1985): 21-42.

21. Bal, "Sexuality," p. 40.

22. Mary Phil Korsak, "Eve, Malignant or Maligned?" *Cross Currents* 44 (1994-95): 453-62.

23. Ilana Pardes, "Beyond Genesis 3: The Politics of Maternal Naming," in Athalya Brenner, editor, *A Feminist Companion to Genesis* (Sheffield: JSOT Press, 1993), pp. 173-93.

24. Korsak, "Eve," pp. 460-61.

25. Pardes, "Beyond Genesis 3," pp. 174-85.

26. Pardes, "Beyond Genesis 3," pp. 185-87.

27. Carol Meyers, *Discovering Eve: Ancient Israelite Women in Context* (Oxford: Oxford University Press, 1988), p. 3.

28. Carol Meyers, "Women and the Domestic Economy of Ancient Israel," in Barbara S. Leski, editor, *Woman's Earliest Records: From Ancient Egypt and Western Asia* (Atlanta: Scholars Press, 1989), p. 277.

29. Meyers, "Women and the Domestic Economy," p. 266.

30. Meyers, *Discovering Eve*, p. 4.

31. Meyers, *Discovering Eve*, p. 132.

GENESIS: SELECTIONS AND COMMENTARY

The Seven Days of Creation

The creation account below is traditionally assigned to the Priestly writers (c. 500s-400s BCE). (Source: New Revised Standard Version of the Bible.)

Genesis 1:1–2:4a

[1:1]In the beginning when God created the heavens and the earth, [2]the earth was a formless void and darkness covered the face of the deep, while a wind from God swept over the face of the waters. [3]Then God said, "Let there be light"; and there was light. [4]And God saw that the light was good; and God separated the light from the darkness. [5]God called the light Day, and the darkness he called Night. And there was evening and there was morning, the first day.

[6]And God said, "Let there be a dome in the midst of the waters, and let it separate the waters from the waters." [7]So God made the dome and separated the waters that were under the dome from the waters that were above the dome. And it was so. [8]God called the dome Sky. And there was evening and there was morning, the second day.

[9]And God said, "Let the waters under the sky be gathered together into one place, and let the dry land appear." And it was so. [10]God called the dry land Earth, and the waters that were gathered together he called Seas. And God saw that it was good. [11]Then God said, "Let the earth put forth vegetation: plants yielding seed, and fruit trees of every kind on earth that bear fruit with the seed in it." And it was so. [12]The earth brought forth vegetation: plants yielding seed of every kind, and trees of every kind bearing fruit with the seed in it. And God saw that it was good. [13]And there was evening and there was morning, the third day.

[14]And God said, "Let there be lights in the dome of the sky to separate the day from the night; and let them be for signs and for seasons and for days and years, [15]and let them be lights in the dome of the sky to give light upon the earth." And it was so. [16]God made the two great lights—the greater light to rule the day and the lesser light to rule the night—and the stars. [17]God set them in the dome of the sky to give light upon the earth, [18]to rule over the day and over the night, and to separate the light from the darkness. And God saw that it was good. [19]And there was evening and there was morning, the fourth day.

²⁰And God said, "Let the waters bring forth swarms of living creatures, and let birds fly above the earth across the dome of the sky." ²¹So God created the great sea monsters and every living creature that moves, of every kind, with which the waters swarm, and every winged bird of every kind. And God saw that it was good. ²²God blessed them, saying, "Be fruitful and multiply and fill the waters in the seas, and let birds multiply on the earth." ²³And there was evening and there was morning, the fifth day.

²⁴And God said, "Let the earth bring forth living creatures of every kind: cattle and creeping things and wild animals of the earth of every kind." And it was so. ²⁵God made the wild animals of the earth of every kind, and the cattle of every kind, and everything that creeps upon the ground of every kind. And God saw that it was good.

²⁶Then God said, "Let us make humankind in our image, according to our likeness; and let them have dominion over the fish of the sea, and over the birds of the air, and over the cattle, and over all the wild animals of the earth, and over every creeping thing that creeps upon the earth."

²⁷So God created humankind in his image,
    in the image of God he created them;
      male and female he created them.

²⁸God blessed them and God said to them, "Be fruitful and multiply, and fill the earth and subdue it; and have dominion over the fish of the sea and over the birds of the air and over every living thing that moves upon the earth." ²⁹God said, "See, I have given you every plant yielding seed that is upon the face of all the earth, and every tree with seed in its fruit; you shall have them for food. ³⁰And to every beast of the earth, and to every bird of the air, and to everything that creeps on the earth, everything that has the breath of life, I have given every green plant for food." And it was so. ³¹God saw everything that he had made, and indeed, it was very good. And there was evening and there was morning, the sixth day.

²:¹Thus the heavens and the earth were finished, and all their multitude. ²And on the seventh day God finished the work that he had done, and he rested on the seventh day from all the work that he had done. ³So God blessed the seventh day and hallowed it, because on it God rested from all the work that he had done in creation.

⁴These are the generations of the heavens and the earth when they were created.

Commentary: Genesis 1:1–2:4a

¹:²⁶*Then God said, "Let us make humankind in our image, according to our likeness; and let them have dominion over. . . . "*: the Hebrew term translated "humankind" in the NRSV is *'adam*. While it is possible to understand this term either collectively or singularly, the plural verb ("let them have," NRSV) indicates its collective meaning in this verse. The NRSV's use of "humankind"

instead of the generic "man" (King James Version [KJV]) is in keeping with the gender-inclusive possibilities of 'adam (see the discussion of 'adam in the commentary on 2:7a).

The phrase "let us make humankind" is modified by two synonymous adverbial phrases ("in our image" and "according to our likeness") containing the Hebrew terms *selem* ("image," NRSV) and *demut* ("likeness," NRSV). While these phrases distinguish the creation of humankind from the rest of creation (only humankind is made in the image/likeness of God), their precise meaning is open to interpretation. In his commentary on Genesis 1-11, Claus Westermann lists various interpretive options. To be made in God's image has meant:

1. Having certain spiritual qualities or capacities (soul, intellect, will).
2. Having a certain external (corporeal) form (i.e., upright carriage).
3. Having both the spiritual and corporeal features characteristic of humankind.
4. Being God's counterpart on earth; able to enter into partnership with God.
5. Being God's representative on earth (based on royal theology; humankind as God's viceroy/administrator).[1]

While Westermann's treatment of verse 26 is both interesting and helpful (see also his discussion of the plural pronoun for the deity), our interest in gender issues prompts us to move on to verses 27-28.

[1.27]*So God created humankind in his image, in the image of God he created them; male and female he created them*: the three parts (or "cola") of verse 27 are parallel to each other. The first two are synonymously parallel (they repeat the same idea) and are arranged chiastically (the second reverses the order of the first):

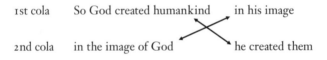

1st cola   So God created humankind   in his image

2nd cola   in the image of God   he created them

The third cola ("male and female he created them") raises several literary and interpretative issues. How should "male and female" be understood? Is there any special connection between "male and female" and the "image of God"? Two suggestions concerning the parallelism found in verse 27 offer significant answers to these questions:

1. If the third cola of verse 27 is *synonymously* parallel to the second—

    2nd cola   in the image of God   he created them

    3rd cola   male and female   he created them

    —then the image of God may have something to do with sexual differentiation (being male and female). Usually this is understood as either saying something about God (that God is both male and female) or something about humans (that both sexes share equally in God's image or that heterosexual marriage is divinely imaged).

2. If the third cola in v. 27 is *synthetically* parallel to the second cola (that is, it adds to
the idea in the second cola rather than repeating it)—

| 2nd cola | in the image of God | he created them |
| 3rd cola ⟶ | male and female | he created them |

—then "male and female" may not refer to the "image of God." Phyllis Bird, for
example, suggests that the couplet forms a bridge between the statements on divine
likeness (vv. 26 and 27aa), and the pronouncement of fertility (v. 28). Like God,
humankind is made in the image of God. Unlike God, humankind is male and female. According to Bird, the phrase "male and female" does not define "image of
God" but simply denotes sexual differentiation and "anticipates and prepares for"
the blessing of fertility in verse 28.[2]

While the two positions outlined above understand "male and female" in
terms of the parallelism of verse 27 or the relationship between verses 26-28,
David Clines argues that the phrase simply brings into correspondence the
creation of *'adam* with that of the plants and animals. As plants (vv. 11-12)
and animals (vv. 21-22, 24-25) are created "according to their kinds," so the
"kinds" of humans are mentioned—"male and female."[3]

The phrase "in his image" in reference to God is also worthy of mention.
Throughout the Hebrew Scriptures, the masculine pronoun is used to refer
to Israel's God. This usage has to be understood in light of the following:
(1) Hebrew has only two pronominal forms for the third person singular—
male and female. Therefore, pronominal references to God that are in the singular form must use a gendered pronoun. (2) Personal, gendered metaphors
for God in the Hebrew Scriptures are male, though there are similes that image God as female (e.g., God is like a woman in childbirth). (3) A polemic
against goddess worship is found throughout the Hebrew Scriptures. Thus the
writers of the Hebrew Scriptures favor the use of the masculine singular pronoun to refer to Yahweh, God of Israel. Modern inclusive-language versions
of the Bible tend to replace such pronouns with the word *God* or *Yahweh* (e.g.,
"in God's image" for "in his image") or to rearrange the syntax of the sentence
to eliminate the need for a pronoun.

[1.28]*God blessed them, and God said to them, "Be fruitful and multiply, and fill the
earth"*: the action described in verse 27 is expanded in verse 28 to include a
blessing and a chain of commands concerning fertility and production—be
fruitful, multiply, and fill (see v. 22, where the same blessing and command to
procreate are given to the fish and birds). The coupling of these commands
with the pronouncement "God saw . . . it was very good" (v. 31) can be seen as
a celebration of human (reproductive?) sexuality.

and subdue it; and have dominion over . . . : whereas the first three commands in verse 28 deal with fertility and reproduction, the last two deal with
domination and function.[4] Their significance for gender issues is dependent
upon how one understands the object of the blessing in verse 28. God blessed
"them" and then gave "them" a series of commands. What is the referent to
"them"?

If "them" refers to *'adam*/humankind (see v. 26 for this collective usage), then it could be argued that the writer is simply referring to humankind as a species. As a species, humans are both like and unlike other species. Like the birds and fish, they are blessed and commanded to be fertile and reproduce. Unlike the birds and fish, they are given dominion and authority. While the writer understands that human females participate in this authority because they are human, the writer shows no significant effort in this verse to make any statement about the mutuality of males and females concerning function or position.

If "them" refers to the "male and female" mentioned in the last cola of verse 27, then it could be argued that the writer is drawing attention to the mutuality of the command and authority given by God. Both male *and* female are "to subdue" and "have dominion."

A Garden in Eden

The selection below is the first part of a longer story that continues in Genesis 3. Usually assigned to the Yahwist, the story is traditionally dated to c. 900s–700s BCE. More recent attempts at dating, however, place it as late as the 500s. (Source: New Revised Standard Version of the Bible.)

Genesis 2:4b–25

[2:4]In the day that the LORD God made the earth and the heavens, [5]when no plant of the field was yet in the earth and no herb of the field had yet sprung up—for the LORD God had not caused it to rain upon the earth, and there was no one to till the ground; [6]but a stream would rise from the earth, and water the whole face of the ground— [7]then the LORD God formed man from the dust of the ground, and breathed into his nostrils the breath of life; and the man became a living being. [8]And the LORD God planted a garden in Eden, in the east; and there he put the man whom he had formed. [9]Out of the ground the LORD God made to grow every tree that is pleasant to the sight and good for food, the tree of life also in the midst of the garden, and the tree of the knowledge of good and evil.

[10]A river flows out of Eden to water the garden, and from there it divides and becomes four branches. [11]The name of the first is Pishon; it is the one that flows around the whole land of Havilah, where there is gold; [12]and the gold of that land is good; bdellium and onyx stone are there. [13]The name of the second river is Gihon; it is the one that flows around the whole land of Cush. [14]The name of the third river is Tigris, which flows east of Assyria. And the fourth river is the Euphrates.

[15]The LORD God took the man and put him in the garden of Eden to till it and keep it. [16]And the LORD God commanded the man, "You may freely eat of every tree of the garden; [17]but of the tree of the knowledge of good and evil you shall not eat, for in the day that you eat of it you shall die."

[18]Then the LORD God said, "It is not good that the man should be alone;

I will make him a helper as his partner." [19]So out of the ground the LORD God formed every animal of the field and every bird of the air, and brought them to the man to see what he would call them; and whatever the man called every living creature, that was its name. [20]The man gave names to all cattle, and to the birds of the air, and to every animal of the field; but for the man there was not found a helper as his partner. [21]So the LORD God caused a deep sleep to fall upon the man, and he slept; then he took one of his ribs and closed up its place with flesh. [22]And the rib that the LORD God had taken from the man he made into a woman and brought her to the man. [23]Then the man said,

> "This at last is bone of my bones
> and flesh of my flesh;
> this one shall be called Woman,
> for out of Man this one was taken."

[24]Therefore a man leaves his father and his mother and clings to his wife, and they become one flesh. [25]And the man and his wife were both naked, and were not ashamed.

Commentary: Genesis 2:4b–25

[2:7]*then the LORD God formed man from the dust of the ground*: in the Hebrew there is a word play (paronomasia) between the terms *'adam* ("man," NRSV) and *'adamah* ("ground," NRSV). Scholars disagree, however, on how *'adam* should be translated and whether or not this word play is significant enough to be retained in translations. There are:

1. those who are sensitive to gender issues and argue that *'adam* is gender-inclusive in this particular context (see "human being" in 2:7, Revised English Bible [REB]).
2. those who argue that the terms are linked by substance as well as assonance and that both should be preserved in translation. Such translations, while being gender-inclusive, stress the creature's organic connectedness with the earth ("earthling/earth,"[5] "earth creature/earth,"[6] "human/humus,"[7] "groundling/ground"[8]). A variant of this approach is Mieke Bal's "clod/earth" which retains the substance of the Hebrew nouns but not their assonance.[9]
3. those who preserve the gender-specific translation of "man" for *'adam* because they think that either:
   a. man's creation had priority over woman's and thus has ontological significance. Therefore it is theologically important to translate *'adam* as "man/male," or
   b. the author of Genesis 2 probably understood and intended *'adam* as "man/male."[10] Therefore this translation should be retained and recognized as one of the "irredeemable" androcentric aspects of the text.[11] It is worthy of note that in Genesis 4:25, the term *'adam* first appears without the definite article and can be understood as the proper noun, "Adam."

and breathed into his nostrils the breath of life; and the man became a living being: the Hebrew term *nephesh* ("being," NRSV) refers to the life force that distinguishes the living from the dead rather than the body/soul dichotomy of postbiblical thought. Translations such as the KJV confused the general understanding of this term by rendering it as "soul." At issue here is the claim, based in part on this verse, that only man (the *'adam* of v. 7a) has a soul. Note that animals also have *nephesh* (see Gen. 2:19).

[2.18a]*Then the LORD God said, "It is not good that the man should be alone"*: the Hebrew term *lo' tob* ("not good," NRSV) in Genesis 2 stands in sharp contrast to the sevenfold affirmation "it was good" of Genesis 1 (vv. 4, 10, 12, 18, 21, 25, 31). Moreover, in the seventh affirmation (v. 31), the deity declares that humankind is "very" good. This is a marked difference from the *'adam* of chapter 2 who is clearly deficient—in need of something.

"I will make him a helper as his partner": the Hebrew phrase *'ezer kenegdo* ("a helper as his partner," NRSV) raises two important translation issues. What is an *'ezer*, and how should one understand its connection to the term *kenegdo*?

The masculine noun *'ezer* is often traced to the root verb *'zr*, "to help." There is little agreement, however, as to how this term should be understood in relation to the *'adam*. For example:

1. Yes, *'ezer* means "helper." Since "helpers" are subordinate to those they help, the relationship between the *'adam* and the *'ezer* is unequal, the *'ezer* serving the *'adam*.[12]
2. Yes, *'ezer* means "helper." In other biblical passages the term refers to God (Pss. 33:20, 115:9-11, 121:2, 124:8; Exod. 18:4; Deut. 33:7, 26, 29) or a human prince or army (Ps. 146:3; Isa. 30:5; Ezek. 12:14; Dan. 11:34; Hos. 13:9) all of whom are superior in status to the ones they help. Therefore, the relationship between the *'adam* and the *'ezer* is unequal, the *'ezer* being superior to the *'adam*.
3. Yes, *'ezer* means "helper." By itself, however, the term denotes neither superiority nor inferiority.[13]
4. No, *'ezer* should not be translated "helper." Since the English term carries overtones of subordination not found in the Hebrew term, it is better to translate *'ezer* as either "companion" or "partner".[14]

Another approach is to argue that *'ezer* should not be traced to the root word *'zr* (to help) but *gre* (to be strong). Thus *'ezer* should be translated as "power" and the verse should read: "a power equal to him."[15]

Understanding the meaning of *'ezer kenegdo* is further compounded because the prepositional phrase *kenegdo* ("as his partner," NRSV) is a *hapax legomenon*—a phrase appearing only once in the entire Hebrew Bible. Juxtaposed with *'ezer* in v. 18, it is translated in a variety of ways: "a help *meet for him*" (KJV); "a helper *fit for him*" (RSV); "a partner *suited to him*" (NEB); "a power *equal to man*"[16]; "a helper *against him*"[17]; "a companion *corresponding to it*"[18]; "a help *as its counterpart*."[19]

In the above examples, *kenegdo* functions to clarify the relationship between the *'ezer* and the *'adam*. But as can be seen, there is a wide variety of opinions as to what *kenegdo* means. Indeed, its interpretation is as difficult as its translation. Some of the most commonly adopted positions are:

1. *kenegdo* should be understood as "less than," thus indicating that the *'ezer* is subordinate to the needs and desires of the *'adam*.
2. *kenegdo* should be understood as "parallel with" or "on a par with" or "corresponding to," thus indicating a mutual and nonhierarchical relationship between the *'ezer* and the *'adam*.
3. *kenegdo* should be understood as "greater than," indicating that the *'ezer* surpasses the *'adam*.
4. *kenegdo* means "against" or "in opposition to," thus indicating a tension between the *'ezer* and *kenegdo*, a tension inherent in all relations between the sexes.
5. *kenegdo* means simply a "complimentary creature," one who is like another (of the same species). It says nothing of the relationship between male and female.

Thus the translation and interpretation of *kenegdo* can affect how one understands the relationship between the *'ezer* and the *'adam*. Depending upon which of the above is adopted, this relationship can be viewed as: (1) subordinating the woman to the man, (2) subordinating the man to the woman, (3) affirming equality and mutuality between the sexes, or (4) indicating a relationship filled with inherent tension. Note that the phrase *'ezer kenegdo* is repeated in verse 20, where the reader is informed that no *'ezer kenegdo* for the *'adam* was found among the animals.

[2:21b-22a]*then he took one of his ribs and closed up its place with flesh. And the rib that the LORD God had taken from the man he made into a woman*: the Hebrew term *sela'* ("rib," NRSV) also means "side" (e.g., the tabernacle's side, Exod. 25-26; the Temple's side, 1 Kings 6:5; or a mountainside, 1 Sam. 16:13). Thus the term *sela'* gave rise to two traditions concerning woman's origins: (1) that she was fashioned out of a "rib" and (2) that she was taken/separated from the "side" of the *'adam*. (According to Bal, if *sela'* is understood as "side," then it might refer to "womb." As "feet" are euphemistic of "testicles" in the Hebrew Scriptures, so "side," Bal suggests, may be euphemistic for "belly" and thus refer to a womb and an "apparent reversal of sexual function."[20])

Two aspects of woman's creation—its order and its method—are often topics of discussion. If we understand *sela'* as rib, then it could be argued that woman was created *after* man, *from* man. While some assume that this makes woman's creation derivative and secondary, others suggest that the last can be first, and argue for the superiority of woman's creation. If we understand *sela'* as side or if we see in this verse sexual differentiation (the creation of man and woman from a single androgynous being), then we might conclude that this verse describes a simultaneous rather than sequential creation. Since neither the man's creation nor the woman's creation would then precede the other, neither man nor woman could argue for superiority based on the order of creation.[21]

For those who see in this verse the creation of woman (as opposed to the creation of man in 2:7), attention is sometimes drawn to the method by which God creates woman. While the verbal activity used to describe *'adam*'s creation employs pottery imagery, woman's creation utilizes the vocabulary of building/architecture. Bal, for example, concludes from this that woman's creation is on a higher level than man's—it is more difficult, more sophisticated, and requires more differentiated material.[22]

2:23 *Then the man said, "This at last is bone of my bones and flesh of my flesh*: the phrase "bone of my bones and flesh of my flesh" can be understood as a kinship formula or one that indicates a covenant or alliance. It is repeated in Genesis 29:14 when Jacob and his uncle Laban meet and recognize the bonds of blood that connect them.

"this one shall be called Woman, for out of Man this one was taken": in the Hebrew there is a word play between the terms *'ish* (man) and *'ishshah* (woman). Although these Hebrew words sound similar, they are not etymologically related (the word *'ishshah* is not derived from *'ish*). While there is no problem with the translation of these terms ("woman" and "man"), there is debate over the identification of the phrase, "this one shall be called woman." Does it reflect the word pattern associated with the act of naming (a "naming formula")? There are two clear positions on this question:

1. No, it is not a naming formula. A naming formula usually follows the pattern "X called his name Y" (subject + the verb "to call" [Heb: *qara*] + noun "name" [Heb: *shem*] + proper noun) (see also Gen. 4:17, 25, 26). Since the term "name" is missing in verse 23 and since the term "woman" is a common noun not a proper noun, then verse 23 does not contain a "naming formula."[23]
2. Yes, naming does take place. The action of naming does not necessarily follow the pattern described above (see Gen. 1). Moreover, since "woman" is a noun, not an adjective, it can function as a name even though it is not a proper noun.[24]

The significance of the above debate revolves around the implications of "naming." Naming, it is argued, implies domination in the ancient world.[25] If woman's naming takes place in verse 23b, then it might suggest that a hierarchical relationship existed between man and woman as part of the created order (not the result of their disobedience). If woman's naming by man does not take place until 3:20 ("The man named his wife Eve") then hierarchy can be seen as perversion of creation's original order.[26] It should be mentioned that not all scholars who find "naming" in 2:23 find "dominance." For them, naming simply indicates a discernment of the true nature of the thing named.

2:24 *Therefore a man leaves his father and his mother and clings to his wife, and they become one flesh*: the Hebrew term *l-ken* ("therefore," NRSV) often concludes an etiological tale (see, e.g., Gen. 11:9, 16:14). While some scholars see verse 24 as the logical conclusion to verses 18-23, others argue that the creation of woman is complete by verse 23 and that verse 24 should be viewed as a gloss (a secondary addition, an insert).[27] What is clear, in either case, is that the verse functions etiologically; in other words, it explains something. Just what it explains, however, is debatable. Some suggestions are:

1. Verse 24 explains the change of tribal identity connected with marriage.[28]
2. Verse 24 explains marriage as an institution (whether patriarchal/patrilocal or matriarchal/matrilocal is debated).

3. Verse 24 explains marriage as a personal experience (love/attraction).
4. Verse 24 explains love as a "force of nature" apart from any legal institution.[29]

2:25And the man and his wife were both naked, and were not ashamed: there is a word play in the Hebrew between the terms *'arummim* ("naked," NRSV) in 2:25 and *'arum* ("crafty," NRSV) in 3:1. For a continuation of the themes of nakedness see Genesis 3:7, 10, and 11.

The fact that "nakedness" brings no "shame" in verse 25 raises questions. How should we understand "nakedness"? If it indicates "powerlessness," then it might refer to a state of vulnerability/helplessness (yet unashamed of this fact).[30] If it refers to sexuality, then the absence of shame might indicate a lack of sexual awareness.

Sent from the Garden

Genesis 3 is the continuation of the Yahwist account in Genesis 2. While Genesis 2 centers on creation, Genesis 3 introduces the themes of disobedience and punishment. (Source: New Revised Standard Version of the Bible.)

Genesis 3:1–24

[3:1]Now the serpent was more crafty than any other wild animal that the LORD God had made. He said to the woman, "Did God say, 'You shall not eat from any tree in the garden'?" [2]The woman said to the serpent, "We may eat of the fruit of the trees in the garden; [3]but God said, 'You shall not eat of the fruit of the tree that is in the middle of the garden, nor shall you touch it, or you shall die.' " [4]But the serpent said to the woman, "You will not die; [5]for God knows that when you eat of it your eyes will be opened, and you will be like God, knowing good and evil." [6]So when the woman saw that the tree was good for food, and that it was a delight to the eyes, and that the tree was to be desired to make one wise, she took of its fruit and ate; and she also gave some to her husband, who was with her, and he ate. [7]Then the eyes of both were opened, and they knew that they were naked; and they sewed fig leaves together and made loincloths for themselves.

[8]They heard the sound of the LORD God walking in the garden at the time of the evening breeze, and the man and his wife hid themselves from the presence of the LORD God among the trees of the garden. [9]But the LORD God called to the man, and said to him, "Where are you?" [10]He said, "I heard the sound of you in the garden, and I was afraid, because I was naked; and I hid myself." [11]He said, "Who told you that you were naked? Have you eaten from the tree of which I commanded you not to eat?" [12]The man said, "The woman whom you gave to be with me, she gave me fruit from the tree, and I ate." [13]Then the LORD God said to the woman, "What is this that you have done?" The woman said, "The serpent tricked me, and I ate." [14]The LORD God said to the serpent,

"Because you have done this,
    cursed are you among all animals
    and among all wild creatures;
upon your belly you shall go,
    and dust you shall eat
    all the days of your life.
[15]I will put enmity between you and the woman,
    and between your offspring and hers;
he will strike your head,
    and you will strike his heel."

[16]To the woman he said,

"I will greatly increase your pangs in childbearing;
in pain you shall bring forth children,
yet your desire shall be for your husband,
    and he shall rule over you."

[17]And to the man he said,

"Because you have listened to the voice of your wife,
and have eaten of the tree about which I commanded you,
'You shall not eat of it,'
    cursed is the ground because of you;
    in toil you shall eat of it all the days of your life;
[18]thorns and thistles it shall bring forth for you;
    and you shall eat the plants of the field.
[19]By the sweat of your face you shall eat bread
    until you return to the ground,
        for out of it you were taken;
    you are dust,
        and to dust you shall return."

[20]The man named his wife Eve, because she was the mother of all living. [21]And the LORD God made garments of skins for the man and for his wife, and clothed them. [22]Then the LORD God said, "See, the man has become like one of us, knowing good and evil; and now, he might reach out his hand and take also from the tree of life, and eat, and live forever"—[23]therefore the LORD God sent him forth from the garden of Eden, to till the ground from which he was taken. [24]He drove out the man; and at the east of the garden of Eden he placed the cherubim and a sword flaming and turning to guard the way to the tree of life.

Commentary: Genesis 3:1–24

[3:1]*Now the serpent was more crafty than any other wild animal that the LORD God had made*: the difficulty with the Hebrew term *nahesh* ("serpent," NRSV) is not its translation but its interpretation. In the ancient Near East the serpent symbolized life, death, wisdom, nature, chaos, and fertility. It was only later, in postbiblical thought, that the serpent became identified as Satan or one of Satan's minions.

He said to the woman: the text contains no explanation of the serpent's motivations or why it addressed the woman first. Therefore, questions such as "Why did the serpent tempt Eve?" or "Why did it speak to her first?" cannot be answered from the text. Attempts to answer such questions (the serpent spoke to Eve first because she was more gullible, untrustworthy, or stupid than the man) are purely speculative and need to be recognized as such.

'You shall not eat from any tree of the garden': note that the Hebrew that stands behind the term "you" (NRSV) in this verse is the second person plural. This indicates that both man *and* woman are included in the command.

3:3 but God said, 'You shall not eat of the fruit of the tree that is in the middle of the garden, nor shall you touch it, or your shall die.' These are the first words spoken by the woman. Although she quotes Yahweh's command, her words do not match Yahweh's words in Genesis 2:16-17. Some readers view this discrepancy as significant, an indication of Eve's stupidity, immorality, or lack of confidence in God's words.[31] According to Bal, however, this "alleged error" simply indicates Eve's confusion of the tree of knowledge with the tree of life—an understandable mistake.[32]

The fact that it is the woman not the man who enters into a lengthy dialogue with the serpent is understood positively (Eve taking the initiative)[33] or negatively (Eve assuming the initiative properly belonging to Adam).

3:6 So when the woman saw that the tree was good for food, and that it was a delight to the eyes: the woman's first two observations concerning the tree deal with the senses (seeing, tasting). Because of this, some interpreters concluded that Eve (and thus all women) were inclined to the senses/sensual.

and the tree was desired to make one wise: frequently overlooked is the woman's third observation—that the tree could "make one wise"—from which one could conclude, using the same logic above, that Eve was also inclined to rational/intellectual pursuits.

she took of its fruit and ate; and she also gave some to her husband, who was with her, and he ate: the prepositional phrase *'immah* can be understood "with-her" if understood as having the attribute of a noun (see NRSV, KJV, Jerusalem Bible [JB], New Authorized Version [NAV]). If it is understood adverbially as "gave it to her husband [also]" then it does not have to be translated (see RSV, NEB, Vulgate/Douai). The former position is supported by the following narrative elements: (1) the woman is at the man's side at the end of Genesis 2 and the she is never said to have left, (2) the serpent reports the command in the plural and Eve answers using "we," and (3) the eyes of both are opened simultaneously (instead of the woman's first and then the man's).[34]

Adam's location during the dialogue between Eve and the serpent is significant in terms of his characterization. Since verse 17 contains a reference to Adam listening to Eve's voice, some conclude that Eve said (or did) something to persuade Adam. Thus parallels are made between the serpent's dialogue with Eve and this implied dialogue between Eve and Adam. From such speculation emerges the image of Eve (thus all women) as temptress luring Adam (thus all men) into disobedience. If Adam is portrayed as with Eve (the nominal understanding of *'immah*), then the image of Eve as tempter loses some of its credibility. An Adam by Eve's side looks more like a willing participant than an unsuspecting victim.

3:7Then the eyes of both were opened, and they knew that they were naked: speculation arose as to what "knowledge" resulted from Adam and Eve's eyes being "opened." Why is their reaction to their nakedness here different than in Genesis 2:25, where they are "not ashamed"? Frequently it was suggested that Adam and Eve either lost something (i.e., the clothing of glory that they originally wore, their virginity, their sexual innocence, their immortality) or else gained something (an awareness of their bodies).

3:12The man said, "The woman whom you gave to be with me, she gave me fruit from the tree, and I ate": when questioned by God, the man blames the woman for giving him the fruit and blames Yahweh for woman's creation.

3:13Then the LORD God said to the woman, "What is this that you have done?": these are God's first direct words to the woman. Before this, the woman was only implicitly addressed in the second person plural pronoun of the prohibition.

The woman said, "The serpent tricked me, and I ate": like the man, the woman evades responsibility for her actions by blaming another character—the serpent. Unlike the man, she does not blame God for creating the source of her temptation.

3:16To the woman he said, "I will greatly increase your pangs in childbearing: Yahweh's words begin with the infinitive absolute of the verb "to increase" which intensifies its meaning ("greatly increase," NRSV). There are problems, however, with the translation and syntax of the remaining words.

One point of debate surrounds the translation of the terms *issabon* and *heron*. The term *issabon* is usually translated "pain" or "toil." Since the term occurs again in man's punishment (v. 17) and is usually translated "toil" or "work" in that context, scholars like Meyers argue that it should be understood as "toil" in verse 16 as well.[35] Thus, according to Meyers, verse 16 describes childbirth as "hard work," but it does not mandate that it be "painful."

The term *heron* is more difficult to translate. If understood as coming from the Hebrew root *hry*, then it is translated "to conceive, become pregnant." Other suggestions are: (1) from the Hebrew root *hrr* (to tremble) or *hgy* (to groan), or (2) from the Ugaritic root *hrr* (to desire).[36]

The syntactical problem in this verse concerns the relationship between the two nouns *issabon* ("pangs," NRSV) and *heron* ("childbearing," NRSV). Are they independent concepts or does the second term modify the first (a hendiadys)? If they are separate concepts, then (depending on the translations of the terms) the phrase might read like this:

"your pains and your groaning" (LXX)
"your sorrows and your conceptions" (Vulgate [Vg], Peshitta [Pes])

"your labor and your groaning" (NEB)
"your toil and your pregnancies"[37]

If the second term modifies the first, the phrase might read like this:

"the pain of thy conception" (ICC)
"your pain in childbearing" (RSV)
"great labor in childbearing" (REB)
"the pangs of your childbearing" (NAV)
"your trouble in childbearing" (TEV)
"(I shall give you) intense pain in childbearing" (New Jerusalem Bible [NJB])

yet your desire shall be for your husband, and he shall rule over you: the Hebrew term *tesuqa* ("desire," NRSV), while fairly easy to translate, is much harder to understand. The term occurs in Song of Songs 7:11-14, where it refers to the man's "desire" for a woman. It also occurs in an enigmatic phrase in Genesis 4:7 ("its [sin's] desire is for you, but you can master it").

What constitutes woman's desire? Suggestions range widely: (1) sexual attraction for her husband, (2) psychological dependency on her husband, or (3) marital subservience (she desires whatever her husband desires).[38] While many translations underscore woman's subordination ("and he shall be your master" [NAB, NEB, AB (Authorized Bible)], "yet you will be subject to him" [TEV], "and he shall rule over you" [NJV], "he will dominate you [NJB]"), it is not clear as to whether verse 16 represents a disruption of, or a return to, the divine intent for male and female relationships. Some of the explanations of this verse include:

1. Verse 16 mandates women's subordination in the post-Edenic world as part of woman's punishment; gender hierarchy now becomes the norm in life after the "fall."
2. Verse 16 describes the gender relations of the writer's world, relations that are implicitly critiqued by the placement of this pronouncement in chapter 3 (life after disobedience) instead of chapter 2 (the ideal); the norm is represented by the egalitarian relationship of chapter 2 not the hierarchical one of chapter 3.
3. Woman's desire to control her husband (v. 16) is a departure from the subordinate position mandated by Genesis 2; the norm is subordination and verse 16 (read as resistance to that norm) signals the beginning of the war between the sexes. Thus the husband's rule is the natural order (not a punishment), and all verse 16 indicates is that now woman will fight it.
4. Verse 16 refers to a return to normalcy. Woman was created subordinate in Genesis 2 but reversed that order when she presumed to speak to the serpent. With the pronouncement in Genesis 3:16, God realigns the couple with the hierarchical ideal of Genesis 2.
5. Verse 16 represents a perversion of the divinely established order of benevolent hierarchy. While the norm is woman's subordination to her husband, verse 16 indicates that men's leadership of women will now be tyrannical rather than the benevolent protection ordained in chapter 2.

Adrien Bledstein offers a significant departure from the above options by suggesting, on the basis of the term's usage in Genesis 4:7, that *tesuqa* should be translated as "desirable" rather than "desire." Thus, the woman will be attractive/ desirable to her husband.[39] Nevertheless, for Bledstein, the end result of woman's subordination remains unchanged.

Bledstein's exegesis raises the issue of the relationship of Genesis 3:16 to Genesis 4:7. J. Oosten and David Moyer suggest that the enigmatic phrase in 4:7 (its [sin's] desire is for you, but you must master it) is out of place in the Cain story and originally belonged in Genesis 3:16. Such a reading would make the "desire" and "dominion" of verse 16 reciprocal. Woman's desire will be for her husband, and he will rule over her (v. 16b as it now stands), while man's desire shall be for his wife and she shall rule over him (adding the phrase from 4:7).[40]

One final remark before we leave verse 16: there is no curse formula in God's address to the woman (see the curse on the serpent in v. 14) nor is there a motivation clause explaining the cause for her punishment ("Because you have . . . "; see God's words to the serpent in v. 14 and to the man in v. 17).

[3:17]*And to the man he said, "Because you have listened to the voice of your wife, and have eaten of the tree"*: this is the only reference to any speech between Eve and Adam. According to Jean Higgins, this reference should be understood as an allusion to 3:12, where Adam blames both God and the woman for his plight. Whereas in verse 12 Adam evades responsibility, now he is forced to assume it—*you* listened and *you* ate.[41]

[3:20]*The man named his wife Eve.* Eve is the only character explicitly given a proper name in chapters 2 and 3. (See note on the differentiation of the sexes in Gen. 2:23 and the issue of "naming.") Trible sees this as witness to a break in the egalitarian relations of Genesis 2.[42] For Bal the naming of Eve marks the climax of her characterization—her fall into subordination is now complete.[43]

because she was the mother of all living. The Hebrew *hay* ("living," NRSV) is often understood as part of an honorific title: The Mother of all Living. Mary Phil Korsak, however, prefers to retain the Hebrew wordplay of verse 20: "The groundling called his woman's name Life (Eve) for she is the mother of all the living."[44] Korsak's translation retains the assonance between the Hebrew terms *hawwa* ("Eve," NRSV) and *hay* ("living," NRSV). She believes that, understood in this manner, Eve's name ("life") shows how Genesis "pays a great tribute to woman."[45] According to Bal, however, the name Eve/life reflects the "sexual and social role" of woman. Thus in giving her this particular name, the man determines that Eve will now be "imprisoned in motherhood."[46]

Life after Eden

Although many accounts of Eve's story stop with her expulsion from the garden, references to "Eve" (4:1) and Adam's "wife" (4:25) occur in Genesis 4 where life continues—east of Eden. (Source: New Revised Standard Version of the Bible.)

Genesis 4:1–2, 25

4:1Now the man knew his wife Eve, and she conceived and bore Cain, saying, "I have produced a man with the help of the LORD." 2Next she bore his brother Abel. Now Abel was a keeper of sheep, and Cain a tiller of the ground.

25Adam knew his wife again, and she bore a son and named him Seth, for she said, "God has appointed for me another child instead of Abel, because Cain killed him."

Commentary: Genesis 4:1–2, 25

4:1*Now the man knew his wife Eve*: the Hebrew verb *yada* (the root of "knew" NRSV) sometimes refers to sexual intimacy. Since the result of this "knowing" is the conception/birth of Cain, then its use in this verse may represent the first unambiguous sexual reference in Genesis. This is the second and last time the name "Eve" occurs in the Hebrew Scriptures (see Gen. 3:20 for the first reference).

and she conceived and bore Cain: Cain is the first child born in the Hebrew Scriptures. While the phrase "I will greatly increase," in Genesis 3:16a, implies that childbirth has already taken place, Cain's is the first birth explicitly mentioned.

"I have produced a man with the help of the LORD": the meaning and intent of Eve's declaration are not clear. Ilana Pardes identifies Eve's words as a "maternal naming speech" and emphasizes that, while Eve was the object of naming in 3:20, she now is the subject of her son's naming. As such, Pardes suggests that Eve now defines herself as a "creatress."[47]

Although the narrative provides no insight into Eve's emotional state as she speaks in verse 1, her "mood" is often supplied by commentators. U. Cassuto concludes, for example, that Eve's "joy at giving birth to her first son" prompts her to boast of "her generative power" that places her on par with the Divine Creator.[48] Isaac Kikawada, on the other hand, hears a note of humility behind Eve's words.[49]

4:2*Next she bore his brother Abel*: Abel is the second of three sons the Hebrew Scriptures ascribe to Eve.

4:25*and she bore a son and named him Seth: for she said, "God has appointed for me another child instead of Abel, because Cain killed him"*: these words signal the birth of Eve's third and final son, and are the last words recorded in Eve's "voice." As in verse 1, commentators often impute "mood" to these words. Cassuto, for example, insists that Eve's mood here is "one of mourning and calamity." While he notes the similarity of form and content between 4:1-2 and 4:25, he nevertheless insists that Eve's words in verse 25 are "uttered meekly with humility and modesty" in contrast to the joy and pride of verses 1-2.[50] Westermann, however, who hears Eve's "voice" in verses 1-2 as one of joy and praise (not inordinate pride), finds in verse 25 the same emotional note.[51] Pardes sees the change from verse 1 to 25 (Eve moves from an active to a more passive role in her child's naming) as evidence of Eve's "fall," for the "son who was the object of her (pro)creative pride turns out to be the destroyer of her creation."[52]

Adam's Descendants

Although the last mention of Eve by name occurs in Genesis 4:2, there is one final allusion to the first woman of Genesis 1:28 in Genesis 5:2 with its reference to the "male and female" created by God. (Source: New Revised Standard Version of the Bible.)

Genesis 5:1–5

[1]This is the list of the descendants of Adam. When God created humankind, he made them in the likeness of God. [2]Male and female he created them, and he blessed them and named them "Humankind" when they were created.

[3]When Adam had lived one hundred thirty years, he became the father of a son in his likeness, according to his image, and named him Seth. [4]The days of Adam after he became the father of Seth were eight hundred years; and he had other sons and daughters. [5]Thus all the days that Adam lived were nine hundred thirty years: and he died.

Commentary: Genesis 5:1–5

[5:1]*When God created humankind*: The *'adam* is translated "humankind" (NRSV) in recognition of its gender-inclusive content in this verse.

[5:1-2]*he made them in the likeness of God. [2]Male and female he created them*: an allusion to Genesis 1:27, this represents the last reference to the first woman in the Hebrew Scriptures.

he blessed them and named them "Humankind" when they were created: a naming formula indicating humankind's formal naming by Elohim.

[5:3]*Adam . . . became the father of a son in his likeness, according to his image*: note the similarity between this statement and Genesis 1:27. As God made humankind in God's image, so now it is Adam who fathers a son in his image. No mention is made of Eve.

[5:4]*and he had other sons and daughters*: these children are neither named or otherwise mentioned in the biblical text. The inclusion of "daughters" here is unusual because biblical genealogies often mention only sons.

[5:5]*and he died*: there is no comparable note in the Hebrew Scriptures marking the end of Eve's life.

NOTES TO CHAPTER I, SELECTIONS AND COMMENTARY

1. Claus Westermann, *Genesis 1-11: A Commentary* (Minneapolis: Augsburg, 1984), pp. 148-55.

2. Phyllis A. Bird, " 'Male and Female': Gen 1:27b in the Context of the Priestly Account of Creation," *Harvard Theological Review* (1981): 147-50.

3. David Clines, " 'What Does Eve Do to Help?' And Other Readerly Questions in the Old Testament," Journal for the Study of the Old Testament, Supplement Series 94 (Sheffield: JSOT Press, 1990), p. 38.

4. Bird, "Male and Female," p. 150.

5. Carol Meyers, *Discovering Eve: Ancient Israelite Women in Context* (New York: Oxford University Press, 1988), p. 81.

6. Phyllis Trible, *God and the Rhetoric of Sexuality* (Philadelphia: Fortress Press, 1978), p. 76.

7. Meyers, *Discovering Eve*, p. 82.

8. Mary Phil Korsak, "Genesis: A New Look," in Athalya Brenner, editor, *A Feminist Companion to Genesis* (Sheffield: JSOT Press, 1993), p. 47.

9. Mieke Bal, *Lethal Love: Feminist Literary Readings of Biblical Love Stories* (Bloomington: Indiana University Press, 1987), pp. 112-14.

10. David Jobling, "Myth and Limits in Gen. 2:4b-3:24," in *The Sense of Biblical Narrative: Structural Analyses in the Hebrew Bible* (Sheffield: JSOT Press, 1987), vol. 2, p. 41.

11. Clines, " 'What Does Eve Do,' " p. 40.

12. Clines, " 'What Does Eve Do,' " pp. 38-41.

13. Lyn M. Bechtel, "Rethinking the Interpretation of Genesis 2.4b-3.24," in Athalya Brenner, editor, *A Feminist Companion to Genesis* (Sheffield: JSOT Press, 1993), p. 113.

14. Trible, *God and the Rhetoric*, pp. 88-90.

15. R. David Freedman, "Woman, A Power Equal to Man," *Biblical Archeology Review* (1983): 56-58.

16. Freedman, "Woman," pp. 56-57.

17. Athalya Brenner, *The Israelite Woman: Social Role and Literary Type in Biblical Narrative* (Sheffield: JSOT Press, 1985), p. 126.

18. Mieke Bal, "Sexuality, Sin and Sorrow: The Emergence of the Female Character (A Reading of Genesis 1-3)," *Poetics Today* 6 (1985): 26.

19. Korsak, "Genesis: A New Look," p. 47.

20. Bal, "Sexuality, Sin and Sorrow," p. 27.

21. Trible, *God and the Rhetoric*, pp. 98-99.

22. Bal, "Sexuality, Sin and Sorrow," p. 27.

23. Trible, *God and the Rhetoric*, pp. 99-102.

24. Clines, " 'What Does Eve Do,' " pp. 38-39.

25. Gerhard von Rad, *Genesis: A Commentary*, The Old Testament Library (Philadelphia: Westminster Press, 1972), p. 83.

26. Trible, *God and the Rhetoric*, pp. 130-34.

27. Angelo Tosato, "On Genesis 2:24," *Catholic Biblical Quarterly* 52 (1990): 389-409.

28. A. F. L. Beeston, "One Flesh," *Vetus Testamentum* 36 (1986): 115-17.

29. Von Rad, *Genesis: A Commentary*, p. 85.

30. A. J. Hauser, "Genesis 2-3: The Theme of Intimacy and Alienation," in D. J. A. Clines et al., editors, *Art and Meaning: Rhetoric in Biblical Literature* (Sheffield: JSOT Press, 1982), p. 25.

31. R. W. L. Moberly, "Did the Serpent Get It Right?" *Journal of Theological Studies* 39 (1988): 7.

32. Bal, *Lethal Love*, pp. 121-22.

33. Mary Phil Korsak, "Eve, Malignant or Maligned," *Cross Currents* 44 (1994-95): 458.

34. Jean M. Higgins, "The Myth of the Temptress," *Journal of the American Academy of Religion* 44 (1976): 645-47.

35. Meyers, *Discovering Eve*, pp. 95-121.

36. See the discussion of C. Rabin and M. Dahood's association of *heron* with the Ugaritic term *hrr* meaning "sexual desire" in David Toshio Tsumura, "A Note on *heron* (Gen 3,16)," *Biblica* 75 (1994): 398-400.

37. Meyers, *Discovering Eve*, p. 105.

38. Susan T. Foh, "What Is the Woman's Desire?" *Westminster Theological Journal* 37 (1974-75): 376-77.

39. Adrien Janis Bledstein, "Was Eve Cursed?" *Bible Review* 9 (1993): 44-45.

40. J. Oosten and David Moyer, "De mythisch omkering; een analyse van de sociale code van de scheppingsmythen van Genesis 2:4b-11" as discussed in Bal, "Sexuality, Sin and Sorrow," p. 37.

41. Higgins, "Myth of the Temptress," pp. 644-45.

42. Trible, *God and the Rhetoric*, pp. 133-34.

43. Bal, "Sexuality, Sin and Sorrow," pp. 38-40.

44. Korsak, "Genesis: A New Look," p. 41.

45. Korsak, "Genesis: A New Look," p. 49.

46. Bal, *Lethal Love*, p. 128.

47. Ilana Pardes, "Beyond Genesis 3," *Hebrew University Studies in Literature and the Arts* 9 (1989): 168-75.

48. U. Cassuto, *A Commentary on the Book of Genesis* (Jerusalem: Magnes Press, 1961), p. 201.

49. Isaac M. Kikawada. "Two Notes on Eve," *Journal of Biblical Literature* 91 (1972): 35.

50. Cassuto, *A Commentary*, pp. 245-46.

51. Westermann, *Genesis 1-11*, p. 338.

52. Pardes, "Beyond Genesis 3," p. 187.

CHAPTER TWO

Jewish Postbiblical Interpretations
(200S BCE–200 CE)

INTRODUCTION

Jewish literature from 200 BCE to 200 CE reflects an interest in Eve and Adam far beyond that found in the Hebrew Scriptures. Writings of the Apocrypha (Deuterocanon) and Pseudepigrapha (c. 200 BCE-200 CE) and of such intellectuals as Philo (c. 20 BCE-50 CE) and Josephus (c. 37-100 CE) retell, expand, and comment on Genesis 1-5. While many support hierarchical readings that subordinate Eve to Adam, others offer a more ambiguous, or at least less negative, interpretation of the first woman/Eve.

Philo's Eve: Woman in Need of a Master

The most pejorative presentation of Eve in this period is found in the writings of Philo of Alexandria. Philo's treatment of Eve is riddled with damning observations about women:

1. Woman is the beginning of man's trouble (*Opificio Mundi* [*Op.*] 151).
2. Mortality is the result of sexual desire, and sexual desire is the result of woman (*Op.* 151-52).
3. Rather than bringing Life (as her name seems to indicate), Eve brought Adam's death (*Quis Rerum Divinarum Heres sit* [*Heres*] 52).
4. Woman rules over death and vile things (*Quaestiones et Solutiones in Genesin* [*QG*] 1.37).

5. Woman is more accustomed to deception (*QG* 1.33) and thus more easily deceived (*QG* 1.46).
6. Woman is less honorable than man (*QG* 1.27).
7. Man's sin was that he gave up his rightful position as master to subordinate himself to woman (*Op.* 165).
8. The created order is hierarchical, the woman being subordinate to the man (*Op.* 165).

Two elements of Philo's treatment of Genesis 1-3 are particularly important for our interest in gender issues: his treatment of the two creation accounts in Genesis 1-2 and his allegory of Adam and Eve in Genesis 2-3. According to Philo, Genesis 1-2 provides two creation accounts because there were two creations (*Op.* 134). The first creation (Gen. 1) described a noncorporeal, spiritual being made in the image of God (*Op.* 69). The second account (Gen. 2) detailed the origin of man/male, the corporeal being (*Heres* 138-39). Thus the woman, who comes from man, has secondary ontological status. She is two steps removed (being both corporeal and female) from the immortal image of God found in Genesis 1.[1]

Philo also explored the allegorical (that is, symbolic) dimensions of Genesis 2-3. According to Philo, Adam and Eve were archetypes of the husband/wife relation. Since hierarchy stabilized marriage[2] then Adam's sin was that he upset the normal balance of gender relations by leaving his family (Gen. 2:24) and by listening to his wife (Gen. 3:17) (*Legum Allegoriae* [*LA*] 3.222-45).

Genesis 1-3 also represented for Philo an allegory of the tripartite individual: (1) Adam = mind/rationality, (2) Eve = sense perception/irrationality, and (3) the serpent = pleasure (*Op.* 165). Philo arranged these elements in a hierarchy with the mind foremost (followed by sense perception and pleasure). Although sense perception has value for Philo (*LA* 2.7ff), it is clearly inferior to the mind (*LA* 3.222). Since sense perception needs supervision so that pleasure will not dominate it, it is the mind's responsibility to see that this control is achieved (*LA* 2.49ff).

Eve's Account: The Rest of the Story

In contrast to Philo, the *Apocalypse of Moses* (chaps. 15-30) provides readers with a more sympathetic image of Eve. In these chapters, Eve tells her side of the story. It is a story that, as John Levison notes, exonerates Eve in a number of ways:[3]

1. Eve is given authority to present her own autobiography.
2. Eve is a victim of Satan's deception—he appears to her as an angel and sings hymns to God (17.1-2).
3. Twice Eve resists Satan because she is afraid (18.2 and 6).
4. Eve takes an oath to give Adam the fruit and, although she wants to break it, she stands by her word (19.1-2; 20.3).
5. When Eve speaks to Adam, it is not she but Satan who speaks instead (21.3).

6. Satan entered the Garden through Adam's portion, which was left unguarded (15.1-3).
7. Eve relates God's words without adding the command about touching the tree, and thus gets the command "correct" (17.5).
8. Rather than accuse Eve to God, Adam asks Eve about her actions (23.4-5).
9. Adam accepts sole responsibility for the disobedience (27.1).

Since the image of Eve in chapters 15 through 30 of the *Apocalypse of Moses* differs radically from the one in chapters 1 through 14 and 31 through 51 (where Eve is repeatedly denigrated), Levison suggests that chapters 15 through 30 were originally independent from their current context. The importance of this, according to Levison, is significant:

> What results from reading *Apoc. Mos* 15-30 independently? It is a fresh hearing of a voice sympathetic to the first woman which was long obscured by its negative context. Contemporary analyses of the Apocalypse of Moses invariably point out that Eve is blamed for the primeval sin. . . . Obviously, the predominance of negative statements about Eve in the Apocalypse of Moses has blocked from these contemporary authors' view the positive evaluation of Eve contained in her testament.[4]

Adam and Eve's Disobedience

No other source from this period presents Eve in such a sustained sympathetic light as that found in the *Apocalypse of Moses* 15-30. Nevertheless, the contemporary reader, so conditioned to hearing Eve blamed for the "original sin" of all humankind, will be surprised at the lack of consensus in this period concerning: (1) the nature of humankind's disobedience (what they did wrong), (2) the significance of the disobedience (what happened as a result), and (3) the party primarily responsible (who was to blame).

Twentieth-century readers are familiar with the idea that humankind's first "sin" involved either the desire for sex or the desire for knowledge. While the roots of these explanations are clearly visible in the writings of this period, there is a remarkable lack of consensus as to whether or not desire for knowledge (sexual or otherwise) was humankind's disobedience. In *Jubilees*, for example, Adam "knows" (has intercourse with) Eve before they enter the Garden (3.6) and thus before they disobeyed God (3.20-22). A different sequence of events is found in 2 *Baruch* 56.5-6 where the conception of children and the passion of parents are a result (not cause) of humankind's first disobedience. Nor did all see the thirst for wisdom as the motivating factor behind Adam and Eve's disobedience. The writer of Sirach, for example, describes knowledge and wisdom as God's gifts. Although linked to creation, they are not something forbidden to humankind and acquired through stealth (17:7 and 11).

One explanation of humankind's disobedience, largely unknown to twentieth-century readers, is its identification with drunkenness. In *3 Baruch* (Slavonic), for example, various angels are responsible for planting the Garden's trees (i.e., Michael, the olive; Uriel, the nut; 4.7). The vine is planted by the angel Satanael and is identified with "sinful desire." Thus eating the fruit (of the vine) is understood as the excessive drinking of wine (*3 Bar.* 4.8, 17).

As ancient writers speculated on what the first couple did wrong, so they commented on the significance of that disobedience. While many viewed it as catastrophic for all creation, there was little agreement as to what that catastrophe entailed. Suggestions raised by writers were quite diverse: moral corruption (*Vita Adae et Evae* [*VAE*] 44); change of diet (*VAE* 1-4); sorrow (*VAE* 47; *Apoc. Mos.* 39); loss of dominion (*Apoc. Mos.* 11.1-2) and glory (*Apoc. Mos.* 21.6); loss of the animals' ability to talk (*Jub.* 3.28); loss of spiritual joy (*VAE* 10.4); disruption of the natural world (*4 Ezra* 7.11-12; *2 Bar.* 56.6); pain and illness (*VAE* 34.1-3; *Apoc. Mos.* 8.2; *2 Bar.* 56.6); death (*VAE* 26.2; *Apoc. Mos.* 14.2-3); and ultimately God's judgment by water and fire (*VAE* 49.3).

Viewing death as punishment (*VAE* 26.2; *Apoc. Mos.* 14.2-3), however, presupposed that humankind was originally created immortal, an assumption not shared by writers such as Sirach and Josephus. For Sirach, death was part of the natural order, not a divine punishment (33:7-13; 41:3-4; but see 25:24 for a different view). For Josephus, it was not death per se that was humankind's punishment, but an early or untimely death. Thus, as a result of Adam and Eve's disobedience, humankind's longevity (not their immortality) was curtailed (*Ant.* 1.46) (see also *2 Bar.* 17.2-3, 56.6).

Moreover, instead of Adam and Eve's disobedience resulting in moral/ inherited corruption (*VAE* 44), the writers of Sirach, *4 Ezra*, and *2 Baruch* suggested that individual free will and moral responsibility were functional in life after Eden (Sir. 15:11-20; *2 Bar* 54.15-19; *4 Ezra* 7.19-24; 8.55-62; 14.34; but for an exception to this see *4 Ezra* 3.21-22, 25-26; 7.62-72).

Not surprisingly, since there was little consensus on either the nature or significance of the disobedience, writers of this period also disagreed on who they held ultimately responsible. While the writer of *1 Enoch* presented Adam and Eve as equally culpable (98.4ff), other writers focused on Eve as the primary culprit (*VAE* 3.1). In support of Eve's culpability, Sirach 25:24 is often cited as the first mention of Eve's sin and the death it brought upon humankind. (Scholars such as Jack Levison, however, question whether the "woman" referred to in this verse is really Eve. Other candidates, Levison suggests, might be the "bad" wife of the surrounding verses, or the "daughters of men" in Genesis 6:1-4.[5] Other selections in this chapter make Adam primarily responsible for human suffering. It was Adam's "evil heart" that made the post-Edenic world what it was (*4 Ezra* 3:20-26). Or, it was Adam's drunkenness that stood behind the first disobedience (*3 Bar.* 4.8). Still others looked to the snake as the ultimate culprit in Genesis 3. It was envy (Wis. 2:24) or the desire for revenge (*Apoc. Mos.* 16; *VAE* 12-17) that prompted the serpent to approach Eve. Thus, it is the serpent (understood as Satan or Satan's minion) that is ultimately to blame for the Garden catastrophe.

A few writers went beyond Genesis 1-3 to find their foundational myth of human suffering. Genesis 6:1-4, with its report of the intermarriage of the sons of God with the daughters of men, became crucial for the traditions preserved in *Jubilees* (5.1-11; 10.1-5) and *1 Enoch* (6-11).

Eve and Jewish Women in Postbiblical Judaism

It is difficult to reconstruct how images of this period's Eve influenced Jewish women's daily lives. In part this is due to the heterogeneous nature of Judaism in this period. Indeed, the approaches to Eve's story presented in this chapter's selections, in some ways, reflect the variety of this period's Judaisms. As Tal Ilan remarks:

> In the Second Temple period Jewish society was highly heterogeneous. Different groups lived by different versions of Jewish law. *Tannaitic halakhah* was not fully adhered to in that period, both because it was not yet fully developed, part of it being written after the destruction of the Temple, and because only a particular group attempted to live by it before the Destruction. After the Destruction, adherence to *tannaitic halakhah* did not become more widespread, despite the disappearance of many other competing groups.[6]

None of the selections in this chapter had the lasting effect on Judaism that the Talmud and Midrash would make (200-600 CE; see the next chapter of this book). This is not to say, however, that the writings in this chapter had no impact, either on their immediate audience, or on subsequent generations. The fact that they were written, in itself, points to their writers' attempts to shape women's lives through Eve's story. While we do not know the immediate effect of Philo's Eve on women's lives, for example, we do know that she was more widely received by Hellenistic Judaism than by Rabbinic Judaism. We also know that Christians accepted Philo's Eve, and that later Maimonides resurrected it for his medieval Jewish audience.[7] Moreover, the influence of works such as the *Life of Adam and Eve* would be immortalized for future generations in the words of John Milton's *Paradise Lost* (see chapter six of this book).

Background to the Selections

The works collected in this chapter can be grouped into three broad categories: (1) Apocrypha/Deuterocanon (Sirach, 2 Esdras [= *4 Ezra*]); (2) Pseudepigrapha (*Jubilees*, *2 Baruch*, *1 Enoch*, *Life of Adam and Eve/Apocalypse of Moses*); and (3) Jewish Philosophers and Historians (Philo, Josephus).

The term Apocrypha (also called Deuterocanon) refers to the thirteen works contained in old Greek manuscripts of the Old Testament (*Codex Vaticanus*, *Codex Sinaiticus*, and *Codex Alexandrinus*) but not found in the Hebrew text (*Biblia Hebraica*). These works date from about 300 BCE to 70 CE and were considered by many Jews during this period to be authoritative. They were part of the Christian Old Testament until the sixteenth century when Martin Luther and subsequent Protestants rejected them as noncanonical. At the Council of Trent (1546), the Roman Catholic Church affirmed their inspired status, labeling them the Deuterocanon ("second canon").[8]

The term "pseudepigrapha" is a term used by scholars to refer to a contemporary grouping of ancient texts. James H. Charlesworth suggests the following criteria as guidelines for including works in this collection:

> First, the work must be at lest partially, and preferably totally, Jewish or Jewish Christian. Second, it should date from the period 200 B.C. to A.D. 200. Third, it should claim to be inspired. Fourth, it should be related in form or content to the Old Testament. Fifth, it ideally is attributed to an Old Testament figure, who often claims to be the speaker or author.[9]

Since the Pseudepigrapha represents a type of biblical interpretation, Charlesworth also identifies the various ways that pseudepigraphical material relates to the biblical text:

> 1. *Inspiration.* The Old Testament serves primarily to inspire the author, who then evidences considerable imagination, perhaps sometimes under influences from nonbiblical writings (ranging from the *Books of Enoch* to the *Arda Viraf*).
>
> 2. *Framework.* The Old Testament provides the framework for the author's own work. The original setting of the Old Testament work is employed for appreciably other purposes.
>
> 3. *Launching.* A passage or story in the Old Testament is used to launch another, considerably different reflection. The original setting is replaced.
>
> 4. *Inconsequential.* The author borrows from the Old Testament only the barest facts, names especially, and composes a new story.
>
> 5. *Expansions.* Most of these documents, in various ways and degrees, start with a passage or story in the Old Testament, and rewrite it, often under the imaginative influence of oral traditions linked somehow to the biblical narrative.[10]

Of the works treated in this chapter, five are commonly included in collections of Pseudepigrapha: *Jubilees, 1 Enoch, 2 Baruch, Life of Adam and Eve*, and the *Apocalypse of Moses*.

Besides selections from the Apocrypha/Deuterocanon and the Pseudepigrapha, this chapter also contains material from two Jewish intellectuals of the first century CE: the soldier turned historian, Flavius Josephus (whose Jewish name was Joseph ben Mattathias); and the philosopher, Philo of Alexanderia (sometimes called Philo Judaecus). Of Philo's many writings, three in particular are important for his treatment of Genesis 1-3: *De Opificio Mundi* 24-25, 64-88, 134-69; *Legum Allegoriae* 1.31-42, 2.4+; and *Quaestiones et Solutiones in Genesin*. Since our space is limited, only portions from the last are presented in this chapter.

Although the selections in this chapter represent a broad range of literary genre, they have one thing in common—a fascination with Genesis 1-3 and the significance of Adam and Eve's story.

NOTES TO CHAPTER 2, INTRODUCTION

1. Philo did not read the phrase "male and female" in Genesis 1:27c as the conclusion to v. 27 a and b, but as the beginning of a new idea. One must keep in mind that the punctuation we have today for the Septuagint was not in place in the first century CE. Judith Romney Wegner, "Philo's Portrayal of Women—Hebraic or Hellenic?" in Amy-Jill Levine, editor, *"Women Like This": New Perspectives on Jewish Women in the Greco-Roman World*, Society of Biblical Literature: Early Judaism and Its Literature, 1 (Atlanta: Scholars Press, 1991), p. 45.

2. According to Philo, each gender had its appropriate role and sphere of activity: husbands that of activity, leadership, and the public realm; and wives that of passivity, obedience, and the home (*QG* 1.26).

3. John Levison, "The Exoneration of Eve in the Apocalypse of Moses 15-30," *Journal for the Study of Judaism in the Persian, Hellenistic and Roman Period* 20 (1978): 135-50.

4. John Levison, "The Exoneration of Eve," p. 150.

5. Jack Levison, "Is Eve to Blame? A Contextual Analysis of Sirach 25:24," *Catholic Biblical Quarterly* 47 (1985): 617-23.

6. Tal Ilan, *Jewish Women in Greco-Roman Palestine* (Peabody, Mass.: Hendrickson, 1996), p. 228.

7. Daniel Boyarin, *Carnel Israel: Reading Sex in Talmudic Culture* (Berkeley: University of California Press, 1993), pp. 31-106.

8. James H. Charlesworth, "Apocrypha," in David Noel Freedman, editor, *The Anchor Bible Dictionary* (New York: Doubleday, 1992), vol. 1, pp. 292-94.

9. James H. Charlesworth, *LXX: The Pseudepigrapha and Modern Research*, Septuagint and Cognate Studies 7 (Ann Arbor: Scholars Press, 1981), p. 21.

10. James H. Charlesworth, "In the Crucible: The Pseudepigrapha as Biblical Interpretation," in D. R. G. Beattie and M. J. McNamara, editors, *The Aramaic Bible: Targums in Their Historical Context*, Journal for the Study of the Old Testament, Supplement Series 166 (Sheffield: JSOT Press, 1994), p. 29.

APOCRYPHA (DEUTEROCANON)
AND PSEUDEPIGRAPHA

1 Enoch

The tradition in Genesis 5:24 that Enoch did not die gave rise to much speculation. *1 Enoch* (sometimes referred to as the *Ethiopic Book of Enoch*) is the oldest of the three pseudepigraphs that bear Enoch's name and reflect this speculation. *1 Enoch* is a composite work, stemming from at least five authors and periods: The Astronomical Book (chaps. 72-82, c. 200s BCE); The Book of the Watchers (chaps. 1-36, c. 200s BCE); Epistle of Enoch (chaps. 91-107, c. 170

BCE); The Book of Dreams (chaps. 83-90, date uncertain); and The Book of Parables (chaps. 37-71, date uncertain). Our selection (32.3-6) is taken from the second oldest section, The Book of the Watchers. This book describes the angels' disobedience (chaps. 6-11, based on Genesis 6:1-4) and Enoch's two angelically guided journeys throughout creation (chaps. 17-19 and 20-36).

In the passage below (32.3-6), Enoch (on his journey to the East) visits a beautiful garden that his angelic companion Raphael identifies as Eden. Neither Adam nor Eve is singled out for blame in Raphael's comments concerning the first couple. Moreover, the only punishment associated with their disobedience is their expulsion from the Garden. (Source: "*1 Enoch*," translated by E. Isaac, in James H. Charlesworth, editor, *The Old Testament Pseudepigrapha*, Garden City, N.Y.: Doubleday, 1983, vol. 1, p. 28.)

1 Enoch 1–36 (c. 200s BCE)

32.3–6

32.3And I came to the garden of righteousness and saw beyond those trees many (other) large (ones) growing there—their fragrance sweet, large ones, with much elegance, and glorious. And the tree of wisdom, of which one eats and knows great wisdom, (was among them). 4It looked like the colors of the carob tree, its fruit like very beautiful grape clusters, and the fragrance of this tree travels and reaches afar. 5And I said, "This tree is beautiful and its appearance beautiful and pleasant!" 6Then the holy angel Raphael, who was with me, responded to me and said, "This very thing is the tree of wisdom from which your old father and aged mother, they who are your precursors, ate and came to know wisdom; and (consequently) their eyes were opened and they realized that they were naked and (so) they were expelled from the garden."

Sirach

Sirach (also known as Ben Sira or Ecclesiasticus) is the longest and one of the oldest books in the Apocrypha (Deuteroncanon). Patterned after the book of Proverbs, it contains observations about life presented in various wisdom forms (e.g., proverbs). According to its prologue, it was written in Hebrew by the translator's grandfather (Ben Sira) and later translated into Greek by the grandson (c. 132 BCE). The purpose of Sirach is to address the clash of cultures (Hellenism versus Judaism) experienced by the writer's second-century audience.

Although the selections below mention neither Adam nor Eve explicitly, they represent a discussion of concepts that are often associated with Genesis 1-3. The first two passages (15:11-20; 17:1-10) emphasize wisdom as God's gift, human free will, and death as part of the natural order. These emphases stand in tension with those of later writers who identified the sin of the Garden as the desire for wisdom, and the punishment for that sin as moral corruption and death. The last selection below (25:16-26) makes a causal connection between woman, sin, and death. Whether or not the "woman" to which the author refers is Eve, or the "evil wife" of the surrounding verses, or even the "daughters of men" of Genesis 6:1-4, however, is not clear. If it refers to Eve, then this is the earliest post-Genesis association of Eve with the entrance of sin and death into the world. (Source: New Revised Standard Version of the Bible.)

Sirach (c. 180 BCE)

15:11–20

^{15:11}Do not say, "It was the Lord's
        doing that I fell away";
    for he does not do what he hates.
¹²Do not say, "It was he who led me astray";
    for he has no need of the sinful.
¹³The Lord hates all abominations;
    such things are not loved by
        those who fear him.
¹⁴It was he who created humankind
        in the beginning,
    and he left them in the power
        of their own free choice.
¹⁵If you choose, you can keep the commandments,
    and to act faithfully is a matter
        of your own choice.
¹⁶He has placed before you fire and water;
    stretch out your hand for
        whichever you choose.
¹⁷Before each person are life and death,
    and whichever one chooses will be given.
¹⁸For great is the wisdom of the Lord;
    he is mighty in power and sees everything;
¹⁹his eyes are on those who fear him,
    and he knows every human action.
²⁰He has not commanded anyone to be wicked,
    and he has not given anyone
        permission to sin.

17:1–11

^{17:1}The Lord created human beings out of earth,
    and makes them return to it again.
²He gave them a fixed number of days,
    but granted them authority
        over everything on the earth.
³He endowed them with strength like his own,

and made them in his own image.
⁴He put the fear of them in all living beings,
    and gave them dominion over beasts and birds.
⁶Discretion and tongue and eyes,
    ears and a mind for thinking he gave them.
⁷He filled them with knowledge and understanding,
    and showed them good and evil.
⁸He put the fear of him into their hearts
    to show them the majesty of his works.
¹⁰And they will praise his holy name,
    ⁹to proclaim the grandeur of his works.
¹¹He bestowed knowledge upon them,
    and allotted to them the law of life.

25:16–26

²⁵:¹⁶I would rather live with a lion
    and a dragon than live with an evil woman.
¹⁷A woman's wickedness changes her appearance,
    and darkens her face like that of a bear.
¹⁸Her husband sits among the neighbors,
    and he cannot help sighing bitterly.
¹⁹Any iniquity is small compared to a woman's iniquity;
    may a sinner's lot befall her!
²⁰A sandy ascent for the feet of the aged—
    such is a garrulous wife to a quiet husband.
²¹Do not be ensnared by a woman's beauty,
    and do not desire a woman for her possessions.
²²There is wrath and impudence and great disgrace
    when a wife supports her husband.
²³Dejected mind, gloomy face,
    and wounded heart come from an evil wife.
  Drooping hands and weak knees
    come from the wife who does
        not make her husband happy.
²⁴From a woman sin had its beginning,
    and because of her we all die.
²⁵Allow no outlet to water,
    and no boldness of speech to an evil wife.
²⁶If she does not go as you direct,
    separate her from yourself.

Jubilees

The book of *Jubilees*, written sometime in the second century BCE, is one of
the earliest Jewish pseudepigraphs from the Second Temple period. Based on
an alleged revelation from the Angel of the Presence to Moses at Mt. Sinai
(1:29–2:1), the book retells the biblical account found in Genesis 1:1 to

Exodus 12:50. Much of the creative and editorial activity in *Jubilees* can be understood as a response to second century threats to Judaism (by overt acts such as those of Antiochus IV Ephiphanes and by more covert pressures exerted on Judaism by the surrounding Hellenistic culture). The author counters Hellenistic influence by emphasizing the Jewish Law and calendar and by focusing on Israel's ancestors as models of virtue. Thus in *Jubilees*, the Garden becomes holy ground (and the foundation for the purity legislation in Leviticus 12), Adam becomes a virtuous ancestor who performs priestly functions, and the Genesis 6:1-4 story (with its mixture of humans and angels) becomes the arch sin of the angelic hosts and the cause for humankind's ongoing misery.

The selections below are "rewritten" portions of Genesis 1-4 that differ from the biblical text in significant ways. Some of the differences that concern gender issues are: God's command to "be fruitful and multiply" is missing (2.14); dominion is granted to Adam only (2.14); Adam realizes his loneliness upon seeing the animals in pairs (3.3); Eve's creation takes place outside of the garden (3.5-9); Adam and Eve have sex before entering the garden (3.6); marriage is given ontological status (3.6); the laws of women's impurity are linked to creation (3.8-14); Eve's "shame" requires cover (3.21); Eve covers herself before giving Adam the fruit (3.21); the laws against nudity are linked to Adam and Eve's expulsion (3.31); Eve has two daughters, 'Awan (4.1) and 'Azurah (4.8); and Eve bears Adam a total of fourteen children (4.1-10). (Sources: "*Jubilees*," translated by O. S. Wintermute, in James H. Charlesworth, editor, *The Old Testament Pseudepigrapha*, Garden City, N.Y.: Doubleday, 1985, vol. 2, pp. 55-61.)

Jubilees (c. mid-100s BCE)

2.1, 13–16

[2.1]And the angel of the presence spoke to Moses by the word of the LORD, saying, "Write the whole account of creation, that in six days the LORD God completed all his work and all that he created. And he observed a sabbath the seventh day, and he sanctified it for all ages. And he set it (as) a sign for all his works."

[13]And on the sixth day he made all of the beasts of the earth and all of the cattle and everything which moves upon the earth. [14]And after all of this, he made man—male and female he made them—and he gave him dominion over everything which was upon the earth and which was in the seas and over everything which flies, and over beasts and cattle and everything which moves upon the earth or above the whole earth. And over all this he gave him dominion. And these four kinds he made on the sixth day. [15]And the total was twenty-two kinds. [16]And he completed all of his work on the sixth day, everything which is in the heavens and the earth and the seas and the depths and in the light and in the darkness and in every place.

3.1–35

^{3.1}And in six days of the second week, by the word of the LORD, we brought to Adam all of the beasts, and all of the cattle, and all of the birds, and everything which moves on the earth, and everything which moves in the water, each one according to its kind, and each one according to its likeness: the beasts on the first day, and cattle on the second day, and the birds on the third day, and everything which moves upon the earth on the fourth day, and whatever moves in the water on the fifth day. ²And Adam named all of them, each one according to its name, and whatever he called them became their names. ³And during these five days Adam was observing all of these, male and female according to every kind which was on the earth, but he was alone and there was none whom he found for himself, who was like himself, who would help him.

⁴And the LORD said to us, "It is not good that the man should be alone. Let us make for him a helper who is like him." ⁵And the LORD our God cast a deep sleep upon him, and he slept. And he took one bone from the midst of his bones for the woman. And that rib was the origin of the woman from the midst of his bones. And he built up the flesh in place of it, and he constructed a woman.

⁶And he awakened Adam from his sleep, and when he awoke, he stood up on the sixth day. And he brought her to him and he knew her and said to her, "This is now bone of my bone and flesh from my flesh. This one will be called my wife because she was taken from her husband."

⁷Therefore a man and woman shall be one. And therefore it shall be that a man will leave his father and his mother and he will join with his wife and they will become one flesh.

⁸In the first week Adam was created and also the rib, his wife. And in the second week he showed her to him. And therefore the commandment was given to observe seven days for a male, but for a female twice seven days in their impurity.

⁹And after forty days were completed for Adam in the land where he was created, we brought him into the garden of Eden so that he might work it and guard it. And on the eighth day his wife was also brought in. And after this she entered the garden of Eden. ¹⁰And therefore the command was written in the heavenly tablets for one who bears, "If she bears a male, she shall remain seven days in her impurity like the first seven days. And thirty-three days she shall remain in the blood of her purity. And she shall not touch anything holy. And she shall not enter the sanctuary until she has completed these days which are in accord with (the rule for) a male (child). ¹¹And that which is in accord with (the rule for) a female is two weeks—like the two first weeks—in her impurity. And sixty-six days she shall remain in the blood of her purity. And their total will be eighty days."

¹²And when she finished those eighty days, we brought her into the garden of Eden because it is more holy than any land. And every tree which is planted

in it is holy. [13]Therefore the ordinances of these days were ordained for anyone who bears a male or female that she might not touch anything holy and she might not enter the sanctuary until these days are completed for a male or female. [14]This is the law and testimony which is written for Israel so that they might keep it always.

[15]And during the first week of the first jubilee Adam and his wife had been in the garden of Eden for seven years tilling and guarding it. And we gave him work and we were teaching him to do everything which was appropriate for tilling. [16]And he was tilling. And he was naked, but he neither knew it nor was he ashamed. And he was guarding the garden from the birds and beasts and cattle and gathering its fruit and eating. And he used to set aside the rest for himself and his wife. And what was being guarded he set aside.

[17]At the end of seven years which he completed there, seven years exactly, in the second month on the seventeenth day, the serpent came and drew near to the woman. And the serpent said to the woman, "The LORD commanded you, saying, 'You shall not eat from any tree which is in the garden.' " [18]And she said to him, "The LORD said, 'Eat from all of the fruit of the trees which are in the garden.' But the LORD said to us, 'You shall not eat from the fruit of the tree which is in the midst of the garden, and you shall not touch it lest you die.' " [19]And the serpent said to the woman, "It is not (true) that you shall surely die because the LORD knows that on the day you eat of it your eyes will become opened and you will become like gods, and you will know good and evil."

[20]And the woman saw the tree that it was pleasant and it was pleasing to the eye and its fruit was good to eat and she took some of it and she ate. [21]And she first covered her shame with a fig leaf, and then she gave it to Adam and he ate and his eyes were opened and he saw that he was naked. [22]And he took a fig leaf and sewed it and made an apron for himself. And he covered his shame.

[23]And the LORD cursed the serpent and he was angry with it forever. And he was angry with the woman also because she had listened to the voice of the serpent and had eaten. And he said to her, [24]"I will surely multiply your grief and your birth pangs. Bear children in grief. And to your husband is your return and he will rule over you." [25]And to Adam he said, "Because you listened to the voice of your wife and you ate from that tree from which I commanded you that you should not eat, the land shall be cursed because of you. Thorns and thistles shall sprout up for you. And eat your bread in the sweat of your face until you return to the earth from which you were taken because you are earth and to the earth you will return."

[26]And he made for them garments of skin and he dressed them and sent them from the garden of Eden. [27]And on that day when Adam went out from the garden of Eden, he offered a sweet-smelling sacrifice—frankincense, galbanum, stacte, and spices—in the morning with the rising of the sun from the day he covered his shame. [28]On that day the mouth of all the beasts and cattle and birds and whatever walked or moved was stopped from speaking because all of them used to speak with one another with one speech and one

language. ²⁹And he sent from the garden of Eden all of the flesh which was in the garden of Eden and all of the flesh was scattered, each one according to its kind and each one according to its family, into the place which was created for them. ³⁰But from all the beasts and all the cattle he granted to Adam alone that he might cover his shame. ³¹Therefore it is commanded in the heavenly tablets to all who will know the judgment of the Law that they should cover their shame and they should not be uncovered as the gentiles are uncovered.

³²And on the first of the fourth month Adam and his wife went out from the garden of Eden and dwelt in the land of 'Elda, in the land of their creation. ³³And Adam named his wife Eve. ³⁴They had no son until the first jubilee but after this he knew her. ³⁵And he tilled the land as he had been taught in the garden of Eden.

4.1–2, 7–10

^{4.1}And in the third week in the second jubilee, she bore Cain. And in the fourth she bore Abel. And in the fifth she bore 'Awan, his daughter. ²And at the beginning of the third jubilee, Cain killed Abel because the sacrifice of Abel was accepted, but the offering of Cain was not accepted.

⁷And Adam and his wife were mourning four weeks of years on account of Abel. And in the fourth year of the fifth week they rejoiced. And Adam again knew his wife and she bore a son for him. And he named him Seth because he said, "The LORD has raised up another seed for us upon the earth in place of Abel because Cain killed him." ⁸And in the sixth week he begat 'Azura, his daughter.

⁹And Cain took his sister, 'Awan, as a wife, and she bore for him Enoch at the end of the fourth jubilee. And in the first year of the first week of the fifth jubilee, buildings were constructed in the land. And Cain built a city and he named it with the name of his son, Enoch. ¹⁰And Adam knew Eve, his wife, and she bore nine more children.

Wisdom of Solomon

Written in Greek by a Hellenized Jew in Alexandria, the Wisdom of Solomon defends the intellectual dimension of Jewish faith against the "pagan" faith of the Egyptians. The work, often classified as an "exhortation" (a protreptic), is divided into three parts: Wisdom and immortality (1:1-6:21), Solomon and his quest for Wisdom (6:22-10:21), and Wisdom and the Exodus (11-19). Our selection is from the first section, and concludes a diatribe in which the ungodly speak for themselves. Two important themes of the book are the immortality of the soul and the nature of (and quest for) Sophia (Wisdom).

In the selection below (2:21-25), we have the earliest biblical references to the devil and Genesis 3, and "envy" as a motive for the devil's actions. The passage also blames the devil, rather than Adam and Eve, for the entry of death into the world. (Source: New Revised Standard Version of the Bible.)

Wisdom of Solomon (c. 30s BCE–100 CE)

2:21–25

²:²¹Thus they reasoned,
      but they were led astray,
     for their wickedness blinded them,
²³and they did not know
     the secret purposes of God,
  nor hoped for the wages of holiness,
   nor discerned the prize for blameless souls;
²⁴for God created us for incorruption,
      and made us in the image of his own eternity,
²⁵but through the devil's envy
      death entered the world,
  and those who belong to his company
     experience it.

2 Esdras

2 Esdras 3–14 is a Jewish apocalypse composed of seven visions (3:1–5:20; 5:21–6:34; 6:35–9:25; 9:26–10:59; 11–12; 13; 14). Set in the fictional world of sixth-century Babylonia, it uses the Babylonian defeat of Jerusalem and the destruction of the Temple in 587 BCE as a literary vehicle to address the Roman defeat of Jerusalem and the Temple's destruction in 70 CE.

In the selection below (3:20–26), Adam's "evil heart" (not Eve's) is blamed for his transgression. Like Adam, Adam's descendants also have this "evil heart" and transgress. (Source: New Revised Standard Version of the Bible.)

2 Esdras 3–14 [4 Ezra] (c. 100 CE)

3:20–26

³:²⁰"Yet you did not take away their evil heart from them, so that your law might produce fruit in them. ²¹For the first Adam, burdened with an evil heart, transgressed and was overcome, as were also all who were descended from him. ²²Thus the disease became permanent; the law was in the hearts of the people along with the evil root; but what was good departed, and the evil remained. ²³So the times passed and the years were completed, and you raised up for yourself a servant, named David. ²⁴You commanded him to build a city for your name, and there to offer you oblations from what is yours. ²⁵This was done for many years; but the inhabitants of the city transgressed, ²⁶in every-

thing doing just as Adam and all his descendants had done, for they also had the evil heart.

2 Baruch

2 Baruch (otherwise known as the *Syriac Apocalypse of Baruch*) is a second-century CE pseudepigraph written in response to the destruction of Jerusalem in 70 CE. Like 2 Esdras 3-14 (*4 Ezra*), 2 Baruch is set within a sixth-century BCE story world. This fictional setting is the vehicle through which the author addresses the Roman defeat of Jerusalem and the Temple's destruction in 70 CE. The question of inherited corruption versus moral choice and responsibility is one of the book's key themes.

The first two of the four selections below suggest that, although Adam's disobedience ushered in death and other physical ills (described in detail in 56.6), it did not take away individual moral choice and responsibility. The third selection describes the "dark waters" of catastrophe unleashed on the world as a result of Adam's actions. Although conversant with Eve's part in the disobedience (see 48.42) the author focuses primarily on Adam. In the eschatological vision contained in the fourth selection, the "dark waters" give way to the "bright waters" as the punishments given to the man and woman in Genesis 3 are rescinded. (Source: "2 Baruch," translated by A. F. J. Klijn, in James H. Charlesworth, editor, *The Old Testament Pseudepigrapha*, Garden City, N.Y.: Doubleday, 1983, vol. 1, pp. 637, 640, 646.)

2 Baruch (c. early 100s CE)

48.42-47

[48.42]And I answered and said:

O Adam, what did you do to all who were born after you? And what will be said of the first Eve who obeyed the serpent, [43]so that this whole multitude is going to corruption? And countless are those whom the fire devours.

[44]But again I shall speak before you.

[45]You, O Lord, my Lord, you know that which is in your creation, [46]for you commanded the dust one day to produce Adam; and you knew the number of those who are born from him and how they sinned before you, those who existed and who did not recognize you as their Creator. [47]And concerning all of those, their end will put them to shame, and your Law which they transgressed will repay them on your day.

54.13-19

[54.13]For with your counsel, you reign over all creation which your right hand has created, and you have established the whole fountain of light with yourself, and you have prepared under your throne the treasures of wisdom. [14]And those who do not love your Law are justly perishing. And the torment of judgment will fall upon those who have not subjected themselves to your power. [15]For, although Adam sinned first and has brought death upon all who were not in his own time, yet each of them who has been born from him has prepared for himself the coming torment. And further, each of them has chosen for himself the coming glory. [16]For truly, the one who believes will receive reward.

[17]But now, turn yourselves to destruction, you unrighteous ones who are living now, for you will be visited suddenly, since you have once rejected the understanding of the Most High. [18]For his works have not taught you, nor has the artful work of his creation which has existed always persuaded you. [19]Adam is, therefore, not the cause, except only for himself, but each of us has become our own Adam.

56.6–9

[56.6]For when he transgressed, untimely death came into being, mourning was mentioned, affliction was prepared, illness was created, labor accomplished, pride began to come into existence, the realm of death began to ask to be renewed with blood, the conception of children came about, the passion of the parents was produced, the loftiness of men was humiliated, and goodness vanished. [7]What could, therefore, have been blacker and darker than these things? [8]This is the beginning of the black waters which you have seen. [9]And from these black waters again black were born, and very dark darkness originated.

73.7–74.4

[73.7]And women will no longer have pain when they bear, nor will they be tormented when they yield the fruits of their womb.

[74.1]And it will happen in those days that the reapers will not become tired, and the farmers will not wear themselves out, because the products of themselves will shoot out speedily, during the time that they work on them in full tranquillity. [2]For that time is the end of that which is corruptible and the beginning of that which is incorruptible. [3]Therefore, the things which were said before will happen in it. Therefore, it is far away from the evil things and near to those which do not die. [4]Those are the last bright waters which have come after the last dark waters.

Life of Adam and Eve

The *Life of Adam and Eve* is preserved in both a Latin text (*Vita Adae et Evae*) and a Greek text (known also as the *Apocalypse of Moses*). Although dated as late as the fourth century CE, the tradition behind them is usually located within the first two centuries of the common era.

In the passage from the Latin text below (chaps. 30-44), a dying Adam recounts to his children his expulsion from Eden, and commissions Eve and Seth to return there for some oil from the tree of mercy. The subsequent trip is a disaster: a serpent bites Seth on the way, and when Eve and Seth arrive the angels refuse them pain relief for Adam. Some of the significant developments concerning Eve's characterization are: the blaming of Eve for Adam's pain (by Eve 35.2-3; 37.2; by the beast/serpent 38.1-3; and by Adam 44.1-2); the addressing of Adam, not Eve, by the divine speakers (41.1-43.3); and the emphasis on Seth's identity as the "image of God" (37.3; 39.2-3) and "man of God" (41.2) while no such favorable epithet is used of Eve. This characterization, when combined with the rest of the work, serves to elevate the status of the male characters (Adam/Seth) while lowering that of the female (Eve).

In our second selection (chaps. 15-30 of the Greek text [*Apocalypse of Moses*]), Eve presents her account of the first couple's expulsion from Eden. Its sympathetic portrayal of Eve (see the discussion in the general introduction to this chapter) stands in contrast to her imaging in the surrounding materials. Moreover, there is no parallel to these chapters in the tradition's Latin version. (Source: "*Life of Adam and Eve*," translated by M. D. Johnson, in James H. Charlesworth, editor, *The Old Testament Pseudepigrapha* Garden City, N.Y.: Doubleday, 1985, Vol. 2, pp. 270-87.)

Life of Adam and Eve (c. late 100s–400 CE)

Latin Text, Vita Adae et Evae, *30–44*

30.1 After Adam had lived 930 years, he knew his days were at an end and therefore said, "Let all my sons be gathered to me, that I may bless them before I die, and speak with them." 2 And they assembled in three parts in his sight at the oratory where they used to worship the LORD God. 3 And they asked him, "What is it with you, Father, that you should gather us together? And why are you lying on your bed?" 4 And Adam answered and said, "My sons, I am sick with pains." And all his sons said to him, "What is it, Father, to be sick with pains?"

31.1 Then his son Seth said, "Lord, perhaps you have longed for the fruit of Paradise of which you used to eat, and that is why you are lying in sadness. 2 Tell me and I will go to the vicinity of the entrances to Paradise 3 and will put dust on my head and throw myself to the ground before the gates of Paradise and mourn with great lamentation, entreating the LORD. Perhaps he will hear me and send his angel to bring me the fruit which you desire." 4 Adam answered and said, "No, my son, I do not long for (that); but I have weakness and great pain in my body." 5 Seth responded, "What is pain, O lord Father? I do not know; do not hide it from us, but tell us."

32.1 And Adam answered and said, "Listen to me, my sons. When God made us, me and your mother, and placed us in Paradise and gave us every tree bearing fruit to eat, he forbade us (saying), 'Regarding the tree of the knowledge of good and evil, which is in the midst of Paradise, do not eat of it.' 2 Moreover, God gave a part of Paradise to me and (a part) to your mother. The trees of the eastern part and over against the north he gave to me, and to your mother he gave the southern and western parts.

^{33.1}"The LORD God appointed two angels to guard us. ²The hour came when the angels ascended to worship in the presence of God. ³Immediately the adversary, the devil, found opportunity while the angels were away and deceived your mother so that she ate of the illicit and forbidden tree. And she ate and gave to me.

^{34.1}"And immediately the LORD God was angry with us and the LORD said to me, 'Because you have forsaken my commandment and have not kept my word which I set for you, behold, I will bring upon your body seventy plagues; ²you shall be racked with various pains, from the top of the head and the eyes and ears down to the nails of the feet, and in each separate limb.' ³These he considered to be the scourge of pain from one of the trees. Moreover, the LORD sent all these to me and to all our generations."

^{35.1}Adam said this to all his sons while he was seized with great pains, and he cried out with a loud voice, saying, "Why should I suffer misery and endure such agony?" ²And when she saw him weeping, Eve herself began to weep, saying, "O LORD, my God, transfer his pain to me, since it is I who sinned." ³And Eve said to Adam, "My lord, give me a portion of your pain, for this guilt has come to you from me."

^{36.1}And Adam said to Eve, "Rise and go with my son Seth to the regions of Paradise and put dust on your heads and prostrate yourselves to the ground and mourn in the sight of God. ²Perhaps he will have mercy and send his angel to the tree of his mercy, from which flows the oil of life, and will give you a little of it with which to anoint me, that I might have rest from these pains by which I am wasting away."

^{37.1}And Seth and his mother went toward the gates of Paradise; and while they were walking, behold suddenly there came a serpent, a beast, and attacked and bit Seth. ²And when Eve saw it, she cried out and said, "Woe is me for I am cursed, since I have not kept the command of the LORD. ³And Eve said to the serpent in a loud voice, "Cursed beast! How is it that you were not afraid to throw yourself at the image of God, but have dared to attack it? And how were your teeth made strong?"

^{38.1}The beast answered in a human voice, "O Eve, is not our malice against *you*? Is not our fury against *you*? ²Tell me, Eve, how was your mouth opened that you ate of the fruit which the LORD God commanded you not to eat? ³Now, however, are you not able to bear it if I begin to reproach you?"

^{39.1}Then Seth said to the beast, "May the LORD God rebuke you. Stop; be quiet; close your mouth, cursed enemy of truth, chaotic destroyer. ²Stand back from the image of God until the day when the LORD God shall order you to be brought to judgment." ³And the beast said to Seth, "See, I stand back from the presence of the image of God, as you have said." Immediately he left Seth, who was wounded by (his) teeth.

^{40.1}But Seth and his mother walked toward the regions of Paradise for the oil of mercy, to anoint the sick Adam. ²And they arrived at the gates of Paradise, took dust from the earth, and put it on their heads, prostrated themselves to the ground on their faces and began to mourn with loud sighs, ³begging the

LORD God to pity Adam in his pains and to send his angel to give them the oil from the tree of mercy.

[41.1]But when they had prayed and entreated for many hours, behold, the angel Michael appeared to them, saying, "I have been sent to you from the LORD; I have been set by the LORD over the bodies of men. [2]I say to you, Seth, man of God, do not weep, praying and begging for the oil of the tree of mercy to anoint your father Adam for the pains of his body.

[42.1]Truly I say to you that you are by no means able to take from it, except in the last days.

[43.1]But you, Seth, go to your father Adam, for the span of his life is completed. [2]Six days from now his soul shall leave the body; and as it leaves, you shall see great wonders in heaven and on the earth and in the lights of heaven." [3]Having said this, Michael immediately withdrew from Seth. [4]And Eve and Seth turned back and brought with them aromatics, namely, nard, crocus, calamine, and cinnamon.

[44.1]And when Seth and his mother reached Adam, they told him how the beast, the serpent, bit Seth. [2]And Adam said to Eve, "What have you done? You have brought upon us a great wound, transgression and sin in all our generations. [3]And you shall relate what you have done to your children after my death, for those who rise up from us shall labor, not being adequate, but failing, and they shall curse us, saying, [4]'Our parents who were from the beginning have brought upon us all evils.' " [5]When Eve heard this she began to weep and groan.

Greek text, **Apocalypse of Moses, *15–30***

[15.1]Then Eve said to them, "Listen, all my children and my children's children, and I will tell you how our enemy deceived us. [2]It happened while we were guarding Paradise, each his portion allotted from God. Now I was watching in my share, the South and West, [3]and the devil came into Adam's portion, where the male animals were, since God divided the animals among us, and all the males he gave to your father, and all the females to me, and each of us kept his own.

[16.1]"And the devil spoke to the serpent, saying, 'Rise and come to me, and I will tell you something to your advantage.' [2]Then the serpent came to him, and the devil said to him, 'I hear that you are wiser than all the beasts; so I came to observe you. I found you greater than all the beasts, and they associate with you; but yet you are prostrate to the very least. [3]Why do you eat of the weeds of Adam and not of the fruit of Paradise? Rise and come and let us make him to be cast out of Paradise through his wife, just as we were cast out through him.' [4]The serpent said to him, 'I fear lest the LORD be wrathful to me.' [5]The devil said to him, 'Do not fear; only become my vessel, and I will speak a word through your mouth by which you will be able to deceive him.'

[17.1]"And immediately he suspended himself from the walls of Paradise about the time when the angels of God went up to worship. Then Satan came in the form of an angel and sang hymns to God as the angels. ²And I saw him bending over the wall, like an angel. ³And he said to me, 'Are you Eve?' And I said to him, 'I am.' And he said to me, 'What are you doing in Paradise?' I replied, 'God placed us to guard it and eat from it.' ⁴The devil answered me through the mouth of the serpent, 'You do well, but you do not eat of every plant.' ⁵And I said to him, 'Yes, we eat from every plant except one only, which is in the midst of Paradise, concerning which God commanded us not to eat of it, else *you shall most surely die.*'

¹⁸·¹"Then the serpent said to me, 'May God live! For I am grieved over you, that you are like animals. For I do not want you to be ignorant; but rise, come and eat, and observe the glory of the tree.' ²And I said to him, 'I fear lest God be angry with me, just as he told us.' ³He said to me, 'Fear not; for at the very time you eat, *your eyes will be opened and you will be like gods, knowing good and evil.* ⁴But since God knew this, that you would be like him, he begrudged you and said, "Do not eat of it." ⁵But come to the plant, and see its great glory.' ⁶And I turned to the plant and saw its great glory. And I said to him, 'It is pleasing to consider with the eyes'; yet I was afraid to take of the fruit. And he said to me, 'Come, I will give it to you. Follow me.'

¹⁹·¹"And I opened (the gate) for him, and he entered into Paradise, passing through in front of me. After he had walked a little, he turned and said to me, 'I have changed my mind and will not allow you to eat.' He said these things, wishing in the end to entice and ruin me. And he said to me, 'Swear to me that you are giving (it) also to your husband.' ²And I said to him, 'I do not know by what sort of oath I should swear to you; however, that which I do know I tell you: By the throne of the LORD and the cherubim and the tree of life, I shall give (it) also to my husband to eat.' ³When he had received the oath from me, he went, climbed the tree, and sprinkled his evil poison on the fruit which he gave me to eat which is his covetousness. For covetousness is the origin of every sin. And I bent the branch toward the earth, took of the fruit, and ate.

²⁰·¹"And at that very moment my eyes were opened and I knew that I was naked of the righteousness with which I had been clothed. ²And I wept saying, 'Why have you done this to me, that I have been estranged from my glory with which I was clothed?' ³And I wept also about the oath. But that one came down from the tree and vanished. ⁴I looked for leaves in my region so that I might cover my shame, but I did not find (any) from the trees of Paradise, since while I ate, the leaves of all the trees of my portion fell, except (those) of the fig tree only. ⁵And I took its leaves and made for myself skirts; they were from the same plants of which I ate.

²¹·¹"And I cried out with a loud voice, saying, 'Adam, Adam, where are you? Rise, come to me and I will show you a great mystery.' ²And when your father came, I spoke to him unlawful words of transgression such as brought us down from great glory. ³For when he came, I opened my mouth and the devil was speaking, and I began to admonish him, saying, 'Come, my lord

Adam, listen to me and eat of the fruit of the tree of which God told us not to eat from it, and you shall be as God.' ⁴Your father answered and said, 'I fear lest God be angry with me.' And I said to him, 'Do not fear; for as soon as you eat, you shall know good and evil.' ⁵Then I quickly persuaded him. He ate, and his eyes were opened, and he also realized his nakedness. ⁶And he said to me, 'O evil woman! Why have you wrought destruction among us? You have estranged me from the glory of God.'

²²·¹"And in the same hour we heard the archangel Michael sounding his trumpet, calling the angels, saying, ²'Thus says the LORD, "Come with me into Paradise and hear the sentence which I pronounce on Adam." ' ³And as we heard the archangel sounding the trumpet, we said, 'Behold, God is coming into Paradise to judge us.' We were afraid and hid. And God returned to Paradise, seated on a chariot of cherubim, and the angels were praising him. When God came into Paradise, all the plants, both of the portion of Adam and also of my portion, bloomed forth and were established. ⁴And the throne of God was made ready where the tree of life was.

²³·¹"And God called Adam, saying, 'Adam, where did you hide, thinking that I would not find you? Can a house hide from its builder?' ²Then your father answered and said, 'O LORD, we are not hiding thinking that we would not be discovered by you, but rather I am afraid because I am naked, and I stood in awe of your might, O LORD.' ³God said to him, 'Who showed you that you are naked, unless you have forsaken my commandment which I delivered to you to keep?' ⁴Then Adam remembered the word which I spoke to him, when I wanted to deceive him, 'I will make you safe from God.' ⁵And he turned and said to me, 'Why have you done this?' And I also remembered the word of the serpent, and I said, 'The serpent deceived me.'

²⁴·¹"God said to Adam, 'Because you transgressed my commandment and listened to your wife, cursed is the ground in your labors. ²For when you work it, it will not give its strength; *it shall yield you brambles and thistles* and *with sweat on your brow shall you eat your bread*. You will suffer many a hardship:

> You will grow weary and not rest;
> >   be afflicted with bitterness and not taste sweetness;
> ³be oppressed by heat and burdened by cold;
> >   you will toil much and not gain wealth;
> >   you will grow fat and finally not be.

⁴And the animals over which you ruled will rise up against you in disorder, because you did not keep my commandment.'

²⁵·¹"Turning to me, the LORD said to me, 'Since you have listened to the serpent and ignored my commandment, you shall suffer birth pangs and unspeakable pains; ²with much trembling you shall bear children and on that occasion you shall come near to lose your life from your great anguish and pains, ³and you shall confess and say "LORD, LORD, save me and I will never again turn to the sin of the flesh." ⁴And by this, according to your word I will

judge you, because of the enmity which the enemy has placed in you. And yet you shall turn again to your husband, and he shall rule over you.'

26.1"And after he had told me these things, he spoke to the serpent in great wrath, saying to him, 'Since you have done this and become an ungrateful vessel, so far as to lead astray the careless of heart, *accursed* are you *beyond all wild beasts.* ²You shall be deprived of the food which you used to eat, and shall *eat dust every day of your life. You shall crawl on your belly* and you shall be deprived of your hands as well as your feet. ³There shall be left for you neither ear nor wing nor one limb of all that with which you enticed (them) in your depravity and caused them to be cast out of Paradise. ⁴And I will put enmity between you and his seed; he shall beware of your head and you his heel until the day of judgment.'

27.1"Having said these things, he ordered his angels to cast us out of Paradise. ²While we were being expelled and lamenting, your father Adam begged the angels, 'Let me be a little while so that I may beseech God that he might have compassion and pity me, for I alone have sinned.' ³And they ceased driving him out. And Adam cried out with weeping and said, 'Forgive me, LORD, what I have done.' ⁴Then the LORD said to his angels, "Why have you stopped driving Adam out of Paradise? Is the guilt mine, or did I judge badly?' ⁵Then the angels fell on the ground and worshiped the LORD, saying, 'You are righteous, LORD, and you judge uprightly.'

28.1"And the LORD turned and said to Adam, 'From now on I will not allow you to be in Paradise.' ²And Adam answered and said, 'LORD, give me from the tree of life that I might eat before I am cast out.' ³Then the LORD spoke to Adam, 'You shall not now take from it; for it was appointed to the cherubim and the flaming sword which turns to guard it because of you, that you might not taste of it and be immortal forever, but that you might have the strife which the enemy has placed in you. ⁴But when you come out of Paradise, if you guard yourself from all evil, preferring death to it, at the time of the resurrection I will raise you again, and then there shall be given to you from the tree of life, and you shall be immortal forever.'

29.1"When the LORD had said these things, he ordered us cast out of Paradise. ²And your father wept before the angels opposite Paradise, and the angels said to him, "What do you want us to do for you, Adam?' ³Your father answered and said to the angels, 'See, you are casting me out; I beg you, let me take fragrances from Paradise, so that after I have gone out, I might bring an offering to God so that God will hear me.' ⁴And they came to God and said, 'Jael, eternal king, command that fragrant incenses from Paradise be given to Adam.' ⁵And God ordered Adam to come that he might take aromatic fragrances out of Paradise for his sustenance. ⁶When the angels allowed him, he gathered both kinds: crocus, nard, reed, cinnamon; and other seeds for his food. And he took these and went out of Paradise. And (so) we came to be on the earth.'

30.1"Now then, my children, I have shown you the way in which we were deceived. But you watch yourselves so that you do not forsake the good."

JEWISH PHILOSOPHERS AND HISTORIANS

Philo of Alexandria

Philo (20 BCE-50 CE) was a wealthy member of the Jewish community in Alexandria, Egypt. He received a classical Greek education and is a good example of Hellenistic Diaspora Judaism.

The selections below are taken from Philo's exegetical commentary on Genesis. Arranged in a question-and-answer format, this commentary reveals what types of questions concerned first-century CE readers of Genesis. Within his answers, Philo's use of allegory unfolds to reveal his belief that Adam, Eve, and the serpent are symbolic of the tripartite individual (man representing soul/intellect; woman representing body/emotion; and the serpent representing pleasure). (Source: Philo, *Questions and Answers on Genesis*, translated by Ralph Marcus, Loeb Classical Library: Philo, Supplement 1, Cambridge, Mass.: Harvard University Press, 1953.)

Quaestiones et Solutiones in Genesin (C. 20S–40S CE)
PHILO

1.26 (Gen. 2:22) Why does Scripture call the likeness of the woman "a building"?

The harmonious coming together of man and woman and their consummation is figuratively a house. And everything which is without a woman is imperfect and homeless. For to man are entrusted the public affairs of state; while to a woman the affairs of the home are proper. The lack of her is ruin, but her being near at hand constitutes household management.

1.27 (Gen. 2:21) Why was not woman, like other animals and man, also formed from earth, instead of the side of man?

First, because woman is not equal in honour with man. Second, because she is not equal in age, but younger. Wherefore those who take wives who have passed their prime are to be criticized for destroying the laws of nature. Third, he wishes that man should take care of woman as of a very necessary part of him; but woman, in return, should serve him as a whole. Fourth, he counsels man figuratively to take care of woman as of a daughter, and woman to honour man as a father. And this is proper; for woman changes her habitation from her family to her husband. Wherefore it is fitting and proper that one who receives something should in return show goodwill to those who have given it, but one (i.e., the woman) who has made a change should give to him who has taken her the honour which she showed those who begot her. For man has a wife entrusted to him as a deposit from her parents, but woman (takes a husband) by law. . . .

1.29 (Gen. 2:24) Why does (Scripture) say, "Wherefore man shall leave his father and mother, and cleave to his wife, and they shall be two in one flesh?"

(Scripture) commands man to act toward his wife with the most extreme exaggeration in partnership, so that he may endure to abandon even his parents. Not as though this is proper, but as though they would not be causes of goodwill to the wife. And most excellent and careful was it not to say that the woman should leave her parents and be joined to her husband—for the audacity (of man) is bolder than the nature of woman—but that for the sake of woman man is to do this. Since with a very ready and prompt impulse he is brought to a concord of knowledge. Being possessed and foreseeing the future, he controls and stills his desires, being fitted to his spouse alone as if to a bridle. And especially because he, having the authority of a master, is to be suspected of arrogance. But woman, taking the rank of servant, is shown to be obedient to his life. But when Scripture says that the two are one flesh, it indicates something very tangible and sense-perceptible, in which there is suffering and sensual pleasure, that they may rejoice in, and be pained by, and feel the same things and, much more, may think the same things. . . .

1.33 (Gen. 3:1) Why does the serpent speak to the woman and not to the man?

In order that they may be potentially mortal he deceives by trickery and artfulness. And woman is more accustomed to be deceived than man. For his judgment, like his body, is masculine and is capable of dissolving or destroying the designs of deception; but the judgment of woman is more feminine, and because of softness she easily gives way and is taken in by plausible falsehoods which resemble the truth. Accordingly, since in old age the serpent casts off his skin from the top of his head to his tail, by casting it, he reproaches man, for he has exchanged death for immortality. From his bestial nature he is renewed and adjusts himself to different times. Seeing this, she was deceived, though she ought to have looked, as if at an example, at him who practiced stratagems and trickery, and to have obtained ageless and unfading life. . . .

1.37 (Gen. 3:6) Why does the woman first touch the tree and eat of its fruit, and afterwards the man also take of it?

According to the literal meaning the priority (of the woman) is mentioned with emphasis. For it was fitting that man should rule over immortality and everything good, but woman over death and everything vile. In the allegorical sense, however, woman is a symbol of sense and man, of mind. Now of necessity sense comes into contact with the sense-perceptible; and by the participation of sense, things pass into the mind; for sense is moved by objects, while the mind is moved by sense. . . .

1.43 (Gen. 3:8) Why, when they hid themselves from the face of God, was not the woman, who first ate of the forbidden fruit, first mentioned, but the man; for (Scripture) says "Adam and his wife hid themselves"?

It was the more imperfect and ignoble element, the female, that made a beginning of transgression and lawlessness, while the male made the beginning of reverence and modesty and all good, since he was better and more perfect. . . .

1.45 (Gen. 3:9) Why does He, who knows all things, ask Adam, "Where art thou?", and why does He not also ask the woman?

The things said appear to be not a question but a kind of threat and reproach: where art thou now, from what good hast thou removed thyself, O man!; giving up immortality and a blessed life, thou hast gone over to death and unhappiness, in which thou hast been buried. But the woman He did not consider it fitting to question, although she was the beginning of evil and led him (man) into a life of vileness. But this passage also has a more apt allegory. For the sovereign and ruling element in man, having reason, when it listens to anyone, introduces the vice of the female part also, that is, perception. . . .

1.49 (Gen. 3:16) Why does the curse on the woman consist of an increase in sorrow and lamentation and in giving birth in pain and in turning to her husband and being under his rule?

This experience comes to every woman who lives together with a man. It is (meant) not as a curse but as a necessity. But symbolically the senses of man have difficult labours and suffering, being treated badly and scourged by domestic ills. And these are the offspring of sense: seeing, of the organ of sight; hearing, of the organ of hearing; smelling, of the nostrils; tasting, of the organ of taste; contact, of the organ of touch. And since the life of the worthless and evil man is sorrowful and necessitous, it is necessary that whatever is acted upon by sense should be mixed with fear and suffering. But according to the deeper meaning, there takes place a turning of sense to the man, not as to a helper, for it is a subject of no worth, but as to a master, since it prizes force more than righteousness.

Josephus

Josephus (c. 37-100 CE) (otherwise known by his Hebrew name, Joseph ben Mattathias or his Roman name, Flavius Josephus) was general of the Jewish forces in Palestine during the war with Rome (66-70 CE). After his capture, he became a Roman citizen. The selections below are taken from Josephus's multivolume work, *Antiquitates Judaicae* (or *Jewish Antiquities*). In it, Josephus surveys Jewish history from its biblical beginnings up to the war with Rome. Written to justify Jewish culture and religion to interested Roman readers, the work is a combination of expansions, additions, and omissions on the biblical text.

In his account of Genesis 1-3, Josephus makes several significant changes to the biblical story of Eve: Eve receives the prohibition directly from God; God's prohibition includes the touching of the tree; Eve's role as "mate" is emphasized; Adam is punished for taking the advice of a woman; and Eve and the serpent are paralleled. (Source: Josephus, *Jewish Antiquities*, translated by

H. St. J. Thackeray, Loeb Classical Library: *Jewish Antiquities, Books 1-4.* Cambridge, Mass.: Harvard University Press, 1952.)

Jewish Antiquities (c. 90s CE)
JOSEPHUS

1.34–36

And here, after the seventh day, Moses begins to interpret nature, writing on the formation of man in these terms: "God fashioned man by taking dust from the earth and instilled into him spirit and soul." Now this man was called Adam, which in Hebrew signifies "red," because he was made from the red earth kneaded together; for such is the colour of the true virgin soil. And God brought before Adam the living creatures after their kinds, exhibiting both male and female, and gave them the names by which they are still called to this day. Then seeing Adam to be without female partner and consort (for indeed there was none), and looking with astonishment at the other creatures who had their mates, He extracted one of his ribs while he slept and from it formed woman; and when she was brought to him Adam recognized that she was made from himself. In the Hebrew tongue woman is called *essa*; but the name of that first woman was Eve, which signifies "mother of all (living)."

1.40–51

Now God bade Adam and his wife partake of the rest of the plants, but to abstain from the tree of wisdom, forewarning them that, if they touched it, it would prove their destruction. At that epoch all the creatures spoke a common tongue, and the serpent, living in the company of Adam and his wife, grew jealous of the blessings which he supposed were destined for them if they obeyed God's behests, and, believing that disobedience would bring trouble upon them, he maliciously persuaded the woman to taste of the tree of wisdom, telling her that in it resided the power of distinguishing good and evil, possessing which they would lead a blissful existence no whit behind that of a god. By these means he misled the woman to scorn the commandment of God: she tasted of the tree, was pleased with the food, and persuaded Adam also to partake of it. And now they became aware that they were naked and, ashamed of such exposure to the light of day, bethought them of a covering; for the tree served to quicken their intelligence. So they covered themselves with fig-leaves, and, thus screening their persons, believed themselves the happier for having found what they lacked before. But, when God entered the garden, Adam, who ere then was wont to resort to His company, conscious of his crime withdrew; and God, met by action so strange, asked for what reason he who once took delight in His company now shunned and avoided it. But when he spoke not a word, conscious of having transgressed the divine

command, God said, "Nay, I had decreed for you to live a life of bliss, unmo-
lested by all ill, with no care to fret your souls; all things that contribute to
enjoyment and pleasure were, through my providence, to spring up for you
spontaneously, without toil or distress of yours; blessed with these gifts, old
age would not soon have overtaken you and your life would have been long.
But now thou hast flouted this my purpose by disobeying my commands; for
it is through no virtue that thou keepest silence but through an evil conscience." Adam then began to make excuse for his sin and besought God not
to be wroth with him, laying the blame for the deed upon the woman and
saying that it was her deception that had caused him to sin; while she, in her
turn, accused the serpent. Thereupon God imposed punishment on Adam for
yielding to a woman's counsel, telling him that the earth would no more produce anything of herself, but, in return for toil and grinding labour, would but
afford some of her fruits and refuse others. Eve He punished by child-birth
and its attendant pains, because she had deluded Adam, even as the serpent had
beguiled her, and so brought calamity upon him. He moreover deprived the
serpent of speech, indignant at his malignity to Adam; He also put poison beneath his tongue, destining him to be the enemy of men, and admonishing
them to strike their blows upon his head, because it was therein that man's
danger lay and there too that his adversaries could most easily inflict a mortal
blow; He further bereft him of feet and made him crawl and wriggle along the
ground. Having imposed these penalties upon them, God removed Adam and
Eve from the garden to another place.

CHAPTER THREE

Rabbinic Interpretations
(200–600s CE)

INTRODUCTION *Grp#1*

Talmudic and midrashic treatments of Genesis 1-3 combine an intense interest and curiosity about the text with a remarkable openness to interpretive
options. No aspect of Genesis 1-3 escapes scrutiny and rabbinic comment; no
gap in the story line goes unfilled. Modern readers of these compilations are
likely to be overwhelmed by the plethora of opinions offered and the dissonance between authoritative rabbinic "voices."

Looking through the Rabbinic Lens:
A Many-Faceted Eve

*Diff.
understandings
not
one
voice*

Looking at Eve through the lens of rabbinic discussions and arriving at an
image of her likeness is like trying to connect dozens of puzzle pieces, each
with its own shape and emphasis, in hopes of arriving at a single, cohesive
picture. The task is difficult, if not impossible, to accomplish. First, there are
no systematic, linear expositions of Genesis 1-3 in the Talmuds or in the
majority of midrashic compilations. (An exception to this is *Genesis Rabbah*,
though at times this work is only marginally linear.) Thus, to construct a single "picture" of the rabbinic Eve we have to collect and then connect rabbinic
comments scattered throughout our sources. Such an image of Eve, however,
is inescapably forced and artificial. Second, each rabbinic comment on Adam

and Eve has its own context and concerns. Comments in the *Talmud* are connected (however tentatively) to the *Mishnah*, while those in *Midrash Rabbah* are tied (though often loosely) to the Scriptures. Thus individual comments on Genesis 1–3 are often crafted in response to an immediate literary context rather than being part of a unified systematic presentation. Lastly, rabbinic materials do not display the unicity that readers often expect of authoritative writings. That is, the rabbinic "voices" readers "hear" frequently differ quite vociferously in their understanding of Eve's story.

A prime example of this interpretive diversity is found in explanations of the differences between woman's creation in Genesis 1:27 and that in Genesis 2:21–22. As the reader will remember from our first chapter, Genesis 1 recounts the simultaneous creation of man and woman, while in Genesis 2, woman is created after man from one of his body parts. Nineteenth-century historical critical scholars explained this difference by suggesting that there were two different sources behind (and hence two different stories within) Genesis 1–2. The ancient rabbis also struggled with these differences and arrived at their own readings:

1. God changed God's mind about creating woman (Genesis 1 contains God's intentions, while Genesis 2 contains what God finally did), or
2. God created two Eves, one in Genesis 1 and the other in Genesis 2 (God removed the first before creating the second), or
3. At first God created an androgynous creature (Gen. 1) that was later divided (Gen. 2).

Nor was the creation of woman the only topic on which the rabbis differed. According to Genesis 2, God created woman from one of man's body parts. But which one? Rabbinic answers to this question ranged from Adam's rib to his tail, face, and side. Another question arose concerning the garden's forbidden fruit. While Western legends identified it as an apple, rabbinic lore suggested figs, grapes, and even wheat.

From the above examples it is clear that the interpretive options offered by the rabbis are often mutually exclusive. For example, it is not plausible (in terms of story logic) that God changed God's mind *and* that there were two Eves any more than it is plausible to say that Eve was created from Adam's face *and* tail or that the fruit was a fig *and* a grape. It is at this point that contemporary non-Jewish readers may be perplexed, wanting to know which answer is "correct." While scholarly disagreements are certainly common to contemporary readers, some attempt is usually made by the person reporting the debate to indicate which is the better or more accurate position. But the compilers of the *Talmud* and *Midrash Rabbah* are quite comfortable in presenting a range of interpretive options without demanding that readers arrive at a specific, monolithic reading. Within the rabbinic worldview, even dissonance has its place as a pathway to learning. As the writer of the Talmudic tractate *Hagigah* 3b so aptly pointed out,

> Just as a plant grows and increases, so the words of Torah grow and increase.

[What does the phrase] "the masters of assemblies" [mean?] [T]hese are the disciples of the wise, who sit in assemblies and occupy themselves with the Torah, some pronouncing unclean and others pronouncing clean, some prohibiting and others permitting, some declaring unfit . . . and others declaring fit.

Should a man say: How in these circumstances shall I learn Torah? Therefore the text says: "All of them are given from one Shepherd." One God gave them; one leader uttered them from the mouth of the Lord of all creation, blessed be He; for it is written 'And God spoke all these words.' . . . [M]ake thine ear like the hopper and get thee a perceptive heart to understand the words of those who pronounce unclean and the words of those who pronounce clean. . . .

Thus even voices raised in disagreement are pathways to Torah and truth!

The Rabbinic Eve: Subordinate or Equal?

Is the targumic, talmudic, and midrashic image of Eve pejorative or complementary? Does it support a vision of mutuality or subordination between the sexes? One way to answer these questions is to examine the rabbinic references to Eve and Adam, analyze their content, amass a list of story elements which can be identified as either pejorative or complementary, and finally, look to see which list is the longer. A representative list, taken solely from the readings in this chapter, would look something like this:

Elements Pejorative of Eve

The glorification of Adam (in contrast to Eve)
The first Eve's repulsiveness
The connection between Eve's creation and Satan's
Eve's creation by theft
Eve's crookedness linked to the rib's curve
Eve's creation from Adam's tail
Eve's creation from the face that looks backward, not forward
Eve's creation from bone smelling like the grave
Eve's creation and the birth of the evil inclination
Eve's curiosity
The folly of Adam (husbands) listening to Eve (wives)
Eve the temptress
Eve's copulation with the serpent
Eve's subordination to Adam (via the order of the punishments)
Woman's bodily functions as punishment for Eve's sin
Motherhood a source of pain and punishment for Eve's sin
Eve blamed for the disobedience
Adam repents and is forgiven (Eve does not)
Eve as the source of Cain and Abel's fatal argument
Eve, the mother of demons

Less Pejorative Elements

The androgyny of the first human being
Superiority not linked to order of creation

Eve's creation from Adam's side more "equal"
Adam incomplete without Eve
Eve's beauty a gift from God
Eve an improvement on Adam
Eve a victim of serpent's lust
Eve swayed by a reasoned, logical argument (not simply an appeal to the senses)
Sex is part of the natural order
Adam blamed for garden disobedience
Adam imaged as a whiner, complainer
Adam refused to repent when given a chance
Eve repents of what she did
Ironic reversal of desire: man now desires woman

While the above list is far from exhaustive—even limited as it is to the readings in this chapter—it is sufficient to reveal the difficulties encountered in this approach. The most obvious problem is that our list contains discrepancies. Adam both repents *and* refuses to repent. Mention is either *made* or *not made* of Eve's repentance. Eve's creation is either *a bad thing* or else *an improvement* on Adam's.

A more subtle problem emerges with elements that, on the surface, seem unequivocally egalitarian. Take, for instance, the image of the androgyne. Does androgyny constitute an egalitarian or hierarchical imaging of the first human? One could argue that being created male and female is an egalitarian vision of creation because it undermines arguments of women's subordination based on her status as a secondary, derivative creation. Moreover, the androgyne recovers the egalitarian vision of Genesis 1:28 ("male and female he created them") that is frequently overlooked in favor of the Genesis 2-3 account. But since some rabbis envisioned the androgyne as having two faces, one looking forward (male) and one looking backward (female), evaluating this element of Eve's story becomes more complex than we originally anticipated. Does the image of the female face looking backward negate the more positive image of a human who is both male and female? How can we assess whether an element is pejorative or not?

Another example is found in Eve's "improvement" over Adam. God gives Eve, we are told, more "understanding" than Adam. But what is meant by "understanding"? And is understanding a good thing to have? What does one "do" with it? Is its main effect on domestic or public affairs? Questions such as these reveal the problems in evaluating the subtleties of the rabbinic Eve's characterization. It should not surprise us then that scholars differ as to what the rabbinic Eve really "looks" like.

According to Nehama Aschkenasy, "if the biblical Eve is the instrument through which civilization comes into being, the midrashic Eve is, to use Freud's words, a retarding element, a force opposed to the progress of civilization."[1] Although rabbinic midrash can be sympathetic toward women, Aschkenasy argues that it is essentially patriarchal.[2] Contrary, however, to later depictions of Eve as the quintessential evil woman, Aschkenasy finds the rabbinic Eve neither dangerous nor evil—merely silly and childish.[3] Eve is a "mundane housewife, frivolous and jealous, who needs a man's wise guidance and often tries his immense patience."[4] For the rabbis to arrive at this characterization of Eve, Aschenasy argues, they had to suppress aspects of the biblical story that did not conform to patriarchal norms (i.e., Eve as an intellectually curious person) in favor of those that supported rabbinic values (i.e., domesticity and subordination). In general, however, Aschkenasy finds "the rabbis' overall attitude to Eve, and to women in general, more 'condescending' than 'condemning.' "[5]

Another scholar of rabbinic culture, Daniel Boyarin, views the rabbinic Eve as a mixture of the good and bad, with neither one predominating. While it is true that some rabbis are virulent in blaming Eve for humankind's disobedience,[6] others present her in a more sympathetic light—victim rather than victimizer. Moreover, to appreciate the more positive aspects of the rabbis' Eve, Boyarin argues that one must understand the cultural context out of which she emerged. Unlike the Eve of Hellenistic Judaism or Patristic Christianity, there is no "fall into sexuality" for the rabbis' Eve.[7] According to Boyarin, this means that the rabbis' Eve presents a more positive image of women's bodies. Since the rabbis "do not disavow their corporeality, they do not construct it as feminine."[8] Indeed, according to Boyarin "open misogyny" is "rare" in rabbinic writings—at least in comparison "with Philo, on the one hand, or Patristic culture on the other."[9]

According to Leila Leah Bronner,[10] talmudic and midrashic materials are "male discourses that depict Eve as the tempter of Adam" and "concentrate on formulating guides to daily observance and conduct for women to follow in order to atone for Eve's sin and to achieve the modesty required for the fulfillment of their roles in marriage and matrimony."[11] Nevertheless, Bronner admits to a certain amount of ambiguity in rabbinic treatments of Eve. She therefore cautions readers to avoid stereotyping the ancient rabbis, for "by assuming that rabbis merely stereotyped women, we in turn stereotype the rabbis."[12] While some readers, she admits, will no doubt find the pejorative dimensions of the rabbis' Eve too pervasive for comfort, others may take advantage of this ambiguity to fashion "a reconstructed view [of Eve] that recuperates the tradition's overall power and beauty."[13]

Reading the Rabbis' Eve:
Helpful or Hazardous to Women's Health?

What role did the rabbinic Eve play in the shaping of Jewish women's lives from 200 to 600 CE? Reconstructions of Jewish women's history for this period have traditionally been heavily dependent upon rabbinic sources. Read in this way, the rabbinic Eve's characterization is examined and then "read back" into Jewish women's lives. Bronner, however, raises some insightful words of caution concerning this approach: "How much of their [the rabbis'] reading into the biblical text was based on the actual status of women of their own times? How much was an idealized attempt to communicate to women the values and models they thought appropriate?"[14] Judith Wegner expresses a similar concern:

[handwritten margin note: rabbinic understanding does not give us actual life of women]

Since the social reality reflected in the Mishnaic and Talmudic texts is unavoidably distorted by the perspective of the framers and interpreters, rabbinic statements about the nature and role of women cannot provide an objective view of women's history; rather, they offer us an androcentric vision, sometimes colored by men's fears or wishful thinking about female sexuality.[15]

If, as Bronner and Wegner suggest, the rabbinical sources are suspect when it comes to reconstructing Jewish women's lives during this period, then we must turn to other sources for our information. Scholars like Ross Kraemer suggest, for example, that archaeological and epigraphical materials furnish us with an important corrective to rabbinic sources.[16] Indeed, Kraemer goes so far as to suggest that *Genesis Rabbah*, a key rabbinic work on Genesis, "reflects some rabbinic opposition to the power and prestige of women in Jewish communities previously outside the influence and authority of rabbinic traditions."[17]

Another fact to keep in mind concerning the rabbinic Eve's effect on ancient women's lives is that rabbinic Judaism was not the only form of Judaism in the ancient world. Boyarin astutely reminds us that

[handwritten margin note: Rabbi. Jud. not only dominant]

> Rabbinic Judaism is a particular Jewish formation of late antiquity. Although this is the type of Judaism that became the historical ancestor of virtually all later groups that call themselves Jewish, in the early centuries of our era it was just one form of Judaism. Various types of Hellenistic Judaism, apocalyptic groups such as the one at Qumran, and the early Christianity were all competing with the Judaism of the Rabbis and their followers for hegemony.[18]

Kraemer voices this caution as well. Since rabbinic Judaism became the norm for later generations, historians often assume it was the norm for this period. According to Kraemer, rabbinic Judaism at best may reflect "the opinions and writings of a small number of Jewish men living in a relatively isolated portion of the Roman Empire mostly in the third century CE and beyond."[19]

Whether or not we can solve the historical dilemma of which came first—the rabbinic Eve or her Jewish sisters' lived experiences—it cannot be denied that the rabbinic Eve became tremendously important to Jewish women in subsequent centuries. For these women, and perhaps for some of those in rabbinic times as well, Eve's story became the basis of *halakah* and women's values. As Bronner observes, it ultimately provided "the rationale for rules and regulations guiding women's behavior, a Jewish catechism of do's and don't's for females."[20]

Background to the Selections

This chapter includes three types of materials: Targums, Talmud, and midrashic collections. While each represents a distinct genre, they all employ at times a similar approach to the reading of scripture—an approach called "midrash." Since this type of exposition may be unfamiliar to some readers, it will be useful for us to digress a moment and talk about the dynamics of midrash before discussing the actual sources of this chapter's selections.

The term "midrash" can mean either a type of rabbinical biblical exegesis, a collection of these interpretations, or a general term for the genre as a whole. As a type of exegesis, midrash has been described as "playful" in the sense that it displays a remarkable flexibility in the way it treats the meaning, relationships, and referents of words. Indeed, midrashic approaches to biblical texts assume not only that every biblical verse has something to teach, but that all biblical texts are interrelated and have a limitless plurality of meaning.[21]

The word "midrash" comes from the word *darash* (to seek, to ask). There are two types of midrash: *halakic* and *aggadic*. Whereas the former deals with comments on legal texts or judicial practices, the latter comments on nonlegal materials and displays a homiletical dimension. Both types of midrash are found in the selections in this chapter. All the selections in this chapter—Targums, Talmud, and midrashic compilations—employ midrash as a mode of biblical interpretation. Of the three types of materials in this chapter, only the Targums (and *Genesis Rabbah* to some extent) follow a linear unfolding of the biblical account. The Targums are Aramaic translations of the Hebrew Scriptures. There are five Targums of Genesis: *Targum Onqelos, Targum Pseudo-Jonathan, Codex Neofiti I*, the Fragmentary Targum, and the Cairo Genizah Fragments. Of these, excerpts from two—*Targum Onqelos* and *Targum Pseudo-Jonathan*—are included in this chapter. While the *Targum Onqelos* is a bit early (c. 100s CE) for the period covered in this chapter (200-600s CE), we include it so that readers can compare it with, and thus better recognize the expansive character of, the *Targum Pseudo-Jonathan* (c. 600s CE). While the *Targum Onqelos* stays fairly close to the biblical account, the *Targum Pseudo-Jonathan* reflects the midrashic and speculative approach found in the *Talmud* and *Midrash Rabbah*. Unlike the Targums, which are translations, the Talmuds are basically commentaries. They contain interpretive discussions (called *Gemara*) of the *Mishnah*—a second-century collection of 63 sections or "tractates" that contain commentary on the written laws found in the Torah/Pentateuch. Thus, in a sense, the Talmuds are commentaries on a commentary.

There are two Talmuds, each identified by their geographical point of origin: the *Palestinian Talmud* (pre-500s CE) and the *Babylonian Talmud* (pre-600s CE). We have included in this chapter selections from only the *Babylonian Talmud* for two reasons: (1) space did not permit us to present an exhaustive collection of both Talmuds, and (2) of the two, the *Babylonian Talmud* occupies a privileged position in subsequent Jewish tradition. Since the two Talmuds are different, we would encourage interested readers to survey the appropriate passages in the *Palestinian Talmud* as a supplement to the materials in this chapter.

In reading excerpts from talmudic sources it is helpful to keep in mind that:

1. Rabbinical materials are not always arranged in a linear, systematic form; they are often only loosely connected to the topic of comment.
2. Although sayings are often attributed to a named sage, scholars argue that the authors and editors of such sayings are in reality, unknown.
3. In commenting on a subject, opinions are included that are repetitive, complementary, or contradictory without an attempt to signal the "correct" opinion.
4. There is no set form of rabbinical comment.

Like talmudic materials, midrashic collections are types of commentary. Unlike the Talmuds, they comment on Scripture not Mishnah. For this anthology we have included selections from what is called the "Midrash Rabbah" or the "Great Midrash." It is a collection of works that reflect different writers, genres, and periods. The selections are from:

Genesis Rabbah (c. 400s CE) [exegetical midrash]
Lamentations Rabbah (c. 400s CE) [exegetical midrash]
Leviticus Rabbah (c. 400s-500s CE) [homiletical midrash]
Deuteronomy Rabbah (c. 400s-800s CE) [homiletical midrash]
Song of Songs Rabbah (c. 500s CE) [exegetical midrash]
Exodus Rabbah (c. 900s-1100s CE) [homiletical midrash]
Numbers Rabbah (c. 800s-1100s CE) [homiletical midrash]

Since *Genesis Rabbah* presents the most sustained treatment of Genesis it should not be surprising that many of our selections are taken from it. Wherever possible we also include cross-references to other talmudic and midrashic passages that are a witness to each selection's theme.

NOTES TO CHAPTER 3, INTRODUCTION

1. Nehama Aschkenasy, *Eve's Journey: Feminine Images in Hebraic Literary Tradition* (Philadelphia: University of Pennsylvania Press, 1986), p. 12.
2. Aschkenasy, *Eve's Journey*, p. 14.
3. Aschkenasy, *Eve's Journey*, p. 43.
4. Aschkenasy, *Eve's Journey*, p. 45.
5. Aschkenasy, *Eve's Journey*, p. 45.
6. Daniel Boyarin, *Carnal Israel: Reading Sex in Talmudic Culture* (Berkeley: University of California Press, 1993), pp. 88-90.
7. Boyarin, *Carnal Israel*, pp. 82-83.
8. Boyarin, *Carnal Israel*, p. 106.
9. Boyarin, *Carnal Israel*, pp. 82-83.
10. Leila Leah Bronner, *From Eve to Esther: Rabbinic Reconstructions of Biblical Women* (Louisville: John Knox Press, 1994).
11. Bronner, *From Eve to Esther*, p. 36.
12. Bronner, *From Eve to Esther*, p. 185.
13. Bronner, *From Eve to Esther*, p. 36.
14. Bronner, *From Eve to Esther*, p. xiii.
15. Judith Romney Wegner, "The Image and Status of Women in Classical Rab-

binic Judaism," in Judith R. Baskin, editor, *Jewish Women in Historical Perspective* (Detroit: Wayne State University Press, 1991), p. 69.

16. For an example of this kind of research see Ross S. Kraemer, "Jewish Women in the Diaspora World of Late Antiquity," in Judith R. Baskin, editor, *Jewish Women in Historical Perspective* (Detroit: Wayne State University Press, 1991), pp. 43-67.

17. Ross S. Kraemer, *Her Share of the Blessings: Women's Religion among Pagans, Jews, and Christians in the Greco-Roman World* (Oxford: Oxford University Press, 1992), p. 100.

18. Boyarin, *Carnal Israel*, pp. 230-31.

19. Ross S. Kraemer, "Hellenistic Jewish Women: The Epigraphical Evidence," *Society of Biblical Literature Seminar Papers* (1986): 183.

20. Bronner, *From Eve to Esther*, p. 22.

21. Paul Morris, "Exiled from Eden: Jewish Interpretations of Genesis," in Paul Morris and Deborah Sawyer, editors, A *Walk in the Garden: Biblical, Iconographical and Literary Images of Eden*, Journal for the Study of the Old Testament, Supplement Series 136 (Sheffield: JSOT Press, 1992), pp. 117-66.

MIDRASH AND TALMUD

Since comments on Adam and Eve are scattered throughout the *Midrash Rabbah* (a multivolume midrash on the biblical text) and the *Babylonian Talmud* (a multivolume exposition of the Mishnah), the selections below are arranged thematically. Representative selections are given for each theme and, where possible, additional references are given for those readers interested in more exhaustive coverage. (Sources: *The Babylonian Talmud*, I. Epstein, editor, vols. 1-35, London: Soncino Press, 1983; *The Midrash Rabbah*, H. Freedman and M. Simon, editors, vols. 1-10, London: Soncino Press, 1939.)

Humankind's Creation

new bir

Adam the Androgyne

Genesis 1:27 and 5:2 describe humankind as "male and female." Although some rabbis understood this phrase to mean two individuals (a man and a woman), others envisioned a being *both* male and female—an androgyne. Rabbis who viewed Adam as an androgyne suggested that Adam's male and female parts were connected at the back (needing separation like "Siamese twins").

Adam a hermaphrodite

Genesis Rabbah 8.1

R. Jeremiah b. Leazar said: When the Holy One, blessed be He, created Adam, He created him an hermaphrodite ... for it is said, *Male and female created He them and called their name Adam* (Gen. 5:2). R. Samuel b. Nahman said: When the Lord created Adam He created him double-faced, then He split him and made him of two backs, one back on this side and one back on the other side.

Leviticus Rabbah 14.1

R. Levi said: When man was created, he was created with two body-fronts, and He sawed him in two, so that two backs resulted, one back for the male and another back for the female. (See also *Berakoth* 61a, *'Erubin* 18a.)

A Change of Mind

One way of reconciling the creation of "male and female" in Genesis 1:27c with the masculine singular pronoun of verse 27b ("[God] created *him*") is to understand verse 27c as what God intended to do and verse 27b as what God actually did. The selection below explains how God, who originally intended to create both male and female, created only the male instead.

Berakoth 61a

It is written, *Male and female created He them*, and it is also written, *For in the image of God made He man*. How are these statements to be reconciled? At first the intention was to create two, but in the end only one was created. (See also: *'Erubin* 18a, *Kethuboth* 8a.)

Eve I and II

One tradition suggested that there were two Eves, the first of which God re-moved because Adam found her repugnant.

Genesis Rabbah 18.4

AND THE MAN SAID: THIS IS NOW (ZOTH HA-PA'AM), etc. (2.23). R. Judah b. Rabbi said: At first He created her for him and he saw her full of discharge and blood; thereupon He removed her from him and recreated her a second time. Hence he said: THIS TIME SHE IS BONE OF MY BONE.

Genesis Rabbah 22.7

Out of this argument, CAIN ROSE UP AGAINST HIS BROTHER ABEL, etc. Judah b. Rabbi said: Their quarrel was about the first Eve. Said R. Aibu: The first Eve had returned to dust. Then about what was their quarrel? (See also *Genesis Rabbah* 17.7.)

Larger than Life

Some rabbinic traditions exaggerated Adam's original size, capabilities and ap-pearance. They described him as having cosmic proportions and supernatural knowledge, skill, and glory.

Genesis Rabbah 24.2

Thine eyes did see mine unformed substance, and in Thy book they were all writ-ten (Ps. 139:16). R. Joshua b. R. Nehemiah and R. Judah b. R. Simon in R. Eleazar's name said: When the Holy One, blessed be He, created Adam, He created him extending over the whole world. How do we know that he extended from east to west? Because it is said, *Thou hast formed me behind and before* (Ps. 139:5). From north to south? Because it is said, *And from the one end of heaven unto the other* (Deut. 4:32). And how do we know that he filled the hollow spaces of the world? From the verse, *And hast laid Thy hand upon me* (Ps. 139:5). R. Tanhuma in R. Banayah's name, and R. Berekiah in R. Eleazar's name said: He created him a shapeless mass, and he lay stretching from one end of the world to the other; as it is written, "*Thine eyes did see my shapeless mass.*" R. Judah b. R. Simon said: While Adam lay a shapeless mass before Him at whose decree the world came into existence, He showed him every generation and its Sages, every generation and its judges, scribes, interpreters, and leaders.

Pesahim 54a

For it was taught, R. Jose said: Two things He decided to create on the eve of the Sabbath, but they were not created until the termination of the Sabbath, and at the termination of the Sabbath the Holy One, blessed be He, inspired Adam with knowledge of a kind similar to Divine [knowledge], and he procured two stones and rubbed them on each other, and fire issued from them; he also took two [heterogenous] animals and crossed them, and from them came forth the mule. (See also: *Sanhedrin* 38b, 100a; *Genesis Rabbah* 8.1, 11.2, 21.3; *Exodus Rabbah* 32.1; *Leviticus Rabbah* 14.1, 16.2; *Hagigah* 12a.)

The Adorable Adam

The original Adam was so splendid that even the angels confused him with God. To guarantee that adoration was reserved solely for God, God made some changes in Adam and created sleep. (For a more negative interpretation of sleep, see *Genesis Rabbah* 17.5.)

Genesis Rabbah 8.10

R. Hoshaya said: When the Holy One, blessed be He, created Adam, the ministering angels mistook him [for a divine being] and wished to exclaim 'Holy' before him. . . . What did the Holy One, blessed be He, do? He caused sleep to fall upon him, and so all knew that he was [but mortal] man; thus it is written, *Cease ye from man, in whose nostrils is a breath, for how little is he to be accounted* (Isa. 2:22)! (See also: *Ecclesiastes Rabbah* 6.1,10.)

Last Is Sometimes Least

While some rabbis envisioned a hierarchical creation with the last being the most important, the selection below cautions against having too much pride in being the last created.

Sanhedrin 38a

Our Rabbis taught: Adam was created [last of all beings] on the eve of Sabbath. And why? . . . In order that, if a man's mind becomes [too] proud, he may be reminded that the gnats preceded him in the order of creation. (See also *Leviticus Rabbah* 14.1.)

Adam's Inclinations

The rabbinical theory of "two inclinations" explained the dilemma of human morality. Choosing one's actions was linked to two inclinations, resident in each person: the desire to do good and the desire to do evil. In the selections below, the evil inclination came into being either at Adam's creation, or with the creation of Eve. (In the latter tradition only the good inclination exists before Eve's creation.)

Berakoth 61a

R. Nahman b. R. Hisda expounded: What is meant by the text, *Then the Lord God formed* [wa-yizer] *man*? [The word *wa-yizer*] is written with two *yods*, to show that God created two inclinations, one good and the other evil.

Genesis Rabbah 21.5

The view of R. Berekiah in R. Hanan's name is that as long as there was [only] Adam he was one, but when his rib was taken from him, it was *To know good and evil.*

Eve—Made from Stolen Goods?

Since there is no indication in Genesis 2:21 that Adam is aware of or approved of his rib's removal, a question arose concerning God's integrity. Was God a thief? In the selections below, R. Gamaliel and R. Jose challenge the idea that God's actions constituted "theft" and explain *why* secrecy was necessary in Eve's creation.

Sanhedrin 39a

The Emperor once said to Rabban Gamaliel: Your God is a thief, for it is written, *And the Lord God caused a deep sleep to fall upon the man* [Adam] *and he slept* [*and He took one of his ribs, etc.*]. Thereupon his [the Emperor's] daughter said to him: Leave him to me and I will answer him, and [turning to the Emperor] said: "Give me a commander." "Why do you need him?" asked he. "Thieves visited us last night and robbed us of a silver pitcher, leaving a golden one in its place." "Would that such visited us every day!" he exclaimed. "Ah!" she retorted, "was it not to Adam's gain that he was deprived of a rib and a wife presented to him in its stead to serve him?" He replied: "This is what I mean: he should have taken it from him openly." Said she to him: "Let us have a piece of raw meat." It was given to her. She placed it under her armpit, then took it out and offered it to him to eat. "I find it loathsome," he exclaimed. "Even so would she [Eve] have been to Adam had she been taken from him openly," she retorted.

Genesis Rabbah 17.7

A [Roman] lady asked R. Jose: "Why [was woman created] by a theft?" "Imagine," replied he, "a man depositing an ounce of silver with you in secret, and you return him a *litra* [= 12 ounces] of silver openly; is that theft!" "Yet why in secret?" she pursued. "At first He created her for him and he saw her full of discharge and blood; thereupon He removed her from him and created her a second time."

What's So Special about a Rib?

Why did God use Adam's rib and not some other body part to create Eve? Speaking in R. Levi's name, R. Joshua explains the rib's significance by providing a glimpse into the mind of God.

Genesis Rabbah 18.2

R. Joshua of Siknin said in R. Levi's name: *WAYYIBEN* is written, signifying that He considered well (*hithbonnen*) from what part to create her. Said He: "I will not create her from [Adam's] head, lest she be swelled-headed; nor from the eye, lest she be a coquette; nor from the ear, lest she be an eavesdropper; nor from the mouth, lest she be a gossip; nor from the heart, lest she be prone to jealousy; nor from the hand, lest she be light-fingered; nor from the foot, lest she be a gadabout; but from the modest part of man, for even when he stands naked, that part is covered." And as He created each limb He ordered her, "Be a modest woman." Yet in spite of all this, *But ye have set at nought all My counsel, and would none of My reproof* (Prov. 1:25). I did not create her from the head, yet she is swelled-headed, as it is written, *They walk with stretched-forth necks* (Isa. 3:16); nor from the eye, yet she is a coquette: *And wanton eyes* (Isa. 3:16); nor from the ear, yet she is an eavesdropper: *Now Sarah listened in the tent door* (Gen. 18:10); nor from the heart, yet she is prone to jealousy: *Rachel envied her sister* (Gen. 30:1); nor from the hand, yet she is light-fingered: *And Rachel stole the teraphim* (Gen. 31:19); nor from the foot, yet she is a gadabout: *And Dinah went out*, etc. (Gen. 34:1). (See also *Genesis Rabbah 80.5, Deuteronomy Rabbah 6.11*.)

Eve, a Bone of Contention

Did it matter that Eve was made from bone? Some rabbis saw a connection between women's behavior and the substance from which Eve was created. They explained diverse actions such as wearing perfume, determining a baby's sex, and establishing coital positions, by reference to the earth and bone used in humankind's creation.

Genesis Rabbah 17.8

R. Joshua was asked: "Why does a man come forth [at birth] with his face downward, while a woman comes forth with her face turned upwards?" "The man looks towards the place of his creation [viz. the earth], while the woman looks towards the place of her creation [viz. the rib]," he replied. "And why must a woman use perfume, while a man does not need perfume?" "Man was created from earth," he answered, "and earth never putrefies, but Eve was created from a bone. For example: if you leave meat three days unsalted, it immediately goes putrid." "And why has a woman a penetrating [shrill] voice, but not a man?" "I will give you an illustration," replied he. "If you fill a pot with meat it does not make any sound, but when you put a bone into it, the sound [of sizzling] spreads immediately." "And why is a man easily appeased, but not a woman?" "Man was created from the earth," he answered, "and when you pour a drop of water on it, it immediately absorbs it; but Eve was created from a bone, which even if you soak many days in water does not become saturated."

new bit

Niddah 31b

And why does the man lie face downwards and the woman face upwards towards the man? He [faces the elements] from which he was created and she [faces the man] from whom she was created. And why is a man easily pacified and a woman is not easily pacified? He [derives his nature] from the place from which he was created and she [derives hers] from the place from which she was created. Why is a woman's voice sweet and a man's voice is not sweet? He [derives his] from the place from which he was created and she [derives hers] from the place from which she was created. (See also: *Exodus Rabbah* 1.14.)

What Side Is Eve From?

Not all rabbis understood Eve to be taken from Adam's "rib." An alternative translation suggested that Eve was created from one of Adam's two "sides," either from a face or from a tail.

Berakoth 61a

And the rib which the Lord God had taken from man made he a woman. Rab and Samuel explained this differently. One said that [this "*rib*"] was a face, the other that it was a tail. (See also *'Erubin* 18a, *Genesis Rabbah* 8:1.)

Without Eve, Adam's Incomplete

Significance of marriage

Apart from the physical connectedness inherent in the idea of androgyny, many rabbis viewed Adam and Eve as connected on sexual and social levels as well. Heterosexual bonding within marriage—the rabbinic ideal—defined the "complete" person.

Niddah 31b

R. Dostai son of R. Jannai was asked by his disciples: Why does a man go in search of a woman and no woman goes in search of a man? This is analogous to the case of a man who lost something. Who goes in search of what? He who lost the thing goes in search of what he lost.

Yebamoth 63a

R. Eleazar said: Any man who has no wife is no proper man; for it is said, *Male and female created He them and called their name Adam.* . . .

R. Eleazar further stated: What is meant by the Scriptural text, *This is now bone of my bones, and flesh of my flesh?* This teaches that Adam had intercourse with every beast and animal but found no satisfaction until he cohabited with Eve.

Genesis Rabbah 17.2

IT IS NOT GOOD. It was taught: He who has no wife dwells without good, without help, without joy, without blessing, and without atonement. "Without good": IT IS NOT GOOD THAT THE MAN SHOULD DWELL ALONE. "Without help": *I will make him a help meet for him.* "Without joy": *And thou shalt rejoice, thou and thy household* (Deut. 14:26). "Without a blessing": *To cause a blessing to rest on thy house* (Ezek. 44:30). "Without atonement": *And he shall make atonement for himself, and for his house* (Lev. 16:11). R. Simon said in the name of R. Joshua b. Levi: Without peace too, for it is said: *And peace be to thy house* (1 Sam. 25:6). R. Joshua of Siknin said in the name of R. Levi: Without life too, for it is said, *Enjoy life with the wife whom thou lovest* (Eccles. 9:9). R. Hiyya b. Gomdi said: He is also incomplete, for it is written, *And He blessed them, and called their name Adam*—i.e., man (Gen. 5:2). Some say: He even impairs the Divine likeness: thus it is written, *For in the image of God made He man* (Gen 9:6), which is followed by, *And you, be ye fruitful, and multiply* (Gen 9:7). (See also *Genesis Rabbah* 17.4, *Berakoth* 62b.)

Is Eve a Help?

According to certain rabbis, whether or not Eve was a "help" depended on Adam's worth and luck.

Yebamoth 63a

R. Eleazar further stated: What is the meaning of the Scriptural text, *I will make him a help meet for him?* If he was worthy she is a help to him; if he was not worthy she is against him.

Others say: R. Eleazar pointed out a contradiction: It is written *kenegedo* but we read *kenegedo!*—If he was worthy she is *meet for him*; if he was not worthy she chastises him.

Genesis Rabbah 17.3

I WILL MAKE HIM A HELP ('EZER) AGAINST HIM (KE-NEGDO): if he is fortunate, she is a help; if not, she is against him.

Two Can Subdue!

In the passage below, R. Ile'a draws attention to the fact that God commanded *both* the man and the woman to have dominion over creation.

Yebamoth 65b

R. Ile'a replied in the name of R. Eleazar son of R. Simeon: Scripture stated, *And replenish the earth, and subdue it*, it is the nature of a man to *subdue* but it is not the nature of a woman to subdue. On the contrary! *And subdue it* implies two!

Jewelry and Clothes—God's Gifts

One well-attested rabbinic tradition portrays God as Eve's personal attendant who adorns her, clothes her, and fixes her hair in preparation for her introduction to Adam.

Genesis Rabbah 18.1

R. Aibu—others state the following in R. Bannayah's name, and it was also taught in the name of R. Simeon b. Yohai—said: He [God] adorned her like a bride and brought her to Him, for there are places where coiffure is called building. R. Hama b. R. Hanina said: What think you, that He brought her to him from under a carob tree or a sycamore tree! Surely He first decked her out with twenty-four pieces of finery and then brought her to him! Thus it is written, *Thou wast in Eden the garden of God; every precious stone was thy covering, the carnelian, the topaz, and the emerald, the beryl, the onyx, and the jasper, the sapphire, the carbuncle, and the smaragd, and gold; the workmanship of thy settings and of thy sockets was in thee, in the day that thou wast created they were prepared* (Ezek. 28:13).

'Erubin 18a

For R. Simeon b. Menassia made the following exposition: *And the Lord God builded the side* teaches that the Holy One, blessed be He, plaited Eve's hair and then brought her to Adam, for in the sea-towns a plait is called "building." (See also: *Berakoth* 61a, *Niddah* 45b, *Shabbath* 95a.)

The Most Beautiful Woman in the World

[handwritten margin note: hierarchy in beauty]

Although biblical accounts do not describe the first woman's physical appearance, rabbinic traditions portrayed her as beautiful—the standard for all female beauty. Eve's beauty, however, was subordinate to Adam's, while Adam's was subordinate to the Shechinah's (God's divine presence).

Genesis Rabbah 40.5

R. 'Azariah and R. Jonathan in R. Isaac's name said: Eve's image was transmitted to the reigning beauties of each generation. Elsewhere it is written, *And the damsel was very fair—'ad me'od* (1 Kings 1:4), which means that she attained to Eve's beauty; but here in truth it is written, THE EGYPTIANS BEHELD THE WOMAN THAT SHE WAS VERY FAIR (ME'OD)— which means, even more beautiful than Eve's image.

Baba Bathra 58a

Compared with Sarah, all other people are like a monkey to a human being, and compared with Eve Sarah was like a monkey to a human being, and compared with Adam Eve was like a monkey to a human being, and compared with the *Shechinah* Adam was like a monkey to a human being.

Eve, the Improved Version of Adam

Good version to women

According to one tradition, when God "built" Eve, God added something "extra"—more understanding.

Niddah 45b

Our Rabbis taught: These are the rulings of Rabbi R. Simeon b. Eleazar stated, The age limits that were assigned to the girl apply to the boy while those assigned to the boy apply to the girl. R. Hisda stated: What is Rabbi's reason? Because it is written in Scripture, *And the Lord God built the rib* which teaches that the Holy One, blessed be He, endowed the woman with more understanding than the man. (See also *Genesis Rabbah* 18.1.)

The Disobedience

Satan and Eve Share a Birthday

Attempts to connect Eve with the serpent in Genesis 3 take a variety of forms. One of the more unusual rabbinic traditions is R. Hanina's reference to Satan's simultaneous creation with Eve.

Genesis Rabbah 17.6

R. Hanina, son of R. Adda, said: From the beginning of the Book until here no *samech* is written, but as soon as she [Eve] was created, Satan was created with her.

Why Did the Serpent Do It?

Although "envy" of Adam's greatness played an important part in at least one rabbinic explanation of the serpent's actions (*Sanh.* 59b), another explanation added an erotic element by imaging Eve as the object of the serpent's lustful attention.

Genesis Rabbah 20.4

R. Hoshaya said: [The Almighty said to the serpent:] "All that thou didst do was on account of this woman; was not all thy labour for her sake?"

Genesis Rabbah 18.6

Said R. Joshua b. Karhah: It teaches you through what sin that wicked creature inveigled them, viz. because he saw them engaged in their natural functions, he [the serpent] conceived a passion for her.

Sotah 9b

We thus find it with the primeval serpent [in the Garden of Eden] which set its eyes on that which was not proper for it; what it sought was not granted to it and what it possessed was taken from it. The Holy One, blessed be He, said, I declared, Let it be king over every animal and beast; but now, *Cursed art thou above all cattle and above every beast of the field.* I declared, let it walk with an erect posture; but now it shall go upon its belly. I declared, Let its food be the same as that of man; but now it shall eat dust. It said, I will kill Adam and marry Eve; but now, *I will put enmity between thee and the woman, and between thy seed and her seed.*

The Cunning Conversationalist

How did the serpent convince Eve to eat the forbidden fruit? According to Genesis 3, it promised that she would be like God, knowing "good and evil" (v. 5). Rabbinic accounts elaborated on this conversation, the serpent insisting that while touching the tree was indeed harmless, eating its fruit was the gateway to power and a guarantee that humankind could maintain their dominance of creation.

Genesis Rabbah 19.3

Thus, the Holy One, blessed be He, had said, *For in the day that thou eatest thereof thou shalt surely die* (Gen. 2:17); whereas she did not say thus, but, GOD HATH SAID: YE SHALL NOT EAT OF IT, NEITHER SHALL YE TOUCH IT; when he [the serpent] saw her thus lying, he took and thrust her against it. "Have you then died?" he said to her; "just as you were not stricken through touching it, so will you not die when you eat it, but *For God doth know that in the day ye eat thereof,*" etc. (Gen. 2:5).

Genesis Rabbah 19.4

R. Joshua of Siknin said in R. Levi's name: He [the serpent] began speaking slander of his Creator, saying, "Of this tree did He eat and then create the world; hence He orders you, ye shall not eat thereof, so that you may not create other worlds, for every person hates his fellow craftsmen." R. Judah b. R. Simon said: He argued: "Whatever was created after its companion dominates it. Thus: heaven was created on the first day and the firmament on the second: does it not bear its weight? The firmament was created on the second and herbs on the third: do they not interrupt its waters? Herbs were created on the third day and the luminaries on the fourth; the luminaries on the fourth and the birds on the fifth." R. Judah b. R. Simon said: The *ziz* is a clean bird, and when it flies it obscures the orb of the sun. "Now you were created after everything in order to rule over everything; make haste and eat before He creates other worlds which will rule over you." Hence it is written, *And the woman saw that it was good*, etc. (Gen. 3:6): she saw [how plausible were] the words of the serpent. (See also *Deuteronomy Rabbah* 19.10.)

Eve and Pandora: Sisters in Crime

Like Hesiod's Pandora, the story below ascribes Eve's disobedience to her curiosity.

Genesis Rabbah 19.10

AND HE SAID: I HEARD THY VOICE . . . AND HE SAID: WHO TOLD THEE, etc. (Gen. 3:11f)? R. Levi said: Imagine a woman borrowing vinegar, who went in to the wife of a snake-charmer and asked her, "How does your husband treat you?" "He treats me with every kindness," she replied, "save that he does not permit me to approach this cask which is full of serpents and scorpions." "It contains all his finery," said the other; "he wishes to marry another woman and give it to her." What did she do? She inserted her hand into it, and they began biting her. When her husband came he heard her crying out [with pain]. "Have you touched that cask?" he demanded. Similarly, HAST THOU EATEN OF THE TREE, WHEREOF I COMMANDED THEE, etc.?

The Folly of Listening to Your Wife *new bsp*

Although Genesis 3 contains no reference to Eve's coercion of Adam, some Rabbis puzzled over *why* Adam ate the forbidden fruit. Taking a clue from God's criticism of Adam in verse 17 (Adam "listened" to his wife), they concluded that Eve must have done or said *something* to make Adam disobey.

Genesis Rabbah 19.5

R. Simlai said: She came upon him with her answers all ready, saying to him: "What think you: that I will die and another Eve will be created for you?"— *There is nothing new under the sun* (Eccles. 1:9). Or do you think that I will die while you remain alone? *He created it not a waste, He formed it to be inhabited* (Isa. 45:18). The Rabbis said: She began weeping and crying over him.

Deuteronomy Rabbah 4.5

The Holy One, blessed be He, said: "Hearken unto Me, for no man who hearkens unto Me loses thereby." The Rabbis say: You find occasions when a man listened to his wife and lost thereby, and when a man listened to his wife and profited thereby. For example, Adam listened to his wife and lost thereby. Whence this? For it is said, *And unto Adam He said: Because thou hast hearkened unto the voice of thy wife*, etc. (Gen. 3:17). R. Isaac said: This can be compared to a king who said to his servant: "Do not taste any food until I return from the bath"; but his wife said unto him: "Taste the dish so that the king will not need to put in salt or sauce." The king returned and found him smacking his lips, and he said to him: "Did I not forbid you to eat, and yet you have eaten?" He replied: "Sire, your maidservant gave it to me." Whereupon the king exclaimed: "And have you listened to my maidservant rather than to me?" So God commanded Adam, *But of the tree of the knowledge of good and evil, thou shalt not eat of it* (Gen. 2:17). What did Eve do? She did give him to eat of it. R. Abin said: She merely had to weep and wail over him, whereupon he ate of it, for so it is written, "*Unto the* voice *of thy wife.*" . . . Here, then, is an instance of a man listening to his wife and losing thereby. (See also: *Genesis Rabbah* 20.8.)

The Serpentine Eve

It was argued that, as the serpent persuaded Eve, so Eve persuaded Adam. In later centuries, such parallels between Eve and the serpent would ultimately result in images of Eve as tempter and seducer.

Genesis Rabbah 20.11
AND THE MAN CALLED HIS WIFE'S NAME EVE—HAWWAH, i.e., life (Gen. 3:2). She was given to him for an adviser, but she played the eavesdropper like the serpent. [Another interpretation]: He showed her how many generations she had destroyed. R. Aha interpreted it: The serpent was thy [Eve's] serpent [i.e., seducer], and thou are Adam's serpent.

Genesis Rabbah 22.2
AND THE MAN KNEW, etc. . . . He knew how he had been robbed of his tranquillity; he knew what his serpent [i.e., Eve, his tempter] had done to him. R. Aha observed: The serpent was thy serpent, and thou wast Adam's serpent.

Sleeping with a Snake

As we saw in an earlier section in this chapter, one strand of rabbinic tradition portrayed Eve as the object of the serpent's sexual desires. R. Johanan takes this idea to its logical conclusion with his reference to the serpent's sexual union with Eve.

Eve || to idolaters

Yebamoth 103b
For R. Johanan stated: When the serpent copulated with Eve, he infused her with lust. The lust of the Israelites who stood at Mount Sinai, came to an end, the lust of the idolaters who did not stand at Mount Sinai did not come to an end. (See also *Shabbath* 145b-46a, *Abodah Zarah* 22b.)

Sex in the Garden

What role did sexuality play in the garden narrative? In the previous reading describing the serpent's union with Eve, illicit sex pollutes Eve and her descendents. But was all sex considered illicit? In rabbinical lore, three traditions concerning Adam and Eve's sexuality stand out as intriguing: their role as sex educators for the rest of creation, their licit sexual encounters in the garden before their expulsion, and the fecundity they experienced in their union.

Genesis Rabbah 22.2

AND THE MAN KNEW, etc. R. Huna and R. Jacob in R. Abba's name said: No creature ever copulated before Adam: it is not written, man knew, but AND THE MAN; KNEW intimates that he made known sexual functions to all.

Genesis Rabbah 18.6

Said R. Joshua b. Karhah: It teaches you through what sin that wicked creature inveigled them, viz. because he saw them engaged in their natural functions, he [the serpent] conceived a passion for her.

Genesis Rabbah 19.3

AND THE WOMAN SAID UNTO THE SERPENT: OF THE FRUIT OF THE TREES OF THE GARDEN WE MAY EAT (Gen. 3:2). Now where was Adam during this conversation? Abba Halfon b. Koriah said: He had engaged in his natural functions [intercourse] and then fallen asleep.

Sanhedrin 38b

R. Johanan b. Hanina said: The day consisted of twelve hours. In the first hour, his [Adam's] dust was gathered; in the second, it was kneaded into a shapeless mass; in the third, his limbs were shaped; in the fourth, a soul was infused into him; in the fifth, he arose and stood on his feet; in the sixth, he gave [the animals] their names; in the seventh, Eve became his mate; in the eighth, they ascended to bed as two and descended as four; in the ninth, he was commanded not to eat of the tree; in the tenth, he sinned; in the eleventh, he was tried; and in the twelfth he was expelled [from Eden] and departed, for it is written, *Man abideth not in honour.*

Genesis Rabbah 22.2

AND SHE CONCEIVED AND BORE CAIN. R. Eleazar b. 'Azariah said: Three wonders were performed on that day: on the very day they were created, on that very day they cohabited, and on that very day they produced offspring. R Joshua b. Karhah said: Only two entered the bed, and seven left it: Cain and his twin sister, Abel and his two twin sisters.

Genesis Rabbah 22.3

AND AGAIN (WA-TOSEF) SHE BORE HIS BROTHER ABEL (Gen. 4:2). This supports what R. Joshua b. Karhah said: They ascended the bed two and descended seven, for AND SHE AGAIN BORE implies an additional birth, but not an additional pregnancy.

Adam the Drunkard

Other than a reference to the tree from which the fruit is taken ("the tree of the knowledge of good and evil" 2:17), Genesis 2-3 never identifies the type of fruit eaten. Not surprisingly, various traditions arose concerning its identity. In *Sanhedrin* 70a, for example, the rabbis suggested that Eden's "forbidden fruit" was either wheat, figs, or grapes. The last suggestion—the grape—had ramifications for determining the first "sin" of humankind—drunkenness. Most rabbinic traditions identified only Adam as the drunkard (but see *Numbers Rabbah* 10.2 for an exception to this).

Berakoth 40a

For it has been taught: R. Meir holds that the tree of which Adam ate was the vine, since the thing that most causes wailing to a man is wine, as it says, *And he drank of the wine and was drunken.*

Leviticus Rabbah 12.1

They that go to search mixed wine, that is he who, on hearing that So-and-So has good wine, goes after him. What is written of such a person in the end?—*At last it biteth like a serpent, and stingeth* (parash) *like a basilisk* (Prov. 23:32). Even as the basilisk divides (*parash*) between death and life, so did wine cause a separation (*parash*) between Adam and Eve, as R. Judah b. Ila'i said: The tree from which Adam, the first man, ate was a vine, [since it is said], *Their grapes, the grapes of the first* [man]; *were bitter clusters for them* (Deut. 32:32), they brought bitterness into the world.

Numbers Rabbah 10.4

And have not the understanding of a man—adam (Prov. 30:2); that is, of Adam; since owing to the wine which he drank the world was cursed on his account. For R. Abin said: Eve mingled wine for Adam and he drank; as it says, *And when the woman saw* (wa-tere) *that the tree was good for food* (Gen. 3:6), and it is written, *Look not thou* (al tere) *upon the wine when it is red,* etc. (Prov. 23:31). (See also *Genesis Rabbah* 19.5, *Numbers Rabbah* 10.2, *Esther Rabbah* 5.1, *Sanhedrin* 70a-b.)

The Voice of Adam: Whine, Whine, Whine

When confronted by God in Genesis 3, Adam shifts the blame for his actions to the woman and God (v. 12). This evasion of responsibility did not go unnoticed by some rabbis who depicted Adam as a petty complainer.

Lamentations Rabbah 3.39

WHEREFORE DOTH A LIVING MAN COMPLAIN? (Lam. 3:39). It is sufficient for him that he lives. R. Levi said: The Holy One, blessed be He, declared: "Your existence is in My hand, and being alive you complain!"

R. Huna said: Let him stand up like a brave man, acknowledge his sins, and not complain. R. Berekiah said: [The verse is to be interpreted thus:] Wherefore doth a man complain against Him who lives eternally? If a man wishes to complain, let it be about his sins. Rabbi [Judah ha-Nasi] says [Israel] are the children of murmurers. [God said:] "After all the favour I showed to Adam he complained before Me and said, *The woman whom Thou gavest to be with me, she gave me of the tree, and I did eat*" (Gen. 3:12). (See also *'Abodah Zarah* 5a-b, *Genesis Rabbah* 38.9.)

You Asked for Her

The rabbinic tradition below suggests that Adam had no grounds for his complaint (see the previous section). God gave him a mate, but only after Adam asked for one.

Genesis Rabbah 17.4

Said he, "Every one has a partner, yet I have none": thus, BUT FOR ADAM THERE WAS NOT FOUND A HELP MEET FOR HIM! And why did He not create her for him at the beginning? Because the Holy One, blessed be He, foresaw that he would bring charges against her, therefore He did not create her until he expressly demanded her. But as soon as he did so, forthwith THE LORD GOD CAUSED A DEEP SLEEP TO FALL UPON THE MAN, AND HE SLEPT (2:21).

The Hierarchy of Punishment

In Genesis 3:8-13 God first confronts the man (who blames the woman and God) and then the woman (who blames the serpent). This order, man then woman, is reversed in the punishments described in 3:14-19. For some rabbis, this chiastic literary structure (man/woman/serpent/woman/man) was proof that men were more important than women or snakes.

Taanith 15b

AND ON THE HEAD OF THE NASI: And afterwards [the Mishnah] states, EVERYONE ELSE PUTS ASHES UPON HIS OWN HEAD. But is it so? Has it not been taught: Rabbi says: Where it is a case of doing honour we begin at the most distinguished, but where it is a case of censuring we begin at the least important; as it is said, *And Moses said unto Aaron, and unto Eleazar and unto Ithamar*; but where it is a case of censuring we begin at the least important, (for a Master said:) First the serpent was cursed, and afterwards Eve and [only] then Adam? (See also *Berakoth* 61a, *Genesis Rabbah* 20.3.)

The Pain of Parenting

According to Genesis 3:16a, woman is punished with "pain" or "toil" in childbirth. For the rabbis, this pain/work began before, and extended far beyond, the act of parturition (childbirth). Moreover, it entailed both physical and emotional suffering.

Genesis Rabbah 20.6

THY PAIN refers to the pain of conception; THY TRAVAIL, to the discomfort of pregnancy; IN PAIN, to the sufferings of miscarriages; SHALT THOU BRING FORTH, to the agony of childbirth; CHILDREN, to the suffering involved in the upbringing of children.

'Erubin 100b

. . . R. Isaac b. Abdimi stated: Eve was cursed with ten curses, since it is written: *Unto the woman He said, and I will greatly multiply,* which refers to the two drops of blood, one being that of menstruation and the other that of virginity, *"thy pain"* refers to the pain of bringing up children, *"and thy travail"* refers to the pain of conception, *"in pain thou shalt bring forth children"* is to be understood in its literal meaning, *"and thy desire shall be to thy husband"* teaches that a woman yearns for her husband when he is about to set out on a journey, *"and he shall rule over thee"* teaches that while the wife solicits with her heart the husband does so with his mouth, this being a fine trait of character among women?—What was meant is that she ingratiates herself with him. But are not these only seven?—When R. Dimi came he explained: She is wrapped up like a mourner, banished from the company of all men and confined within a prison. What is meant by "banished from the company of all men"? If it be suggested: That she is forbidden to meet a man in privacy, is not the man also, [it could be retorted,] forbidden to meet a woman in privacy?—The meaning rather is that she is forbidden to marry two men.

Song of Songs Rabbah 2.14

R. Hunyi said in the name of R. Meir: Why were the matriarchs so long barren? In order that their husbands might enjoy their beauty. For when a woman conceives, she becomes clumsy and stout. The proof is that so long as Sarah was barren she sat in her house like a bride in her bridal chamber, but when she became pregnant her charm faded; and so it says, *In pain thou shalt bring forth children* (Gen. 3:16). (See also *Numbers Rabbah* 10.2.)

Piety and Painless Childbirth

While apocalyptic visions of the future promised women that the punishment decreed in Genesis 3:16a would be reversed, the rabbinic tradition below suggested that women could be exempt from childbirth pain through piety and righteousness.

Sotah 12a

And the woman conceived and bare a son. But she had already been pregnant three months! R. Judah b. Zebina said: It compares the bearing of the child to its conception; as the conception was painless so was the bearing painless. Hence [it is learnt] that righteous women were not included in the decree upon Eve. (See also *Exodus Rabbah* 1.20.)

Who Works Harder, Adam or Eve?

Although the root for the Hebrew term used to describe woman's pain/toil (Gen. 3:16a) is the same term used to describe the pain/toil of man (Gen. 3:17), some rabbis saw a quantitative difference in the pain/toil described.

Genesis Rabbah 20.9

IN TOIL (*BE-'IZZABON*) SHALT THOU EAT OF IT. R. Issi said: The difficulties of earning a livelihood are twice as great as those of childbirth. In respect of birth it is written, "*In pain* (be-'ezeb) *shalt thou bring forth children*," whereas in respect of a livelihood it is written IN GREAT PAIN (*BE-'IZZABON*) SHALT THOU EAT OF IT. (See also *Pesahim* 118a, *Genesis Rabbah* 97.3.)

On Desiring Your Husband

Genesis 3:16b refers to a woman's desire for her husband and her husband's subsequent "rule" over her. In the rabbinic remarks below, it is woman's "desire" that draws the most comment.

Genesis Rabbah 20.7

Another interpretation of AND THY DESIRE SHALL BE TO THY HUSBAND: When a woman sits on the birthstool, she declares, "I will henceforth never fulfil my marital duties," whereupon the Holy One, blessed be He, says to her: "Thou wilt return to thy desire, thou wilt return to the desire for thy husband." R. Berekiah and R. Simon in the name of R. Simeon b. Yohai said: Because she fluttered in her heart, she must bring a fluttering sacrifice [i.e., a bird]: *She shall take two turtle-doves, or two young pigeons* (Lev. 12:8).

'Erubin 100b

. . . "*and thy desire shall be to thy husband*" teaches that a woman yearns for her husband when he is about to set out on a journey, "*and he shall rule over thee*" teaches that while the wife solicits with her heart the husband does so with his mouth, this being a fine trait of character among women?—What was meant is that she ingratiates herself with him. (See also *Yebamoth* 62b, *Song of Songs Rabbah* 7.11,1.)

It's All Adam's Fault

However the repercussions from the first disobedience were understood, the spotlight of blame fell on more than one character in the story (e.g., *Numbers*

Rabbah 10.2, which blames the serpent). The rabbinic traditions below, however, mention only Adam.

Numbers Rabbah 10.2

This applies to the ancient Adam, who was the first of all mankind, and who, through wine, received the penalty of death and caused the pangs of death to be brought upon the world.

Deuteronomy Rabbah 9.8

So Moses pleaded: "Master of the Universe, there are thirty-six transgressions punishable by extinction enumerated in the Torah, for the commission of any one of which a man is liable to be put to death. Have I then trangressed any one of them? Why dost Thou decree death upon me?" God replied: "You are to die because of the sin of the first man who brought death into the world."

It's All Eve's Fault

In the passage below, Eve—not Adam—is culpable for Adam's corruption and death.

Genesis Rabbah 17.8

"Why do they [the women] walk in front of the corpse [at a funeral]?" "Because they brought death into the world, they therefore walk in front of the corpse, [as it is written], *For he is borne to the grave . . . and all* men *draw* after *him, as there were innumerable* before *him*" (Job 21:32f). "And why was the precept of menstruation given to her?" "Because she shed the blood of Adam [by causing death], therefore was the precept of menstruation given to her." "And why was the precept of "dough" given to her?" "Because she corrupted Adam, who was the dough (*hallah*) of the world, therefore was the precept of dough given to her." "And why was the precept of the Sabbath lights given to her?" "Because she extinguished the soul of Adam, therefore was the precept of the Sabbath lights given to her."

You Have No One to Blame But Yourself

Rabbinic teachings that stressed individual responsibility, like the selection below, stood in some tension with those blaming Adam and Eve.

Numbers Rabbah 19.18

BECAUSE YE REBELLED AGAINST MY WORD (Num. 20:24). This bears on what Scripture says, *The Lord will not suffer the soul of the righteous to famish* (Prov. 10:3). It applies to Adam. All the righteous men that are to spring from him, and against whom death is decreed, will not depart this life without beholding the presence of the *Shechinah*, and they will reprove Adam by saying to him: "You have brought mortality upon us." Adam will answer them: "As for me, I have only one sin to my account, while in your case there is not a single man among you who has not at least four transgressions to his account!" How do we know that they behold the presence of the *Shechinah* and reprove Adam? Because the text has it, *I said: I shall not see the Lord, even the Lord in the land of the living; I shall behold man* (adam) *no more with the inhabitants of the world* (Isa. 38:11). The righteous are punished with death for slight transgressions. This is in order that Adam might not be called to account by them; as it says, "*The Lord will not suffer the soul of the righteous to famish.*" This is the reason why it says, BECAUSE YE REBELLED AGAINST MY WORD.

Did Adam Say He Was Sorry?

Diverse rabbinic traditions refer to God giving Adam an opportunity to repent. There was no rabbinic consensus, however, as to whether or not Adam availed himself of this opportunity. Both Adam the rebel and Adam the saint are images found in the selections below.

Genesis Rabbah 21.6

AND NOW LEST (PEN) HE PUT FORTH HIS HAND. R. Abba b. Kahana said: This teaches that the Holy One, blessed be He, provided him with an opportunity of repentance.

Genesis Rabbah 22.13

AND CAIN WENT OUT, etc. . . . . Adam met him and asked him, "How did your case go?" "I repented and am reconciled," replied he. Thereupon Adam began beating his face, crying, "So great is the power of repentance, and I did not know!" Forthwith he arose and exclaimed, *A Psalm, a song for the Sabbath day: It is a good thing to make confession unto the Lord* (Ps. 92:1).

'Erubin 18b

R. Meir said Adam was a great saint. When he saw that through him death was ordained as a punishment he spent a hundred and thirty years in fasting, severed connection with his wife for a hundred and thirty years, and wore clothes of fig [leaves] on his body for a hundred and thirty years.

Abodah Zarah 8a

Our Rabbis taught: When Adam, on the day of his creation, saw the setting of the sun he said, "Alas, it is because I have sinned that the world around me is becoming dark; the universe will now become again void and without form—this then is the death to which I have been sentenced from Heaven!" So he sat up all night fasting and weeping and Eve was weeping opposite him. When however dawn broke, he said: "This is the usual course of the world!" He then arose and offered up a bullock whose horns were developed before its hoofs, as it is said [by the Psalmist], *And it [my thanksgiving] shall please the Lord better than a bullock that hath horns and hoofs.*

Numbers Rabbah 13.3

AND HE THAT PRESENTED HIS OFFERING . . . WAS, etc. (7:12). This bears on the text, *A man's pride shall bring him low; but he that is of a lowly spirit shall attain to honour* (Prov. 29:23). Tanhuma b. Abba expounded: "*A man's pride shall bring him low*" applies to Adam. How? When Adam transgressed the commandment of the Holy One, blessed be He, and ate of the tree, the Holy One, blessed be He, desired that he should repent, and He gave him an opening, but Adam did not do so. Hence it is written, *And the Lord God said: Behold, the man is become as one of us . . . and now*, etc. (Gen. 3:22). What, asked R. Abba b. Kahana, is the import of "*And now*"? Simply this: that the Holy One, blessed be He, said to Adam, "Repent even now, and I shall accept thee." But Adam replied: "I will not." . . . This explains "*A man's pride shall bring him low*," because since he was too proud in the face of the Holy One, blessed be He, to repent, He brought him low and drove him from the Garden of Eden. (See also *Leviticus Rabbah* 10.5.)

Adam and Eve after Eden

The Pious Priest Adam

In the materials below God forgives Adam (no such forgiveness is extended to Eve!) and Adam becomes God's priest. Thus, it should not be surprising that in the last selection below, Adam becomes a hero who keeps company with the Messiah.

Leviticus Rabbah 29.1

Thus you are left to conclude that on New Year's Day, in the first hour the idea of creating man entered his mind, in the second he took counsel with the Ministering Angels, in the third He assembled Adam's dust, in the fourth he kneaded it, in the fifth he shaped him, in the sixth he made him into a lifeless body, in the seventh He breathed a soul into him, in the eighth He brought him into the Garden of Eden, in the ninth he was commanded [against eating of the fruit of the tree of knowledge], in the tenth he transgressed, in the eleventh he was judged, in the twelfth he was pardoned.

Genesis Rabbah 34.9

AND HE OFFERED BURNT-OFFERINGS ON THE ALTAR. R. Eliezer b. Jacob said: That means on the great altar in Jerusalem, where Adam sacrificed, as it is written, *And it shall please the Lord better than a bullock that hath horns and hoofs* (Ps. 69:32). (See also *Leviticus Rabbah* 2.7.)

Numbers Rabbah 4:8

There is proof that the firstborn offered the sacrifices before the tribe of Levi took office. Go back to the beginning of the creation of the world. Adam was the world's firstborn. When he offered his sacrifice, as it says: *And it pleased the*

Lord better than a bullock that hath horns and hoofs (Ps. 69:32)—he donned high priestly garments; as it says: *And the Lord God made for Adam and for his wife garments of skins, and clothed them* (Gen. 3:21). They were robes of honour which subsequent firstborn used. When Adam died he transmitted them to Seth.

Song of Songs Rabbah 8.9,3

If you see a Persian horse tethered to a grave in the land of Israel, look for the coming of the Messiah. Why so? Because it says, *And this shall be peace: when the Assyrian shall come into our land, and when he shall tread in our palaces, then shall we raise against him seven shepherds*, etc. (Mic. 5:4). These are the seven shepherds: David, in the centre, Adam, Seth, and Methuselah on his right hand, Abraham, Jacob, and Moses on his left.

The First Fratricide

What caused the ill will between Cain and his brother Abel? One rabbinic tradition blamed the "first" Eve for the fatal encounter between brothers.

Genesis Rabbah 22.7

AND CAIN SPOKE UNTO ABEL HIS BROTHER, etc. (Gen. 4:8). About what did they quarrel? . . . Judah b. Rabbi said: Their quarrel was about the first Eve.

Adam and Eve Separate

The biblical text records a 130-year gap between Cain and Abel's birth and that of Seth's. The rabbis explained this "gap" by suggesting that Adam slept apart from Eve.

Numbers Rabbah 14.12

THE WEIGHT THEREOF A HUNDRED AND THIRTY SHEKELS. This was in allusion to the one hundred and thirty years during which he had kept away from his wife, and at the end of which he begat Seth who was the first of this generation; as it says, *And Adam lived a hundred and thirty years, and begot a son in his own likeness, after his image; and called his name Seth* (Gen. 5:3). (See also *Genesis Rabbah* 20.11, 21.9.)

Affairs of the Loins

Two traditions arose to explain what happened during Adam and Eve's 130-year separation. While one imaged Adam as an abstemious saint (see earlier section of this chapter, "Did Adam Say He Was Sorry?"), the other developed the idea of Adam and Eve's sexual license.

Genesis Rabbah 20.11

R. Simon said: THE MOTHER OF ALL LIVING means, the mother of all life. For R. Simon said: Throughout the entire one hundred and thirty years during which Adam held aloof from Eve the male demons were made ardent by her and she bore, while the female demons were inflamed by Adam and they bore, as it is written, *If he commit iniquity, I will chasten him with the rod of men, and with the afflictions of the children of man—Adam* (2 Sam. 7:14) which means, the children of the first man. (See also *'Erubin* 18b, *Genesis Rabbah* 24.6.)

Getting Back Together

To the rabbis, the birth of Seth marked the reunion of Adam and Eve. Ironically, this tradition presents readers with a reversal of the punishment of Genesis 3:16b ("your desire shall be for your husband"). In the passage below, we find out that it is man's desire for woman that is increased.

Genesis Rabbah 23.4–5

Said he [Lamech] to them [his wives]: "Come let us go to Adam [and consult him]." So they went to him. He said to them: "Do you do your duty, while the Holy One, blessed be He, will do His." "Physician, physician, heal thine own limp!" retorted the other. "Have you kept apart from Eve a hundred and thirty years for any reason but that you might not beget children by her!" On hearing this, he [Adam] resumed his duty of begetting children and forthwith, *And Adam knew his wife again* (Gen. 4:25).

   5. [AND ADAM KNEW HIS WIFE FURTHERMORE.] Desire was added to his desire. Formerly he had experienced no desire when he did not see her, but now he desired her whether he saw her or not. (See also *Genesis Rabbah* 21.9.)

Humankind in the Post-Edenic World

Humankind Cut Down to Size

Since some rabbinic traditions imaged Adam as larger than life (see earlier section of this chapter, "Larger than Life"), it is not surprising that post-Edenic humankind is often imaged as diminished in stature, ability, and glory.

Sanhedrin 38b

Rab Judah said in Rab's name: The first man reached from one end of the world to the other, as it is written, *Since the day that God created man upon the earth, even from the one end of Heaven unto the other.* But when he sinned, the Holy One, blessed be He, laid His hand upon him and diminished him, as it is written, *Thou has hemmed me in behind and before, and laid Thy hands upon me.*

Genesis Rabbah 11.2

He blessed it in respect of the luminaries. R. Simeon b. Judah said: Though the luminaries were spoilt on the eve of the Sabbath, yet they were not smitten until the termination of the Sabbath. This agrees with the Rabbis but not with R. Assi, who maintained: Adam's glory did not abide the night with him. What is the proof? *But Adam passeth not the night in glory* (Ps. 49:13). The Rabbis mantain: His glory abode with him, but at the termination of the Sabbath He deprived him of his splendour and expelled him from the Garden of Eden, as it is written, *Thou changest his countenance, and sendest him away* (Job 14:20).

Genesis Rabbah 12.6

GENERATIONS (*TOLEDOTH*). All *toledoth* found in Scripture are defective, except two, viz. *These are the toledoth* (generations) *of Perez* (Ruth 4:18), and the present instance. And why are they defective? R. Judan said in R. Abun's name: The six [which they lack] corresponds to the six things which were taken away from Adam, viz., his lustre, his immortality [lit. 'life'], his height, the fruit of the earth, the fruit of trees, and the luminaries. Whence do we know this of his lustre?—*Thou changest his countenance, and sendest him away* (Job 14:20). His immortality?—*For dust thou art, and unto dust shalt thou return* (Gen. 3:19). His height?—For it says, *And the man and his wife hid themselves* (Gen. 3:8). R. Aibu said: His height was cut down and reduced to one hundred cubits. The fruit of the earth and the fruit of the tree?—*Cursed is the ground for thy sake*, etc. (Gen. 3:17). Luminaries?— R. Simeon b. Judah said: Though the luminaries were cursed on the eve of the Sabbath, they were not smitten until the termination of the Sabbath. This agrees with the Rabbis but not with R. Assi, who maintained: Adam did not retain his glory for a night. What is the proof? *But Adam passeth not the night in glory* (Ps. 49:13). The Rabbis maintain: He passed the night in his glory, but at the termination of the Sabbath, He deprived him of his splendour and expelled him from the Garden of Eden, as it is written, "*Thou changest his countenance, and sendest him away*" (Job 14:20). (See also *Genesis Rabbah* 21.3, *Leviticus Rabbah* 18.2, Numbers Rabbah 13.2, Song of Songs Rabbah 3.7,5, Hagigah 12a.)

Death in the World

In the passages below, death is understood as the result of Adam and Eve's sin (see also *Genesis Rabbah* 19.5, where Eve gives the fruit to the animals and, by implication, brings death to the animal world as well).

Genesis Rabbah 21.5

R. Berekiah said in R. Hanina's name: Like Elijah: just as he did not experience the taste of death, so [Adam] too was not meant to experience death.

Numbers Rabbah 10.2

"*Or as he that lieth upon the top of a mast*" (Prov. 23:34). This applies to the ancient Adam, who was the first of all mankind, and who, through wine, received the penalty of death and caused the pangs of death to be brought upon the world.

Exodus Rabbah 30.3

But you find, with the exception of two places—"*These are the generations of the heaven and the earth*" (Gen. 2:4) and *Now these are the generations of Perez* (Ruth 4:18)—the word '*toledoth*' whenever it occurs in the bible is spelt defectively, and for a very significant reason. Thus the word is spelt fully [with a *waw*] in the case of "*These are the generations of the heaven and the earth*," because when God created His world, there was no Angel of Death in the world, and on this account is it spelt fully; but as soon as Adam and Eve sinned, God made defective all the '*toledoth*' mentioned in the Bible. (See also *Genesis Rabbah* 21.5, *Exodus Rabbah* 38.2, *Numbers Rabbah* 23.13, *Deuteronomy Rabbah* 9.8, *Shabbath* 55b.)

Israel, Polluted until Sinai

[handwritten margin note: Torah cleansed the world of the C&E sin]

For some Rabbis, the serpent's copulation with Eve resulted in a limited "inherited pollution" for Israel. This pollution was cleansed by the giving of Torah at Mt. Sinai.

Yebamoth 103b

For R. Johanan stated: When the serpent copulated with Eve, he infused her with lust. The lust of the Israelites who stood at Mount Sinai came to an end, the lust of the idolaters who did not stand at Mount Sinai did not come to an end. (See also *Shabbath* 145b-46a, *Abodah Zarah* 22b.)

The Departure of God's Presence

According to some rabbis, one result of the disobedience in the Garden was that God's presence (the Shechinah) left the earth.

Genesis Rabbah 19.7

The real home of the *Shechinah* was in the nether sphere; when Adam sinned it departed to the first *rakia'* [firmament]. (See also *Numbers Rabbah* 12.6, 13.2, *Song of Songs Rabbah* 5.1,1.)

TARGUMS

Targum Onqelos

The *Targum Onqelos* account of Genesis, while interpretive, remains reasonably close to the Hebrew text. (Source: Bernard Grossfeld, translator, *The*

Targum Onqelos to Genesis: Translated, with a Critical Introduction, Apparatus, and Notes, Wilmington: Michael Glazier, 1988.)

Targum Onqelos to Genesis (c. 100s CE)

Genesis 1:26–31

[26]Then the Lord said, "Let us make man in our image according to our like-ness and they shall rule over the fish of the sea and over the fowl of the sky, and over the cattle and over all the earth as well as (over) every crawling thing that crawls upon the earth." [27]Now the Lord created Adam in His image, in the image of God He created him, male and female He created them. [28]And the Lord blessed them and the Lord said to them, "Be many and increase and fill the earth and have power over it, and rule over the fish of the sea and over the fowl of the sky and over every living creature that crawls upon the earth." [29]And the Lord said, "Here, I have given you every plant whose seed can be sown which is upon the face of all the earth, and every tree which has the fruit whose seed can be sown, for you it shall be to eat. [30]And to every beast of the earth, and to every fowl of the sky, and to everything that crawls upon the earth which has the breath of life in it, (I have given) every plant to eat," and it was so. [31]Then the Lord perceived that all that He had made was very proper, and it was evening and it was morning the sixth day.

Genesis 2:7–25

[7]Now the Lord God created Adam (as) dust from the earth and breathed into the {nostrils of} his face the breath of life and it became in Adam a spirit ut-tering speech. [8]And the Lord God planted a garden in Eden, in ancient times and He made Adam whom He created, dwell there. [9]And the Lord God caused to grow from the earth every tree that was desirable to look upon and good for eating; with the tree of life in the midst of the garden and the tree of which (those who eat its fruit) are perceptive (to know) good from evil. [10]Now, a river emanated from Eden to water the garden, and from there it divided into four main rivers. [11]The name of one is Pishon; it encompasses the whole land of Havilah, where there is gold. [12]And the gold of that land is good, there is bdellium there and the onyx stone. [13]And the name of the second river is Gihon; it encompasses the whole land of Kush. [14]And the name of the third river is Tigrith, it flows east of Ashur; and the fourth river is the Euphrates. [15]Now the Lord God took Adam and made him dwell in the garden of Eden to cultivate it and guard it. [16]And the Lord God commanded Adam as follows: "Of every tree of the garden you may eat freely. [17]But from the tree, of which those who eat its fruit are perceptive (to know) good from evil, you shall not eat from it; for on the day you eat from it you shall surely die." [18]Then the Lord God said, "It is not right that Adam should be alone; I will make him a support alongside of him." [19]And the Lord God created from the earth every wild beast and every fowl of the heaven, and brought them to Adam to see

what he would call them; and whatever Adam called each living creature, that was its name. [20]So Adam gave names to all the cattle and to the fowl of the heaven and to all the wild beasts, but for Adam no support alongside of him was found. [21]And the Lord cast a sleep upon Adam and he fell asleep; then He took one of his ribs and filled flesh in its place. [22]Then the Lord God fashioned the rib, which He had taken from Adam, into a woman and brought her to Adam. [23]And Adam said, "This time it is the bone of my bones and the flesh of my flesh; this one shall be called Woman, because from her husband was this one taken." [24]Therefore, a man should leave the sleeping abode of his father and his mother, and should cling to his wife, so that they become one flesh. [25]Now they were both naked, Adam and his wife yet they were not ashamed.

Genesis 3:1–24

[1]Now the serpent was more cunning than any wild beast which the Lord God had made; and it said to the woman, "Is it true that the Lord God said 'You shall not eat of any tree of the garden?' " [2]Whereupon the woman said to the serpent, "Of the fruit of the trees of the garden we may eat. [3]But concerning the fruit of the tree which is in the middle of the garden the Lord said, 'You shall not eat of it, and you shall not touch it, lest you die.' " [4]Then the serpent said to the woman, "You will surely not die. [5]For it is revealed before the Lord that on the day you eat of it your eyes will be opened, and you will be like angels perceptive (to know) good from evil." [6]Now when the woman realized that the tree was good for eating, and that it was a cure for the eyes, and the tree was desirable to become wise therewith, she took of its fruit and also gave to her husband (who was) with her, and he ate. [7]Then the eyes of both of them were opened and they perceived that they were naked, so they sewed fig leaves together for themselves and made girdles for themselves. [8]Then they heard the voice of the Memra of the Lord God walking in the garden towards the decline of the day; so Adam and his wife hid themselves from before the Lord God within a tree of the garden. [9]Whereupon the Lord God called out to Adam and said to him, "Where are you?" [10]And he said, "I heard the voice of Your Memra in the garden, but I was afraid because I was naked, so I hid." [11]Then He said, "Who told you that you were naked? Did you eat of the tree about which I commanded you not to eat of it?" [12]So Adam said, "The woman whom you gave (to be) with me, she gave me of the tree, and I ate." [13]Then the Lord God said to the woman, "What is this you have done?" And the woman said, "The serpent led me astray, and I ate." [14]So the Lord God said to the serpent, "Because you have done this, cursed are you more than all the cattle and more than all the wild beasts; on your belly you shall crawl, and dust you shall eat all the days of your life. [15]And I will place enmity between you and (between) the woman, and between your children and (between) her children; it will remember what you did to it in ancient time and you will sustain (your hatred) for it to the end (of time)." [16]And to the woman He said, "I will greatly

increase your pregnancy pains and inconveniences; with pain you shall bear children, yet to your husband shall be your desire and he shall dominate you." [17]And to Adam He said, "Because you have obeyed the word of your wife and you ate of the tree concerning which I commanded you, saying, 'You shall not eat from it'; cursed be the earth on your account; through toil you shall eat from it all the days of your life. [18]And thorns and thistles it shall sprout forth to you, and you shall eat the plants of the earth. [19]By the sweat of your face you shall eat bread until you are returned to the earth from which you were created, for dust you are and to dust you shall return." [20]Then Adam called the name of his wife Eve because she was the mother of all humanity. [21]And the Lord God made for Adam and his wife garments of honor for the skin of their flesh, and He clothed them. [22]Then the Lord God said, "Here, Adam has become the only one in the world knowing good from evil, and now perhaps he will stretch out his hand and also take from the tree of life and eat, and live forever." [23]So the Lord God banished him from the garden of Eden to till the soil whence he was created. [24]Then He expelled Adam and stationed to the east of Eden the cherubim and the sharp revolving sword to guard the way to the tree of life.

Genesis 4:1–2

[1]Now Adam knew Eve his wife, and she conceived and gave birth to Cain, saying, "I have acquired a man from before the Lord." [2]Then she gave birth again, to his brother Abel. Now Abel was a shepherd of flock, while Cain was a tiller of the soil.

Genesis 5:1–5

[1]This is the record of the generations of Adam; on the day when the Lord created man He made him in the likeness of God. [2]He created them male and female; and blessed them and called their name Adam on the day that they were created. [3]Now Adam lived 130 years, then begot (a son) in his likeness, who resembled him; and he called his name Seth. [4]And Adam's days after he begot Seth were 800 years, and he begot sons and daughters. [5]Now all the days that Adam lived were 930 years, then he died.

Targum Pseudo-Jonathan

Unlike *Targum Onqelos*, *Targum Pseudo-Jonathan* contains a wealth of haggadic expansions on the Genesis account of Adam and Eve. Many of the story elements found in this Targum are similar to those midrashic and talmudic themes discussed earlier in this chapter. (Source: Michael Maher, translator, *Targum Pseudo-Jonathan: Genesis*. Collegeville: Michael Glazier, 1992.)

Targum Pseudo-Jonathan: Genesis (pre-600 CE)

Genesis 1:26–31

[26]And God said to the angels who minister before him, who were created on the second day of the creation of the world, "Let us make man in our image, in our likeness, and let them have dominion over the fish of the sea, and over the birds that are in the air of the heavens, and over the cattle, and over all the earth, and over every creeping thing that creeps upon the earth." [27]And God created Adam in his own likeness, in the image of God he created him, with two hundred and forty-eight members, with six hundred and sixty-five nerves, and he formed a skin over him, and filled it with flesh and blood; male and female in their appearance he created them. [28]God blessed them, and God said to them, "Increase and multiply and fill the earth with sons and daughters, and become powerful in possessions upon it, and have dominion over the fish of the sea and over the birds of the heavens, and over every creeping animal that creeps upon the earth." [29]God said, "Behold I have given to you every plant whose seed is sown, that is upon the face of all the earth, and every unfruitful tree for the requirements of building and for burning; and (every tree) on which there is fruit whose seed is sown shall be yours for food. [30]To every beast of the earth, to every bird of the heavens, and to everything that creeps upon the earth, in which there is the breath of life, (I give) every green plant." And it was so. [31]And God saw all that he had made, and behold, it was very good. And there was evening and there was morning, a sixth day.

Genesis 2:7, 18–25

[7]The Lord God created Adam with two inclinations. And he took dust from the site of the sanctuary and from the four winds of the world, and a mixture of all the waters of the world and created him red, black and white. And he breathed into his nostrils the breath of life, and the breath became in the body of Adam a spirit capable of speech, to give light to the eyes and to give hearing to the ears. . . .

[18]And the Lord God said, "It is not right that Adam should sleep alone; I will make for him a woman who will be a support alongside him." [19]So the Lord God created from the ground every beast of the field and every bird of the heavens, and brought (them) to Adam to see what name he would call them; and whatever Adam called each living creature, that was its name. [20]And Adam gave their names to all the cattle and to all the birds of the heavens, and to all the beasts of the field; but for Adam, no support alongside him was yet found. [21]The Lord God cast a deep sleep upon Adam, and he slept. And he took one of his ribs—it was the thirteenth rib of the right side—and he closed its place with flesh. [22]And the Lord God built the rib he had taken from Adam into a woman and brought her to Adam. [23]And Adam said, "This time, but never again will woman be created from man as this one has been created from me—bone of my bones and flesh of my flesh. It is fitting to call this one

woman, for she has been taken from man." [24]Therefore a man shall leave and be separated from the bedroom of his father and of his mother, and he shall be united to his wife, and the two of them shall become one flesh. [25]And the two of them were wise, Adam and his wife, but they did not remain in their glory.

Genesis 3:1–24

[1]Now the serpent was more skilled in evil than all the beasts of the field which the Lord God had made. And he said to the woman, "Is it true that the Lord God said, 'You shall not eat of any tree of the garden'?" [2]And the woman said to the serpent, "We are allowed to eat of the fruit of the other trees of the garden; [3]but of the fruit of the tree in the middle of the garden the Lord said, 'You shall not eat of it and you shall not touch it, lest you die.' " [4]At that moment the serpent spoke slander against his creator, and said to the woman, "You shall not die. But every craftsman hates his fellow craftsman. [5]For it is manifest before the Lord that on the day on which you eat of it you shall be like the great angels, who are able to distinguish good from evil." [6]And the woman saw Sammael the angel of death and she was afraid. She knew that the tree was good to eat, that it was a cure for the light of the eyes, and that the tree was desirable as a source of wisdom. And she took of its fruit and ate; and she also gave to her husband (who was) with her, and he ate. [7]Then the eyes of both of them were enlightened and they knew that they were naked because they were stripped of the clothing of fingernails in which they had been created, and they saw their shame; and they sewed fig leaves for themselves, and they made girdles for themselves. [8]They heard the voice of the Memra of the Lord God strolling in the garden at the decline of the day; and Adam and his wife hid themselves from before the Lord God in the midst of the trees in the garden. [9]The Lord God called to Adam and said to him, "Is not the whole world which I created manifest before me, the darkness as well as the light? How then do you imagine in your heart that you can hide yourself from before me? Do I not see the place where you are hiding? And where are the commandments that I commanded you?" [10]He said, "I heard the voice of your Memra in the garden and I was afraid, for I was naked, because I neglected the commandment you gave me, and I hid myself for shame." [11]He said, "Who told you that you were naked? Perhaps you have eaten of the fruit of the tree from which I commanded you not to eat?" [12]And Adam said, "The woman you put beside me, she gave me of the fruit of the tree and I ate." [13]The Lord God said to the woman. "What is this you have done?" And the woman said, "The serpent lured me with his cleverness and led me astray in his wickedness, and I ate." [14]Then the Lord God brought the three of them to judgment, and he said to the serpent, "Because you have done this, cursed are you above all cattle, and above all beasts of the field. Upon your belly you shall go about, and your feet shall be cut off, and you will cast off your skin once every seven years, and the poison of death will be in your mouth, and you shall eat dust all the days of your life. [15]And I will put enmity between you and the woman,

between the offspring of your children and the offspring of her children. And when the children of the woman keep the commandments of the Law, they will take aim and strike you on your head. But when they forsake the commandments of the Law you will take aim and wound them on their heels. For them, however, there will be a remedy; but for you there will be no remedy; and they are to make peace in the end, in the days of the King Messiah." [16]To the woman (he said), "I will greatly multiply your affliction in the blood of virginity and (in) your pregnancies; in pain you shall bear children, yet your desire shall be for your husband; he shall rule over you both for righteousness and for sin." [17]And to Adam he said, "Because you listened to the word of your wife, and ate of the fruit of the tree concerning which I commanded you saying, 'You shall not eat of it,' cursed be the earth because it did not show you your guilt; by toil you shall eat of it all the days of your life. [18]Thorns and thistles it shall sprout and produce because of you; and you shall eat the plants that are upon the surface of the field." Adam answered and said, "I beseech by the mercy before you, O Lord, Let me not be reckoned before you as cattle, that I should eat the grass of the surface of the field. I will rise and labor with the labor of my hands, and I will eat of the food of the earth; and thus let there be a distinction before you between the children of men and the offspring of cattle." [19]"By the labor of your hand you shall eat food until you return to the dust from which you were created, because dust you are, and to dust you will return; but from the dust you are destined to arise to render an account and a reckoning of all you have done, on the day of great judgment." [20]Adam named his wife Eve, because she was the mother of all human beings. [21]And the Lord God made garments of glory for Adam and for his wife from the skin which the serpent had cast off (to be worn) on the skin on their flesh, instead of their (garments of) fingernails of which they had been stripped, and he clothed them. [22]And the Lord God said to the angels who minister before him, "Behold, Adam was alone on the earth as I am alone in the heavens on high. From him there will arise those who will know how to distinguish between good and evil. If he had kept the commandments (which) I commanded him he would have lived and endured like the tree of life forever. But now, since he has not observed what I commanded him, let us decree against him, and let us banish him from the Garden of Eden, before he puts forth his hand and takes (also) of the fruit of the tree of life. For behold, if he eats of it, he will live and endure forever." [23]And the Lord God drove him out of the Garden of Eden, and he went and settled on Mount Moriah to till the soil from which he had been created. [24]And he drove Adam out of (the place) where, from the beginning, he had caused the Glory of his Shekinah to dwell between the two cherubim. Before he had yet created the world, he created the Law. He established the garden of Eden for the righteous, that they might eat and take delight in the fruit of the tree, for having during their lives cherished the instruction of the Law in this world and fulfilled the precepts. For the wicked he established Gehenna, which is like a sharp two-edged sword. Within it he established sparks of fire and burning coals with which to judge the wicked, who during their lives rebelled against the instruction of the Law. The Law is better for him who toils in it than the fruit of the tree of life, (that Law) which the Memra of the Lord established to be kept so that people might endure and walk in the paths of the way of life in the world to come.

Genesis 4:1–2

[1]Adam knew his wife Eve who had conceived from Sammael, the angel of the Lord. [2]Then, from Adam her husband she bore his twin sister and Abel.

Genesis 5:1–3

[1]This is the record of the genealogical line of Adam. On the day that the Lord created Adam, in the likeness of the Lord he made him. [2]Male and female he created them. He blessed them in the name of his Memra, and called their name Adam on the day they were created. [3]When Adam had lived a hundred and thirty years, he begot Seth, who resembled his image and likeness. For before that, Eve had borne Cain, who was not from him and who did not resemble him. Abel was killed by Cain, and Cain was banished, and his descendants are not recorded in the book of the genealogy of Adam. But afterwards he begot one who resembled him and he called his name Seth.

CHAPTER FOUR

Early Christian Interpretations
(50–450 CE)

INTRODUCTION

Early Christian interpretations of Genesis 1-3 comprise a variety of texts. New Testament references of note range from the relatively early letters of Paul to the Pastoral Epistles (especially 1 Timothy) of the second century. In addition to the New Testament treatments, extracanonical sources such as the various gnostic scriptures and the Apocryphal Acts of the Apostles, as well as the writings of the Church "Fathers" (male writers who represented the view of Christianity eventually defined as orthodoxy), commented extensively on Genesis 1-3. Though the egalitarian model had its advocates, particularly in the earliest Christian communities, for the most part the New Testament authors and the Fathers found in the creation account a hierarchical universe that subordinated women to men.

New Testament Interpretations

Scholars have long debated how accurately the subordinate position frequently accorded women in the New Testament reflected the status of women in the earliest Christian communities. From Hans von Campenhausen[1] in 1953 to Elisabeth Schussler Fiorenza[2] among contemporary authorities, scholars have argued for decades that the earliest Christian communities, as illegal sects of persons called out from the larger culture, tended to be less hierarchical and more open to charismatic leadership than was the later institutionalized church. The New Testament makes a number of references to women leaders in the early community of believers. Some scholars consider some of the references rather oblique—such as the role of proclaiming the resurrection entrusted to Mary Magdalene and other women in the Gospels, or promises given to women at the day of Pentecost that God's Spirit will be poured "upon all flesh, and your sons and your daughters shall prophesy" (Acts 2:17, NRSV). Other references are more straightforward. Romans 16 identifies a woman named Phoebe as a deacon and another woman called Junia as an apostle. Philemon and Colossians mention by name women who were leaders in the early Christian movement, and the apostle Paul recognizes several women—such as Mary, Tryphena, Tryphosa, and Persis in Romans (16:6, 12) and Euodia and Syntyche in Philippians (4:2 ff.)—as missionaries of the gospel.[3]

Wayne Meeks has argued that such references indicate that "in the Pauline school women could enjoy a functional equality in leadership roles that would have been unusual in Greco-Roman society as a whole and quite astonishing in comparison with contemporary Judaism."[4] The creation account in Genesis was central to that egalitarian understanding of gender. In Galatians 3:27-28, Paul wrote: "As many of you as were baptized in Christ have clothed yourselves with Christ. There is no longer Jew or Greek, there is no longer *male and female*; for all of you are one in Christ Jesus" (NRSV; emphasis added). Paul's reference in verse 28 to the creation account of Genesis 1:27[5] indicated that early Christians construed baptism ("as many of you as were baptized into Christ") as a reunification ritual. Galatians 3:28 suggested, as Meeks explained, "that somehow the act of Christian initiation reverses the fateful division of Genesis 2:21-22. Where the image of God is restored, there, it seems, man [sic] is no longer divided—not even by the most fundamental division of all, male and female."[6]

Christian baptism, according to this view, was a dramatic ritual. Initiates disrobed and were immersed in water. They then donned new clothing symbolic of putting on Christ and becoming new creations conformed to the image of the Creator, in whom there were no gender distinctions. Divided among themselves no longer by social discriminations, early Christian converts heard the pronouncement of their unity in Christ as a statement of objective reality. The dishonorable clothing of animal skins that Eve and Adam had worn after the first sin had been replaced by the clothing of Christ, the redeemer who remade believers in the divine image. Such symbolism had the power (and was intended) to create among believers new attitudes and behaviors. Hierarchical social roles had no place in the new order of being.[7]

In time, however, believers came to define the "new creation" less in terms of the individual's experience of redemption in Christ and more as a metaphor for the unity the community of believers shared with Christ.[8] Egalitarian gender roles lost their significance as signs of the new order, and hierarchical roles resumed. Accordingly, a second Pauline consideration of Genesis 1-3 came to dominate exegetical discussions. In the midst of pondering the proper attire for women leading public prayer, Paul argued in 1 Corinthians 11:7-12 that man "is the image and reflection of God; but woman is the reflection of man." Paul's explanation for this distinction was that "man was not made from woman, but woman from man." Paul then moderated this hierarchy with the admonition that "in the Lord woman is not independent of man or man independent of woman," concluding that "all things come from God" (NRSV).

While the consequence of man having been created before woman was not entirely clear in 1 Corinthians, the more the church became institutionalized, the more Christians came to believe that the order of creation *was* theologically significant—and the more Christians came to rely upon Genesis 2 as the authoritative account of creation. As a result, man, as "head" of woman, came to be identified with Christ, the "head" of the church. In addition, New Testament texts such as Ephesians 5:22-6:10, Colossians 3:18-4:1, Titus 2:4-10, and 1 Peter 2:13-3:12 offered household codes instructing Christians how to order their home lives. These texts instructed wives to be subject to husbands, children to be subject to parents, and slaves to be subject to masters at the same time that the texts admonished the superior partners— the husbands, parents, and masters—to be wise and compassionate heads. Love bound all believers, but status distinctions remained.

1 Timothy 2:11-15, presumed by scholars to be a second-century document, provided the interpretation of Paul that became most influential for subsequent defenders of orthodoxy in the church's first five centuries. Noting that Paul in 1 Corinthians gave theological precedence to Adam because, according to the second creation account, Adam was created before Eve, the writer of 1 Timothy commanded women to exercise no authority over men. Women, the writer claimed, should be silent during worship. "For Adam was formed first, then Eve; and Adam was not deceived, but the woman was deceived and became a transgressor. Yet she will be saved through childbearing . . . " (NRSV). Both the notion that Eve (and, by implication, all women) was solely responsible for sin and the idea that woman's salvation depended upon bearing children would prove crucial to discussions throughout the early church period.

Early Christian Interpretations: Gnostic Readings

Discussions continued apace. From the beginning (and long before the famous trinitarian and christological controversies of the fourth and fifth centuries), competing groups of believers battled one another for control of the church. As a new religion, Christianity experienced an extended period of debate and division before reaching (or enforcing) a rough consensus on what constituted definitive Christian doctrine and practice. The "orthodox" groups who eventually gained supremacy tended to minimize the authority of women in the church. "Heretical" factions who disagreed often appealed to the earliest practices of the church to justify their views. Second-century groups like the Marcionites and Montanists, both of whom gave considerably more leadership and authority to women than did the emerging orthodox church, claimed to be reviving the religion of the apostles over against the unhealthy innovations of the orthodox.

The group (or, to be precise, groups) of believers that posed the strongest opposition to the orthodox were the assorted bands of gnostic Christians. From the earliest days of the church, the gnostics and the orthodox were embroiled in a battle to create the definitive form of Christianity. At the heart of that contention lay a conflict over the meaning of Genesis 1-3. Indeed, Elaine Pagels has asserted that it "is an oversimplification—but not much—to look at the whole controversy between orthodox and gnostic Christians as a battle over the disputed territory of the first three chapters of Genesis."[9]

According to Pagels, gnostic Christians, unlike the orthodox, did not read Genesis 1-3 as though it were "history with a moral." Rather, gnostic Christians read the text as "myth with a meaning." Interested in symbolic explications, gnostic Christians interpreted Genesis 1-3 as a story of the interaction within the individual between the human *psyche* (ordinary consciousness) and the *spirit* (spiritual consciousness, or higher self). In some gnostic texts, Adam represented the higher self; in other texts (such as the *Apocryphon of John* and the *Hypostasis of the Archons*), Eve represented the higher power who emerged from Adam as he slept, urging him to awaken to the spiritual enlightenment dormant within him.[10]

Gnostic cosmologies were far more complicated than those of the orthodox. For gnostic Christians, the creation was never the work of a single deity, but always the complicated outworking of ranks of various cosmic powers. But like Paul in Galatians 3:28, gnostic Christians were attracted to the notion that redemption in Christ was a return to a primordial union that existed prior to Adam's separation from Eve. The gnostic *Gospel According to Philip* contended that in "the days when Eve was [in] Adam, death did not exist. When she was separated from him, death came into existence. If he [reenters] and takes it unto himself death will not exist."[11] Gnostic literature also echoed the Pauline concern that believers clothe themselves with Christ. Thus, where Colossians spoke of putting off the body of flesh in order to clothe "yourselves with the new self, which is being renewed in knowledge according to the image of its creator,"[12] the *Gospel According to Philip* warned that "no one can obtain this grace without putting on the perfect light [and] becoming, as well, perfect light."[13]

Other gnostic writings depicted the return to the archetypal union of male and female as a choice to lead an ascetic lifestyle. In the *Gospel According to Thomas*, Jesus told the disciples that "when you make the two one . . . that you might make the male and the female be one and the same," then they would "enter the kingdom of heaven." At the end of the book, Peter asked Jesus to send Mary Magdalene away, since she, as a woman, was not worthy of life. But Jesus answered that "I am going to attract her to make her male so that she too might become a living spirit that resembles you males. For every female (element) that makes itself male will enter the kingdom of heavens."[14]

Wayne Meeks has contended that the ideal of "singleness" advocated in the *Gospel According to Thomas* signified both celibacy and asocial isolation. The reference to Mary becoming "a living spirit" may be an allusion to the creation of Adam in Genesis 2:7. But the book's emphasis on salvation as self-knowledge[15] suggested to Meeks that the categories of male and female were metaphors for aspects of the believer's personality. For the two to become one, or the female to become male, the believer must advance in virtue and spiritual consciousness. The path of transformation demanded that the believer renounce all social ties. The *Gospel According to Thomas* promised believers that those who declared war on their parents, their siblings, and their children "will stand at rest by being solitaries." Proclaiming that "whoever has become acquainted with the world has found a corpse," Jesus warned his followers that "buyers and traders [will] not enter the places of my father." Meeks concluded that for ascetics "in these circles the union of male and female represents not a heightened or even a spiritualized libido, but a neutralization of sexuality, and therewith a renunciation of all ties which join the 'unified' individual with society."[16]

Orthodox and Apocryphal Uses of Genesis 1–3

While gnostic Christians were interested in reading Genesis 1-3 metaphorically, using it as a guide for spiritual enlightenment, orthodox Christians read the text as history, seeking in it a guide to moral behavior.[17] Almost universally, the orthodox subsumed the first creation account in Genesis 1 under the second account in Genesis 2-3. They saw in Genesis 2-3 a hierarchical universe in which men were superior to women, and they argued that the text functioned as a practical guide to gender relations. Woman was, by most accounts, a subservient partner created to serve man and to bear him children. She was not man's equal in proclaiming the gospel, and, in general, she served God best by being silent. The leadership roles that women played in the earliest days of the Christian movement faded from memory, as the church Fathers fashioned a church structure in which authority adhered to offices (such as priest and bishop) that only men could hold.

The orthodox isolated a number of significant themes in Genesis 1-3. Quoting 1 Corinthians 11:7-10 with approval, they noted that God created man first as a sign of man's superiority to woman. The fact that God formed Eve from Adam's side to be Adam's "helper" proved once again that woman was the inferior partner. Most church Fathers assumed that God created Eve for one reason only: that humanity might be able to procreate. Augustine commented that for any other purpose, a man would have provided Adam better company; therefore, he concluded, "I cannot think of any reason for woman's being made as man's helper, if we dismiss the reason of procreation."[18]

The orthodox also made much of Eve having fallen into sin before Adam. 1 Timothy's insistence that the serpent had deceived Eve, but not Adam, carried great significance. The Fathers concluded that women were less rational than men and more prone to evil. They identified the original sin with disorder in the divinely ordained hierarchy of gender relations. In persuading Adam to eat forbidden fruit, Eve had usurped Adam, and Adam had failed to exercise leadership. The consequences were far-reaching, as John Chrysostom observed:

> The woman taught once and for all, and upset everything. Therefore he [1 Timothy] says, "Let her not teach." Then does it mean something for the rest of womankind, that Eve suffered this judgment? It certainly does concern other women! For the female sex is weak and vain, and here this is said of the whole sex.[19]

Though the orthodox consoled themselves that women afforded men the possibility of fathering children, the orthodox feared the lust and loss of rational control that they identified with sexuality. Associating virginity with divine incorruptibility, the orthodox preferred celibacy to marriage. Some, like Chrysostom, insisted that if there had never been a Fall, God would have accomplished reproduction by asexual means. Others, like Augustine, contended that God always intended for humanity to reproduce sexually, but that sexual intercourse prior to sin would have been a dispassionate and rational activity not unlike that of a farmer planting crops. In associating women with sin and sexual desire, the church Fathers came close to despising women. It was difficult to follow Augustine's admonition to love in one's wife "what is human," while hating in her "what pertains to a wife."[20]

Nevertheless, egalitarian interpretations of Genesis 1–3 did not disappear in the church. At times, the church Fathers themselves revived the egalitarian model. Chrysostom, for example, suggested that, as bone of Adam's bone and flesh of Adam's flesh (Genesis 2:23), Eve was originally "equal in honor" to Adam. She was not subject to subordination, Chrysostom contended, until she "misused her power . . . and ruined everything."[21] Given their admiration for the celibate life, the church Fathers also viewed asceticism as an avenue for women (as well as men) to recapture the perfection of the original creation. They depicted Mary as the obedient virgin who reversed the cycle of sin and death initiated by Eve's disobedience. Gregory of Nyssa argued that the helper given to humanity in Genesis 2:18 was not Eve, but virginity. Finally, some offices of spiritual authority remained available to women. Though the priesthood was closed to them, women whose husbands had died could exercise a number of pastoral duties in the order of widows and, at least in the Eastern church, women could also aspire to the order of deaconesses.[22]

Women who filled the office of widow or deaconess were required to be celibate as well as submissive to male clergy. Widows and deaconesses did not preach. Yet they could, by renouncing their sexuality, raise their status within the church. Women who aspired to higher status in the church were depicted in the Apocryphal Acts, a form of Christian literature that arose in the late second and third centuries, and in accounts of martyrdom.[23] The Apocryphal Acts, like gnostic literature such as the *Gospel According to Thomas*, made explicit what orthodoxy's emphasis on celibacy and asceticism implied: in embracing the rigorous spiritual life, women became "like men," reclaiming the archetypal union of male and female that preceded the fall into sin.

Women played vigorous roles in the accounts of martyrs. In *The Martyrdom of Perpetua and Felicitas*, Perpetua gave up her baby and underwent martyrdom rather than renounce her faith as a Christian. The text made clear, in a dream sequence described by her fellow martyr Saturus, that God honored Perpetua's sacrifice. In Saturus's dream, he and Perpetua were permitted to meet God face to face, while outside the divine presence a priest and a bishop knelt before the two martyrs, humbly seeking their advice. Before the day she was to be martyred, Perpetua had a vision of herself in the arena, stripped of clothing and suddenly becoming a man, as she successfully battled an Egyptian gladiator. When the day of martyrdom actually came, Perpetua faced her "second baptism" with such fortitude that the writer insisted that the Holy Spirit that had in fullness of grace moved "sons and daughters to prophesy" in the ancient church "even in our day . . . is still efficaciously present."[24]

The motifs of baptism and of a reuniting of male and female were even more obvious in the apocryphal *Acts of Paul and Thecla*. Converted by Paul, the virgin Thecla refused to marry the man to whom she was engaged. When attempts to burn her and to feed her to wild beasts failed to harm her, she threw herself into a pit of water filled with dangerous seals, saying, "In the name of Jesus Christ, I baptize myself on the last day." A flash of fire killed the seals, and Thecla, surrounded by a cloud of fire, was not "perceived as naked." Thus Thecla reversed the shame that had, ever since the Fall, been associated with human nakedness. Yearning to see Paul again, Thecla dressed in men's clothing and sought him out, informing him that "the One who worked together with you in the Gospel also worked with me for my being baptized."[25]

Thecla was a model for the woman who, through baptism and asceticism, was restored to the image of a God who was neither male nor female. Thus, Galatians 3:27-28 continued to undergird the relatively egalitarian interpretations of Genesis 1-3 that had been more prevalent in the earliest days of the Christian movement. For the majority of the orthodox who strove to define Christianity in the postapostolic age, however, Genesis 1-3 constructed a hierarchical creation that subordinated women to men. Though asceticism offered women the possibility of greater spiritual status, redemption in Christ did not alter women's subservience to men.

NOTES TO CHAPTER 4, INTRODUCTION

1. Hans von Campenhausen, *Kirchliches Amt und geistliche Vollmacht in den ersten drei Jahrhunderten* (Tübingen, Germany: Mohr, 1953). For an English version, see

J. A. Baker, translator, *Ecclesiastical Authority and Spiritual Power* (Stanford: Stanford University Press, 1969).

2. See, among many other of her works, Elisabeth Schussler Fiorenza, *In Memory of Her*.

3. Elisabeth Schussler Fiorenza, "Women in the Early Christian Movement," in Carol P. Christ and Judith Plaskow, editors, *Womanspirit Rising: A Feminist Reader in Religion* (San Francisco: Harper & Row, 1979); pp. 89-91; and *In Memory of Her*, pp. 168-84.

4. Wayne A. Meeks, "The Image of the Androgyne: Some Uses of a Symbol in Earliest Christianity," *History of Religions* 13 (1973): 198.

5. "So God created humankind in his own image; *male and female* he created them" (NRSV; emphasis added). The phrase is repeated in Genesis 5:1-2: "When God created humankind, he made them in the likeness of God. *Male and female* he created them . . . " (NRSV; emphasis added).

6. Meeks, "The Image of the Androgyne," p. 185. Schussler Fiorenza notes that a return to a presexual state did not necessarily connote androgyny. It could simply indicate that "sexual dimorphism, and gender roles based on it, must be relinquished to enter the kingdom." Thus, she interprets the phrase "no longer male and female" to mean that "patriarchal marriage—and sexual relationships between male and female—is no longer constitutive of the new community in Christ" (*In Memory of Her*, pp. 212, 211).

7. Meeks, "The Image of the Androgyne," pp. 182-89.

8. Meeks, "The Image of the Androgyne," pp. 204-206. Meeks noted that an example of the changed emphasis can be seen in Ephesians 5: 22-33. First the text states that wives should be subject to husbands as the church is subject to Christ, its head. Then the text appeals to husbands and wives to love each other as much as they love themselves. For just as Christians are members of one body—Christ's—so too a husband and wife become (and here the text cites Genesis 2:24) one flesh. "This," the text concludes, "is a great mystery." But what is mysterious is *not*, as in Galatians, that the distinctions of male and female have passed away. Rather, the mystery is that, in spite of (or in the midst of) status distinctions based upon gender, wife and husband nevertheless love each other as they love themselves. The unity in Galatians is a unity of status; all are recreated, and former distinctions have passed away. In Ephesians, the unity is of love; differences not only remain, but they are theologically significant. The husband is like Christ, who rules the church; the obedient wife is a symbol of the church, which is submissive to its head.

9. Elaine Pagels, "Adam and Eve and the Serpent in Genesis 1-3," in Karen L. King, editor, *Images of the Feminine in Gnosticism* (Philadelphia: Fortress Press, 1988), p. 413.

10. Pagels, "Adam and Eve and the Serpent in Genesis 1-3," pp. 414-15.

11. *The Gospel According to Philip* (63). Quoted from Bentley Layton, translator, *The Gnostic Scriptures* (Garden City, N.Y.: Doubleday & Company, 1987), p. 342. All subsequent quotations from the gnostic gospels will be taken from this volume.

12. Colossians 2:11 and 3:10. See Meeks, "The Image of the Androgyne," pp. 183-89.

13. Layton, *The Gospel According to Philip* (90), p. 348. See also Pagels, "Pursuing the Spiritual Eve," pp. 199-204. Probably the most famous example in gnostic literature of clothing representing both the pure self as well as the image of the divine is the *Hymn of the Pearl*. There, a young man descended from the heavenly realm of his parents in order to capture a pearl in the land of Egypt. On his arrival, he donned the attire of the Egyptians, and immediately forgot his true identity. Only the receipt of a message from his parents reminded him of his mission. After snatching the pearl, the young man shed the clothing of the Egyptians and reclaimed the royal robe of his childhood. Of that robe, he said, "I perceived in it my whole self," as well as "the image of the King of Kings" that "was (woven) all through it" (Layton, pp. 371-75).

14. Layton, *The Gospel According to Thomas* (22, 114), pp. 384, 399.

15. Layton, *The Gospel According to Thomas* (3): "The kingdom is inside of you. And it is outside of you. When you become acquainted with yourselves, then you will be recognized. And you will understand that it is you who are children of the living father. But if you do not become acquainted with yourselves, then you are in poverty, and it is you who are the poverty."

16. Meeks, "The Image of the Androgyne," pp. 193-97. Quotations from Layton, *The Gospel of Thomas* (16, 57, 64), pp. 383, 390-92.

17. Pagels, "Adam and Eve and the Serpent in Genesis 1-3," p. 413.

18. Augustine, *On the Good of Marriage*, quoted in Elizabeth A. Clark, editor, *Women in the Early Church*, Message of the Fathers of the Church, 13 (Wilmington, Del.: Michael Glazier, 1983), p. 29.

19. John Chrysostom, *Homily 9 on 1 Timothy*, quoted in Clark, *Women in the Early Church*, p. 158.

20. Clark, pp. 122-31, 58-60, 64-65. The quotation comes from Augustine's *On the Sermon on the Mount*.

21. Chrysostom, *Homily 26 on 1 Corinthians*, quoted in Clark, *Women in the Early Church*, p. 42. See also pp. 43-44.

22. Clark, *Women in the Early Church*, pp. 120, 175-81.

23. Clark, *Women in the Early Church*, pp. 77-78.

24. *The Martyrdom of Perpetua*, in Patricia Wilson-Kastner, G. Ronald Kastner, Ann Millin, Rosemary Rader, and Jeremiah Reedy, *A Lost Tradition: Women Writers of the Early Church* (Lanham, Md.: University Press of America, 1981), pp. 19-30. The document's insistence that the Holy Spirit continued to guide and empower believers just as it did in the earliest Christian communities prompts scholars to associate it with North African Montanist Christianity (p. 2). See also Clark, *Women in the Early Church*, p. 97.

25. *The Acts of Paul and Thecla*, in Clark, *Women in the Early Church*, pp. 78-88; Meeks, "The Image of the Androgyne," p. 196.

NEW TESTAMENT

The following texts are arranged into two categories. The first category consists of New Testament passages that might be construed to support an egalitarian reading of Genesis 1-3. These passages suggest either that redemption in Christ meant being remade according to God's image and returning to the original created order, in which social status distinctions were nonexistent, or, more minimally (as in the case of 1 Corinthians 15:21-22), that the blame for the Fall rested upon Adam. Commentators among the early church Fathers characteristically avoided the latter passage in favor of 1 Timothy 2:8-15, which blamed Eve for the Fall and exonerated Adam.

The second category consists of New Testament texts that employ a hierarchical interpretation of Genesis 1-3. Such passages assume that the cosmos constitutes a hierarchy (or chain) of being, with God at the head, Christ below God, and the church below Christ. Because man was created first, according to these texts, he functioned as woman's head. Ephesians 5:21-29 represents a "household code," or advice on how to order a household. Such household codes were a common genre in the Hellenistic world. Ephesians appealed to a patriarchal worldview typical of Greco-Roman culture: husbands above wives, parents above children, masters above slaves. The passages from 2 Corinthians and from 1 Timothy are notable for singling out Eve as the person responsible for the Fall. Later Christian commentators who favored a hierarchical interpretation of Genesis 1-3 would repeatedly cite such New Testament texts. (Source: The New Revised Standard Version of the Bible.)

"Egalitarian" Texts
(c. 50–150 CE)

1 Corinthians 15:21–22

²¹For since death came through a human being, the resurrection of the dead has also come through a human being; ²²for as all die in Adam, so all will be made alive in Christ.

Galatians 3:27–28

²⁷As many of you as were baptized into Christ have clothed yourselves with Christ. ²⁸There is no longer Jew or Greek, there is no longer slave or free, there is no longer male and female; for all of you are one in Christ Jesus.

Ephesians 4:22–24

²²You were taught to put away your former way of life, your old self, corrupt and deluded by its lusts, ²³and to be renewed in the spirit of your minds, ²⁴and to clothe yourselves with the new self, created according to the likeness of God in true righteousness and holiness.

Colossians 3:9–11

⁹Do not lie to one another, seeing that you have stripped off the old self with its practices ¹⁰and have clothed yourselves with the new self, which is being renewed in knowledge according to the image of its creator. ¹¹In that renewal there is no longer Greek and Jew, circumcised and uncircumcised, barbarian, Scythian, slave and free; but Christ is all in all!

"Hierarchical" Texts
(c. 50–150 CE)

1 Corinthians 11:3–12

³But I want you to understand that Christ is the head of every man, and the husband is the head of his wife, and God is the head of Christ. ⁴Any man who prays or prophesies with something on his head disgraces his head, ⁵but any woman who prays or prophesies with her head unveiled disgraces her head—it is one and the same thing as having her head shaved. ⁶For if a woman will not

veil herself, then she should cut off her hair; but if it is disgraceful for a woman to have her hair cut off or to be shaved, she should wear a veil. [7]For a man ought not to have his head veiled, since he is the image and reflection of God; but woman is the reflection of man. [8]Indeed, man was not made from woman, but woman from man. [9]Neither was man created for the sake of woman, but woman for the sake of man. [10]For this reason a woman ought to have a symbol of authority on her head, because of the angels. [11]Nevertheless, in the Lord woman is not independent of man or man independent of woman. [12]For just as woman came from man, so man comes through woman; but all things come from God.

2 Corinthians 11:2–6

[2]I feel a divine jealousy for you, for I promised you in marriage to one husband to present you as a chaste virgin to Christ. [3]But I am afraid that as the serpent deceived Eve by its cunning, your thoughts will be led astray from a sincere and pure devotion to Christ. [4]For if someone comes and proclaims another Jesus than the one we proclaimed, or if you receive a different spirit from the one you received, or a different gospel from the one you accepted, you submit to it readily enough. [5]I think that I am not in the least inferior to these super-apostles. [6]I may be untrained in speech, but not in knowledge; certainly in every way and in all things we have made this evident to you.

Ephesians 5:21–6:9

[21]Be subject to one another out of reverence for Christ.

[22]Wives, be subject to your husbands as you are to the Lord. [23]For the husband is the head of the wife just as Christ is the head of the church, the body of which he is the Savior. [24]Just as the church is subject to Christ, so also wives ought to be, in everything, to their husbands.

[25]Husbands, love your wives, just as Christ loved the church and gave himself up for her, [26]in order to make her holy by cleansing her with the washing of water by the word, [27]so as to present the church to himself in splendor, without a spot or wrinkle or anything of the kind—yes, so that she may be holy and without blemish. [28]In the same way, husbands should love their wives as they do their own bodies. He who loves his wife loves himself. [29]For no one ever hates his own body, but he nourishes and tenderly cares for it, just as Christ does for the church, [30]because we are members of his body. [31]"For this reason a man shall leave his father and mother and be joined to his wife, and the two will become one flesh."[32] This is a great mystery, and I am applying it to Christ and the church. [33]Each of you, however, should love his wife as himself, and a wife should respect her husband.

[6:1]Children, obey your parents in the Lord, for this is right. [2]"Honor your father and mother"—this is the first commandment with a promise: [3]"so that it may be well with you and you may live long on the earth."

[4]And, fathers, do not provoke your children to anger, but bring them up in the discipline and instruction of the Lord.

[5]Slaves, obey your earthly masters with fear and trembling, in singleness of heart, as you obey Christ; [6]not only while being watched, and in order to please them, but as slaves of Christ, doing the will of God from the heart. [7]Render service with enthusiasm, as to the Lord and not to men and women, [8]knowing that whatever good we do, we will receive the same again from the Lord, whether we are slaves or free.

[9]And, masters, do the same to them. Stop threatening them, for you know that both of you have the same Master in heaven, and with him there is no partiality.

1 Timothy 2:8–15

[8]I desire, then, that in every place the men should pray, lifting up holy hands without anger or argument; [9]also that the women should dress themselves modestly and decently in suitable clothing, not with their hair braided, or with gold, pearls, or expensive clothes, [10]but with good works, as is proper for women who profess reverence for God. [11]Let a woman learn in silence with full submission. [12]I permit no woman to teach or to have authority over a man; she is to keep silent. [13]For Adam was formed first, then Eve; [14]and Adam was not deceived, but the woman was deceived and became a transgressor. [15]Yet she will be saved through childbearing, provided they continue in faith and love and holiness, with modesty.

EXTRACANONICAL SOURCES

The Gospel According to Thomas

The *Gospel of Thomas* was, according to its prologue, a collection of Jesus's "obscure" sayings. It promised that "Whoever finds the meaning of these sayings will not taste death." Scholars do not know the name of its compiler, and estimates of the date of its composition range from the middle of the first century to the middle of the second century. Scholars postulate that the compiler had access to the "Q" source—a document of Jesus's sayings that the writers of the Gospel of Matthew and the Gospel of Luke are also presumed to have used.

Unlike the gospels in the New Testament, the *Gospel of Thomas* does not provide a "life" of Jesus. Instead, it presents a corpus of wise sayings attributed to Jesus. To understand this wisdom was to receive eternal life—a message typical of gnosticism. It is not known, however, which branch of gnosticism produced the *Gospel of Thomas*. In the first four centuries of Christianity, the *Gospel of Thomas* competed with other Christian writings for canonical status.[1]

Themes of importance relating to our present study include *Thomas's* discussion of singleness. Jesus argued, in this gospel, that the renunciation of worldly ties allowed believers to become "solitaries." Ascetic devotion to the truth erased the distinction between male and female, so that the primordial unity and integrity of human identity was restored. The archetypal reunion of male and female restored the conditions of the original creation. As Jesus noted, "when you make the two one . . . that you might make the male and the female be one and the same . . . then you will enter [the kingdom]." (Source: *The Gospel of Thomas*, in Bentley Layton, translator, *The Gnostic Scriptures*, Garden City, N.Y.: Doubleday & Company, 1987, pp. 383, 384, 389, 390, 391, 393, 398, 399.)

The Gospel of Thomas (c. 50–150 CE)

(16): Jesus Has Come to Impose Divisions

JESUS said, "People probably think that it is peace that I have come to impose upon the world. And they do not recognize that it is divisions that I have come to impose upon the earth—fire, sword, battle. Indeed, there will be five in a house. There will be three over two and two over three, parent over child and child over parent. And they will stand at rest by being solitaries."

(22): Those Who Enter the Kingdom Resemble Little Ones

JESUS saw some little ones nursing. He said to his disciples, "What these little ones who are nursing resemble is those who enter the kingdom." They said to him, "So shall we enter the kingdom by being little ones?" Jesus said to them, "When you (plur.) make the two one and make the inside like the outside and the outside like the inside and the above like the below, and that you might make the male and the female be one and the same, so that the male might not be male nor the female be female, when you make eyes in place of an eye and a hand in place of a hand and a foot in place of a foot, an image in place of an image—then you will enter [the kingdom]."

(49): Solitaries Have Come from the Kingdom

JESUS said, "Blessed are those who are solitary and superior, for you (plur.) will find the kingdom; for since you come from it you shall return to it."

(56): The World Is a Corpse

JESUS said, "Whoever has become acquainted with the world has found a corpse, and the world is not worthy of the one who has found the corpse."

(61): Jesus on Salome's Couch

JESUS said, "Two will repose on a couch: one will die, one will live."

Salome said, "Who are you, O man? Like a stranger (?) you have gotten upon my couch and you have eaten from my table." Jesus said to her, "It is I who come from that which is integrated. I was given (some) of the things of my father."[. . .] "I am your female disciple."[. . .]

"Therefore I say that such a person, once integrated, will become full of light; but such a person, once divided, will become full of darkness."

(75): Solitaries Will Enter the Bridal Chamber

JESUS said, "There are many standing at the door, but it is the solitaries who will enter the bridal chamber."

(110): The Rich Should Renounce

JESUS said, "The one who has found the world and become rich should renounce the world."

(106): The Power of Wholeness

JESUS said, "When you (plur.) make the two into one you will become sons of man, and when you say, 'O mountain, go elsewhere!' it will go elsewhere."

(114): The Female Element Must Make Itself Male

SIMON PETER said to them, "Mary should leave us, for females are not worthy of life." Jesus said, "See, I am going to attract her to make her male so that she too might become a living spirit that resembles you males. For every female (element) that makes itself male will enter the kingdom of heavens."

NOTE TO CHAPTER 4, EXTRACANONICAL SOURCES, THE GOSPEL ACCORDING TO THOMAS

1. Layton, *The Gnostic Scriptures*, pp. 376-78.

The Gospel According to Philip

The *Gospel of Philip* represented the Valentinan school of gnosticism. Valentinus was a second-century Christian who revised classic gnostic theology in light of Christian themes. Neither the identity of the compiler of the *Gospel of Philip* nor its date of compilation is known. The earliest manuscript is dated at 350 CE. In the first four centuries of Christianity, the *Gospel of Philip* competed with other Christian writings for canonical status.[1]

Philip did not present a "life" of Jesus, and was not even primarily devoted to sayings attributed to Jesus. The text functioned as an anthology of theological discussions, some related to Jesus, and others addressed to broader themes. Of particular interest is the *Gospel of Philip's* reworking of the story of

Adam and Eve. According to *Philip*, the Genesis account of creation presented the original humanity as an androgyne. *Philip* describes the separation of Eve from Adam (Genesis 2:21-23) as a symbol for the entry of death into the world. The solution, for *Philip*, was in Christ: "The anointed (Christ) came to rectify the separation that had been present since the beginning and join the two (components); and to give life unto those who had died by separation and join them together."

For *Philip*, this process of reunion involved being "reborn by the holy spirit." As in Colossians, where believers were urged to put off the flesh and clothe themseves "with the new self, which is being renewed in knowledge according to the image of its creator" (Col. 2:11; 3:10), the compiler of the *Gospel of Philip* exhorted those who would be perfect to put on "the perfect light" in order to become the "perfect light." Truly to see Christ was to become Christ; it was to move beyond the distinctions of male and female and return to the unity and integrity of the original humanity. (Source: *The Gospel of Philip*, in Bentley Layton, translator, *The Gnostic Scriptures*. Garden City, N.Y.: Doubleday & Company, 1987, pp. 337, 342-43, 348.)

The Gospel of Philip (pre–350 CE)

(38): Only Like Can See Like

PEOPLE cannot see anything in the real realm unless they become it. In the realm of truth, it is not as human beings in the world, who see the sun without being the sun, and see the sky and the earth and so forth without being them. Rather, if you have seen any things there, you have become those things: if you have seen the spirit, you have become the spirit; if you have seen the anointed (Christ), you have become the anointed (Christ); if you have seen the [father, you] will become the father. Thus [here] (in the world), you see everything and do not [see] your own self. But there, you see yourself; for you shall [become] what you see.

(63): Separation of Eve from Adam

IN THE DAYS when Eve was [in] Adam, death did not exist. When she was separated from him, death came into existence. If he [reenters] and takes it unto himself death will not exist.

(67): Baptism

WE ARE reborn by the holy spirit. And we are born by the anointed (Christ) through two things. We are anointed by the spirit. When we were born we were joined. No one can see himself in the water or in a mirror without light. Nor, again, can you see by the light without water or a mirror. For this reason it is necessary to baptize with two things—light and water. And light means chrism.

(69): *The Garment of Light*

THE FORCES do not see those who have put on the perfect light and cannot seize them. One will put on the light in a mystery, through the act of joining.

(70): *Reunion in the Bridal Chamber*

IF THE FEMALE had not separated from the male, she and the male would not die. That being's separation became the source of death. The anointed (Christ) came to rectify the separation that had been present since the beginning and join the two (components); and to give life unto those who had died by separation and join them together. Now, a woman joins with her husband in the bridal bedroom, and those who have joined in the bridal bedroom will not reseparate. Thus Eve became separate from Adam because it was not in the bridal bedroom that she joined with him.

(90): *The Garment of Light*

THE PERFECT human being not only cannot be restrained, but also cannot be seen—for if something is seen it will be restrained. In other words, no one can obtain this grace without putting on the perfect light [and] becoming, as well, perfect light.

NOTE TO CHAPTER 4, EXTRACANONICAL SOURCES, THE GOSPEL ACCORDING TO PHILIP

1. Layton, *The Gnostic Scriptures*, pp. xv-xxii, 325-26.

The Acts of Paul and Thecla

The *Acts of Thecla* was, according to scholarly judgment, an independent narrative that a later editor came to insert into another document: *The Acts of Paul*.[1] Both works represent second-century examples of "apocryphal" accounts of the apostles. *The Acts of Paul and Thecla* circulated widely among Christians in the early church. Thecla became such a popular figure that a cult developed in her honor, and writers like Jerome urged Christians to imitate her zeal for Christ. Other Christian writers disagreed. In 203 CE, Tertullian denounced *The Acts of Thecla*—or a work similar to it—on the grounds that it encouraged women to circumvent priestly authority and baptize themselves.[2]

Thecla epitomized the ascetical ideal that early Christianity promoted as the appropriate lifestyle for believers who wished to recapture the perfection of the original creation. *The Acts of Thecla* also made explicit what orthodoxy's celebration of celibacy and asceticism implied: that women who chose to practice rigorous Christian discipline could become "like men" and reclaim the archetypal union of male and female that preceded the Fall. Thecla, against constant opposition from male advisers, not only refused to marry but also withstood considerable persecution. She proved impervious to death by fire and, when faced with execution by wild beasts, threw herself into a ditch of water filled with dangerous seals, proclaiming, "In the name of Jesus Christ, I baptize myself on the last day." God confirmed her proclamation, as a flash of lightning killed the seals, and a cloud of fire hid Thecla's nakedness. Having thus reversed the shame associated with nakedness ever since the Fall, Thecla donned men's clothing. Announcing to Paul that "the One who worked together with you in the Gospel also worked with me for my being baptized," Thecla exemplified the ascetical woman restored to the image of a God who was neither male nor female. (Source: *The Acts of Thecla*, in "Thecla of Iconium, An Ascetic Christian and the Prototypical Convert," in Ross Kraemer, editor, *Maenads, Martyrs, Matrons, Monastics: A Sourcebook on Women's Religions in the Greco-Roman World*, Philadelphia: Fortress Press, 1988, pp. 280-88.)

The Acts of Thecla (c. 100s CE)

7. And while Paul was speaking so in the middle of the assembly in the house of Onesiphorus, a certain virgin named Thecla (her mother was Theocleia) who was engaged to a man named Thamyris, sat at a nearby window in her house and listened night and day to what Paul said about the chaste life. And she did not turn away from the window but pressed on in the faith, rejoicing exceedingly. Moreover, when she saw many women and virgins going in to Paul she wished that she too be counted worthy to stand before Paul and hear the word of Christ, for she had not yet seen Paul in person but only heard him speak.

8. But since she did not move from the window, her mother sent to Thamyris. He came joyfully as if he were already taking her in marriage. So Thamyris said to Theocleia, "Where is my Thecla, that I may see her?" And Theocleia said, "I have something new to tell you, Thamyris. Indeed, for three days and three nights Thecla has not risen from the window either to eat or to drink but, gazing intently as if on some delightful sight, she so devotes herself to a strange man who teaches deceptive and ambiguous words that I wonder how one so modest in her virginity can be so severely troubled.

9. "Thamyris, this man is shaking up the city of the Iconians, and your Thecla too. For all the women and the young men go in to him and are taught by him that it is necessary, as he says, 'to fear one single God only and live a pure life.' And my daughter also, like a spider bound at the window by his words, is controlled by a new desire and a terrible passion. For the virgin concentrates on the things he says and is captivated. But you go and speak to her, for she is engaged to you."

10. And Thamyris went to her, loving her and yet fearing her distraction, and said, "Thecla, my fiancée, why do you sit like that? And what sort of passion holds you distracted? Turn to your Thamyris and be ashamed." And her mother also said the same thing: "Child, why do you sit like that, looking down and not answering, like one paralyzed?" And they wept bitterly, Thamyris for the loss of a wife, Theocleia for a daughter, the female servants for a mistress. So there was a great commingling of grief in the house. And while that was going on Thecla did not turn away but was concentrating on Paul's word. . . .

15. When Thamyris had heard this from them, he rose up early in the morning full of jealousy and wrath and went to the house of Onesiphorus, with rulers and officials and a great crowd, with clubs. He said to Paul, "You have corrupted the city of the Iconians, and my fiancée so that she does not want me. Let us go to governor Castellius!" And the whole crowd shouted, "Away with the *magus!* For he has corrupted all our women." And the crowds were persuaded.

16. And standing before the judgment seat Thamyris cried out, "Proconsul, this man—we don't know where he comes from—who does not allow virgins to marry, let him declare before you the reasons he teaches these things." And Demas and Hermogenes said to Thamyris, "Say that he is a Christian, and so you will destroy him." But the governor kept his wits and called Paul, saying to him, "Who are you and what do you teach? For they bring no light accusation against you."

17. Paul lifted up his voice and said, "If today I am interrogated as to what I teach, then listen, Proconsul. The living God, the God of vengeance, the jealous God, the God who has need of nothing has sent me since he longs for the salvation of humanity, that I may draw them away from corruption and impurity, and from all pleasure and death, that they may sin no more. Wherefore God sent his own child, the one whom I proclaim and teach that in him humanity has hope, he who alone had compassion upon a world gone astray, that humanity may no longer be under judgment but have faith, fear of God, knowledge of dignity, and love of truth. If then I teach the things revealed to me by God, what wrong do I do, Proconsul?" When the governor heard this, he commanded Paul to be bound and to be led off to prison until he could find a convenient time to give him a more careful hearing.

18. But during the night Thecla removed her bracelets and gave them to the doorkeeper, and when the door was opened for her she headed off to the prison. Upon giving a silver mirror to the jailer, she went in to Paul and sitting at his feet she heard about the mighty acts of God. And Paul feared nothing but continued to live with full confidence in God; and her faith also increased, as she kissed his fetters. . . .

20. He [the governor] ordered Paul to be brought to the judgment seat. But Thecla rolled around in the place where Paul was teaching as he sat in the prison, so the governor commanded that she too be brought to the judgment seat. And she headed off joyfully exulting. But when Paul was brought forward again, the crowd shouted out even more, "He is a *magus!* Away with him!"

But the governor gladly listened to Paul concerning the holy works of Christ. When he had taken counsel he called Thecla, saying, "Why do you not marry Thamyris according to the law of the Iconians?" But she just stood there looking intently at Paul. And when she did not answer, Theocleia, her mother, cried out, saying, "Burn the lawless one! Burn her who is no bride in the midst of the theater in order that all the women who have been taught by this man may be afraid!"

21. And the governor was greatly moved. He had Paul whipped and threw him out of the city, but Thecla he sentenced to be burned. And immediately the governor arose and went off to the theater, and all the crowd went out to the inevitable spectacle. But Thecla, as a lamb in the wilderness looks around for the shepherd, so she sought for Paul. And looking over the crowd, she saw the Lord sitting in the form of Paul and said, "As if I were not able to bear up, Paul has come to look after me." And she looked intently at him, but he took off into the heavens.

22. Now, the young men and the virgins brought wood and straw for burning Thecla. And as she was brought in naked, the governor wept and marveled at the power in her. The executioners spread out the wood and ordered her to mount the pyre, and making the sign of the cross she mounted up on the wood pile. They put the torch underneath the pile, and although a great fire blazed up, the flame did not touch her. For God in compassion produced a noise below the earth, and a cloud above full of water and hail overshadowed (the theater), and all its contents poured out, so that many were in danger and died. The fire was extinguished, and Thecla was saved.

23. Now, Paul was fasting with Onesiphorus and his wife and the children in an open tomb on the road by which they go from Iconium to Daphne. . . .

24. Now, when she [Thecla] came to the tomb, Paul was kneeling in prayer and saying, "Father of Christ, do not let the fire touch Thecla, but be present with her, for she is yours!" And standing behind him, she cried out, "Father, maker of heaven and earth, the Father of your beloved child Jesus Christ, I bless you because you saved me from the fire that I might see Paul." And rising up, Paul saw her and said, "God, the knower of hearts, Father of our Lord Jesus Christ, I bless you that you have so quickly (accomplished) what I asked, and have listened to me."

25. And inside the tomb there was much love, with Paul leaping for joy, and Onesiphorus, and everyone. They had five loaves, and vegetables and water, and they were rejoicing over the holy works of Christ. And Thecla said to Paul, "I shall cut my hair short and follow you wherever you go." But he said, "The time is horrible, and you are beautiful. May no other temptation come upon you worse than the first and you not bear up but act with cowardice." And Thecla said, "Only give me the seal in Christ, and temptation will not touch me." And Paul said, "Have patience, Thecla, and you will receive the water." . . . [Thecla and Paul then journeyed to Antioch, where Thecla refused to marry a Syrian named Alexander. Shamed at her refusal, Alexander had Thecla condemned to fight the beasts in the arena. The women of Antioch

protested, and a wealthy woman named Tryphaena opened her home to Thecla until it was time to battle the beasts.]

28. When the beasts were led in procession, they bound her to a fierce lioness, and the queen Tryphaena followed her. And as Thecla sat upon the lioness's back, the lioness licked her feet, and all the crowd was astounded. Now the charge on her inscription was Sacrilegious. But the women with their children cried out from above, saying, "O God, an impious judgment is come to pass in this city!" . . .

33. Now, when Thecla was taken out of Tryphaena's hands, she was stripped, given a girdle, and thrown into the stadium. And lions and bears were thrown at her, and a fierce lioness ran to her and reclined at her feet. Now, the crowd of women shouted loudly. And a bear ran up to her, but the lioness ran and met it, and ripped the bear to shreds. And again a lion trained against men, which belonged to Alexander, ran up to her, and the lioness wrestled with the lion and perished with it. So the women mourned all the more, since the lioness that helped her was dead.

34. Then they sent in many beasts while she stood and stretched out her hands and prayed. And when she had finished her prayer, she turned and saw a great ditch full of water and said, "Now is the time for me to wash." And she threw herself in, saying, "In the name of Jesus Christ, I baptize myself on the last day!" And when they saw it, the women and the whole crowd wept, saying, "Do not throw yourself into the water!"—so that even the governor wept that such a beauty was going to be eaten by seals. So then she threw herself into the water in the name of Jesus Christ, but the seals, seeing the light of a lightning flash, floated dead on the surface. About her there was a cloud of fire so that neither could the beasts touch her nor could she be seen naked. . . .

37. The governor summoned Thecla from among the beasts and said to her, "Who are you? And what have you about you that not one of the beasts touched you?" She answered, "I am a servant of the living God. As to what I have about me, I have believed in him in whom God is well pleased, his Son, on account of whom not one of the beasts touched me. For he alone is the goal of salvation and the foundation of immortal life. For to the storm-tossed he is a refuge, to the oppressed relief, to the despairing shelter; in a word, whoever does not believe in him shall not live but die for ever."

38. When the governor heard this, he ordered clothing to be brought and said, "Put on the clothing." But she said, "The one who clothed me when I was naked among the beasts, this one shall clothe me with salvation in the day of judgment." And taking the clothing, she got dressed.

And the governor issued a decree immediately, saying, "I release to you Thecla, the God-fearing servant of God." So all the women cried out with a loud voice and as with one mouth gave praise to God, saying, "One is God who has saved Thecla!"—so that all the city was shaken by the sound.

39. And when Tryphaena was told the good news, she came to meet her with a crowd. She embraced Thecla and said, "Now I believe that the dead are raised up! Now I believe that my child lives! Come inside, and I will transfer

everything that is mine to you." So Thecla went in with her and rested in her house for eight days, instructing her in the word of God, so that the majority of the female servants also believed. And there was great joy in the house.

40. Yet Thecla longed for Paul and sought him, sending all around in every direction. And it was made known to her that he was in Myra. So taking male and female servants, she got herself ready, sewed her *chiton* into a cloak like a man's, and headed off to Myra. She found Paul speaking the word of God and threw herself at him. But he was astonished when he saw her and the crowd that was with her, wondering whether another temptation was not upon her. So realizing this, she said to him, "I have taken the bath, Paul, for he who worked with you for the gospel has also worked with me for my washing."

41. And taking her by the hand, Paul led her into the house of Hermias and heard everything from her, so that Paul marveled greatly and those who heard were strengthened and prayed on behalf of Tryphaena. And standing up, Thecla said to Paul, "I am going to Iconium." So Paul said, "Go and teach the word of God!" Now, Tryphaena sent her a lot of clothing and gold, so it could be left behind for Paul for the ministry of the poor.

43. . . . And when she had given this witness she headed off to Seleucia, and after enlightening many with the word of God, she slept with a fine sleep.

NOTES TO CHAPTER 4, EXTRACANONICAL SOURCES, THE ACTS OF THECLA

1. The redactor may also have revised *The Acts of Thecla*. Sheila E. McGinn has argued that "the author/redactor of the text was a well-placed male member of the mainline Christian church in Asia Minor who took a woman's folktale about Thecla and 'domesticated' it, giving Paul more prominence in the story, and transforming it from the *Acts of Thecla* into the *Acts of Paul and Thecla*." "The Acts of Thecla," in Elisabeth Schussler Fiorenza, editor, *Searching the Scriptures: A Feminist Commentary* (New York: Crossroad, 1994), vol. 2, p. 805.

2. Elizabeth A. Clark, *Women in the Early Church*, p. 78; Ross S. Kraemer, editor, *Maenads, Martyrs, Matrons, Monastics: A Sourcebook on Women's Religions in the Greco-Roman World* (Philadelphia: Fortress Press, 1988), p. 407.

CHURCH FATHERS

Theophilus

Theophilus lived in the Syrian city of Antioch—a city important to the Roman Empire but also to early Christianity. According to Acts 11:26, Antioch was where followers of Jesus were called "Christian" for the first time. Theophilus was a Christian "Apologist," meaning that he sought to defend the intellectual and ethical integrity of his faith to non-Christians. He became bishop of Antioch, perhaps in 168 CE if the date provided by the early historian Eusebius is correct.[1]

The following selection comes from an "apology" Theophilus addressed to Autolycus. This apology is the only extant writing of Theophilus. In it, he recommends the Christian faith by contrasting it to Greek religion and mythology. The doctrine of creation forms the context for our passage; discussions of the first six days as well as of the first sin and the expulsion from Paradise precede this consideration of Eve; a discussion of Cain follows it.

In this selection Theophilus assigns monotheistic significance to one deity creating both man and woman, and identifies the first sin as polytheism. Although he speaks relatively extensively of God's design for "mutual affection" between husbands and wives, he also describes Eve as "the author of sin." Some scholars contend that his reference near the selection's conclusion to "invoking Eve" alludes to a practice of shouting "Eva" during bacchanalian orgies and thus stresses the sinfulness of this ritual.[2] (Source: Theophilus, "Theophilus to Autolycus," translated by Marcus Dods, in Alexander Roberts and James Donaldson, editors, *The Ante-Nicene Fathers*, Buffalo: Christian Literature Publishing Company, 1885, vol 2, p. 105.)

"Apology to Autolycus" (late 100s CE)
THEOPHILUS

Book 2, Chapter 28: Why Eve Was Formed of Adam's Rib

And Adam having been cast out of Paradise, in this condition knew Eve his wife, whom God had formed into a wife for him out of his rib. And this He did, not as if He were unable to make his wife separately, but God foreknew that man would call upon a number of gods. And having this prescience, and knowing that through the serpent error would introduce a number of gods which had no existence,—for there being but one God, even then error was striving to disseminate a multitude of gods, saying, "Ye shall be as gods;"— lest, then, it should be supposed that one God made the man and another the woman, therefore He made them both; and God made the woman together with the man, not only that thus the mystery of God's sole government might be exhibited, but also that their mutual affection might be greater. Therefore said Adam to Eve, "This is now bone of my bones, and flesh of my flesh." And besides, he prophesied, saying, "For this cause shall a man leave his father and his mother, and shall cleave unto his wife; and the two shall be one flesh;" which also itself has its fulfillment in ourselves. For who that marries lawfully does not despise mother and father, and his whole family connection, and all his household, cleaving to and becoming one with his own wife, fondly preferring her? So that often, for the sake of their wives, some submit even to death. This Eve, on account of her having been in the beginning deceived by the serpent, and become the author of sin, the wicked demon, who also is called Satan, who then spoke to her through the serpent, and who works even to this day in those men that are possessed by him, invokes as Eve. And he is called "demon" and "dragon," on account of his revolting from God. For at first he was an angel. And concerning his history there is a great deal to be said; wherefore I at present omit the relation of it, for I have also given an account of him in another place.

NOTES TO CHAPTER 4, CHURCH FATHERS, THEOPHILUS

[1. See the "Introductory Note to Theophilus of Antioch" by Marcus Dods in *The Ante-Nicene Fathers* (Buffalo: Christian Literature Publishing Company, 1885), vol. 2, p. 88.]

[2. See "Theophilus to Autolycus," in *The Ante-Nicene Fathers* (Buffalo: Christian Literature Publishing Company, 1885), vol. 2, p. 105, note 4.]

Anastasius Sinaita

As Jean M. Higgins has noted, this selection is remarkable in its reading of Genesis 2-3. It argues that Adam, not Eve, was the weaker partner. Eve, the passage claims, was stronger than Adam; she argued with the serpent and ate only because she was persuaded by the serpent's duplicity. Moreover, since she had not talked with God directly, she could not be certain that Adam, rather than God, had not issued the command not to eat the fruit of the tree of the knowledge of good and evil. Adam, on the other hand, offered no resistance. Eve, a mere human being, convinced Adam, whom God had explicitly told to avoid the forbidden fruit, to disobey. The passage contends that Eve thus proved herself the be the man's "boethius" (superior helper).

Such a text is extraordinary for the patristic age, a period in which the dominant mode of interpretation cast Eve as Adam's inferior and blamed her for introducing sin and death into the world. Scholars have traditionally assumed the author to be Anastasius Sinaita, a seventh-century Orthodox monk. The text is a manuscript fragment appended to the works of the renowned church father Irenaeus and is presumed to have been excerpted from Anastasius Sinaita's *Anagogicarum Contemplationum*.

Few scholars have devoted attention to the text. Higgins argues that it presents such a striking interpretation of Eve that it is hard to imagine that either Irenaeus or Anastasius Sinaita composed it. Neither Irenaeus nor Anastasius Sinaita adopted a feminist tone in their other works. Higgins suggests that it was probably the work of Irenaeus's opponents and points to the Nag Hammadi documents (the gnostic scriptures) as literature that also depicted strong female figures. Nowhere in early orthodoxy do we find such a spirited argument for the superiority of Eve to Adam other than in this fragment. Whoever was the author, the text, as Higgins observes, "stands as an ancient witness with striking affinities to some contemporary exegesis."[1] (Source: Jean M. Higgins, "Anastasius Sinaita and the Superiority of the Woman," *Journal of Biblical Literature* 97 [2] [1978]: 53-56.)

Anagogicarum Contemplationum (c. 150–250 CE)
ANASTASIUS SINAITA

Why did the serpent not attack the man, rather than the woman? You say he went after her because she was the weaker of the two. On the contrary. In the transgression of the commandment, she showed herself to be the stronger, truly the man's "assistance" (*boethos*).

For she alone stood up to the serpent. She ate from the tree, but with resistance and dissent, and after being dealt with perfidiously. But Adam partook of the fruit given by the woman, without even beginning to make a fight, without a word of contradiction—a perfect demonstration of consummate weakness and a cowardly soul.

The woman, moreover, can be excused; she wrestled with a demon and was thrown. But Adam will not be able to find excuse in having been defeated by a woman; he had himself personally received the commandment from God.

The woman, finally, even when she did hear the command from Adam, must have felt she was being made little of; either because she had not been judged worthy to converse with God herself; or because she suspected there was an even chance that Adam had given her the command on his own.

NOTE TO CHAPTER 4, CHURCH FATHERS, ANASTASIUS SINAITA

1. Jean M. Higgins, "Anastasius Sinaita and the Superiority of the Woman," *Journal of Biblical Literature* 97 (2) (1978): 53-56.

Tertullian

Tertullian (c. 160-c. 225 CE) was a Christian from the North African city of Carthage whose ideas and terminology have greatly influenced Western or Latin Christianity. Little is known about Tertullian's biography. His writings, however, show his attraction to asceticism. Historian Peter Brown has described Tertullian's "Exhortation to Chastity" as "the first consequential statement" in the Latin West "of the belief that abstinence from sex was the most effective technique with which to achieve clarity of soul."[1] On the basis of such beliefs, Tertullian eventually was attracted to Montanism, a Christian sectarian movement that stressed a rigorous asceticism along with a perfectionist understanding of the church.

Tertullian wrote his treatise "On the Apparel of Women" to a female audience, perhaps to women who recently had converted to Christianity. In our selection from the treatise's introduction, Tertullian makes repeated connections between Eve and all other women. Telling his audience "you are the devil's gateway," he rebukes women for the ways they tempt men by their alluring appearances. He further urges that women adopt a humble—and even penitent—style of dress since their sex brought sin into the world and thereby necessitated the death of God's Son. Ascribing vanity and envy to Eve and her daughters, the selection closes with a funereal description of woman in "her dead and condemned state." (Source: Tertullian, "On the Apparel of Women," translated by S. Thelwall, in Alexander Roberts and James Donaldson, editors, *The Ante-Nicene Fathers*, New York: Christian Literature Company, 1890, vol. 4, p. 14.)

"On the Apparel of Women" (c. 202 CE)
TERTULLIAN

Book 1, Chapter 1

If there dwelt upon earth a faith as great as is the reward of faith which is expected in the heavens, no one of you at all, best-beloved sisters, from the time that she had first "known the Lord" and learned (the truth) concerning her own (that is woman's) condition, would have desired too gladsome (not to say too ostentatious) a style of dress; so as not rather to go about in humble garb, and rather to affect meanness of appearance, walking about as Eve mourning and repentant, in order that by every garb of penitence she might the more fully expiate that which she derives from Eve,—the ignominy, I mean, of the first sin, and the odium (attaching to her as the cause) of human perdition. "In pains and in anxieties dost thou bear (children), woman; and toward thine husband (is) thy inclination, and he lords it over thee." And do you not know that you are (each) an Eve? The sentence of God on this sex of yours lives in this age: the guilt must of necessity live too. *You* are the devil's gateway: *you* are the unsealer of that (forbidden) tree: *you* are the first deserter of the divine law: *you* are she who persuaded him whom the devil was not valiant enough to attack. *You* destroyed so easily God's image, man. On account of *your* desert—that is, death—even the Son of God had to die. And do you think about adorning yourself over and above your tunics of skins? Come, now; if from the beginning of the world the Milesians sheared sheep, and the Serians spun trees, and the Tyrians dyed, and the Phrygians embroidered with the needle, and the Babylonians with the loom, and pearls gleamed, and onyx-stones flashed; if gold itself also had already issued, with the cupidity (which accompanies it), from the ground; if the mirror, too, already had license to lie so largely, Eve, expelled from paradise, (Eve) already dead, would also have coveted *these* things, I imagine! No more, then, ought she *now* to crave, or be acquainted with (if she desires to live again), what, when she *was* living, she had neither had nor known. Accordingly these things are all the baggage of woman in her condemned and dead state, instituted as if to swell the pomp of her funeral.

1. Peter Brown, *The Body and Society: Men, Women, and Sexual Renunciation in Early Christianity* (New York: Columbia University Press, 1988), p. 78. Emphasizing Tertullian's description of the body as a "unified organism" with direct connections to the soul, Brown warns against attributing Tertullian's stress on asceticism to "dualism"; see p. 77.

Origen

Origen (c. 185-250/254 CE) was a Christian scholar of scripture and theology. He has greatly influenced Western exegesis, particularly through his understanding that biblical passages have multiple meanings. According to Origen, scriptural texts not only have a literal sense but also have moral and allegorical meanings. Born in Egypt, he was raised by Christian parents in Alexandria. Origen's adult life was marked by controversy. He taught at the catechetical school in Alexandria, but conflicts with the bishop of Alexandria increased until Origen eventually left Alexandria around 232. Origen was imprisoned and tortured during the persecution launched by the emperor Decius. He either died during this persecution in 250 or survived for a few years afterward.

Although Origen was a prolific writer, most of his texts have perished. Our selection comes from sermons he delivered, probably in the Palestinian seaport of Caesarea around 240 CE.[1] Both Homily 1 and Homily 6 show his use of allegorical interpretation. When discussing the *imago dei*, or image of God, in Homily 1, Origen uses allegory to posit that each human being is both male/spirit and female/soul. Note here his descriptions of the female/soul's propensity for carnal matters and lesser goods. In the selection from Homily 6, Origen brings Genesis 3:16 into his reflection on Genesis 21:12.[2] An allegorical interpretation of Sarah as virtue allows him to speak of how it is that husbands like Abraham should listen to their wives, even as he upholds the hierarchy of husbands over wives on the literal level of "physical marriage." (Source: Origen, "Homily 1" and "Homily 6," translated by Ronald E. Heine, in *Homilies on Genesis and Exodus*, The Fathers of the Church series, Washington, D.C.: Catholic University of America Press, 1982, vol. 71, pp. 67-68, 122.)

"Homilies on Genesis" (c. 240 CE)
ORIGEN

Homily 1

(14) "Male and female he made them, and God blessed them saying: 'Increase and multiply and fill the earth and have dominion over it.' "

It seems to be worth inquiring in this passage according to the letter how, when the woman was not yet made, the Scripture says, "Male and female he made them." Perhaps, as I think, it is because of the blessing with which he blessed them saying, "Increase and multiply and fill the earth." Anticipating what was to be, the text says, "Male and female he made them," since, indeed, man could not otherwise increase and multiply except with the female. Therefore, that there might be no doubt about his blessing that is to come, the text says, "Male and female he made them." For in this manner man, seeing the consequence of increasing and multiplying to be from the fact that the female was joined to him, could cherish a more certain hope in the divine blessing. For if the Scripture had said: "Increase and multiply and fill the earth and have dominion over it," not adding this, "Male and female he made them," doubtless he would have disbelieved the divine blessing, as also Mary said in response to that blessing which was pronounced by the angel, "How shall I know this, since I know not a man?"[3]

Or perhaps, because all things which have been made by God are said to be united and joined together, as heaven and earth, as sun and moon, so, therefore, that it might be shown that man also is a work of God and has not been brought forth without harmony or the appropriate conjunction, therefore, the text says in anticipation: "Male and female he made them."

These things have been said on that question, which can be raised about the literal meaning.

(15) But let us see also allegorically how man, made in the image of God, is male and female.

Our inner man consists of spirit and soul. The spirit is said to be male; the soul can be called female. If these have concord and agreement among themselves, they increase and multiply by the very accord among themselves and they produce sons, good inclinations and understandings or useful thoughts, by which they fill the earth and have dominion over it. This means they turn the inclination of the flesh, which has been subjected to themselves, to better purposes and have dominion over it, while the flesh, of course, becomes insolent in nothing against the will of the spirit. But now if the soul, which has been united with the spirit and, so to speak, joined in wedlock, turn aside at some time to bodily pleasures and turn back its inclination to the delight of the flesh and at one time indeed appear to obey the salutary warnings of the spirit, but at another time yield to carnal vices, such a soul, as if defiled by adultery of the body, is said properly neither to increase nor multiply, since indeed Scripture designates the sons of adulterers as imperfect. Such a soul, to be sure, which prostrates itself totally to the inclination of the flesh and bodily desires, having forsaken conjunction with the spirit, as if turned away from God will shamelessly hear, "You have the face of a harlot; you have made yourself shameless to all."[4] She will be punished, therefore, like a harlot and her sons will be ordered to be prepared for slaughter.

Homily 6

(1) . . . I think therefore, that Sara, which means prince or one who governs empires, represents "*aretē*," which is the virtue of the soul. This virtue, then,

is joined to and clings to a wise and faithful man, even as that wise man who said of wisdom: "I have desired to take her for my spouse."[5] For this reason, therefore, God says to Abraham: "In all that Sara has said to you, hearken to her voice." This saying, at any rate, is not appropriate to physical marriage, since that well known statement was revealed from heaven which says to the woman of the man: "In him shall be your refuge and he shall have dominion over you."[6] If, therefore, the husband is said to be lord of his wife, how is it said again to the man: "In all that Sara has said to you, hearken to her voice"?[7] If anyone, therefore, has married virtue, let him hearken to her voice in all which she shall counsel him.

NOTES TO CHURCH FATHERS, CHAPTER 4, ORIGEN

[1. See Ronald E. Heine's Introduction to *Origen: Homilies on Genesis and Exodus* (Washington, D.C.: Catholic University of America Press, 1981), p. 20.]

[2. Commentators often have discussed God's intentions for gender relations in light of the relationship between Sarah and Abraham. Particularly important have been the descriptions of God telling Abraham to "do whatever Sarah says to you" (Gen. 21:12) and of Sarah referring to Abraham as "lord." On the latter, see 1 Peter 3:6.]

3. Luke 1:34.

4. Jer. 3:3.

5. Wis. 8:2.

[6. This translation of Genesis 3:16b derives from the wording of the Greek Septuagint.]

7. Gen. 21:12.

Ambrose

Ambrose (339-97 CE) is one of the four traditional doctors of the Latin church. The son of aristocratic parents, he spent part of his youth in Rome. He began his career as an "Advocatus," an advocate in the Roman law courts. He later became governor of a province whose seat was located in Milan. He was elected bishop of Milan in 374, before he had been baptized. From this position he emerged as an important church leader in the West. Famous as a preacher, he stressed Christian morality. He also wrote hymns, encouraged monasticism, and argued for the church's independence from civil power. On the basis of his knowledge of Greek, Ambrose introduced themes from Eastern theology into the Latin church.

Our selection comes from an early work of St. Ambrose which was composed shortly after his election as bishop.[1] Although Ambrose is known for his ascetical writings, here he stresses human reproduction—citing it as the reason for woman's creation—and offers a positive assessment of conjugal unions when he connects contemplating them with recognizing God's kingdom.

Ambrose's hierarchical interpretation of Eve and Adam's relation is seen in his explanation of Eve's inferiority despite her creation inside paradise, in his stress that Eve learned the command about the tree from Adam, and in his allegorical interpretation at the conclusion of this selection. Thus it is no surprise that he would describe Eve's punishment in Genesis 3:16 as the "milder sentence." Also significant for our theme are Ambrose's ambivalent assessments of Eve's character amid the scenes of temptation and God's interrogation, including his understanding that she admits to her misdeed. (Source: Ambrose, "Paradise," translated by John J. Savage, in Hexameron, *Paradise, and Cain and Abel*, The Fathers of the Church series, Washington, D.C.: Fathers of the Church, Inc., 1961, vol. 42, pp. 301-302; 311-12; 325-29; 336-37; 349-52.)

"Paradise" (c. 375 CE)
AMBROSE

Chapter 4

(24) "And God took the man whom he had created and placed him in the Garden of Eden to till it and keep it." Note, now, the person who was taken and the land where he was formed. The virtue of God, therefore, took man and breathed into him, so that man's virtue will advance and increase. God set him apart in Paradise that you may know that man was taken up, that is to say, was breathed upon by the power of God. Note the fact that man was created outside Paradise, whereas woman was made within it. This teaches us that each person acquires grace by reason of virtue, not because of locality or of race. Hence, although created outside Paradise, that is, in an inferior place, man is found to be superior, whereas woman, created in a better place, that is to say, in Paradise, is found to be inferior. She was first to be deceived and was responsible for deceiving the man. Wherefore the Apostle Paul has related that holy women have in olden times been subject to the stronger vessel and recommends them to obey their husbands as their masters. And Paul says: "Adam was not deceived, but the woman was deceived and was in sin."[2] This is a warning that no one ought to rely on himself, for she who was made for assistance needs the protection of a man. The head of the woman is man, who, while he believed that he would have the assistance of his wife, fell because of her. Wherefore, no one ought to entrust himself lightly to another unless he has first put that person's virtue to the test. Neither should he claim for himself in the role of protector one whom he believes is subservient to him. Rather, a person should share his grace with another. Especially is this true of one who is in the position of greater strength and one who plays the part of protector. We have advice of the Apostle Peter, wherein he recommends that husbands pay honor to their wives: "Husbands, in like manner, dwell with your wives considerately, paying honor to the woman as to the weaker vessel and as co-heir of the grace of life that your prayers be not hindered."[3] . . .

Chapter 6

(33) One more point. The circumstances connected with the tree of the knowledge of good and evil were such as to convince us that both good and evil were recognized. We are led to believe from the evidence of Scripture that such was the case: "When they both ate, their eyes were opened and they realized that they were naked," that is, the eyes of their mind were opened and they realized the shame of being naked. For that reason, when the woman ate of the tree of the knowledge of good and evil she certainly sinned and realized that she had sinned. On realizing this, she should not have invited her husband to share in her sin. By enticing him and by giving him what she herself had tasted she did not nullify her sin; rather, she repeated it. Certainly it stands to reason that she did intend to lure the person whom she loved to share in her punishment. She should be expected to ward off from one who was unaware of it the danger of falling into a sin of which she had knowledge. Yet this woman, knowing that she could not remain in Paradise after the Fall, seems to have had a fear that she alone would be ejected from the Garden. Hence, after the Fall, they both went into hiding. Being aware, therefore, that she would have to be separated from the man she loved, she had no desire to be deceived. . . .

Chapter 10

(46) Still another question arises, that concerning the saying of the Lord: "It is not good for man to be alone." Recognize the fact, first of all, that, when God created man from the slime of the earth, He did not add: "God saw that it was good," as He did in the case of each of His works. If He had said at that time that the creation of man was good, then the other statement that "it is not good" would be a contradiction in terms, although He had said that the creation of what preceded the formation of man was good. That was the situation at the time of the creation of Adam. But, when He perceived that man and woman were joined together in creation, He did not treat each even then in a special manner, for He soon after states: "God saw that all he had ever made was very good." The meaning is clear. The creation of both man and woman is considered to be good.

(47) From this question another problem arises. How did it happen that, when Adam alone was created, it was not said that it was good, but when a woman also was made, then are we to understand that everything was good? Whereas God in one case commended the whole of creation, as well as every creature in it (including man who is held to be a part of nature), a special reference to man did not then seem necessary. Wherefore, when Adam alone was created, an assertion that this work was good was not thought to be by any means a fitting climax to a satisfactory achievement. It was said, moreover, that it was not good for man to be alone. Yet we know that Adam did not commit sin before woman was created. However, after creation, she was the

first to disobey the divine command and even allured her husband to sin. If, therefore, the woman is responsible for the sin, how then can her accession be considered a good? But, if you consider that the universe is in the care of God, then you will discover this fact, namely, that the Lord must have gained more pleasure for Himself in being responsible for all creation than condemnation from us for providing the basis for sin. Accordingly, the Lord declared that it was not good for man to be alone, because the human race could not have been propagated from man alone. God preferred the existence of more than one whom He would be able to save than to have to confine this possibility to one man who was free from error. Inasmuch as He is the Author of both man and woman, He came into this world to redeem sinners. Finally, He did not permit Cain, a man accused of parricide, to perish before he brought forth sons. For the sake, therefore, of the successive generations of men it followed that woman had to be joined to man. Thus we must interpret the very words of God when He said [that] it was not good for man to be alone. If the woman was to be the first one to sin, the fact that she was the one destined to bring forth redemption must not be excluded from the operations of Divine Providence. Although "Adam was not deceived, the woman was deceived and was in sin." Yet woman, we are told, "will be saved by childbearing,"[4] in the course of which she generated Christ.

(48) Not without significance, too, is the fact that woman was made out of the rib of Adam. She was not made of the same earth with which he was formed, in order that we might realize that the physical nature of both man and woman is identical and that there was one source for the propagation of the human race. For that reason, neither was man created together with a woman, nor were two men and two women created at the beginning, but first a man and after that a woman. God willed it that human nature be established as one. Thus, from the very inception of the human stock He eliminated the possibility that many disparate natures should arise. He said: "Let us make him a helper like himself." We understand that to mean a helper in the generation of the human family—a really good helper. If we take the word "helper" in a good sense, then the woman's co-operation turns out to be something of major import in the process of generation, just as the earth by receiving, confining, and fostering the seed causes it to grow and produce fruit in time. In that respect, therefore, woman is a good helper even [though] in an inferior position. We find examples of this in our own experience. We see how men in high and important offices often enlist the help of men who are below them in rank and esteem. . . .

Chapter 11

(50) "And God cast Adam into a deep sleep and he slept." What does the phrase "deep sleep" signify? Does it not mean that when we contemplate a conjugal union we seem to be turning our eyes gradually in the direction of God's kingdom? Do we not seem, as we enter into a vision of this world, to partake a little of things divine, while we find our repose in the midst of what

is secular and mundane? Hence, after the statement, "He cast Adam into a deep sleep and he slept," there follows: "The rib which God took from Adam he built into a woman." The word "built" is well chosen in speaking of the creation of a woman because a household, comprising man and wife, seems to point toward a state of full perfection. One who is without a wife is regarded as being without a home. As man is considered to be more skillful in public duties, so woman is esteemed to be more adaptable to domestic ministrations. Reflect on the fact that He did not take a part from Adam's soul but a rib from his body, that is to say, not soul from a soul, but "bone of my bone and flesh of my flesh" will this woman be called.

Chapter 12

(55) . . . No addition therefore—not even a good one—is called for. What is, therefore, at first sight objectionable in the addition made by the woman: "Neither shall you touch anything of it"? God did not say this, but, rather: "you must not eat." Still, we have here something which leads to error. There are two possibilities to the addition she made: Either it is superfluous or because of this personal contribution she had made God's command only partly intelligible. John in his writings has made this clear: "If anyone shall add to them, God will add unto him the plagues that are written in this book. And if anyone shall take away from these words of the book of this prophecy, God will take away his portion from the tree of life."[5] If this is true in this case, how much truer is it that nothing should be taken away from the commands laid down by God! From this springs the primary violation of the command. And many believe that this was Adam's fault—not the woman's. They reason that Adam in his desire to make her more cautious had said to the woman that God had given the additional instruction: "Neither shall you touch it." We know that it was not Eve, but Adam, who received the command from God, because the woman had not yet been created. Scripture does not reveal the exact words that Adam used when he disclosed to her the nature and content of the command. At all events, we understand that the substance of the command was given to the woman by the man. What opinions others have offered on this subject should be taken into consideration. It seems to me, however, that the initial violation and deceit was due to the woman. Although there may appear to be an element of uncertainty in deciding which of the two was guilty, we can discern the sex which was liable first to do wrong. Add to this the fact that she stands convicted in court whose previous error is afterward revealed. The woman is responsible for the man's error and not vice-versa. Hence Paul says: "Adam was not deceived, but the woman was deceived and was in sin."[6] . . .

Chapter 14

(70) . . . Perhaps you are disturbed by the fact that Adam is the first to be rebuked, although the woman was the first to eat the fruit. But the weaker sex begins by an act of disobedience, whereas the stronger sex is more liable

to feelings of shame and forgiveness. The female furnished the occasion for wrongdoing; the male, the opportunity to feel ashamed.

(71) And the woman said: "The serpent deceived me and I ate." That fault is pardonable which is followed by an admission of guilt. The woman, therefore, is not to be despaired of, who did not keep silent before God, but who preferred to admit her sin—the woman on whom was passed a sentence that was salutary. It is good to suffer condemnation for our sins and to be scourged for our crimes, provided we are scourged along with other men. Hence, Cain, because he wanted to deny his guilt, was judged unworthy to be punished in his sin. He was forgiven without a prescribed penalty, not, perhaps, for having committed such a serious crime as parricide—he was responsible for his brother's death—as one of sacrilege, in that he thought he had deceived God when he said: "I do not know. Am I my brother's keeper?"[7] And so the accusation is reserved for his accuser, the Devil, prescribing that he be scourged along with his angels, since he did not wish to be scourged with men. Of such, therefore, has it been said: "There is no regard for their death and they shall not be scourged like other men."[8] The woman's case is, accordingly, of a different character. Although she incurred the sin of disobedience, she still possessed in the tree of Paradise food for virtue. And so she admitted her sin and was considered worthy of pardon. . . .

(72) Because Eve has admitted her crime, she is given a milder and more salutary sentence, which condemned her wrong-doing and did not refuse pardon. She was to serve under her husband's power, first, that she might not be inclined to do wrong, and, secondly, that, being in a position subject to a stronger vessel, she might not dishonor her husband, but on the contrary, might be governed by his counsel. I see clearly here the mystery of Christ and His Church. The Church's turning toward Christ in times to come and a religious servitude submissive to the Word of God—these are conditions far better than the liberty of this world. Hence it is written: "Thou shalt fear the Lord thy God and shall serve him only."[9] Servitude, therefore, of this sort is a gift of God. Wherefore, compliance with this servitude is to be reckoned among blessings. . . .

Chapter 15

(73) "The serpent urged me," she said. This seemed to God to be pardonable, inasmuch as He knew that the serpent found numerous ways to deceive people. "Satan disguises himself as an angel of light" and "his ministers as ministers of justice,"[10] imposing false names on individual things, so as to call "rashness" a virtue and avarice "industry." The serpent, in fact, deceived the woman and the woman led the man away from truth to a violation of duty. The serpent is a type of the pleasures of the body. The woman stands for our senses and the man, for our minds. Pleasure stirs the senses, which, in turn, have their effect on the mind. Pleasure, therefore, is the primary source of sin. For this reason, do not wonder at the fact that by God's judgment the serpent

was first condemned, then the woman, and finally the man. The order of condemnation, too, corresponded to that of the crimes committed, for pleasure usually captivates the senses and the senses, the mind. . . .

NOTES TO CHAPTER 4, CHURCH FATHERS, AMBROSE

[1. John J. Savage discusses the date in his Introduction to his translation of *Hexameron, Paradise, and Cain and Abel*, p. ix.]
2. 1 Tim. 2:14.
3. 1 Pet. 3:7.
4. 1 Tim. 2:14.
5. Rev. 22:18-19.
6. 1 Tim. 2:14.
7. Gen. 4:9.
8. Ps. 72:4,5.
9. Deut. 6:13; Luke 4:8.
10. 2 Cor. 11:14, 15.

John Chrysostom

John Chrysostom (c. 347-407 CE) gained the name "Chrysostom"—or "golden mouth"—because of his oratorical skills. A Greek-writing theologian, he has influenced the theologies of both the Eastern and the Western churches through his enormous literary production. Chrysostom was born in Antioch. Early in his life he was attracted to Christian asceticism. As a youth, he lived according to monastic discipline and eventually lived as a hermit. Ordained deacon in 381, he became a priest five years later. In 398 he was made Patriarch of Constantinople against his wish. As priest and bishop, he used his oratorical skills to urge the moral reformation of the nominal Christianity of Antioch. Having incurred the displeasure of the Empress Eudoxia and others, he was unseated as bishop in 404 and sent into exile. He died in 407 while serving a second sentence of exile.

Our selection from Chrysostom's sermons on Genesis involves several distinctive themes. As an example of "Antiochene exegesis," its accent on a literal reading of the story stands in contrast to allegorical forms of interpretation. Further, it shows Chrysostom's ambivalence concerning what Eve signifies about God's original intention for women. On the one hand, he offers a distinctive stress on Eve's original equality with Adam as seen in his portrayal that she was "like man in every detail" and his description of Eve and Adam's "equality of status." From this vantage point, Eve's subordinate status becomes an effect of sin. On the other hand, Chrysostom depicts Eve as being inferior to Adam from the beginning, for example, in his descriptions of her innate weakness when she spoke with the serpent. Another important feature of the selection involves Chrysostom's understandings that the *imago dei* signifies the ability to govern (in distinction from the tradition of interpreting it as "rationality") and that the primary sin involves carelessness (in distinction from the tradition that portrays it as pride). Further, his interpretation of Genesis 4:1 portrays his conviction that sexual intercourse was not God's original design for relations between woman and man.[1] (Source: John Chrysostom, "Homilies on Genesis," translated by Robert C. Hill, in *Homilies on Genesis 1-17*, The Fathers of the Church series, Washington, D.C.: Catholic University of America Press, 1985, vol. 74, pp. 110-11; 134; 197; 198; 200-201; 208-13; 215; 238-42. Also in *Homilies on Genesis 18-45*, The Fathers of the Church series, Washington, D.C.: Catholic University of America Press, 1990, vol. 85, pp. 10-11.)

"Homilies on Genesis" (c. 386 CE)
JOHN CHRYSOSTOM

Homily 8

(9) . . . So "image" refers to the matter of control, not anything else, in other words, God created the human being as having control of everything on earth, and nothing on earth is greater than the human being, under whose authority everything falls.

(10) Yet if, despite such great precision in terms, there are still those spoiling for a fight who would want to say "image" is used in terms of form, we will say to them: that means he is not only man but also woman, for both have the same form. But this would make no sense. I mean, listen to Paul's words: "It is not proper for a man to cover his head, being image and glory of God whereas the woman is man's glory."[2] One is in command, the other is subordinate, just as God had also said to woman from the beginning, "your yearning will be for your husband and he will be your master." You see, since it is on the basis of command that the image was received and not on the basis of form, man commands everything whereas woman is subservient—hence Paul's words about man, that he is constituted God's image and glory, whereas woman is man's glory. If, however, he had been speaking about form, he would not have distinguished between them, man and woman being identical in type, after all.

Homily 10

(9) So, after saying, "Male and female he made them" as though to bestow a blessing on each of them, he goes on, "God blessed them in the words, 'Increase and multiply, fill the earth and gain dominion over it, and have control of the fish of the sea.' " Behold the remarkable character of the blessing! I mean, those words, "Increase and multiply and fill the earth," anyone could see are said of the brute beasts and the reptiles alike, whereas "Gain dominion and have control" are directed to the man and woman. See the Lord's loving

kindness: even before creating her he makes her sharer in this control and bestows on her the blessing.

Homily 15

(5) . . . So in case you think it was in reference to [the animals] it was said above, "Let us make him a helpmate," it now begins its statement with the words, "For Adam, however, there proved to be no helpmate of his kind," as if blessed Moses were teaching us in saying these words that, while all these animals were created and received from Adam the assignment of names, nevertheless none of them proved to be adequate for helping him. Accordingly he wants to teach us about the formation of the being about to be brought forth and the fact that this being due for creation is the one he was speaking about. "Let us make him a helpmate like himself," meaning of his kind, with the same properties as himself, of equal esteem, in no way inferior to him. Hence his words, "For Adam, however, there proved to be no helpmate of his kind," by which this blessed author shows us that whatever usefulness these irrational animals bring to our service, the help provided for Adam by woman is different and immeasurably superior.

(7) . . . "God caused drowsiness to come upon Adam," the text says, "and he slept." It wasn't simply drowsiness that came upon him nor normal sleep; instead, the wise and skillful Creator of our nature was about to remove one of Adam's ribs. Lest the experience cause him pain and afterwards he be badly disposed towards the creature formed him from his rib, and through memory of the pain bear a grudge against this being at its formation, God induced in him this kind of sleep: He caused a drowsiness to come upon him and bid him be weighed down as though by some heavy weight. . . .

(11) "The Lord God," the text says, "fashioned the rib he had taken from Adam into a woman." See the precision of Scripture. I mean, it no longer said, He formed, but "He fashioned," since he took part of what was already formed and, so to say, made up for what was lacking. Hence it says, "He fashioned:" he didn't perform further shaping, but took some small part of the shaping already done, fashioned this part and made a complete being. How great the power of God, the master craftsman, making a likeness of those limbs from that tiny part, creating such wonderful senses, and preparing a creature complete, entire and perfect, capable both of speaking and of providing much comfort to man by a sharing of her being. For it was for the consolation of this man that this woman was created. Hence Paul also said, "Man was not created for woman, but woman for man."[3] Do you see how everything is made for him? I mean, after the act of creation, after the brute beasts were brought forth, some suited for eating and some capable of assisting with man's service, the human being that had been formed stood in need of someone to talk to and able to offer him much comfort by a sharing of her being. So, from man's rib God creates this rational being, and in his inventive wisdom he makes it complete and perfect, like man in every detail—rational, capable of rendering

him what would be of assistance in times of need and the pressing necessities of life. . . . "The Lord God," the text says, "fashioned the rib he had taken from Adam into a woman, and led her to Adam," showing that it was for him that he had made her. He led her to Adam, it says. That is, since among all the other creatures there proved to be no helpmate of his kind (so the text says), lo, the promise I made (having guaranteed as I did to provide you with a help-mate of your kind) I kept by giving you one.

Homily 16

(3) . . . "The serpent said to the woman: 'Why is it that God said, Do not eat of any tree of the garden?' " See the evil spirit's envy and devious scheming. I mean, he saw that the human being, creature though he was, had the good fortune to enjoy the highest esteem and was scarcely inferior in any respect to the angels, as blessed David also says, "You have placed him on a level scarcely lower than the angels,"[4] and even this "scarcely lower" was the result of dis-obedience, the inspired author, after all, uttering this after the disobedience. The author of evil, accordingly, seeing an angel who happened to live on earth, was consumed by envy, since he himself had once enjoyed a place among the powers above but had been cast down from that pinnacle on ac-count of his depravity of will and excess of wickedness. So he employed con-siderable skill so as to pluck the human being from God's favor, render him ungrateful and divest him of all those goods provided for him through God's loving kindness. What did he do? He discovered this wild animal, namely, the serpent, overcoming the other animals by his cunning, as blessed Moses also testified in the words, "The serpent was the wiliest of all the beasts on the earth made by the Lord God." He made use of this creature like some instrument and through it inveigled that naive and weaker vessel, namely, woman, into his deception by means of conversation. "The serpent spoke to the woman," the text says.

(4) . . . People, following Scripture, need to consider the fact that the words came from the devil, who was spurred on to this deception by his own ill-will, while this wild animal he employed like some convenient instrument so as to be able to set the bait for his own deception and thus upset the woman first of all, being ever more readily susceptible of deception, and then, through her, man the first-formed. So he employs this irrational animal for laying his plan, and by means of it he speaks to the woman in these words: "Why is it that God said, Do not eat of any tree of the garden?" Notice in this case the extreme subtlety of his malice: in the unfolding of his planning and inquiry he introduces words not spoken by God and acts as though motivated by care for them. . . . "Why is it that God said?" What, he is saying, is the reason for this? What is the advantage of life in the garden when you aren't free to enjoy the things in it, but are even worse off in incurring the more intense pain of having sight of things but missing out on the enjoyment that comes from pos-sessing them?

(5) Do you see how he uses the words like a bait to inject his poison? The woman should have been able from his very approach to recognize the extremity of his frenzy and the fact that he deliberately said what was not the case and made a pretense of care for them as part of his plan so as to be in a position to find out the instructions they had been given by God, and thus lead them to their downfall. So he did not want her to be able to recognize his trickery immediately and thus abandon converse with him as being idle speech and so avoid being dragged down to a low level. After all, there was no need for her to get involved in conversation with him in the first place; she should rather have conversed with the person for whose sake she came into being, with whom she shared everything on equal terms, and whose helpmate she had been made.

(6) But acting impetuously—how, I know not—she got involved in conversation with the serpent and through him as through an instrument she took in the devil's deadly words. . . . In fact, through her grave negligence she not only failed to turn away but revealed the whole secret of the Lord's direction, thus casting pearls before swine and fulfilling what was said by Christ: "Don't cast your pearls before swine, lest they trample them underfoot, turn on you and tear you to pieces,"[5] as in fact happened in this case. I mean, she exposed to swine, to that evil beast, that is, to the demon acting through it, the divine pearls; he not only trampled on them and opposed them with his words, but turned and led into the rupture of disobedience not only her but also the first-formed man with her. Such is the evil of idly and casually exposing to all and sundry the divine mysteries. . . .

(9) . . . She revealed the secret of the instruction and told him what God had said to them, and thus received from him a different kind of advice, bringing ruin and death. . . . Then, not being satisfied with contradicting the words of God, he goes on to misrepresent the Creator as jealous so as to be in a position to introduce deceit by this means, get the better of the woman and carry out his own purpose. "You will not truly die," he said. "God, you see, knows that on the day that you eat of it, your eyes will be opened and you will be like gods, knowing good and evil." See all the bait he offered: he filled the cup with a harmful drug and gave it to the woman, who did not want to recognize its deadly character. She could have known this from the outset, had she wanted; instead, she listened to his word, that God forbade their tasting the fruit for that reason—"He knows that your eyes will be opened and you will be like gods, knowing good from evil"—puffed up as she was with the hope of being equal to God and evidently dreaming of greatness.

(13) Our text says, "She gave it to her husband also, and they both ate it. Their eyes were opened." Great was the man's indifference, too: even though like him she was human and his wife as well, still he should have kept God's law intact and given it preference before her improper greed, and not joined her as a partner in her fall nor deprived himself of such benefits on account of a brief pleasure, offending his benefactor who had also shown him so much loving kindness. . . .

Homily 17

(30) . . . Since it was the serpent that was the cause of the deception, accordingly he was the first to incur punishment; and since he deceived her first, and she then dragged her husband down with her, she is punished first. . . .

(31) I will ensure, [God] is saying, that the generation of children, a reason for great satisfaction, for you will begin with pain so that each time without fail you will personally have a reminder, through the distress and the pain of each birth, of the magnitude of this sin of disobedience, and may not in the course of time allow the event to slip into oblivion. . . .

(32) Nevertheless, however, the loving God offered comfort with the pain, so that the satisfaction of bearing the child equally matched those pangs that tortured the womb all those months. . . .

(36) As if to explain his reasons to the woman, the loving God said this, meaning, In the beginning I created you equal in esteem to your husband, and my intention was that in everything you would share with him as an equal, and as I entrusted control of everything to your husband, so did I to you; but you abused your equality of status. Hence I subject you to your husband: "Your yearning will be for your husband, and he will be your master." Because you abandoned your equal, who was sharer with you in the same nature and for whom you were created, and you chose to enter into conversation with that evil creature the serpent, and to take the advice he had to give, accordingly I now subject you to him in future and designate him as your master for you to recognize his lordship, and since you did not know how to rule, learn well how to be ruled. "Your yearning will be for your husband, and he will be your master." It is better that you be subject to him and fall under his lordship than that enjoying freedom and authority, you would be cast into the abyss. It would be more useful also for a horse to carry the bit and travel under direction than without this to fall down a cliff. Accordingly, considering what is advantageous, I want you to have yearning for him and, like a body being directed by its head, to recognize his lordship pleasurably.

(37) I know that you are wearied by the excess of words, but stir yourselves a little, I beseech you, lest we leave the sentence incomplete and depart while the judge is still sitting. We are in fact close to the end now. So let us see what he says to the man after the woman, and what kind of punishment he inflicts on him. . . . Since you listened to your wife, he is saying, and ate from the tree, and put the advice from her ahead of my command and weren't prepared to keep away from this one single tree which I told you not to eat from (surely, after all, I didn't bid you keep away from many? one only, and yet you couldn't keep away from that, but forgot my commands and were overborne by your wife). Hence you are to learn through your very labors how much evil you have committed.

(38) Let men give good heed, let women give good heed—the former, that they may have nothing to do with those people advising evil actions, and the latter, that they may advise nothing of the sort. . . .

Homily 18

(12) "Now Adam had intercourse with his wife Eve." Consider when this happened. After their disobedience, after their loss of the garden, then it was that the practice of intercourse had its beginning. You see, before their disobedience they followed a life like that of the angels, and there was no mention of intercourse. How could there be, when they were not subject to the needs of the body? So, at the outset and from the beginning the practice of virginity was in force; but when through their indifference disobedience came on the scene and the ways of sin were opened, virginity took its leave for the reason that they had proved unworthy of such a degree of good things, and in its place the practice of intercourse took over for the future. Accordingly, consider, I ask you, dearly beloved, how great the esteem of virginity, how elevated and important a thing it is, surpassing human nature and requiring assistance from on high.

NOTES TO CHAPTER 4, CHURCH FATHERS, JOHN CHRYSOSTOM

[1. For further examples, see Chapters 14 through 17 of John Chrysostom's "On Virginity," in *On Virginity; Against Remarriage*, translated by Sally Rieger Shore, with an introduction by Elizabeth A. Clark, Studies in Women and Religion series (New York and Toronto: Edwin Mellen Press, 1983), vol. 9. Excerpts of these texts—and of his "Homily on 1 Corinthians 7:2"—also are found in Elizabeth A. Clark's *Women in the Early Church*, Message of the Fathers of the Church series (Wilmington, Del.: Michael Glazier, 1983), vol. 13, pp. 63-64; 122-26; 153-57.]

    2. 1 Cor. 11:7.
    3. 1 Cor. 11:9.
    4. Ps. 8:5.
    5. Matt. 7:6.

Augustine

Augustine (354-430 CE) was born in North Africa. His influence on Western Christianity has been tremendous. Yet Augustine resisted Christianity for many years, even though his mother was a Christian. As a young man, he embraced Manicheanism, a dualistic religion that divided reality into good and evil, and that stressed releasing the good spirit from the degradations of evil matter through asceticism. Augustine eventually became disillusioned with Manicheanism. In Milan, he came under the influence of Ambrose; he was baptized there in 387. In 388 he returned to Africa and wrote a commentary on the opening chapters of Genesis in which he opposed Manicheanism by stressing the fundamental goodness of creation, including the goodness of physicality, marriage, and sexual intercourse.[1] Yet Augustine also appraised human sexuality with caution, maintaining that ever since the Fall, it has been distorted by the uncontrollability of lust. In 391, he became a priest; a few years later he became bishop of Hippo Regius, a position he held until his death.

Augustine wrote commentaries on the opening chapters of Genesis several times in his life.[2] Our selection comes from *The Literal Meaning of Genesis: A Commentary in Twelve Books*. He began writing this text in 401, and worked on it for the next 14 years. In this text, Augustine wanted to offer a "literal" interpretation of Genesis, a task he had begun and left unfinished about 10 years earlier. His use of "literal" interpretation involved telling what happened rather than offering a "symbolic" or "figurative" interpretation which would stress the text's spiritual or allegorical meaning. At one point in our selection he ventured into a symbolic interpretation when he located the origins of slavery in God's postlapsarian pronouncement that Eve would be ruled by her husband.

Our selection involves several other features of Augustine's narration. The initial entries show how he distinguished Genesis 1 from Genesis 2 so that Genesis 1 describes a "first creation" in terms of potentials and causal principles, and Genesis 2 portrays a later production whereby God brings the potentialities of the original creation into visible form.[3] When discussing the first creation, Augustine affirmed that woman as a rational being was made in the image of God. When discussing Genesis 2, he dwelt on woman's procreative significance, offering what became a classic definition for why God created women. His descriptions of Eve's temptation and of the excuses proffered by Adam and Eve show Augustine's stress that pride constitutes the primary sin. Yet the final entry's consideration of what tempted Adam indicates Augustine's concern for the disorder caused by loving another human being. (Source: Augustine, *St. Augustine: The Literal Meaning of Genesis*, 2 vols., John Hammond Taylor, translator, Ancient Christian Writers series, Number 41, New York and Ramsey, N.J.: Newman Press, 1982, pp. 98-99, 183; Number 42, New York and Ramsey, N.J.: Newman Press, 1982, pp. 73-75, 161-62, 167-71, 174-76.)

The Literal Meaning of Genesis (begun c. 401 CE)
AUGUSTINE

*Book III, Chapter 22: "*Woman, in so far as she has a rational mind, is made to the image and likeness of God.*"*

34. Some have conjectured that at this point the interior man was created, but that his body was created afterwards where Scripture says, *And God formed man of the slime of the earth*. We should then take the expression, *God created man*, to refer to his spirit; whereas the statement *God formed man* would apply to his body. But they do not realize that there could have been no distinction of male and female except in relation to the body. There is, of course, the sub-

tle theory that the mind of man, being a form of rational life and precisely the part in which he is made to the image of God, is partly occupied with the contemplation of eternal truth and partly with the administration of temporal things, and thus it is made, in a sense, masculine and feminine, the masculine part as the planner, the feminine as the one that obeys. But it is not in this double function that the image of God is found, but rather in that part which is devoted to the contemplation of immutable truth. With this symbolism in mind, Paul the Apostle declares that only man is the image and glory of God, *But woman*, he adds, *is the glory of man.*[4]

Hence, although the physical and external differences of man and woman symbolize the double role that the mind is known to have in one man, nevertheless a woman, for all her physical qualities as a woman, is actually renewed in the spirit of her mind in the knowledge of God according to the image of her Creator, and therein there is no male or female. Now women are not excluded from this grace of renewal and this reformation of the image of God, although on the physical side their sexual characteristics may suggest otherwise, namely, that man alone is said to be the image and glory of God. By the same token, in the original creation of man, inasmuch as woman was a human being, she certainly had a mind, and a rational mind, and therefore she also was made to the image of God. But because of the intimate bond uniting man and woman, Scripture says merely, *God made man to the image of God.* And, lest anyone think that this refers only to the creation of man's spirit, although it was only according to the spirit that he was made to the image of God, Scripture adds, *Male and female He made him*, to indicate that the body also was now made.

Moreover, lest anyone suppose that this creation took place in such a way that both sexes appeared in one single human being (as happens in some births, in the case of what we call hermaphrodites), the sacred writer shows that he used the singular number because of the bond of unity between man and woman, and because woman was made from man, as will be shown shortly when the brief account of this passage will be elaborated in greater detail. Hence he immediately added the plural number when he said, *He made them . . . and He blessed them.*

*Book VI, Chapter 5: "*Second hypothesis: In the first creation of the six days God created all living beings, including Adam and Eve, potentially and in their causes. From these causes God later created them in their visible forms."

8. It cannot be said that the male was made on the sixth day and the female in the course of days following. On the sixth day it is explicitly said, *Male and female He made them, and He blessed them*, and so forth, and these words are said about both and to both. The original creation, therefore, of the two was different from their later creation. First they were created in potency through the word of God and inserted seminally into the world when He created

all things together, after which He rested from these works on the seventh day. From these creatures all things are made, each at its own proper time throughout the course of history. Later the man and the woman were created in accordance with God's creative activity as it is at work throughout the ages and with which He works even now; and thus it was ordained that in time Adam would be made from the slime of the earth and the woman from the side of her husband.

Book IX, Chapter 3: "The woman as a helper. God's plan for procreation."

5. If one should ask why it was necessary that a helper be made for man, the answer that seems most probable is that it was for the procreation of children, just as the earth is a helper for the seed in the production of a plant from the union of the two. This purpose was declared in the original creation of the world. *Male and female He made them. And God blessed them and said, "Increase and multiply and fill the earth and subdue it."* This reason for creation and union of male and female, as well as this blessing, was not abrogated after the sin and punishment of man. It is by virtue of this blessing that the earth is now filled with human beings who subdue it.

6. Although it was after the expulsion of the man and woman from Paradise that they came together in sexual intercourse and begot children, according to Scripture, nevertheless I do not see what could have prohibited them from honorable nuptial union and the "bed undefiled"[5] even in Paradise. God could have granted them this if they had lived in a faithful and just manner in obedient and holy service to Him, so that without the tumultuous ardor of passion and without any labor and pain of childbirth, offspring would be born from their seed. . . .

Book IX, Chapter 5: "In what sense Eve was made as a helper for Adam."

9. Now, if the woman was not made for the man to be his helper in begetting children, in what was she to help him? She was not to till the earth with him, for there was not yet any toil to make help necessary. If there were any such need, a male helper would be better, and the same could be said of the comfort of another's presence if Adam were perhaps weary of solitude. How much more agreeably could two male friends, rather than a man and woman, enjoy companionship and conversation in a life shared together. And if they had to make an arrangement in their common life for one to command and the other to obey in order to make sure that opposing wills would not disrupt the peace of the household, there would have been proper rank to assure this, since one would be created first and the other second, and this would be further reinforced if the second were made from the first, as was the case with the woman. Surely no one will say that God was able to make from the rib of the man only a woman and not also a man if He had wished to do so. Consequently, I do not

see in what sense the woman was made a helper for the man if not for the sake of bearing children.

Book XI, Chapter 30: "The exchange between the serpent and the woman."

38. Therefore, *The serpent said to the woman: "Why did God say, You shall not eat of every tree in Paradise?" And the woman said to the serpent: "We may eat of the fruit of trees that are in Paradise, but regarding the fruit of the tree in the middle of Paradise, God said: 'You shall not eat of it nor shall you touch it, lest you die.'"*

The serpent, then, first asked the question, and the woman replied, so that her transgression would be inexcusable, and no one would be able to say that the woman had forgotten the command of God. Of course, forgetting a command, especially this unique command which was so necessary, would involve culpable negligence and serious sin. But the sin is more evident when the command is retained in memory and God as present in His command is despised. . . .

39. Then *The serpent said to the woman: "You will not die the death. For God knew that on the day on which you would eat of it your eyes would be open, and you would be like gods, knowing good and evil."* How could these words persuade the woman that it was a good and useful thing that had been forbidden by God if there was not already in her heart a love of her own independence and a proud presumption on [sic] self which through that temptation was destined to be found out and cast down? Finally, not content with the words of the serpent, she also gazed on the tree and saw that it *was good for food and a delight to behold*; and since she did not believe that eating it could bring about her death, I think she assumed that God was using figurative language when He said, *If you eat of it, you shall die.* And so she took some of the fruit and ate and gave some also to her husband, who was with her, using perhaps some persuasive words which Scripture does not record but leaves to our intelligence to supply. Or perhaps there was no need to persuade her husband, since he saw that she was not dead from eating the fruit.

Book XI, Chapter 34: "Adam, hiding himself in shame, is called forth by God."

45. *And the Lord God called Adam and said to him: "Where are you?"* This question is uttered by One who is admonishing, not by one who is ignorant. And there is surely some special meaning in the fact that just as the command was given to the man, and through him transmitted to the woman, so the man is questioned first. For the command came from the Lord through the man to the woman, but sin came from the Devil through the woman to the man. This is full of mystical meanings, not intended by the persons in whom these actions took place, but intended by the all-powerful Wisdom of God. Our purpose now, however, is not to unfold hidden meanings but to establish what actually happened. . . .

Book XI, Chapter 35: "The excuses of Adam and Eve."

47. . . . *And Adam replied, "The woman whom Thou gavest to be my companion gave me fruit of the tree, and I ate."* What pride! Did he say, "I have sinned"? He has the deformity of confusion, not the humility of confession. This interrogation has been written down precisely because it took place in order to be recorded truthfully for our instruction (if it were not recorded truthfully, it would not instruct), so that we may see how men today are suffering from the disease of pride as they try to make their Creator responsible for any sin they commit, while they want attributed to themselves any good they do. Adam said, *The woman whom Thou gavest with me*, that is, *to be my companion, gave me fruit of the tree, and I ate.* As if she had been given to Adam for this purpose, and not rather that she should obey her husband and that both of them should obey God!

48. *Then the Lord God said to the woman, "What is this that you have done?"* And she replied, *The serpent beguiled me, and I ate.* She too fails to confess her sin. She shifts the blame to another, and although her sex is different from Adam's, her pride is the same. . . .

Book XI, Chapter 37: "The sentence pronounced on the woman."

50. *To the woman He said: "I will greatly multiply your sorrows and your anguish. With sorrows you shall bring forth children, and you shall be subject to your husband, and he shall rule over you."* These words that God spoke to the woman are also more appropriately understood in a figurative and prophetic sense. The woman, of course, had not yet given birth. Furthermore, the pain and anguish of childbirth belong solely to this body of death (a death engendered by the transgression), in which the members from the beginning were those of a natural body, which, if man had not sinned, were destined not to die but to live in that other more blessed state until they would deserve to be transformed, after a life of virtue, into a better condition, as I have already stated above in several places. The punishment, then, given to the woman is also understood in a literal sense; and furthermore we must give consideration to the statement, *And you shall be subject to your husband, and he shall rule over you*, to see how it can be understood in the proper sense.

For we must believe that even before her sin woman had been made to be ruled by her husband and to be submissive and subject to him. But we can with reason understand that the servitude meant in these words is that in which there is a condition similar to that of slavery rather than a bond of love (so that the servitude by which men later began to be slaves to other men obviously has its origin in punishment for sin). St. Paul says, *Through love serve one another.*[6] But by no means would he say, "Have dominion over one another." Hence married persons through love can serve one another, but St. Paul does not permit a woman to rule over a man. The sentence pronounced by God gave this power rather to man; and it is not by her nature but rather by her sin that woman deserved to have her husband for a master. But if this order is not maintained, nature will be corrupted still more, and sin will be increased.

Book XI, Chapter 41: "Theories about the nature of the sin of Adam and Eve."

56. I am aware of the fact that some exegetes have thought that the first couple were in a hurry to satisfy their desire for a knowledge of good and evil and that they wished to have before due time what was being postponed and kept for a more opportune occasion, and that the tempter induced them to offend God by anticipating what was not yet intended for them. Thus by their expulsion and condemnation they were said to have been deprived of the advantage of that which they might have enjoyed to their spiritual advancement had they sought it at the proper time as God intended. Now if these writers should wish to understand the tree not in the proper sense as a real tree with real fruit but in a figurative sense, their interpretation could result in a theory apparently consistent with faith and reason.

57. There is also the opinion of those who say that the first couple anticipated marriage by a kind of theft and that they had sexual intercourse before they were united by their Creator. And hence they say that sexual intercourse was signified by the word "tree," and that it had been forbidden them until they would be joined in due time.

I suppose we must assume that Adam and Eve had been created at such a young age that they were required to wait until they would reach puberty! Or perhaps the union was not allowed as soon as it was possible? If it was impossible, it certainly would not take place! Or maybe the bride had to be given away by her father, and they had to wait for the solemn pronouncing of vows, the celebration of the wedding banquet, the appraisal of the dowry, and the signing of the contract! This is ridiculous, and furthermore it is taking us away from the literal meaning of what happened, which we undertook to explain and which we have explained in so far as God has wished to help us.

Book XI, Chapter 42: "Did Adam believe the words spoken through the serpent? How was he tempted to sin?"

58. There is a more serious problem to be considered. If Adam was a spiritual man, in mind though not in body, how could he have believed what was said through the serpent, namely, that God forbade them to eat of the fruit of that one tree because He knew that if they did they would be gods in their knowledge of good and evil? As if the Creator would grudge so great a good to His creatures! It is surely strange if a man endowed with a spiritual mind could have believed this. Was it because the man would not have been able to believe this that the woman was employed on the supposition that she had limited understanding, and also perhaps that she was living according to the spirit of the flesh and not according to the spirit of the mind?

Is this the reason that St. Paul does not attribute the image of God to her?

For he says, *A man indeed ought not to cover his head, since he is the image and glory of God, but woman is the glory of man.*[7] This is not to say that the mind of woman is unable to receive that same image, for in that grace St. Paul says we are neither male nor female.[8] But perhaps the woman had not yet received the gift of the knowledge of God, but under the direction and tutelage of her husband she was to acquire it gradually. It is not without reason that St. Paul said, *For Adam was formed first, then Eve; and Adam was not seduced, but the woman was seduced and fell into sin.*[9] In other words, it was through her that man sinned. For Paul calls him a sinner also when he says, *in the likeness of the sin of Adam, who is a type of the One to come.*[10] But he says that Adam was not seduced. In fact, Adam under interrogation did not say, "The woman whom Thou gavest to be my companion seduced me and I ate"; but, *She gave me fruit of the tree and I ate.* On the other hand, the woman said, *The serpent seduced me.*

59. Can we imagine that Solomon, a man of incredible wisdom, believed that there was any advantage in the worship of idols? But he was unable to resist the love of women drawing him into this evil, and he did what he knew should not be done lest he should inhibit the deadly delights in which he was being wasted away. So it was in the case of Adam. After the woman had been seduced and had eaten of the forbidden fruit and had given Adam some to eat with her, he did not wish to make her unhappy, fearing she would waste away without his support, alienated from his affections, and that this dissension would be her death. He was not overcome by the concupiscence of the flesh, which he had not yet experienced in the law of the members at war with the law of his mind, but by the sort of attachment and affection by which it often happens that we offend God while we try to keep the friendship of men. That he should not have acted thus is clear from the just sentence which God pronounced on him.

NOTES TO CHAPTER 4, CHURCH FATHERS, AUGUSTINE

[1. John Hammond Taylor assesses Augustine's position: "In guarding himself against the errors of the Manichees, who held that sexual desire and procreation were from the Evil Principle, he came to a balanced view of human sexuality which is remarkable in a writer of that period." See *The Literal Meaning of Genesis* (New York and Ramsey, N.J.: Newman Press, 1982), vol. 2, p. 267, note 15. For alternative assessments, see Elizabeth A. Clark's "Vitiated Seeds and Holy Vessels: Augustine's Manichean Past," in Karen L. King, editor, *Images of the Feminine in Gnosticism*, Studies in Antiquity and Christianity Series (Philadelphia: Fortress Press, 1988), pp. 367-401, as well as Paula Fredriksen's "Response to 'Vitiated Seeds and Holy Vessels: Augustine's Manichean Past' by Elizabeth A. Clark" in the same volume, pp. 402-409.]

[2. For examples, see Books 12 and 13 of Augustine's *Confessions* and Book 2 of his *The City of God*.]

[3. See John Hammond Taylor's discussion in *St. Augustine: The Literal Mean-*

ing of Genesis, vol. 1, p. 262, note 18. For a more extended discussion, see Susan E. Schreiner's "Eve, The Mother of History: Reaching for the Reality of History in Augustine's Later Exegesis of Genesis," in Gregory Allen Robbins, editor, *Genesis 1-3 in the History of Exegesis: Intrigue in the Garden* (Lewiston and Queenston: Edwin Mellen Press, 1988), pp. 135-86.]

4. 1 Cor. 11:7.
5. Heb. 13:4.
6. Gal. 5:13.
7. 1 Cor. 11:7.
8. Gal. 3:28.
9. 1 Tim. 2:13-14.
10. Rom. 5:14.

CHAPTER FIVE

Medieval Readings: Muslim, Jewish, and Christian (600–1500 CE)

INTRODUCTION

The medieval era[1] produced a variety of portrayals of Eve and Adam. While most accounts proposed hierarchical readings, a number of egalitarian readings emerged as well. This chapter continues our discussion of Jewish and Christian interpretations while adding a third significant partner: Islamic interpretations. In this time period, Islam enters the scene as a distinct religious tradition; thus we open this chapter with Muslim portrayals of Eve or—as she is known in Arabic—"Hawwa'."

Islam

It is no accident that discussions of the character and activity of women play a significant role in Islam. Islam emphasizes the need for persons to bring their lives into conformity to the will of God.[2] The terms "Islam" and "Muslim" indicate this emphasis because their shared Arabic root, "s-l-m," contains concepts of "submission and "surrender." Such stress on obeying God makes it important to know God's will, including God's intentions for women, for men, and for the relationships that are established between them.

For Muslims, the Qur'an constitutes the primary source for knowing God's intentions. This foundational status of the Qur'an makes it important to highlight several aspects of Islam's understanding of its scripture.[3] First, according to Islam, the Qur'an reveals God's intentions and designs for human life, including those concerning gender relations, because it contains the revelations—or recitations—that the Prophet Muhammad received across a twenty-two-year span. According to Islamic orthodoxy, God conveyed the text of the Qur'an to an angel, who, in turn, recited it to Muhammad. These revelations disclose God's will as well as impart God's promises and judgments. Second, because God conveyed these revelations in Arabic, Arabic is understood to be the language of revelation. Thus any translation of the Qur'an into a language other than Arabic is seen as an *interpretation* of the Qur'an rather than the Qur'an itself. Third, the major parts of the Qur'an are called "surahs." As a reference to literary structure, "surah" is akin to the English term "chapter." No other Islamic book, however, is divided into surahs. Fourth, each surah is subdivided into "ayat" ("ayah" in the singular). This term functions similarly to the English term "verse"; yet in Arabic one of its meanings is "sign," which highlights the Qur'an's status as sacred text.

The influence of Eve on Islamic understandings of women far exceeds the number of times she appears in the Qur'an. The name "Hawwa' "—the Arabic counterpart for Eve—appears nowhere in Islam's scripture. Yet the Qur'an mentions the first woman several times, often by referring to her as Adam's mate or wife (e.g., Q.2:35; Q.20:117). These references provide scriptural support for how Muslims understand the character and activities of the first woman/Eve, and through her, understand God's designs for the character and responsibilities of all women.

The Qur'an's distinctive renderings of the first woman/Eve are less commonly known than some of its other descriptions of gender relations. Persons often know that the Qur'an holds open the possibility of polygyny, a man marrying more than one woman (Q.4:3). It also is well known that the Qur'an endorses modesty, especially in female attire (Q.24:3of.). Less well known is the fact that the Qur'an never describes the first woman/Eve as having been created inferior or secondarily to Adam. Indeed the Qur'an gives no precise indication of how God created the first woman or even of why God created her. Although the Qur'an describes God's desire for providing "rest" or "repose" as the reason God created spouses, this repose is not gender specific.[4] The Qur'an never correlates this provision only with what women offer to men. Rather, Islam's scripture sounds a note of mutuality through its proclamation that God wills all spouses to offer rest to one another (Q.30:21). Further, while the Qur'an offers several depictions of the first human temptation and disobedience (Q.2:29f.; 7:19f.; 20:115f.), it never assigns primary culpability for this downfall to the first woman (Q.7:2of; 20:121).

In this chapter, the selections from the Qur'an relate either specifically to the first woman or more generally to all women in terms of their characteristics and situations. These selections are arranged according to their order in the Qur'an. The heading that follows each surah's number is the title for that surah. A surah's title usually accords with a distinctive feature of that surah, perhaps a distinctive word or phrase. Titles rarely indicate the theme of the entire surah. For example, Surah 2 covers more topics than its title "The Cow" indicates.

After the passages from the Qur'an, our exploration of medieval Muslim interpretations continues by setting out selections that represent three genres of interpretation: formal exegetical commentary, folklore, and mystical contemplation. These subsequent Muslim interpretations of the first woman probe, amplify, and also obscure many of the Qur'an's distinctive renderings of Eve.

The selection by Abu Ja'far Muhammad ibn Jarir al-Tabari (839-923 CE) provides a window for looking at discussions of Eve that occurred during Islam's formative centuries. Our selection comes from al-Tabari's exegetical commentary on the Qur'an, a large-scale work that is understood to sum up the first three centuries of Muslim exegetical activity.[5] Born in what is now northern Iran, al-Tabari wrote this text after traveling to important centers of Islamic learning, where he collected exegetical traditions.[6] He recorded the traditions that he deemed authoritative, indicating their reliability by reporting their "isnad"—a list of names showing the sequence of persons who transmitted a particular tradition. Frequently he provides multiple traditions concerning the interpretation of a single word or phrase.

In our selection, al-Tabari traces two of the traditions back to the "Companions," persons who have great authority because they lived during the time of Muhammad. These two traditions depict Eve in ways that make her character more subservient and menacing than her portrayals in the Qur'an. One, a discussion of Q.2:35, contends that God created Eve to be a source of rest for Adam; it thereby narrows the Qur'an's more inclusive stress on spouses as sources of rest.[7] This tradition from the Companions also portrays Eve as created secondarily to Adam, maintaining that the word for "life" provides the etymological root of her name "because she was created from something living."[8]

The other tradition from the Companions included in our selection from al-Tabari's commentary discusses Q.2:36 and its description of the first human rebellion against God.[9] This tradition attributes the first disobedience to Eve. It underscores her culpability by presenting Adam as initially refusing to eat from the forbidden tree. Moreover, it portrays Eve as responsible for Adam's sin by having her successfully tempt him to follow her disobedient example. Other interpretations that al-Tabari records of this ayat or verse show that the Companions are not unique in blaming Eve. Additional exegetical comments he collected also fault Eve, using motifs such as wine or beauty as the tools she employs to sway Adam.[10] Near the conclusion of this selection, al-Tabari offers his own interpretation.[11] It appears prudent and reserved when compared to the more embellished interpretations set forth in the traditions he preserved.

Our next Muslim text, a selection from *The Tales of the Prophets of al-*

Kisa'i, also consists of a collection of traditions.[12] But in this selection the as-sembled traditions arise from the legends of popular culture rather than from the more schooled literature of Qur'anic commentary gathered by al-Tabari. Little is known about al-Kisa'i, the collector of these legends. Even the dating of the collection offered by their English translator, W. M. Thackston, Jr., as "not long before 1200" remains vague.[13] Thackston argues that this genre of folklore communicated tales that were used to entertain people and to guide their conduct. He also points to the popularity enjoyed by these tales, noting that they appear in several different Islamic regions.[14]

This collection of legends includes many stories about Adam and Eve. The sustained character of these stories contrasts with the disjointed texture of the Qur'an and of al-Tabari's exegetical commentary. Some of the *Tales* re-iterate themes we saw in al-Tabari's commentary. Others provide new themes, such as a depiction of Iblis/Satan taking on the disguise of a slave as a way to deceive Eve.[15] In keeping with an egalitarian presentation, descriptions in "The Creation of Eve" portray her as being as tall as Adam and at least as beautiful as he was.[16] Further, the *Tales* ascribe qualities of tenderness and care to the first couple's relationship, particularly in the portrayals of their actions and reflections when, following their disobedience, God separated them from each other.[17]

Yet all is not well. The *Tales* also promote a hierarchical rendering of gen-der relations. They report that God created Eve from a crooked rib out of Adam's left side.[18] Further, they characterize greed as her motivation for eat-ing the fruit—she is prompted to eat by being told that "whoever eats first has precedence."[19] Moreover, the *Tales* speak of Eve as being "deficient in reason, religion, ability to bear witness, and in inheritance."[20] Some ambiguity exists over whether these specific traits belonged to her from the time of her crea-tion (as indicated in "Eve's Query") or represent divine punishments (as sug-gested in God's speech in "The Address of Eve").[21] But the subordinate place of Eve and her daughters is underscored regardless of the particular time when God assigns women these deficiencies. Moreover, "Eve's Query" and "The Address of Eve" list additional character flaws and punishments for women, including moral malformation, menstruation, and seclusion. It is little won-der that God's recital of the punishments inflicted upon women concludes by maintaining of Eve and her daughters: "God will never make a prophet or a wise person from among them."[22]

The final medieval Muslim selection in this chapter comes from *The Bezels of Wisdom* by Muhammad b. 'Ali b. Muhammad Ibn al-Arabi al-Ta'i al-Hatimi or, as he usually is named, Ibn al-Arabi (1165-1240 CE).[23] Ibn al-Arabi was a Sufi philosopher. Sufism, the branch of Islam that represents its mystical tradition, arose in various parts of the Islamic empire alongside the development of state-supported orthodoxy during Islam's early centuries. In accord with the mystical branches of other religious traditions, Sufism envi-sions union with God as the goal for human life; also it emphasizes contemplation and self-discipline as the means for reaching this goal. Ibn al-Arabi was born in Spain, where he studied under Sufi masters as a youth; two of his masters were women.[24]

The *Bezels of Wisdom* is a work from Ibn al-Arabi's later years. It presents his reflections on the line of prophets, beginning with Adam. Our selection comes from his discussion of Muhammad at the book's conclusion. Here, rather than in his study of Adam, he sets out his interpretation of the significance of gender and of what it means for humanity to be created in God's image.[25]

Ibn al-Arabi's mystical exegesis can make for difficult reading because he is alert to meanings that are not readily apparent when one simply looks at the surface level of a text. Yet this speculative discussion merits serious attention. It presents a strong challenge to positions that disparage women, even though it does not advocate the equality of women and men.[26] While portraying the contemplation of women as a way to gain "perfect contemplation of the Reality," it endorses women's subordination through its descriptions of women as passive and of lower rank as well as through its portrayal of a *syzygy* in which the sexes are in complementary opposition.[27] Yet it also places women over men through its discussions of God's feminine dimensions and its celebration of women's spiritual capacities. On the basis of the latter, Leila Ahmed describes Ibn al-Arabi as having a "countercultural understanding of Islam with respect to women," maintaining that he was "probably unique among major Muslim scholars and philosophers in regarding women sympathetically."[28]

In contrast to the claim of *The Tales of the Prophets of al-Kisa'i* that God would never make a woman a wise person, Sufism often has respected women as spiritual guides and saints.[29] Rabi'a al-Adawiyya (d. 801), for example, is a prominent Sufi saint; several stories about her stress how she surpassed her male colleagues in piety and wisdom. Often promoting celibacy (especially for women), Sufism has offered many of its female adherents greater autonomy than orthodox Islam's stress on women's subordination to their husbands. Such untraditional roles for women do not mean Sufism only presents a positive assessment of women; Sufi literature contains many negative statements about women. Yet the wider role for women within Sufism constitutes an important contribution for gaining insight into Muslim understandings of God's will for the character and activities of women. Ahmed notes that the Sufi movement's break with orthodox conventions about women shows that "there were ways of reading the Islamic moment and text that differed from those of the dominant culture and that such readings had important implications for the conceptualization of women and the social arrangements concerning gender."[30]

The hadith offer another countervoice to the assumption that Islam—particularly in its formative period—prohibits women from assuming positions of authority. These reports of deeds or sayings of the Prophet are held in such esteem within orthodox Islam that they serve as a "second scripture" after the Qur'an. The irony of the hadith in terms of the conceptualization of women has just begun to be explored. On the one hand, these narrations set forth many hierarchical assumptions and prescriptions for gender relations, as seen in the statements attributed to the Companions in our selection from al-Tabari. On the other hand, the chain of transmission for a number of these reports concludes with the name of a woman. It is no small matter that the locus of authority for these reports resides in the testimony of particular women. As Ahmed points out: "The very fact of women's contribution to this important literature indicates that at least the first generation of Muslims . . . and their immediate descendants had no difficulty in accepting women as authorities."[31]

Judaism

Contrary to the popular image of the "dark ages," the years 600 CE to 1500 CE saw a flourishing of Jewish literary activity. Four approaches to Eve's characterization can be seen in this period: (1) compilations that continue themes and literary forms found in traditional midrashic and talmudic treatments of Eve (e.g., *Pirke de Rabbi Eliezer*, *The Chronicles of Jerahmeel*), (2) commentaries that supplement (and sometimes challenge) rabbinical explanations of Genesis 1–3 with philological and historical exegesis (e.g., Rashi's commentary on the Pentateuch), (3) philosophical treatises that employ allegorical and rational explanations of Eve and Adam (e.g., Maimonides, *Guide for the Perplexed*), and (4) mystical treatments that use esoteric symbol systems to understand Genesis 1–3 (e.g., *Zohar*).

The approaches outlined above often reiterate or challenge the materials included in chapter 3 of this volume. They also expand these traditions, frequently introducing new themes and utilizing methods other than midrash. Like the writers of preceding periods, medieval Jewish writers produced interpretations of Eve that contain both hierarchical and egalitarian elements.

Eve and Medieval Midrash

Many of the extrabiblical themes about Eve in the targumic, midrashic, and talmudic materials we read about in chapter 3 surface again in medieval treatments. But the writers of this period did more than simply repeat what they inherited. Like the sages upon whose work their own depended, medieval writers explicated and expanded the traditions they received. New story elements appeared, once again pushing back Genesis 1–3's interpretive boundaries. Since space in this introduction does not permit an exhaustive identification and analysis of these elements, we will focus on two examples as case studies—the expansion of the snake's conversation with Eve and reflections on woman's creation in Genesis 1-2.

In Genesis 3, when Eve reports God's instructions to the serpent (vv. 2–3), she includes a command prohibiting the touching of the tree (a command not given in Genesis 2). No explanation is given as to how Eve knows God's command, since technically she is not yet created when it is given in chapter 2 (unless one understands Adam as an androgyne). Midrashic and talmudic treatments supplemented the biblical account of Eve's conversation with the serpent by adding various story elements (e.g., the serpent's motivation, an explanation of why Eve was addressed first). When the author of *The Fathers According to Rabbi Nathan* (*ARN*) reports Eve's conversation with the serpent, however, he not only explains how Eve learned of God's prohibition, but goes on to suggest that ultimately Eve was not to blame for what happened in the Garden.

According to *ARN* (version A, chap. 1), the serpent touches the tree and its fruit without getting hurt. The serpent then suggests to Eve, quite logically, that if touching the tree is harmless then eating its fruit will likewise be harmless. Since Eve, we are now told, originally received the command from Adam, not God, Eve concludes that Adam somehow got God's command wrong and proceeds to eat the fruit. The writer completes the episode by censoring Adam for adding to God's original command, placing a "hedge" around it. Adam's "hedge" makes Adam ultimately culpable for Eve's actions. Thus *ARN*'s treatment of the serpent's conversation with Eve exonerates Eve in three ways: (1) Eve falls victim to a reasoned, logical argument supported by visible, credible proofs, (2) Eve assumes Adam was mistaken and thus does not deliberately break God's command, and (3) Adam is held responsible for Eve's actions. While previous rabbinical treatments of the conversation mentioned Adam's hedge and the snake's touching of the tree, none exonerated Eve and censored Adam to this degree.

A second example of midrashic expansion in this period can be found in the development of the character "Lilith." Not all expansions of rabbinical themes in *ARN* and other writings of this period were as kind to women as *ARN*'s exoneration of Eve. Indeed, of all the midrashic expansions to emerge from the medieval period, none can parallel the horrific imaging of women found in Lilith's story.

The origin of the character "Lilith" is not clear. Some scholars identify her with the "night hag" of Isaiah 34:14 (RSV),[32] while others look to Mesopotamian demons for her origin.[33] Though references to Lilith occur four times in the Babylonian Talmud (*Nid.* 24b,[34] *Sabb.* 151b,[35] *B. Bat.* 73a,[36] *'Erub.* 100b[37]), they appear in contexts unrelated to Adam. It is not until the medieval period that interpreters connect Lilith intimately with Adam. Prior to this, talmudic and midrashic writers struggled with the discrepancies concerning woman's creation in Genesis 1-2. One suggestion offered was that there were originally two Eves. Since Adam was disgusted by the first Eve's creation, God removed her and created a second one (the Eve of Gen. 2). Medieval writers combined the rabbinic tradition of the two Eves with that of the demon Lilith to arrive at the story of Lilith, Adam's first wife.

The Alphabet of Ben Sira (c. 800s-900s) preserves the first clearly articulated account of Adam's relationship with Lilith. In several important ways, the account differs from the earlier two-Eve story. Whereas before, God removed the first Eve due to Adam's displeasure, now Lilith leaves Adam on her own accord. While the first Eve disgusted Adam, Lilith rebels against him, refusing to assume the coital position Adam assigned her.[38] Moreover, unlike the first Eve, Lilith survives her initial encounter with Adam and proceeds to interact with him and with others.

What happens to Lilith after she leaves Adam? According to legend she: (1) endangers newborns, (2) gives birth to demons, (3) sexually stalks men who sleep alone at night, and (4) marries, in her various aspects, the highest echelon of demonic leadership. Such descriptions of Lilith's exploits elevated fears of the demonic/dangerous aspects of women to new heights in Jewish literature.

The Midrashic Eve Challenged

By the tenth century, the midrashic approach to scripture, so prevalent in classical rabbinical materials (and the source of a great deal of Eve's literary development), came under attack both internally and externally. Internally, the Jewish sectarian group known as the Karaites ("scripturalists") questioned the authority of the Oral Torah with its expansionistic treatment of scripture and advocated a return to the Written Torah's literal meaning.

Externally, midrashic expansions of scripture became especially problematic as Jews felt compelled to defend their faith to Christians and Muslims. Even though, as Paul Morris astutely points out, "Jewish scholars familiar with Christian exegesis generally found it as bizarre as anything propounded in midrashic sources," challenges from Christians caused medieval Jews to reflect on the midrashic method. In addition, Muslim rationalistic and philological approaches to the study of the Qur'an contrasted sharply with the expansive extravagance of rabbinic midrash. It was pressures such as these, Morris suggests, that "led Jewish scholars back to the Hebrew of the biblical text and the creation of a 'new' hermeneutic of the 'plain meaning' of Scripture."[39] As additional ways of approaching the text emerged, so did new ways of reading Eve and Adam's story.

This is not say that midrashic treatments of Genesis 1-3 disappeared from Jewish literature after the tenth century. Quite the contrary. As we have already shown, writers preserved both the content and the method of earlier midrash while continuing to produce new midrashic treatments. What it does mean, however, is that apologetic necessities arising from Judaism's interaction with Christianity and Islam, plus the resulting infusion into Judaism of new hermeneutical stances, caused Jewish scholars both to challenge and to preserve older traditions. In quite different ways, commentators like Rashi and Nahmanides and philosophers like Maimonides attempted to integrate the old with the new.

The two most influential commentaries to emerge from the medieval period were those written by the French exegete Rashi (Rabbi Shlomo ben

Yitzhaki, 1040-1105) and the Spanish exegete Nahmanides (Rabbi Moses ben Nahman, Ramban, 1195-1270).

Rashi, famous for his exegetical goal of recovering the text's "plain" sense,[40] often employed philological insights in his commentary on Torah. For example, Rashi's response to Genesis 2:23 ("this shall be called woman, because this was taken out of man") is to observe simply that "Here we have a kind of play upon words (the words *ishshah* and *ish* sounding similar)" (Rashi on Genesis 2:23).

For Rashi, the subordination of women in marriage was part of the created order. Rashi suggests that God's command in Genesis 1:28 ("to be fruitful and multiply") is given to the male only and that the phrase "subdue it" should be understood as "and subdue her [the woman]." To appreciate the importance of Rashi's interpretation, one should realize that his commentary became almost canonical in later Judaism. Compilers of the *Mikra'ot Gedolot* (literally, "Great Readings"; otherwise known as the "Rabbinic Bible") included Rashi's commentary alongside the Hebrew text and its targumic version.[41] The *Mikra'ot Gedolot* (and thus Rashi's commentary) became a standard reference for scripture study. Thus, Rashi's hierarchical reading of Genesis 1:28 had far-reaching consequences for generations of later readers who found in it a blueprint for gender relations.

Like Rashi, Nahmanides also wrote a commentary on the Torah.[42] Nahmanides's commentary, however, challenged previous interpretations of Genesis 1-3, such as those produced by Rabbi Abraham Ibn Ezra (biblical exegete, 1089-1164) and Rashi. According to Nahmanides, Adam originally possessed a spiritualized body that was subsequently lost after his disobedience. Aside from the loss of this body, Adam's disobedience also resulted in the emergence of human will. Thus, for Nahmanides, the knowledge of good and evil is not sexual desire (as argued by some commentators) but the desire to choose between good and evil. Nor was woman's subordination part of the created order (as argued by Rashi) but instead belonged to the post-Garden human experience.

Philosophers like Maimonides (Moses ben Maimon, Rambam, 1135/8-1204) also addressed the meaning of Genesis 1-3. In his monumental work, *The Guide for the Perplexed*, Maimonides discusses Adam and Eve in section 1.2 (where he "answers" objections raised to the Genesis 2-3 account) and in 2.30 (which is part of a philosophical discussion of Genesis 1-4). In these sections, Maimonides allegorizes the Adam and Eve story. For Maimonides, Adam and Eve represent "male" and "female," which in turn stand for "form" and "matter." While both are components of human existence, matter is subordinate to form. Thus, Maimonides discerns in Genesis 1-3 a philosophical anthropology, the likes of which had not been seen in Judaism since the writings of Philo in the first century CE.[43] Indeed, Daniel Boyarin suggests that "Maimonides's reading of the story of the creation of Adam and Eve introduces into the later rabbinic culture the very dualisms from which the midrashic Rabbis escaped in theirs."[44]

Eve and the Esoteric: The Kabbalah

Perhaps the most distinctive Jewish reading of Genesis 1–3 to emerge from the medieval period came out of the kabbalistic tradition. While a comprehensive study of the gender imagery of Jewish mysticism could easily fill a volume of its own, we will sketch some of the elements having a direct bearing on our study—the nature of God and the relationship between the divine and human realms. The following discussion represents a synthesis of various kabbalistic writers and schools.

Medieval Jewish mystical treatments of God maintain that there are two parts to God: the *Ein-Sof* (literally, "No End"), which is hidden and not accessible to human knowledge, and the *sefirot*, a series of ten emanations or spheres that flow out from the *Ein-Sof*. Each *sefira* represents a distinct part of God.[45] The *Ein-Sof* and the *sefirot* constitute the upper world of reality. Originally, the various parts of God interacted harmoniously and peace reigned in the upper world.

Parallel to the upper world of peace and harmony is a world of separation—the lower world. Located below the ten *sefirot*, it is a flawed material world that came into existence because Adam disobeyed God. Adam's actions affected himself (he lost his spiritual body) and the upper realm as well. Since the upper and lower worlds were not only parallel but also dynamically connected, actions in one world had consequences in the other. Thus Adam and Eve's separation in the lower world mirrored the separation of God's male and female parts—the *Tiferet* (masculine) and the *Malkhut* (feminine)—in the upper world. Humankind's task, therefore, is to reunite the female with the male. Such gender integration in the lower realm becomes effective in the upper realm, restoring cosmic harmony and balance. Thus humankind is given the job of repairing not only its own gender schism, but that of God's as well.

Twentieth-century readers of Kabbalah have often praised its imagery for God (male and female) and its reading of the human task (to reintegrate the male and female) as an egalitarian vision of gender relations that is refreshingly liberating. Not all modern readers, however, agree with this evaluation. Elliot Wolfson, for example, suggests that the "oneness" of the kabbalistic system is simply the reconstructed rabbinical androgyne. For Wolfson this implies a merging of sexes that subordinates the female to the male.[46] Thus for Wolfson, the rich gender imagery of the Jewish Kabbalah "reflects the androcentric and patriarchical norms of medieval society in general and that of rabbinic culture more particularly."[47]

Eve and Her Medieval Jewish Daughters

To what extent did the images of Eve mentioned in this chapter shape medieval Jewish women's lives? This question is difficult to answer for several reasons. First, we are not sure how many people read these texts during this period, or, having read them, accepted their teachings as authoritative. We know that texts like the *Alphabet of Ben Sira*, *The Guide for the Perplexed*, and the *Zohar* were critiqued and suppressed by portions of their medieval audiences. Nevertheless, each text managed to survive and win enthusiastic acceptance in later generations.

Negative medieval responses to the *Alphabet of Ben Sira*, for example, ranged from cautions against reading, copying, or even mentioning it, to the extravagant claim that if one burned the *Alphabet* on a Sabbath Yom Kippur, one performed a "blessed act." Yet the *Alphabet*, with its virulent image of Lilith, went on to become one of the "most copied of popular texts of medieval Jewish society."[48] The same was true, on an intellectual level, of Maimonides's writings. Although Maimonides would later be remembered as "the greatest figure in the intellectual history of medieval Jewry,"[49] his work evoked open hostility both during his lifetime and after his death. Jews who did not accept Aristotelianism, or who accepted Maimonides's Aristotelianism but not his religious commitment, or who thought his work undermined traditional rabbinic and scriptural authority, all raised their voices in protest of Maimonides's ideas.[50] As for the Kabbalah, while it would later become a foundation of popular Jewish spirituality, it originally represented the esoteric beliefs of only a small group of educated men, and was considered dangerous by others.[51]

Thus, while these three texts became important to future generations of Jews, they evoked a mixed review from medieval readers. This makes it difficult to know how these texts affected the lives of particular women. In addition, few women during this period were literate and thus able to read these works. While later Jewish women, both orthodox and liberal, would appeal to the Kabbalah's female imagery, and while twentieth-century Jewish feminists would find in Lilith a role model, it is difficult to recover how the *Zohar* and the *Alphabet* immediately affected medieval Jewish women. The absence of texts written for and by women during this period unfortunately limits our chances of hearing firsthand how women responded to these texts.

Finally, there is a geopolitical element of medieval Jewish women's lives that adds complexity to the issue of women's history during this period. That is, a Jewish woman living in Christian Europe experienced a different social reality than a Jewish woman in Muslim-governed regions. At the very least, this factor cautions us against speaking monolithically of medieval Jewish women's experience.

Yiddish texts from the sixteenth and seventeenth centuries, however, give us entree into one segment of Jewish women's experience. Although a bit beyond our period of study in this chapter, these materials reveal an interesting development in the relationship between Eve's story and Jewish women's lives. By the late medieval-early modern period, some Jewish women in central and eastern Europe could read and write in Yiddish. Texts written expressly for women appeared in two genres: ethical instructions (*musar*) and devotional prayers (*tkhines*). While the *musar* were written exclusively by men to women, the *tkhines* could contain prayers written by women. In the *Brantshpigl* [The burning mirror] by Moses Henoch Altshuler (1596) and in the *Sefer mitsvas ha-noshim* [The book of women's commandments] by R. Benjamin Aaron Solnik (1577)—both examples of Yiddish ethical admonitions to women— we see a link forged between women's bodies and Eve's story. Both authors interpret the three "women's commandments" (*hallah*, *niddah*, and *haddlaqah*) as a necessary atonement for Eve's transgression.[52] Moreover, women's bodily functions are imaged as symbolic of, and punishment for, Eve's disobedience. As Solnik writes:

> After Eve ate of the apple, and knew she must die, she wanted her husband to eat of it as well. She said, If I have to die, you have to die with me. And she gave it to him so that he would also have to eat of the apple. Adam, poor thing, at first didn't want to eat of the apple. So she took a tree branch in her hand and beat him until he also ate of the apple. As the verse says, "She gave me of the tree, and I ate" [Gen. 3:12 *Hi natnah li min ha-ez va-okhel*]. She gave [it] to me with the tree, and I ate. And because that foolish Adam let his wife beat him, God, blessed be his name, cursed him, for he should not have let a woman beat him, but he should have beaten her . . . for God made the man to rule over the woman. . . .
>
> Therefore the woman must also . . . suffer torment and misfortune. And therefore she must have her period every month, and must fast once or twice [a month], so that she will always remember her sin and remain in a constant state of repentance. Just as a murderer continuously does, who must all his days fast once or twice a month, so that he will think about repentance, and regret his sin, so must the woman do as well. Every month she immerses herself in the ritual bath, so that she will remember her sins, and be pious. . . . Therefore, it is fitting for her to recite the prayers for a repentant sinner.[53]

Altshuler, in his *Brantshpigl*, went even further than Solnik by suggesting that the blood of women's menstrual cycle and of childbirth is connected to the snake's venom originally deposited within Eve during the Garden copulation.[54] Thus both documents imaged women's domestic ritual responsibilities and their bodily functions negatively, as ongoing atonement for Eve's (and their) disobedience.

The *tkhines*, on the other hand, stress Jewish women's rewards for their obedience and present a more positive image of their ritual activities. Chava Weissler, a modern scholar of *tkhine* literature, asserts, "I have yet to discover a *tkhine* that links the three women's *mitzvot* to Eve's sin . . . in the *tkhines*, the observance of the women's *mitzvot* is connected with fertility, rather than with penance."[55] Moreover, while the *tkhines* connect women's pain in childbirth with Eve's disobedience, no poisonous parallel is drawn between the snake's venom and women's monthly cycle or childbirth blood.

Thus, by the sixteenth and seventeenth centuries, women who could read Yiddish had available to them two discussions of women's commandments and Eve. One discussion heightened women's culpability and tied women's ritual obligation to the notion of penance, while the other acknowledged the pain and suffering resultant from Eve's actions, but presented women's *mitzvot* in a more positive light.[56] Unfortunately, we lack similar materials for the period covered in this chapter.

Background to the Selections

The readings on medieval Judaism we have included in this chapter represent a variety of genres. Some, quite intentionally, carry on the form of earlier rabbinical materials. *The Fathers According to Rabbi Nathan*, a commentary on the Mishnaic tractate *Abot*, is an extracanonical Minor Tractate to the Babylonian Talmud. Existing in two forms (*ARN* A and *ARN* B), its final date of compilation is usually assigned to c. 600-700s. Most scholars consider the work pseudonymous.

We have also included selections from three other pseudonymous works: *Alphabet of Ben Sira* (c. 800s-900s), *Pirke de Rabbi Eliezer* (c. 700-800s), and *The Chronicles of Jerahmeel* (c. 1300s). While the first deals with the supposed exploits of Ben Sira,[57] the second and third present midrashic readings of Genesis. *Pirke de Rabbi Eliezer* (*PRE*) is reported to be the work of Rabbi Eliezer, son of Hurkanos (c. 50-100s CE). Of its 53 chapters, 9 deal with creation (chapters 12-20). The *Chronicles of Jerahmeel* is the name given by its translator (M. Gaster) to a compilation of legendary materials. Gaster explained that he chose the name "Jerahmeel" because Jerahmeel's work (next to Yosippon) "forms the most interesting and the most remarkable portion of this compilation." According to Gaster, however, the text probably could be called the "Chronicle of Eleasar ben Asher the Levite," whom Gaster identifies as its fourteenth-century compiler. The *Chronicles of Jerahmeel* covers the period from Creation to the death of Judah Maccabeus.[58] Both *PRE* and the *Chronicles of Jerahmeel* arrange their materials sequentially, presenting a more readable narrative than earlier midrashic collections.

As mentioned previously, the tenth century witnessed the emergence of the commentary as a literary genre in Jewish literature. Although heavily indebted to midrashic and talmudic materials, these commentaries often presented a verse-by-verse exposition of the scripture that drew heavily on its philological and grammatical dimensions. The commentaries we have included in this chapter—those from Rashi (c. late 1000s) and Nahmanides (c. 1200s)—are often considered the two most significant medieval examples of this genre.

Philosophical treatises also became fertile grounds for discussions on Eve and Adam. As representative of this arena of discussion we have included selections from Maimonides's *The Guide for the Perplexed*, composed somewhere around the last decades of the twelfth century. Though Maimonides wrote this work for his student, Yosef ben Yehuda Sham'un, he also directed it toward the Jewish intellectual who wanted to hold both philosophy and the Jewish faith together—an individual Maimonides designated as the "perplexed."

As representative of Jewish mystical approaches to Genesis 1-3, we have included three types of materials: a pre-*Zohar* text by Isaac Kohen, selections from the *Zohar*, and portions of Nahmanides's commentary (though his commentary contains only veiled allusions to symbols).

In the pre-*Zohar* period, kabbalistic thinking flourished in Provence (southern France), Gerona (Spain), and Castile (Spain). Isaac Kohen is representative of the Castilian kabbalistic school. According to Lawrence Fine, this school was distinguished for "the development of an elaborate theory of a demonic emanation of the ten *sefirot* paralleling the ten holy *sefirot*."[59] The selections we have included from Kohen's treatment of this "left emanation" describe these demonic *sefirot* in detail. Such was the effect of Kohen's work on Jewish mysticism that Joseph Dan credits it with the introduction of "a full blown Gnostic dualism into Kabbalistic symbolism."[60]

The *Zohar*, the classic text of esoteric Jewish mysticism, was published by the Castilian kabbalist, Moses ben Shemtov de Leon (c. 1280s). Leon claimed to have access to an ancient manuscript that preserved the teachings of Rabbi Shimon bar Yohai, a second-century rabbi from Palestine.[61] Modern scholars have challenged this claim, and Lawrence Fine, for example, labels it a "literary ploy." Along with other features it "ultimately assured the *Zohar*'s near-canonical status by the sixteenth century."[62] Like other great Jewish classics, the *Zohar* went on to inspire a branch of literature devoted to its interpretation. It was and remains, as Fine correctly notes, "a genuinely unique book without parallel in the whole history of Judaism."[63]

Christianity

Genesis 1–3 was a crucial text for medieval Christians. It provided, as Barbara Newman has noted, "the touchstone for all meditation on man and woman."[64] Though medieval thinkers were heavily influenced by Augustine's discussion of the Genesis account, they were not bound by it. Thomas Aquinas introduced Aristotelian theories of sexuality into the conversation. Female writers offered novel syntheses of traditional notions of the creation and fall. And the male writers of the *Malleus Maleficarum*, a fifteenth-century guide for inquisitors, argued that women were, from their creation, imperfect and lustful beings who posed grave dangers to men. While medieval Christians tended to find a hierarchy of gender in Genesis 1–3, some notable exceptions emerged. Readings that were egalitarian or that merely sought to correct the Augustinian tendency entirely to blame women for the Fall existed alongside the misogyny of the *Malleus Maleficarum*.

Thomas Aquinas, the most significant Christian medieval theologian, saw in Genesis 1–3 a hierarchy of gender. Thomas assumed that God created woman as man's subordinate in order to allow humanity to reproduce. Appealing to Aristotelian notions of biology, Thomas argued that males, as the "active power" in procreation, provided the "form" (the rational soul, or defining principle) of the child conceived during intercourse, whereas females, as passive principles, provided only the matter. If all went well during the procreative act, a male would be conceived. If, on the other hand, the active force was insufficient or the passive matter unready for the task—or even if a south wind were blowing—a female, or "misbegotten male" would result.[65]

Despite defining females as defective males, Thomas added a number of points that softened his views on gender hierarchy. Against Chrysostom, Thomas insisted that Adam and Eve would have engaged in sexual inter-course even if they had not fallen into sin. Against Augustine, he asserted that sex in Eden would have been pleasurable—more pleasurable, in fact, than it would prove to be after the Fall. Against those who argued that in an ideal creation, no women would have existed, Thomas countered that women, though inferior to men, were necessary to complete the perfection of the hu-man race. Had there been no fall into sin, Thomas maintained, husbands and wives would still (by their own choice) have conceived females as well as males.[66]

Writings of and about medieval women mystics also contributed recon-siderations of hierarchical readings of Genesis 1-3. In the church's first three centuries, Christians celebrated those women who were courageous enough to suffer martyrdom for the faith. After Constantine made Christianity the official religion of the Roman empire in the fourth century, however, martyr-dom could no longer enhance individual women's spiritual status. Lives de-voted to asceticism and virginity, on the other hand, did continue to offer hope for women to attain a spiritual status higher than that accorded to the ordinary daughters of Eve. In the Middle Ages, a significant number of Chris-tian women experienced mystical visions. Denied both the vocation of the priesthood and the vocation of the university scholar, women discovered in mysticism an experience that could invest them with spiritual authority.

Spiritual authority, however, did not invariably accompany mysticism. Mystical experiences that led women into heresy or that positioned them as rivals to priestly authority could prompt the church to denounce and even persecute such women. For those female mystics whose visionary experiences allowed them to continue to recognize the authority of church officials, on the other hand, mysticism continued the pentecostal age announced in Acts 2:17-18, where the Holy Spirit empowered both women and men to prophesy. Biographers of female mystics often described miraculous phenomena associ-ated with their lives. Christina Mirabilis (1150-1224), for example, was said to have flown like a bird and to have repeatedly thrown herself into fires—without suffering bodily harm—in order to do penance on behalf of souls suf-fering in purgatory.[67] Such hagiographies, or lives of the saints, used super-natural phenomena to depict women's bodies as the sites of God's redemptive activities.

One female mystic named Hildegard of Bingen (1098-1179) made explicit the notion that women's bodies, previously identified by Christian tradition as the locus of the fall into sin, now functioned as a source of redemption. Gene-sis 1:26 had stated that God created humanity in the divine image and likeness. Hildegard identified the image of God with the body, while the likeness of God was the rational soul. That exegesis was reminiscent of Philo, except that Hildegard, in identifying man with rationality and woman with bodiliness, argued that woman's association with the body tied her more closely to the Incarnation than was man. Eve was the mother of all humanity, and Mary was the mother of God incarnate. For its very form, then, humanity was dependent upon woman; and for recreation through divine humanity in Christ, humanity was again dependent upon woman. Thus, Hildegard presented Eve, and not Adam, as the representative human being. Only woman could give to human beings their participation in the divine image.[68]

Another female writer who questioned hierarchical readings of Genesis 1–3 was Christine de Pizan. Well known today for her *Book of the Ladies*, in which she offered for public consideration the examples of numerous noteworthy women, Christine in 1399 wrote a poem entitled "Letter of the God of Love." Decrying her culture's predilection for depicting women as evil simply because some individual women fell short of perfection, Christine countered: "When God on high created angels, made / The cherubim, archangels, seraphim, / Now weren't there some bad ones in the lot? / Because of that must one call angels bad?" She complained that clerics indoctrinated schoolboys with the stories of Adam and other men supposedly deceived by women so that the boys would grow up believing that women were evil. Such tales, Christine contended, were based upon books "which tell more lies than any drunkard does."[69]

In answer to such slander, Christine noted that the gospels depicted women as the most faithful followers of Jesus, and that women should rejoice to share the same "form" as Mary, the mother of Jesus. Christine described woman's majestic form in these words: "God has never formed another thing / Of equal dignity, nor quite as good, / Excepting Jesus' own humanity." Moreover, Christine asserted, Christian tradition was wrong to claim that Eve deceived Adam; rather, Eve innocently accepted the serpent's words as true and then guilelessly shared that information with Adam. For those who would denigrate woman's goodness, Christine argued that an honest comparison of men and women would not be advantageous to men. Unlike men, Christine said, women did not wage war, cheat others of their inheritance, or create political intrigue. Neither did women murder or resort to arson for political and financial gain. "Thus I can say, and it's no heresy," she concluded, "That God on High did them a courtesy / When He created them without those traits / That lead one into great calamity."[70]

In depicting Mary as God's "mother and his spouse," enthroned in heaven adjacent to Jesus and at the right hand of God the Father,[71] Christine challenged traditional readings of Genesis 1–3 that subordinated woman to man and condemned women as temptresses who sought to rob men of their sexual purity. Yet the *Malleus Maleficarum*, the 1496 manual for inquisitors, proved that the tendency to blame women for inflicting sexual desires upon men had by no means disappeared. Even in their most hierarchical readings of Genesis 1-3, the church Fathers had depicted Eve as God's good creation—perhaps not equal to Adam, but good in her own right. The *Malleus* disputed that claim, insisting that "there was a defect in the formation of the first woman, since she was formed from a bent rib . . . which is bent as it were in a contrary direction to man. And since through this defect she is an imperfect animal, she always deceives."[72]

Maintaining that Eve seduced Adam and that woman was "a wheedling and secret enemy" more "bitter than death," the *Malleus* concluded that women's insatiable lust was the source of witchcraft.[73] In warning men to beware lest they fall victim to women's malignant designs, the *Malleus* set the stage for two centuries of brutal persecution of presumed witches. The *Malleus* indicated the depths of misogyny that Genesis 1-3 could be called upon to justify. Prior to the thirteenth century, the church had condemned belief in witches as pagan; the burning of presumed witches was punishable by death under the emperor Charlemagne. The systematic persecution of women suspected of witchcraft from 1450 to 1750, accompanied by the execution of anywhere from tens of thousands to hundreds of thousands of accused witches,[74] could not provide a clearer example of interpreters first reading cultural presuppositions into Genesis 1-3 and then using Genesis 1-3 to confirm their prior understanding of gender roles. In this instance, the interaction between text and culture was deadly.

Conclusion

By separating Islam, Judaism, and Christianity in this introduction and the selections that follow, we may have failed to demonstrate the connections among traditions that existed during this period. Commentators like the French exegete Rashi, for example, stood in debt to medieval Qur'anic scholars who developed philological and grammatical aids in their Qur'anic studies. Moreover, since a large number of Jews resided in Arabic-speaking, Muslim-governed territories, it is not surprising to find Muslim influence on other Jewish writers.

The Jewish philosopher Maimonides offers a good example of the interplay among all three traditions. Maimonides worked and wrote against the backdrop of Islamic rationalism. Not only were his works published in Arabic, and his Aristotle (as well as other classical writers) obtained through Arabic translations, but his thought and methodology were shaped in conversation with the Islamic context in which he lived and wrote.[75] When, after his death, Maimonides's work was translated into Latin and read by Christian theologians such as Thomas Aquinas, the boundaries between Muslim, Jewish, and Christian thought truly began to blur. Thus, while the selections in this chapter are divided according to traditions, it is good to remember that there was cultural and scholarly interplay among these traditions that is regrettably lost in this arrangement.

NOTES TO CHAPTER 5, INTRODUCTION

1. Islam marks historical eras uniquely, designating the first year of the Hijra (Hegira), when the community migrated from Mecca to Medina in 622 CE, as the first year of the Islamic Era. Thus Islam's formative period—its own "Classical Period"— overlaps with what is known as the "Middle Ages" of Europe. Islam's own "Medieval Period" commences at least a century later. Bruce Lawrence, for example, dates Islam's "Middle Period" as 750 CE to 1500 CE. See his entry "Islam," in Keith Crim, editor, *Abingdon Dictionary of Living Religions* (Nashville: Abingdon, 1981), p. 345.

2. For an introduction to Islam's basic tenets as well as its origin and development, see John Esposito's entry, "Islam: An Overview," in John L. Esposito, editor, *The Oxford Encyclopedia of the Modern Islamic World* (New York and Oxford: Oxford University Press, 1995), vol. 2, pp. 243-54.

3. For a helpful discussion of the Qur'an and its interpretation, see Jane Dammen McAuliffe's *Qur'anic Christians: An Analysis of Classical and Modern Exegesis* (Cambridge: Cambridge University Press, 1991), especially Part I, "Qur'anic Commentary and Commentators."

4. See the discussion of Jane I. Smith and Yvonne Yazbeck Haddad, "Eve: Islamic Image of Woman," in Azizah al-Hibri, editor, *Women and Islam*, vol. 5 of the Women's Studies International Forum (Oxford:Pergamon Press, 1982), p. 137.

5. Abu Ja'far Muhammad ibn Jarir al-Tabari, *The Commentary on the Qur'an*, vol. 1, with an introduction and notes by John Cooper; Wilfred F. Madelung and Alan Jones, editors (Oxford University Press and Hakim Investment Holdings (M.E.) Limited, 1987).

6. See Barbara Freyer Stowasser's discussion of al-Tabari in *Women in the Qur'an, Traditions, and Interpretation* (Oxford: Oxford University Press, 1994), pp. 28-30.

7. Al-Tabari, *Commentary on the Qur'an*, vol. 1, p. 245.

8. Al-Tabari, *Commentary on the Qur'an*, vol. 1, p. 245.

9. Al-Tabari, *Commentary on the Qur'an*, vol. 1, p. 252.

10. Al-Tabari, *Commentary on the Qur'an*, vol. 1, pp. 253, 254.

11. Al-Tabari, *Commentary on the Qur'an*, vol. 1, pp. 257-58; see also vol. 1, pp. 248, 255.

12. Muhammad ibn 'Abd Allah al-Kisa'i, *The Tales of the Prophets of al-Kisa'i*, translated and with notes by W. M. Thackston, Jr.; Library of Classical Arabic Literature, vol. 2, Ilse Lischenstadler, editor (Boston: G. K. Hall and Company, 1978).

13. See Thackston, the translator of these tales into English, in his introduction to *The Tales of the Prophets of al-Kisa'i*, p. xix. Compare with Serenity Young's eleventh-century date for the collection in *An Anthology of Sacred Texts By and About Women* (New York: Crossroad, 1993), p. 99.

14. Thackston, *The Tales of the Prophets*, pp. xvii-xviii.

15. Al-Kisa'i, *The Tales of the Prophets*, p. 39.

16. Al-Kisa'i, *The Tales of the Prophets*, p. 31.

17. Al-Kisa'i, *The Tales of the Prophets*, pp. 55, 65.

18. Al-Kisa'i, *The Tales of the Prophets*, pp. 31, 54.

19. Al-Kisa'i, *The Tales of the Prophets*, p. 40.

20. Al-Kisa'i, *The Tales of the Prophets*, pp. 44, 54.

21. In *The Tales of the Prophets*, see pp. 54f. for the section entitled "Eve's Query" and pp. 44f. for the section entitled "The Address of Eve."

22. Al-Kisa'i, *The Tales of the Prophets*, p. 44.

23. Muhammad b. 'Ali b. Muhammad Ibn al-Arabi al-Ta'i al-Hatimi, *Ibn al' Arabi: The Bezels of Wisdom*, translated and with an introduction by Ralph W. J. Austin; preface by Titus Burckhardt, The Classics of Western Spirituality series, Richard J. Payne, editor (New York: Paulist Press, 1980).

24. Leila Ahmed, *Women and Gender in Islam: Historical Roots of a Modern Debate* (New Haven: Yale University Press, 1992), pp. 99-100.

25. For one discussion of these interpretations, see R. W. J. Austin's "The Feminine Dimensions in Ibn 'Arabi's Thought," *Muhhydin Ibn'Arabi Society Journal* 2 (1984): 5-14.

26. Concerning women's place in Sufi theosophy, Jamal J. Elias states, "On a scale of perfection she exists above the male and below the male; however she is never equal to him." See his "Female and Feminine in Islamic Mysticism," *Muslim World* 77 (1988): 224.

27. *Syzygy*, which means "yoked together," often carries the sense of holding together contrasting—or at least dissimilar—entities. Ibn al-Arabi's use of the term is found on p. 274 of *Bezels of Wisdom*.

28. Ahmed, *Women and Gender in Islam*, p. 99.

29. See Annemarie Schimmel's "Women in Mystical Islam," in al-Hibri, editor, *Women and Islam*, pp. 145-51.

30. Ahmed, *Women and Gender in Islam*, pp. 100-101.

31. Ahmed, *Women and Gender in Islam*, p. 47.

32. Isaiah 34:1-17 is a postexilic oracle of judgment against Edom. Verse 14 describes Edom after Yahweh's day of vengeance. Where the RSV translated "night hag" in the second half of v. 14, the NRSV translates "Lilith." Within the verse's context, some type of wasteland denizen is indicated.

> 34:14   Wildcats shall meet with hyenas,
> goat-demons shall call to each other;
> there too Lilith shall repose,
> and find a place to rest. (NRSV)

33. Jo Milgrom, for example, suggests that "lilith" is the female counterpart of "Lillu," a vampire-like Sumerian demon who is depicted with wings and talons. According to Milgrom, four such demons made up a Sumerian fraternity of incubi-succubae. Jo Milgrom, "Some Second Thoughts about Adam's First Wife," in Gregory Allen Robbins, editor, *Genesis 1-3 in the History of Exegesis: Intrigue in the Garden* (Lewiston and Queenston: Edwin Mellen Press, 1988), pp. 226-29.

Other scholars, such as Lowell K. Handy, agree that Lilith is derived from Mesopotamian demons but argue against finding evidence of the Hebrew Lilith in many of the epigraphical and artifactual sources frequently cited as such (e.g., the Sumerian Gilgamesh fragment, the Sumerian incantation from Arshlan-Tash). Lowell K. Handy, "Lilith," in David Noel Freedman, editor, *The Anchor Bible Dictionary* (New York: Doubleday, 1992) vol. 4, pp. 324-25.

34. *Niddah* 24b discusses the issue of the abnormal fetus and the category of uncleanness:

> Rab Judah citing Samuel ruled: If an abortion had the likeness of Lilith its mother is unclean by reason of the birth, for it is a child, but it has wings. So it was also taught: R. Jose stated, It once happened at Simoni that a woman aborted the likeness of Lilith, and when the case came up for a decision before the Sages they ruled it was a child but that it also had wings.

35. *Shabbat* 151b warns of the perils that await the man who sleeps alone: "R. Hanina said: One may not sleep in a house alone, and whoever sleeps in a house alone is seized by Lilith."

36. *Baba Batra* 73a-b contains a reference to Lilith's son, Hormin:

> Rabbah said: I saw how Hormin the son of Lilith was running on the parapet of the wall of Mahuza, and a rider, galloping below on horseback could not overtake him. Once they saddled for him two mules which stood

on two bridges of the Rognag; and he jumped from one to the other, backward and forward, holding in his hands two cups of wine, pouring alternately from one to the other, and not a drop fell to the ground. [Furthermore], it was [a stormy] day [such as that on which] they [that go down to the sea in ships] mounted up to the heaven; they went down to the deeps. When the government heard [of this] they put him to death.

37. *'Erubin* 100b discusses Eve's ten curses, and comments on the eighth curse, which refers to her being "banished from the company of all men": "In a Baraitha it was taught: She grows long hair like Lilith, sits when making water like a beast, and serves as a bolster for her husband."

38. According to the *Alphabet of Ben Sira*: "Adam said, 'You shall lie below' and Lilith said, 'You shall lie below, for we are equal and both of us were [created] from the earth.' " Eli Yassif, "Pseudo Ben Sira, the Text, Its Literary Character and Status in the History of the Hebrew Story in the Middle Ages," 2 vols. (in Hebrew), Ph.D. diss., Hebrew University, 1977, pp. 64-65, in Joseph Dan, "Samuel, Lilith, and the Concept of Evil in Early Kabbalah," *Association for Jewish Studies Review* 5 (1980): 21.

39. Paul Morris, "Exiled from Eden: Jewish Interpretations of Genesis," in Paul Morris and Deborah Sawyer, editors, *A Walk in the Garden: Biblical, Iconographical and Literary Images of Eden, Journal for the Study of the Old Testament*, Supplement Series, 136 (Sheffield: JSOT Press, 1992), p. 137.

40. Although Rashi claims to prefer the text's plain sense (*peshat*) over its homiletical dimension (*derash*), he nevertheless makes ample use of rabbinical traditions. Indeed, Rashi's allusions to midrashim and his occasional preference for *derash* over *peshat* is a fascinating study in itself, albeit beyond the scope of our interests in this volume.

41. Edward L. Greenstein, "Medieval Bible Commentaries" in Barry W. Holtz, editor, *Back to the Sources: Reading the Classic Jewish Texts* (New York: Summit Books, 1984), p. 228.

42. Besides being the first major scripture commentary to contain hints of Jewish mysticism, Nahmanides's commentary also employed allegorical methods to unlock the text's various levels of meaning (Greenstein, "Medieval Bible Commentaries," p. 254).

43. For an extensive analysis in Hebrew of Maimonides's treatment of Adam and Eve, see Sarah Klein-Braslavy, *Maimonides' Interpretation of the Adam Stories in Genesis: A Study in Maimonides' Anthropology* (Jerusalem: Magnes Press, 1986). A much shorter treatment in English is Klein-Braslavy's "The Creation of the World and Maimonides' Interpretation of Gen. I-IV," in Shlomon Pines and Yiriyahu Yovel, editors, *Maimonides and Philosophy: Papers Presented at the Sixth Jerusalem Philosophical Encounter, May 1985* (Dordrecht: Martinus Nijhoff Publishers, 1986), pp. 65-78.

44. Daniel Boyarin, *Carnal Israel: Reading Sex in Talmudic Culture* (Berkeley: University of California Press, 1993), p. 57.

45. Although the names given to the *sefirot* vary, the following are seen frequently:

1. *Keter Elyon*, the Supreme Crown. (The Zohar refers to this sefirah as *Ratzon*, "Divine Will");
2. *Hokmah* (Wisdom), the primordial, undifferentiated divine thought;
3. *Binah* (Understanding); in contrast to *Hokmah*, *Binah* is the principle of intellect that makes distinctions;
4. *Gedullah* (Greatness), sometimes called *Hesed* (God's Overflowing Love);
5. *Gevurah* (Power), often called *Din* (Rigorous Judgment);
6. *Tiferet* (Beauty), often called *Rahamim* (Compassion);

7. *Netzah* (Endurance);
8. *Hod* (Majesty);
9. *Yesod* (Foundation), called *Zaddik* (Righteous One); [and]
10. *Malkhut* (kingdom), often called by the traditional term *Shekhinah* (Divine Presence) and considered the divine archetype of *Knesset Yisrael* (the Community of Israel).

(Robert M. Seltzer, *Jewish People, Jewish Thought: The Jewish Experience in History* [New York: Macmillan Publishing Co., 1980], p. 430.)

46. Some Rabbis imaged the androgynous *'adam* as having two faces, one looking forward and one looking backward. Since the face looking forward was male and the one looking backward was female, scholars suggest that such an arrangement implicitly subordinated the female. See our discussion of this matter in the introduction to chapter 3 of this volume.

47. Elliot R. Wolfson, "On Becoming Female: Crossing Gender Boundaries in Kabbalistic Ritual and Myth," in T. M. Rudavsky, editor, *Gender and Judaism: The Transformation of Tradition* (New York: New York University Press, 1995), p. 210.

48. According to Yassif, over 150 copies of *The Alphabet* from the eleventh to the seventeenth centuries are extant. Eli Yassif, "The Body Never Lies: The Body in Medieval Jewish Folk Narratives," in Howard Eilberg-Schwartz, editor, *People of the Body: Jews and Judaism from an Embodied Perspective* (Albany: State University of New York Press, 1992), p. 205.

49. Seltzer, *Jewish People, Jewish Thought*, p. 393.

50. Seltzer, *Jewish People, Jewish Thought*, pp. 407-418.

51. Seltzer, *Jewish People, Jewish Thought*, pp. 419-450.

52. Traditionally, Jewish men were obliged to keep 613 *mitzvot* (commandments) while women were responsible for only 3: (1) *Hallah*: the setting aside of the dough, (2) *Niddah*, menstrual purity legislation (including such ordinances as those prohibiting intercourse during menstruation or those requiring women to take ritual baths after their menstrual cycles), and (3) *Haddlaqah*, the lighting of the Sabbath candles.

53. Solnik (1602) as cited in Chava Weissler, "*Mizvot* Built into the Body: *Tkhines* for *Niddah*, Pregnancy, and Childbirth," in Eilberg-Schwartz, *People of the Body*, p. 104.

54. Weissler, "*Mizvot*," p. 110.

55. Weissler, "*Mizvot*," p. 106.

56. This can readily be seen in a comparison of their treatments of women's commandments. Solnik, for example, declares that:

> women must kindle the lights, for they have extinguished our light. And for that reason they must also suffer the pain of menstruation, because they shed our blood. Therefore they have the suffering of menstruation and must immerse themselves. For the immersion is like the repentance of a penitent sinner who was a murderer. And so it is with *hallah*, too. For she has spoiled things for us, we who are called "Israel was holy to the Lord, the first fruits of his harvest" [Jer. 2:3]; this means in Yiddish, Hallow, Israel, to God the firstling of his fruit. Therefore she must "take *hallah*." For she is commanded, "As the first yield of your baking, you shall set aside a loaf [*hallah*] as a gift [Num. 15:20]; this means in Yiddish, the first part of your dough shall you separate as *hallah*. Therefore the woman must keep the three commandments." (Solnik 1602:4a, as cited in Weissler, "*Mizvot*," p. 105)

A *tkhine* covering the lighting of the Sabbath candles, however, states:

> We must kindle lights for the holy day, to brighten it and to rejoice on it; therewith may we be worthy of the light and joy of eternal life. . . . Lord of the world, I have done all my work in the six days, and will now rest, as you have commanded, and will kindle two lights, according to the require-

ment of our holy Torah, as interpreted by our sages, to honor you and the holy Sabbath. . . . And may the lights be, in your eyes, like the lights that the priest kindled in the Temple. And let our lights not be extinguished, and let your light shine upon us. Deliver our souls into the light of paradise together with other righteous men and women. . . . (*Seder tkhines* 1650:5b; as cited in Weissler, "*Mizvot*," p. 107).

57. Strack and Stemberger describe *The Alphabet of Ben Sira* as "a pungent satire on the Bible and rabbinic religiosity composed of biblical and haggadic elements." According to them, it was "widely circulated but also frequently censored." H. L. Strack and G. Stemberger, *Introduction to the Talmud and Midrash* (Minneapolis: Fortress Press, 1992), pp. 372-73.

58. M. Gaster, "Introduction," in *The Chronicles of Jerahmeel* (London: Royal Asiatic Society, 1899), p. xxi.

59. Lawrence Fine, "Kabbalistic Texts" in Barry W. Holtz, *Back to the Sources: Reading the Classic Jewish Texts*, p. 309.

60. Joseph Dan, "Samael, Lilith, and the Concept of Evil," p. 37.

61. In talmudic literature, Rabbi Simeon bar Yohai is a Palestinian rabbi who lived in Galilee after the Bar Kokhba revolt. He is not associated, however, with any mystical traditions.

62. Fine, "Kabbalistic Texts," p. 311.

63. Fine, "Kabbalistic Texts," p. 310.

64. Barbara Newman, *Sister of Wisdom: St. Hildegard's Theology of the Feminine* (Berkeley: University of California Press, 1987), p. 89.

65. Thomas Aquinas, *Summa Theologiae*, vol. 13, Question Ia, 92, 99, Blackfriars edition (New York: McGraw-Hill Book Company and London: Eyre & Spottiswoode, 1964), pp. 35-39, 165.

66. Thomas Aquinas, *Summa Theologiae*, vol. 13, Question Ia, 92, pp. 35-39, 151-59.

67. Thomas de Cantimpre, "The Life of Christina of St. Trond, Called Christina Mirabilis," in Elizabeth Alvida Petroff, editor, *Medieval Women's Visionary Literature* (London: Oxford University Press, 1986), pp. 184-89.

68. Barbara Newman, *Sister of Wisdom*, pp. 90-95. Hildegard is currently a rather popular figure. Numerous editions of selected portions of her work are in print, and at least one compact disk of her musical compositions may be purchased. Unfortunately, the passages in which Hildegard discusses Genesis 1-3 are not available in translation and are thus not included in this anthology. Nevertheless, Newman's *Sister of Wisdom* provides an excellent discussion, as well as translations of a number of passages, of Hildegard's treatment of Genesis.

69. Christine de Pizan, "Letter of the God of Love," in Thelma S. Fenster and Mary Carpenter Erler, editors, *Poems of Cupid, God of Love* (Leiden: E. J. Brill, 1990), pp. 43, 45, 47.

70. Christine de Pizan, "Letter of the God of Love," pp. 47, 61, 63, 65, 67, 69.

71. Christine de Pizan, "Letter of the God of Love," p. 63.

72. Heinrich Kramer and James Sprenger, in Reverend Montague Summers, translator, *The Malleus Maleficarum* (New York: Dover, 1971), p. 44.

73. Kramer and Sprenger, *Malleus Maleficarum*, p. 47.

74. Elizabeth Clark and Herbert Richardson, *Women and Religion: A Feminist Sourcebook of Christian Thought* (New York: Harper & Row, 1977), pp. 116-17; revised and expanded as *Women and Religion: The Original Sourcebook of Women in Christian Thought* (HarperSanFrancisco, 1996), p. 119. Unless otherwise indicated, references to Clark and Richardson cite the first edition.

75. Alfred L. Ivry, "Islamic and Greek Influences on Maimonides' Philosophy,"

in S. Pines and Y. Yovel, editors, *Maimonides and Philosophy* (Boston: Martinus Nijhoff Publishers, 1986), pp. 139-56.

ISLAM

The Qur'an

The Qur'an is the scripture of Islam. According to Muslim understanding, Islam came into being as a religious institution when God called Muhammad to prophethood by revealing the Qur'an to him. Muslims understand these revelations to stand in continuity with the revelations God made through earlier prophets. Islam sees Muhammad as the final prophet—the so-called "Seal of the Prophets"—because the revelations he received from 610 to 632 CE both correct and complete the revelations that the other "people of the book" received through the succession of prophets that had begun with Adam.

There is no book named "Genesis" in the Qur'an. Yet across the span of its chapters, or "surahs," the Qur'an offers many depictions of the "genesis" or beginnings of the human race. At several other junctures, the Qur'an mentions gender matters without specifically talking about creation. These more general discussions of gender have a bearing on Muslim interpretations of humanity's creation because they often are connected to God's initial design for women, for men, and for relationships between them.

Our selection from the Qur'an involves portions of nine surahs. The arrangement of these "ayat," or verses, will follow their order in the Qur'an. Yet, for the purpose of offering a brief description of the texts, they can be characterized as falling into three broad categories. First, several of the passages we selected refer generally to humanity's creation. Some of these speak of humanity's creation from a single soul (Q.4:1; 7:189). Others refer to such original material as earth or dust (Q.23:12f.; 30:20). Still others highlight initial diversities within humanity: some refer to differences in color and language (Q.30: 20, 22); others refer to differences in nation and tribe (Q.49:13).

A second type of Qur'anic passage refers to humanity's creation by telling stories about the beginning that involve some configuration of the particular characters of Adam, his mate, and the antagonist of Iblis or Satan (Q.2:29-38; 7:19-27; 7:190; 15:26-45; 20:115-23). These accounts display the Qur'an's distinctive renderings of the first woman. There is no mention of God creating woman out of a rib; indeed there is no story singling out how God created woman. Moreover, the woman is never presented as particularly culpable for humanity's downfall.

A third kind of Qur'anic text that is important for Muslim interpretations of the first human beings talks about gender matters in general terms without speaking directly about creation. These texts often have been correlated with the creation accounts so that their descriptions have had significant bearing on Muslim understandings of God's intentions for women and men. Some of the passages we selected concern specific aspects of women's lives such as menstruation or attire (Q.2:222; 24:30-31). Others describe features of gender relations such as marriage and divorce (Q.2:228; 4:128-30; 24:32-33). Furthermore, passages about polytheism and about slavery also are relevant to our examination of gender and hierarchy (Q.4:116; 7:190; 24:33). (Source: *The Meaning of the Glorious Koran: An Explanatory Translation*, Mohammed Marmaduke Pickthall, translator, New York and Scarborough, Ontario: Mentor Books, New American Library, n.d., pp. 36, 53, 79, 83, 90-91, 123, 136, 192, 233-34, 248, 253, 255-56, 291, 369.)

Selections from the Qur'an (c. 610–632 CE)

Surah 2, The Cow: 2:29–38, 222–23, 228

2:29. He it is Who created for you all that is in the earth. Then turned He to the heaven, and fashioned it as seven heavens. And He is Knower of all things.

2:30. And when thy Lord said unto the angels: Lo! I am about to place a viceroy in the earth, they said: Wilt Thou place therein one who will do harm therein and will shed blood, while we, we hymn Thy praise and sanctify Thee? He said: Surely I know that which ye know not.

2:31. And He taught Adam all the names,[1] then showed them to the angels, saying: Inform me of the names of these, if ye are truthful.

2:32. They said: Be glorified! We have no knowledge saving that which Thou hast taught us. Lo! Thou, only Thou, art the Knower, the Wise.

2:33. He said, O Adam! Inform them of their names, and when he had informed them of their names, He said: Did I not tell you that I know the secret of the heavens and the earth? And I know that which ye disclose and which ye hide.

2:34. And when We said to the angels: Prostrate yourselves before Adam, they fell prostrate, all save Iblis. He demurred through pride, and so became a disbeliever.

2:35. And We said: O Adam! Dwell thou and thy wife in the Garden, and eat ye[2] freely (of the fruits) thereof where ye will; but come not nigh this tree lest ye become wrongdoers.

2:36. But Satan caused them to deflect therefrom and expelled them from the (happy) state in which they were; and We said: Fall down,[3] one of you a foe unto the other! There shall be for you on earth a habitation and provision for a time.

2:37. Then Adam received from his Lord words (of revelation), and He relented toward him. Lo! He is the Relenting, the Merciful.

2:38. We said: Go down, all of you, from hence; but verily there cometh unto you from Me a guidance; and whoso followeth My guidance, there shall no fear come upon them neither shall they grieve.

2:222. They question thee (O Muhammad) concerning menstruation.

Say: It is an illness, so let women alone at such times and go not in unto them till they are cleansed. And when they have purified themselves, then go in unto them as Allah hath enjoined upon you. Truly Allah loveth those who turn unto Him, and loveth those who have a care for cleanness.

2:223. Your women are a tilth for you (to cultivate) so go to your tilth as ye will, and send (good deeds) before you for your souls, and fear Allah, and know that ye will (one day) meet Him. Give glad tidings to believers (O Muhammed).

2:228. Women who are divorced shall wait, keeping themselves apart, three (monthly) courses. And it is not lawful for them that they should conceal that which Allah hath created in their wombs if they are believers in Allah and the Last Day. And their husbands would do better to take them back in that case if they desire a reconciliation. And they (women) have rights similar to those (of men) over them in kindness, and men are a degree above them. Allah is Mighty, Wise.

Surah 4, Women: 4:1, 3, 34–36, 116–20, 128–30

In the name of Allah the beneficent, the Merciful.

4:1. O mankind! Be careful of your duty to your Lord Who created you from a single soul and from it created its mate and from them twain hath spread abroad a multitude of men and women. Be careful of your duty toward Allah in Whom ye claim (your rights) of one another, and toward the wombs (that bare you). Lo! Allah hath been a Watcher over you.

4:3. And if ye fear that ye will not deal fairly by the orphans, marry of the women, who seem good to you, two or three or four; and if ye fear that ye cannot do justice (to so many) then one (only) or (the captives) that your right hands possess. Thus it is more likely that ye will not do injustice.

4:34. Men are in charge of women, because Allah hath made the one of them to excel the other, and because they spend of their property (for the support of women). So good women are the obedient, guarding in secret that which Allah hath guarded. As for those from whom ye fear rebellion, admonish them and banish them to beds apart, and scourge them. Then if they obey you, seek not a way against them. Lo! Allah is ever High Exalted, Great.

4:35. And if ye fear a breach between them twain (the man and wife) appoint an arbiter from his folk and an arbiter from her folk. If they desire   ·
amendment Allah will make them of one mind. Lo! Allah is ever Knower, Aware.

4:36. And serve Allah. Ascribe no thing as partner unto Him. (Show) kindness unto parents, and unto near kindred, and orphans, and the needy, and unto the neighbour who is of kin (unto you) and the neighbour who is not of kin, and the fellow-traveler and the wayfarer and (the slaves) whom your right hands possess. Lo! Allah loveth not such as are proud and boastful.

4:116. Lo! Allah pardoneth not that partners should be ascribed unto him.

He pardoneth all save that to whom He will. Whoso ascribeth partners unto Allah hath wandered far astray.

4:117. They invoke in His stead only females;[4] they pray to none else than Satan, a rebel

4:118. Whom Allah cursed, and he said: Surely I will take of Thy bondmen an appointed portion,

4:119. And surely I will lead them astray, and surely I will arouse desires in them, and surely I will command them and they will cut the cattle's ears, and surely I will command them and they will change Allah's creation. Whoso chooseth Satan for a patron instead of Allah is verily a loser and his loss is manifest.

4:120. He promiseth them and stirreth up desires in them, and Satan promiseth them only to beguile.

4:128. If a woman feareth ill-treatment from her husband, or desertion, it is no sin for them twain if they make terms of peace between themselves. Peace is better. But greed hath been made present in the minds (of men). If ye do good and keep from evil, lo! Allah is ever Informed of what ye do.

4:129. Ye will not be able to deal equally between (your) wives, however much ye wish (to do so). But turn not altogether away (from one), leaving her as in suspense. If ye do good and keep from evil, lo! Allah is ever Forgiving, Merciful.

4:130. But if they separate, Allah will compensate each out of His abundance. Allah is ever All-Embracing, All-Knowing.

Surah 7, The Heights: 7:19–27, 189–90

7:19. And (unto man): O Adam! Dwell thou and thy wife in the Garden and eat from whence ye will, but come not nigh this tree lest ye become wrongdoers.

7:20. Then Satan whispered to them that he might manifest unto them that which was hidden from them of their shame, and he said: Your Lord forbade you from this tree only lest ye should become angels or become of the immortals.

7:21. And he swore unto them (saying): Lo! I am a sincere adviser unto you.

7:22. Thus did he lead them on with guile. And when they tasted of the tree their shame was manifest to them and they began to hide (by heaping) on themselves some of the leaves of the Garden. And their Lord called them, (saying): Did I not forbid you from that tree and tell you: Lo! Satan is an open enemy to you?

7:23. They said: Our Lord! We have wronged ourselves. If Thou forgive us not and have not mercy on us, surely we are of the lost!

7:24. He said: Go down (from hence), one of you a foe unto the other. There will be for you on earth a habitation and provision for a while.

7:25. He said: There shall ye live, and there shall ye die, and thence shall ye be brought forth.

7:26. O Children of Adam! We have revealed unto you raiment to conceal your shame, and splendid vesture, but the raiment of restraint from evil, that is best. This is of the revelations of Allah, that they may remember.

7:27. O Children of Adam! Let not Satan seduce you as he caused your (first) parents to go forth from the Garden and tore off from them their robe (of innocence) that he might manifest their shame to them. Lo! he seeth you, he and his tribe, from whence ye see him not. Lo! We have made the devils protecting friends for those who believe not.

7:189. He it is who did create you from a single soul, and therefrom did make his mate that he might take rest in her. And when he covered her she bore a light burden, and she passed (unnoticed) with it, but when it became heavy they cried unto Allah, their Lord, saying: If thou givest unto us aright we shall be of the thankful.

7:190. But when He gave unto them aright, they ascribed unto Him partners in respect of that which He had given them. High is He exalted above all that they associate (with Him).

Surah 15, Al-Hijr: 15:26–45

15:26. Verily We created man of potter's clay of black mud altered,

15:27. And the Jinn did We create aforetime of essential fire.

15:28. And (remember) when thy Lord said unto the angels: Lo! I am creating a mortal out of potter's clay of black mud altered,

15:29. So, when I have made him and have breathed into him of My spirit, do ye fall down, prostrating yourselves unto him.

15:30. So the angels fell prostrate, all of them together

15:31. Save Iblis. He refused to be among the prostrate.

15:32. He said: O Iblis! What aileth thee that thou art not among the prostrate?

15:33. He said: Why should I prostrate myself unto a mortal whom Thou hast created out of potter's clay of black mud altered?

15:34. He said: Then go thou forth from hence, for verily thou art outcast.

15:35. And lo! the curse shall be upon thee till the Day of Judgement.

15:36. He said: My Lord! Reprieve me till the day when they are raised.

15:37. He said: Then lo! thou art of those reprieved

15:38. Till an appointed time,

15:39. He said: My Lord! Because Thou has sent me astray, I verily shall adorn the path of error for them in the earth, and shall mislead them every one,

15:40. Save such of them as are Thy perfectly devoted slaves.

15:41. He said: This is a right course incumbent upon Me:

15:42. Lo! as for My slaves, thou hast no power over any of them save such of the froward as follow thee.

15:43. And lo! for all such, hell will be the promised place.

15:44. It hath seven gates, and each gate hath an appointed portion.

15:45. Lo! those who ward off (evil) are among gardens and watersprings.

Surah 20, Ta Ha: 20:115–23

20:115. And verily We made a covenant of old with Adam, but he forgot, and We found no constancy in him.

20:116. And when We said unto the angels: Fall prostrate before Adam, they fell prostrate (all) save Iblis; he refused.

20:117. Therefor[e] We said: O Adam! This is an enemy unto thee and unto thy wife, so let him not drive you both out of the Garden so that thou come to toil.

20:118. It is (vouchsafed) unto thee that thou hungerest not therein nor art naked.

20:119. And thou thirstest not therein nor art exposed to the sun's heat.

20:120. But the Devil whispered to him, saying: O Adam! Shall I show thee the tree of immortality and power that wasteth not away?

20:121. Then they twain ate thereof, so that their shame became apparent unto them, and they began to hide by heaping on themselves some of the leaves of the Garden. And Adam disobeyed his Lord, so went astray.

20:122. Then his Lord chose him, and relented toward him, and guided him.

20:123. He said: Go down hence, both of you, one of you a foe unto the other. But if there come unto you from Me a guidance, then whoso followeth My guidance, he will not go astray nor come to grief.

Surah 23, The Believers: 23:12–14

23:12. Verily We created man from a product of wet earth;

23:13. Then placed him as a drop (of seed) in a safe lodging;

23:14. Then fashioned We the drop a clot, then fashioned We the clot a little lump, then fashioned We the little lump bones, then clothed the bones with flesh, and then produced it as another creation. So blessed be Allah, the Best of Creators!

Surah 24, Light: 24:30–33

24:30. Tell the believing men to lower their gaze and be modest. That is purer for them. Lo! Allah is Aware of what they do.

24:31. And tell the believing women to lower their gaze and be modest, and to display of their adornment only that which is apparent, and to draw their veils over their bosoms, and not to reveal their adornment save to their own husbands or fathers or husbands' fathers, or their sons or their husbands' sons, or their brothers or their brothers' sons or sisters' sons, or their women, or their slaves, or male attendants who lack vigour, or children who know naught of women's nakedness. And let them not stamp their feet so as to reveal what they hide of their adornment. And turn unto Allah together, O believers, in order that ye may succeed.

24:32. And marry such of you as are solitary and the pious of your slaves and maid-servants. If they be poor, Allah will enrich them of His bounty. Allah is of ample means, Aware.

24:33. And let those who cannot find a match keep chaste till Allah give them independence by His grace. And such of your slaves as seek a writing (of emancipation), write it for them if ye are aware of aught of good in them, and bestow upon them of the wealth of Allah which He hath bestowed upon you. Force not your slave-girls to whoredom that ye may seek enjoyment of the life of the world, if they would preserve their chastity. And if one force them, then (unto them), after their compulsion, Lo! Allah will be Forgiving, Merciful.

Surah 30, The Romans: 30:20–22

30:20. And of His signs is this: He created you of dust, and behold you human beings, ranging widely!

30:21. And of His signs is this: He created for you helpmeets from yourselves that ye might find rest in them, and He ordained between you love and mercy. Lo, herein indeed are portents for folk who reflect.

30:22. And of His signs is the creation of the heavens and the earth, and the difference of your languages and colours. Lo! herein indeed are portents for men of knowledge.

Surah 49, The Private Apartments: 49:13

49:13. O mankind! Lo! We have created you male and female, and have made you nations and tribes that ye may know one another. Lo! the noblest of you, in the sight of Allah, is the best in conduct. Lo! Allah is Knower, Aware.

NOTES TO CHAPTER 5, ISLAM, THE QUR'AN

1. Translator's note: "Some, especially Sufis, hold 'the names' to be the attributes of Allah; others, the names of animals and plants."

2. Translator's note: "Here the command is in the dual, as addressed to Adam and his wife."

3. Translator's note: "Here the command is in the plural, as addressed to Adam's race."

4. Translator's note: "The idols which the pagan Arabs worshipped were all female."

Al-Tabari

Abu Ja'far Muhammad ibn Jarir al-Tabari (c. 839–923) was an authoritative historian and Qur'an commentator.[1] The name "al-Tabari" derives from the region where he was born—an area then known as Tabaristan, which was located in what is now northern Iran.[2] Although al-Tabari traveled extensively, his work as a student and as a teacher was centered in his adopted city of Baghdad. He belonged to the Sunni branch of Islam, which often is described as "orthodox" Islam. His "tafsir" or commentary on the Qur'an holds a distinguished place because he wrote this massive text after traveling to important centers of Islamic learning and gathering exegetical traditions.[3] He often preserved multiple traditions concerning the interpretation of a passage or phrase. He indicated the reliability of the traditions he collected by recording their "isnad" or chain of transmission. He also included his own assessments of interpretations. Although al-Tabari's commentary is the standard source for all subsequent Sunni commentary, it contains much material that can also be found in later Shi'i and Sufi commentaries.

Our selection involves interpretations of Q.2:35 and Q.2:36 that discuss important matters concerning the first woman: how and why she was created, why she was named "Hawwa," how Iblis caused the downfall of the first couple, and the effects of this downfall, including the punishments that God meted out. Through these discussions we see that numerous non-Qur'anic motifs concerning the first woman were circulating in Islamic centers of learning. Moreover, we see that some of these motifs had prevailed over the Qur'an's distinctive portrait of her. For example, al-Tabari records several opinions of "the learned" concerning the way Iblis caused the first human beings to "slip." Most of these opinions underscore that Hawwa/Eve was the means by which Iblis was able to get Adam to fall, even though they may differ in exact details such as whether she lured him with beauty or wine. This repeated faulting of the first woman presents a stark contrast to the Qur'an, which never ascribes primary culpability to her. The exegetical reserve that al-Tabari displays when, near the selection's conclusion, he offers his own assessment of how the downfall occurred conforms more closely to the Qur'an than most of the opinions he collected.

Here is a key to the symbols found in this selection:

⇒   Tabari's chain of transmission omitted; only the source authority given.

« »   Qur'anic quotations.

(. . .)   in text, passage(s) omitted and not summarized; hadith(s) may or may not be included in the omission.

⌈ ⌉   translator's addition.

★   join between two verses.

(Source: Abu Ja'far Muhammad ibn Jarir al-Tabari, *The Commentary on the Qur'an*, John Cooper, translator, Wilfred Madelung and Alan Jones, editors, Oxford: Oxford University Press, 1987, vol. 1, pp. 244-46, 251-55, 257-58.)

Commentary on the Qur'an (c. late 800s CE)
ABU JA'FAR MUHAMMAD IBN JARIR AL-TABARI

Surah 2:35

And We said: "Adam, dwell, you and your wife, in the Garden, and eat thereof easefully where you desire; but do not draw near this tree, lest you become evil-doers."

In this verse there is a clear indication of the correctness of the opinion of those who say that Iblis was exiled from the Garden after he had arrogantly refused to prostrate before Adam, and that Adam was put to dwell there before Iblis fell to earth. Do you not hear God saying: «And We said: "Adam, dwell, you and your wife, in the Garden, and eat thereof easefully where you desire; but do not draw near this tree, lest you become evil-doers."★ Then Satan caused them to slip therefrom, and brought them out of that wherein they were.» It is clear that Iblis caused them to slip from obedience to God after he had been cursed and had demonstrated ⌈his⌉ arrogance, because the angels' prostration before Adam came after the spirit had been breathed into him, and then Iblis refused to prostrate before him, and for the refusal to do this the curse came down upon him. . . .

The Circumstances in which Adam's Wife Was Created for Him, and the Time at which She Was Made a Means of Repose (Sakan) for Him:

First Opinion
⇒Ibn 'Abbas, ⇒ Ibn Mas'ud, and ⇒ A group of Companions:

> Then Iblis was exiled from the Garden when he was cursed, and Adam was put to dwell in the Garden. He went around alone with no wife in whom he could find repose. Then he fell asleep and woke up to find a woman sitting beside his head whom God had created from his rib. So he asked her: "Who are you?" And she said: "A woman." He said: "Why were you created?" She said: "So that you could find repose in me." Then the angels asked him, to see how much he knew: "What is her name, Adam?" He said: "Hawa' (Eve)." They said: "Why is she called Hawa?" He said: "Because she was created from something living (*haiy*)." Then God said to him «"Adam, dwell, you and your wife, in the Garden, and eat thereof easefully where you desire."»

This Tradition states that Eve was created after Adam had been dwelling in the Garden, and that she was created to be a means of repose for him.

Second Opinion

Others said that she was created before Adam dwelt in the Garden.

⇒Ibn Ishaq:

> When God had finished reprimanding Iblis, He turned to Adam and taught
> him all the names. Then He said «"Adam, tell them their names"»—up to
> (*sic*)—«"Surely You are the All-knowing, the All-wise."(...) Then He cast
> slumber upon Adam—according to what has reached us from the people of
> the Torah among the people of scripture, and from other people of knowl-
> edge, through 'Abd Allah b. Abbas and others—and then He took one of his
> ribs from his left side, and joined together the place where it had been with
> flesh. ⌈Meanwhile⌉ Adam slept, and he did not stir from his sleep until God
> had created his wife, Eve, from this rib of his. And He arranged her as a
> woman in whom ⌈Adam⌉ could find repose. When his slumber was lifted
> from him, and he stirred from his sleep, he saw her beside him, and he said—
> according to what they claim, and God knows best—: "My flesh, my blood,
> and my wife." And he found repose in her. When God had duplicated him,
> and made a means of repose for him from himself, He spoke to him face to
> face: «"Adam, dwell, you and your wife, in the Garden and eat thereof ease-
> fully where you desire; but do not draw near this tree, lest you become evil-
> doers."» . . .

Surah 2:36

Then Satan caused them to slip therefrom, and brought them out of that they
were in; and We said: "Get you down, each of you an enemy of each; and in
the earth a sojourn shall be yours, and enjoyment for a time."

QUESTION: How did Iblis cause Adam and his wife to slip, so that their
expulsion from the Garden became attributed to him?

REPLY: The learned have voiced several opinions about this, and we shall
mention some of them.

⇒'Umar b. 'Abd al-Rahman b. Muhrib:

> I heard Wahb b. Munabbih say: When God settled Adam and his off-
> spring—or "his wife," the doubt is from Abu Ja'far ⌈al-Tabari⌉ in the original
> copy of whose book is "his offspring"—and forbade him the tree, it was a tree
> whose branches were entangled, and which has fruit which the angels eat for
> their eternity; this was the fruit which God had forbidden Adam and his
> wife. When Iblis desired to make them slip, he entered into the belly of the
> serpent. Now the serpent had four legs, as if it had been a Bactrian camel, one
> of the most beautiful beasts God created. When the serpent entered the
> Garden, Iblis came out of its belly, took from the tree which God had forbid-
> den Adam and his wife, and brought it to Eve. He said: "Look at this tree!
> How fragrant it is, how delicious it is, what a beautiful colour it has!" So Eve
> took and ate of it, and then took it to Adam, and said: "Look at this tree! How
> fragrant it is, how delicious it is, what a beautiful colour it has!" So Adam ate
> of it, and their shameful parts became conspicuous to them.

Then Adam went inside the tree, and his Lord called out: "Adam, where are you?" (. . .) He said: "I am here, O Lord." He said: "Are you not coming out?" He said: "I feel ashamed before You, O Lord." He said: "Cursed be the earth from which you were created, may its fruit turn into thorns!" (. . .) Then there was no tree in the Garden or on earth which was better than the gum acacia and the Christ's thorn. Then He said: "Eve, you who misled My servant, may your pregnancies all be painful, and when you wish to give birth to what is in your womb, may you more than once look down on death!" Then He said to the serpent: "You, into whose belly the cursed one entered so that he could mislead My servant, cursed be you! May your legs withdraw into your abdomen. You shall have no sustenance but dust. You shall be the enemy of the children of Adam, and they shall be your enemies: when you meet one of them you will seize him by the heel, and when he meets you he will crush your head."

⇒Ibn 'Abbas, ⇒ Ibn Mas'ud, and ⇒ A Group of Companions:

When God said to Adam: «"⌈D⌉well, you and your wife, in the Garden, and eat thereof easefully where you desire, but draw not near this tree, lest you become evil-doers"», Iblis desired to enter the Garden with them, but the guardians prevented him. So he came to the serpent, who was a beast with four legs, as if it were a camel, and was like the handsomest of beasts, and talked to it so that it would let him enter its mouth and would go in with him to Adam. So it let him enter its *fuqm*—Abū Ja'far ⌈al-Tabari⌉ said: "The *fuqm* is the side of the mouth." The serpent passed the guardians and entered, but they did not notice, because God willed it so. ⌈Iblis⌉ spoke with ⌈Adam⌉ from the side of ⌈the serpent's⌉ mouth but ⌈Adam⌉ paid no attention to what he said, so he came out to him and said: «"Adam, shall I point you to the tree of eternity, and a Kingdom that decays not?"» (Q.20:120), meaning "Shall I point you to a tree which, if you eat thereof, you will be a sovereign like God? Or the two of you will be immortals who never die?" And he swore by God to ⌈Adam and Eve⌉: «"Truly, I am a sincere adviser to you"» (Q.7:21), and he meant by that to reveal to them their shameful parts, which were hidden from their sight, by tearing off their garments. He knew that they had shameful parts, since he had read it in the books of the angels, but Adam did not know this. Their garments were ⌈made of⌉ horn. Adam refused to eat from it; then Eve went forward and ate from it, and said: "Adam, eat. I have eaten and it has done me no harm." And when Adam ate «their shameful parts became conspicuous to them, and they straightway stitched upon themselves leaves of the Garden» (Q.7.22). . . .

⇒Ibn Ishaq, from one of the people of knowledge:

When Adam entered the Garden, and saw the munificence therein and what God had given him of it, he said: "If only ⌈I could⌉ dwell ⌈here⌉ forever!" Satan found signs of weakness here from him when he heard him say this, and approached him from the angle of ⌈his desire for⌉ immortality.

⇒Ibn Ishaq:

I was told: When ⌈Iblis⌉ first started his trickery with ⌈Adam and Eve⌉, he wept before them so that they grieved when they heard it. They said: "What makes you cry?" He said: "I am crying because of you. You will die, and will be separated from the blessings and munificence you enjoy." This had an effect on their souls. Then he came to them and tempted (*waswasa*) them, saying: «"Adam, shall I point you to the tree of eternity, and a Kingdom that decays not?"» Then he said: «"Your Lord has only prohibited you from this tree lest you become angels, or lest you become immortals." And he swore to them: "Truly, I am a sincere adviser to you"» ⌈meaning⌉: "You will become angels, or will remain eternally—if you will not be angels—in the blessings of the Garden, and you will not die." God said: «So he led them on by delusion» (Q.7:22).

⇒Ibn Wahb:

Ibn Zaid said: "Satan tempted Eve with the tree and eventually brought her it ⌈'s fruit⌉, then he made her beautiful in Adam's sight. (. . .) So Adam called her out of desire. She said: 'No! Not unless you come here.' When he came to her, she said: 'No! Not until you eat from this tree.' (. . .) So he ate from it and their shameful parts became conspicuous to them. (. . .) Then Adam became a fugitive in the Garden, and his Lord called to him: 'Adam, are you running away from Me?' He said: 'No my Lord, but I am ashamed before You.' He said: 'Adam, from where were you approached?' He said: 'From Eve, Lord.' So God said: 'I shall cause her to bleed once every month, just as you have caused this tree to bleed. I shall make her foolish, although I ⌈originally⌉ created her mild tempered. I shall make her have a painful pregnancy and childbirth, although I ⌈originally⌉ made her have an easy pregnancy and childbirth.' "

Ibn Zaid said: "If it were not for the affliction which befell Eve, the women of this world would not menstruate, and they would be mild tempered, and have easy pregnancies and childbirths."

⇒Yazid b. 'Abd Allah b. Qusait:

I heard Sa'id b. Al-Musaiyib swear by God: "Adam did not eat of the tree as long as he was in his senses, but Eve gave him wine to drink, so that when he was drunk, she led him to it and he ate. . . . "

These Traditions have been narrated, from those of the Companions, Followers, and others we have narrated them from, concerning the description of how Iblis, the enemy of God, caused Adam and his wife to slip so that he brought them out of the Garden. The soundest of these is, in our view, that which agrees with the Book of God. Now God stated that Iblis tempted Adam in order to show the two of them their shameful parts which were masked from them, and that he said to them: «"Your Lord has only prohibited you from this tree lest you become angels, or lest you become immortals"» (Q.7:20), and that «he swore to them: "Truly, I am a sincere adviser to you"», causing them to fall through a deception. . . .

 . . . As for the interpretation of «and ⌈he⌉ brought them out», He means: Satan brought Adam and his wife out «of that they were in», i.e., from the comfortable life in the Garden which Adam and his wife were ⌈enjoying⌉, ⌈and from⌉ its abundant ease in which they ⌈found themselves⌉. It is clear that God ascribed their expulsion to Satan, although it was God who brought them out, because their leaving it was due to a cause ⌈which came⌉ from Satan, and He attributes this to him because he mediated it. . . .

These words from God make it clear that what we said about God being the one who expelled Adam from the Garden is correct, and that God's attributing to Iblis their expulsion is as we have described. It also shows that the fall of Adam, his wife, and their enemy, Iblis, all happened at one time, because God combines them in His statement about their fall, after the sin of Adam and his wife, and Satan's causing them ⌈to commit⌉ this, according to what our Lord has said about them.

NOTES TO CHAPTER 5, ISLAM, MUSLIM INTERPRETATIONS, AL-TABARI

1. For an example of al-Tabari's work as a historian, see *The History of al-Tabari*, vol. 1, *From the Creation to the Flood*, translated and annotated by Franz Rosenthal, SUNY Series in Near Eastern Studies (Albany: State University of New York Press, 1989).
2. See John Cooper's "Translator's Introduction" to al-Tabari's *The Commentary on the Qur'an* (Oxford: Oxford University Press, 1987), vol. 1, p. ix.
3. For a more extensive sketch of al-Tabari's life and work, see Jane Dammen McAuliffe's *Qur'anic Christians: An Analysis of Classical and Modern Exegesis* (Cambridge: Cambridge University Press, 1991), pp. 37-45. See also the "Translator's Introduction" to al-Tabari's *The Commentary on the Qur'an*, vol. 1, pp. ix-xxxvi.

Al-Kisa'i

There can be no doubt that Muhammad ibn 'Abd Allah al-Kisa'i was a great storyteller. His collection of prophetic tales—or Qisas, as they are known in Arabic—attests to his skill. Although little is known about al-Kisa'i himself, the tales he preserved stand as "one of the best-loved versions of the prophetic tales," according to W. M. Thackston, Jr., who translated these tales into English.[1]

Thackston provides a helpful description of the genre of prophetic tales. He points out that this genre originated within the storytelling of popular culture when people wanted to know more about persons and events than the hints and suggestions of the Qur'an conveyed.[2] Legendary traditions developed as persons—especially professional storytellers—elaborated upon Qur'anic allusions, supplying details and unfolding narratives. These legends served devotional purposes. Yet they also were designed to entertain. Indeed, after highlighting some of the so-called "fantastic material" in al-Kisa'i's tales, Thackston maintains that the version of the tales rendered by al-Kisa'i "is basically designed for popular entertainment and should ideally be recited by a professional raconteur."[3]

The tales that al-Kisa'i collected have a sustained quality that contrasts with the disjointed texture of the Qur'an. In selecting tales that concern Eve, we have sought to preserve this sustained character. Our selection first provides excerpts of tales that describe such episodes as God's creation of Eve and the temptation and disobedience of Eve and Adam. The selection then turns to stories concerning the aftermath of the first sin. These later tales relate events that happen after the disobedience of Eve and Adam, including their departure or "fall" from the heights of Paradise to the lower realm of earth, their separation from one another, and their reunion. Tucked within these events are rich descriptions concerning God's responses to the first sin, including decisions God made about punishments and about provisions for the first human beings and their offspring. These tales also provide captivating portrayals of the responses of Eve and Adam as they grapple with what is happening to them. (Source: Muhammad ibn 'Abd Allah al-Kisa'i, *The Tales of the Prophets of al-Kisa'i*, translated and with notes by W. M. Thackston, Jr., Library of Classical Arabic Literature, vol. 2, Ilse Lischenstadler, editor, Boston: G. K. Hall and Company, 1978, pp. 31-32, 38-41, 44-45, 54-55, 60-62, 65-67, 72-74.)

The Tales of the Prophets (collected c. 1200 CE)
MUHAMMAD IBN 'ABD ALLAH AL-KISA'I

14. The Creation of Eve

While Adam slept, God created Eve from one of his left ribs, which was crooked. She was called Eve (*Hawa*) because she was made from a living being (*hayy*), as He hath said: "*O men, fear your Lord, who hath created you out of one man, and out of him created his wife*" (Q.4:1).

Eve was as tall and as beautiful as Adam and had seven hundred tresses studded with gems of chrysolite and incensed with musk. She was in the prime of her life. She had large, dark eyes; she was tender and white; her palms were tinted, and her long, shapely, brilliantly colored tresses, which formed a crown, emitted a rustling sound. She was of the same form as Adam, except that her skin was softer and purer in color than his was, and her voice was more beautiful. Her eyes were darker, her nose more curved, and her teeth whiter than his were.

When God had created her, He seated her at Adam's side. Adam saw her in his sleep on that long-ago day and loved her in his heart.

"O Lord," he asked, "who is this?"

"She is my handmaiden Eve," He said.

"O Lord," asked Adam, "for whom hast thou created her?"

"For one who will take her in trust and will persevere in thanks for her," said God.

Then Adam said, "O Lord, I will take her on one condition, that thou marry me to her." And so Adam was married to Eve before entering Paradise.

It is related on the authority of Ali ibn Abi Talib[4] that Adam saw her while he was asleep and that she spoke to him, saying, "I am the handmaiden of God, and you are the servant of God. Seek my hand from your Lord." Ali also said, "Do not hold marriage to be a good thing, for women can control themselves neither for profit nor for loss; nonetheless, you hold them in trust from God, so do them no harm!" . . .

17. The Serpent, and Iblis's Entry into Paradise

. . . Kaab said that at that time the serpent was shaped like a camel and, like the camel, could stand erect. She had a multicolored tail, red, yellow, green, white, black, a mane of pearl, hair of topaz, eyes like the planets Venus and Jupiter, and an aroma like musk blended with ambergris. Her dwelling was in the aqueous Paradise, and her pond was on the shore of the River Cawthar. Her food was saffron, and she drank from that river; and her speech was exaltation of God, the Lord of the Universe. God had created her two thousand years before he created Adam, and she had told Adam and Eve about every tree in Paradise. . . .

But Iblis spoke from the serpent's mouth, saying, "O Eve, Beauty of Paradise, haven't I been with you in Paradise and told you about everything that is here? Haven't I told the truth in all I have said to you?"

"Yes," said Eve, "I have only known you to be truthful in your speech."

"Eve," said Iblis, "tell me what God permitted to you of this Paradise and what he forbade you." And she told him what God had forbidden them.

"Why did your Lord forbid you the Tree of Eternity?" asked Iblis.

"I do not know," said Eve.

"But I know!" cried Iblis. "He forbade it to you because He wanted to make you like that slave whose place is under the Tree of Eternity and whom God brought to Paradise two thousand years before you!"

Eve jumped up from her dais to look at the slave, whereupon Iblis leapt out of the serpent's mouth like a streak of lightning and sat down under the tree. Eve saw *him* and thought he was the slave. Calling to him, she asked, "Who are you?"

"I am a creature of my Lord, who created me from fire. I have been in this Paradise two thousand years. He created me as He created you two, with his own hand and breathed his breath into me. He caused the angels to bow down before me, then He established me in Paradise and forbade me to eat from this tree. I did not eat from it until one of the angels, who swore to me that he was giving me good advice, told me to do so, saying that whosoever ate from it would have everlasting life in Paradise. I trusted him and ate from it. As you can see, I am still in Paradise and have been safe from old age, illness, death and expulsion." Then he added, as God hath said: "*Your Lord hath not forbidden you this tree, for any other reason but lest ye should become angels, or lest ye become immortal*" (Q.7:19). Then he cried to her, "Eve, eat from it! It is good and edible—of the fruits of Paradise! Hurry and eat before your husband Adam, for whoever eats first will have precedence over his companion."

Then Eve said to the serpent, "You have been with me since I entered this Paradise, but you have not told me anything about this tree." And the serpent was silent, fearing Ridwan[5] and desirous of the words Iblis had promised to teach her.

Ibn Abbas said: Were it not for her alarm over death, she would not have desired the words; but she did what she did.

Thereupon, Eve, bright with good news, came to Adam and told him of the serpent and the person who had sworn to her that he was giving her sound advice, as He hath said: "*And he swore to them saying, 'Verily I am one of those who counsel you aright'* " (Q.7:20). Then destiny was added to Iblis's speech and vow.

So Eve drew near to the tree. It had innumerable branches, and on each branch were ears that contained seeds like Tell Hujur (or, as it is also said, like ostrich eggs). They had a fragrance like musk and were whiter than milk and sweeter than honey. Eve plucked seven ears from seven branches of the tree, ate one and hid one away; the other five she took to Adam.

It has been related from Ibn Abbas that Adam had nothing to do with the act, neither in denial nor in acquiescence, but that it was predestined, as He hath said: "*When thy Lord said unto the angels, I am going to place a substitute on earth; they said, Wilt thou place the one who will do evil therein, and shed blood? but we celebrate thy praise, and sanctify thee? God answered, Verily I know that which ye know not*" (Q.2:30).

Then Adam took the ears from her hand, having forgotten the covenant binding upon him, as He hath said: "*But he forgot; and we found not in him a firm resolution*" (Q.20:115), that is, he did not keep the covenant and tasted of the tree as Eve had done, as He hath said: "*And when they had tasted of the tree, their nakedness appeared unto them*" (Q.7:22).

Ibn Abbas said: And by Him in whose hand is my soul, no sooner had Adam tasted one of the ears of grain than the crown flew off his head, his rings squirmed off his hand and everything that had been on both him and Eve fell off—their clothes, jewelry and ornaments. Each article, as it flew from them, cried out, "O Adam! O Eve! Long may you sorrow and may your affliction be great! Peace be with you until the Day of Resurrection, for we made a covenant with God that we should clothe only obedient, humble servants."

19. The Address of Eve

. . . "My God and Master, it is mine own sin, which I was made to do," she said. "Iblis led me astray with his deception and evil whisperings and swore to me by thy Majesty that he was advising me well. I never thought that anyone would swear by Thee if he were lying."

"Depart now from Paradise, deceived forever henceforth," said God. "I make thee deficient in mind, religion, ability to bear witness and inheritance. I make thee morally malformed, with glazed eyes, and make thee to be imprisoned for the length of days of thy life and deny thee the best things, the Friday congregation, mingling in public, and giving greeting. I destine thee to menstruation and the pain of pregnancy and labor, and thou wilt give birth only by tasting the pain of death along with it. Women shall experience more sorrow, more tears shall flow from them, they shall have less patience, and God will never make a prophet or a wise person from among them."

"O God," cried Eve, "how can I leave Paradise? Thou hast denied me all blessings."

Then the Voice of God cried out: "Leave! For I have bent the hearts of my servants in sympathy with thee."

Ibn Abbas said: God created affection and familiarity between men and women, so keep them at home and be kind toward them insofar as you are able; for every woman who is pious, worships her Lord, performs her religious obligations, and obeys her husband will enter Paradise.

Then God called to Eve, saying, "Depart! For I expel through thee those with whom I shall fill Paradise: the prophets, the pious, the martyrs, those who will be pardoned, and those among your progeny who pray for and ask forgiveness for you two." . . .

25. Eve's Query

Then Eve began to question, saying, "My God, thou didst create me from a crooked rib-bone. Thou didst create me deficient in reason, religion, ability to bear witness and in inheritance. Thou has afflicted me with impurity and denied me the right to assemble at the Friday congregational prayer and further burdened me with divorce and bearing children. I beseech thee, O Lord, to grant me something as Thou has granted these others."

"Verily," said God, "I have given thee life, mercy and kindness. I decree such a reward for thee, upon performance of ritual ablutions after menstruation and birthing, that, were thou to see it, would give thee satisfaction. Furthermore, if a woman die during childbirth, her place shall be among the ranks of the martyrs."

"That is sufficient for me," said Eve. . . .

When their lots had been meted out, they were commanded to descend to the earth, as He hath said: "*Get ye down, the one of you an enemy unto the other; and there shall be a dwelling place for you on earth, and a provision for a season*" (Q.2:36, 38) (the "dwelling place" is the grave and the "season" the Day of Resurrection).

Adam went down by way of the Gate of Repentance, Eve by the Gate of Mercy, Iblis by the Gate of Malediction, the peacock by the Gate of Wrath, and the serpent by the Gate of Ire. This was in the late afternoon. . . .

Kaab said: Adam came down to India, on top of a mountain called

Serendip, which surrounds India. Eve came down to Jidda, Iblis to the land of Maysan, the peacock to Egypt, and the serpent to Isphahan. God separated them one from another so that they were unable to see each other. On the day of his fall, Adam had only a leaf from the garden that had stuck to his body; the wind, however, carried it off to India, where it became the source of perfume.

Thereupon Adam wept day and night for a hundred years. He did not raise his head toward heaven until God had caused aloe-wood, ginger, sandalwood, camphor, ambergris and all types of scents to grow from his tears. And the valleys became filled with trees.

Eve too wept, and from her tears God caused carnations and herbs to grow.

The wind carried Adam's voice to Eve and Eve's to Adam, and each thought that he was near the other, although between them were distant lands.

Ibn Abbas said: Eve remained fixed in the heavens for a long time, so she put her hands on her head, thus transmitting that custom to her daughters until the Day of Resurrection.

Wahb said: When Adam stood erect his head was in the heavens and he could hear the angels praising God, so he praised along with them. It was then that God caused his hair and beard to grow, as before he had been bald and his head had glistened like silver.

28. Adam's Repentance

. . . When Adam prayed with these words, he was told, "Adam, thou art truly my friend, for I have forgiven thee thy transgression. Ask and it shall be given thee."

"My God," he said, "forgive any of the faithful among my children who does not associate anything with thee, and forgive any servant who desires thy forgiveness using these words." When Adam spoke thus, his voice was carried to the distant horizons; and the earth, the mountains and the trees set up a great clamor, saying, "Adam, God has given you relief and has blessed you through your repentance."

Then God commanded these words to be taken to Eve, and the breeze carried them to her. Thus she too received the glad tidings and said, "No one will hear these words but that God will have made them forgiveness and mercy, for He is the Most Merciful." Thereupon she spoke the words and fell down in prostration. . . .

To Eve God sent Michael, and he gave her the glad tidings of repentance and forgiveness and garbed her. She said, "Praise be to God for His excellence and sanction." When she learned that her repentance had been accepted, she removed herself to the seashore and bathed herself and said, "Has not God accepted my repentance? When then shall I find Adam?" And she began to weep out of longing for Adam. Every drop of her tears that fell into the sea was transformed into pearl and coral.

When she returned to her dwelling place, she began to look for Adam, who was at the time asking Gabriel about her. He was told that God had accepted her repentance and would bring them together in the most noble of all places, Mecca. He also told him that God commanded him to build there His House, which is the Kaaba,[6] which he should circumambulate and in which he should offer prayer as he had seen the angels do at the Visited House.[7] There He would offer him Iblis to stone as the angels had done when he refused to prostrate himself. . . .

Then God spoke to Adam, saying, "Build now My House, which I placed on the earth two thousand years before I created thee. I have commanded the angels to aide thee in building it. When thou shalt have completed it, circumambulate, shout hallelujah, glorify me and bless my name, and lift up thy voice in proclaiming my oneness, in praising me, and in thanking me. Grieve not over thy wife, for I shall join thee to her in the bowers of my House, which I shall make the Great *Qibla*[8] the *qibla* of the Prophet Muhammad, who shall be the greatest source of honor for thee. I know what thou feelest in thy heart for Eve and she in hers for thee, so when thou seest her, be kind to her, for I have destined her to be the mother of boys and girls."

29. Mankind Undertakes the Covenant

. . . An angel then approached Eve, who was seated by the sea, and said, "Take these your garments, go forth and enter the Sanctuary in submissiveness to your Lord." He gave her a chemise and a veil from Paradise and turned away while she was putting on the chemise and covering herself with the veil. She entered the Sanctuary from the east of Mecca on a Friday in the month of Muharram, weeping over the loss of her beauty and comeliness. Then the angel sat her on Mount Marwa (which was so named because womankind [*mar'a*] sat there). Eve entered the Sanctuary seven days prior to Adam.

Adam entered from the west of Mecca. When he had gone up onto Mount Safa, the mountain cried out, saying, "Welcome, O Chosen of God" (and it was thus called Safa because Adam was known as the Chosen [*safwa*] of God).

Then Adam cried out to his Lord, saying, "Here am I. Here am I. Thou hast no partner. Here am I. Praise, glory and the kingdom are Thine. Thou hast no partner. Here am I" (and it became part of the ritual to say these words during the major and minor pilgrimages).

God answered him, saying, "Adam, today have I sanctified Mecca and all that surrounds it, and it shall be sacred until the Day of Resurrection" (that is, those who enter therein become so sanctified that they will not burn in Hell).

"O Lord," said Adam, "thou has promised me that thou wouldst join Eve and me in this place. Where is she?"

"O Adam," came the reply, "she is before thee on Mount Marwa. Thou art on Mount Safa. Look upon her, but touch her not until thou hast performed the rites of pilgrimage." Adam then went down to Eve, and they met and rejoiced, for, as Eve was setting out from Marwa and Adam from Safa, they had seen each other across the valley. They met during the day and spoke of Paradise and the primeval fate that had befallen them. By night Eve returned to Marwa and Adam to Safa, where they remained until the month of Dhu'l-Hijja, when Gabriel came to Adam and taught him the pilgrimage rites. . . .

After Gabriel taught him the rites, Adam rose and was vested with the pilgrimage garb. Gabriel took him by the hand and circumambulated the House seven times, taught him all the rites of pilgrimage and made him stand at all the stations. Afterwards he returned him to the House and commanded him to circumambulate seven times. When he had finished, Gabriel said, "This is sufficient for you, Adam. You are absolved, your repentance has been accepted, and your wife has also been absolved. Pray to your Lord to heed your prayer." Adam then prayed for all believers who ascribe no partner to God and asked Him to edify the House with His visitation, and God granted his prayer.

Adam went to Eve, with the angels aligned in ranks and saying, "God grant you mercy, Adam! We have performed the pilgrimage to this House two thousand years before you." Adam and Eve came together on a Friday eve, for which reason, to the exclusion of all other nights, He grants coition on Friday eve. And Eve conceived that very night.

Kaab said: Eve did not conceive until after she had menstruated. When she first experienced it, she was frightened; but Adam said, "It is in fulfillment of your Lord's promise to afflict you with impurity. But Eve," he continued, "where is your beauty and comeliness? You have been transformed."

"It is on account of my transgression," she said. So Adam denied her the right to pray during the days of her menstrual period until the blood should have stopped. Then there came unto her an angel, who stood before the well of Zemzem and said to Adam, "Run about in this place!" When he ran, the earth, with God's permission, burst forth with a spring filled with water that was colder than ice, sweeter than honey and more redolent than musk. Eve wished to drink the water, but Adam said, "Do not drink until God gives me permission." Eve bathed in it, however; and from her tresses the musk spread throughout the earth. . . .

31. Eve's First Conception

Then Adam lay with Eve on a Friday eve, and she conceived twins, a male and a female. In the eighth month she aborted, and this was the first miscarriage in this world. Then she again conceived male and female but was likewise afflicted, and Adam and Eve were grief-stricken. Then she conceived for the third time, as He hath said: "*And when he had known her, she carried a light burden for a time, wherefore she walked easily therewith*" (that is, until her pregnancy was obvious). "*But when it became more heavy, she cried upon God their Lord, saying, 'If thou give us a child rightly shaped* (that is, if this pregnancy ends sound), *we will surely be thankful*'" (Q.7:189).

Iblis came to Eve and said, "Do you want what is in your womb to live?

"Yes," she replied.

"Then name him Abdul-Harith," said Iblis, as He hath said: "*Yet when he had given them a child rightly shaped, they attributed companions unto him, for that which he had given them*" (Q.7:190) (that is, they gave Iblis association in the name by calling him Abdul-Harith, for the Harith is Iblis).[9]

When she gave birth to a healthy child, she called him Abdul-Harith. An angel came to them with God's permission and asked them, "Why did you call this babe by that name?"

"So he would live," said Eve, whereupon the angel said, "Why did you not name him Abdullah, or Abdul-Rahman or Abdul-Rahim?" Adam and Eve became extremely frightened and said, "We do not need this child." So God caused it to die.

Eve again conceived twins, male and female; and when she bore them she called them Abdullah and Amatullah. Then she conceived another pair of male and female twins and called them Abdul-Rahman and Amatul-Rahman. She continued to bear until she had given birth to twenty sets of male and female twins. Then she bore the prophet of God Abel and his sister, then Cain and his sister, then Siboe and his sister, then Sandal and his sister. She continued to give birth until she had borne one hundred and twenty times, each time to male and female twins. And they begat generations and multiplied.

32. Adam's Mission

. . . Kaab al-Ahbar said: Then, on the first night of Ramadan,[10] God revealed to Adam twenty-two leaves, on which were several chapters written in disjointed letters, none of which were joined together. This was the first book God revealed to Adam. It contained a thousand words, comprising duties, traditions, legislation, the foreboding threat, and accounts of this world. In it God showed him the actions of the people of every age, their shapes and careers, their kings and prophets and what they would do upon the earth, even their food and drink.

Adam looked upon all of that and knew what his children would do after him. And Adam read it to his children.

Then God commanded him to write it with the pen, so he took sheepskins and tanned them until they were soft. On them he wrote the twenty-eight letters which are in the Torah, the Gospel, the Psalms and the Koran. . . .

NOTES TO CHAPTER 5, ISLAM, MUSLIM INTERPRETATIONS, AL-KISA'I

[1. W. M. Thackston, Jr., "Introduction," in *The Tales of the Prophets of al-Kisa'i* (Boston: G. K. Hall, 1978), p. xix.]

[2. Thackston, "Introduction," pp. xi–xxxiv.]

[3. Thackston, "Introduction," p. xxiv.]

[4. Ali ibn Abi Talib, a cousin of Muhammad, married Muhammad's daughter Fatima. Ali is recognized as the fourth Caliph by Sunni Muslims and the first Iman of the Shi'ites.]

[5. Ridwan in this context is identified as the "gatekeeper of heaven" according to Thackston, in note 29, p. 342 of *The Tales of the Prophets of al-Kisa'i*.]

[6. The Kaaba or Ka'ba, known as "the House of Allah" by Muslims, stands at the center of the Mosque at Mecca.]

[7. The "Visited House" is the heavenly prototype of the Kaaba.]

[8. *Qibla* is the direction of the Kaaba in Mecca, toward which all Muslims turn when praying.]

[9. Noting that "al-Harith" means "the tiller of the soil," Thackston points out that this discussion reflects "the antiagricultural prejudice of presedentary nomads"; see note 56, p. 345 of *The Tales of the Prophets of al-Kisa'i*.]

[10. Ramadan is the ninth month of the Islamic lunar calendar. Muslims observe this sacred time by fasting from dawn until sunset and performing other acts of piety that are understood to be particularly efficacious during this time.]

Ibn al-Arabi

"Ibn al-Arabi" and "Ibn Arabi" are shortened forms of the name of one of Islam's most famous mystics, Muhammad b. Ali b. Muhammad Ibn al-Arabi al-Ta'i al-Hatimi (1165-1240).[1] Ibn al-Arabi was born and raised in Spain; after extensive travels, he settled in Damascus. As a youth, he studied under several Sufi masters, two of whom were women. As an adult, he taught theology to his daughter Zainab who, reportedly, at one year of age was able to answer theological questions.[2]

Sufism represents Islam's mystical tradition. In accord with the mystical branches of other religious traditions, Sufism envisions union with God as the goal for human life. It calls for gaining a constant awareness of God's presence by developing a personal piety that is marked by contemplation, self-discipline, and moral zeal. Sufism arose during Islam's early centuries in various parts of the Islamic empire alongside the development of state-supported orthodoxy. It repudiated the moral laxity and tepid spirituality it saw being practiced. The Arabic term *sufi* signifies "wool-clad"; some scholars maintain that this designation highlights Sufism's protest of "the silks and satins of the Damascus court."[3]

The work and thought of Ibn al-Arabi portray the theoretical and philosophical dimensions of Sufism. A prolific author, Ibn al-Arabi wrote over 250 works. Although his writing can make for difficult reading, it also provides a good example of the theoretical facets of Sufism: its esoteric speculations and its elaborate poetic imagery. Our selection comes from his reflection on the Prophet Muhammad in the final chapter of his *The Bezels of Wisdom*, which is also known as *The Wisdom of the Prophets*. Concerning this book, Bruce Lawrence has stated, "Revealed to Ibn Arabi in a single night at age sixty-five [it] is a brilliant, insightful book without parallel in Sufi history."[4] (Source: Ibn al-Arabi, *Ibn al'Arabi: The Bezels of Wisdom*, translated and with an introduction by Ralph W. J. Austin, preface by Titus Burkhardt, The Classics of Western Spirituality series, Richard J. Payne, editor, New York: Paulist Press, 1980, pp. 272-77.)

The Bezels of Wisdom (c. 1200s)
MUHAMMAD B. ALI B. MUHAMMAD IBN AL-ARABI

The Wisdom of Singularity in the Word of Muhammad

His is the wisdom of singularity because he is the most perfect creation of this humankind, for which reason the whole affair [of creation] begins and ends with him. He was a prophet when Adam was still between the water and the clay[5] and he is, by his elemental makeup, the Seal of the Prophets, first of the three singular ones, since all other singulars derive from it.

He was the clearest of evidence for his Lord, having been given the totality of the divine words, which are those things named by Adam, so that he was the closest of clues to his own triplicity, he being himself a clue to himself. Since, then, his reality was marked by primal singularity and his makeup by triplicity, he said concerning love, which is the origin of all existent being, "Three things have been made beloved to me in this world of yours," because of the triplicity inherent in him. Then he mentioned women and perfume, and added that he found solace in prayer.[6]

He begins by mentioning women and leaves prayer until last, because, in the manifestation of her essence, woman is a part of man. Now, man's knowledge of himself comes before his knowledge of his Lord, the latter being the result of the former, according to his saying, "Whoso knows himself, knows his Lord." From this one may understand either that one is not able to know and attain, which is one meaning, or that gnosis is possible. According to the first [interpretation] one cannot know oneself and cannot, therefore, know one's Lord, while, according to the second, one may know oneself and therefore one's Lord. Although Muhammad was the most obvious evidence of his Lord, every part of the Cosmos is a clue to its origin, which is its Lord, so understand.

Women were made beloved to him and he had great affection for them because the whole always is drawn toward its part. This he explains as coming from the Reality, in His saying regarding the elemental human makeup, "*And I breathed into him of My spirit!*"[7] God describes Himself as having a deep longing for contact with man when He says to those who long [for Him], "O David, I long for them even more." That is a special meeting. . . .

Then God drew forth from him a being in his own image, called woman, and because she appears in his own image, the man feels a deep longing for her, as something yearns for itself, while she feels longing for him as one longs for that place to which one belongs. Thus, women were made beloved to him, for God loves that which He has created in His own image and to which He made His angels prostrate, in spite of their great power, rank and lofty nature. From that stemmed the affinity [between God and man], and the [divine] image is the greatest, most glorious and perfect [example of] affinity. That is because it is a syzygy that polarizes the being of the Reality, just as a woman, by her coming into being, polarizes humanity, making of it a syzygy. Thus we have a ternary, God, man, and woman, the man yearning for his Lord Who is his origin, as woman yearns for man. His Lord made women dear to him, just as God loves that which is in His own image. Love arises only for that from which one has one's being, so that man loves that from which he has his being, which is the Reality, which is why he says, "were made beloved to me,"[8] and not "I love," directly from himself. His love is for his Lord in Whose image he is, this being so even as regards his love for his wife, since he loves her through God's love for him, after the divine manner. When a man loves a woman, he seeks union with her, that is to say the most complete union possible in love, and there is in the elemental sphere no greater union than that between the sexes. It is [precisely] because such desire pervades all his parts that man is commanded to perform the major ablution. Thus the purification is total, just as his annihilation in her was total at the moment of consummation. God is jealous of his servant that he should find pleasure in any but Him, so He purifies him by the ablution, so that he might once again behold Him in the one in whom he was annihilated, since it is none other than He Whom he sees in her.

When man contemplates the Reality in woman he beholds [Him] in a passive aspect, while when he contemplates Him in himself, as being that from which woman is manifest, he beholds Him in an active aspect. When, however, he contemplates Him in himself, without any regard to what has come from him, he beholds Him as passive to Himself directly. However, his contemplation of the Reality in woman is the most complete and perfect, because in this way he contemplates the Reality in both active and passive mode, while by contemplating the Reality only in himself, he beholds Him in a passive mode particularly.

Because of this the Apostle loved women by reason of [the possibility of] perfect contemplation of the Reality in them. Contemplation of the Reality without formal support is not possible, since God, in His Essence, is far beyond all need of the Cosmos. Since, therefore, some form of support is necessary, the best and most perfect kind is the contemplation of God in women. The greatest union is that between man and woman, corresponding as it does to the turning of God toward the one He has created in His own image, to make him His vicegerent, so that He might behold Himself in him. Accordingly, He shaped him, balanced him, and breathed His spirit into him, which is His Breath, so that his outer aspect is creaturely, while his inner aspect is divine. Because of this He describes it [the spirit] as being the disposer of this human structure by which God *disposes of things from the heaven*, which is elevation, *to the earth*,[9] which is the lowest of the low, being the lowest of the elements.

He calls them women [*nisa'*], a word that has no singular form. The Apostle therefore said, "Three things have been made beloved to me in this world, women . . . ,"[10] and not "woman," having regard to the fact that they came into being after him [man]. Indeed, the word *nus'ah* means "coming after." He says, "*The postponed month* [nasi'] *is an increase in unbelief*,"[11] as also selling by *nasi'ah*, that is, "by postponement." Thus he says "women." He loves them only because of their [lower] rank and their being the repository of passivity. In relation to him they are as the Universal Nature is to God in which He revealed the forms of the Cosmos by directing toward it the divine Will and Command, which, at the level of elemental forms, is symbolized by conjugal union, [spiritual] concentration in the realm of luminous spirits, and the ordering of premises toward a conclusion [in the realm of thought], all of which correspond to the consummation of the Primordial Singularity in all these aspects.

Whoever loves women in this way loves with a divine love, while he whose love for them is limited to natural lust lacks all [true] knowledge of that desire. For such a one she is mere form, devoid of spirit, and even though that form be indeed imbued with spirit, it is absent for one who approaches his wife or some other woman solely to have his pleasure of her, without realizing Whose the pleasure [really] is. Thus he does not know himself [truly], just as a stranger does not know him until he reveals his identity to him. As they say,

> They are right in supposing that I am in love,
> Only they know not with whom I am in love.[12]

Such a man is [really] in love with pleasure itself and, in consequence, loves its repository, which is woman, the real truth and meaning of the act of being lost on him. If he knew the truth, he would know Whom it is he is enjoying and Who it is Who is the enjoyer; then he would be perfected.

Just as woman [ontologically] is of a lower rank than man, according to His saying, "*Men enjoy a rank above them*,"[13] so also is the creature inferior in rank to the One Who fashioned him in his image, despite his being made in His image. . . .

He places women first because they are the repository of passivity, just as the Universal Nature, by its form, comes before those things that derive their being from her. . . .

Then the Apostle goes on to give precedence to the feminine over the masculine, intending to convey thereby a special concern with and experience of women. Thus he says *thalath* [three] and not *thalathah*, which is used for numbering masculine nouns. This is remarkable, in that he also mentions perfume, which is a masculine noun, and the Arabs usually make the masculine gender prevail. . . .

Now, although the Apostle was an Arab, he is here giving special attention to the significance of the love enjoined on him, seeing that he himself did not choose that love. It was God Who taught him what he knew not, and God's bounty on him was abundant. He therefore gave precedence to the feminine over the masculine by saying *thalath*. How knowledgeable was the Apostle concerning [spiritual] realities and how great was his concern for proper precedence.

Furthermore, he made the final term [prayer] correspond to the first [women] in its femininity, placing the masculine term [perfume] between them. He begins with "women" and ends with "prayer," both of which are feminine nouns, [the masculine noun] perfume coming in between them, as is the case with its existential being, since man is placed between the Essence [a feminine noun] from which he is manifested, and woman who is manifested from him. Thus he is between two feminine entities, the one substantively feminine, the other feminine in reality, women being feminine in reality, while prayer is not. Perfume is placed between them as Adam is situated between the Essence, which is the source of all existence, and Eve, whose existence stems from him. . . .

NOTES TO CHAPTER 5, ISLAM, IBN AL-ARABI

[1. For a more extensive account of Ibn al-Arabi's life and thought, see Ralph W. J. Austin's introduction to *Ibn al'Arabi: The Bezels of Wisdom*, translated by Ralph W. J. Austin, preface by Titus Burkhardt, The Classics of Western Spirituality series, Richard J. Payne, editor (New York: Paulist Press, 1980), pp. 1-41.]

[2. See Leila Ahmed, *Women and Gender in Islam*, p. 99.]

[3. Kenneth Cragg, *The House of Islam*, 2nd ed., Religious Life of Man series, Frederick J. Streng, editor (Encino, Calif., and Belmont, Calif.: Dickenson Publishing Company, 1975), p. 67.]

[4. Bruce Lawrence, "{IBN ARABI, MUHYI D-DIN}," in Keith R. Crim, editor, *Abingdon Dictionary of Living Religions* (Nashville: Abingdon, 1981), p. 332. For an alternative view of the book's composition, see R. W. J. Austin's introduction to *Ibn al'Arabi: The Bezels of Wisdom*, pp. 13, 17-18.]

5. Bukhari 78:119.
6. Nasa'i 36:1.
7. Qur'an 15:29.
8. Nasa'i 36:1.
9. Qur'an 32:5.
10. Nasa'i 36:1.
11. Qur'an 9:37.
12. R. W. J. Austin points out that he was unable to locate this quotation. See footnote 525, page 276 of his translation of *Ibn al'Arabi: The Bezels of Wisdom*.
13. Qur'an 2:228.

JUDAISM

Midrashic Themes (c. 600–1300s CE)

While the talmudic and midrashic themes covered in chapter 3 of this volume appear in many medieval collections, new themes and significant reworkings of older themes emerged as well. The selections below are a sample of new interpretive developments concerning Adam and Eve that emerged during the medieval period. (Sources: Eli Yassif, "Pseudo Ben Sira, The Text, Its Literary Character and Status in the History of the Hebrew Story in the Middle Ages," 2 vols. (in Hebrew), Ph.D. diss., Hebrew University, 1977, pp. 64-65, in Joseph Dan, "Samuel, Lilith and the Concept of Evil in Early Kabbalah," *Association for Jewish Studies Review* 5 [1980]: 21; Gerald Friedlander, translator, *Pirke de Rabbi Eliezer*, New York: Hermon Press, 1965; M. Gaster, translator, *The Chronicles of Jerahmeel*, London: Royal Asiatic Society, 1899; Judah Goldin, translator, *The Fathers According to Rabbi Nathan*, New Haven: Yale University Press, 1955; The Fathers According to Rabbi Nathan (ARNB) as cited in Claude G. Montefiore and H. Loewe, editors, *A Rabbinic Anthology*, New York: Schocken Books, 1974, p. 507.)

The Creation of Lilith

The account below represents the earliest cohesive presentation of Lilith as Adam's first wife.

Alphabet of Ben Sira

When God created His world and created Adam, He saw that Adam was alone, and He immediately created a woman from earth, like him, for him, and named her Lilith. He brought her to Adam, and they immediately began to fight: Adam said, "You shall lie below" and Lilith said, "You shall lie below, for we are equal and both of us were [created] from earth." They did not listen to each other. When Lilith saw the state of things, she uttered the Holy Name and flew into the air and fled. Adam immediately stood in prayer before God and said: "Master of the universe, see that the woman you gave me has already fled away." God immediately sent three angels and told them: "Go and fetch Lilith; if she agrees to come, bring her, and if she does not, bring her by force." The three angels went immediately and caught up with her in the [Red] Sea, in the place that the Egyptians were destined to die. They seized her and told her: "If you agree to come with us, come, and if not, we shall drown you in the sea." She answered: "Darlings, I know myself that God created me only to afflict babies with fatal disease when they are eight days old; I shall have permission to harm them from their birth to the eighth day and no longer; when it is a male baby; but when it is a female baby, I shall have permission for twelve days." The angels would not leave her alone, until she swore by God's name that wherever she would see them or their names in an amulet, she would not possess the baby [bearing it]. They then left her immediately. This is [the story of] Lilith who afflicts babies with disease.

Woman: God's Answer to God's Problem

An earlier solution to the problem of distinguishing humankind from God was God's creation of sleep (see *Gen. Rab.* 8.10). In the *Pirke de Rabbi Eliezer*, however, God solves this problem by creating woman and making propagation possible.

Pirke de Rabbi Eliezer, Chapter 12

And (Adam) was at his leisure in the garden of Eden, like one of the ministering angels. The Holy One, blessed be He, said: I am alone in My world and this one (Adam) also is alone in his world. There is no propagation before Me and this one (Adam) has no propagation in his life; hereafter all creatures will say: Since there was no propagation in his life, it is he who has created us. It is not good for man to be alone, as it is said, "And the Lord God said, It is not good for man to be alone; I will make him an help meet for him . . . " (Gen. 2:18).

Adam Had One Wife, Not Ten!

In the selection below, the practice of monogamy is defended by an appeal to Adam and Eve's monogamous marriage.

The Fathers According to Rabbi Nathan (Version B), Chapter 2

Job said, "I made a covenant with mine eyes that I would not look upon a maid" (31:1). R. Judah b. Bathyra said: Job was entitled to look upon an unmarried woman, since he could have married her himself, or given her as wife to one of his sons or relations, but he said, "If it had been fitting for Adam to have been given ten wives, God would have given them to him, yet He gave him but one. So I, too, will be satisfied with one wife and my one portion."

Prince Sammael and the Serpent

In the *Pirke de Rabbi Eliezer* the Satanic figure of Sammael is the skillful hand behind the serpent's actions. The passage below details Sammael's appearance and actions.

Pirke de Rabbi Eliezer, Chapter 13

Sammael was the great prince in heaven; the Chajjoth had four wings and the Seraphim had six wings, and Sammael had twelve wings. What did Sammael do? He took his band and descended and saw all the creatures which the Holy One, blessed be He, had created in His world and he found among them none so skilled to do evil as the serpent, as it is said, "Now the serpent was more subtle than any beast of the field" (Gen. 3:1). Its appearance was something like that of the camel, and he mounted and rode upon it. The Torah began to cry aloud, saying, Why, O Sammael! now that the world is created, is it the time to rebel against the Omnipresent? Is it like a time when thou shouldst lift up thyself on high? The Lord of the world "will laugh at the horse and its rider" (Job 39:18).

Adam: The Cause of Eve's Disobedience

In talmudic and earlier midrashic sources, Adam is described as making a "hedge" around God's command in Genesis 2. In *The Fathers According to Rabbi Nathan*, however, Adam's "hedge" is clearly blamed for Eve's actions.

The Fathers According to Rabbi Nathan (Version A), Chapter 1

What is the hedge which Adam made about his words? Lo, it says, *And the Lord God commanded the man, saying: Of every tree of the garden thou mayest freely eat; but of the tree of the knowledge of good and evil, thou shalt not eat of it; for in the day that thou eatest thereof thou shalt surely die* (Gen. 2:16-17). Adam, however, did not wish to speak to Eve the way the Holy One, blessed be He, had spoken to him. Rather, this is what he said to her: *But of the fruit of the tree which is in the midst of the garden, God hath said: Ye shall not eat of it, neither shall ye touch it, lest ye die* (Gen. 3:3).

At that time the wicked serpent thought in his heart as follows: Since I cannot trip up Adam, I shall go and trip up Eve. So he went and sat down beside her, and entered into a long conversation with her. He said to her, "If it is against touching the tree thou sayest the Holy One, blessed be He, commanded us—behold, I shall touch it and not die. Thou, too, if thou touch it, shalt not die!" What did the wicked serpent do? He then arose and touched the tree with his hands and feet, and shook it until its fruits fell to the ground.

. . . Furthermore, the serpent said to her, "If it is against eating of the fruit of the tree thou sayest the Holy One, blessed be He, commanded us, behold I shall eat of it and not die. Thou too, if thou eat of it shalt not die!" What did Eve think in her mind? "All the things about which my master admonished me at first are false"—for at first Eve addressed Adam only as "my master." Forthwith she took of the fruit and ate. . . .

What led to Eve's touching the tree? It was the hedge which Adam put around his words.

Sammael and Eve Punished

Pirke de Rabbi Eliezer ascribes the fall of the angelic hosts to Sammael's role in Adam and Eve's disobedience. It also expands Eve's curses by adding several new punishments.

Pirke de Rabbi Eliezer, Chapter 14

He cast down Sammael and his troop from their holy place in heaven, and cut off the feet of the serpent. . . . He gave the woman nine curses and death: the afflictions arising from menstruation and the tokens of virginity; the affliction of conception in the womb; and the affliction of child-birth; and the affliction of bringing up children; and her head is covered like a mourner, and it is not shaved except on account of immorality, and her ear is pierced like (the ears of) perpetual slaves; and like a hand-maid she waits upon her husband; and she is not believed in (a matter of) testimony; and after all these (curses comes) death.

The Children of Eve and Sammael

While talmudic sources suggest a sexual union between Eve and the serpent, *Pirke de Rabbi Eliezer* presents Eve coupling with Sammael, and Cain as the fruit of this illicit union.

Pirke de Rabbi Eliezer, Chapters 21–22

(Sammael) riding on the serpent came to her, and she conceived; afterwards Adam came to her, and she conceived Abel. . . .

"And Adam lived an hundred and thirty years, and he begat in his own likeness after his image" (Gen. 5:3). Hence thou mayest learn that Cain was not of Adam's seed, nor after his likeness, nor after his image.

The Children of Adam and Lilith

As the previous section presented Eve's coupling with Sammael, so the selection from the *Chronicles of Jerahmeel* below presents Adam's illicit union with Lilith and the demonic hordes which it spawned.

Chronicles of Jerahmeel, Chapter 23

(1) Know and understand that, when Adam was separated for 130 years from Eve, he slept alone, and the first Eve—that is, Lilith—found him, and being charmed with his beauty, went and lay by his side, and there were begotten from her demons, spirits, and imps in thousands and myriads, and whomever they lighted upon they injured and killed outright, until Methushelah appeared and besought the mercy of God.

The Children of Adam and Eve

Different traditions suggested different numbers for Adam and Eve's progeny. The selection from the *Chronicles of Jerahmeel* below is unusual in that it not only numbers the children, but provides a complete set of names for the them as well.

Chronicles of Jerahmeel, Chapter 26

(1) Adam begat three sons and three daughters, Cain and his twin wife Qalmana, Abel and his twin wife Deborah, and Seth and his twin wife Noba. (2) And Adam, after he had begotten Seth, lived 700 years, and there were eleven sons and eight daughters born to him. These are the names of his sons: 'Eli, Sheel, Surei, 'Almiel, Berokh, Ke'al, Nahath, Zarhamah, Sisha, Mahtel,

and 'Anat . . . ; and the names of his daughters are: Havah, Gitsh, Hare, Bikha, Zifath, Hekhiah, Shaba, and 'Azin.

Rashi

The commentary of Rashi (Rabbi Shlomo ben Yitzhaki, 1040-1105) on the Torah/Pentateuch is the most widely studied of all the medieval Jewish commentaries. Famous for his interest in the "plain" sense of scripture, Rashi nevertheless makes ample reference to midrashic and talmudic sources. Some of his more interesting observations for our study include: comments on hierarchical relationships (Gen. 1:26); the subject and object of God's command "to subdue" (Gen. 1:28); the meaning of "naked" (Gen. 3:7); and the serpent's plot to kill Adam (Gen. 3:15). (Source: Morris Rosenbaum and Abraham M. Silbermann, translators, *Pentateuch with Targum Onkelos, Haphtaroth and Prayers for Sabbath and Rashi's Commentary: Genesis*, London: Shapiro, Vallentine & Co., 1946.)

Commentary on the Pentateuch (c. late 1000s CE)
RASHI

Genesis 1:26–28

26 . . . WE WILL MAKE MAN—The meekness of the Holy One, blessed be He, they (the Rabbis) learned from here; because the man is in the likeness of the angels and they might envy him, therefore He took counsel with them (see *Gen. Rab.* 8). And when He judges the kings He likewise consults His heavenly council, for thus we find in the case of Ahab to whom Micha said, (1 Kings 22:19) "I saw the Lord sitting on His throne, and all the host of heaven standing by Him on His right hand and on His left." Has God, then, a right hand and a left hand? But it means that some stood on the right side to plead in favour of the accused and others stood on the left side to accuse; and similarly we read (Dan. 4:14), "the matter is by the decree of the watchers, and the sentence by the word of the holy ones,"—here, also, He consulted His heavenly council and asked permission of them, saying to them: "There are in the heavens beings after My likeness; if there will not be on earth also beings after My likeness, there will be envy among the beings that I have created." . . . WE WILL MAKE MAN—Although they did not assist Him in forming him (the man) and although this use of the plural may give the heretics an occasion to rebel (i.e. to argue in favour of their own views); yet the verse does not refrain from teaching proper conduct and the virtue of humbleness, namely, that the greater should consult, and take permission from the smaller; for had it been written, "I shall make man," we could not, then, have learned that He spoke to His judicial council but to Himself. And as a refutation of the heretics it is written immediately after this verse "And God created the man"; and it is not written "and they created.". . . IN OUR IMAGE—

in our type. . . . AFTER OUR LIKENESS—with the power to comprehend and to discern. . . . AND THEY SHALL HAVE DOMINION OVER THE FISH . . . [AND OVER THE BEASTS]—. . . may imply dominion as well as descending—if he is worthy, he dominates over the beasts and cattle, if he is not worthy he will sink lower than them, and the beast will rule over him. (27) . . . SO GOD CREATED THE MAN IN HIS IMAGE—in the type that was specially made for him, for everything else was created by a creative fiat, whilst he was brought into existence by a creative act (lit. by hand), as it is said (Ps. 139:5) "And Thou hast laid thy hand upon me." He was made by a seal as a coin that is made by a die that is called in O.F. coin. It is similarly said, (Job 38:14) "it is changed as clay under the seal." . . . IN THE IMAGE OF GOD CREATED HE HIM—It explains to you that the form prepared for him was the form of the image of his Creator. . . . MALE AND FEMALE CREATED HE THEM—And further on (2:21) it is said: "and He took one of his ribs etc." (The two passages appear to be contradictory.) But according to a Midrashic explanation ('Erub. 18a), He created him at first with two faces, and afterwards He divided him. But the real sense of the verse is: here it tells you that both of them were created on the sixth day, but it does not explain to you how their creation took place; this it explains to you in another place (2:8). (28) . . . AND SUBDUE IT—The word . . . may be read as meaning: and subdue her (i.e. the woman), thereby teaching you that the male controls the female in order that she may not become a gad-about; teaching you also that to the man, whose nature is to master, was given the Divine command to have issue, and not to the woman.

Genesis 2:18, 20–25

(18) . . . IT IS NOT GOOD etc.—I shall make an help meet for him in order that people may not say that there are two Deities, the Holy One, blessed be He, the only One among the celestial Beings without a mate, and this one (Adam), the only one among the terrestrial beings, without a mate (Pirke d'R. Eliezer 12). . . . A HELP MEET FOR HIM—(kenegdo lit., opposite, opposed to him). If he is worthy she shall be a help to him; if he is unworthy she shall be opposed to him, to fight him.

(20–21) . . . FOR THE MAN HE HAD NOT FOUND A HELP MEET FOR HIM . . . AND THE ETERNAL GOD CAUSED AN OVERPOWERING SLEEP TO FALL—When He brought them, He brought them before him male and female of each and every kind. Thereupon he said: all these have a mate, but I have no mate! Immediately He caused to fall [an overpowering sleep upon him] (Gen. R. 17). (21) . . . OF HIS RIBS—The word means of his sides, similar to (Exod. 26:20) . . . "and for the second side of the tabernacle"; this has a bearing upon what they (the Sages) say ('Erub. 18a): They were created with two faces (sides). . . . AND HE CLOSED UP the place where it was cut. . . . AND HE SLEPT AND then HE TOOK in order that he should not see the piece of flesh out of which she was created, for she might be despised by him (*Sanh.* 39a). (22) . . . AND HE FORMED (lit. He built)—as a structure, wide below and narrower above for bearing the child, just as a wheat-store is wide below and narrower above so that its weight should not strain the walls. . . . AND HE MADE THE RIB INTO A WOMAN. . . . (23) . . . THIS NOW—This teaches that Adam endeavored to find a companion among all cattle and beasts, but found no satisfaction except in Eve (*Yebam.* 63a). . . . THIS SHALL BE CALLED WOMAN, BECAUSE THIS WAS TAKEN OUT OF MAN—Here we have a kind of play upon words (the words *ishshah* and *ish* sounding similar): hence we may learn that the language used at the time of the Creation was the Holy Tongue (Hebrew). (24) . . . THEREFORE A MAN LEAVETH—The Divine Spirit says this, thus prohibiting immoral relationship to the "Sons of Noah" also (*Sanh.* 57b). . . . ONE FLESH—Both parents are united in the child. (25) . . . AND THEY WERE NOT ASHAMED—for they did not know what modestly meant, so as to distinguish between good and evil. Although he (Adam) had been endowed with knowledge to give names to all creatures, yet the evil inclination did not become an active principle in him until he had eaten of the tree, when it entered into him and he became aware of the differences between good and evil.

Genesis 3:1–16

(1) . . . AND THE SERPENT WAS MORE SUBTLE—What connection is there between the following narrative and the statement just made? The latter should have been followed by: "and He [the Lord God] made for Adam and his wife garments of skin and clothed them" (3:21), but Scripture informs you with what plan the serpent assailed them: he saw them naked and unashamed and he coveted her (Eve) (*Gen. R.* 18). . . . MORE SUBTLE THAN ALL—Corresponding with his subtleness and his greatness was his downfall; "more subtle than all"—"more cursed than all" (see v. 14), (*Gen. R.* 19). . . . ALTHOUGH GOD HATH SAID—The meaning is, "Perhaps He has said unto you" . . . YE SHALL NOT EAT OF EVERY TREE OF THE GARDEN—And although he saw them eating of the other fruits yet he entered into a long conversation with her so that she should answer him, and so that he might then have an opportunity to talk about that particular tree. (3) . . . NEITHER SHALL YE TOUCH IT—She added to God's command (which did not forbid touching the tree, but only eating of its fruit) therefore she was led to diminish from it. It is to this that the text refers (Prov. 30:6): "Add thou not unto His words" (*Gen. R.* 19). (4) . . . YE SHALL NOT SURELY DIE—He pushed her until she touched it. He then said to her, "Just as there is no death in touching it, so there is no death in eating it" (*Gen. R.* 19). (5) . . . FOR [GOD] KNOWS—Every artisan detests his fellow-artisans ("Two of a trade never agree"). The serpent suggested to her: God ate of the tree and created the world (*Gen. R.* 19) so if you eat . . . YE WILL BE AS GOD—Creators of worlds. (6) . . . AND THE WOMAN SAW—She ap-

proved the words of the serpent—they pleased her and she believed him (*Gen. R.* 19). . . . THAT THE TREE WAS GOOD to make her become like God. . . . AND THAT IT WAS A DELIGHT TO THE EYES—even as he had said to her: "then your eyes shall be opened". . . . AND IT WAS TO BE DESIRED TO MAKE ONE WISE—even as he had said to her: "knowing good and evil". . . . AND SHE GAVE ALSO TO HER HUSBAND so that she should not die and he remain alive to take another wife (*Gen. R.* 19). The word . . . also, may be understood to include cattle and beasts (that is, that she gave to these and also to her husband). (7) . . . [AND THE EYES OF BOTH OF THEM] WERE UNCLOSED—Scripture speaks here with reference to intelligence (the mind's eye) and not with reference to actual seeing; the end of the verse proves this for it states, . . . AND THEY KNEW THAT THEY WERE NAKED—Even a blind person knows when he is naked! What then does "and they knew that they were naked" signify? One charge had been entrusted to them and they now knew they had stripped themselves of it (*Gen. R.* 19). . . . FIG LEAVES—This was the tree of which they had eaten; by the very thing through which their ruin had been caused was some improvement effected in their condition (*Sanh.* 70b). The other trees however prevented them from taking of their leaves. And why is not the name of the tree clearly mentioned? Because the Holy One, blessed be He, never wishes to grieve anything He has created: hence its name is not mentioned in order that it might not be put to shame by people saying, "This is the tree through which the world suffered" (*Midrash R. Tanchuma*). (8) . . . AND THEY HEARD— There are many Midrashic explanations and our Teachers have already collected them in their appropriate places in *Bereshith Rabbah* and in other Midrashim. I, however, am only concerned with the plain sense of Scripture and with such Agadoth that explain the words of Scripture in a manner that fits in with them. . . . AND THEY HEARD—What did they hear? They heard the sound of the Holy One, blessed be He, as He walked in the garden (see *Gen. R.* 19). . . . IN THE WIND OF THE DAY—(*ruah* is used also in the meaning of direction, north, east, etc.) in that direction in which the sun travels . . . which is the west, for towards evening the sun is in the west, and they committed the sin in the tenth hour (*Sanh.* 38b). (9) . . . WHERE ART THOU—He knew where he was, but He asked this in order to open up a conversation with him that he should not become confused in his reply, if He were to pronounce punishment against him all of a sudden. Similarly in the case of Cain, He said to him, (4:9) "where is Abel thy brother?" Similarly with Balaam, (Num. 22:9) "what men are these with thee?"—to open up a conversation with them; so, also, in the case of Hezekiah with reference to the messengers of Merodach-baladan (Isa. 39:3). (11) . . . WHO TOLD THEE?— Whence has the knowledge come to you what shame there is in standing naked? . . . HAST THOU EATEN OF THE TREE. . . . (12) . . . WHOM THOU GAVEST TO BE WITH ME—Here he showed his ingratitude (*Ab. Zar.* 5b). (13) . . . HE DECEIVED ME; we find the word in the same meaning in (2 Chron. 32:15), "Now therefore let not Hezekiah beguile you" (*Gen.*

R. 19). (14) ... BECAUSE THOU HAST DONE THIS—From here we infer that we should not occupy ourselves with what may be in favour of one who seduces people to idolatry, for had He asked it, "Why hast thou done this?", it could have answered Him, "When the words of the teacher and those of the pupil are contradictory whose orders should be obeyed?" (*Sanh.* 29a) (i.e. if You told them one thing and I another, should they not have obeyed You?). ... FROM AMONG (or, MORE THAN) ALL CATTLE AND ALL THE BEASTS OF THE FIELD—If it was cursed more than the cattle whose period of gestation is longer than that of beasts does it not necessarily follow that it was cursed more than the beasts? Our Rabbis have definitely established the correctness of the following deduction in treatise *Berakoth* (8a), that is (viz., the use of these apparently superfluous words "and more than all the beasts of the field") teaches that the period of gestation of the serpent is seven years. ... UPON THY BELLY SHALT THOU GO—It had feet but they were cut off (*Gen. R.* 20). (15) ... AND I WILL SET ENMITY—Your sole intention was that Adam should die by eating it first and that you should then take Eve for yourself, and you came to speak to Eve first only because women are easily influenced and know how to influence their husbands; therefore "I shall put enmity [between thee and the woman]." ... HE WILL BRUISE (or, POUND) THEE—Like (Deut. 9:21), "And I beat in pieces" which Onkelos translates ... "I pounded it." ... AND THOU SHALT BRUISE HIS HEEL—As you will have no height (not stand erect) you will be able to bite him only on the heel, but even at that spot you will kill him. ... (16) ... THY PAIN—viz., the trouble of rearing children (*'Erub.* 100b). ... AND THY CONCEPTION—viz., the pain of pregnancy. ... IN PAIN THOU SHALT BEAR CHILDREN—This refers to the pangs of childbirth (Erub. 100b). ... THY DESIRE—Similar to (Isa. 29:8), ... "and his soul hath appetite" (desires).

Genesis 4:1

(1) ... AND THE MAN KNEW already before the events related above took place—before he sinned and was driven out of the Garden of Eden. So, also, the conception and birth of Cain took place before this. ... she meant to say: when He created me and my husband He created us by Himself, but in the case of this one we are copartners with Him (cf. *Niddah* 31a). ... —The threefold *'t* signify extension of the scope of the text, teaching that a twin sister was born with Cain, and that with Abel two were born; consequently the text states ... "and she bore more" than the previous time (*Gen. R.* 22).

Nahmanides

An outstanding Talmudist of his day, Nahmanides (Rabbi Moses ben Nahman, "Ramban" 1195-1270) often refutes Rashi's conclusions. A good example of this can be seen below in Nahmanides's insistence that women's subordination to men was not part of the created order (see Rashi on Genesis 1:28) but a result of woman's disobedience. Other significant comments on gender by Nahmanides concern sexual intercourse (before and after the disobedience) and the interpretation of "one flesh" in Genesis 2:24. (Source: Jacob Newman, translator, *The Commentary of Nahmanides on Genesis Chapters 1-6*, Leiden: E. J. Brill, 1960.)

Commentary on the Torah (c. 1200s CE)
NAHMANIDES

Genesis 1:26

In Gen. R. they have said: " 'Let the earth bring forth the living creature after its kind': says R. Eliezer, by *'nephesh haya'* (living souls) is meant the spirit of the first man." Now we cannot suppose for a moment that R. Eliezer means that the words "let the earth bring forth" should be explained as referring to the soul of the first man. He means, however, what I have mentioned, namely, that the formation of the man with his breath, that is to say, the soul which is in the blood, was (made) from the earth by means of the same command as produced the beasts, and the cattle. For all the motion-giving souls were made together, and afterwards He created for them bodies. He made first the bodies of the cattle and the beasts, and afterwards the body of the man, and placed in him this soul. Later again He breathed into him a higher soul (*neshamah*). It is concerning that separable soul in him that a special commandment was issued and ascribed to God who bestowed it, as it is written "and He breathed into his nostrils the breath of life." The explanation of this in the way of truth will be known to the person who understands the following verse. It may be that R. Eliezer had this in mind when in explanation of the words "let the earth bring forth" he added the remark, "the earth of life," meaning that it should bring forth a living soul of its kind enduring for ever. So also we explain "male and female created He them," to mean that creation was in the first instance male and female and his soul was included in them, but the formation was a formation for man and building of a rib for a woman, as is related subsequently. That is why he uses here the term "creation" and in the later chapter the term "formation." And the wise person will understand.

Genesis 2:9

9. *The tree of life also in the midst of the garden, and the tree of knowledge of good and evil. . . .* The tree of life was a tree the fruit of which gave to those that ate it long life. Of the tree of knowledge of good and evil, the commentators say that its fruit produced the desire for sexual intercourse, and therefore they covered their nakedness after they had eaten thereof. They quote as a parallel to this expression, the words used by Barzillai the Gileadite, "Can I discern between good and bad," because the sexual desire was no longer felt by him. But

in my opinion this is not correct. For it says "and ye shall be as God, knowing good and evil." And if you should say that he lied to her, we have the verse: "And the Lord God said: 'Behold, the man is become as one of us, to know good and evil.' " And besides they have said: "Three spoke the truth and perished from the world, and these are they: the serpent, the spies, and Doeg the Edomite." The proper explanation in my eyes is, that the man used to do naturally what it is fitting to do according to nature, as is done by the heavens and all their hosts which are faithful workers whose work is faithfully done and who do not deviate from their prescribed task, and in whose work there is no love nor hatred. The fruit of this tree, however, produced in those that ate it the will and the desire to chose between a thing and its opposite, whether for good or for evil. It is called, therefore, "the tree of knowledge of good and evil," because the word "knowledge" is used in our language for "will." . . .

Now at that time intercourse between the man and his wife was not to gratify desire. They came simply together at the time of begetting and propagated. Therefore all the limbs were in their eyes like the face and the hands and they were not ashamed of them. But after he had eaten from the tree, choice was in his hand and it depended on his own will to do evil or good either to himself or to others.

Genesis 2:18

18. *It is not good that the man should be alone*: It is not likely that the man had been created from the beginning to be alone in the world and that he should not beget children, because all that were created were created male and female of all flesh created to propagate seed. The herb and the tree also have their seed in them. The most probable opinion is that of him who says, "They were created with two faces"; they were made in such a way that there should be in them a natural impulse bringing a generative force into the organs of propagation from the male to the female, or you may explain "seed" on the lines of the well-known dispute concerning pregnancy, and that the second face was a help to the first in its propagation. The Holy One b.b.H. [blessed be He] saw that it was good that the help should face the man and that he should see it and separate from it or join it according to his will. And this is what he says: "I will make him a help meet for him." The point of the words "It is not good that the man should be alone" is that it cannot be said of him "that it is good" when he is alone, because in this way he will not be preserved, for in the work of creation good means preservation, as I have explained on the words "and God saw that it was good."

Genesis 2:24

24. *Therefore shall a man leave his father and his mother and shall cleave unto his wife, etc.*: The holy spirit says this in order to prohibit forbidden degrees of marriage to the "Sons of Noah" (also) *That they may become as one flesh*: "the child is formed through both of them and there their flesh becomes one." So

Rashi. This, however, is pointless. For cattle and beasts also become one flesh in their offspring. The correct (interpretation) in my opinion is, that the cattle and the beast have no attachment to their females, but the male will copulate with any female he finds and they will bear to them. For this reason the verse says that because the female of the man was bone of his bones and flesh of his flesh and he cleaved unto her and she clung to his bosom like his own flesh and he desired to have her continually with him, and as this was the case with Adam, so was his nature implanted in his offspring so that the males among them should cleave to their wives, leaving their father and their mother and looking upon their wives as if they were with them one flesh. For "one flesh" compare "for he is our brother, our flesh," and "to any that is near of kin to him," i.e. those who are near in the family. Thus a man should leave the kinship of his father and his mother and his female relatives and he should see to it that his wife is nearer to him than they are.

Genesis 3:12

12. By the words: *The woman Thou gavest to be with me*: Adam meant to say that the woman whom your Honour gave to me to be of help, she gave me of the tree, and I thought that everything she would say to me would be of help and advantage to me. Hence God said when punishing him: "Because thou hast hearkened unto the voice of thy wife" you had no right to transgress my commandments on account of her advice.

Our Rabbis call him here "Unappreciative of kindness." They would have us understand that he (Adam) answered Him: You have caused me this downfall, for you have given me a wife to be a help and she advised me to do evil.

Genesis 3:16

16. *And thy desire shall be to thy husband*: "for intercourse, and yet you will not have the face to ask for it with your mouth, but 'he shall rule over thee,' everything shall be from him and not from you"; so Rashi. But it is not correct, for this is praiseworthy in a woman, as they have said: "and this is a good quality in women." R. Abraham explains that: "Thy desire shall be to thy husband" means "thy obedience." The meaning is that you will have to hearken to all the commands he will give you, for you are under his control to do his will. But I have not found the word "*teshuqah*" (desire) save as applied to desire and lust. In my opinion the correct explanation is that He punished her (by decreeing) that she should long exceedingly for her husband and not pay heed to the pains of pregnancy and childbirth, and that he should keep her like maidservant; and it is not the custom of a servant to desire to obtain a master for himself, but he would rather be able to escape from him whenever he wants, and this is measure for measure, for she gave to her husband also and he ate at her command, and so her punishment was that so far from her commanding him but he should command her, to do whatever he pleased.

Maimonides

Without question, Maimonides (Moses ben Maimon, "Rambam" 1135-1204) is the most significant Jewish philosopher of the medieval period. His treatise, *The Guide for the Perplexed*, from which we have included two selections below, reflects his use of rationalism and allegory in his interpretation of Genesis 1-3. For Maimonides, Adam is both first and every human. (Source: Moses Maimonides, *The Guide for the Perplexed*, translated by M. Friedländer, 2nd ed., New York: Dover, 1956 [1904].)

The Guide for the Perplexed (c. late 1100s CE)
MAIMONIDES

On Genesis 3.5, part I, chap. 2

Some years ago a learned man asked me a question of great importance; the problem and the solution which we gave in our reply deserve the closest attention. Before, however, entering upon this problem and its solution I must premise that every Hebrew knows that the term *Elohim* is a homonym, and denotes God, angels, judges, and the rulers of countries, and that Onkelos the proselyte explained it in the true and correct manner by taking *Elohim* in the sentence, "and ye shall be like *Elohim*" (Gen. 3:5) in the last mentioned meaning, and rendering the sentence "and ye shall be like princes." Having pointed out the homonymity of the term "*Elohim*" we return to the question under consideration. "It would at first sight," said the objector, "appear from Scripture that man was originally intended to be perfectly equal to the rest of the animal creation, which is not endowed with intellect, reason, or power of distinguishing between good and evil: but that Adam's disobedience to the command of God procured him that great perfection which is the peculiarity of man, viz., the power of distinguishing between good and evil—the noblest of all the faculties of our nature, the essential characteristic of the human race. It thus appears strange that the punishment for rebelliousness should be the means of elevating man to a pinnacle of perfection to which he had not attained previously. This is equivalent to saying that a certain man was rebellious and extremely wicked, wherefore his nature was changed for the better, and he was made to shine as a star in the heavens." Such was the purport and subject of the question, though not in the exact words of the inquirer. Now mark our reply, which was as follows: —You appear to have studied the matter superficially, and nevertheless you imagine that you can understand a book which has been the guide of past and present generations, when you for a moment withdraw from your lusts and appetites, and glance over its contents as if you were reading a historical work or some poetical composition. Collect your thoughts and examine the matter carefully, for it is not to be understood as you at first sight think, but as you will find after due deliberation; namely, the intellect which was granted to man as the highest endowment, was bestowed on him before his disobedience. With reference to this gift the Bible states that "man was created in the form and likeness of God." On account of this gift of intellect man was addressed by God, and received His commandments, as it is said: "And the Lord God commanded Adam" (Gen. 2:16)—for no commandments are given to the brute creation or to those who are devoid of understanding. Through the intellect man distinguishes between the true and the false. This faculty Adam possessed perfectly and completely. The right and the wrong are terms employed in the science of apparent truth (morals), not in that of necessary truths, as e.g., it is not correct to say, in reference to the proposition "the heavens are spherical," it is "good" or to declare the assertion that "the earth is flat" to be "bad"; but we say of the one it is true, of the other it is false. Similarly our language expresses the idea of true and false by the terms *emet* and *sheker*, of the morally right and the morally wrong, by *tob* and *ra'*. Thus it is the function of the intellect to discriminate between the true and the false—a distinction which is applicable to all objects of intellectual perception. When Adam was yet in a state of innocence, and was guided solely by reflection and reason—on account of which it is said: "Thou hast made him (man) little lower than the angels" (Ps. 8:6)—he was not at all able to follow or to understand the principles of apparent truths; the most manifest impropriety, viz., to appear in a state of nudity, was nothing unbecoming according to his idea: he could not comprehend why it should be so. After man's disobedience, however, when he began to give way to desires which had their source in his imagination and to the gratification of his bodily appetites, as it is said, "And the wife saw that the tree was good for food and delightful to the eyes" (Gen. 3:6), he was punished by the loss of part of that intellectual faculty which he had previously possessed. He therefore transgressed a command with which he had been charged on the score of his reason; and having obtained a knowledge of the apparent truths, he was wholly absorbed in the study of what is proper and what improper. Then he fully understood the magnitude of the loss he had sustained, what he had forfeited, and in what situation he was thereby placed. Hence we read, "And ye shall be like *elohim*, knowing good and evil," and not "knowing" or "discerning the true and false": while in necessary truths we can only apply the words "true and false," not "good and evil." Further observe the passage, "And the eyes of both were opened, and they knew they were naked" (Gen. 3:7): it is not said, "And the eyes of both were opened, and they *saw*"; for what the man had seen previously and what he saw after this circumstance was precisely the same; there had been no blindness which was now removed, but he received a new faculty whereby he found things wrong which previously he had not regarded as wrong. Besides, you must know that the Hebrew word *pakah* used in this passage is exclusively employed in the figurative sense of receiving new sources of knowledge, not in that of regaining the sense of sight. Comp., "God opened her eyes" (Gen. 21:19). "Then shall the eyes of the blind be opened" (Isa. 38:8). "Open ears, he heareth not" (Isa. 42:20), similar in sense to the verse, "Which have eyes to see, and see not" (Ezek. 12:2). When, however,

Scripture says of Adam, "He changed his face (*panav*) and thou sentest him forth" (Job 14:20), it must be understood in the following way: On account of the change of his original aim he was sent away. For *panim*, the Hebrew equivalent of face, is derived from the verb *panah*, "he turned," and signifies also "aim," because man generally turns his face towards the things he desires. In accordance with this interpretation, our text suggests that Adam, as he altered his intention and directed his thoughts to the acquisition of what he was forbidden, he was banished from Paradise: this was his punishment; it was measure for measure. At first he had the privilege of tasting pleasure and happiness, and of enjoying repose and security; but as his appetites grew stronger, and he followed his desires and impulses (as we have already stated above), and partook of the food he was forbidden to taste, he was deprived of everything, was doomed to subsist on the meanest kind of food, such as he never tasted before, and this even only after exertion and labour, as it is said, "Thorns and thistles shall grow up for thee" (Gen. 3:18), "By the sweat of thy brow," etc., and in explanation of this the text continues, "And the Lord God drove him from the Garden of Eden, to till the ground whence he was taken." He was now with respect to food and many other requirements brought to the level of the lower animals; comp., "Thou shalt eat the grass of the field" (Gen. 3:18). Reflecting on his condition, the Psalmist says, "Adam unable to dwell in dignity, was brought to the level of the dumb beast" (Ps. 49:13).

"May the Almighty be praised, whose design and wisdom cannot be fathomed."

On Genesis 1–4, part II, chap. 30

The following point now claims our attention. The account of the six days of creation contains, in reference to the creation of man, the statement: "Male and female created he them" (1:27), and concludes with the words: "Thus the heavens and the earth were finished, and all the host of them" (2:1), and yet the portion which follows describes the creation of Eve from Adam, the tree of life, and the tree of knowledge, the history of the serpent and the events connected therewith, and all this as having taken place after Adam had been placed in the Garden of Eden. All our Sages agree that this took place on the sixth day, and that nothing new was created after the close of the six days. None of the things mentioned above is therefore impossible, because the laws of Nature were then not yet permanently fixed. There are, however, some utterances of our Sages on this subject [which apparently imply a different view]. I will gather them from their different sources and place them before you, and I will refer also to certain things by mere hints, just as has been done by the Sages. You must know that their words, which I am about to quote, are most perfect, most accurate, and clear to those for whom they were said. I will therefore not add long explanations, lest I make their statements plain, and I might thus become "a revealer of secrets," but I will give them in a certain order, accompanied with a few remarks, which will suffice for readers like you.

One of these utterances is this: "Adam and Eve were at first created as one being, having their backs united; they were then separated, and one half was removed and brought before Adam as Eve." The term *mi-zal'otav* (lit. "of his ribs") signifies "of his sides." The meaning of the word is proved by referring to *zel'a*, "the side" of the tabernacle (Exod. 26:20), which Onkelos renders *setar* ("side"), and so also *mi-zal'otav* is rendered by him "*mi-sitrohi*" (of his sides). Note also how clearly it has been stated that Adam and Eve were two in some respects, and yet they remained one, according to the words, "Bone of my bones, and flesh of my flesh" (Gen. 2:23). The unity of the two is proved by the fact that both have the same name, for she is called *ishshah* (woman), because she was taken out of *ish* (man), also by the words, "And shall cleave unto his wife, and they shall be one flesh" (2:24). How great is the ignorance of those who do not see that all this necessarily includes some [other] idea [besides the literal meaning of the words]. This is now clear.

Another noteworthy Midrashic remark of our Sages is the following: "The serpent had a rider, the rider was as big as a camel, and it was the rider that enticed Eve; this rider was Samael." Samael is the name generally applied by our Sages to Satan. Thus they say in several places that Satan desired to entice Abraham to sin, and to abstain from binding Isaac, and he desired also to persuade Isaac not to obey his father. At the same time they also say, in reference to the same subject, viz., the *Akedah* ("the binding of Isaac"), that *Samael* came to Abraham and said to him, "What! hast thou, being an old man, lost thy senses?" etc. This shows that Samael and Satan are identical. There is a meaning in this name [Samael], as there is also in the name *nahash* ("serpent"). In describing how the serpent came to entice Eve, our Sages say: "Samael was riding on it, and God was laughing at both the camel and its rider." It is especially of importance to notice that the serpent did not approach or address Adam, but all his attempts were directed against Eve, and it was through her that the serpent caused injury and death to Adam. The greatest hatred exists between the serpent and Eve, and between his seed and her seed; her seed being undoubtedly also the seed of man. More remarkable still is the way in which the serpent is joined to Eve, or rather his seed to her seed; the head of the one touches the heel of the other. Eve defeats the serpent by crushing its head, whilst the serpent defeats her by wounding her heel. This is likewise clear.

The following is also a remarkable passage, most absurd in its literal sense; but as an allegory it contains wonderful wisdom, and fully agrees with real facts, as will be found by those who understand all the chapters of this treatise. When the serpent came to Eve he infected her with poison; the Israelites, who stood at Mount Sinai, removed that poison; idolaters, who did not stand at Mount Sinai, have not got rid of it. Note this likewise. Again they said: "The tree of life extends over an area of five hundred years' journey, and it is from beneath it that all the waters of the creation sprang forth"; and they added the explanation that this measure referred to the thickness of its body, and not to the extent of its branches, for they continue thus: "Not the extent of the branches thereof, but the stem thereof [*korato*, lit. 'its beam,' signifying here 'its stem'] has a thickness of five hundred years' journey." This is now sufficiently clear. Again: "God has never shown the tree of knowledge [of good and evil] to man, nor will He ever show it." This is correct, for it must be so according to the nature of the Universe. Another noteworthy saying is this: "And the Lord God took the man, i.e., raised him, and placed him in the Garden of Eden," i.e., He gave him rest. The words "He took him," "He gave him," have no reference to position in space, but they indicate his position in rank among transient beings, and the prominent character of his existence. Remarkable and noteworthy is the great wisdom contained in the names of Adam, Cain, and Abel, and in the fact that it was Cain who slew Abel in the field, that both of them perished, although the murderer had some respite, and that the existence of mankind is due to Seth alone. Comp. "For God has appointed me another seed" (4:25). This has proved true.

Isaac Kohen

A Treatise on the Left Emanation by Isaac Kohen (Rabbi Isaac ben Jacob Ha-Kohen, c. 1200s) represents the earliest dated Jewish work in which Lilith is presented as the Satan's consort. As part of the pre-Zohar Kabbalistic tradition, Kohen's work presents a detailed description of the concept of evil. (Source: Joseph Dan, editor, and Ronald C. Kiener, translator, *The Early Kabbalah*, New York: Paulist Press, 1986, pp. 165-82.)

A Treatise on the Left Emanation (c. 1200s CE)
ISAAC KOHEN

6.

I will now set down the names of the princes of jealousy and enmity. Yet since their essence and their service is true and pure, their mouths are free from mendacity and neither lies nor falsehoods pass between them.

The first prince and accuser, the commander of jealousy, is evil Samael, accompanied by his retinue. He is called "evil" not because of his nature but because he desires to unite and intimately mingle with an emanation not of his nature, as we shall explain.

The second prince is called his deputy, and his name is Za'afi'el accompanied by his entourage.

The third prince is called third-in-command, and his name is Za'ami'el, accompanied by his staff.

The fourth prince is Qasfi'el, accompanied by his retinue.

The fifth prince is Ragzi'el, accompanied by his staff.

The sixth prince is 'Abri'el, accompanied by his staff.

The seventh is Meshulhi'el, accompanied by his staff. These latter comprise the delegation of evil angels.

Now I shall allude to you the reason for all the jealousy between these latter princes and the former princes of the seven groups of holy angels which are called "the guardians of the walls." A form destined for Samael stirs up enmity and jealousy between the heavenly delegation and the forces of the supernal army. This form is Lilith, and she is in the image of a feminine form. Samael takes on the form of Adam and Lilith the form of Eve. They were both born in a spiritual birth as one, as a parallel to the forms of Adam and Eve above and below: two twinlike forms. Both Samael and [Lilith, called] Eve the Matron—also known as the Northern One—are emanated from beneath the Throne of Glory. It was the Sin which brought about this calamity, in order to bring her shame and disgrace to destroy her celestial offspring. The calamity was caused by the Northern One, who was created beneath the Throne of Glory and it resulted in a partial collapse and weakening of the legs of the Throne. Then, by means of Gamali'el and the primeval snake Nahashi'el, the scents of each intermingled: the scent of man reached the female, and the scent of woman reached the male. Ever since then the snakes have increased and have taken on the form of biting snakes. Thus it is written, "The Lord sent fiery snakes among the people" (Num. 21:6). This requires a full explanation in a separate treatise for it is very deep—no one can find it out.

12.

We shall now discuss the third ether. The scholars of tradition said that it is a received tradition from their fathers that this ether is divided into three parts: an upper part, a middle part, and a lower part. The upper part was given over to Asmodeus, the great king of the demons. He does not have permission to accuse or cause confusion except on Mondays. We will expand on this in the treatise as best we can.

Even though Asmodeus is called the great king, he is subservient to Samael. He is called the great prince with reference to the emanations above him and the king of kings with reference to the emanations underneath him. Asmodeus is governed by him and is subservient to him.

Samael, the great prince and great king over all the demons, cohabits with the great Matron Lilith. Asmodeus, the king of the demons, cohabits with the Lesser [Younger] Lilith. The scholars of this tradition admit to many horrendous details concerning the forms of Samael and Asmodeus and the images of Lilith the bride of Samael and Lilith the bride of Asmodeus. Happy is he who merits this knowledge.

19.

In answer to your question concerning Lilith, I shall explain to you the essence of the matter. Concerning this point there is a received tradition from the ancient Sages who made use of the *Secret Knowledge of the Lesser Palaces*, which is the manipulation of demons and a ladder by which one ascends to the prophetic levels. In this tradition it is made clear that Samael and Lilith were born as one, similar to the form of Adam and Eve who were also born as one, reflecting what is above. This is the account of Lilith which was received by the Sages in the *Secret Knowledge of the Palaces*. The Matron Lilith is the mate of Samael. Both of them were born at the same hour in the image of Adam and Eve, intertwined in each other. Asmodeus the great king of the demons has as a mate the Lesser (younger) Lilith, daughter of the king whose name is Qafsefoni. The name of his mate is Mehetabel daughter of Matred, and their daughter is Lilith.

This is the exact text of what is written in *The Chapters of the Lesser Palaces* as we have received it, word for word and letter for letter. And the scholars of this wisdom possess a very profound tradition from the ancients. They found it stated in those *Chapters* that Samael, the great prince of them all, grew exceedingly jealous of Asmodeus the king of the demons because of this Lilith who is called Lilith the Maiden (the young). She is in the form of a beautiful woman from her head to her waist. But from the waist down she is burning fire—like mother like daughter. She is called Mehetabel daughter of Matred, and the meaning is something immersed (*mahu tabal*). The meaning here is that her intentions are never for the good. She only seeks to incite wars and various demons of war and the war between Daughter Lilith and Matron Lilith.

The Zohar

In the selections below, biblical verses are interpreted using midrashic traditions set against the backdrop of the kabbalah's symbol system. Three interesting ideas concerning gender issues are: (1) the image of God as Mother and Father, (2) the human task of gender integration, and (3) Adam's praise of woman/Eve. (Source: Harry Sperling and Maurice Simon, translators, *The Zohar: Volume 1*, London: Soncino Press, 1973.)

The Zohar (c. late 1200s CE)

Bereshith, 35a

We have stated that Adam and Eve were created side by side. Why were they not created face to face? Because "the Lord God had not yet caused it to rain upon the earth" (Gen. 2:5), and the union of heaven and earth was not yet firmly established. When the lower union was perfected and Adam and Eve were turned face to face, then the upper union was consummated. We know this from the case of the Tabernacle, of which we have learnt that another tabernacle was erected with it, and that the upper one was not raised till the lower one was raised; and similarly here. Further, since all was not yet in order above, Adam and Eve were not created face to face. The order of verses in the Scripture proves this: for first we read, "For the Lord God had not caused it to rain upon the earth," and then "there was not a man to till the ground,"

the meaning being that man was still defective, and only when Eve was perfected was he also perfected.

Bereshith, 36b

When they begat children, the first-born was the son of the (serpent's) slime.
For two beings had intercourse with Eve, and she conceived from both and
bore two children. Each followed one of the male parents, and their spirits
parted, one to this side and one to the other, and similarly their characters. On
the side of Cain are all the haunts of the evil species, from which come evil
spirits and demons and necromancers. From the side of Abel comes a more
merciful class, yet not wholly beneficial—good wine mixed with bad. The
right kind was not produced until Seth came, who is the first ancestor of all
the generations of the righteous, and from whom the world was propagated.

Bereshith, 47a

LET US MAKE MAN IN OUR IMAGE, AFTER OUR LIKENESS, i.e.
partaking of six directions, compounded of all, after the supernal pattern,
with limbs arranged so as to suggest the esoteric Wisdom, altogether an exceptional creature. "Let us make man": the word *adam* (man) implies male and
female, created wholly through the supernal and holy Wisdom. "In our image,
after our likeness": the two being combined, so that man should be unique in
the world and ruler over all.

Bereshith, 48b

The function of lighting the Sabbath light has been entrusted to the women
of the holy people: as the colleagues put it, "woman put out the light of the
world and brought darkness, etc."; and so we agree. There is, however, a more
esoteric reason. This tabernacle of peace is the Matron of the world, and the
souls which are the celestial lamp abide in her. Hence it behooves the matron
to kindle the light, because thereby she is attaching herself to her rightful
place and performing her rightful function. A woman should kindle the
Sabbath light with zest and gladness, because it is a great honour for her, and,
further, she qualifies herself thereby to become the mother of holy offspring
who will grow to be shining lights of learning and piety and will spread peace
in the world, and she also procures long life for her husband. . . .

AND THE LORD GOD BUILT (*vayiven*) THE SIDE WHICH HE
HAD TAKEN FROM THE MAN, ETC. . . . INTO A WOMAN: to be
linked with the flame of the left side, because the Torah was given from the
side of *Geburah*. Further, *ishah* (woman) may be analysed into *esh he* (fire of *he*),
signifying the union of the two. AND HE BROUGHT HER TO THE
MAN: as much as to say that the Oral Torah must not be studied by itself, but
in conjunction with the Written Torah, which then nourishes and supports it
and provides all its needs. . . . We learn from this passage that when a man

women
side
by side
w/man

gives his daughter in marriage, up to the time of the wedding the father and mother are responsible for her upkeep, but once she is married the husband has to support her and provide all her necessaries. For it first says here that the Lord God built up the side, i.e. that the Father and Mother provided for her, but afterwards "he brought her to the man," that they might be closely united to one another, and the man might thenceforth provide all her requirements.

Bereshith, 49a

AND THE LORD GOD FORMED THE MAN. At this point he was completely formed so as to partake both of the Right and of the Left. We laid down before that he was wholly under the aegis of the good inclination: now God formed him with both good and evil inclination—with the good inclination for himself, and the evil inclination to turn towards the female. Esoterically speaking, we learn from here that the North is always attracted to the female and attaches itself to her, and therefore she is called *isha* (i.e. *esh he*, fire of *he*). Observe this. The good inclination and the evil inclination are in harmony only because they share the female, who is attached to both, in this way: first the evil inclination sues for her and they unite with one another, and when they are united the good inclination, which is joy, rouses itself and draws her to itself, and so she is shared by both and reconciles them. Hence it is written, "and the Lord God formed man," the double name being made responsible both for the good and the evil inclination. THE MAN: as we have explained, male and female, together and not separated, so as to turn face to face. . . .

AND THE LORD GOD BUILT. Here also the full name of the Deity is used, indicating that the father and mother provided for her until she came to her husband.

Bereshith, 49b

Observe that it says here AND THE MAN SAID, THIS TIME, ETC., to show that he spoke to her lovingly so as to draw her to him and to win her affections. See how tender and coaxing is his language—"bone of my bone and flesh of my flesh"—to prove to her that they were one and inseparable. Then he began to sing her praises: THIS SHALL BE CALLED WOMAN, this is the peerless and incomparable one; this is the pride of the house, who surpasses all other women as a human being surpasses an ape. This one is perfect in all points, and alone merits the title of woman. Every word is inspired by love, like the verse "Many daughters have done valiantly, but thou excellest them all" (Prov. 31:29). THEREFORE A MAN SHALL LEAVE HIS FATHER AND HIS MOTHER AND CLEAVE TO HIS WIFE, AND THEY SHALL BE ONE FLESH: all this, too, was to win her affection and to draw her closer.

AND THE SERPENT WAS SUBTLE. After the man had addressed all these words to the woman, the evil inclination awoke, prompting him to seek to unite with her in carnal desire, and to entice her to things in which the evil

praise
of
women

inclination takes delight, until at last THE WOMAN SAW THAT THE TREE WAS GOOD FOR FOOD, AND THAT IT WAS A DELIGHT FOR THE EYES AND SHE TOOK OF THE FRUIT THEREOF AND ATE—giving ready admission to the evil inclination—AND GAVE ALSO UNTO HER HUSBAND WITH HER: it was she now who sought to awaken desire in him, so as to win his love and affection.

Bereshith, 55b

MALE AND FEMALE HE CREATED THEM. R. Simeon said: Profound mysteries are revealed in these two verses. The words "male and female he created them" make known the high dignity of man, the mystic doctrine of his creation. Assuredly in the way in which heaven and earth were created man was also created; for of heaven and earth it is written, "these are the generations of the heaven and the earth," and of man it is written, "these are the generations of man"; of heaven and earth it is written, "when they were created," and of man it is written, "on the day when they were created"; "Male and female he created them." From this we learn that every figure which does not comprise male and female elements is not a true and proper figure, and so we have laid down the esoteric teaching of our Mishnah. Observe this. God does not place His abode in any place where male and female are not found together, nor are blessings found save in such a place, as it is written, AND HE BLESSED THEM AND CALLED THEIR NAME MAN ON THE DAY THAT THEY WERE CREATED: note that it says *them* and *their* name, and not *him* and *his* name. The male is not even called man till he is united with the female.

CHRISTIANITY

Thomas Aquinas

Thomas Aquinas (c. 1225-1274) was a Dominican philosopher and theologian whose thought has been tremendously influential, particularly on Roman Catholicism. When Thomas was five years of age, his parents sent him to a Benedictine monastery. As a teenager, he became interested in seeking admission to the then-recently founded Dominican Order. Opposing this idea, his family kidnapped him and held him prisoner for over a year. Yet they could not dissuade Thomas; he joined the Dominican Order in 1244. In 1245, he enrolled at the University of Paris, where he came under the influence of Albertus Magnus. Albert introduced Thomas to the controversial subject of Aristotle's philosophy, which had become increasingly available in the Latin West in part through the preservation of Aristotle's writings by Muslim scholars. Although many Christians dismissed Aristotle's philosophy as anti-Christian, Thomas agreed with Albert that Christian theology needed to offer an account of Aristotle's thought. Thus in his *Summa Theologiae*, Thomas used careful analysis to demonstrate points of agreement between Aristotle's teachings and those of Augustine and other Christian theologians. This work, which was begun in the late 1260s, remained unfinished at the time of Thomas's death in 1274.

Thomas's *Summa Theologiae* provides a compendium of questions and answers that reflect topics being debated within university settings. The "Parts" of the *Summa* are divided into "Questions." Each Question identifies a broad topic that is further subdivided into "Articles." The query posed in the Article is deliberated upon first by identifying "Objections" to it and then by posing a counterobjection as "On the contrary." Thomas's own reply follows as "I answer that." The discussion of the Article concludes with Thomas responding to each Objection cited at the start of the Article.

Our selection consists of excerpts from seven Questions. At the beginning of our selection, Question 92 from Part 1 opens with concerns about whether woman should have been created at the original creation of things. At the close of our selection, Question 163 from Part 2-2 considers whose sin was more serious: Eve's or Adam's. Between these, we highlight Thomas's deliberations on humanity's creation in God's image (Q. 93), on social hierarchies and slavery (Q. 96), on sexual intercourse (Q. 98), on the birth of female children (Q. 99), and on the transmission of original sin (Q. 81 from Part 1-2). Throughout his discussions we see the influence of Aristotle, whom Thomas often referred to as "the Philosopher." Particularly vivid are Aristotle's understanding of woman as a defective male, his antithesis of matter and form, and his equations of woman with matter and man with form. (Source: Thomas Aquinas, *The "Summa Theologica" of St. Thomas Aquinas*, translated by Fathers of the English Dominican Province, London: Burns Oates & Washbourne, 1914f, vol. 4, pp. 274-80, 288-89, 330-34, 346-48, 352-54; vol. 7, pp. 412-13; vol. 13, pp. 259-61.)

Summa Theologiae (begun late 1260s CE)
THOMAS AQUINAS

Question 92 of Part 1: The Production of the Woman

We must next consider the production of the woman. Under this head there are four points of inquiry: (1) Whether the woman should have been made in that first production of things? (2) Whether the woman should have been made from man? (3) Whether of man's rib? (4) Whether the woman was made immediately by God?

First Article: Whether the Woman Should Have Been Made in the First Production of Things?
We proceed thus to the First Article:—

Objection 1. It would seem that the woman should not have been made in the first production of things. For the Philosopher [Aristotle] says (*De Gener.*

Animal. [*On the Generation of Animals*] 2.3), that the *female is a misbegotten male.* But nothing misbegotten or defective should have been made in the first production of things. Therefore woman should not have been made at that first production.

Obj. 2. Further, subjection and limitation were a result of sin, for to the woman was it said after sin (Gen. 3:16): *Thou shalt be under the man's power;* and Gregory [of Nyssa] says that *Where there is no sin, there is no inequality.* But woman is naturally of less strength and dignity than man; *for the agent is always more honourable than the patient,* as Augustine says (*Gen. ad lit.* [*The Literal Meaning of Genesis*] 12.16). Therefore woman should not have been made in the first production of things before sin.

Obj. 3. Further, occasions of sin should be cut off. But God foresaw that the woman would be an occasion of sin to man. Therefore He should not have made woman.

On the contrary, It is written (Gen. 2:18): *It is not good for man to be alone; let us make him a helper like to himself.*

I answer that, It was necessary for woman to be made, as the Scripture says, as a *helper* to man; not, indeed, as a helpmate in other works, as some say, since man can be more efficiently helped by another man in other works; but as a helper in the work of generation. This can be made clear if we observe the mode of generation carried out in various living things. Some living things do not possess in themselves the power of generation, but are generated by some other specific agent, such as some plants and animals by the influence of the heavenly bodies, from some fitting matter and not from seed; others possess the active and passive generative power together; as we see in plants which are generated from seed; for the noblest vital function in plants is generation. Wherefore we observe that in these the active power of generation invariably accompanies the passive power. Among perfect animals the active power of generation belongs to the male sex, and the passive power to the female. And as among animals there is a vital operation nobler than generation, to which their life is principally directed; therefore the male sex is not found in continual union with the female in perfect animals, but only at the time of coition; so that we may consider that by this means the male and female are one, as in plants they are always united; although in some cases one of them preponderates, and in some the other. But man is yet further ordered to a still nobler vital action, and that is intellectual operation. Therefore there was greater reason for the distinction of these two forces in man; so that the female should be produced separately from the male; although they are carnally united for generation. Therefore directly after the formation of woman, it was said: *And they shall be two in one flesh* (Gen. 2:24).

Reply Obj. 1. As regards the individual nature, woman is defective and misbegotten, for the active force in the male seed tends to the production of a perfect likeness in the masculine sex; while the production of woman comes from defect in the active force or from some material indisposition, or even from some external influence; such as that of a south wind, which is moist, as the Philosopher observes (*De Gener. Animal.* 4.2). On the other hand, as regards human nature in general, woman is not misbegotten, but is included in nature's intention as directed to the work of generation. Now the general intention of nature depends on God, Who is the universal Author of nature. Therefore, in producing nature, God formed not only the male but also the female.

Reply Obj. 2. Subjection is twofold. One is servile, by virtue of which a superior makes use of a subject for his own benefit; and this kind of subjection began after sin. There is another kind of subjection, which is called economic or civil, whereby the superior makes use of his subjects for their own benefit and good; and this kind of subjection existed even before sin. For good order would have been wanting in the human family if some were not governed by others wiser than themselves. So by such a kind of subjection woman is naturally subject to man, because in man the discretion of reason predominates. Nor is inequality among men excluded by the state of innocence, as we shall prove (Q. 96., A. 3).

Reply Obj. 3. If God had deprived the world of all those things which proved an occasion of sin, the universe would have been imperfect. Nor was it fitting for the common good to be destroyed in order that individual evil might be avoided; especially as God is so powerful that He can direct any evil to a good end.

Second Article: Whether Woman Should Have Been Made From Man?
We proceed thus to the Second Article: . . .

I answer that, When all things were first formed, it was more suitable for the woman to be made from the man than (for the female to be from the male) in other animals. First, in order thus to give the first man a certain dignity consisting in this, that as God is the principle of the whole universe, so the first man, in likeness to God, was the principle of the whole human race. Wherefore Paul says that *God made the whole human race from one* (Acts 17:26). Secondly, that man might love woman all the more, and cleave to her more closely, knowing her to be fashioned from himself. Hence it is written (Gen. 2:23, 24): *She was taken out of man, wherefore a man shall leave father and mother, and shall cleave to his wife.* This was most necessary as regards the human race, in which the male and female live together for life; which is not the case with other animals. Thirdly, because, as the Philosopher says (*Ethic.* [*Nicomachean Ethics*] 8.12), the human male and female are united, not only for generation, as with other animals, but also for the purpose of domestic life, in which each has his or her particular duty, and in which the man is the head of the woman. Wherefore it was suitable for the woman to be made out of man, as out of her principle. Fourthly, there is a sacramental reason for this. For by this is signified that the Church takes her origin from Christ. Wherefore the Apostle says (Eph. 5:32): *This is a great sacrament; but I speak in Christ and in the Church.* . . .

Third Article: Whether the Woman Was Fittingly Made from the Rib of Man?

We proceed thus to the Third Article: . . .

Obj. 2. Further, in those things which were first created there was nothing superfluous. Therefore a rib of Adam belonged to the integrity of his body. So, if a rib was removed, his body remained imperfect; which is unreasonable to suppose. . . .

I answer that, It was right for the woman to be made from a rib of man. First, to signify the social union of man and woman, for the woman should neither *use authority over man,* and so she was not made from his head; nor was it right for her to be subject to man's contempt as his slave, and so she was not made from his feet. Secondly, for the sacramental signification; for from the side of Christ sleeping on the Cross the Sacraments flowed—namely, blood and water—on which the Church was established. . . .

Reply Obj. 2. The rib belonged to the integral perfection of Adam, not as an individual, but as the principle of the human race; just as the semen belongs to the perfection of the begetter, and is released by a natural and pleasurable operation. Much more, therefore, was it possible that by the Divine power the body of the woman should be produced from the man's rib. . . .

Question 93 of Part 1: The End or Term of the Production of Man

Fourth Article: Whether the Image of God Is Found in Every Man?

We proceed thus to the Fourth Article:

Objection 1. It would seem that the image of God is not found in every man. For the Apostle says that *man is the image of God, but woman is the image* (Vulg., *glory*) *of man* (1 Cor. 11:7). Therefore, as woman is an individual of the human species, it is clear that every individual is not an image of God. . . .

I answer that, Since man is said to be to the image of God by reason of his intellectual nature, he is the most perfectly like God according to that in which he can best imitate God in his intellectual nature. Now the intellectual nature imitates God chiefly in this, that God understands and loves Himself. Wherefore we see that the image of God is in man in three ways. First, inasmuch as man possesses a natural aptitude for understanding and loving God; and this aptitude consists in the very nature of the mind, which is common to all men. Secondly, inasmuch as man actually or habitually knows and loves God, though imperfectly; and this image consists in the conformity of grace. Thirdly, inasmuch as man knows and loves God perfectly; and this image consists in the likeness of glory. Wherefore on the words, *The light of Thy countenance, O Lord, is signed upon us* (Ps. 4:7), the gloss distinguishes a threefold image, of *creation,* of *re-creation,* and of *likeness.* The first is found in all men, the second only in the just, the third only in the blessed.

Reply Obj. 1. The image of God, in its principal signification, namely the intellectual nature, is found both in man and in woman. Hence after the words, *To the image of God He created him,* it is added, *Male and female He created them* (Gen. 1:27). Moreover it is said *them* in the plural, as Augustine (*Gen. ad. lit.* 3.22) remarks, lest it should be thought that both sexes were united in one individual. But in a secondary sense the image of God is found in man, and not in woman: for man is the beginning and end of woman; as God is the beginning and end of every creature. So when the Apostle had said that *man is the image and glory of God, but woman is the glory of man,* he adds his reason for saying this: *For man is not of woman, but woman of man; and man was not created for woman, but woman for man.* ....

Question 96 of Part 1: Of the Mastership Belonging to Man in the State of Innocence

Third Article: Whether Men Were Equal in the State of Innocence?
We proceed thus to the Third Article:

Objection 1. It would seem that in the state of innocence all would have been equal. For Gregory says (*Moral.* [*Commentary on the Book of Job*] 21.): *Where there is no sin, there is no inequality.* But in the state of innocence there was no sin. Therefore all were equal.

Obj. 2. Further, likeness and equality are the basis of mutual love, according to Ecclus. [Sirach] 13:[14], *Every beast loveth its like; so also every man him that is nearest to himself.* Now in that state there was among men an abundance of love, which is the bond of peace. Therefore all were equal in the state of innocence. ....

I answer that, We must needs admit that in the primitive state there would have been some inequality, at least as regards sex, because generation depends upon diversity of sex: and likewise as regards age; for some would have been born of others; nor would sexual union have been sterile.

Moreover, as regards the soul, there would have been inequality as to righteousness and knowledge. For man worked not of necessity, but of his own free-will, by virtue of which man can apply himself, more or less, to action, desire, or knowledge; hence some would have made a greater advance in virtue and knowledge than others.

There might also have been bodily disparity. For the human body was not entirely exempt from the laws of nature, so as not to receive from exterior sources more or less advantage and help: since indeed it was dependent on food wherewith to sustain life.

So we may say that, according to the climate, or the movement of the stars, some would have been born more robust in body than others, and also greater, and more beautiful, and in all ways better disposed; so that, however, in those who were thus surpassed, there would have been no defect or fault either in soul or body.

Reply Obj. 1. By those words Gregory means to exclude such inequality as exists between virtue and vice; the result of which is that some are placed in subjection to others as a penalty.

Reply Obj. 2. Equality is the cause of equality in mutual love. Yet between those who are unequal there can be a greater love than between equals; although there be not an equal response: for a father naturally loves his son more than a brother loves his brother; although the son does not love his father as much as he is loved by him. . . .

Fourth Article: Whether in the State of Innocence Man Would Have Been Master over Man?

We proceed thus to the Fourth Article:

Objection 1. It would seem that in the state of innocence man would not have been master over man. For Augustine says (*De Civ. Dei* [*The City of God*] 19.15): *God willed that man, who was endowed with reason and made to His image, should rule over none but irrational creatures; not over men, but over cattle.*

Obj. 2. Further, what came into the world as a penalty for sin would not have existed in the state of innocence. But man was made subject to man as a penalty; for after sin it was said to the woman (Gen. 3:16): *Thou shalt be under thy husband's power.* Therefore in the state of innocence man would not have been subject to man. . . .

I answer that, Mastership has a twofold meaning. First, as opposed to slavery, in which sense a master means one to whom another is subject as a slave. In another sense mastership is referred in a general sense to any kind of subject; and in this sense even he who has the office of governing and directing free men, can be called a master. In the state of innocence man could have been a master of men, not in the former but in the latter sense. This distinction is founded on the reason that a slave differs from a free man in that the latter has the disposal of himself, as is stated in the beginning of the *Metaphysics* [Aristotle], whereas a slave is ordered to another. So that one man is master of another as his slave when he refers the one whose master he is, to his own— namely, the master's use. And since every man's proper good is desirable to himself, and consequently it is a grievous matter to anyone to yield to another what ought to be one's own, therefore such dominion implies of necessity a pain inflicted on the subject; and consequently in the state of innocence such a mastership could not have existed between man and man.

But a man is the master of a free subject, by directing him either towards his proper welfare, or to the common good. Such a kind of mastership would have existed in the state of innocence between man and man, for two reasons. First, because man is naturally a social being, and so in the state of innocence he would have led a social life. Now a social life cannot exist among a number of people unless under the presidency of one to look after the common good; for many, as such, seek many things, whereas one attends only to one. Wherefore the Philosopher says, in the beginning of the *Politics*, that wherever many things are directed to one, we shall always find one at the head directing them. Secondly, if one man surpassed another in knowledge and virtue, this would not have been fitting unless these gifts conduced to the benefit of others, according to 1 Pet. 4:10, *As every man hath received grace, ministering the same one to another.* Wherefore Augustine says (*De Civ. Dei* 19.14): *Just men command not by the love of domineering, but by the service of counsel*: and (*Ibid.* 15): *The natural order of things requires this; and thus did God make man.*

From this appear the replies to the objections which are founded on the first-mentioned mode of mastership.

Question 98 of Part 1: Of the Preservation of the Species

Second Article: Whether in the State of Innocence There Would Have Been Generation By Coition?
We proceed thus to the Second Article:

I answer that, Some of the earlier doctors, considering the nature of concupiscence as regards generation in our present state, concluded that in the state of innocence generation would not have been effected in the same way. Thus Gregory of Nyssa says (*De Hom. Opif.* [*On the Making of Man*] 17.) that in Paradise the human race would have been multiplied by some other means, as the angels were multiplied without coition by the operation of the Divine Power. He adds that God made man male and female before sin, because He foreknew the mode of generation which would take place after sin, which He foresaw. But this is unreasonable. For what is natural to man was neither acquired nor forfeited by sin. Now it is clear that generation by coition is natural to man by reason of his animal life, which he possessed even before sin, as above explained (Q. 97., A. 3), just as it is natural to other perfect animals, as the corporeal members make it clear. So we cannot allow that these members would not have had a natural use, as other members had, before sin.

Thus, as regards generation by coition, there are, in the present state of life, two things to be considered. One, which comes from nature, is the union of man and woman; for in every act of generation there is an active and a passive principle. Wherefore, since wherever there is distinction of sex, the active principle is male and the passive is female; the order of nature demands that for the purpose of generation there should be concurrence of male and female. The second thing to be observed is a certain deformity of excessive concupiscence, which in the state of innocence would not have existed, when the lower powers were entirely subject to reason. Wherefore Augustine says (*De Civ. Dei* 14.26): *We must be far from supposing that offspring could not be begotten without concupiscence. All the bodily members would have been equally moved by the will, without ardent or wanton incentive, with calmness of soul and body. . . .*

Question 99 of Part 1: Of the Condition of the Offspring as to the Body

Second Article: Whether, in the Primitive State, Women Would Have Been Born?

We proceed thus to the Second Article:

Objection 1. It would seem that in the primitive state woman would not have been born. For the Philosopher says (*De Gener. Animal.* 2.3) that woman is a *misbegotten male*, as though she were a product outside the purpose of nature. But in that state nothing would have been unnatural in human generation. Therefore in that state women would not have been born.

Obj. 2. Further, every agent produces its like, unless prevented by insufficient power or ineptness of matter: thus a small fire cannot burn green wood. But in generation the active force is in the male. Since, therefore, in the state of innocence man's active force was not subject to defect, nor was there inept matter on the part of the woman, it seems that males would always have been born.

Obj. 3. Further, in the state of innocence generation is ordered to the multiplication of the human race. But the race would have been sufficiently multiplied by the first man and woman, from the fact that they would have lived forever. Therefore, in the state of innocence, there was no need for women to be born.

On the contrary, nature's process in generation would have been in harmony with the manner in which it was established by God. But God established male and female in human nature, as it is written (Gen. 1 and 2). Therefore also in the state of innocence male and female would have been born.

I answer that, Nothing belonging to the completeness of human nature would have been lacking in the state of innocence. And as different grades belong to the perfection of the universe, so also diversity of sex belongs to the perfection of human nature. Therefore in the state of innocence, both sexes would have been begotten.

Reply Obj. 1. Woman is said to be a *misbegotten male*, as being a product outside the purpose of nature considered in the individual case: but not against the purpose of universal nature, as above explained (Q. 92., A. 1 *ad* 2).

Reply Obj. 2. The generation of woman is not occasioned either by a defect of the active force or by inept matter, as the objection supposes; but sometimes by an extrinsic accidental cause; thus the Philosopher says (*De Animal. Histor.* [*The History of Animals*] 6.19): *The northern wind favors the generation of males, and the southern wind that of females*: sometimes also by some impression in the soul (of the parents), which may easily have some effect on the body (of the child). Especially was this the case in the state of innocence, when the body was more subject to the soul; so that by the mere will of the parent the sex of the offspring might be diversified.

Reply Obj. 3. The offspring would have been begotten to an animal life, as to the use of food and generation. Hence it was fitting that all should generate, and not only the first parents. From this it seems to follow that males and females would have been in equal number.

Question 81 of Part 2-1: Of the Cause of Sin, on the Part of Man

Fifth Article: Whether If Eve, and Not Adam, Had Sinned, Their Children Would Have Contracted Original Sin?

We proceed thus to the Fifth Article:

Objection I. It would seem that if Eve, and not Adam, had sinned, their children would have contracted original sin. Because we contract original sin from our parents, in so far as we were once in them, according to the word of the Apostle (Rom. 5:12): *In whom all have sinned.* Now a man pre-exists in his mother as well as in his father. Therefore a man would have contracted original sin from his mother's sin as well as from his father's. . . .

On the contrary, The Apostle says (Rom. 5:12): *By one man sin entered into this world.* Now, if the woman would have transmitted original sin to her children, he should have said that it entered by two, since both of them sinned, or rather that it entered by a woman, since she sinned first. Therefore original sin is transmitted to the children, not by the mother, but by the father.

I answer that, The solution of this question is made clear by what has been said. For it has been stated (A. 1) that original sin is transmitted by the first parent in so far as he is the mover in the begetting of his children: wherefore it has been said (A. 4) that if anyone were begotten materially only, of human flesh, they would not contract original sin. Now it is evident that in the opinion of philosophers, the active principle of generation is from the father, while the mother provides the matter. Therefore original sin is contracted, not from the mother, but from the father: so that, accordingly, if Eve, and not Adam, had sinned, their children would not contract original sin: whereas, if Adam, and not Eve, had sinned, they would contract it.

Reply Obj. I. The child pre-exists in its father as in its active principle, and in its mother, as in its material and passive principle. Consequently the comparison fails. . . .

Question 163 of Part 2-2: Of the First Man's Sin

Fourth Article: Whether Adam's Sin Was More Grievous Than Eve's?

We proceed thus to the Fourth Article:

Objection 1. It would seem that Adam's sin was more grievous than Eve's. For it is written (1 Tim. 2:14): *Adam was not seduced, but the woman being seduced was in the transgression*: and so it would seem that the woman sinned through ignorance, but the man through assured knowledge. Now the latter is the graver sin, according to Luke 12:47, 48, *That servant who knew the will of his lord . . . and did not according to his will, shall be beaten with many stripes: but he that knew not, and did things worthy of stripes, shall be beaten with few stripes.* Therefore Adam's sin was more grievous than Eve's.

Obj. 2. Further Augustine says (*[De Decem Chordis*, a sermon] 3):[1] *If the man is the head, he should live better, and give an example of good deeds to his wife, that she may imitate him.* Now he who ought to do better sins more grievously, if he commit a sin. Therefore Adam sinned more grievously than Eve. . . .

On the contrary, Punishment corresponds to guilt. Now the woman was more grievously punished than the man, as appears from Gen. 3. Therefore she sinned more grievously than the man.

I answer that, As stated (A. 3), the gravity of a sin depends on the species rather than on a circumstance of that sin. Accordingly we must assert that, if we consider the condition attaching to these persons, the man's sin is the more grievous, because he was more perfect than the woman.

As regards the genus itself of the sin, the sin of each is considered to be equal, for each sinned by pride. Hence Augustine says (*Gen. ad. lit.* 11.35): *Eve in excusing herself betrays disparity of sex, though parity of pride.*

But as regards the species of pride, the woman sinned more grievously, for three reasons. First, because she was more puffed up than the man. For the woman believed in the serpent's persuasive words, namely that God had forbidden them to eat of the tree, lest they should become like to Him; so that in wishing to attain to God's likeness by eating of the forbidden fruit, her pride rose to the height of desiring to obtain something against God's will. On the other hand, the man did not believe this to be true; wherefore he did not wish to attain to God's likeness against God's will: but his pride consisted in wishing to attain thereto by his own power.—Secondly, the woman not only herself sinned, but suggested sin to the man; wherefore she sinned against both God and her neighbour.—Thirdly the man's sin was diminished by the fact that, as Augustine says (*Gen. ad. lit.* 11.42), *he consented to the sin out of a certain friendly good-will, on account of which a man sometimes will offend God rather than make an enemy of his friend. That he ought not to have done so is shown by the just issue of the Divine sentence.*

It is therefore evident that the woman's sin was more grievous than the man's.

Reply Obj. 1. The woman was deceived because she was first of all puffed up with pride. Wherefore her ignorance did not excuse, but aggravated her sin, in so far as it was the cause of her being puffed up with still greater pride.

Reply Obj. 2. This argument considers the circumstance of personal condition, on account of which the man's sin was more grievous than the woman's. . . .

[1. A sermon by Augustine, according to an editor's note in the English translation; we have been unable to locate the text.]

Christine de Pizan

Born in Italy in 1364, Christine de Pizan grew up in France, where her father worked as court astrologer for Charles V. Christine married at age fifteen and bore three children. Though her marriage was a happy one, Christine suffered a series of losses that pushed her to the brink of financial ruin. Her father died when she was twenty, and her husband died five years later, leaving her to support her three children and her mother. She decided to attempt to provide for her family through her writing, and in the process became the first woman in France to earn her living as an author. She devoted her work to a defense of women. Not surprisingly, she preferred an egalitarian interpretation of Genesis 1-3.

In 1399 Christine wrote "Letter of the God of Love," from which the selection in this section is excerpted. "Letter of the God of Love" anticipated arguments she would later make in her famous *Book of the City of Ladies*, published around 1405.[1] There she contended that God created Eve to be "a most noble creature" who should "stand at his [Adam's] side as a companion and never lie at his feet like a slave." Christine even found a way to use Genesis 2 to her advantage, noting that God created Adam before creating Paradise. Since Eve was created last, she—and she alone—could claim Paradise as her proper home. Christine refuted the Aristotelian assumption that femaleness was a sign of defective conception, insisting that God gave to both Eve and Adam "wholly similar souls, equally good and noble."

And even if Eve were the first to sin, Christine asserted, humanity gained more through the virgin Mary—who in Jesus united humanity and divinity—than it lost through Eve. Since the Fall led to the glory of the incarnation, the Fall was a fortunate event. Moreover, it was clear that Jesus held women in high regard. For Jesus not only was born of a woman but also entrusted to women the responsibility of being the first witnesses to the resurrection.[2]

Such themes are also evident in *Poems of Cupid, the God of Love*. In addition, in this earlier work Christine observed that men were fond of denigrating women because of Eve. She then proceeded to catalogue sins of violence and avarice that men regularly committed, noting that women were of a different, gentler nature. Women did not suffer by comparison to men in Christine's work; and in that characteristic she is highly unusual in the history of Christian theology. (Source: Christine de Pizan, *Epistre au dieu d'Amours*, in Thelma S. Fenster and Mary Carpenter Erler, editors, *Poems of Cupid, God of Love*, Leiden: E. J. Brill, 1990, pp. 43-47, 61-69.)

NOTES TO CHAPTER 5, CHRISTIANITY, CHRISTINE DE PIZAN

1. Elizabeth Alvida Petroff, editor, *Medieval Women's Visionary Literature* (New York and Oxford: Oxford University Press, 1986), pp. 303-304.

2. Christine de Pizan, *The Book of the City of Ladies*, Earl Jeffrey Richards, translator, with a foreword by Marina Warner (New York: Persea Books, 1982), pp. 23-30.

"Letter of the God of Love" (1399 CE)
CHRISTINE DE PIZAN

. . . .

Good God, what gossips! God, what gatherings,	[163]
At which a lady's honor's stripped away!	164
And where, in slander, is the profit for	
The very men who ought to arm themselves	
To guard the ladies and defend their name?	
For every man must have a tender heart	168
Toward a woman, she who is his mother dear,	
Who's never wicked, pitiless toward him,	
But rather, she is pleasant, gentle, sweet;	
When he's in need, she understands and helps.	172
She's done and does so many services	
For him; how right her ministrations are	
Gently to serve the creature needs of man.	
At birth, in life, and at his time of death	176
Women, always willing, help and assist.	
Compassionate and kind, obliging him.	
The man who slanders them is merciless,	
An ingrate, lacking any thought of thanks.	180
So I repeat: that man too much distorts	
His nature who rehearses ugly slurs,	
Or blames a woman, thus reproaching her,	
Whether it's one, or two, or womankind.	184
Now if some women are the foolish kind,	
Brimming with sin of every stamp and type,	
And lacking faith and love and loyalty,	
Or puffed-up, evil, filled with cruelty,	188
Inconstant, loose and low and fickle types,	
Or scheming, false, or practising deceit—	
Must we, because of that, imprison all	
And testify that none deserves respect?	192
When God on high created angels, made	
The cherubim, archangels, seraphim,	
Now weren't there some bad ones in the lot?	

Because of that must one call angels bad?   196
The man who knows an evil woman should
Keep clear of her, and not defame a third
Or fourth of womankind, or charge them all,
Decrying every trait that's feminine.   200
For many do and did and will exist
Who should be praised as good and courteous,
In whom are grace and virtue to be found,
Whose goodness proves their wisdom and their worth.   204

. . . .

    The ladies mentioned here above complain   [259]
Of many clerks who lay much blame to them,   260
Composing tales in rhyme, in prose, in verse,
In which they scorn their ways with words diverse;
They give these texts out to their youngest lads,
To schoolboys who are young and new in class.   264
Examples given to indoctrinate
So they'll retain such doctrine when they're grown.
    Thus, "Adam, David, Samson, Solomon,"
They say in verse, "a score of other men,   268
Were all deceived by women morn and night;
So who will be the man who can escape?"
"They're treacherous," another clerk opines
"And false and cunning; they're no good at all."   272
    "They're dreadful liars," other men pronounce,
"They're faithless, fickle, they are low and loose."
Of many other wrongs they stand accused
And blamed, in nothing can they be excused.   276
And that's what clerks are up to noon and night,
With verses now in Latin, now in French,
They base their words on I don't know what books
Which tell more lies than any drunkard does.   280

. . . .

    And yet, whoever's said or written ill   [557]
Of women, only good is said of them
In books that talk of Jesus, of His life,
Or of His death pursued so jealously;   560
The Gospel says no ill of them, but all
Record their high responsibilities,
Great prudence, great good sense, great constancy,
Their perfect love, their lasting faithfulness,   564
Their ample charity, their fervent will.
With firm and steadfast heart and mind they longed
To serve the Lord, as they indeed did show,
For never did they leave him, live or dead;   568

Except for women was sweet Jesus left
Alone completely, wounded, stricken, dead.
In just one woman all the faith remained.
How foolish is the man who sullies them,   572
If only for the reverence due to her,
The Queen of Heaven, in remembrance of
Her goodness; so noble and dignified,
She earned the right to bear the son of God!   576
Thus God the Father honored woman so,
Who made of her his mother and his spouse;
God's Temple to the Trinity was joined.
A woman should be glad and fill with joy   580
Since she resembles her and has her form;
For God has never formed another thing
Of equal dignity, nor quite as good,
Excepting Jesus' own humanity.   584
How foolish then, is he who charges them,
When woman's seated on so high a throne
Beside her son, and to the Father's right,
An honor to maternal womankind.   588
We find that women never were disdained
By Jesus, rather were they loved and prized.
   Now God created her resembling Him;
He gave to her intelligence and skill   592
To save her soul, and judgment and good sense.
When God created her he gave her form
Majestic, made of very noble stuff:
For not from earthly mud was she derived,   596
But made uniquely from the rib of man,
Whose body was already, summing up,
Among the things of earth the noblest one.
The old and trusted stories that are found   600
Within the Bible, certainly no lies,
Relate that woman was the first to be
Created in the earthly Paradise,
Not man. Now as to the deceitful act   604
For which our mother Eve is brought to blame,
Upon which followed God's harsh punishment,
I say she never did play Adam false,
In innocence she took the enemy's   608
Assertion, which he gave her to believe.
Accepting it as true, sincerely said,
She went to tell her mate what she had heard.
No fraudulence was there, no planned deceit,   612
For guilelessness, which has no hidden spite,

Must not be labeled as deceptiveness.
For none deceives without intending to,
Or else that isn't really called deceit.   616
    What evils can be said of womankind?
And isn't Paradise their recompense?
What awful crimes can one accuse them of?
And if some foolish men prefer to play   620
At love—and may they gain but ill from it—
They can't do else; but let the wise refrain;
For he who planned deceit but was instead
Deceived has but himself alone to blame.   624
And if, on this, I were to say it all,
I'd fear incurring wrath from certain ones,
For very often speaking out the truth
Creates ill feeling and hostility.   628
So I don't want to make comparisons:
Comparisons, at times, just cause more hate.
Let me be satisfied to praise not blame,
For one can call some people good without   632
Comparing, saying who is bad or worse.
For he who blames another just to praise
Himself casts doubt on his integrity.
It's certainly far better not to speak.   636
And so I hold my tongue. Let each be judge,
And heeding truth, adjudicate the case.
He'll find, if he will try it honestly,
Her greatest fault can cause but little harm   640
    She doesn't kill or wound or mutilate,
Or foster any treasonous misdeeds;
Or dispossess another; set afire;
Or poison; pilfer silver, steal one's gold;   644
Or cheat of wealth or one's inheritance
Through bogus contracts; nor does she bring harm
To empires or to duchies or to realms.
Ill barely follows, even from the worst.   648
Commonly, one alone won't prove the rule.
    And so whoever would search history
Or in the Bible just to prove me wrong,
With instances of one or two or more   652
Who've been immoral women and corrupt,
Will find those cases are abnormal ones.
I'm speaking of the great majority,
For very few are those who use such tricks.   656
    And if there's someone who would say to me
That women's traits and qualities are not
Inclined toward things like that, toward making war,

Or murdering, or fashioning the torch   660
To set the blaze, or any of those things,
And thus no special credit, praise, or pay
Belongs to them, nor can nor should apply,
For struggling to abstain from all of that,   664
With due respect to those who hold that view,
I quite agree, indeed, that women's hearts
Are not so made, disposed toward wickedness!
For woman's nature is but sweet and mild,   668
Compassionate and fearful, timorous
And humble, gentle, sweet and generous,
And pleasant, pious, meek in time of peace,
Afraid of war, religious, plain at heart.   672
When angry, quickly she allays her ire,
Nor can she bear to see brutality
Or suffering. It's clear those qualities
By nature make a woman's character.   676
And she who's lacking them by accident
Corrupts her nature, goes against the grain.
In women cruelty's to be reproved,
And gentleness alone should be approved.   680
    Now since it's not their temper or their way
To kill or bring about some bloody act,
Nor have they other ugly, awful sins,
They're innocent of them, completely free,   684
Indeed, of flagrant and enormous sins,
Now each of us is tainted by some sin,
But women won't be marked as culpable
For great misdeeds in which they're not ensnared.   688
Nor will they have, through suffering and pain,
The punishment for sins that aren't theirs.
Thus I can say, and it's no heresy,
That God on high did them a courtesy   692
When He created them without those traits
That lead one into grave calamity.

.   .   .   .

Malleus Maleficarum

Heinrich Kramer and James Sprenger, two Dominican inquistors, compiled
the *Malleus* (the "Hammer against Witches") in 1496, circulating it with copies of a papal bull that denounced witches and mandated the inquisitors to
eradicate them. The *Malleus* included detailed instructions on how to identify
witches and devoted considerable attention to torture techniques that could
aid inquisitors in soliciting confessions from alleged witches. The *Malleus*
helped set off a wave of persecution that lasted for two centuries. One of

the most notable aspects of the *Malleus*, as Elizabeth Clark and Herbert Richardson have observed, was "its preoccupation with sexual functions and its broad and vicious attack on women."[1]

Of particular interest in this selection is the claim that Eve was a defective creation, by nature inclined to deceive. The *Malleus* disregarded the traditional understanding that in Genesis God declared all of the creation good. The *Malleus* pointed to Eve's (and therefore to all women's) sexuality, or "carnal lust," as the root of women's sinfulness. "Insatiable" lust made women particularly dangerous to men. Ruled by desire rather than by reason, women were, asserted the *Malleus*, far quicker than men to desert the faith and turn to Satan for carnal pleasures. The *Malleus* warned that ambitious women would unite with Satan to overthrow men from their divinely ordained roles as leaders of the human race. Women would also seek to ravage men's sexuality. When men experienced inordinate passion or when they were unable to perform sexually, the *Malleus* asserted, it was highly likely that they were under the spell of a witch. Thus the *Malleus* invited men to project their own dysfunctions and fears onto women.

In virtually equating women with the demonic, the *Malleus* interpreted the creation of woman in Genesis 2 as a cautionary tale, not as an act of divine goodness. (Source: Heinrich Kramer and James Sprenger, *The Malleus Maleficarum*, translated and with an introduction by the Reverend Montague Summers, New York: Dover Publications, Inc., 1971, pp. 41-48, 55.)

NOTE TO CHAPTER 5, CHRISTIANITY, *MALLEUS MALEFICARUM*

1. Clark and Richardson, *Women and Religion*, revised and expanded edition, p. 123.

Malleus Maleficarum (1496 CE)

HEINRICH KRAMER AND JAMES SPRENGER

Part I, Question VI: Concerning Witches Who Copulate with Devils

Why It Is that Women Are Chiefly Addicted to Evil Superstitions.
There is also, concerning witches who copulate with devils, much difficulty in considering the methods by which such abominations are consummated. On the part of the devil: first, of what element the body is made that he assumes; secondly, whether the act is always accompanied by the injection of semen received from another; thirdly, as to time and place, whether he commits this act more frequently at one time than at another; fourthly, whether the act is invisible to any who may be standing by. And on the part of the women, it

has to be inquired whether only they who were themselves conceived in this filthy manner are often visited by devils; or secondly, whether it is those who were offered to devils by midwives at the time of their birth; and thirdly, whether the actual venereal delectation of such is of a weaker sort. But we cannot here reply to all these questions, both because we are only engaged in a general study, and because in the second part of this work they are all singly explained by their operations, as will appear in the fourth chapter, where mention is made of each separate method. Therefore let us now chiefly consider women; and first, why this kind of perfidy is found more in so fragile a sex than in men. And our inquiry will first be general, as to the general conditions of women; secondly, particular, as to which sort of women are found to be given to superstition and witchcraft; and thirdly, specifically with regard to midwives, who surpass all others in wickedness.

Why Superstition Is Chiefly Found in Women.
As for the first question, why a greater number of witches is found in the fragile feminine sex than among men; it is indeed a fact that it were idle to contradict, since it is accredited by actual experience, apart from the verbal testimony of credible witnesses. And without in any way detracting from a sex in which God has always taken great glory that His might should be spread abroad, let us say that various men have assigned various reasons for this fact, which nevertheless agree in principle. Wherefore it is good, for the admonition of women, to speak of this matter; and it has often been proved by experience that they are eager to hear of it, so long as it is set forth with discretion. . . .

Now the wickedness of women is spoken of in *Ecclesiasticus* xxv: There is no head above the head of a serpent: and there is no wrath above the wrath of a woman. I had rather dwell with a lion and a dragon than to keep house with a wicked woman. And among much which in that place precedes and follows about a wicked woman, he concludes: All wickedness is but little to the wickedness of a woman. Wherefore S. John Chrysostom says on the text, It is not good to marry (*S. Matthew* xix): What else is woman but a foe to friendship, an unescapable punishment, a necessary evil, a natural temptation, a desirable calamity, a domestic danger, a delectable detriment, an evil of nature, painted with fair colours! Therefore if it be a sin to divorce her when she ought to be kept, it is indeed a necessary torture; for either we commit adultery by divorcing her, or we must endure daily strife. . . .

Others again have propounded other reasons why there are more superstitious women found than men. And the first is, that they are more credulous; and since the chief aim of the devil is to corrupt faith, therefore he rather attacks them. See *Ecclesiasticus* xix: He that is quick to believe is light-minded, and shall be diminished. . . .

There are also others who bring forward yet other reasons, of which preachers should be very careful how they make use. For it is true that in the Old Testament the Scriptures have much that is evil to say about women, and this because of the first temptress, Eve, and her imitators; yet afterwards in the New Testament we find a change of name, as from Eva to Ave (as S. Jerome says), and the whole sin of Eve taken away by the benediction of Mary. Therefore preachers should always say as much praise of them as possible.

But because in these times this perfidy is more often found in women than in men, as we learn by actual experience, if anyone is curious as to the reason, we may add to what has already been said the following: that since they are feebler both in mind and body, it is not surprising that they should come more under the spell of witchcraft.

For as regards intellect, or the understanding of spiritual things, they seem to be of a different nature from men; a fact which is vouched for by the logic of the authorities, backed by various examples from the Scriptures. Terence says: Women are intellectually like children. And Lactantius (*Institutiones*, III): No woman understood philosophy except Temeste. And *Proverbs* xi, as it were describing a woman, says: As a jewel of gold in a swine's snout, so is a fair woman which is without discretion.

But the natural reason is that she is more carnal than a man, as is clear from her many carnal abominations. And it should be noted that there was a defect in the formation of the first woman, since she was formed from a bent rib, that is, a rib of the breast, which is bent as it were in a contrary direction to a man. And since through this defect she is an imperfect animal, she always deceives. For Cato says: When a woman weeps she weaves snares. And again: When a woman weeps, she labours to deceive a man. And this is shown by Samson's wife, who coaxed him to tell her the riddle he had propounded to the Philistines, and told them the answer, and so deceived him. And it is clear in the case of the first woman that she had little faith; for when the serpent asked why they did not eat of every tree in Paradise, she answered: Of every tree, etc.—lest perchance we die. Thereby she showed that she doubted, and had little faith in the word of God. And all this is indicated by the etymology of the word; for *Femina* comes from *Fe* and *Minus*, since she is ever weaker to hold and preserve the faith. And this as regards faith is of her very nature; although both by grace and nature faith never failed in the Blessed Virgin, even at the time of Christ's Passion, when it failed in all men.

Therefore a wicked woman is by her nature quicker to waver in her faith, and consequently quicker to abjure the faith, which is the root of witchcraft. . . .

And indeed, just as through the first defect in their intelligence they are more prone to abjure the faith; so through their second defect of inordinate affections and passions they search for, brood over, and inflict various vengeances, either by witchcraft, or by some other means. Wherefore it is no wonder that so great a number of witches exist in this sex. . . .

If we inquire, we find that nearly all the kingdoms of the world have been overthrown by women. Troy, which was a prosperous kingdom, was, for the rape of one woman, Helen, destroyed, and many thousands of Greeks slain. The kingdom of the Jews suffered much misfortune and destruction through the accursed Jezebel, and her daughter Athaliah, queen of Judah, who caused her son's sons to be killed, that on their death she might reign herself; yet each of them was slain. The kingdom of the Romans endured much evil through Cleopatra, Queen of Egypt, that worst of women. And so with others. Therefore it is no wonder if the world now suffers through the malice of women.

And now let us examine the carnal desires of the body itself, whence has arisen unconscionable harm to human life. Justly may we say with Cato of Utica: If the world could be rid of women, we should not be without God in our intercourse. For truly, without the wickedness of women, to say nothing of witchcraft, the world would still remain proof against innumerable dangers. Hear what Valerius said to Rufinus: You do not know that woman is the Chimaera, but it is good that you should know it; for that monster was of three forms; its face was that of a radiant and noble lion, it had the filthy belly of a goat, and it was armed with the virulent tail of a viper. And he means that a woman is beautiful to look upon, contaminating to the touch, and deadly to keep.

Let us consider another property of hers, the voice. For as she is a liar by nature, so in her speech she stings while she delights us. Wherefore her voice is like the song of the Sirens, who with their sweet melody entice the passersby and kill them. For they kill them by emptying their purses, consuming their strength, and causing them to forsake God. Again Valerius says to Rufinus: When she speaks it is a delight which flavours the sin; the flower of love is a rose, because under its blossom there are hidden many thorns. See *Proverbs* v, 3-4: Her mouth is smoother than oil; that is, her speech is afterwards as bitter as absinthium. [Her throat is smoother than oil. But her end is as bitter as wormwood.]

Let us consider also her gait, posture, and habit, in which is vanity of vanities. There is no man in the world who studies so hard to please the good God as even an ordinary woman studies by her vanities to please men. An example of this is to be found in the life of Pelagia, a worldly woman who was wont to go about Antioch tired and adorned most extravagantly. A holy father, named Nonnus, saw her and began to weep, saying to his companions, that never in all his life had he used such diligence to please God; and much more he added to this effect, which is preserved in his orations.

It is this which is lamented in *Ecclesiastes* vii, and which the Church even now laments on account of the great multitude of witches. And I have found a woman more bitter than death, who is the hunter's snare, and her heart is a net, and her hands are bands. He that pleaseth God shall escape from her; but he that is a sinner shall be caught by her. More bitter than death, that is, than the devil: *Apocalypse* vi, 8, His name was Death. For though the devil tempted Eve to sin, yet Eve seduced Adam. And as the sin of Eve would not have brought death to our soul and body unless the sin had afterwards passed on to Adam, to which he was tempted by Eve, not by the devil, therefore she is more bitter than death.

More bitter than death, again, because that is natural and destroys only the body; but the sin which arose from woman destroys the soul by depriving it of grace, and delivers the body up to the punishment for sin.

More bitter than death, again, because bodily death is an open and terrible enemy, but woman is a wheedling and secret enemy.

And that she is more perilous than a snare does not speak of the snare of hunters, but of devils. For men are caught not only through their carnal desires, when they see and hear women: for S. Bernard says: Their face is a burning wind, and their voice the hissing of serpents: but they also cast wicked spells on countless men and animals. And when it is said that her heart is a net, it speaks of the inscrutable malice which reigns in their hearts. And her hands are as bands for binding; for when they place their hands on a creature to bewitch it, then with the help of the devil they perform their design.

To conclude. All witchcraft comes from carnal lust, which is in women insatiable. See *Proverbs* xxx: There are three things that are never satisfied, yea, a fourth thing which says not, It is enough; that is, the mouth of the womb. Wherefore for the sake of fulfilling their lusts they consort even with devils. More such reasons could be brought forward, but to the understanding it is sufficiently clear that it is no matter for wonder that there are more women than men found infected with the heresy of witchcraft. And in consequence of this, it is better called the heresy of witches than of wizards, since the name is taken from the more powerful party. And blessed be the Highest Who has so far preserved the male sex from so great a crime: for since He was willing to be born and to suffer for us, therefore He has granted to men this privilege.

What Sort of Women Are Found to
Be above All Others Superstitious and Witches.

As to our second inquiry, what sort of women more than others are found to be superstitious and infected with witchcraft; it must be said, as was shown in the preceding inquiry, that three general vices appear to have special dominion over wicked women, namely, infidelity, ambition, and lust. Therefore they are more than others inclined towards witchcraft, who more than others are given to these vices. Again, since of these three vices the last chiefly predominates, women being insatiable, etc., it follows that those among ambitious women are more deeply infected who are more hot to satisfy their filthy lusts; and such are adulteresses, fornicatresses, and the concubines of the Great.

Now there are, as it is said in the Papal Bull, seven methods by which they infect with witchcraft the venereal act and the conception of the womb: First, by inclining the minds of men to inordinate passion; second, by obstructing their generative force; third, by removing the members accommodated to that act; fourth, by changing men into beasts by their magic art; fifth, by destroying the generative force in women; sixth, by procuring abortion; seventh, by offering children to devils, besides other animals and fruits of the earth with which they work much harm. And all these will be considered later; but for the present let us give our minds to the injuries towards men.

And first concerning those who are bewitched into an inordinate love or hatred, this is a matter of a sort that it is difficult to discuss before the general intelligence. Yet is must be granted that it is a fact. For S. Thomas (IV, 34), treating of obstructions caused by witches, shows that God allows the devil greater power against men's venereal acts than against their other actions; and gives this reason, that this is likely to be so, since those women are chiefly apt to be witches who are most disposed to such acts.

For he says that, since the first corruption of sin by which man became the slave of the devil came to us through the act of generation, therefore greater power is allowed by God to the devil in this act than in all others. Also the power of witches is more apparent in serpents, as it is said, than in other animals, because through the means of a serpent the devil tempted woman. For this reason also, as is shown afterwards, although matrimony is a work of God, as being instituted by Him, yet it is sometimes wrecked by the work of the devil: not indeed through main force, since then he might be thought stronger than God, but with the permission of God, by causing some temporary or permanent impediment in the conjugal act.

And touching this we may say what is known by experience; that these women satisfy their filthy lusts not only in themselves, but even in the mighty ones of the age, of whatever state and condition; causing by all sorts of witchcraft the death of their souls through the excessive infatuation of carnal love, in such a way that for no shame or persuasion can they desist from such acts. And through such men, since the witches will not permit any harm to come to them either from themselves or from others once they have them in their power, there arises the great danger of the time, namely, the extermination of the Faith. And in this way do witches every day increase. . . .

Part I, Question VIII: Whether Witches Can Hebetate the Powers of Generation or Obstruct the Venereal Act

. . . For it has been shown that witchcraft does not exist only in men's imaginations, and not in fact; but that truly and actually innumerable bewitchments can happen, with the permission of God. It has been shown, too, that God permits it more in the case of the generative powers, because of their greater corruption, than in the case of other human actions. But concerning the method by which such obstruction is procured, it is to be noted that it does not affect only the generative powers, but also the powers of the imagination or fancy.

And as to this, Peter of Palude (III, 34) notes five methods. For he says that the devil, being a spirit, has power over a corporeal creature to cause or prevent a local motion. Therefore he can prevent bodies from approaching each other, either directly or indirectly, by interposing himself in some bodily shape. In this way it happened to the young man who was betrothed to an idol and nevertheless married a young maiden, and was consequently unable to copulate with her. Secondly, he can excite a man to that act, or freeze his desire for it, by the virtue of secret things of which he best knows the power.

Thirdly, he can so disturb a man's perception and imagination as to make the woman appear loathsome to him: since he can, as has been said, influence the imagination. Fourthly, he can directly prevent the erection of that member which is adapted to fructification, just as he can prevent a local motion. Fifthly, he can prevent the flow of the vital essence to the members in which lies the motive power; by closing as it were the seminary ducts, so that it does not descend to the generative channels, or falls back from them, or does not project from them, or in any of many ways fails in its function.

And he continues in agreement with what has been treated of above by other Doctors. For God allows the devil more latitude in respect of this act, through which sin was first spread abroad, than of other human acts. Similarly, serpents are more subject to magic spells than are other animals. And a little later he says: It is the same in the case of a woman, for the devil can so darken her understanding that she considers her husband so loathsome that not for all the world would she allow him to lie with her.

Later he wishes to find the reason why more men than women are bewitched in respect of that action; and he says that such obstruction generally occurs in the seminal duct, or in an inability in the matter of erection, which can more easily happen to men; and therefore more men than women are bewitched. It might also be said that, the greater part of witches being women, they lust more for men than for women. Also they act in the despite of married women, finding every opportunity for adultery when the husband is able to copulate with other women but not with his own wife; and similarly the wife also has to seek other lovers.

CHAPTER SIX

Interpretations from the Protestant Reformation (1517–1700 CE)

INTRODUCTION

The Protestant Reformation restructured the medieval church in ways that had the potential radically to transform Christian understandings of sexuality and gender roles. Since the days of the early church Fathers, theologians had argued that chastity was spiritually superior to marriage. Church vocations such as the priesthood or the various monastic callings were predicated upon celibacy. Moreover, the Fathers—and the medieval theologians who succeeded them—frequently argued that God created woman to enable humanity to procreate. Medieval theology valued celibacy above marriage and contrasted woman's procreative power with man's presumed lofty spiritual temperament. It is not hard to understand, given that worldview, that male theologians not infrequently depicted women as temptresses who sought to rob godly men of their sexual purity.

In initiating far-reaching reformulations of church doctrine and practice in the sixteenth century, however, Protestants found themselves rethinking traditional notions of what it meant to be male and female. Protestant reformers rejected the medieval assumption that celibacy was essential to the highest form of spirituality and abolished the long-standing requirement that the clergy must be unmarried. Protestant theologians developed the notion of the "priesthood of the believer," insisting that clergy and laity were spiritually equal before God and that God had instituted marital relations as a part of the divine plan for human life. Though Protestants did not require their clergy to marry, they did put an end to monasticism.

Medieval Christians had understood the priesthood as a visible sign of the spiritual union between Christ and the church. Protestant reformers could not point to celibate clerics "wed" to Christ as an image of the Church's relationship to its savior. Instead, they pointed to the family. There, they said, was a microcosm of the faithfulness and spiritual unity manifested between believers and Christ in the larger church. Father, mother, and children living in right order with one another and with God were an essential way in which God manifested God's governance in human society.

Such rethinking about the function of sexuality in the Christian life created the possibility of reformulating gender roles in the church as well. The doctrine of the priesthood of the believer was democratizing on the spiritual level, reducing a distinction between the presumed "purity" of the clergy and the inferior spirituality of the laity that had been very real to medieval Christians. If Protestants applied the priesthood of the believer to questions of social status as well as those of spiritual status, the doctrine could prompt them to adopt more egalitarian gender relations.

But not necessarily. In celebrating the family, rather than a celibate male clergy, as the institution in which God's rule was clearly reflected on earth, Protestants were not obliged to depict women as men's equals. It was possible, instead, to define the family as a hierarchy ruled by the father, so that the "headship" of men was the defining mark of appropriate family discipline. Spiritual equality between Christians, in other words, was not necessarily accompanied by social equality.

Similarly, the Protestant decision to end monasticism could be, but was not necessarily, a sign that Protestants would value women's participation in the church more highly than medieval Christians had. Medieval Christianity, with its tendency to regard women as sexual temptresses, did offer one official avenue that recognized women's calling to minister in Christ's name: monasticism. Admittedly women monastics were subject to male clerics for ultimate oversight, as well as for the benefit of the sacraments. Nevertheless, women's monastic communities enjoyed a significant degree of autonomy, offering women opportunities for Christian service and producing some of the most remarkable theological works of the Middle Ages.

In abolishing monasticism and upholding marriage as a Christian vocation, Protestants rejected, at least in theory, the presupposition that women were innately less spiritual than men. Yet in dismantling monasticism, Protestants deprived women of the one institution that had traditionally provided them an official outlet for serving God. Was the ending of monasticism a gain for Protestant women, or were Catholic women better served by its continuance?

The answer to that question would depend upon the ways in which Protestants defined new roles for women in their churches. One thing was certain: in reconsidering the roles of men and women, Protestant theologians would go to the Scriptures for guidance. From Luther onward, Protestants complained that the church had for centuries been guided overmuch by tradition and far too little by the actual words of the Bible. Insisting on the centrality of Scripture for authentic faith and practice, Protestants pored over Genesis 1-3, as well as over New Testament commentary on Genesis, to determine the proper roles for men and women in church and society. At times, Protestant interpretation of Genesis 1-3 was remarkably egalitarian; at other times, Protestants echoed the hierarchical readings that had predominated for centuries.

Our readings in this chapter will come from three groups of Protestants: "magisterial" reformers (who worked in cooperation with their rulers to establish state-supported Protestant churches), as represented by Martin Luther and John Calvin; Anabaptists (who rejected state-supported Christianity in favor of voluntary churches composed of regenerated believers), as represented by Balthasar Hubmaier; and English Protestants who dissented from Anglicanism, as represented by John Milton and Margaret Fell.

The Magisterial Reforms of Luther and Calvin

Luther and Calvin led reforms that created Protestant churches aligned with secular governments. Both reformers were clerics who extolled the virtues of marriage. Historian Steven Ozment has noted that

> no institutional change brought about by the Reformation was more visible, responsive to late medieval pleas for reform, and conducive to new social attitudes than the marriage of Protestant clergy. Nor was there another point in the Protestant program where theology and practice corresponded more successfully.[1]

In rethinking the nature of human sexuality, both Calvin and Luther interpreted Genesis 1-3 in ways that significantly challenged the traditional hierarchical model of gender roles. Yet neither ultimately produced a social ethic that accorded equal status to women. In the end, the godly households they envisioned were hierarchical units headed by males. The magisterial reformers, in hailing the establishment of pious family life, produced an age, as Ozment has put it, "when fathers ruled."

The first of the major Protestant reformers, Martin Luther wrote commentaries on Genesis that were startling, both in his insistence that Eve was originally "in no respect inferior to Adam,"[2] and in his conclusions that that primordial equality was irrelevant to present social ordering. Luther argued that Aristotle's definition of woman as a "maimed man" was incorrect. He also disputed earlier readings of Genesis that depicted Adam alone as created in God's image. For Luther, God intended Adam and Eve together to rule the creation. Eve, contended Luther, had the same mental gifts as Adam and was by nature able to know, understand, and obey God's Word. Luther admitted there were distinctions between Eve and Adam; though Eve "was a most extraordinary creature," still "she was nevertheless a woman." Adam excelled her in glory and prestige. That distinction notwithstanding, Eve was Adam's partner, not his subordinate, in exercising dominion over the original creation.[3]

With the Fall, however, the relationship between man and woman changed forever. In the original creation, Luther explained, government was unnecessary; human beings by nature could know, love, and obey God. With the fall into sin, however, humanity lost its knowledge of God and no longer cared to know and do God's will. In listening to the serpent rather than to God's commands, Eve was not, as some interpreters had argued, inflamed with desire for the fruit. Rather, Luther explained, Eve chose to listen to a word other than God's Word, and as a result she, and Adam after her, fell into unbelief. The loss of the knowledge and love of God was so complete that, "to this sin," Luther concluded, "our entire nature has succumbed."[4]

Once corrupted by sin, people could not obey God. God therefore instituted government as a "remedy" for sin. For Luther, government was not a part of God's original plan for the creation. Rather, government was an order of preservation, falling short of the ethical perfection both of the original creation and of the gospel delivered by Christ. Government depended on coercion and the threat of violence to institute its laws, and in wielding the sword the state abided by an ethic far less pure than that of Jesus, who had commanded his followers to turn the other cheek rather than resort to violence. Because sinful people, left to their own devices, would turn upon one another, God commanded the state to exercise the sword in order to protect the lawful and deter the lawless. Given the sinfulness of human society, no government that followed Jesus's nonresistant love could survive. Therefore, Luther said, God compelled the state to use the sword.

Just as God had responded to the Fall by establishing the state to govern people in the political sphere, Luther contended, so God had instituted patriarchal marriage to govern fallen people in their households. God punished Eve, and thus all women, for the original sin especially harshly, subjecting them to pain in childbirth as well as to the rule of their husbands. Like Augustine, Luther believed that prior to the Fall, sexual intercourse would have been a passionless activity. In humanity's sinful state, however, sexual activity was marked by lust. In the same way, then, that God had instituted the state as a "remedy" for sin, so God also instituted marriage as a "remedy" for lust.[5]

Marriage also served as a way to regulate the behavior of women. Once "in no respect the inferior of her husband," woman was now, Luther argued, "compelled to obey him by God's command." It was irrelevant, Luther explained, that, had Eve never fallen into sin, women would "have been a partner in the rule which is now entirely the concern of males." Eve did sin; and God did subject her to her husband's authority. The husband, Luther noted, ruled the home and the state. He waged wars, defended his possessions, and was responsible for planting and harvesting crops. But "the woman, on the other hand, is like a nail driven into the wall. She sits at home. . . . " Still, Luther concluded, even this condition of subordination had its rewards. Women could find joy in motherhood; and enough remnants of mutuality between man and woman had survived the Fall that marriage could be both an experience of joy and a sign of God's love.[6]

Unlike the majority of commentators before him, Luther assumed that God's original intent was for men and women to rule the creation together. Luther's insistence on this point was one of the strongest egalitarian readings of Genesis 1-3 in the history of Christian thought through the sixteenth century. But his understanding of the Fall as utterly devastating to human nature meant that that original equality was irrelevant to gender relations after the Fall. Even redemption in Christ did not change the fact that God commanded husbands to rule their wives. Luther was disinclined to discuss redemption as an experience of regeneration. He described God's grace primarily as forgiving and only secondarily as transforming.

Moreover, unlike Catholic theologians, Luther did not categorize marriage as a sacrament but as a form of government. And, in outlining his famous doctrine of "two kingdoms," Luther was careful to distinguish the ethic appropriate to the state from the gospel ethic. As private individuals, he said, Christians were bound to follow the ethic of Christ. They should return no one evil for evil. Like Christ, they would suffer injury and death rather than fall short of the perfection of the gospel. Christians lived in peace with their neighbors out of gratitude for the love Christ had poured out upon the world; they did not need secular laws or punishments to coerce them into good behavior.

As public citizens, however, Christians were obliged to support the state. Until the world was populated entirely by true Christians—which, Luther asserted, would never occur short of the final judgment—the state would have to rely upon the sword to coerce the wayward to obey the law. God had established the state to protect the good and to punish the wicked, and God commanded Christians, as citizens, to aid the state in its work. Thus, as private believers Christians were to follow the gospel in its perfection; as public citizens, they were to support government even though its methods fell short of the purity of the gospel.

Had Luther categorized marriage as an institution subject to the perfection of the gospel, he might have argued that the subordination of women to men was unacceptable for Christians. But because Luther identified marriage as a form of government, and thus a remedy for sin, he concluded that husbands should exercise dominion over their wives. Though patriarchal marriage fell short of the perfection of the gospel, Luther insisted that Christians continue to subordinate wives to husbands.

Calvin's reading of Genesis 1-3 was equally paradoxical. He rejected four features typical of the hierarchical interpretation: (1) the claim that God created Eve solely for the purpose of allowing Adam to procreate, (2) the claim that Eve was not created fully in the image God, (3) the claim that Adam fell into sin because Eve seduced him, and (4) the claim that Eve alone was responsible for plunging humanity into sin. Calvin responded to the first point by arguing that human beings were, by nature, social creatures. God created humanity as male and female not simply so that procreation would be possible, but in order to bond husband and wife through physical as well as spiritual intimacy. Second, Calvin contended, the Genesis text was clear in stating that God created both male and female in the divine image and likeness.

Third, Calvin praised Eve for her initial determination to resist the serpent. Eve had no experience with evil, Calvin noted, and therefore had no reason to consider the serpent anything other than a domestic animal. Thus, Calvin concluded that in initially rejecting the serpent's suggestion that she eat the forbidden fruit, "it was impossible for Eve more prudently or more courageously to repel the assault of Satan. . . . " Eve eventually yielded to the serpent because she became infected with the "poison of cupiscence," desiring to exalt herself in the place of God.

Finally, Calvin argued that Adam ate the fruit that Eve gave him not because he was captivated by her charms, but for precisely the same reason that Eve ate: Adam was persuaded that, as the serpent had promised, he could be like God. Calvin conceded that 1 Timothy 2:14 suggested that the serpent deceived Eve alone, and that Adam ate not because he was deceived, but because he wrongly chose to submit to his wife. Calvin also acknowledged that in eating the fruit Adam had in fact heeded his wife; but, Calvin insisted, Adam ate for other reasons as well—because, like Eve, he was ambitious and wished to usurp God. In any case, Calvin concluded, the Timothy text spoke only "comparatively" about Eve as the origin of evil. Ultimately, sin entered the world not through Eve, but through Adam, as Paul himself stated in Romans 5:12. Interpretations that gave Eve sole blame for the Fall were, for Calvin, unpersuasive.[7]

In spite of rejecting four elements typical of the hierarchical model of interpretation of Genesis 1–3, Calvin did not embrace an egalitarian reading of Genesis 1–3. He stressed the mutuality that Adam and Eve enjoyed in Eden, describing Eve as Adam's "inseparable associate." But even prior to the Fall, he argued, Eve was subject to Adam. For this reason, Paul in 1 Corinthians 11 had noted that man was the image of God, but woman the image of man. That claim, Calvin reasoned, was not an ontological one, since according to Genesis 1 both Eve and Adam reflected the divine image. Rather, Paul must have been discussing the image of God in *government*. God had created male and female so that the male had superiority over the wife. Originally, this superiority indicated nothing more than a higher degree of honor. But after the Fall, God punished Eve by changing the original "liberal and gentle subjection" into genuine "servitude" so that "Thou shall desire nothing but what thy husband wishes."[8]

Calvin's analysis of woman's subordination to man after the Fall led him to some curious positions. As Jane Dempsey Douglass has noted, Calvin restricted woman's subordination to the political realm. In institutions of human ordering, such as the state or the family, women were bound to accede to men; but Calvin did not apply this subordination to the theological realm. In the church, where God's reign was made real, men and women were spiritually equal. Calvin felt free to interpret New Testament passages bidding women to be silent or to cover their heads in church as advice appropriate to the social context of the New Testament era, not as eternally binding admonitions. Indeed, as Dempsey Douglass explained, Calvin insisted that under special circumstances God could call women to teach and govern within the church.[9]

But it is important to see that Calvin limited gender equality to the theological realm. When he discussed marriage, he insisted that wives must obey their husbands. He cautioned husbands not to abuse their authority, noting that marriage ought to be an experience of love and support for each partner. Still, regardless of how much (or little) compassion that a husband demonstrated for his wife, she was bound to submit to him. Dempsey Douglass has documented Calvin's correspondence with women who sought his advice on how to respond to husbands who did not share their faith. Calvin was eminently clear in admonishing the women to "bear with patience the cross which God has seen fit to place upon" them, even if their husbands resorted to violence. If their husbands commanded them to sin against God, they should resist; otherwise, Calvin concluded: "We do not find ourselves permitted by the Word of God . . . to advise a woman to leave her husband, except by force of necessity, and we do not understand this force to be operative when a husband behaves roughly, and uses threats to his wife, nor even when he beats her, but when there is imminent peril to her life. . . . "[10]

Admonishing women to submit to domestic violence until they were certain that the next beating posed a threat to their lives is not the sort of advice that might endear Calvin to contemporary readers. It is paradoxical that both Calvin and Luther, who self-consciously rejected many of the features typical of traditional hierarchical readings of Genesis 1-3, in the end used Genesis 3 to justify the subjection of women to men in marriage. Since Luther posited an equality of status between Adam and Eve prior to the Fall, his insistence that God's original intent for gender relations was irrelevant to a post-Fall world, even within the church, was all the more ironic. Calvin, on the other hand, saw gender hierarchy as present even before the Fall—which made his insistence upon distinguishing between the hierarchy appropriate to government and the theological equality all the more notable. Neither Luther nor Calvin propounded significant egalitarian applications of Genesis 1-3; yet neither did they accept many of the readings of Genesis 1-3 typical of the hierarchical model.

Anabaptist Readings

Anabaptists formed part of the "Radical Reformation," that branch of Protestantism that rejected infant baptism and failed to gain state support. In distinction from the magisterial reformers like Luther and Calvin, Anabaptist groups (such as the Mennonites, the Hutterites, and the Swiss Brethren) rejected the notion that the Fall had so corrupted human beings that they were unable, apart from the assistance of God's grace, to wish to love and obey God. Rather, the Anabaptists argued, people were free to seek God's grace or to reject it. Those who sought grace received God's transforming spirit, which regenerated them into persons who delighted in doing God's will. The true church, for Anabaptists, consisted of regenerated Christians who, through submitting themselves to adult baptism, had indicated that they had forsaken the sinful world and yielded themselves to Christ. Anabaptists paid a heavy price for their beliefs; both Catholics and magisterial Protestants persecuted and killed them.

Anabaptists placed even more stress on the priesthood of all believers than did the magisterial reformers. Anabaptist pastors were chosen from the body of believers. They did not receive special theological education, nor were they ordained. Anabaptists emphasized humility as a basic Christian virtue and opposed the special status that both magisterial reformers and Catholics awarded their clergy.

In their readings of Genesis 1-3, Anabaptists did not indulge in vituperative attacks upon Eve. For example, Menno Simons—the leader for whom the Mennonites were named—conceded that Eve sinned first because she was "the weaker vessel," but he also insisted that Adam and Eve shared equally in the divine image and that it was through Adam, not Eve, that the rest of humanity inherited a sinful nature.[11] Like many other radical reformers, Menno accepted the Aristotelian notion that men supplied to their offspring all genetic material, whereas women merely provided a nurturing environment for the fetus. Thus, original sin infected humanity not because of Eve, but because of Adam. Men, not women, were responsible for the transmission of sin.

Regeneration, on the other hand, accrued to men and women equally. Menno argued that the church of Christ—the community of saints—originated from both Adam and Eve and that all those who chose to follow Christ were reborn into the spotless humanity that Eve and Adam enjoyed before the Fall. The community of men and women who followed Christ became one body, just as many grains came together to form one loaf of bread. United in faith, true believers were joined together in harmony and peace; thus, Menno claimed, the "true and living members of the body of Christ" became "one heart, one mind, and one soul."[12]

Unlike explicators of explicitly hierarchical interpretations of Genesis 1-3, Anabaptists were not inclined to dwell upon the distinctions between the virtues of men and the virtues of women. Rather, Anabaptists were more interested in discussing the differences between the "world" and the community of true faith. Anabaptists insisted on regeneration and obedience as marks of the church—and they made those claims in full knowledge that their faith made them subject to persecution and death. Swiss Brethren leader Dirk Philips summarized the Anabaptist position when he noted that from the time Cain murdered Abel until the present, "there were two kinds of people, two kinds of children, two kinds of congregations on earth, namely, the people of God and the devil's people."[13]

The true church, Dirk claimed, was a "*congregation* of holy beings" descended from Eve. God promised in Genesis 3 that Jesus, the seed of Eve, would provide rebirth to those who loved God, whereas those who shunned God would ally themselves with Satan. Dirk argued that the persecution of the Anabaptists was a proof that God's prophecy had been realized. "All believers," he said, "are the seed of the spiritual Eve, just as the unbelievers are the seed of the crooked old serpent, and that in a spiritual sense. And between the children of the aforementioned Eve and the serpent has been put an eternal enmity by God so that the children of the devil all the time hate, envy, and persecute the children of God (Gen. 3:15)." For Dirk, Eve was not a figure to be reviled; she was, rather, the source of the true church.

In a similar vein, Balthasar Hubmaier railed against Christians (such as Luther) who argued that humanity was mired in sin and unable to choose to be yielded to God. Such reasoning, Hubmaier insisted, was specious. True, without God's transforming grace, no one could experience the new birth; but to argue that humanity was helpless to ask for grace to live in obedience to God's will was to "cover all license of the flesh and lay all our sin and guilt on God, as Adam did on his Eve, and Eve on the serpent."[14] Hubmaier was not so much interested in blaming Eve for the Fall as in asserting that individuals were responsible for their own choices.

In light of the Anabaptists' commitment to regeneration, obedience, humility, and community, some scholars such as Roland Bainton have speculated that Anabaptists, alone of all the Reformation factions, established equality between men and women.[15] More recently, scholars like M. Lucille Marr have argued that the gap between theological theory (which seemed to support gender equality) and actual practice was not inconsiderable. Anabaptist leaders like Menno Simons and Dirk Philips argued that rejecting celibacy in favor of married life was a sign of woman's importance; she was not merely an object of lust to be shunned, but a partner in the life of faith whom man ought to treasure. Men and women were equally called to be faithful to radical Christianity; both could—and did—witness to their faith when persecuted, tortured, and killed by Catholic or magisterial Protestant officials. Nevertheless, Menno and Dirk expected wives to be submissive to their husbands; and Hubmaier faulted Adam for failing to "master his rib."[16]

Anabaptist life and thought, in short, combined both hierarchical and egalitarian readings of Genesis 1-3. Many of the harsher elements of a hierarchical interpretation were unimportant to Anabaptist interpretations of Genesis. Anabaptists did not hold Eve solely responsible for the Fall; they assumed that men, not women, transmitted original sin to new generations; they celebrated God's triumph over sin through Jesus, Eve's seed; they assumed that the holy company of believers originated in Eve and Adam; and they used images like the "seed of Eve" to describe the faithful. Yet Anabaptists tacitly assumed that men would act as women's heads, and they attributed the Fall to such causes as Eve's weaker nature or Adam's failure to master Eve. Thus, the Anabaptist uses of Genesis 1-3 were not fully egalitarian; but Anabaptists refuted many of the elements that had traditionally composed a hierarchical reading.

English Dissidents: Puritans and Quakers

Protestant movements in England precipitated decades of theological and political controversy, both before and after Queen Elizabeth I (who reigned from 1558 to 1603) established Anglicanism as the state church of England, and thus the official form of English Protestantism. In this chapter, we are particularly interested in examining representatives from two dissident groups of English Protestants: Puritans and Quakers. No interpretation of Genesis 1-3 in Christian history has been more influential than its 1667 Puritan retelling, *Paradise Lost*; and no reformulation of the theological roots of power and authority among Christians was more far-reaching than that of the Quakers.

In *Paradise Lost*, John Milton challenged some of the classic features of a hierarchical reading of Genesis 1-3, but his reconstruction of the Garden of Eden was thoroughly patriarchal. Milton left no doubt that Eve was a good creation. "Godlike erect, with native Honour clad / In naked Majestie," both Eve and Adam to him "seemd Lords of all, / And worthy seemed, for in their looks divine / The image of thir glorious Maker shon . . . " (IV, 288-92). Milton was also convinced of the goodness of sexuality, describing the "conjugal attraction unreprov'd" that Eve and Adam felt for each other prior to the Fall. With "kisses pure," they were "imparadis't in one another's arms," innocently enjoying "their fill / Of bliss on bliss" (IV, 492-508). So right was the pleasure that Eve and Adam found in each other, Milton said, that all of nature rejoiced at their "Nuptial Bowre" (VIII, 506-32).

Though Milton saw the mutuality enjoyed by Eve and Adam as God's good gift, he did not posit Eve as Adam's equal. God created Adam "for God only, shee for God in him." Eve was created for subjection, but Adam's rule was so benevolent that Eve found it easy to heed his will (IV, 299-310). Ultimately, however, Eve's charms were so disarming that in her presence Adam was unable to remember that he, as the more rational of the two, was created to rule, and she to follow:

> For well I understand in the prime end
> Of Nature her th' inferiour, in the mind
> And inward Faculties, which most Excell;
> . . . yet when I approach
> Her loveliness, so absolute she seems
> And in her self compleat, so well to know
> Her own, that what she wills to do or say
> Seems wisest, vertuousest, discreetest, best;
> All higher knowledge in her presence falls
> Degraded. . . . (VIII, 540-52)

Adam's inability to rule his passions set the stage for the Fall. Milton depicted Eve's decision to disobey God as an act of lust. Eve sought not knowledge, but pleasure, as "greedily she ingorg'd without restraint" the forbidden fruit (IX, 791). Once having eaten, Eve wished to share the fruit with Adam, that he might be her equal in this experience of pleasure. Adam saw that disobedience had defaced and deflowered Eve, yet he could not bear to be separated from the woman who was bone of his bone and flesh of his flesh. Adam made a chivalrous decision to join Eve in her disobedience, not, according to Milton, because she deceived Adam, but because, against his better knowledge, he was "fondly overcome with Femal charm" (IX, 896-999).

Only after the Fall did Adam question his earlier conviction that Eve was the "last and best / Of all God's works" (IX, 896-897). Disillusioned by the loss of paradise, Adam was no longer sure that God's decision to give him a woman for a partner was a good choice. Why, he asked, had God created

> This noveltie on Earth, this fair defect
> Of Nature, and not fill the World at once
> With Men as Angels without Feminine,
> Or find some other way to generate
> Mankind? this mischief had not then befall'n,
> And more that shall befall, innumerable
> Disturbances on Earth through Femal snares. . . . (X, 891-897)

Such deprecations of woman were the product of Adam's fallen reasoning. Nevertheless, Milton's point was that the Fall had occurred because Adam had failed to rule Eve. In the end, *Paradise Lost* presented a thoroughly hierarchical interpretation of Genesis 1-3.

In Margaret Fell (1614-1702), however, English Protestantism offered a thinker who rejected the hierarchical model. Fell belonged to the Quakers, a dissident Protestant group founded by George Fox in the 1640s. By its very existence, Quakerism was a threat to traditional social hierarchies. Quakers did not have a formal clergy; they addressed each other as "thee" and "thou," refusing to use titles of status that set some persons above others; their marriage vows did not require wives to obey their husbands; and they insisted that an "Inner Light" indwelled each person and could empower any one—regardless of gender, class, or race—to speak God's Word.[17] To the dismay of the English mainstream, Quakers permitted women to testify in their religious meetings.

Such a worldview was subversive to the hierarchical presuppositions basic to most Christian theology. Accordingly, Fell's reading of Genesis 1-3 was radically egalitarian. She insisted that Adam and Eve shared the image of God equally and found little significance in the fact that Eve was first to eat the forbidden fruit. Though Eve had sinned first, Fell argued, God had promised that in Eve's seed the serpent would be rebuked. The Scriptures were clear that the Church was female—the church was, after all, the bride of Christ—so, if the female were not to speak in opposition to Satan, there would be none left to testify on God's behalf. Fell noted that it was women who first preached

the resurrection of Christ and that it was male disciples who initially rejected their testimony. Thus, those who "despise and oppose the Message of
the Lord God that he sends by Women" rejected the gospel itself.[18]

Fell also pointed to numerous New Testament instances of women's
preaching the gospel. She dismissed Paul's instruction (1 Corinthians 14) that
women refrain from speaking in church as an admonition for women who
were under the law, not the gospel. And she characterized 1 Timothy 2 as a
discussion of domestic relations. Wives, she concluded from the text, should
not dress immodestly for worship services, and in that sense ought not usurp
authority over their husbands; but that directive was irrelevant to the question
of women speaking in worship.

Fell's admission that wives should submit to their husbands by dressing
modestly was the only explicit remnant of the hierarchical reading of Genesis
1-3. For the rest, her interpretation was remarkably egalitarian. She insisted
that the Holy Spirit gave the message of the gospel to men and women alike
and concluded that Christendom had fallen so far into apostasy that its opposition to women's speaking in church "had arisen out of the bottomless Pit."[19]
Only when Christians freely accepted the Scriptural claim that the truths of
the gospel were revealed through women as well as men, she concluded, would
the revelations of God once more become clear to the Christian world. The
egalitarian reading of Genesis 1-3 had, in the 16 centuries since Jesus's death,
no more eloquent advocate than Margaret Fell.

NOTES TO CHAPTER 6, INTRODUCTION

1. Steven Ozment, *The Age of Reform, 1250-1550* (New Haven and London: Yale
University Press, 1980), p. 381. See also his *When Fathers Ruled: Family Life in Reformation Europe* (Cambridge: Harvard University Press, 1983).

2. Martin Luther, *Lectures on Genesis: Chapters 1-5,* translated by George V.
Schick and edited by Jaroslav Pelikan, *Luther's Works* (Saint Louis: Concordia Publishing House, 1958), vol. 1, p. 115.

3. Luther, *Lectures on Genesis,* pp. 62-71.

4. Luther, *Lectures on Genesis,* pp. 147-62.

5. Luther, *Lectures on Genesis,* pp. 115-19, 137-38.

6. Luther, *Lectures on Genesis,* pp. 198-203, 132-35.

7. John Calvin, *Commentaries on The First Book of Moses Called Genesis,* translated
by Rev. John King (Grand Rapids: Wm. B. Eerdmans Publishing Company, 1948), vol.
1, pp. 95-96, 128-31, 145-54.

8. Calvin, *Commentaries,* vol. 1, pp. 95-96, 128-31, 172.

9. Jane Dempsey Douglass, "Christian Freedom: What Calvin Learned at the
School of Women," *Church History* 53 (2) (June 1984): 160-66. See also John Lee
Thompson, *John Calvin and the Daughters of Sarah: Women in Regular and Exceptional
Roles in the Exegesis of Calvin, His Predecessors, and His Contemporaries,* Travaux
d'Humanisme et Renaissance 259 (Geneva: Librairie Droz, 1992). As Dawn DeVries
noted in a review of Thompson's book, neither Thompson nor Douglass interpreted
Calvin as sympathetic to feminism or to women's ordination; *Church History* (March
1995): 114-15.

10. Jane Dempsey Douglass, "Women and the Continental Reformation," in
Rosemary Radford Ruether, editor, *Religion and Sexism: Images of Woman in the Jewish
and Christian Traditions* (New York: Simon and Schuster), pp. 299-301.

11. Menno Simons, *The Incarnation of Our Lord*, in J. C. Wenger, editor, and Leonard Verduin, translator, *The Complete Writings of Menno Simons* (Scottdale, Penn.: Herald Press, 1956), pp. 816, 800.

12. Menno Simons, *Reply to Gellius Faber*, p. 742; *Foundation of Christian Doctrine*, p. 145, both in *The Complete Writings*.

13. Dirk Philips, "The Word of God," in George H. Williams and Angel M. Mergal, editors, *Spiritual and Anabaptist Writers*, The Library of Christian Classics, Ichthus Edition (Philadelphia: Westminster Press, 1957), pp. 230-31.

14. Balthasar Hubmaier, "On Free Will," in Williams and Mergal, *Spiritual and Anabaptist Writers*, pp. 114-15.

15. Roland Bainton, *What Christianity Says about Sex, Love, and Marriage* (New York: Association Press, 1957), p. 94. For an excellent analysis of this argument, see M. Lucille Marr, "Anabaptist Women of the North: Peers in the Faith, Subordinates in Marriage," *Mennonite Quarterly Review* 61 (4) (October 1987): 347-62. See also Sherrin Marshall-Wyntjes, "Women and Religious Choices in the Sixteenth Century Netherlands," *Archiv. Ref.* 75 (1984): 776-89; and Merry E. Weisner, "Beyond Women and the Family: Toward a Gender Analysis of the Reformation," *Sixteenth Century Journal* 18 (3) (1987): 311-23.

16. Marr, "Anabaptist Women in Marriage," pp. 350-60; Hubmaier, "On Free Will," p. 130.

17. Barbara J. MacHaffie, *Her Story* (Philadelphia: Fortress Press, 1986), p. 89.

18. Margaret Fell, *Women's Speaking: Justified, Proved, and Allowed of by the Scriptures* (London: Pythia Press, 1989 [1666]), pp. 1-9.

19. Fell, *Women's Speaking Justified*, pp. 9-13.

●

FIVE REFORMATION THINKERS

Balthasar Hubmaier

Born between 1480 and 1485 in Friedberg (Germany), Balthasar Hubmaier was a Catholic priest who served as professor of theology at the University of Ingolstoldt, cathedral preacher at Regensburg, and parish priest in Waldshut. In the 1520s, he fell under the influence of magisterial reformers Martin Luther (in German Wittenberg) and Ulrich Zwingli (in Swiss Zurich), only to ally himself, finally, with the Anabaptist wing of the Protestant Reformation. He and sixty Waldshut parishioners received believer's baptism from the Swiss Brethren pastor Wilhelm Reublin in April of 1525. On the following Easter Sunday, Hubmaier baptized three hundred others, thus providing the first instance of an entire congregation converting to Anabaptism. He then fled Catholic persecution in Waldshut (where he was suspected of supporting the 1525 Peasants' Revolt), only to be imprisoned and tortured in Protestant Zurich. Forced to recant his faith, Hubmaier moved to Moravia, where he published numerous defenses of Anabaptism. Seized by imperial forces, he was tortured and then burned at the stake for treason on March 10, 1528.[1]

Hubmaier departed from the classic Anabaptist doctrine (as articulated in the 1527 *Schleitheim Confession*) that true Christians should separate themselves from the work of government. But his 1527 *Freedom of the Will* was an exemplary defense, against the Lutheran insistence on the bondage of the will to sin, of the Anabaptist assertion that Christians were both able and obliged to seek God's aid in yielding themselves to the rigorous demands of the gospel. Against Luther's contention that Christians remained *simul justis et peccator* (simultaneously justified and sinful), Anabaptists believed in the regenerating power of the new birth. For Anabaptists, God's grace was transforming and empowering, enabling true Christians to follow Jesus in word and deed.

One effect of that doctrine, as Hubmaier's *Freedom of the Will* indicated, was a disinclination to blame Eve for the sinful choices that people make. In distinguishing three divisions within the human being—flesh, spirit, soul— and identifying Eve as a metaphor of the flesh, and Adam as a metaphor of the soul, Hubmaier subordinated Eve to Adam, much as Philo had done centuries earlier. Moreover, Hubmaier regarded Eve, or the flesh, as more blameworthy in the Fall than Adam, the soul. Nevertheless, he insisted that flesh, spirit, and soul were originally entirely good creations and that redemption in Christ restored that goodness. Thus, he claimed, "no one may decry Adam or Eve, nor excuse or gloss over his sins with Adam's Fall since everything which had been lost, wounded, and had died in Adam has been sufficiently restored, healed, and made healthy." In articulating typical Anabaptist understandings of freedom and regeneration, Hubmaier was a countervoice to the long theological tradition that blamed Eve for humanity's continuing woes. (Source: Balthasar Hubmaier, *Freedom of the Will* in *Balthasar Hubmaier: Theologian of Anabaptism*, translated and edited by H. Wayne Pipkin and John H. Yoder, Classics of the Reformation series, Scottdale, Penn., and Kitchener, Ontario: Herald Press, 1989, vol. 5, pp. 429-36, 439, 440, 442-43, 445-46.)

NOTE TO CHAPTER 6, BALTHASAR HUBMAIER

1. See Christof Windhurst, "Balthasar Hubmaier: Professor, Preacher, Politician," in Hans-Jurgen Geertz, editor, *Profiles of Radical Reformers* (Scottdale, Penn., and Kitchener, Ontario: Herald Press, 1982), pp. 144-57; Donald F. Durnbaugh, *The Believers' Church* (Scottdale, Penn., and Kitchener, Ontario: Herald Press, 1985), pp. 70-72; and David C. Steinmetz, *Reformers in the Wings* (Grand Rapids: Baker Books, 1971), pp. 199-202.

Freedom of the Will (1527 CE)
BALTHASAR HUBMAIER

The human being is a corporal and rational creature, created by God as body, spirit, and soul, Gen. 2:7. These three elements are found essentially and in varying ways in every human being, as the Scripture thoroughly proves.

When the Lord God made the human being out of the dust from the earth, he blew a living breath into his face and thus the human being became a living soul, Gen. 2:7. Here Moses points to three things with distinct names. First, the flesh or the body is made out of the earth, which clod of earth or lump of clay, *aphar* and *erets* in the Hebrew, is translated in German as "dust," "ashes," or "mud taken from the earth." Second, notice the living breath, *neshamah* in the Hebrew, translated as "blowing on," "breathing on," "blowing upon," or "spirit." Third, the soul, called *nephesh*, is expressed separately; it is that which makes the body alive. . . .

Now since with scriptural authority no one can deny these three essential things, substances, or essences, it follows that one must confess also three kinds of will in human beings, namely, the will of the flesh, the will of the soul, and the will of the spirit. However, so that I might teach in clear writing the different divisions of these three wills, the Spirit of God speaks in John 1:13 of the will of the flesh, which does not want to suffer; the will of the soul, willing to suffer, but due to the flesh seeks not to; and the will of the spirit which strongly desires to suffer (cf. John 1:13). . . . Now we are once born, but in original sin and wrath, as Paul laments to the Romans and Ephesians, also David, Job, and Jeremiah, Rom. 7:5; Eph. 2:3; Ps. 51:7; Job 3:1. Accordingly we must be born again or we cannot see the kingdom of God, nor enter it. . . .

That is the true rebirth of which Christ speaks in John 3:3, whereby our Adam, who had become a woman and an Eve through the Fall, now again becomes a man; and the soul, which had become flesh, now again becomes spirit. . . . Note here, dear Christian, how the soul, which has become flesh through the disobedience of Adam, must through the Spirit of God and his living Word be reborn to a new spirit and become spirit, for what is born of the Spirit is spirit, John 3:6. . . .

How the Human Being Was before the Fall of Adam

Before the transgression of Adam all three substances in the human being—flesh, soul, and spirit—were good, Gen. 1:31. For God considered all the things which he had made and they were very good—indeed, especially the human being made in the image of God, Gen. 1:31. The three substances were also wholly free to choose good or evil, life or death, heaven or hell. . . .

How the Human Being Has Become after the Fall of Adam Concerning the Flesh

After our first father Adam transgressed the commandment of God by his disobedience, he lost this freedom for himself and all his descendants. . . . When Eve, who is a figure of our flesh, desired to eat and did eat of the forbidden fruit, she thereby lost the knowledge of good and evil, indeed of wanting and doing the good, and had to pay for this loss with death, so that as soon as a person is conceived and born, he is conceived and born in sin. . . .

Concerning the Spirit

The spirit of the human being, however, has before, during, and after the Fall remained upright, whole, and good. For it has neither with counsel nor deed, will nor action, been disobedient in any way in allowing the flesh to eat the forbidden fruit. Indeed, like a prisoner in the body, it had to eat against its will. However, the guilt was not its own, but that of the flesh and the soul, which also became flesh. . . .

Concerning the Soul

However, the soul, the third part of the human being, has through this disobedience of Adam been wounded in the will in such a way and become sick unto death so that it can on its own choose nothing good. Nor can it refuse evil since it has lost the knowledge of good and evil, Gen. 2; 3. There is nothing left to it but to sin and to die. Yes, as far as doing good goes, the soul has become entirely powerless and ineffective, Rom. 7. Only the flesh can act, without which the soul is outwardly able to do nothing, for the flesh is its instrument. Since, however, the instrument is incapable of doing anything, how can anything good be done with it, even if the soul gladly wanted to and made every effort. Nevertheless this Fall of the soul is reparable through the Word of God, Ps. 119:7; which teaches us again what it is to will or not will good or evil, and that after this life through the resurrection of the flesh, the body will become a heavenly, imperishable, noble, and spiritual one for action and fulfillment, 1 Cor. 15:44. Yes, it is the body of these people born again of the water and the Spirit, as the first human Adam was created into the natural life and the last Adam into the spiritual life. The first human is of the earth and is earthly; the second is from heaven and is heavenly.

That, however, this Fall of the soul is also reparable and harmless here on earth, while that of the flesh irreparable and even deadly, is due to the following: Adam, a figure of the soul—as Eve is a figure of the flesh—would have preferred not to eat of the forbidden tree, 1 Tim. 2:14. He was not seduced by the snake but Eve was, Gen. 3:6. Adam knew well that the word of the serpent contradicted the Word of God. Nevertheless, he willed to eat of this fruit against his own conscience in order not to grieve or anger his rib and flesh, Eve. He would have preferred not to do it. Thus, since he was more obedient to his Eve than to God, he lost the knowledge of good and evil. So he cannot will or choose good, nor can he not will or flee something evil, for he does not know what is truly good or evil before God, Ps. 14:3; 32:5; 53:2. Nothing tastes good to him but that which tastes and seems good to his Eve, that is, his flesh. For he has lost the right sense of taste. . . .

How the Human Being Is after the Restoration

If the human being after the restoration by Christ is considered, one finds clearly that the flesh is still good for nothing and wholly ruined, as all the Scriptures lament. The spirit is happy, willing, and ready to do all good. The soul, sad and troubled, standing between the spirit and the flesh, knowing not what to do, is in its natural powers blind and ignorant of heavenly things. However, since it has been awakened by the heavenly Father through words of comfort, threats, promises, good things, punishment, and in other ways prodded, admonished, and drawn, as well as made whole by his dear Son, and enlightened by the Holy Spirit—as the three main articles of our Christian faith concerning God the Father and the Son and the Holy Spirit show—by this the soul now again knows what is good and evil. Now it has again obtained its lost freedom. It can now freely and willingly be obedient to the spirit, can will and choose good, as well as it was able in Paradise. It can also reject evil and flee it. . . .

The soul stands between the spirit and the flesh, as Adam stood between God, who tells him he should not eat of the tree of the knowledge of good and evil, and his Eve, who tells him he should eat of the tree, Gen. 2: 3. The soul is now free and may follow the spirit or the flesh. However, if it follows Eve, that is, the flesh, then it becomes an Eve and flesh. If it is obedient to the spirit, then it becomes a spirit. . . .

From this passage it is easy to note how the law is given in different ways: to the flesh for the recognition of its sins; to the spirit as an aid and witness against sin; to the soul for a light whereby it can see and learn the way of righteousness and flee sin and evil. Thus, when the flesh hears the law, it is frightened and its hair stands on end in terror. The spirit leaps for joy. The believing soul thanks God and praises him for the lamp and light to his feet, Ps. 119:105. For as the devil neither wishes to nor can do good, but is stuck in his evil, so likewise our flesh, since it has sinned out of willfulness when it saw that the forbidden fruit was good to eat and was appealing to the eyes and lovely to the sight. However, the soul did not sin out of its own willfulness but out of weakness and the impulse of the flesh since Adam did not want to grieve Eve, who was his flesh. As he then excused himself and said: "The woman, whom you gave me for a mate, gave me from the tree and I ate," Gen. 3:6. Only the spirit has remained upright in this Fall; therefore it will return to the Lord, who gave it, Eccles. 12:7. . . .

From the things said above one notes clearly and surely that the human being received two wounds by the Fall of Adam. The first is an inner one which is ignorance of good and evil; therefore Adam was more obedient to the voice of his Eve than to the voice of God. The second wound is external, in doing and acting. Thus the human being cannot wholly complete and hold the commandments of God on account of the inborn evil of his flesh; rather, in all his works he is a useless servant, Luke 17:10. This weakness or lack originates from the fact that Adam has not rightly mastered his rib Eve according to the command of God, but against the same has also eaten of the tree which was forbidden him on penalty of death.

The first wound is healed by the wine poured on it by the Samaritan Christ, Luke 10:34, that is, through the law in which the human being by a new grace is again taught anew what is truly good and evil before God. The second wound is healed by the oil, that is, with the gospel. . . .

Here one grasps with both hands how Christ has made the Fall of Adam wholly innocuous for us and incapable of condemning, and how he crushed the head of the old serpent through the seed of the woman, Gen. 3:15, how he took away the sting and made its poison no longer lethal to us, 1 Cor. 15:30f. Thus, henceforth, no one may decry Adam or Eve nor excuse or gloss over his sins with Adam's Fall since everything which had been lost, wounded, and had died in Adam has been sufficiently restored, healed, and made healthy. For Christ with his Spirit has acquired for our spirit from the heavenly Father that the prison is not harmful to our spirit. And with his soul he has acquired for our soul that through his divine Word it is again taught and enlightened as to what good and evil is. Yes, also by his flesh he earns for our flesh that after it has become ashes it may again be resurrected in honor and be immortal, 1 Cor. 15:22. Accordingly, henceforth every soul that sins will bear its sin itself since it is willingly responsible for its own sin and not Adam, not Eve, not the flesh, sin, death or the devil, for all these things are already captured, bound, and overcome in Christ. To him we say, with Paul, be praise, honor, and thanks for eternity.

Martin Luther

Martin Luther (1483-1546) was a pivotal figure in the Protestant Reformation. A German Catholic priest on the faculty of Wittenberg University, he first came to wider attention with the circulation of his 1517 *Ninety-Five Theses*, a series of propositions intended to stir academic debate on the issues of sin, repentance, and papal indulgences. Luther's *Theses* and his subsequent writings emphasized the devastating effects of the Fall and insisted that trust in God's forgiving grace—rather than futile attempts to perform meritorious actions—was the sole path of salvation. This fact, he claimed, was grounded in Scripture, an authority which was superior to church traditions and papal practices. Luther was excommunicated in 1521 and, after a period in hiding, returned to Wittenberg to lead the Lutheran Reformation.

His notable achievements and publications are too numerous to mention. His translations of the New Testament and the Hebrew Bible into German proved pivotal for the shaping of the modern German language, and his innovations in worship (such as congregational singing, communion in two kinds, and the use of the vernacular) continue to influence Protestantism. Luther also abolished monasticism, arguing that enforced celibacy was unnatural. The truest form of Christian society, he argued, was not a community of celibate monks or nuns. Rather, with the pious father as its head and the rest of the members in submission to the father's authority, it was the family that most vividly exemplified the body of Christ. In recognizing marriage as an expression of the love of Christ, Luther rejected medieval theological traditions that had celebrated celibacy and denigrated women as threats to men's sexual purity. But by describing the godly family as one ruled by the father, Luther continued the medieval pattern of subordinating women to men.

This ambivalence about the status of women is nowhere clearer than in Luther's *Lectures on Genesis*. Here he argued, in contradiction to much of Christian tradition, that Eve had originally shared with Adam dominion over the creation. Eve was Adam's partner, not his subordinate. But the Fall, Luther contended, had devastated human nature, so that the original gender equality was irrelevant to current life. Seeing humanity mired in sin, God had instituted government as a "remedy" to curb the most vicious effects of sin. Luther understood marriage as a form of government, in which God commanded the wife to obey her husband. Nothing on earth—not even the experience of redemption in Christ—could alter that hierarchy of gender. Husbands commanded; wives obeyed. Though women could seek consolation in the joys of motherhood, the consequences of the Fall were dire and irreparable. (Source: *Luther's Works*, vol. 1: *Lectures on Genesis, Chapters 1-5*, translated by George V. Schick, edited by Jaroslav Pelikan, St. Louis: Concordia Publishing House, 1958, vol. 1, pp. 66-70, 117, 118, 131-34, 137, 150-51, 155, 160, 162-64, 178-79, 184-85, 198-203.)

Lectures on Genesis (begun 1535 CE)
MARTIN LUTHER

[Gen. 1:26] "Let him have dominion over the fish of the sea," *etc.*

Here the rule is assigned to the most beautiful creature, who knows God and is the image of God, in whom the similitude of the divine nature shines forth through his enlightened reason, through his justice and wisdom. Adam and Eve become the rulers of the earth, the sea, and the air. But this dominion is given to them not only by way of advice but also by express command. . . .

If, then, we are looking for an outstanding philosopher, let us not overlook our first parents while they were still free from sin. They had a most perfect knowledge of God, for how would they not know Him whose similitude they had and felt within themselves? Furthermore, they also had the most dependable knowledge of the stars and of the whole of astronomy.

Eve had these mental gifts in the same degree as Adam, as Eve's utterance shows when she answered the serpent concerning the tree in the middle of Paradise. There it becomes clear enough that she knew to what end she had been created and pointed to the source from which she had this knowledge; for she said (Gen. 3:3): "The Lord said." Thus she not only heard this from Adam, but her very nature was pure and full of the knowledge of God to such a degree that by herself she knew the Word of God and understood it. . . .

[Gen. 1:27] "Male and female He created them."

. . . However, here Moses puts the two sexes together and says that God created male and female in order to indicate that Eve, too, was made by God as a partaker of the divine image and of the divine similitude, likewise of the rule over everything. Thus even today the woman is the partaker of the future life, just as Peter says that they are joint heirs of the same grace (1 Peter 3:7). In the household the wife is a partner in the management and has a common interest in the children and the property, and yet there is a great difference between the sexes. The male is like the sun in heaven, the female like the moon, the animals like the stars, over which sun and moon have dominion. In the first place, therefore, let us note from this passage that it was written that this sex may not be excluded from any glory of the human creature, although it is inferior to the male sex. About marriage we shall have something to say below. . . .

Lyra also relates a Jewish tale, of which Plato, too, makes mention somewhere, that in the beginning man was created bisexual and later on, by divine power, was, as it were, split or cut apart, as the form of the back and of the spine seems to prove. Others have expanded these ideas with more obscene details. But the second chapter refutes these babblers. For if this is true, how can it be sure that God took one of the ribs of Adam and out of it built the woman? These are Talmudic tales, and yet they had to be mentioned so that we might see the malice of the devil, who suggests such absurd ideas to human beings.

This tale fits Aristotle's designation of woman as a "maimed man"; others declare that she is a monster. But let them themselves be monsters and sons of monsters—these men who make malicious statements and ridicule a creature of God in which God Himself took delight as in a most excellent work, moreover, one which we see created by a special counsel of God. These pagan ideas show that reason cannot establish anything sure about God and the works of God but only thinks up reasons against reasons and teaches nothing in a perfect and sound manner. . . .

[Gen. 2:18] "The Lord God also said: It is not good that man is alone; I shall make him a help which should be before him."

. . . What appears in the Latin text as "like unto himself" is in Hebrew "which should be about him." With this expression the text also makes a difference between the human female and the females of all the remaining animals, which are not always about their mates: the woman was so created that she should everywhere and always be about her husband. Thus imperial law also calls the life of married people an inseparable relationship. The female of the brutes has a desire for the male only once in a whole year. But after she has become pregnant, she returns to her home and takes care of herself. For her young born at another time she has no concern, and she does not always live with her mate.

But among men the nature of marriage is different. There the wife so binds herself to a man that she will be about him and will live together with him as one flesh. If Adam had persisted in the state of innocence, this intimate relationship of husband and wife would have been most delightful. The very work of procreation also would have been most sacred and would have been held in esteem. There would not have been that shame stemming from sin which there is now, when parents are compelled to hide in darkness to do this. No less respectability would have attached to cohabitation than there is to sleeping, eating, or drinking with one's wife. . . .

So the woman was a helper for Adam; for he was unable to procreate alone, just as the woman was also unable to procreate alone. Moreover, these are the highest praises of sex, that the male is the father in procreation, but the woman is the mother in procreation and the helper of her husband. When we look back to the state of innocence, procreation, too, was better, more delightful, and more sacred in countless ways. . . .

[Gen. 2:22] "And the Lord God built the rib which He had taken from Adam into a woman, and He brought her to Adam."

Here Moses uses a new and unheard-of expression, not the verb "form" and "create," as above, but "build." This induced all the interpreters to suspect that there is some underlying mystery here. Lyra, in common with his Rabbi Solomon, believes that the reference is to the novel form of the woman's body. As the shape of buildings is wider in the lower part but narrower in the upper, so, he says, the bodies of women are thicker in their lower part but more drawn together in the upper, while men have broader shoulders and larger chests. But these are nonessential features of the body. . . .

This living-together of husband and wife—that they occupy the same home, that they take care of the household, that together they produce and bring up children—is a kind of faint image and a remnant, as it were, of that blessed living-together because of which Moses calls the woman a building. . . .

But in addition to the countless other troubles which it has because of sin, this living-together is marred to an astonishing degree by wicked persons. There are not only men who think it is clever to find fault with the opposite sex and to have nothing to do with marriage but also men who, after they have married, desert their wives and refuse to support their children. Through their baseness and wickedness these people lay waste God's building, and they are really abominable monsters of nature. Let us, therefore, obey the Word of God and recognize our wives as a building of God. Not only is the house built through them by procreation and other services that are necessary in a household; but the husbands themselves are built through them, because wives are, as it were, a nest and a dwelling place where husbands can go to spend their time and dwell with joy. . . .

[Gen. 2:23] "This one will be called Woman, because she has been taken from the man."

. . . We are altogether unable to imitate the nicety of the Hebrew language. 'Ish denotes a man. But he says that Eve must be called 'ishshah, as though for "wife" you would say "she-man" from man, a heroic woman who performs manly acts.

Moreover, this designation carries with it a wonderful and pleasing description of marriage, in which, as the jurist also says, the wife shines by reason of her husband's rays. Whatever the husband has, this the wife has and possesses in its entirety. Their partnership involves not only their means but children, food, bed, and dwelling; their purposes, too, are the same. The result is that the husband differs from the wife in no other respect than in sex; otherwise the woman is altogether a man. Whatever the man has in the home and is, this the woman has and is; she differs only in sex and in something that Paul mentions (1 Tim. 2:13), namely, that she is a woman by origin, because the woman came from the man and not the man from the woman. . . .

[Gen. 3:1] "Who said to the woman: Did God really command you not to eat from every tree of Paradise?"

. . . At first Eve resists the tempter admirably. For she is still being led by that Spirit who was lighting her path, just as we showed above that man was created perfect and according to the likeness of God. But in the end she allows herself to be persuaded. . . .

Secondly, consideration must be given also to his extraordinary cleverness, which becomes evident immediately, when Satan assails the greatest strength of man and battles against the very likeness of God, namely, the will that was properly disposed toward God. The serpent's cleverness, says the text, was greater than that of all the animals on earth. . . .

Satan's cleverness is perceived also in this, that he attacks the weak part of the human nature, Eve the woman, not Adam the man. Although both were created equally righteous, nevertheless Adam had some advantage over Eve. Just as in all the rest of nature the strength of the male surpasses that of the other sex, so also in the perfect nature the male somewhat excelled the female. Because Satan sees that Adam is the more excellent, he does not dare assail him; for he fears that his attempt may turn out to be useless. And I, too, believe that if he had tempted Adam first, the victory would have been Adam's. He would have crushed the serpent with his foot and would have said: "Shut up! The Lord's command was different." Satan, therefore, directs his attack on Eve as the weaker part and puts her valor to the test, for he sees that she is so dependent on her husband that she thinks she cannot sin. . . .

[Gen. 3:2] To this the woman answered: "Of the fruit of the trees which are in Paradise we eat;
[Gen. 3:3] "but of the fruit which is in the midst of Paradise God commanded us not to eat or to touch it, lest perchance we die."

The beginning is rather favorable: she makes a distinction between the remaining trees and this one, and she quotes God's command. But she begins to waver when she comes to the mention of the punishment. She does not mention the punishment as God had stated it. He had simply stated (Gen. 2:17): "On whatever day you will eat from it, you will surely die." Out of this absolute statement she herself makes one that is not absolute when she adds: "Lest perchance we shall die." . . .

For this reason our text here, too, has been poorly translated. It reads as though Eve were quoting her own words; actually, she is quoting God's words, and on her own she is adding to God's Word the little word "perchance." And so the deceit of the lying spirit met with success. What he sought to achieve above all—to lead Eve away from the Word and faith—this he has now achieved to the extent that Eve distorts the Word of God; that is, to use Paul's language, he has turned her away from the divine will, so that she goes after Satan (1 Tim. 5:15). But it is the beginning of one's ruin to turn away from God and to turn to Satan, that is, not to remain constant in the Word and in faith. When Satan sees these beginnings, he now exerts himself with his utmost power, as though against a leaning wall, in order to overwhelm her altogether. . . .

[Gen. 3:6] "And so the woman saw that the tree was good for eating and beautiful for the eyes and delightful, because it made wise. She took of its fruit and ate, and she gave to her husband, and he ate."

. . . The emphasis, therefore, lies on what the Latin text nevertheless has omitted, namely, that the tree appeared delightful because it would make people wise. This is what the devil is wont to bring about in all his temptations, that the farther man draws away from the Word, the more learned and the wiser he appears to himself. . . .

And this also reveals Satan's cunning. He does not immediately try to allure Eve by means of the loveliness of the fruit. He first attacks man's greatest strength, faith in the Word. Therefore the root and source of sin is unbelief and turning away from God, just as, on the other hand, the source and root of righteousness is faith. Satan first draws away from faith to unbelief. When he achieved this—that Eve did not believe the command which God had given—it was easy to bring this about also, that she rushed to the tree, plucked the fruit, and ate it. The outward act of disobedience follows sin, which through unbelief has fully developed in the heart. Thus the nature of sin must be considered in accordance with its true immensity, in which we have all perished. Now follows the disclosure of the sin together with its punishments.

[Gen. 3:7] "Then the eyes of both were opened; and when they realized that they were naked, they sewed together leaves of the fig tree and made themselves girdles."

. . . But before this revelation, while sin is being committed, Eve's eyes are not open; otherwise she would have died rather than touch the fruit. But because her eyes are not yet open and unbelief remains, there remain both the delight in the forbidden fruit and the eagerness and the desire to acquire a wisdom which was also forbidden. Poor Eve is so engrossed in unbelief both in spirit and in body that she does not realize that she is doing evil. . . .

[Gen. 3:12] "The woman whom Thou gavest me as a companion gave me from the tree, and I ate."

. . . Therefore the statement "The woman whom Thou didst give to me" is full of resentment and anger against God, as if Adam were saying: "Thou hast burdened me with this trouble. If thou hadst given the woman some garden of her own and hadst not burdened me by making me live with her, I would have remained without sin. Therefore the guilt for my having sinned is Thine, since Thou didst give me a wife." Here Adam is presented as a typical instance of all sinners and of such as despair because of their sin. They cannot do otherwise than accuse God and excuse themselves, inasmuch as they see that God is omnipotent and could have prevented those sins. Such an awful evil is sin when hearts are not given encouragement in time through the promise of the forgiveness of sins. And such is the working of the Law that, when the Law stands alone without the Gospel and the knowledge of grace, it leads to despair and ultimate impenitence.

[Gen. 3:13] "And the Lord God said to the woman: Why did you do this? And she answered: The serpent deceived me, and I ate."

Now Eve, too, is put before us as an example; and when she is corrupted by sin, she is not one whit better than Adam. Adam wanted to appear innocent; he passed on his guilt from himself to God, who had given him his wife. Eve also tries to excuse herself and accuses the serpent, which was also a creature of God. Indeed, she confesses that she ate the fruit. "But the serpent," says she, "which Thou hast created and which Thou hast permitted to move about in Paradise, deceived me." Is not this accusing the Creator and pushing off one's guilt from oneself? So we see that sin is and acts the same everywhere. It does not want to be sin; it does not want to be punished because of sin. It wants to be righteousness. When it cannot achieve this, it puts the guilt on God, so that it accuses God of a lie when He accuses sin. Thus out of a human sin comes a sin that is clearly demonic; unbelief turns into blasphemy, disobedience into contempt of the Creator. . . .

[Gen. 3:14] "And the Lord God said to the serpent: Because you did this, you are cursed among all living things and beasts of the earth: on your belly you will walk, and dust you will eat all the days of your life."

. . . I am excusing Lyra, who appears to have been a good man but yields too much to the authority of the fathers. And so he allows himself to become involved through St. Augustine in a most absurd allegory, which Gregory also adopts in his *Moralia*. The woman must be taken to mean the lower reason; her seed, to mean its good working; the seed of the devil, his corrupt prompting. Moreover, the words of the Lord, "I shall put enmity between you and her seed," must be understood of that conflict which occurs when the devil, by means of his evil prompting, assails the lower reason, which is the woman. If she should yield to her lusts, then through her Satan hopes also to topple the man, that is, the higher reason. Furthermore, this is said to be the meaning of the statement that the serpent is lying in wait for the heel; for Satan does not make his attacks except from below, by setting before the senses the things that delight them. . . .

Then there is also something absurd in making Eve the lower part of reason, although it is sure that in no part, that is, neither in body nor in soul, was Eve inferior to her husband Adam. This ridiculous interpretation is the source of the familiar secular discussions about free will and about reason's striving toward the supreme good, which finally turn the whole of theology into philosophy and into specious prattle. . . .

. . . Thus I adhere simply to the historical and literal meaning, which is in harmony with the text. In accordance with this meaning, the serpent remains a serpent, but one dominated by Satan; the woman remains a woman; Adam remains Adam, just as the following events prove. For it is not the lower and the higher reason that beget Cain and Abel, but Adam and Eve, that is, the first human beings, who had fallen into death through their sin and had been put under the rule of Satan.

[Gen. 3:16] "But to the woman He said: I will greatly multiply your sorrow when you are pregnant. In pain you will bear children, and you will be under your husband's power; and he will rule over you."

. . . Therefore truly happy and joyful is this punishment if we correctly appraise the matter. Although these burdens are troublesome for the flesh, yet the hope for a better life is strengthened together with those very burdens or punishments, because Eve hears that she is not being repudiated by God. Furthermore, she also hears that in this punishment she is not being deprived of the blessing of procreation, which was promised and granted before sin. She sees that she is keeping her sex and that she remains a woman. She sees that she is not being separated from Adam to remain alone and apart from her husband. She sees that she may keep the glory of motherhood, if I may use the phrase. All these things are in addition to the eternal hope, and without a doubt they greatly encouraged Eve. Above all, there remains also a greater and more genuine glory. Not only does she keep the blessing of fruitfulness and remain united with her husband, but she has the sure promise that from her will come the Seed who will crush the head of Satan.

Without a doubt, therefore, Eve had a heart full of joy even in an apparently sad situation. Perhaps she gave comfort to Adam by saying: "I have sinned. But see what a merciful God we have. How many privileges, both temporal and spiritual, He is leaving for us sinners! Therefore we women should bear the hardship and wretchedness of conceiving, of giving birth, and of obeying you husbands. His is a fatherly anger, because this stands: that the head of our enemy will be crushed, and after the death of our flesh we shall be raised to a new and eternal life through our Redeemer. These abundant good things and endless kindnesses far surpass whatever curse and punishments our Father has inflicted on us." These and similar conversations Adam and Eve undoubtedly carried on often in order to mitigate their temporal adversities. . . .

Moreover, the word *rab* appears here; it denotes a quantity which is both extensive and varied. This means that Eve's sorrows, which she would not have had if she had not fallen into sin, are to be great, numerous, and also of various kinds. The threat is directed particularly at birth and conception. But conception designates the entire time during which the fetus, after being conceived, is carried in the womb, a time beset with severe and sundry ailments. From the beginning of that time a woman suffers very painful headaches, dizziness, nausea, an amazing loathing of food and drink, frequent and difficult vomiting, toothache, and a stomach disorder which produces a craving, called pica, for such foods from which nature normally shrinks. Moreover, when the fetus has matured and birth is imminent, there follows the most awful distress, because only with utmost peril and almost at the cost of her life does she give birth to her offspring.

When the heathen, who have no knowledge of God and of His works, see this, it displeases them. Because of these discomforts, they maintain that a prudent man should not marry. The female sex has been greatly humbled and afflicted, and it bears a far severer and harsher punishment than the men. For what is there of such things that a man suffers on his own body? But because through marriage the husband transfers, as it were, a part of those punishments upon himself (for he cannot without grief see those things in his wife), it has come about that wicked men prefer fornication to marriage. . . .

The second part of the curse has to do with cohabitation. . . . Now there is also added to those sorrows of gestation and birth that Eve has been placed under the power of her husband, she who previously was very free and, as the sharer of all the gifts of God, was in no respect inferior to her husband.

This punishment, too, springs from original sin; and the woman bears it just as unwillingly as she bears those pains and inconveniences that have been placed upon her flesh. The rule remains with the husband, and the wife is compelled to obey him by God's command. He rules the home and the state, wages war, defends his possessions, tills the soil, builds, plants, etc. The woman, on the other hand, is like a nail driven into the wall. She sits at home, and for this reason Paul, in Titus 2:5, calls her an *oikourgos*. The pagans have depicted Venus as standing on a seashell; for just as the snail carries its house with it, so the wife should stay at home and look after the affairs of the household, as one who has been deprived of the ability of administering those affairs that are outside and that concern the state. She does not go beyond her most personal duties.

If Eve had persisted in the truth, she would not only not have been subjected to the rule of her husband, but she herself would also have been a partner in the rule which is now entirely the concern of males. Women are generally disinclined to put up with this burden, and they naturally seek to gain what they have lost through sin. If they are unable to do more, they at least indicate their impatience by grumbling. However, they cannot perform the functions of men, teach, rule, etc. In procreation and in feeding and nurturing their offspring they are masters. In this way Eve is punished; but, as I said in the beginning, it is a gladsome punishment if you consider the hope of eternal life and the honor of motherhood which have been left her.

John Calvin

John Calvin, a second-generation Protestant reformer, lived from 1509 to 1564. Raised in Catholic France, where he studied both law and theology, he came under the influence of Protestant doctrine and was forced to leave France in 1533. He eventually settled in Geneva, and from 1541 was instrumental there in institutionalizing the definitive version of Reformed Protestantism. Calvin shared with Martin Luther an insistence upon the devastating effects of the Fall, but was more concerned than Luther to articulate the ameliorative effects of sanctification. Calvin was convinced that Christian societies should be visibly holy, and his efforts to order Genevan culture according to the demands of Scripture provided a prototype for future Reformed Christians. Preeminent among Calvin's many published works was his *Institutes of the Christian Religion*.

As articulated in his *Commentaries* on the Pentateuch, Calvin's reading of Genesis 1–3 combined elements of hierarchical and egalitarian interpretations. In opposition to earlier commentators who had denigrated Eve, Calvin insisted that Eve was a good creation, sharing fully in the *imago dei*. He denied that God created Eve merely to allow Adam to procreate, noting that the physical and spiritual intimacy provided by marriage was in itself a great gift. Calvin also dismissed the notion that Eve had seduced Adam into sin or that Eve alone was responsible for plunging the human race into sin. Indeed, Calvin indicated his admiration for the ways in which Eve initially attempted to resist the serpent's efforts to prompt her to eat the forbidden fruit.

Despite those claims, Calvin's interpretation of Genesis 1–3 was ultimately hierarchical. He contended that, even before the Fall, Eve had been subordinate to Adam. After the Fall, that subordination became more rigorous; now Eve was reduced to servitude. It was, Calvin explained, as if God had said to Eve: "Thou shalt desire nothing but what thy husband wishes." While Calvin, in other works, noted that it was only in the political realm and not in the spiritual realm that women were subordinated to men, the practical effect of his interpretation of Genesis 1-3 was to reinforce the gender hierarchy of sixteenth-century Europe. (Source: John Calvin, *Commentaries on the First Book of Moses Called Genesis*, translated by John King, Grand Rapids, Mich.: Wm. B. Eerdmans, 1948, vol. 1: 95-96, 128-33, 145-46, 148-49, 151-52, 171-73.)

Commentaries on the First Book of Moses
Called Genesis (c. 1555 CE)
JOHN CALVIN

[Gen. 1:26] **In our image, after our likeness. . . .**

This further difficulty is also to be encountered, namely, why Paul should deny the *woman* to be the image of God, when Moses honours both, indiscriminately, with this title. The solution is short; Paul there alludes only to the domestic relation. He therefore restricts the image of God to *government*, in which the man has superiority over the wife, and certainly he means nothing more than that man is superior in the degree of honour. But here the question is respecting that glory of God which peculiarly shines forth in human nature, where the mind, the will, and all the senses, represent the Divine order. . . .

[Gen. 2:18] **It is not good that the man should be alone.**

Moses now explains the design of God in creating the woman; namely, that there should be human beings on the earth who might cultivate mutual society between themselves. Yet a doubt may arise whether this design ought to be extended to progeny, for the words simply mean that since it was not expedient for man to be alone, a wife must be created, who might be his helper. I, however, take the meaning to be this, that God begins, indeed, at the first step of human society, yet designs to include others, each in its proper place. The commencement, therefore, involves a general principle, that man was formed to be a social animal. Now, the human race could not exist without the woman; and, therefore, in the conjunction of human beings, that sacred bond is especially conspicuous, by which the husband and the wife are combined in one body, and one soul; as nature itself taught Plato, and others of the sounder class of philosophers, to speak. But although God pronounced, concerning Adam, that it would not be profitable for him to be alone, yet I do not restrict the declaration to his person alone, but rather regard it as a common law of man's vocation, so that every one ought to receive it as said to himself, that solitude is not good, excepting only him whom God exempts as by a special privilege. Many think that celibacy conduces to their advantage, and, therefore, abstain from marriage, lest they should be miserable. Not only have heathen writers defined that to be a happy life which is passed without a wife, but the first book of Jerome, against Jovinian, is stuffed with petulant reproaches, by which he attempts to render hallowed wedlock both hateful and infamous. To these wicked suggestions of Satan let the faithful learn to oppose this declaration of God, by which he ordains the conjugal life for man, not to his destruction, but to his salvation.

I will make him an help. It may be inquired, why this is not said in the plural number, *Let us make*, as before in the creation of man. Some suppose that a distinction between the two sexes is in this manner marked, and that it is thus shown how much the man excels the woman. But I am better satisfied with an interpretation which, though not altogether contrary, is yet different; namely, since in the person of the man the human race had been created, the common dignity of our whole nature was without distinction, honoured with one eulogy, when it was said, "Let us make man;" nor was it necessary to be repeated in creating the woman, who was nothing else than an accession to the man. Certainly, it cannot be denied, that the woman also, though in the second degree, was created in the image of God; whence it follows, that what was said in the creation of the man belongs to the female sex. Now, since God assigns the woman as a help to the man, he not only prescribes to wives the rule of their vocation, to instruct them in their duty, but he also pronounces that marriage will really prove to men the best support of life. We may therefore conclude, that the order of nature implies that the woman should be the helper of the man. The vulgar proverb, indeed, is, that she is a necessary evil; but the voice of God is rather to be heard, which declares that woman is given as a companion and an associate to the man, to assist him to live well. I confess, indeed, that in this corrupt state of mankind, the blessing of God, which is here described, is neither perceived nor flourishes; but the cause of the evil must be considered, namely, that the order of nature, which God had appointed, has been inverted by us. . . . On this main point hangs another, that women, being instructed in their duty of helping their husbands, should study to keep this divinely appointed order. It is also the part of men to consider what they owe in return to the other half of their kind, for the obligation of both sexes is mutual, and on this condition is the woman assigned as a help to the man, that he may fill the place of her head and leader. One thing more is to be noted, that, when the woman is here called the help of the man, no allusion is made to that necessity to which we are reduced since the fall of Adam; for the woman was ordained to be the man's helper, even although he had stood in his integrity. But now, since the depravity of appetite also requires a remedy, we have from God a double benefit: but the latter is accidental.

Meet for him. In the Hebrew it is *kenegedo*, "as if opposite to," or "over against him." *Caph* in that language is a note of similitude. But although some of the Rabbies [*sic*] think it is here put as an affirmative, yet I take it in its general sense, as though it were said that she is a kind of counterpart, for the woman is said to be *opposite to* or *over against* the man, because she responds to him. But the particle of similitude seems to me to be added because it is a form of speech taken from common usage. The Greek translators have faithfully rendered the sense *kat'auton*, and Jerome, "Which may be like him," for

Moses intended to note some equality. And hence is refuted the error of some, who think that the woman was formed only for the sake of propagation, and who restrict the word "good," which had been lately mentioned, to the production of offspring. They do not think that a wife was personally necessary for Adam, because he was hitherto free from lust; as if she had been given to him only for the companion of his chamber, and not rather that she might be the inseparable associate of his life. Wherefore the particle *caph* is of importance, as intimating that marriage extends to all parts and usages of life. The explanation given by others, as if it were said, "Let her be ready to obedience," is cold; for Moses intended to express more, as is manifest from what follows. . . .

[Gen. 2:21] And the Lord God caused a deep sleep to fall. . . .

If, however, we should say that the rib out of which he would form another body had been prepared previously by the Creator of the world, I find nothing in this answer which is not in accordance with Divine Providence. Yet I am more in favour of a different conjecture, namely, that something was taken from Adam, in order that he might embrace, with greater benevolence, a part of himself. He lost, therefore, one of his ribs; but, instead of it, a far richer reward was granted him, since he obtained a faithful associate of life; for he now saw himself, who had before been imperfect, rendered complete in his wife. And in this we see a true resemblance of our union with the Son of God; for he became weak that he might have members of his body endued with strength. . . . Moses also designedly used the word "*built*" to teach us that in the person of the woman the human race was at length complete, which had before been like a building just begun. . . .

[Gen. 3:1] And he said unto the woman. . . .

Moreover, the craftiness of Satan betrays itself in this, that he does not directly assail the man, but approaches him, as through a mine, in the person of his wife. This insidious method of attack is more than sufficiently known to us at the present day, and I wish we might learn prudently to guard ourselves against it. For he warily insinuates himself at that point at which he sees us to be the least fortified, that he may not be perceived till he should have penetrated where he wished. The woman does not flee from converse with the serpent, because hitherto no dissension had existed; she, therefore, accounted it simply as a domestic animal. . . .

[Gen. 3:3] Of every tree of the garden. . . .

It was impossible for Eve more prudently or more courageously to repel the assault of Satan, than by objecting against him, that she and her husband had been so bountifully dealt with by the Lord, that the advantages granted to them were abundantly sufficient, for she intimates that they would be most ungrateful if, instead of being content with such affluence, they should desire more than was lawful. When she says, God had forbidden them to eat or to touch, some suppose the second word to be added for the purpose of charging God with too great severity, because he prohibited them even from the *touch*. But I rather understand that she hitherto remained in obedience, and expressed her pious disposition by anxiously observing the precept of God; only, in proclaiming the punishment, she begins to give way, by inserting the adverb "perhaps," when God has certainly pronounced, "Ye shall die the death." For although with the Hebrews "*pen*" does not always imply doubt, yet, since it is generally taken in this sense, I willingly embrace the opinion that the woman was beginning to waver. Certainly, she had not death so immediately before her eyes, should she become disobedient to God, as she ought to have had. She clearly proves that her perception of the true danger of death was distant and cold. . . .

[Gen. 3:6] And gave also unto her husband with her. . . .

From these words, some conjecture that Adam was present when his wife was tempted and persuaded by the serpent, which is by no means credible. Yet it might be that he soon joined her, and that, even before the woman tasted the fruit of the tree, she related the conversation held with the serpent, and entangled him with the same fallacies by which she herself had been deceived. Others refer the particle "*immah*," "with her," to the conjugal bond, which may be received. But because Moses simply relates that he ate the fruit taken from the hands of his wife, the opinion has been commonly received, that he was rather captivated with her allurements than persuaded by Satan's impostures. For this purpose the declaration of Paul is adduced, "Adam was not deceived, but the woman" (1 Tim. 2:14). But Paul in that place, as he is teaching that the origin of evil was from the woman, only speaks comparatively. Indeed, it was not only for the sake of complying with the wishes of his wife, that he transgressed the law laid down for him; but being drawn by her into fatal ambition, he became partaker of the same defection with her. And truly Paul elsewhere states that sin came not by the woman, but by Adam himself (Rom. 5:12). Then, the reproof which soon afterwards follows, "Behold, Adam is as one of us," clearly proves that he also foolishly coveted more than was lawful, and gave greater credit to the flatteries of the devil than to the sacred word of God. . . .

[Gen. 3:16] Unto the woman he said. . . .

In bringing the serpent forward, Eve thought she had herself escaped. God, disregarding her cavils, condemns her. Let the sinner, therefore, when he comes to the bar of God, cease to contend, lest he should more severely provoke against himself the anger of him whom he has already too highly offended. We must now consider the kind of punishment imposed upon the woman. When he says, "I will multiply thy pains," he comprises all the trouble women sustain during pregnancy. . . . It is credible that the woman would have brought forth without pain, or at least without such great suffering, if she had stood in her original condition; but her revolt from God subjected her to inconveniences of this kind. The expression, "pains and conception," is to be taken by the figure *hypallage*, for the pains which they endure in consequence of conception. The second punishment which he exacts is *subjection*. For this form of speech, "Thy desire shall be unto thy husband," is of the same force as if he had said that she should not be free and at her own command, but subject to the authority of her husband and dependent upon his will; or as if he had said, "Thou shalt desire nothing but what thy husband wishes." As it is declared afterwards, "Unto thee shall be his desire," (chap. 4:7). Thus the woman, who had perversely exceeded her proper bounds, is forced back to her own position. She had, indeed, previously been subject to her husband, but that was a liberal and gentle subjection; now, however, she is cast into servitude.

[Gen. 3:17] And unto Adam he said. . . .

In the first place, it is to be observed, that punishment was not inflicted upon the first of our race so as to rest on those two alone, but was extended generally to all their posterity, in order that we might know that the human race was cursed in their person; we next observe, that they were subjected only to temporal punishment, that, from the moderation of the divine anger, they might entertain hope of pardon. God, by adducing the reason why he thus punishes the man, cuts off from him the occasion of murmuring. For no excuse was left to him who had obeyed his wife rather than God; yea, had despised God for the sake of his wife, placing so much confidence in the fallacies of Satan,— whose messenger and servant she was,—that he did not hesitate perfidiously to deny his Maker. But, although God deals decisively and briefly with Adam, he yet refutes the pretext by which he had tried to escape, in order the more easily to lead him to repentance.

Margaret Fell

Born in England in 1614, and married to Puritan judge Thomas Fell, Margaret Fell was a crucial figure in early Quaker history. She customarily kept Swarthmore Hall, the Fell residence, open to itinerant preachers. George Fox, who began the Quaker movement in the 1640s, preached in Swarthmore Hall in 1652 and converted Margaret and several members of the household to the Society of Friends. Fell's seven daughters became Quaker preachers. Thomas Fell died in 1658, and in 1669 Margaret married George Fox. Through her writing, her administrative gifts, and her fund-raising efforts, Margaret Fell was pivotal in the development of the Society of Friends. She, along with other Quakers, occasionally suffered imprisonment for their beliefs. She wrote her 1666 tract, *Women's Speaking: Justified,* from jail. Fell died in 1702 and remains a revered figure in Quaker history.[1]

Quakers believed that each person had access to the divine presence, or Inner Light. They encouraged both men and women, inspired by that Inner Light, to speak in worship meetings, to assist in congregational governance, and to write theological tracts in defense of the Quaker movement. Fell's *Women's Speaking: Justified* endeavored to vindicate Quaker egalitarian gender practices on biblical grounds. She succeeded in composing one of the most outspoken defenses of an egalitarian reading of Genesis 1-3 that the Christian world had yet seen.

Fell cited Genesis 1:26 as proof that both "male and female" shared the divine image. Those who would distinguish between the divine gifts accorded to men and women were, in her opinion, untrue to Genesis 1. She was not discouraged by Eve's sin, since Genesis 3:15 promised that Eve and her seed would exist in enmity toward the serpent and his seed. To Fell, this text proved the necessity for women to speak vigorously on behalf of the gospel: "Let this Word of the Lord . . . stop the mouths of all that oppose Womens Speaking in the Power of the Lord; for he hath put enmity between the Woman and the Serpent; and if the Seed of the Woman speak not, the Seed of the Serpent speaks. . . . " Fell also found New Testament references to the Church as the bride of Christ significant, since the metaphor suggested that the Church was a woman. To oppose the speaking of women, then, would be to silence the testimony of the Church.

Fell did not ignore New Testament passages that had traditionally been understood to support a hierarchical reading of Genesis 1-3; but in her explications those passages lost much of their sting. Paul's admonition in 1 Corinthians 14:34 that women should be silent in church ("they are not permitted to speak, but should be subordinate, as the law also says"), she saw as irrelevant, since Christians lived under the gospel, not the law. And 1 Timothy 2:8-15, in her view, directed woman to dress modestly for worship, but did not prohibit all women from speaking. Forbidding women to speak, Fell concluded, would be self-contradictory, since Paul elsewhere acknowledged and praised women who labored on behalf of the gospel. (Source: Margaret Fell, *Women's Speaking: Justified, Proved, and Allowed of by the Scriptures,* London: Pythia Press, 1989, pp. 1-4, 6-13, 18-19.)

NOTE TO CHAPTER 6, MARGARET FELL

1. Hugh Barbour, *The Quakers in Puritan England* (New Haven and London: Yale University Press, 1964), p. 46; Hugh Barbour and J. William Frost, *The Quakers,* Denominations in America, Number 3 (New York, Westport, and London: Greenwood Press, 1988), pp. 27-29, 43, 67; Rosemary Radford Ruether and Catherine M.

Prelinger, "Women in Sectarian and Utopian Groups," in Rosemary Radford Ruether and Rosemary Skinner Keller, editors, *Women and Religion in America*, vol. 2: *The Colonial and Revolutionary Periods* (San Francisco: Harper & Row, 1983), pp. 260-61.

Women's Speaking: Justified, Proved, and Allowed of by Scriptures (1666 CE)
MARGARET FELL

WHEREAS it hath been an Objection in the minds of many, and several times hath been objected by the Clergy, or Ministers, and others, against Womens Speaking in the Church; and so consequently may be taken that they are condemned for meddling in the things of God; the ground of which Objection, is taken from the Apostle's words, which he Writ in his first Epistle to the Corinthians, chap. 14, vers. 34, 35. And also what he writ to Timothy in the first Epistle, chap. 2, vers. 11, 12. But how far they wrong the Apostle's intentions in those Scriptures, we shall shew clearly when we come to them in their course and order.

But first let me lay down how God himself hath manifested his Will and Mind concerning Women, and unto Women.

And first, when *God created Man in his own Image; in the Image of God created he them, Male and Female; and God blessed them; and God said unto them, Be fruitful, and multiply: and God said, Behold, I have given you of every Herb, etc.* Gen. 1. Here God joins them together in his own Image, and makes no such distinctions and differences as men do; for though they be weak, he is strong; and as he said to the Apostle, *His Grace is sufficient, and his strength is made manifest in weakness*, 2 Cor. 12:9. And such hath the Lord chosen, even the weak things of the world, to confound the things which are mighty; and things which are despised, hath God chosen, to bring to nought things that are, 1 Cor. 1. And god hath put no such difference between the Male and Female as men would make.

It is true, *The Serpent that was more subtle then any other Beast of the Field*, came unto the Woman, with his Temptations, and with a lie; his subtly discerning her to be more inclinable to harken to him, when he said, *If ye eat, your eyes shall be opened*, and the Woman saw that *the Fruit was good to make one wise*; there the temptation got into her, and *she did eat, and gave to her Husband, and he did eat also*, and so they were both tempted into the transgression and disobedience; and therefore God said unto Adam, when that he hid himself when he heard his voice, *Hast thou eaten of the Tree which I commanded thee that thou shouldst not eat?* And Adam said, *The Woman which thou gavest me, she gave me of the Tree, and I did eat.* And the Lord said unto the Woman, *What is this that thou hast done?* and the Woman said, *The Serpent beguiled me, and I did* eat. Here the Woman spoke the truth unto the Lord: see what the Lord saith, verse 15 after he had pronounced Sentence on the Serpent; *I will put enmity between thee and the Woman, and between thy Seed and her Seed; it shall bruise his heel*, Genesis 3.

Let this Word of the Lord, which was from the beginning, stop the mouths of all that oppose Womens Speaking in the Power of the Lord; for he hath put enmity between the Woman and the Serpent; and if the Seed of the Woman speak not, the Seed of the Serpent speaks; for God hath put enmity between the two Seeds, and it is manifest, that those that speak against the Woman and her Seeds Speaking, speak out of the enmity of the old Serpents Seed; and God hath fulfilled his Word and his Promise, *When the fullness of time was come, he hath sent forth his Son, made of a Woman, made under the Law, that we might receive the adoption of Sons*, Gal. 4:4, 5.

Moreover, the Lord is pleased, when he mentions his Church, to call her by the name of Woman, by his Prophets, saying, *I have called thee as a Woman forsaken, and grieved in Spirit, and as a Wife of Youth*, Isa. 54:6. Again, *How long wilt thou go about, thou back-sliding Daughter? For the Lord hath created a new thing in the earth, a Woman shall compass a Man*, Jer. 31:22. And David, when he was speaking of Christ and his Church, he said, *The Kings Daughter is all glorious within, the clothing is wrought Gold; she shall be brought unto the King: with gladness and rejoicing shall they be brought; they shall enter the Kings Palace*, Psal. 45. And also King Solomon in his Song, where he speaks of Christ and his Church, where she is complaining and calling for Christ, he saith, *If thou knowest not, O thou fairest among women, go thy way by the footsteps of the Flock*, Cant. 1.8.c.5.9. And John, when he saw the wonder that was in Heaven, he saw a *Woman clothed with the Sun, and the Moon under her feet, and upon her head a Crown of twelve Stars; and there appeared another wonder in Heaven, a great red Dragon stood ready to devour her Child*: here the enmity appears that God put between the Woman and the Dragon, Revelations 12.

Thus much may prove that the Church of Christ is a Woman, and those that speak against the Womans Speaking, speak against the Church of Christ, and the Seed of the Woman, which Seed is Christ; that is to say, Those that speak against the Power of the Lord, and the Spirit of the Lord speaking in a Woman, simply, by reason of her Sex, or because she is a Woman, not regarding the Seed, and Spirit, and Power that speaks in her; such speak against Christ, and his Church, and are of the Seed of the Serpent, wherein lodgest the enmity. And God the Father made no such difference in the first Creation, not never since between the Male and Female, but always out of his Mercy and loving kindness, had regard unto the weak. So also, his Son, Christ Jesus, confirms the same thing; when the Pharisees came to him, and asked him, if it were lawful for a man to put away his Wife? He answered and said unto them, *Have you not read, That he that made them in the beginning, made them Male and Female, and said, For this cause shall a Man leave Father and Mother, and shall cleave unto his Wife, and they twain shall be one flesh, wherefore they are no more twin but one flesh. What therefore God hath joined together, let no Man put asunder*, Mat. 19. . . .

Thus we see that Jesus owned the Love and Grace that appeared in Women, and did not despite it; and by what is recorded in the Scriptures, he received as much love, kindness, compassion, and tender dealing towards him from Women, as he did from any others, both in his life time, and also after they had exercised their cruelty upon him; for Mary Magdalene, and Mary the Mother of Jesus, beheld where he was laid; And when the Sabbath was past, Mary Magdalene, and Mary the Mother of James and Salom, had *brought sweet spices that they might anoint him: And very early in the morning, the first day of the week, they came unto the Sepulchre at the rising of the Sun; and they said among themselves, Who shall roll us away the stone from the door of the Sepulchre? And when they looked, the stone was rolled away, for it was very great*; Mark 16:1, 2, 3, 4. Luke 24:1, 2. and they went down into the Sepulchre; and as Matthew saith, *The Angel rolled away the stone; and he said unto the Women, Fear not, I know whom ye seek, Jesus which was Crucified; he is not here, he is risen*, Mat. 28. Now Luke saith thus, That *there stood two men by them in shining apparel, and as they were perplexed and afraid, the men said unto them, He is not here; remember how he said unto you when he was in Galilee, That the Son of Man must be delivered into the hands of sinful men, and be crucified, and the third day rise again; and they remembered his words, and returned from the Sepulchre, and told all these things to the eleven, and to all the rest.*

It was Mary Magdalene, and Joanna, and Mary the Mother of James, and the other Women that were with them, which told these things to the Apostles, *And their words seemed unto them as idle tales, and they believed them not.* Mark this, ye despisers of the weakness of Women, and look upon your selves to be so wise; but Christ Jesus doth not so, for he makes use of the weak: for when he met the Women after he was risen, he said unto them, All Hail, and they came and held him by the Feet, and worshipped him; then said Jesus unto them, *Be not afraid; go tell my Brethren that they go into Galilee, and there they shall see me*, Mat. 28:10, Mark 16:9. And John saith, when Mary was weeping at the Sepulchre, that Jesus said unto her, *Woman, why weepest thou? what seekest thou? And when she supposed him to be the Gardener, Jesus saith unto her, Mary; she turned her self, and saith unto him Rabboni, which is to say Master; Jesus saith unto her, Touch me not, for I am not yet ascended to my Father, but go to my Brethren, and say unto them, I ascend unto my Father, and your Father, and to my God, and your God,* John 20:16, 17.

Mark this, you that despise and oppose the Message of the Lord God that he sends by Women; what had become of the Redemption of the whole Body of Man-kind, if they had not believed the Message that the Lord Jesus sent by these Women, of and concerning his Resurrection? And if these Women had not thus, out of their tenderness and bowels of love, who had received Mercy, and Grace, and forgiveness of sins, and Virtue, and Healing from him; which many men also had received the like, if their hearts had not been so united and knit unto him in love, that they could not depart as the men did, but sat watching, and waiting, and weeping about the Sepulchre until the time of his Resurrection, and so were ready to carry his Message, as is manifested; else how should his Disciples have known, who were not there? . . .

And now to the Apostles words, which is the ground of the great Objection against Womens Speaking; And first 1 Cor. 14. let the Reader seriously read that Chapter, and see the end and drift of the Apostle in speaking these words: for the Apostle is there exhorting the Corinthians unto charity, and to desire Spiritual gifts, and not to speak in an unknown tongue; and not to be Children in understanding, but to be Children in malice, but in understanding to be men; and that the Spirits of the Prophets should be subject to the Prophets; for God is not the Author of Confusion, but of Peace: And then he saith, *Let your Women keep silence in the Church*, etc.

Where it doth plainly appear that the Women, as well as others, that were among them, were in confusion; for he saith, *How is it Brethren? when ye come together, every one of you hath a Psalm, hath a Doctrine, hath a Tongue, hath a Revelation, hath an Interpretation? let all things be done to edifying.* Here was no edifying, but all was in confusion speaking together; Therefore he saith, *If any man speak in an unknown Tongue, let it be by two, or at most by three, and that by course; and let one Interpret; but if there be no Interpreter, let him keep silence in the Church.* Here the Man is commanded to keep silence as well as the Women, when they are in confusion and out of order.

But the Apostle saith further, *They are commended to be in Obedience, as also saith the Law; and if they will learn anything let them ask their Husbands at home; for it is a shame for a Woman to speak in the Church.*

Here the Apostle clearly manifests his intent; for he speaks of Women that were under the Law, and in that Transgression as Eve was, and such as were to learn, and not to speak publicly, but they must first ask their Husbands at home; and it was a shame for such to speak in the Church: And it appears clearly, that such women were speaking among the Corinthian *[sic]*, by the Apostles exhorting them from malice and strife, and confusion, and he preacheth the Law unto them, and he saith, *in the law it is written, With men of other tongues, and other lips, will I speak unto this people,* vers. 2.

And what is all this to Womens Speaking? That have the Everlasting Gospel to preach, and upon whom the Promise of the Lord is fulfilled, and his Spirit poured upon them according to his Word, Acts 2:16, 17, 18. And if the Apostle would have sopped such as had the Spirit of the Lord poured upon them, why did he say just before, *If anything be revealed to another that sitteth by, let the first hold his peace?* And *you may all prophesy one by one.* Here he did not say that such Women should not Prophesy as had the Revelation and Spirit of God poured upon them; but their Women that were under the Law, and in the Transgression, and were in strife, confusion and malice in their speaking; for if he had stopt Womens praying or prophesying, why doth he say, *Every man praying or prophesying, having his head covered, dishonoureth his head; but every Woman that prayeth or prophesieth with her head uncovered, dishonoureth her head? Judge in your selves, It is comely that a Woman pray or prophesy uncovered? For the Woman is not without the Man, neither is the Man without the Woman, in the Lord,* 1 Cor. 11:3,4,13.

Also that other Scripture, in 1 Tim. 2. Where he is exhorting that Prayer and Supplication be made everywhere, lifting up holy Hands without wrath and doubting; he saith in the like manner also, That *Women must adorn themselves in modest apparel, with shamefastness and sobriety, not with broidered hair, or gold, or pearl, or costly array;* He saith, *Let Women learn in silence with all subjection, but I suffer not a Woman to teach, not to usurp authority over the Man, but to be in silence; for Adam was first formed, then Eve; and Adam was not deceived, but the Woman being deceived was in the transgression.*

Here the Apostle speaks particularly to a Woman in Relation to her Husband, to be in subjection to him, and not to teach, nor usurped *[sic]* authority over him, and therefore he mentions Adam and Eve; But let it be strained to the utmost, as the opposers of Womens Speaking would have it, that is, That they should not preach nor speak in the Church, of which there is nothing here; Yet the Apostle is speaking to such as he is teaching to wear their apparel, what to wear, and what not to wear; such as were not come to wear modest apparel, and such as were not come to shamefastness and sobriety, but he was exhorting them from broidered hair, gold, and pearls, and costly array; and such are not to usurped *[sic]* authority over the Man, but to learn in silence with all subjection, as it becometh Women professing Godliness and good works.

And what is all this to such as have the Power and Spirit of the Lord Jesus poured upon them, and have the Message of the Lord Jesus given unto them? Must not they speak the Word of the Lord because of these undecent and unreverent Women that the Apostle speaks of, and to, in these two Scriptures? And how are the men of this Generation blinded, that bring these Scriptures, and pervert the Apostles Words, and corrupt his intent in speaking of them? and by these Scriptures, endeavor to stop the Message and Word of the Lord God in Women, by condemning and despising of them. If the Apostle would have had Womens Speaking stopt, and did not allow of them, why did he entreat his true Yoak-Fellow to help those Women who laboured with him in the Gospel? Phil. 4:3. And why did the Apostles join together in Prayer and Supplication with the Women, and Mary the Mother of Jesus, and with his Brethren, Acts 1:14. if they had not allowed, and had union and fellowship with the Spirit of God, wherever it was revealed in Women as well as others? But all this opposing and gainsaying of Womens Speaking, had risen out of the bottomless Pit, and spirit of Darkness that hath spoken for these many hundred years together in this night of Apostasy, since the Revelations have ceased and been hid: and so that spirit hath limited and bound all up within its bond and compass, and so would suffer none to speak, but such as that spirit of Darkness approved of, Man or Woman. . . .

A further Addition in Answer to the Objection concerning Women keeping silence in the Church; for it is not permitted for them to speak, but to be under obedience; as also saith the Law, If they will learn any thing, let them ask their Husbands at home, for it is a shame for a Woman to speak in the

Church; Now this as Paul writeth in Cor. 14:34 is one with that of 1 Tim. 2:11. Let Women learn in silence with all subjection.

TO WHICH I SAY, If you tie this to all outward Women, then there were many Women that were Widows which had no Husbands to learn of, and many were Virgins which had no Husbands; and Philip had four Daughters that were Prophets; such would be despised, which the Apostle did not forbid: And if it were to all Women, that no Woman might speak, then Paul would have contradicted himself; but they were such Women that the Apostle mentions in Timothy, *That grew wanton, and were busiebodies, and tattlers, and kicked against Christ*: for Christ in the Male and in the Female is one, and he is the Husband, and his Wife is the Church; and God hath said, that his Daughters should Prophesy as well as his Sons; and where he hath poured forth his Spirit upon them, they must prophesy, though blind Priests say to the contrary, and will not permit holy Women to speak.

And whereas it is said, *I permit not a Woman to speak, as saith the Law*: but where Women are led by the Spirit of the God, they are not under the Law, for Christ in the Male and in the Female is one; and where he is made manifest in Male and Female, he may speak, *for he is the end of the Law for Righteousness to all them that believe.* So here you ought to make a distinction what sort of Women are forbidden to speak, such as were under the Law, who were not come to Christ, nor to the Spirit of Prophesy: For Hulda, Miriam, and Hanna, were Prophets, who were not forbidden in the time of the Law, for they all prophesied in the time of the Law; as you may read, in 2 Kings 22 what Hulda said unto the Priest, and to the Ambassadors that were sent to her from the King.

John Milton

The English poet John Milton (1608-1674) is perhaps most widely known for his classic work, *Paradise Lost*, in which he retells the story of Adam and Eve. Employing a wealth of information from earlier Jewish and Christian treatments,[1] Milton's tale mediated the biblical story for generations of readers.

The selections below focus on Milton's characterization of Eve. It is easy to see how elements such as the portrayal of Eve's narcissism and Eve's subordination to Adam have caused some readers to charge Milton with misogynism.[2] Indeed, feminists have attacked Milton's *Paradise Lost* on the grounds that: (1) Milton's God is extremely patriarchal, (2) Adam and Eve's relationship reflects Puritan ideals of women and domesticity, (3) Eve's "voice" echoes the values of the patriarchal system, and (4) Eve is sympathetic to Satan.[3] Other readers have challenged such a monolithic and reductionist reading of Milton's Eve. They suggest that Adam is dependent on Eve, indeed incomplete without her, and that while Eve is imaged as a destroyer she is also the preserver of all humankind. That is, if Milton's Eve is Adam's downfall, she is also Adam's redemption.[4] (Source: H. C. Beeching, *The Poetical Works of John Milton*, Oxford: Clarendon Press, 1900.)

NOTES TO CHAPTER 6, JOHN MILTON

1. An excellent though somewhat dated discussion of possible sources behind Milton's Eve can be found in J. M. Evans's *Paradise Lost and the Genesis Tradition* (Oxford: Clarendon Press, 1968).
2. See, for example, Sandra Gilbert and Susan Gubar's influential work, *The Madwoman in the Attic: The Woman Writer and the Nineteenth-Century Literary Imagination* (New Haven: Yale University Press, 1979).
3. William Shullenberger, "Wrestling with the Angel: Paradise Lost and Feminist Criticism" *Milton Quarterly* 20 (1986): 71.
4. A good example of a more positive reading of Milton's Eve can be found in Diane Kelsey McColley's *Milton's Eve* (Urbana: University of Illinois Press, 1983).

Paradise Lost (1667 CE)
JOHN MILTON

Book IV, ll. 285–535

[Satan descends to earth to view the paradise God has created.]

> the Fiend
> Saw undelighted all delight, all kind
> Of living Creatures new to sight and strange:
> Two of far nobler shape erect and tall,
> Godlike erect, with native Honour clad
> In naked Majestie seemd Lords of all,   290
> And worthie seemd, for in thir looks Divine
> The image of thir glorious Maker shon,
> Truth, Wisdome, Sanctitude severe and pure,
> Severe, but in true filial freedom plac't;
> Whence true autoritie in men; though both
> Not equal, as their sex not equal seemd;
> For contemplation hee and valour formd,
> For softness shee and sweet attractive Grace,
> Hee for God only, shee for God in him:
> His fair large Front and Eye sublime declar'd   300
> Absolute rule; and Hyacinthin Locks
> Round from his parted forelock manly hung
> Clustring, but not beneath his shoulders broad:
> Shee as a vail down to the slender waste
> Her unadorned golden tresses wore

Dissheveld, but in wanton ringlets wav'd
As the Vine curles her tendrils, which impli'd
Subjection, but requir'd with gentle sway,
And by her yeilded, by him best receivd,
Yeilded with coy submission, modest pride,   310
And sweet reluctant amorous delay.
Nor those mysterious parts were then conceald,
Then was not guiltie shame, dishonest shame
Of natures works, honor dishonorable,
Sin-bred, how have ye troubl'd all mankind
With shews instead, meer shews of seeming pure,
And banisht from mans life his happiest life,
Simplicitie and spotless innocence.
So passd they naked on, nor shund the sight
Of God or Angel, for they thought no ill: 320
So hand in hand they passd, the lovliest pair
That ever since in loves imbraces met,
Adam the goodliest man of men since born
His Sons, the fairest of her Daughters *Eve*.
Under a tuft of shade that on a green
Stood whispering soft, by a fresh Fountain side
They sat them down, and after no more toil
Of thir sweet Gardning labour then suffic'd
To recommend coole *Zephyr*, and made ease
More easie, wholsom thirst and appetite   330
More grateful, to thir Supper Fruits they fell,
Nectarine Fruits which the compliant boughes
Yeilded them, side-long as they sat recline
On the soft downie Bank damaskt with flours:
The savourie pulp they chew, and in the rinde
Still as they thirsted scoop the brimming stream:
Nor gentle purpose, nor endearing smiles
Wanted, nor youthful dalliance as beseems
Fair couple, linkt in happie nuptial League,
Alone as they. About them frisking playd   340
All Beasts of th' Earth, since wilde, and of all chase
In Wood or Wilderness, Forrest or Den;
Sporting the Lion rampd, and in his paw
Dandl'd the Kid; Bears, Tygers, Ounces, Pards
Gambold before them, th' unwieldy Elephant
To make them mirth us'd all his might, and wreathd
His Lithe Proboscis; close the Serpent sly
Insinuating, wove with Gordian twine
His breaded train, and of his fatal guile
Gave proof unheeded; others on the grass   350

Coucht, and now fild with pasture gazing sat,
Or Bedward ruminating; for the Sun
Declin'd was hasting now with prone carreer
To th' Ocean Iles, and in th' ascending Scale
Of Heav'n the Starrs that usher Evening rose:
When *Satan* still in gaze, as first he stood,
Scarce thus at length faild speech recoverd sad.
    O Hell! what doe mine eyes with grief behold,
Into our room of bliss thus high advanc't
Creatures of other mould, earth-born perhaps,   360
Not Spirits, yet to heav'nly Spirits bright
Little inferior; whom my thoughts pursue
With wonder, and could love, so lively shines
In them Divine resemblance, and such grace
The hand that formd them on thir shape hath pourd.
Ah gentle pair, yee little think how nigh
Your change approaches, when all these delights
Will vanish and deliver ye to woe,
More woe, the more your taste is now of joy;
Happie, but for so happie ill secur'd   370
Long to continue, and this high seat your Heav'n
Ill fenc't for Heav'n to keep out such a foe
As now is enterd; yet no purpos'd foe
To you whom I could pittie thus forlorne
Though I unpittied: League with you I seek,
And mutual amitie so streight, so close,
That I with you must dwell, or you with me
Henceforth; my dwelling haply may not please
Like this fair Paradise, your sense, yet such
Accept your Makers work; he gave it me,   380
Which I as freely give; Hell shall unfould,
To entertain you two, her widest Gates,
And send forth all her Kings; there will be room,
Not like these narrow limits, to receive
Your numerous ofspring; if no better place,
Thank him who puts me loath to this revenge
On you who wrong me not for him who wrongd.
And should I at your harmless innocence
Melt, as I doe, yet public reason just,
Honour and Empire with revenge enlarg'd,   390
By conquering this new World, compels me now
To do what else though damnd I should abhorre.
    So spake the Fiend, and with necessitie,
The Tyrants plea, excus'd his devilish deeds.
Then from his loftie stand on that high Tree

Down he alights among the sportful Herd
Of those fourfooted kindes, himself now one,
Now other, as thir shape servd best his end
Neerer to view his prey, and unespi'd
To mark what of thir state he more might learn   400
By word or action markt: about them round
A Lion now he stalkes with fierie glare,
Then as a Tiger, who by chance hath spi'd
In some Purlieu two gentle Fawnes at play,
Strait couches close, then rising changes oft
His couchant watch, as one who chose his ground
Whence rushing he might surest seise them both
Grip't in each paw: when *Adam* first of men
To first of women *Eve* thus moving speech,
Turnd him all eare to heare new utterance flow.   410
    Sole partner and sole part of all these joyes,
Dearer thy self then all; needs must the Power
That made us, and for us this ample World
Be infinitly good, and of his good
As liberal and free as infinite,
That rais'd us from the dust and plac't us here
In all this happiness, who at his hand
Have nothing merited, nor can performe
Aught whereof hee hath need, hee who requires
From us no other service then to keep   420
This one, this easie charge, of all the Trees
In Paradise that beare delicious fruit
So various, not to taste that onely Tree
Of knowledge, planted by the Tree of Life,
So neer grows Death to Life, what ere Death is,
Som dreadful thing no doubt; for well thou knowst
God hath pronounc't it death to taste that Tree,
The only sign of our obedience left
Among so many signes of power and rule
Conferred upon us, and Dominion giv'n   430
Over all other Creatures that possesse
Earth, Aire, and Sea. Then let us not think hard
One easie prohibition, who enjoy
Free leave so large to all things else, and choice
Unlimited of manifold delights:
But let us ever praise him, and extoll
His bountie, following our delightful task
To prune these growing Plants, & tend these Flours,
Which were it toilsom, yet with thee were sweet.
    To whom thus *Eve* repli'd. O thou for whom   440

And from whom I was formd flesh of thy flesh,
And without whom am to no end, my Guide
And Head, what thou hast said is just and right.
For wee to him indeed all praises owe,
And daily thanks, I chiefly who enjoy
So farr the happier Lot, enjoying thee
Preëminent by so much odds, while thou
Like consort to thy self canst no where find.
That day I oft remember, when from sleep
I first awak't, and found my self repos'd   450
Under a shade on flours, much wondring where
And what I was, whence thither brought, and how.
Not distant far from thence a murmuring sound
Of waters issu'd from a Cave and spread
Into a liquid Plain, then stood unmov'd
Pure as th' expanse of Heav'n; I thither went
With unexperienc't thought, and laid me downe
On the green bank, to look into the cleer
Smooth Lake, that to me seemd another Skie.
As I bent down to look, just opposite,   460
A Shape within the watry gleam appeerd
Bending to look on me, I started back,
It started back, but pleasd I soon returnd,
Pleas'd it returnd as soon with answering looks
Of sympathie and love, there I had fixt
Mine eyes till now, and pin'd with vain desire,
Had not a voice thus warnd me, What thou seest,
What there thou seest fair Creature is thy self,
With thee it came and goes: but follow me,
And I will bring thee where no shadow staies   470
Thy coming, and thy soft imbraces, hee
Whose image thou art, him thou shall enjoy
Inseparablie thine, to him shalt beare
Multitudes like thy self, and thence be call'd
Mother of human Race: what could I doe,
But follow strait, invisibly thus led?
Till I espi'd thee, fair indeed and tall,
Under a Platan, yet methought less faire,
Less winning soft, less amiablie milde,
Then that smooth watry image; back I turnd,   480
Thou following cryd'st aloud, Return fair *Eve*,
Whom fli'st thou? whom thou fli'st, of him thou art,
His flesh, his bone; to give thee being I lent
Out of my side to thee, neerest my heart
Substantial Life, to have thee by my side

Henceforth an individual solace dear;
Part of my Soul I seek thee, and thee claim
My other half: with that thy gentle hand
Seisd mine, I yeilded, and from that time see
How beauty is excelld by manly grace   490
And wisdom, which alone is truly fair.
  So spake our general Mother, and with eyes
Of conjugal attraction unreprov'd,
And meek surrender, half imbracing leand
On our first Father, half her swelling Breast
Naked met his under the flowing Gold
Of her loose tresses hid: he in delight
Both of her Beauty and submissive Charms
Smil'd with superior Love, as *Jupiter*
On *Juno* smiles, when he impregns the Clouds   500
That shed *May* Flowers; and press'd her Matron lip
With kisses pure: aside the Devil turnd
For envie, yet with jealous leer maligne
Ey'd them askance, and to himself thus plaind.
  Sight hateful, sight tormenting! thus these two
Imparadis't in one anothers arms
The happier *Eden*, shall enjoy thir fill
Of bliss on bliss, while I to Hell am thrust,
Where neither joy nor love, but fierce desire,
Among our other torments not the least,   510
Still unfulfill'd with pain of longing pines;
Yet let me not forget what I have gain'd
From thir own mouths; all is not theirs it seems:
One fatal Tree there stands of Knowledge call'd,
Forbidden them to taste: Knowledge forbidd'n?
Suspicious, reasonless. Why should thir Lord
Envie them that? can it be sin to know,
Can it be death? and do they onely stand
By Ignorance, is that thir happie state,
The proof of thir obedience and thir faith?   520
O fair foundation laid whereon to build
Thir ruine! Hence I will excite thir minds
With more desire to know, and to reject
Envious commands, invented with designe
To keep them low whom knowledge might exalt
Equal with Gods; aspiring to be such,
They taste and die: what likelier can ensue?
But first with narrow search I must walk round
This Garden, and no corner leave unspi'd;
A chance but chance may lead where I may meet   530

Some wandring Spirit of Heav'n, by Fountain side,
Or in thick shade retir'd, from him to draw
What further would be learnt. Live while ye may,
Yet happie pair; enjoy, till I return,
Short pleasures, for long woes are to succeed.

Book VIII, ll. 436–594

[The angel Raphael has descended to Eden to discuss with Adam God's purpose in creating the world. Raphael tells Adam of the rebellion of the fallen
angels and warns him that Satan will attempt to lure Eve and Adam into for-
saking obedience to God. After preparing a dinner of "savory fruits," (V, 304)
Eve arises with "lowliness majestic" (VIII, 42), leaving Adam alone with
Raphael. In the lines below, Adam recounts his recollection of Eve's creation,
and Raphael reminds Adam that Eve is his inferior.]

This answer from the gratious voice Divine,
   Thus farr to try thee *Adam*, I was pleas'd,
And finde thee knowing not of Beasts alone,
Which thou hast rightly nam'd, but of thy self,
Expressing well the spirit within thee free,   440
My Image, not imparted to the Brute,
Whose fellowship therefore unmeet for thee
Good reason was thou freely shouldst dislike,
And be so minded still; I, ere thou spak'st,
Knew it not good for Man to be alone,
And no such companie as then thou saw'st
Intended thee, for trial onely brought,
To see how thou could'st judge of fit and meet:
What next I bring shall please thee, be assur'd,
Thy likeness, thy fit help, thy other self,   450
Thy wish, exactly to thy hearts desire.
   Hee ended, or I heard no more, for now
My earthly by his Heav'nly overpowerd,
Which it had long stood under, streind to the highth
In that celestial Colloquie sublime,
As with an object that excels the sense,
Dazl'd and spent, sunk down, and sought repair
Of sleep, which instantly fell on me, call'd
By Nature as in aide, and clos'd mine eyes.
Mine eyes he clos'd, but op'n left the Cell   460
Of Fancie my internal sight, by which
Abstract as in a transe methought I saw,
Though sleeping, where I lay, and saw the shape
Still glorious before whom awake I stood;
Who stooping op'nd my left side, and took

From thence a Rib, with cordial spirits warme,
And Life-blood streaming fresh; wide was the wound,
But suddenly with flesh fill'd up & heal'd:
The Rib he formd and fashond with his hands;
Under his forming hands a Creature grew,   470
Manlike, but different sex, so lovly faire,
That what seemd fair in all the World, seemd now
Mean, or in her summd up, in her containd
And in her looks, which from that time infus'd
Sweetness into my heart, unfelt before,
And into all things from her Aire inspir'd
The spirit of love and amorous delight.
She disappeerd, and left me dark, I wak'd
To find her, or for ever to deplore
Her loss, and other pleasures all abjure: 480
When out of hope, behold her, not farr off,
Such as I saw her in my dream, adornd
With what all Earth or Heaven could bestow
To make her amiable: On she came,
Led by her Heav'nly Maker, though unseen,
And guided by his voice, nor uninformd
Of nuptial Sanctitie and marriage Rites:
Grace was in all her steps, Heav'n in her Eye,
In every gesture dignitie and love.
I overjoyd could not forbear aloud.   490
     This turn hath made amends; thou hast fulfill'd
Thy words, Creator bounteous and benigne,
Giver of all things faire, but fairest this
Of all thy gifts, nor enviest. I now see
Bone of my Bone, Flesh of my Flesh, my Self
Before me; Woman is her Name, of Man
Extracted; for this cause he shall forgoe
Father and Mother, and to his Wife adhere;
And they shall be one Flesh, one Heart, one Soule.
     She heard me thus, and though divinely brought,   500
Yet Innocence and Virgin Modestie,
Her vertue and the conscience of her worth,
That would be woo'd, and not unsought be won,
Not obvious, not obtrusive, but retir'd,
The more desirable, or to say all,
Nature her self, though pure of sinful thought,
Wrought in her so, that seeing me, she turn'd;
I follow'd her, she what was Honour knew,
And with obsequious Majestie approv'd
My pleaded reason. To the Nuptial Bowre   510

I led her blushing like the Morn: all Heav'n,
And happie Constellations on that houre
Shed thir selectest influence; the Earth
Gave sign of gratulation, and each Hill;
Joyous the Birds; fresh Gales and gentle Aires
Whisper'd it to the Woods, and from thir wings
Flung Rose, flung Odours from the spicie Shrub,
Disporting, till the amorous Bird of Night
Sung Spousal, and bid haste the Eevning Starr
On his Hill top, to light the bridal Lamp.   520
Thus I have told thee all my State, and brought
My Storie to the sum of earthly bliss
Which I enjoy, and must confess to find
In all things else delight indeed, but such
As us'd or not, works in the mind no change,
Nor vehement desire, these delicacies
I mean of Taste, Sight, Smell, Herbs, Fruits, & Flours,
Walks, and the melodie of Birds; but here
Farr otherwise, transported I behold,
Transported touch; here passion first I felt,   530
Commotion strange, in all enjoyments else
Superiour and unmov'd, here onely weake
Against the charm of Beauties powerful glance.
Or Nature faild in mee, and left some part
Not proof enough such Object to sustain,
Or from my side subducting, took perhaps
More then enough; at least on her bestow'd
Too much of Ornament, in outward shew
Elaborate, of inward less exact.
For well I understand in the prime end   540
Of Nature her th' inferiour, in the mind
And inward Faculties, which most excell,
In outward also her resembling less
His Image who made both, and less expressing
The character of that Dominion giv'n
O're other Creatures; yet when I approach
Her loveliness, so absolute she seems
And in her self compleat, so well to know
Her own, that what she wills to do or say,
Seems wisest, vertuousest, discreetest, best;   550
All higher knowledge in her presence falls
Degraded, Wisdom in discourse with her
Looses discount'nanc't, and like folly shewes;
Authoritie and Reason on her waite,
As one intended first, not after made

Occasionally; and to consummate all,
Greatness of mind and nobleness thir seat
Build in her loveliest, and create an awe
About her, as a guard Angelic plac't.
To whom the Angel with contracted brow.   560
    Accuse not Nature, she hath don her part;
Do thou but thine, and be not diffident
Of Wisdom, she deserts thee not, if thou
Dismiss not her, when most thou needst her nigh,
By attributing overmuch to things
Less excellent, as thou thy self perceav'st.
For what admir'st thou, what transports thee so,
An outside? fair no doubt, and worthy well
Thy cherishing, thy honouring, and thy love,
Not thy subjection: weigh with her thy self;   570
Then value: Oft times nothing profits more
Then self-esteem, grounded on just and right
Well manag'd; of that skill the more thou know'st,
The more she will acknowledge thee her Head,
And to realities yeild all her shows;
Made so adorn for thy delight the more,
So awful, that with honour thou maist love
Thy mate, who sees when thou art seen least wise.
But if the sense of touch whereby mankind
Is propagated seem such dear delight   580
Beyond all other, think the same voutsaf't
To Cattel and each Beast; which would not be
To them made common & divulg'd, if aught
Therein enjoy'd were worthy to subdue
The Soule of Man, or passion in him move.
What higher in her societie thou findst
Attractive, human, rational, love still;
In loving thou dost well, in passion not,
Wherein true Love consists not; love refines
The thoughts, and heart enlarges, hath his seat   590
In Reason, and is judicious, is the scale
By which to heav'nly Love thou maist ascend,
Not sunk in carnal pleasure, for which cause
Among the Beasts no Mate for thee was found.

Book IX, ll. 780–1063

[The next day, Adam and Eve set out to tend the garden of Eden. Eve suggests that they will work more efficiently if they separate, but Adam worries that Satan will find them easy prey if work apart from one another. Eve welcomes

the challenge to prove her faithfulness should Satan choose to appear to her,
and Adam consents. Satan then beguiles Eve into eating the forbidden fruit.]

So saying, her rash hand in evil hour   780
Forth reaching to the Fruit, she pluck'd, she eat:
Earth felt the wound, and Nature from her seat
Sighing through all her Works gave signs of woe,
That all was lost. Back to the Thicket slunk
The guiltie Serpent, and well might, for *Eve*
Intent now wholly on her taste, naught else
Regarded, such delight till then, as seemd,
In Fruit she never tasted, whether true
Or fansied so, through expectation high
Of knowledg, nor was God-head from her thought.   790
Greedily she ingorg'd without restraint,
And knew not eating Death: Satiate at length,
And hight'nd as with Wine, jocond and boon,
Thus to her self she pleasingly began.
    O Sovran, vertuous, precious of all Trees
In Paradise, of operation blest
To Sapience, hitherto obscur'd, infam'd,
And thy fair Fruit let hang, as to no end
Created; but henceforth my early care,
Not without Song, each Morning, and due praise   800
Shall tend thee, and the fertil burden ease
Of thy full branches offer'd free to all;
Till dieted by thee I grow mature
In knowledge, as the Gods who all things know;
Though others envie what they cannot give;
For had the gift bin theirs, it had not here
Thus grown. Experience, next to thee I owe,
Best guide; not following thee, I had remaind
In ignorance, thou op'nst Wisdoms way,
And giv'st access, though secret she retire.   810
And I perhaps am secret; Heav'n is high,
High and remote to see from thence distinct
Each thing on Earth; and other care perhaps
May have diverted from continual watch
Our great Forbidder, safe with all his Spies
About him. But to *Adam* in what sort
Shall I appear? shall I to him make known
As yet my change, and give him to partake
Full happiness with mee, or rather not,
But keep the odds of Knowledge in my power   820
Without Copartner? so to add what wants

In Femal Sex, the more to draw his Love,
And render me more equal, and perhaps,
A thing not undesireable, somtime
Superior: for inferior who is free?
This may be well: but what if God have seen,
And Death ensue? then I shall be no more,
And *Adam* wedded to another *Eve*,
Shall live with her enjoying, I extinct;
A death to think. Confirm'd then I resolve,   830
Adam shall share with me in bliss or woe:
So dear I love him, that with him all deaths
I could endure, without him live no life.

So saying, from the Tree her step she turnd,
But first low Reverence don, as to the power
That dwelt within, whose presence had infus'd
Into the plant sciential sap, deriv'd
From Nectar, drink of Gods. *Adam* the while
Waiting desirous her return, had wove
Of choicest Flours a Garland to adorne   840
Her Tresses, and her rural labours crown
As Reapers oft are wont thir Harvest Queen.
Great joy he promis'd to his thought, and new
Solace in her return, so long delay'd;
Yet oft his heart, divine of somthing ill,
Misgave him; hee the faultring measure felt;
And forth to meet her went, the way she took
That Morn when first they parted; by the Tree
Of Knowledge he must pass, there he her met,
Scarse from the Tree returning; in her hand   850
A bough of fairest fruit that downie smil'd,
New gatherd, and ambrosial smell diffus'd.
To him she hasted, in her face excuse
Came Prologue, and Apologie to prompt,
Which with bland words at will she thus addrest.

Hast thou not wonderd, *Adam*, at my stay?
Thee I have misst, and thought it long, depriv'd
Thy presence, agonie of love till now
Not felt, nor shall be twice, for never more
Mean I to trie, what rash untri'd I sought,   860
The paine of absence from thy sight. But strange
Hath bin the cause, and wonderful to heare:
This Tree is not as we are told, a Tree
Of danger tasted, nor to evil unknown
Op'ning the way, but of Divine effect
To open Eyes, and make them Gods who taste;

And hath bin tasted such: the Serpent wise,
Or not restraind as wee, or not obeying,
Hath eat'n of the fruit, and is become,
Not dead, as we are threatn'd, but thenceforth   870
Endu'd with human voice and human sense,
Reasoning to admiration, and with mee
Perswasively hath so prevaild, that I
Have also tasted, and have also found
Th' effects to correspond, opener mine Eyes
Dimm erst, dilated Spirits, ampler Heart,
And growing up to Godhead; which for thee
Chiefly I sought, without thee can despise.
For bliss, as thou hast part, to me is bliss,
Tedious, unshar'd with thee, and odious soon.   880
Thou therfore also taste, that equal Lot
May joyne us, equal Joy, as equal Love;
Least thou not tasting, different degree
Disjoyne us, and I then too late renounce
Deitie for thee, when Fate will not permit.
     Thus *Eve* with Countnance blithe her storie told;
But in her Cheek distemper flushing glowd.
On th' other side, *Adam*, soon as he heard
The fatal Trespass done by *Eve*, amaz'd,
Astonied stood and Blank, while horror chill   890
Ran through his veins, and all his joynts relax'd;
From his slack hand the Garland wreath'd for *Eve*
Down drop'd, and all the faded Roses shed:
Speechless he stood and pale, till thus at length
First to himself he inward silence broke.
     O fairest of Creation, last and best
Of all Gods Works, Creature in whom excell'd,
Whatever can to sight or thought be formd,
Holy, divine, good, amiable, or sweet!
How art thou lost, how on a sudden lost,   900
Defac't, deflourd, and now to Death devote?
Rather how hast thou yeelded to transgress
The strict forbiddance, how to violate
The sacred Fruit forbidd'n! som cursed fraud
Of Enemie hath beguil'd thee, yet unknown,
And mee with thee hath ruind, for with thee
Certain my resolution is to Die;
How can I live without thee, how forgoe
Thy sweet Converse and Love so dearly joyn'd,
To live again in these wilde Woods forlorn?   910
Should God create another *Eve*, and I

Another Rib afford, yet loss of thee
Would never from my heart; no no, I feel
The link of Nature draw me: Flesh of Flesh,
Bone of my Bone thou art, and from thy State
Mine never shall be parted, bliss or woe.
   So having said, as one from sad dismay
Reomforted, and after thoughts disturbd
Submitting to what seemd remediless,
Thus in calme mood his Words to *Eve* he turnd.   920
   Bold deed thou hast presum'd, adventrous *Eve*,
And peril great provok't, who thus hast dar'd
Had it bin onely coveting to Eye
That sacred Fruit, sacred to abstinence,
Much more to taste it under banne to touch.
But past who can recall, or don undoe?
Not God Omnipotent, nor Fate, yet so
Perhaps thou shalt not Die, perhaps the Fact
Is not so hainous now, foretasted Fruit,
Profan'd first by the Serpent, by him first   930
Made common and unhallowd ere our taste;
Nor yet on him found deadly, he yet lives,
Lives, as thou saidst, and gaines to live as Man
Higher degree of Life, inducement strong
To us, as likely tasting to attaine
Proportional ascent, which cannot be
But to be Gods, or Angels Demi-gods.
Nor can I think that God, Creator wise,
Though threatning, will in earnest so destroy
Us his prime Creatures, dignifi'd so high   940
Set over all his Works, which in our Fall,
For us created, needs with us must faile,
Dependent made; so God shall uncreate,
Be frustrate, do, undo, and labour loose,
Not well conceav'd of God, who though his Power
Creation could repeate, yet would be loath
Us to bolish, least the Adversary
Triumph and say; Fickle their State whom God
Most Favors, who can please him long? Mee first
He ruind, now Mankind; whom will be next?   950
Matter of scorne, not to be given the Foe.
However I with thee have fixt my Lot,
Certain to undergoe like doom, if Death
Consort with thee, Death is to mee as Life;
So forcible within my heart I feel
The Bond of Nature draw me to my owne,

My own in thee, for what thou art is mine;
Our State cannot be severd, we are one,
One Flesh; to loose thee were to loose my self.
   So *Adam*, and thus *Eve* to him repli'd.   960
O glorious trial of exceeding Love,
Illustrious evidence, example high!
Ingaging me to emulate, but short
Of thy perfection, how shall I attaine,
Adam, from whose deare side I boast me sprung,
And gladly of our Union heare thee speak,
One Heart, one Soul in both; whereof good prooff
This day affords, declaring thee resolvd,
Rather then Death or aught then Death more dread
Shall separate us, linkt in Love so deare,   970
To undergoe with mee one Guilt, one Crime,
If any be, of tasting this fair Fruit,
Whose vertue, for of good still good proceeds,
Direct, or by occasion hath presented
This happie trial of thy Love, which else
So eminently never had bin known.
Were it I thought Death menac't would ensue
This my attempt, I would sustain alone
The worst, and not perswade thee, rather die
Deserted, then oblige thee with a fact   980
Pernicious to thy Peace, chiefly assur'd
Remarkably so late of thy so true,
So faithful Love unequald; but I feel
Farr otherwise th' event, not Death, but Life
Augmented, op'nd Eyes, new Hopes, new Joyes,
Taste so Divine, that what of sweet before
Hath toucht my sense, flat seems to this, and harsh.
On my experience, *Adam*, freely taste,
And fear of Death deliver to the Windes.
   So saying, she embrac'd him, and for joy   990
Tenderly wept, much won that he his Love
Had so enobl'd, as of choice to incurr
Divine displeasure for her sake, or Death.
In recompence (for such compliance bad
Such recompence best merits) from the bough
She gave him of that fair enticing Fruit
With liberal hand: he scrupl'd not to eat
Against his better knowledge, not deceav'd,
But fondly overcome with Femal charm.
Earth trembl'd from her entrails, as again   1000
In pangs, and Nature gave a second groan,

Skie lowr'd, and muttering Thunder, som sad drops
Wept at compleating of the mortal Sin
Original; while *Adam* took no thought,
Eating his fill, nor *Eve* to iterate
Her former trespass fear'd, the more to soothe
Him with her lov'd societie, that now
As with new Wine intoxicated both
They swim in mirth, and fansie that they feel
Divinitie within them breeding wings   1010
Wherewith to scorn the Earth: but that false Fruit
Farr other operation first displaid,
Carnal desire enflaming, hee on *Eve*
Began to cast lascivious Eyes, she him
As wantonly repaid; in Lust they burne:
Till *Adam* thus 'gan *Eve* to dalliance move.
    Eve, now I see thou art exact of taste,
And elegant, of Sapience no small part,
Since to each meaning savour we apply,
And Palate call judicious; I the praise   1020
Yeild thee, so well this day thou hast purvey'd.
Much pleasure we have lost, while we abstain'd
From this delightful Fruit, nor known till now
True relish, tasting; if such pleasure be
In things to us forbidden, it might be wish'd,
For this one Tree had bin forbidden ten.
But come, so well refresh't, now let us play,
As meet is, after such delicious Fare;
For never did thy Beautie since the day
I saw thee first and wedded thee, adorn'd   1030
With all perfections, so enflame my sense
With ardor to enjoy thee, fairer now
Than ever, bountie of this vertuous Tree.
    So said he, and forbore not glance or toy
Of amorous intent, well understood
Of *Eve*, whose Eye darted contagious Fire.
Her hand he seis'd, and to a shadie bank,
Thick overhead with verdant roof imbowr'd
He led her nothing loath; Flours were the Couch,
Pansies, and Violets, and Asphodel,   1040
And Hyacinth, Earths freshest softest lap.
There they thir fill of Love and Loves disport
Took largely, of thir mutual guilt the Seale,
The solace of thir sin, till dewie sleep
Oppress'd them, wearied with thir amorous play.
Soon as the force of that fallacious Fruit,

That with exhilerating vapour bland
About thir spirits had plaid, and inmost powers
Made erre, was now exhal'd, and grosser sleep
Bred of unkindly fumes, with conscious dreams   1050
Encumberd, now had left them, up they rose
As from unrest, and each the other viewing,
Soon found thir Eyes how op'nd, and thir minds
How dark'nd; innocence, that as a veile
Had shadow'd them from knowing ill, was gon,
Just confidence, and native righteousness,
And honour from about them, naked left
To guiltie shame hee cover'd, but his Robe
Uncover'd more. So rose the *Danite* strong
Herculean Samson from the Harlot-lap   1060
Of *Philistean Dalilah*, and wak'd
Shorn of his strength, They destitute and bare
Of all thir vertue:

Book X, ll. 888b–908

[The final selection is from after the Fall. In his grief, Adam wonders why God created Eve.]

O why did God,
Creator wise, that peopl'd highest Heav'n
With Spirits Masculine, create at last   890
This noveltie on Earth, this fair defect
Of Nature, and not fill the World at once
With Men as Angels without Feminine,
Or find some other way to generate
Mankind? this mischief had not then befall'n,
And more that shall befall, innumerable
Disturbances on Earth through Femal snares,
And straight conjunction with this Sex: for either
He never shall find out fit Mate, but such
As some misfortune brings him, or mistake,   900
Or whom he wishes most shall seldom gain
Through her perverseness, but shall see her gaind
By a farr worse, or if she love, withheld
By Parents, or his happiest choice too late
Shall meet, alreadie linkt and Wedlock-bound
To a fell Adversarie, his hate or shame:
Which infinite calamitie shall cause
To Humane life, and houshold peace confound.

CHAPTER SEVEN

Social Applications in the United States (1800s CE)

INTRODUCTION

This chapter examines applications of Eve and Adam's story to several social issues that were highly contested in the nineteenth century. While the chapter's examination retains the preoccupation with Protestantism of the previous chapter (even as it adds voices from some new religious movements that arose out of Protestantism), it shifts the geographic locus from Europe to the United States. Since never in Western history had a culture produced more innovative readings of Genesis 1-3, or was a culture more determined to use the text in concrete social applications than nineteenth-century North America, this chapter will examine several of those discussions: antebellum debates over slavery and household hierarchies, discussions of sexuality and women's rights, and attempts by new religious movements to produce more egalitarian forms of Christianity. Some descriptions of wider purviews are in order, however, before the chapter focuses in on these areas

Social Applications and Judaism

The nineteenth century was a time of change and challenge for Jewish women around the world.[1] Should Jewish girls celebrate a rite of passage similar to boys at puberty? Should women be granted a writ of divorce even if husbands were unwilling? Should women sit with men during synagogue services and be given full responsibility in communal religious affairs? Should women be responsible for all *mitzvot* (commandments) instead of the three traditionally assigned to them (lighting the Sabbath candles, dividing the dough, and observing menstrual legislation)?[2] Should women be allowed to study Torah and Talmud?

Questions concerning women's social and religious roles were due, in part, to two crises confronting nineteenth-century Jews: assimilation and modernization. In the eighteenth century, Jews in the West had begun to experience a degree of political emancipation, increasingly gaining the right to practice their religion freely and to enjoy enfranchisement as full citizens. By the nineteenth century, this emancipation was, according to Isidore Epstein, "in most countries of Western Europe, as well as in America . . . complete." Yet this newfound freedom threatened the very core of Jewish life. As Epstein notes:

> Wherever Jews were given civic equality, they threw themselves heart and soul into the service of the state, contributing richly into political, social, cultural, and economic life. In all but religion the emancipated Jews identified themselves with the destiny, interests, and endeavors of their fellow citizens. But within this vortex of social and economic change the Jews were caught unawares. . . . A large number of them solved the problem for themselves by deserting to the dominant faith. Many others . . . saw a solution in a process of assimilation . . . [3]

This immersion of Jews into cultures from which they had previously been secluded, if not isolated, raised the issue of *halakah*'s relevance to nineteenth-century Jews. If Jews were to be fully integrated into non-Jewish societies, how could they retain their distinctive social and religious practices? Moreover, if Jews moved freely in "modern" nineteenth-century social circles, how could *halakic* values and practices be defended in light of non-Jewish, post-Enlightenment sensibilities?

Jewish immigrants to North America encountered particularly powerful pressures to assimilate and modernize Jewish customs. Jewish women felt impelled to "Americanize" their religious practices, as well as to respond to the broader issue of women's rights that was so much a part of the nineteenth-century American cultural landscape. Indeed, many issues facing American Jewish women were similar in kind, if not in substance, to those of their Christian counterparts. Women in both traditions encountered questions concerning the public/private dichotomy in their economic, familial, and worship lives. Both groups of women struggled to find their niche in a land "of the free" that promised "liberty and justice for all."

Prior to 1880, the majority of Jews living in the United States were associated with the Reform tradition—a branch of Judaism especially sensitive to aligning Jewish practices with the "spirit of the times." In Germany, for example, the Breslau Conference (1846) contrasted the "civil emancipation" of Jews in the previous century to the lack of such emancipation for nineteenth-century women, concluding that: "The *halachic* position of women must undergo a change, and it is hoped that all members will be unanimous on that subject. . . . [Jewish women] have received assurances of their capabilities for emancipation, without, however, being indeed permitted to become emancipated." Given this reality, the Conference felt a "sacred duty to express most emphatically the complete religious equality of the female sex."[4] Thus, the Conference stated:

> The Rabbinical Conference shall declare the female sex as religiously equal with the male, in its obligations and rights, and pronounce accordingly as *halachic*:
> 1. That women must observe all *mitzvot*, even though they pertain to a certain time, in so far as these *mitzvot* have any strength and vigor at all for our religious consciousness;
> 2. That the female sex has to fulfill all obligations toward the children in the same manner as the male;
> 3. That neither the husband nor the father has the right to absolve a religiously mature daughter or wife from her vow;
> 4. That from now on, the benediction *shele assani ishath* (who has not made me a woman), which was the basis for the religious prejudice against women, shall be abolished;
> 5. That the female sex shall, from earliest youth, be obligated to participate in religious instruction and public worship, and in the latter respect also be counted in a *minyan* [the minimum of ten persons for a public service]; and finally,
> 6. That the religious coming of age for both sexes begin with the age of thirteen.[5]

Immigrants, particularly those from Germany, brought to the United States the egalitarian vision of these European reforms. The American Reform movement, a continuation of its European counterpart, advocated sweeping changes in Jewish women's religious lives. Rabbi Isaac Wise (1819-1900), founder of Hebrew Union College in Cincinnati (1874), and a leading voice in the American Reform movement, declared:

> The principle of justice, and the Law of God inherent in every human being, demand that women be admitted to membership in the congregation and given equal rights with man. . . . We will debate the question with anyone who will show us in what woman is less entitled to the privileges of the synagogue than man, or where her faith is less important to her salvation than man's is to him. Till then, we maintain that women must become active members of the congregation for their own sake, and for the benefit of Israel's sacred cause.[6]

Following in the footsteps of the Breslau Conference, the Pittsburgh platform of 1885[7] articulated the Reform agenda for American Jews.

How did the changes generated by the Reform tradition affect the impact of Eve's story in Reform women's lives? One example can be found in the changing attitudes concerning women's *mitzvot*. Traditional explanations of why Jewish women lit the Sabbath candles, divided the dough, and observed menstrual legislation all referred to the Genesis 3 story of Eve's disobedience. Reform interpretations challenged this association in a number of ways. Jewish women in nineteenth-century America were often unable to procure ritual baths (married women were required to immerse themselves in a bath [*mikvah*] at a specific time following menstruation), and many American Jews increasingly considered menstrual purity legislation outdated. Admittedly, some Jews were sorry to see the custom of ritual bathing fall into disuse—in 1928 a writer looking back on the previous century of American Jewish life lamented that "the daughters of Israel had ceased to guard their purity." Still, as Charles S. Liebman has remarked, "Requirements of family purity . . . were an anachronism in the values of middle-class American culture toward which the immigrants aspired."[8]

While menstrual legislation was no longer meaningful to most American Jewish women, the *mitzvot* of lighting Sabbath candles assumed new significance. Historically, Jews had argued that God required woman to light the Sabbath candles as a penance for Eve's sin. In the nineteenth century, however, American Jews came to view the lighting of the Sabbath candles not as a penance, but as a celebration of woman's contributions to family life and faith. This reassessment and reinterpretation of *halakah* weakened some of the ties between Eve's story and Jewish women's lives. Yet it could be argued that the traditional ties to Eve that Jewish women lost through the modernization of *halakah* were offset by the new connections to Eve that Jews absorbed through contact with nineteenth-century American culture—a culture that was, as the body of this chapter will illustrate, permeated with Eve's presence.

It was not until the immigrations of the late nineteenth and early twentieth centuries, with their influx of Eastern European Jews, that urban Conservative and Orthodox enclaves diversified American Jewry and provided a broader spectrum of responses to *halakah* and women's status.[9]

Social Applications and Islam

Rigorous debates over the status, responsibilities, and rights of women emerged within Islam in the nineteenth century.[10] Contested topics frequently involved such matters as educational opportunities for women and girls, domestic seclusion, face veiling, and polygyny. Because diverse societies and nations constitute Islamic culture, the debates varied widely in content and historical development. Different reactions to modernization as well as different experiences of foreign colonial occupation heightened this variety.[11] Amid the diversity, however, two common traits are evident. First, many Muslim women and men advocated greater equality for women prior to the twentieth century.[12] Second, these advocates often appealed to tenets of Islam as the basis for their reformatory proposals.[13]

Highlighting some moves toward women's equality in two Muslim lands illustrates this growing dissatisfaction with gender inequality. In Turkey, for example, reforms of the Tanzimat Period (1839-1876) included establishing the first secondary school for girls and a women's teacher-training college as well as redressing some inequities concerning women's rights of inheritance.[14] Turkey also was the home of Fatma Aliye Hanim, an Ottoman woman whose advocacy of changes for women eventuated in her publishing the book *Nisvan-i Islam* (Muslim Women) in 1891.[15] In Egypt, strides toward expanding the roles and opportunities for women resulted in the founding of the first state school for girls in 1873 and in the inauguration of a women's press in 1892.[16] Also, greater gender equality was advocated by several Egyptian men including Qasim Amin, who published *The Liberation of the Woman* in 1899, and Amin's teacher Muhammad 'Abduh.[17] While the work of these men has received more attention, Badran and Cooke stress that several Muslim women gave voice to feminist consciousness even earlier in "the poetry, essays, and tales" these women published by the 1860s.[18]

Another set of important factors relating to the focus of this chapter concerns the presence of Muslims in the Americas. Scholars typically point to the late nineteenth century to mark the beginning of Muslim emigration to North America.[19] The "first wave" of Muslim immigrants involved persons from various parts of the Islamic world, but the majority were Arabs from the Ottoman Empire. This immigration, however, was not the first presence of Muslims in the Americas.[20] Instead, Spanish Muslims had come earlier through their participation in the "New World" explorations and settlements of Spain and Portugal. Furthermore, many African Muslims were brought to the Western Hemisphere as slaves. Indeed, possibly one-fifth of the Africans brought in the slave trade were Muslims. We have little information about these African Muslims, in part because many of them were forced to convert to Christianity.[21]

Social Applications and Christianity in the United States

Genesis 1-3 was, from the colonial days, critical in defining gender roles for Americans. In New England, Puritan settlers affirmed a hierarchical model of creation, arguing that Adam and Eve were equally formed in God's image, but that God had created Adam first to indicate women's subordination to men. As Carol Karlsen noted in *The Devil in the Shape of a Woman*, Puritan theologians rejected the assumption of the *Malleus Maleficarum* that women were inherently sinful. In the beginning, Puritans argued, Eve was a good creation; but they blamed her, as the archetypal woman, for seducing Adam and for failing to subordinate herself to him.

Puritans assumed that women, as Eve's daughters, would forever be tempted to disobey male authority. Though Puritans appealed to Scripture to challenge the authority of the British crown, they remained committed to a hierarchical social order. "Puritan men," Karlsen claimed, "worried especially about masterlessness—insubordination in women, children, servants, beggars, and even in themselves." Understanding the world as a great chain of being,

Puritans envisioned each family as a microcosm of the larger society. As rulers over their wives, children, and servants, husbands were, Karlsen noted, elevated to "a godlike position."[22]

That presumed position of mastery provided the grounds for numerous debates. The popularity of lay theologian Anne Hutchinson indicated that Puritans were not unanimous in ascribing spiritual superiority to men,[23] and the ongoing witness of the more egalitarian Quakers provided an alternative theological model for gender construction. The American Revolution, ushered in by a Declaration of Independence proclaiming the "self-evident" truths that "all men are created equal" and "endowed by their Creator with certain unalienable rights" provided an alternative model for understanding social relations. Though the Declaration in practice excluded African American slaves and women of all races from political equality with white males of property, still the notion of an original equality proved intriguing. For those inclined to read Genesis 1-3 as an egalitarian account of gender relations, the Declaration was a handy ally; those committed to hierarchical readings of Genesis 1-3, on the other hand, moved to repudiate the socially leveling implications of the Declaration.

Given the political disputes that marked nineteenth-century North American society, Protestantism of the period provides a particularly apt field of study for those interested in practical applications of Genesis 1-3.[24] We have argued throughout this volume that sacred texts have payoffs. We have suggested as well that interpreters inclined to read Genesis 1-3 as establishing a gender hierarchy may also tend to be sympathetic to other forms of social hierarchies, whereas those who read Genesis 1-3 as establishing gender equality may also be open to other forms of egalitarianism. Antebellum debates about the legitimacy of slavery offer a case study of this thesis, as interpreters read Genesis 1-3 in ways that self-consciously linked racism and sexism. Moreover, nineteenth-century American Protestantism gave rise to a number of novel forms of Christianity which not only proposed radical forms of communitarian living, but also articulated some of the most egalitarian readings of Genesis 1-3 yet delineated. For all of these reasons, we have chosen Protestantism in nineteenth-century North America as a case study in practical applications of Genesis 1-3, illustrating ways in which interpreters linked their reading of Genesis 1-3 to issues such as the gender of God, the status of women, sexual relations, and African American slavery.

To Shape the Nation: Gender, Slavery, and Readings of Genesis

The battle for the creation was particularly important in debates over slavery and women's rights. By 1850, proponents of slavery had developed a multifaceted defense of the peculiar institution. Typically, proslavery orators dismissed the Declaration of Independence's vision of an original equality, turning instead to "the Bible, the whole Bible, and nothing but the Bible."[25] The New Testament proved a rich ground for the justification of slavery. Proslavery advocates interpreted the Golden Rule as an admonition to treat slaves as one would wish to be treated if one were a slave and limited Galatians 3:28 to a call for spiritual unity. New Testament household codes that subordinated wives to husbands, children to parents, and slaves to their masters seemed to provide divine sanction to slavery, as did Paul's letter to Philemon.

Apologists for slavery found support in the Hebrew Bible as well. In addition to various statutes governing Israelite slavery in the law of Moses, texts from the primeval history of Genesis also served to bolster the proslavery interpretations of Scripture. The most popular text was Genesis 9:20-27, where Noah sentenced his grandson Canaan to be the slave of Noah's sons Shem and Japheth and ordered Shem to allow his brother Japheth to dwell in his tents. Southern exegetes interpreted this story as God's blessing of African American slavery (with Canaan and his father Ham representing Africans) and as God's ordering Native Americans (represented by Shem) to give their land to their European brothers (Japheth).[26]

Though Genesis 1-3 was not as frequently cited as Genesis 9 in the proslavery defense, proponents of slavery did not neglect the text. Indeed, it was in proslavery exegesis that the implications of the hierarchical interpretations of Genesis 1-3 came to their fullest realization. Apologists for slavery sought to convince their readers that slavery was just one part of a great chain of being that God intended to encompass all of society. In this interpretation, the subordination of women went hand in hand with the enslavement of African Americans. Distinguishing between essential human rights (the freedom to worship God) and contingent civic rights (such as the right to vote or to own one's labor), Southern clergy like James Henley Thornwell noted it made no sense to argue that the "rights of the citizen" accrued to slaves, for then such rights would belong to women and children, as well as apprentices and convicts—an eventuality Thornwell deemed so ludicrous as to require no further comment.[27]

Defenders of slavery argued that slavery and the subordination of women were the logical consequences of the Fall. In Genesis 3, God cursed men to earn their bread by the sweat of their face and cursed women to be forever subordinate to men. The New Testament dispensation did nothing to alter those divine judgments, though proslavery theologians were quick to point out that, under the gospel dispensation, white male patriarchs were to administer their rule with compassion. Still, as Alabama minister Fred A. Ross noted, the wife, like the slave, was subject to involuntary servitude. How often, Ross conjectured, would the planter's wife

> throw off the yoke if she could! . . . Nevertheless, he [your husband] has authority, from God, to rule over you. You are under service to him. You are bound to obey him in all things. . . . you cannot leave your parlor, nor your bed-chamber, nor your couch, if your husband commands you to stay there![28]

Opponents of slavery called upon both the Bible and their understanding of natural law as grounds for abolishing the peculiar institution. Citing the Declaration of Independence's claim that the inherent equality of all persons was a self-evident truth, some antislavery reformers sought to avoid a debate over Scripture. Recognizing that Scripture provided proslavery advocates with abundant material and that the fight for the Bible would be protracted, these abolitionists appealed to natural law and to the responsibility of each individual to obey the Creator's will as expressed in natural law, as grounds for opposing slavery.

Those antislavery reformers who chose to use the Bible to buttress their critique of slavery countered proslavery exegeses on a number of fronts. They typically viewed the Declaration of Independence as compatible with both the New Testament and with Genesis 1-3. For them, the Golden Rule proscribed slavery, since they could not imagine that anyone would ever wish to be a slave, no matter how kindly treated. As escaped slave and abolitionist Frederick Douglass remarked, "There is not a man beneath the canopy of heaven who does not know that slavery is wrong *for him*."[29] Opponents of slavery argued, in addition, that Galatians 3:28 referred to social equality as well as spiritual equality. Thus, in their reading, the New Testament unequivocally denounced slavery.

Abolitionists found in Genesis 1-3 further warrants against slavery. They argued that slavery usurped God's authority, for it placed the slave owner in the place of the divine creator as Lord of the slave. Slavery was, then, a form of blasphemy. Slavery also negated the Genesis claim that humanity was created in God's image. In reducing the slave to a piece of property, antislavery advocates insisted, the slave owner denied the Bible's central theological claim that human beings were persons of worth, created to know and love God. As Rev. Daniel Payne, bishop of the African Methodist Episcopal Church exclaimed, "*American Slavery brutalizes man—destroys his moral agency, and subverts the moral government of God.*"[30]

As opponents of slavery considered the implications of an egalitarian Eden, some of them concluded that the Bible opposed the subordination of women as well as the enslavement of African Americans. If subjugation rendered null the divine mandate that all should be free to live according to the divine image, and if the redemption offered in the New Testament[31] restored the original order of creation, then advocates for women's rights were ready to rethink hierarchical readings of Genesis. Indeed, they were forced to do so; women who joined the antislavery campaign found themselves the subject of controversy when their desire to denounce slavery ran afoul of Victorian conventions that forbade women to speak in public before "promiscuous" audiences of men and women.

Sarah Grimké's *Letters on the Equality of the Sexes and the Condition of Women* were landmark exegetical arguments for, as she put it, "the original equality of woman." Sarah and her sister Angelina were former slave owners who moved North and converted to Quakerism. They volunteered to deliver abolitionist lectures throughout New England on behalf of the American Anti-Slavery Society in 1837, and were so successful that they were soon drawing as many men as women to their speeches. The Congregational clergy of Connecticut issued a pastoral letter condemning the practice of women addressing promiscuous assemblies, and the Grimké sisters were forced to justify their participation in the antislavery campaign. Among other responses, Sarah Grimké published a series of letters in the *Boston Spectator* on the rights of women. Both Sarah and Angelina were insistent that the cause of freedom, so dear to the hearts of abolitionists, was inseparable from the question of women's rights.

That response raised an uproar among abolitionists. Some argued that the Grimkés, in defending their right to speak on behalf of the slaves, had introduced an "extraneous" issue into antislavery reform. These abolitionists appealed to the Grimkés to drop their discussions of women's rights lest they divert public attention from the antislavery cause. Others urged the Grimkés to tone down their defense of women's rights by appealing not to the issue of human rights, but to their status as Quakers. Quakers, with their doctrine of the Inner Light, had long allowed women to speak in worship settings, and they had been among the first to condemn slavery. The Grimkés, if they chose, could justify their public speaking as a manifestation of Quaker "peculiarity."

Angelina and Sarah Grimké refused to set aside the question of women's rights so as not to "disrupt" the antislavery campaign. "*We* will settle *this right before* we go one step further," retorted Angelina.

> *The time* to assert a right is *the* time when *that* right is denied. . . . You may depend upon it, tho' to meet *this* question *may appear* to be turning out of our road, that *it is not*. IT IS NOT: we must meet it, and meet it *now* and meet it like *women* in the fear of the Lord. . . . What *then* can *woman* do for the slave when she is herself under the feet of man and shamed in *silence*?

The Grimkés also refused to appeal to Quakerism to justify their public speaking on behalf of abolitionism. "Our *right* to labor" on behalf of the slave, Angelina explained, "*must* be firmly established; *not* on the ground of Quakerism, but on the only firm basis of human rights, the Bible."[32]

Indeed, the more the Grimkés considered their predicament, the more convinced they became that the issue of gender hierarchy was critical to the antislavery campaign. If, as abolitionists claimed, their goal was to create an egalitarian society, then they were compelled to challenge the cultural norms that subordinated women to men. Theodore Dwight Weld, their colleague in reform, noted wryly,

> Why! Angelina in yesterdays [sic] letter says she is doubtful whether womans [sic] rights are not the *root*—whether they do not *lie deeper* than the rights involved in our great question!! And adds "The slave may be freed and woman be where she is, but woman cannot be freed and the slave remain where he is."[33]

In her letters to the *Boston Spectator*, Sarah Grimké attacked social hierarchy at its roots, providing perhaps the most egalitarian interpretation of Genesis 1-3 that Christendom had yet witnessed.

For those antislavery reformers who sided with the Grimkés, such as William Lloyd Garrison and his circle, Genesis 1-3 became a text grounded in gender and racial equality. Other abolitionists who agreed that Genesis 1-3 contained no divine mandate for slavery were not ready to conclude with the Grimkés that the original creation established political and social equality between men and women. Numerous abolitionists found the prospect of gender equality profoundly disturbing. Angelina Grimké told of the abolitionist minister who "poured out his sarcasm and ridicule upon our heads and among other things said, he would as soon be caught robbing a hen roost as encouraging a woman to lecture."[34]

Another abolitionist minister, wishing to deny antislavery activist Abby Kelley the right to address the Connecticut Anti-Slavery Society, invoked images of the Fall, depicting woman as temptress and deceiver:

> No woman will speak or vote where I am moderator. It is enough for a woman to rule at home. . . . she has no business to come into this meeting and by speaking and voting lord it over men. Where woman's enticing eloquence is heard, men are incapable of right and efficient action. She beguiles and binds men by her smiles and her bland winning voice. . . . I will not sit in a meeting where the sorcery of a woman's tongue is thrown around my heart. I will not submit to PETTICOAT GOVERNMENT. No woman shall ever lord it over me. *I am Major-Domo in my own house.*[35]

Abolitionists who sought to create a culture in which gender as well as racial egalitarianism would prevail responded by interpreting Genesis through Galatians 3:

> Miss Kelley of Lynn,
> Some esteem it a sin
> And a shame that thou darest to speak;
> Quite forgetting that mind
> Is to sex unconfined.
> That in Christ is nor Gentile nor Greek,
> Abby K!
> That in Christ is nor Gentile nor Greek![36]

Eventually, the American Anti-Slavery Society would suffer a schism over the question of women's rights. Those who wished to enroll women as full members, with speaking and voting privileges, would win control of the Society, and those who opposed the full participation of women would leave to form the American and Foreign Anti-Slavery Society. Clearly, the issue of how American society should be arranged—on a hierarchical or egalitarian basis, divided by race and gender, or oblivious to such distinctions—evoked powerful responses. The battle for the Bible, and particularly for Genesis 1-3, formed the background to the factionalism that led not only to the Civil War, but to the campaign for woman suffrage that persisted for more than five decades after Lee laid down his sword at Appomattox.[37]

Egalitarian Readings of Genesis 1–3: New Religious Movements and the Woman's Bible

Though egalitarian interpretations have always vied for ascendancy, for much of Christian history hierarchical interpretations of Genesis 1-3 have predominated. The United States in the nineteenth century was remarkable for the range and vigor of the egalitarian readings it produced. In addition to the unprecedented egalitarian explication of Genesis 1-3 offered by Sarah Grimké, other noteworthy egalitarian critiques arose. The blossoming of new Christian groups like the Shakers, the Oneida Community, and the Christian Scientists led to innovative interpretations and applications of Genesis 1-3, and the publication of the *Woman's Bible* in the 1890s marked the emergence of a distinctly feminist hermeneutical method.

The Shakers (the United Society of Believers in Christ's Second Coming) were the most successful communitarian movement in American history. They were founded by Ann Lee (1736-1784), who began her ministry in England as a Quaker. Moving her flock to New York in 1774, she and her followers established their first community in upstate New York in 1776. Though "Mother Ann" died in 1784, the movement continued to grow. By 1794, the Shakers had established 12 communities, all in New York and New England. The revivals of the Second Great Awakening garnered converts in what was then the West, so that by 1850 there were about six thousand Shakers living in 19 communities, some as far removed as Ohio, Kentucky, and Indiana. Though the Shakers declined in number in the second half of the nineteenth century, they have not entirely died out even to this day. Their furniture, architecture, and ingenuity continue to draw admirers.[38]

Shaker readings of Genesis 1-3 were unique in Christian history. They interpreted Genesis 1:26 ("Let us make humankind in our image") as a sign of God's plural nature, and noted that Genesis 1:27 described the image of God as "male and female." Shakers concluded from this reference that God was both male and female, both Father and Mother. Since God had first become incarnate in male form (Jesus), the Shakers assumed that, at the second coming, God would be incarnated in female form. Indeed, her followers affirmed that Mother Ann was the second coming of the Christ spirit.

Mother Ann believed that lust, as expressed in sexual intercourse, was *the* original sin. Accordingly, Shaker communities were celibate. Living chastely together as brothers and sisters, Shakers were a source of fascination for outsiders, who rightly saw the Shaker way of life as a repudiation of the hierarchical marriages typical of nineteenth-century Americans. Scholars debate the degree to which Shaker communities escaped the gender conventions of the nineteenth century. On the one hand, the duties assigned to Shaker women were domestic chores typical of those done by women throughout the United States, while Shaker men labored at tasks commonly considered to be men's work. On the other hand, Shakers were, compared to the larger culture, uncommonly egalitarian. Individual Shaker communities as well as the movement as a whole were ruled both by elders and eldresses.[39]

Certainly the development of a theology of God as Mother provided Shakers with a motif, grounded in Genesis 1, that had implications for gender relations. At times, insights from the Shaker writer "Holy Mother Wisdom" revealed that woman was not the "cause" of the Fall, but only the means, and that it was Adam who was negligent in falling asleep rather than staying with Eve to protect her as she attempted to resist the serpent.[40] At other times, Shaker writers followed traditional hierarchical interpretations in blaming Eve for being first to sin, or in arguing that woman was not created in the image of God but only as the glory of man.[41] Because God was incarnate as a woman as well as a man, however, Shaker theology never lent itself to the kinds of misogyny that more standard hierarchical readings had fostered.

Another communitarian movement that rethought the hierarchy of gender typical of the nineteenth century was the Oneida Community, led by John Humphrey Noyes. Noyes first gathered a group of followers in Putney, Vermont, in 1838. In 1848, no longer welcome in Putney, the community moved to western New York, where its members continued to seek Christian perfection. For reasons that will become clear, outside observers were both amazed and appalled at the Oneidans' lifestyles, but for 30 years the community thrived. In 1881, due to external criticism and internal dissension, the Oneidans abandoned community life, forming in its place a thriving corporation, known even today for its distinctive silverware.[42]

Like the Shakers, Noyes believed that the root of human sinfulness was related to sexuality. Unlike Ann Lee, however, Noyes did not contend that lust was the source of original sin, and that celibacy was the answer. Rather, he asserted that sexuality had two benefits: amative and procreative. Originally, he said, God had intended Adam and Eve to enjoy the "amative," or spiritual bond, of sexual activity as an important form of intimacy and pleasure. With the Fall, however, Adam and Eve lost the capacity to live in mutuality with one another. Their sexuality, originally a form of spirituality, degenerated into mere sensuality.

Noyes interpreted the divine decree in Genesis 3:16 ("I will greatly multiply thy sorrow and thy conception") as an indication that, in the absence of sin, Eve and Adam would have enjoyed sex but only rarely conceived children. Bearing many children endangered women's health, and providing financial support for large families increased men's labor. Such labor also isolated men from their wives, who tended the children while their husbands worked long hours outside the home. In short, for Noyes, the Fall produced the typical American marriage, with women condemned to the "curses of involuntary and undesirable procreation" and men condemned to lonely, unremitting toil as the price for sexual intimacy with their wives.

Without reliable forms of birth control, Noyes concluded, the original communion of the "amative" bond was unavailable. Sexual intercourse inevitably subjected women to pregnancy and male domination. Noyes was also concerned about the social consequences of marriage. How could Christians live in genuine mutuality with one another if as husband and wife they formed exclusive couples? Accordingly, Noyes pioneered the practice of "male continence" (in which men engaged in sexual activity with women, but stopped short of ejaculation) and "complex marriage" or "free love." Oneidans saw complex marriage, in which men and women avoided "selfish" attachments by freely choosing to be sexually intimate with any number of community members of the opposite gender, as the antidote to regular marriage. Men and women remained autonomous moral agents, who shared sexual encounters that they might better know and delight in one another.[43]

By all accounts, Oneida women enjoyed unusually satisfying sex lives. Noyes, moreover, had the satisfaction of turning the church Fathers—particularly Augustine—on their heads by finding in Genesis 1-3 a mandate for an ethic of sexual pleasure. But the larger American culture prized marriage, regarded the husband as the head of the household, and considered Oneida to be a threat to its way of life. As historian Sydney Ahlstrom observed, Oneida's demise was hardly surprising, since the community "crashed head on into the most sacred institution in Victorian America: the monogamous family."[44]

Another religious movement that challenged traditional readings of Genesis 1-3 was Christian Science. Founded by Mary Baker Eddy (1821-1910), who in 1875 published the first edition of *Science and Health*, the movement's authoritative commentary on the Bible, Christian Science claimed over 85,000 members by 1906. It was particularly attractive to women, who found in its "science of health" meaningful religious roles denied to them in more traditional Christian settings. Christian Science maintained that God, or Mind, was the only Being, and that the world perceived by human senses was an illusion. People, in their true forms, were the divine reflection of God, but the bodily manifestations available to human senses were, like sin, death, and disease, mere illusions. Through Christian Science, persons could rid themselves of these illusions and encounter truth. Indeed, Eddy argued that the understandings of the divine revealed in *Science and Health* were nothing other than the second coming of Jesus.[45]

Eddy's treatment of Genesis 1-3 was innovative. Genesis 1:27 moved her to describe God as "Father-Mother," adding that it would make more sense to consider God female (since God's highest quality—Love—was associated with the feminine, not the masculine), than male. She also considered the first creation account, which began by depicting the spirit of God on the face of the deep, to be a "brief, glorious history of spiritual creation." The story of Genesis 2-3, on the other hand, struck her as a "material view of God and the universe . . . which is the exact opposite of scientific truth" as recorded in Genesis 1.

Eddy believed that the purpose of Genesis 2-3 was to record allegorically the effects of error. Theologically, she found Genesis 2-3 abhorrent. The notion that God, having already accomplished the creation, would repeat the process on a material level and would even ask Adam, "a prospective sinner," for help in naming the animals (Genesis 2:19) seemed ludicrous. Even worse was the depiction of Eve's creation in Genesis 2:21-22. Eddy described the sleep that, according to the text, God induced in Adam as the first instance of malicious animal magnetism. Contrasting Eve's creation, during Adam's sleep, to Genesis 1, where God created humanity in the light of day, Eddy argued that: "Beginning creation with darkness instead of light—materially rather than spiritually—error now simulates the work of Truth, mocking Love and declaring what great things error has done."

The appearance of a "talking, lying serpent" (Genesis 3:1-3) in what Genesis 1 depicted as a perfectly harmonious creation was for Eddy equally problematic. She decided that the text could not possibly expect readers to believe in the existence of a talking serpent, and concluded that the serpent functioned metaphorically only, as a symbol for evil. Adam she interpreted as a synonym for error, symbolizing belief in the material (rather than the spiritual) mind. That Adam learned of and suffered from evil indicated that materialism invariably created its own punishments, which only spirituality could overcome.

Eddy argued that the two creation accounts were incompatible, forcing readers to make a choice. To choose Truth was to believe Genesis 1, which, she said, "assigns all might and government to God, and endows man out of God's perfection and power." To follow Genesis 2 was to repeat Adam's error, to believe humanity to be "mutable and mortal,—as having broken away from Deity and as revolving in an orbit of his own." Eddy warned readers of the hopelessness of that worldview: "Existence, separate from divinity, Science explains as impossible."[46]

In the history of interpretation, many had used Genesis 2 to show that woman was subordinate to man, but no one more thoroughly established the priority of the first creation account, with its intimations of gender equality, than Mary Baker Eddy. She was not to be alone in that endeavor. At the end of the nineteenth century, a group of women led by Elizabeth Cady Stanton wrote a commentary that attempted to read the Christian scriptures without the lens of male bias that they believed typified previous translations and interpretations.

The Woman's Bible, published in 1895 and 1898, was a watershed study. Its egalitarian reading of Genesis 1-3 continued the line of interpretation that Sarah Grimké had proposed in the 1830s while it also attempted to apply modern scholarship to the study of the Bible. Like the Grimké sisters before them, the contributors to *The Woman's Bible* were suspicious of the male bias that had prejudiced not only the original writers, but subsequent translations of and commentaries on the scriptures. The editors of *The Woman's Bible* identified biblical passages that they found sexist (Stanton, for example, opined that the second creation story was "a mere allegory, symbolizing some mysterious conception of a highly imaginative editor"[47]); they also provided new translations and more egalitarian interpretations of disputed texts. They found in Genesis 1 evidence of God as female as well as male, and concluded that Paul's reading of Genesis 1-3 that subordinated women to men was "a poisonous stream in Church and State" that had "debased marriage and made both canon and civil law a monstrous oppression to woman."[48]

Such an understanding could hardly have been more removed from the gender hierarchy celebrated in proslavery, and even in some abolitionist, writings. Certainly *The Woman's Bible*, like Oneidan free love and Shaker celibacy, met much opposition. Debates among nineteenth-century physicians over the use of ether as an anesthetic to ease the pains of childbirth indicated that many still took God's pronouncements to Eve in Genesis 3:16 seriously. For some doctors, medical efforts to provide anesthetics to make childbirth less painful were disobedient to the divine ordinance that women ought, as punishment for the sin of Eve, to suffer when they delivered children. Other physicians disagreed with that theological assessment. The fact that Oneidans, Shakers, feminists, proslavery apologists, abolitionists, Christian Scientists, and physicians were simultaneously contesting the implications of Genesis 1-3 for social ordering indicated that the lessons of the creation were anything but settled.

NOTES TO CHAPTER 7, INTRODUCTION

1. Those seeking more information about this period should consult the relevant essays in *Jewish Women in Historical Perspective*, edited by Judith Baskin (Detroit: Wayne State University Press, 1991) and *Gender and Judaism: The Transformation of Tradition*, edited by T. M. Rudavsky (New York: New York University Press, 1995). Both contain essays tracing the history of Jewish women from biblical times through the twentieth century. In addition to these secondary sources, a helpful book providing women's religious voices for the modern period is *Four Centuries of Jewish Women's Spirituality: A Sourcebook*, edited by Ellen Umansky and Diane Ashton (Boston: Beacon, 1992).

2. For more information on women's *mitzvot*, see endnote 52 of chapter 5.

3. Isidore Epstein, *Judaism* (London: Penguin, 1959), pp. 290-91.

4. As cited in *The Rise of Reform Judaism* by W. Gunther Plaut (New York: Union of American Hebrew Congregations, 1963), pp. 253-55.

5. As cited in Plaut, *The Rise of Reform Judaism*, pp. 253-55.

6. As cited in Pnina Nave Levinson, "Women and Sexuality: Traditions and Progress," in Jeanne Baker, editor, *Women, Religion and Sexuality* (Philadelphia: Trinity Press International, 1991), p. 53.

7. According to Robert M. Seltzer, "Like European Reform, American Reform had its moderates and radicals, but the more extreme type of antitraditionalism . . . fell on fertile soil in America. Classical Reform reached its apex in the Pittsburgh Platform

of 1885. . . . " *Jewish People, Jewish Thought: The Jewish Experience in History* (New York: Macmillan, 1980), p. 643.

8. Charles S. Liebman, "The Religion of American Jews," in Marshall Sklare, editor, *The Jew in American Society* (New York: Behrman House, 1974), p. 236.

9. Some estimate that by 1820, there were only three thousand Jews in America. While emigration between 1820 and 1880 raised that number to approximately three hundred thousand, it was not until the period between 1880 and 1923 that the American Jewish population rose to almost three million. It was this increase that dramatically diversified American Judaism. See Denise Lardner Carmody, *Women and World Religions* (Englewood Cliffs, N.J.: Prentice-Hall, 1989), p. 218.

10. See the discussion of historical context in the introduction to *Opening the Gates: A Century of Arab Feminist Writing*, edited by Margot Badran and Miriam Cooke (Bloomington and Indianapolis: Indiana University Press, 1990). See also Badran's "Feminism" in *The Oxford Encyclopedia of the Modern Islamic World* (New York and Oxford: Oxford University Press, 1995), vol. 2, pp. 19-23; Sherifa Zuhur's "Women's Movements" in *Oxford Encyclopedia of the Modern Islamic World*, vol. 4, pp. 348-52.

11. For an introduction to these points, see Nadia Hijab's "Overview" as well as the subsequent articles in the entry on "Women and Social Reform" in *Oxford Encyclopedia of the Modern Islamic World*, vol. 4, pp. 332f. For more extended discussions see *Women, Islam, and the State*, edited by Deniz Kandiyoti (Philadelphia: Temple University Press, 1991) and Valentine M. Moghadam's *Modernizing Women: Gender and Social Change in the Middle East* (Boulder and London: Lynne Rienner, 1993). Baroroh Baried explores the particular context and historical development of the women's movement in Indonesia in an essay entitled "Islam and the Modernization of Indonesian Women" in Taufik Abdullan and Sharon Siddique, editors, *Islam and Society in Southeast Asia* (Singapore: Institute of Southeast Asian Studies, 1986), pp. 139-56.

12. The male Egyptian Qasim Amin often receives credit for being among the earliest in the Arab world to advocate greater equality for women. Badran and Cooke, however, show that many Arab women already took such a stance prior to Amin's publication of *The Liberation of Women* in 1899; see their *Opening the Gates*.

13. Badran and Cooke see this strategy as more characteristic of the early feminism of women and the use of extra-Islamic sources as a strategy used more often by profeminist men; see p. xvi of *Opening the Gates*. Albert Hourani, however, describes a shift in Qasim Amin's strategy, maintaining that Amin appeals to Western values and theories after his appeals to Islamic warrants in his first book are attacked; see Hourani's *Arabic Thought in the Liberal Age, 1798-1939* (Cambridge: Cambridge University Press, 1961; reissued 1983), pp. 167f.

14. Deniz Kandiyoti, "End of Empire: Islam, Nationalism and Women in Turkey" in *Women, Islam and the State*, pp. 27-28.

15. Kandiyoti, "End of Empire," p. 26.

16. The first woman's journal in Arabic was established by Hind Nawfal, a Syrian Christian woman who moved to Cairo from Tripoli; see the entry in *Opening the Gates*, pp. 215-19.

17. See Margot Badran's "Competing Agenda: Feminists, Islam and the State in Nineteenth- and Twentieth-Century Egypt," in *Women, Islam and the State*, p. 204. See also Albert Hourani, *Arabic Thought in the Liberal Age*, pp. 166-67.

18. Badran, "Competing Agenda" in *Women, Islam and the State*, p. 202. For a more extensive discussion, see the introduction to *Opening the Gates*, pp. xiv-xvi.

19. See Yvonne Yazbeck Haddad and Jane I. Smith's entry "United States of America" in *Oxford Encyclopedia of the Modern Islamic World*, vol. 4, pp. 277f. See also Frederick Mathewson Denny's entry "Islam in the Americas," *Oxford Encyclopedia of the Modern Islamic World*, vol. 2, pp. 296f.

20. Discussion of these earlier arrivals of Muslims in the Americas include Yvonne Yazbeck Haddad's "A Century of Islam in America," Occasional Paper No. 4 of *The Muslim World Today* (Washington, D.C.: American Institute for Islamic Affairs,

1986), pp. 1-13; Frederick Mathewson Denny's "Islam in the Americas," in *Oxford Encyclopedia of the Modern Islamic World*, vol. 2, pp. 296-300; Yvonne Yazbeck Haddad and Jane I. Smith's "United States of America" in *Oxford Encyclopedia of the Modern Islamic World*, vol. 4, pp. 277-84.

21. See, however, Allan D. Austin, editor, *African Muslims in Antebellum America: A Sourcebook* (New York and London: Garland, 1984). The persistence of Muslim culture differed within the Americas; see descriptions contrasting the North American experience with that of South America and the Caribbean in Marilyn Robinson Waldman's "Reflections on Islamic Tradition, Women, and Family," in Earle H. Waugh, Sharon McIrvin Abu-Laban, and Regula Burckhaardt Qureshi, editors, *Muslim Families in North America* (Edmonton: University of Alberta Press, 1991), pp. 311-12; and Frederick Mathewson Denny's "Islam in the Americas" in *Oxford Encyclopedia of the Modern Islamic World*, vol. 2, pp. 296-300.

22. Carol F. Karlsen, *The Devil in the Shape of a Woman* (New York: Vintage Books, 1987), pp. 153-81; see especially pp. 162-65 and 172-73.

23. Anne Hutchinson held meetings in her home to discuss Puritan sermons, and she also claimed the ability to discern which ministers were of the elect. Despite—or because of—her popularity, Massachusetts authorities banished her from the colony in 1637.

24. We chose to concentrate on nineteenth-century Protestantism in this chapter for several reasons. We were interested in the forceful articulation of egalitarian readings of Genesis that emerged in abolitionism and in the women's rights movement. We were intrigued by the novel egalitarian readings that new religious movements produced. And we believed that the correlations between the status of women and the status of slaves expressed in debates about slavery provided an excellent opportunity to observe connections between gender and racial hierarchies.

We also note that a Protestant focus is consistent with the preeminence that Protestantism enjoyed in the United States in the nineteenth century. Catherine Albanese has argued that

> public Protestantism was and is the dominant religion of the United States. Present from colonial times in Calvinistic Christianity, sheer numbers, political and social prestige, economic power, and an early educational monopoly all contributed to the ascendancy of public Protestantism as the "one religion." The many who were not Protestant also contributed to its ascendancy by their acceptance of its influence and by their imitation of its ways.

Albanese further observed that "nineteenth-century civil religion was rooted in the Puritan and revolutionary heritage" and that "biblical interpretations—and especially biblical millennialism—dominated during times of greatest crisis for the country." Catherine L. Albanese, *America: Religions and Religion*, 2nd ed. (Belmont, Calif.: Wadsworth Publishing, 1992), pp. 429, 450-51.

It is not our desire to celebrate Protestant dominance or to negate the contributions of other religious groups to the development of American culture. But we do believe that public discussion of social reforms in the nineteenth century was shaped by Protestant theology and that a focus on Protestant developments provides a particularly apt case study in practical applications of Genesis 1-3. For an analysis of the influence of Protestant theology upon nineteenth-century social reform, see Valarie H. Ziegler, "A Theology of Reform," in the introduction to *The Advocates of Peace in Antebellum America*, Religion in North America, edited by Catherine L. Albanese and Stephen J. Stein (Bloomington and Indianapolis: Indiana University Press, 1972), pp. 10-17.

25. Thomas Smyth, "The Sin and the Curse; or, the Union: The True Source of Disunion, and our Duty in the Present Crisis" (Charleston, S.C.: Steam Power Presses of Evans and Cogswell, 1860), p. 8, quoted in Richard T. Hughes and C. Leonard

Allen, *Illusions of Innocence: Protestant Primitivism in America, 1630-1875* (Chicago and London: University of Chicago Press, 1988), p. 198. See also Ziegler, *The Advocates of Peace in Antebellum America*, pp. 77-78.

26. See Hughes and Allen, *Illusions of Innocence*, pp. 188-204, for a more complete discussion. Another valuable source is Elizabeth Fox-Genovese and Eugene D. Genovese, "The Divine Sanction of Social Order: Religious Foundations of the Southern Slaveholders' World View," *Journal of the American Academy of Religion* 55 (2) (1987): 210-33.

27. James Henley Thornwell, "The Rights and Duties of Masters. A Sermon Preached at the Dedication of a Church, Erected in Charleston, S. C., for the Benefit and Instruction of the Coloured Population" (Charleston, S. C.: Walker & James, 1850), pp. 26, 40. Partially reprinted in Robert L. Ferm, *Issues in American Protestantism: A Documentary History from the Puritans to the Present* (Gloucester, Mass.: Peter Smith, 1983), pp. 189-99.

28. Fred A. Ross, *Slavery Ordained of God* (Philadelphia: J. B. Lippincott & Co., 1857), pp. 54-56. For additional discussion, see Anne Firor Scott, "Women's Perspective on the Patriarchy in the 1850s," in Jean E. Friedman and William G. Shade, editors, *Our American Sisters: Women in American Life and Thought*, 2nd ed. (Boston: Allyn and Bacon, Inc.), pp. 150-51.

29. Frederick Douglass, "What to the Slave Is the Fourth of July?" in Alice Moore Dunbar, editor, *Masterpieces of Negro Eloquence* (New York: Bookery Publishing Company, 1914), p. 46. Douglass's passionate denunciation of slavery was typical of the abolitionist synthesis of moral and biblical arguments:

> Standing with God and the crushed and bleeding slave on this occasion, I will, in the name of humanity, which is outraged, in the name of liberty, which is fettered, in the name of the Constitution and the Bible, which are disregarded and trampled upon, dare to call in question and to denounce, with all the emphasis I can command, everything that serves to perpetuate slavery—the great sin and shame of America! (p. 44)

30. Douglas C. Stange, "Bishop Daniel Alexander Payne's Protestation of American Slavery, A Document," *The Journal of Negro History* 52 (1) (January 1967): 60.

31. A favorite text here was Acts 2:17-18:

> In the last days, it will be, God declares, that I will pour out my Spirit upon all flesh, and your sons and your daughters shall prophesy. . . . Even upon my slaves, both men and women, in those days I will pour out my Spirit; and they shall prophesy. (NRSV)

32. Angelina Grimké to Theodore Dwight Weld and J. G. Whittier, August 20, 1837, in Gilbert H. Barnes and Dwight L. Dumond, editors, *Letters of Theodore Dwight Weld, Angelina Grimké Weld, and Sarah Grimké, 1822-1844* (Gloucester, Mass.: Peter Smith, 1934), vol. 1, pp. 428-30.

33. Weld to Sarah and Angelina Grimké, October 10, 1837, *Weld-Grimké Letters*, pp. 453-54.

34. Angelina Grimké to Weld and Whittier, August 20, 1837, *Weld-Grimké Letters*, p. 430.

35. Quoted in Dorothy Sterling, *Ahead of Her Time: Abby Kelley and the Politics of Antislavery* (New York: W. W. Norton & Company, 1991), pp. 107-109.

36. Quoted in Sterling, *Ahead of Her Time*, p. 124.

37. For more information on abolitionist debates on the status of women, the biblical case against slavery, and the violence engendered by the Civil War, see Ziegler, *The Advocates of Peace in Antebellum America*, chap. 2-5.

38. Sydney E. Ahlstrom, *A Religious History of the American People* (New Haven and London: Yale University Press, 1972), pp. 492-94.

39. Jean M. Humez, editor, *Mother's First-Born Daughters: Early Shaker Writings*

on Women and Religion (Bloomington and Indianapolis: Indiana University Press, 1993), pp. xx-xxi.

40. Humez, *Mother's First-Born Daughters*, pp. 219-20, 256-58. This account of Adam and Eve was written through a female spirit medium in a document entitled "Holy Mother Wisdom's Fold" (c. 1840s). We have not included this document among the readings for this chapter, both because it is extremely difficult to read and because its points of relevance to our topic are easily summarized.

41. Paula Bates, *Divine Book of Holy and Eternal Wisdom* (1849), in Humez, *Mother's First-Born Daughters*, p. 264.

42. Ahlstrom, *A Religious History of the American People*, pp. 498-99.

43. John Humphrey Noyes, *Male Continence* (Oneida, N.Y.: The Oneida Community, 1872), pp. 10-16; Noyes, *History of American Socialisms* (Philadelphia: J. B. Lippincott & Co., 1870), pp. 626-29, 631-32.

44. Ahlstrom, *A Religious History of the American People*, p. 499.

45. Ahlstrom, *A Religious History of the American People*, pp. 1020-26.

46. Mary Baker Eddy, *Science and Health with Key to the Scriptures* (Boston: Trustees under the Will of Mary Baker Eddy, n.d.), pp. 508, 516-22.

47. Elizabeth Cady Stanton, editor, *The Original Feminist Attack on the Bible (The Woman's Bible)* (New York: Arno Press, 1974), p. 20.

48. *The Woman's Bible*, pp. 14, 163-64.

ANTEBELLUM DEBATES ON HOUSEHOLD HIERARCHIES: PROSLAVERY AND ANTISLAVERY VIEWS

Proslavery and antislavery debates hinged upon two different understandings of how to order society. Advocates of slavery insisted that God intended society to be hierarchical, with each person called to a specific place in the great chain of being. The right to vote or to hold property, or even to own one's own labor, they contended, was consistent with some social stations and inappropriate to others. Duties and rights were contingent upon one's station. Antislavery proponents argued instead for the equality of all persons, insisting that, as the Declaration of Independence put it, "all men are created equal" and possess the inalienable rights of "life, liberty, and the pursuit of happiness."

The question of slave's rights and women's rights quickly proved to be intertwined. Defenders of slavery such as James Henley Thornwell attempted to show the absurdity of arguing for civil rights for all persons by observing that such a state would extend full rights of citizenship to women and children—an eventuality so ludicrous that he did not need to elaborate. The question of women's involvement in antislavery reform proved divisive to the abolitionist movement, as some abolitionists thought women belonged in the home, while others insisted that working for the rights of slaves while denying full civil rights to women made a mockery of the cause of freedom.

The selections in this section explore two of those positions: the proslavery argument, which universally denied full civil rights to slaves and to women, and the more conservative of the antislavery positions, which sought to abolish slavery but did not address the issue of full civil rights for women. The alternative abolitionist position, which argued for the equality of women and men, varied in its interpretation of Genesis 1–3 principally by finding in the text a refutation of sexism as well as of slavery. We will examine Sarah Grimké's gender analysis of Genesis 1–3 in the following section.

Genesis 1–3 functioned for the authors in this section as it did for the other authors we have studied: it revealed to them a divine mandate to establish either a hierarchical or an egalitarian social order. Accustomed to finding gender hierarchy in Genesis 1–3, the proslavery authors found another hierarchy as well—the consignment of some persons to serve as slaves to others. As they reflected upon the divine ordination of slavery, these authors discussed the similarities between the life of slaves and the life of women. God compelled both, the authors argued, to obey their masters without question.

Samuel How turned to Genesis 3 for the origins both of slavery and of woman's subordination. When God sentenced Adam to earn his bread by the sweat of his brow, How argued, slavery was established—for strong men would inevitably compel weaker men to labor for them. How found in Genesis 3:16 the root of woman's subjection to man. Arguing that the passage should read "thy *obedience* shall be to thy husband," rather than the typical translation, "thy *desire* shall be to thy husband," How contended that God condemned woman to subordinate herself to man. Slavery and the subordination of women, How concluded, were divine judgments that even redemption in Christ could not abrogate. Josiah Priest agreed, noting that God established both by judicial decree in response to the first sin and placed them "beyond the reach of the benevolence of the Gospel." For defenders of slavery, Genesis 1–3 was the basis both of the enslavement of African Americans and of the subordination of women.

The antislavery selection, on the other hand, attempts to refute the claim that God mandated slavery. Such a thing was unthinkable, according to Charles Elliott, for it contradicted the Genesis assertion that God created humanity in the divine image. As the image of God, persons could never justifiably be reduced to property; indeed to claim to be "master" of another human being was nothing short of blasphemy. God, the antislavery argument typically insisted, governed individuals through personal relationships with them. Slaveowners, however, usurped God's place as Lord of the slave and deprived slaves of moral agency. For the abolitionist, slavery, rather than being consistent with the divine will, was the vilest of sins.

Slavery Ordained of God (1857 CE)
FRED A. ROSS

These two theories of Right and Wrong,—these two ideas of human liberty,—the right, in the nature of things, or the right as made by God,—the liberty of the individual man, of Atheism, of Red Republicanism, of the devil,—or the liberty of man, in the family, in the State, the liberty from God,—these two theories now make the conflict of the world. This anti-slavery battle is only part of the great struggle: God will be victorious,—and we, in his might.

I now come to particular illustrations of the world-wide law that service shall be rendered by the inferior to the superior. The relations in which such service obtains are very many. Some of them are these:—husband and wife; parent and child; teacher and scholar; commander and soldier,—sailor; master and apprentice; master and hireling; master and slave. Now, sir, all these relations are ordained of God. They are all directly commanded, or they are the irresistible law of his providence, in conditions which must come up in the progress of depraved nature. The relations themselves are all good in certain conditions. And there may be no more of evil in the lowest than in the highest. And there may be in the lowest, as really as in the highest, the fulfilment of the commandment to love thy neighbor as thyself, and of doing unto him whatsoever thou wouldst have him to do unto thee.

Why, sir, the wife everywhere, except where Christianity has given her elevation, *is the slave*. And, sir, I say, without fear of saying too strongly, that for every sigh, every groan, every tear, every agony of stripe or death, which has gone up to God from the relation of master and slave, there have been more sighs, more groans, more tears, and more agony in the rule of the husband over the wife. Sir, I have admitted, and do again admit, without qualification, that every fact in Uncle Tom's Cabin has occurred in the South. But, in reply, I say deliberately, what one of your first men told me, that he who will make the horrid examination will discover in New York City, in any number of years past, more cruelty from husband to wife, parent to child, *than in all the South from master to slave* in the same time. I dare the investigation. And you may extend it further, if you choose,—to all the results of honor and purity. I fear nothing on this subject. I stand on rock,—the Bible,—and therefore, just before I bring the Bible, to which all I have said is introductory, I will run a parallel between the relation of master and slave and that of husband and wife. I will say nothing of the grinding oppression of capital upon labor, in the power of the master over the hireling—the crushed peasant—the chain-harnessed coal-pit woman, a thousand feet under ground, working in darkness, her child toiling by her side, and another child not born; I will say nothing of the press-gang which fills the navy of Britain—the conscription which makes the army of France—the terrible floggings—the awful court-martial—the quick sentence—the lightning-shot—the chain, and ball, and every-day lash—the punishment of the soldier, sailor, slave, who had run away. I pass all this by: I will run the parallel between the slave and wife.

Do you say, The slave is held to *involuntary service?* So is the wife. Her relation to her husband, in the immense majority of cases, is made for her, and not by her. And when she makes it for herself, how often, and how soon, does it become involuntary! How often, and how soon, would she throw off the yoke if she could! O ye wives, I know how superior you are to your husbands in many respects,—not only in personal attraction, (although in that particular, comparison is out of place,) in grace, in refined thought, in passive fortitude, in enduring love, and in a heart to be filled with the spirit of heaven. Oh, I know all this. Nay, I know you may surpass him in his own sphere of boasted prudence and worldly wisdom about dollars and cents. Nevertheless, he has authority, from God, to rule over you. You are under service to him. You are bound to obey him *in all things*. Your service is very, very, very often involuntary from the first, and, if voluntary at first, becomes hopeless necessity afterwards. I know God has laid upon the husband to love you as Christ loved the church, and in that sublime obligation has placed you in the light and under the shadow of a love infinitely higher, and purer, and holier than all talked about in the romances of chivalry. But the husband may not so love you. He may rule you with the rod of iron. What can you do? Be divorced? God forbids it, save for crime. Will you say that you are free,—that you will go where you please, do as you please? Why, ye dear wives, your husbands may forbid. And listen, you cannot leave New York, nor your palaces, any more than your shanties. No; you cannot leave your parlor, nor your bedchamber, nor your couch, if your husband commands you to stay there! What can you do? Will you run away with your stick and your bundle? He can advertise you!! What can you do? You can, and I fear some of you do, wish him, from the bottom of your hearts, at the bottom of the Hudson. Or, in your self-will, you will do just as you please. (Great laughter.)

[A word on the subject of divorce. One of your standing denunciations on the South is the terrible laxity of the marriage vow among the slaves. Well, sir, what does your Boston Dr. Nehemiah Adams say? He says, after giving eighty, sixty, and the like number of applications for divorce, and nearly all granted at individual quarterly courts in New England,—he says he is not sure but that the marriage relation is as enduring among *the slaves in the South* as it is among white people in New England. I only give what Dr. Adams says. I would fain vindicate the marriage relation from this rebuke. But one thing I will say: you seldom hear of a divorce in Virginia or South Carolina.] (Source: Fred A. Ross, *Slavery Ordained of God*, Philadelphia: J. B. Lippincott & Co., 1857, pp. 52–56.)

Slaveholding Not Sinful (1856 CE)
SAMUEL B. HOW

Appendix

I. Slavery Is One of the Penal Effects, or a Part of the Punishment of the Fall and the Wickedness of Man.

The present is not the original state of man. As he came fresh from his Creator's hands, he bore his Creator's likeness, and stood the head and the glory of our world, in the maturity of all his powers of mind and body—a perfectly wise, holy, and happy being. The inspired writer informs us that: "God created man in his own image: in the image of God created he him: male and female created he them."

From this high state man fell by sin. Through the temptation of Satan he deliberately broke a positive command of God, and thus brought upon himself and his descendants death and all our woes. The whole history of the fall teaches us that the government of God is administered on the principle that man's right to life and all its enjoyments depends on his perfectly obeying God's law; and that the transgression of God's law deprives him of his right to life and its enjoyments; that holiness and happiness, sin and wretchedness are inseparably connected. He sinned and forfeited his right to life and the enjoyments of life. Yet God spared his life, because of his designs of mercy towards him, though he pronounced sentence on him.

The sentence on the serpent, reached, we doubt not, that old serpent, the Devil, who used that creature as his instrument, and denoted that he should sink into a lower state of degradation than that in which he was before; that his pursuits and gratifications should be abject and base; and that like the serpent he should be the constant and deadly enemy of man.

The sentence pronounced on the man condemned him to labor, and sorrow, and death. The curse denounced on the ground for man's sake robbed it of its fertility, and caused thorns and thistles spontaneously to grow out of it, rendering incessant toil and labor necessary that he might procure from it food for his sustenance. Here is the origin of his subjection to labor. As the punishment of his sin, God said to him: "In the sweat of thy face shalt thou eat bread, till thou return unto the ground; for out of it wast thou taken: for dust thou art, and unto dust shalt thou return." Here too is the incidental cause of slavery. To escape the labor and toil to which all are condemned, the strong and powerful have compelled the weak and debased to labor for them.

The sentence denounced on the woman placed her in subjection to man. It was this: "Thy desire shall be to thy husband, and he shall rule over thee." (Gen. 3:16.) The marginal reading is: "Thy desire shall be subject to thy husband, and he shall rule over thee." The famous Jewish Rabbi, Aben Ezra, explains the term *teshooqa*, as meaning *obedience*, instead of desire. The words would then be thus translated: "Thy obedience shall be to thy husband, and he shall rule over thee." Professor Stuart, late of Andover, considers this as the correct translation of the passage (See Heb. Chrest. p. 3, Notes on No. 12): Originally woman was the equal of man. But her sin was more aggravated than his in two respects: She was first in committing it, and then tempted him to it. Her punishment was therefore greater than his. She was subjected to the pains of child-birth, and to the rule of man, while authority over her was given to him.

There can be no greater mistake than to suppose that the state of woman in other countries is the same as in ours. We must look to other parts of the world to understand the severity of the sentence which was passed upon her.

The power of the father and the husband over the daughter and the wife, in the times of the Patriarchs and under the Mosaic dispensation, was far greater than it is with us, for then fathers had the power of selling their daughters for wives, and wives who were thus purchased were too apt to be regarded as mere servants by their husbands. (Gen. 29:18-27, 34:11, 12; Joshua 15:16; 1 Sam. 18:23-26.)

A woman in her youth who was in her father's house, could not bind herself by a vow without her father's consent. If he heard and disallowed her vow, it could not stand, and the Lord forgave her, because her father disallowed her. The same was the case with her husband. (Num. 30:6-8.) The Hebrew women were also subject to much hardship through polygamy, concubinage, and the right of divorce, which belonged to their husband.

It is, however, in heathen and savage countries that the rule of man over the woman has been most fearfully abused. There, instead of being his beloved companion, she has been his wretched slave. No bondage among men is deeper, no sufferings are more cruel than she has received from the man who ought to have been her firmest protector, and her highest earthly joy. But we need not refer to the heathen to find instances of deep oppression and cruelty. Should every poor, heart-broken, degraded and crushed in spirit wife or daughter in the proud city of New-York, come in one body to tell of the abominable abuse of their power by drunken or dissipated husbands and fathers, the scenes of cruelty and horror that they would reveal, would, we doubt not, equal the most atrocious cruelties practised on their slaves by any of the most cruel masters of the South. Yet where is the law that provides a punishment any way proportioned to the atrocity of the crimes of these worse than heathen men? Where are the philanthropists who are seriously laboring to protect these down-trodden women from their cruel wrongs? But shall we argue against the marriage connexion as criminal, because of the abuses to which it is subject, and endeavor to break up families, and to abolish the chief earthly blessing that has survived the ruins of the fall? Neither may we reason against the relation of master and slave, because the bad master, like the bad husband, abuses his power.

Far be it from us to teach that the relation between the husband and wife is similar to that which exists between the master and the slave, or that the subjection of the wife to the husband is of the same kind as that of the slave to the master. The marriage union makes the man and woman one—one flesh, one body, united by the closest bonds;—it ought always to be formed and cemented by love founded on the highest esteem, so that it will be the delight of each to promote the happiness of the other. We have adduced the case of the sentence pronounced on the first woman, to show that subjection to the rule of another is a part of the punishment of the fall and sin of man. This subjection is fully recognized under the Gospel dispensation—"Wives, submit yourselves unto your own husbands, as it is fit in the Lord." (Colos. 3:18.) "Wives, submit yourselves unto your own husbands, as unto the Lord. For the husband is the head of the wife, even as Christ is the Head of the church; and he is the Saviour of the body. Therefore, as the church is subject unto Christ, so let the wives be subject to their own husbands in every thing." (Eph. 5:22–24.) These last words, "in every thing," mean in every thing lawful, for neither a husband nor any earthly power has the right to command any one to do what is sinful. Hence the power of the husband is limited by the law of God, and he is taught that his rule should be a rule of love. It says: "Husbands, love your wives, even as Christ also loved the church, and gave himself for it. . . . So ought men to love their wives as their own bodies: he that loveth his wife loveth himself. For no man ever yet hated his own flesh; but nourisheth and cherisheth it, even as the Lord the church." (Eph. 5:28, 29.)

The influence of the Gospel and the Church of Christ in elevating the woman to her proper station, and her proper influence, is clearly shown among us. Though there are many bad husbands, and many wretched wives, this is not the general state of things. No where is woman more loved or honored. When adorned with intelligence, and prudence, and piety, she is the light and the joy of the household. As the wife, she is the companion and the counsellor of the man, his surest and his strongest friend, and the source of his highest earthly bliss;—or she is his darling daughter, his loveliest ornament, and the pride of his heart;—or she is his dear and affectionate sister, the companion of his boyhood, and the counsellor of his riper years;—or she is his mother, his fond and tender and venerated mother, who in the helplessness of his infancy was ever ready to sacrifice her comfort for his; his first instructor and guide in all that was good; who on the Sabbath led his tottering footsteps to the sanctuary, and instilled into his mind his earliest sentiments of piety; who with tender solicitude restrained his wayward passions, and soothed his sorrows, and ministered to his joys, and trained him for all that is high and holy. Happy is that people that has such women, and thanks to God, there are many such in our land; and they have been made such by the grace of God through the Gospel of Christ. They are crowns to their husbands. Their price is far above rubies. To all the charms of beauty, and polish and elegance and sweetness of manners, and high intellectual endowments and accomplishments, they add the higher charms of all the Christian virtues, the beauties of holiness, and the adornments of piety. In the dark season of adversity, such a woman shines beauteous as the morning star, cheering us with the assurance that light, and peace, and day are at hand. Of all earthly objects she is the loveliest, and is but a little lower than an angel of God. And what has made her such? what has given to her this moral as well as intellectual elevation and grandeur? what has raised her so high above yonder ignorant, debased pagan woman, the slave and not the companion of her husband? We repeat it, the Gospel and the Church of Christ; and wherever these come, they come with blessings. They elevate the slave, while they humanize and sanctify his master. They, and only they, are the true remedy for the evils of slavery, and all the penal consequences of sin and the fall.

2. Our second proof that slavery is the punishment of sin is drawn from Gen. 9:24, 25, where the sacred historian having mentioned the wickedness of Ham, the father of Canaan, says: "And Noah awoke from his wine, and knew

what his younger son had done unto him. And he said, Cursed be Canaan; a servant of servants shall he be unto his brethren." The term "servant of servants," means a servant of the lowest and vilest kind.

The term *cursed*, (*aroor*,) here applied by Noah to Canaan, and afterwards by Joshua to the Gibeonites, (Joshua 9:23,) denotes one who is condemned to the penalty of having broken God's law; or subjected to the punishment of sin. (See Gen. 3:14, 17, and 4:11. Deut. 27:15-26. Gal. 3:10.) The particular punishment, therefore, to which Canaan was condemned, was that he should be the most debased of slaves. The term *slave*, as now distinguished by usage from the term *servant*, more exactly expresses the meaning of the original Hebrew word. Gibbon informs us that "the national appellation of the SLAVES (Sclavonians) has been degraded by chance or malice from the signification of glory to that of servitude." In his notes he informs us that "Jordan subscribes to the well-known and probable derivation" of the word slave, "from *Slava, laus, gloria*," and that "this conversion of a national into an appellative name appears to have arisen in the eighth century, in the Oriental France, where the princes and bishops were rich in Sclavonian captives.

It is scarcely necessary to observe that by Canaan is here meant the posterity of Canaan, it being very usual in prophecy to use the name of the father for his posterity. Nor is it at all necessary for us to enquire why the curse is pronounced on Canaan, when Ham his father is mentioned as having sinned; nor whether all the descendants of Ham were included in the curse. It is sufficient for us to remark that Noah, by inspiration of God, pronounced it on Canaan as the punishment of his sin, and is one more proof that subjection to servitude is one of the punishments which God inflicts on the sins of men.

The Canaanites were among the first to introduce idolatry, and they were idolaters of the worst kind. Their character is thus given by God himself: "Every abomination to the Lord which he hateth have they done unto their gods; for even their sons and their daughters they have burnt in the fire to their gods." (Deut. 12:31.) They were as licentious as they were cruel, and the very worst crimes were common among them; till at length God in his wrath gave them up to be destroyed by the Israelites. (Lev. 18:24, 25, and 20:22. Deut. 9:4, and 18:12.)

When the Israelites under Joshua had invaded Canaan, the inhabitants of Gibeon, alarmed at the overthrow of Jericho and Ai, disguised themselves, and having deceived the Israelites by pretending that they had come from a far country, persuaded Joshua and the princes of Israel to make a league with them to let them live. This league they confirmed by an oath. When three days afterwards the Israelites reached their country and discovered their deceit, they were highly displeased, and would have put them all to the sword had not Joshua and the princes resolutely interposed to prevent it. But though they spared their lives, they took them to be slaves. Joshua said to them: "Now therefore ye are cursed; and there shall none of you be freed from being bondmen, and hewers of wood, and drawers of water, for the house of my God. . . . . And Joshua made them hewers of wood, and drawers of water, for the congregation, and for the altar of the Lord, even unto this day, in the place which he should choose." (Josh. 9:23, 27.) The curse of servitude denounced on the Canaanites by Noah was now literally fulfilled by this action of Joshua; and it deserves especial notice that they were made slaves in the House, at the Altar, and for the purpose of assisting in the worship of God. But would God have permitted and sanctioned this if slaveholding is in itself a sin? We think he would not.

3. The Israelites, while they kept the covenant between them and God, and truly worshipped and served him, were permitted to buy bondmen and bondwomen, that is *slaves*, of the heathen that were round about them. (Lev. 25:44-46.) But the Lord warned them that if they apostatized from him, then, as one of the punishments of their sin, they, like the heathen, should be sold into slavery: "The Lord shall bring thee into Egypt again with ships, by the way whereof I spake unto thee, Thou shalt see it no more again: and there ye shall be *sold unto your enemies for bondmen and bondwomen, and no man shall buy you.*" (Deut. 28:68.)

This threatening was partially fulfilled after the Israelites became subject to kings. Towards the close of Samuel's life they insisted that a king should be made for them like all the nations. They doubtless were impatient of the strict enforcement of the law of God by Samuel, and were anxious to have among themselves the pleasures and the splendors of idolatry and royalty. They were guilty, though not of open, yet of heart apostasy. The Lord therefore commanded Samuel to hearken to their voice in all they should say to him, "for they have not rejected thee, but they have rejected me, that I should not reign over them." The Lord through the prophet Hosea, remonstrating with Israel for their sins among them, selects this, and says to them: "I gave thee a king in mine anger, and took him away in my wrath." (Hosea 13:11.) He commanded Samuel to protest solemnly to them, and show them the manner of the king that should rule over them; that they should be his servants, and that he would cruelly oppress them; that he would take from them their sons and daughters and degrade them to servile offices and employments, and rob them of their property and give it to others. (1 Sam. 8:4-18.)

The threatening in Deut. was more fully accomplished in the Babylonian, and afterwards in the Roman captivity of the Jews. Josephus informs us that in the reigns of the two first Ptolemies, many of the Jews were slaves in Egypt. And when Jerusalem was taken by Titus, of the captives who were above seventeen years he sent many bound to the works in Egypt; those under seventeen were sold; but so little care was taken of these captives that eleven thousand of them perished for want. The markets were quite overstocked with them, so that Josephus says in another place that they were sold with their wives and children at the lowest price; there being many to be sold and but few purchasers. . . . We learn from St. Jerome, that "after their last overthrow by Adrian, many thousands of them were sold, and those who could not be sold were transported into Egypt, and perished by shipwreck or famine, or were massacred by the inhabitants.

We think that we have now presented slavery and slaveholding in their true and scriptural light. Had men not apostatized from God their Creator, had they retained holiness of heart and life, and obeyed and worshipped God, they would not have known slavery. But they have sinned, and when they sink into gross impiety, and idolatry, and wickedness, as their punishment they are subjected to slavery. (Source: Samuel B. How, *Slaveholding Not Sinful. Slavery, The Punishment of Man's Sin, Its Remedy, The Gospel of Christ*, 2nd ed., New Brunswick, N.J.: J. Terhune's Press, 1856, pp. 53-65.)

Bible Defence of Slavery (1851 CE)
JOSIAH PRIEST

Fifteenth Section

In the following pages, we are to meet a few more objections of abolitionism, as well as present the reader with some other matters, when we shall finish the labor of this work. It is said, by this class of men, that the *benevolence* of the Gospel contemplates the personal happiness of every human being; and as *individual freedom* is an item in the sum of mortal enjoyments, therefore, the Gospel, in its *spirit* and tendencies, is against slavery of every description, and demands its abolishment.

But, we answer this position, by saying, that, although the spirit and tendencies of the Christian religion most assuredly does contemplate the entire and perfect *moral* happiness of the whole human race, upon certain *conditions*, as obedience to its commands, &c., yet it does *not*, and *cannot* interfere, as we have before said, with the *judgments, decrees,* or *judicial* acts of God, until the *purposes* of such acts are accomplished in the earth. Although the Gospel, as announced in the New Testament, is a message of benevolence from Heaven toward the sufferers of the earth, yet *death* is not, and cannot be counteracted, as yet, by its influence, because death came by the appointment or judicial act of God, on the account of *sin*, placing the direful circumstance *beyond* the redeeming nature of that great system of atonement. Neither can it affect matters of less importance, such as the circumstance of man's being *compelled* by a *Divine judgment* to get his bread in the sweat of his face, with pain, toil, and uncertainty. The case of the woman, who was placed by the *same* power, *judicially*, in a certain circumstance, which is that of great pain and danger, is also placed beyond the reach of the benevolence of the spirit of the Gospel, because she hearkened to the voice of the serpent, in the matter of the forbidden tree. Does the Gospel, and its benevolent *principles*, remove one item of the vast amount of what is called *natural evil*, which the human race now is heir to, such as sickness, poverty, accidents, mistakes, difference of men's opinions, which are all the effects of the *judicial* proceedings of the Creator toward man, on the account of *sin*.

Now, if the *spirit* and *tendencies* of religion, can not, as yet, remove these disabilities or obstacles to man's happiness in this world, how, therefore, can it be expected that it can alter the doom of the negro race, which, as the Bible establishes, is founded on the same foundation, that of the decree of God, and raises a barrier which is impassable and insurmountable to all earthly power: even the famous words of our Lord called the *Golden Rule*, cannot apply *here*. Neither does this rule appear with power to break down any *civil* establishment of society; it was not so intended or understood, by the first disciples and writers of the New Testament. It was not intended by that great and good doctrine, that *servants* and *masters, debtors* and *creditors, rich* and *poor*, should change condition, or even to be put on a *par* with each other by that precept of the Lord. It signified nothing more than that all men, under *all* circumstances of trouble, should do by each other in all kindness, just what they would reasonably desire done to themselves in like circumstances. This precept, therefore, was not meant to reach the case of slavery, as to its *abolishment*, any more than it was the other cases, as above named. It enjoined on masters to extend to servants, minors, and slaves all needed tenderness and consideration, as they themselves could *reasonably* desire were they in a like condition. (Source: Josiah Priest, *Bible Defence of Slavery*, 6th ed., Louisville, Ky.: printed and published by J. F. Brennan for Willis A. Bush, Gallatin, Tenn., 1851, pp. 396-98.)

Sinfulness of American Slavery (1851 CE)
REV. CHARLES ELLIOTT

Chapter III. Slavery vs. Scriptural Principles and Privileges.

Slavery is contrary to many Scriptural *principles* and *privileges*, which secure to the whole race of man certain rights which can not be invaded without guilt and wrong.

1. Slavery is contrary to the original grant which God gave to man at the creation, as the original charter gave no grant of property in man. This grant is contained in the following words: "And God blessed them, and God said unto them, Be fruitful, and multiply, and replenish the earth, and subdue it: and have dominion over the fish of the sea, and over the fowl of the air, and over every living thing that moveth upon the earth. And God said, Behold, I have given you every herb bearing seed, which is upon the face of all the earth, and every tree, in the which is the fruit of a tree yielding seed; to you it shall be for meat," Gen. i, 28, 29. This grant is recognized and reasserted to the human race after the flood. (Gen. ix, 1, 2.) It is referred to and repeated by the Psalmist as the established truth of God, still unrepealed, and never to be repealed: "For thou hast made him a little lower than the angels, and hast crowned him with glory and honor. Thou madest him to have dominion over the works of thy hands; thou hast put all things under his feet: all sheep and oxen, yea, and the beasts of the field; the fowl of the air, and the fish of the sea, and whatsoever passeth through the paths of the seas," Psalm viii, 5-8. This is the original charter on which the right of all property is founded. Slavery

contradicts this grant in two respects: first, by one portion of the human family claiming and securing another portion of the human family as property; and secondly, by depriving that portion of mankind of their right to enjoy a portion of the common property bestowed on the whole race of mankind.

(1.) Slavery is at variance with this original grant, because some claim property in others, and exercise the dominion vested in property over them. We no where find that God has given the Saxon a right of property in the Indian or African—the rich and powerful in the poor and defenseless. God only is the lawful *despotes*—the lord, or possessor of unlimited authority over all mankind. The human *despotes*, or slaveholder, claims a power which alone can belong to almighty God. No such dominion of man over man, or property in man, was granted to man, such as the dominion and property of man in the earth and its productions; and in the renewal of this grant to Noah, and in the repetition of it by the Psalmist, there is no such grant of man in man recognized. Indeed, there are many Scriptural declarations, denouncing any such claims, and pronouncing them to be robbery, man-stealing, violence, oppression, and condemning all these acts as truly sinful: "He that stealeth a man and selleth him, or if he be found in his hand, he shall surely be put to death," Ex. xxi, 16; and when God gave all mankind a right of property in inanimate and irrational creatures, he declares that one man has no right of property in the person of another.

(2.) Slavery is at issue with this original grant of property in irrational and inanimate creatures to all men, because it deprives the portion who are enslaved of their just portion: 1. It deprives the slaves of the right of being fruitful in a lawful way, by separating husbands and wives, and dividing and scattering families. 2. Slavery is a usurpation of that great original charter from God—of all the gifts of Providence to all mankind; for it monopolizes the whole to the slaveholders themselves, and robs the slaves of their just rights. 3. God gave the grant of the whole earth to all mankind, to be possessed and enjoyed; but slavery robs a great part of mankind of this right. It prevents them from the right of property in the earth or its productions. All men, in virtue of the original grant, which is still the unrepealed law of God, have a moral right to possess property of their own by such ways as the moral law and just civil regulations sanction; but slavery cuts off the slave from this provision, by declaring, in opposition to the law of God, "that slaves have no legal rights of property in things real or personal; and whatever property they may acquire belongs, in point of law, to their masters." (Stroud, pp. 45-50.) Slavery is, therefore, the complicated crime of avarice and robbery—avarice, in monopolizing the land and other property of our neighbors; and robbery, in doing it by violence, without the shadow of justice.

2. Slavery sinks the divine image of God, in which man was created, to the level of brutality.

Of all the creatures which God created, he impressed his own image upon none except man. The creation of man was the subject of particular deliberation, so to speak, in the Godhead: "And God said, Let us make man in our image, after our likeness: and let them have dominion over the fish of the sea, and over the fowl of the air, and over the cattle, and over all the earth, and over every creeping thing that creepeth upon the earth. So God created man in his own image, in the image of God created he him; male and female created he them," Gen. i, 26, 27. In Gen. v, 1, we find it again: "In the likeness of God made he him." This image consisted of knowledge, righteousness, and true holiness. (Eph. iv, 24.) And because man was created in the image of God, no satisfaction could be taken for the life of a murderer: "Whoso sheddeth man's blood, by man shall his blood be shed; for in the image of God made he man," Gen. ix, 6. So in Lev. xxiv, 17, 18, 21, "He that killeth any man shall surely be put to death; and he that killeth a beast shall make it good, beast for beast; and he that killeth a man shall be put to death." The attempt, however fruitless, to destroy the image of God in man, is an indirect attack on God himself—on his being and on his sovereignty. How wicked, then, is it, to degrade the image of God in man, by sinking man into the degradation of a brute! God made man only a little lower than the angels; but slavery associates him with the beasts. God "crowned man with glory and honor;" but slavery tears off the crown of honor and glory, and places him under the *yoke*. God made man to have "dominion over the works of his hands;" but slavery casts him down *among* or *beneath* those works. God "put all things under his feet;" but slavery puts man under the feet of his owner.

Man is a rational, moral, immortal being, because created in God's image. He is, therefore, the child or son of God, because created to unfold Godlike faculties, and to govern himself by a divine law, written on his heart and re-published in his word. Thought, reason, intelligence, conscience, the capacity of virtue, the capacity of Christian love, immortality, the idea and obligation of duty, the perception of truth, the hope of happiness, the capacity of endless improvement—all these moral and intellectual attributes declaring a moral connection with God, reduce to insignificance all outward distinctions, and make every human being unspeakably dear to his Creator. The capacity of improvement allies the most ignorant to the more instructed of his race, and places within his reach the knowledge and happiness of the higher world. Such a being was not made to be a thing. He is a person—not a thing.

But slavery fights against the image of God in man. It first unmans him by making him a thing of mere property as far as possible. It can not unman him so far as to deprive him of immortality, or totally imbrute him, and in its rage to undo him wholly, but is compelled, while endeavoring to make him a chattel or thing, to call him a "chattel personal," because God himself hath set limits to man's wickedness, so that he "can not kill the soul," though he may imbrute the body and crush the spirit within man. It is needless here to enlarge. Slavery degrades and attempts to efface the moral image of God from man, consisting of knowledge, righteousness, and true holiness. The slave-holder may feed and clothe the body to preserve its health, and thereby secure the more labor. He may even so far cultivate mind as to give profitable direction to the bodily powers, that they may profit him the more. Here is the utmost limit of slavery. The intellectual powers are crushed, and the master slave state, South Carolina, denounces "all *mental improvement* in slaves." And this is the first law of the code of slavery every-where, and it can never be changed till slavery is destroyed. All the morality of the decalogue is set aside by slavery; and if any of it lives among the slaves, it is because there are some slaveholders who, in spite of the system, do much to counteract it, by acknowledging the ten commandments as obligatory on themselves and their slaves, and promoting the practice of them as they can. A volume would not contain the atrocities of slavery, as it operates against the image of God in man alone, to say nothing of its other legion sins.

3. All men are redeemed by the same blood of Christ; and therefore, this common and general redemption by the blood of Christ is at variance with slavery.

"God so loved the world, that he gave his only-begotten son, that whosoever believeth on him should not perish, but have everlasting life," John iii, 16. This redemption is so extensive as to reach, in its provisions and influence, to all and every one of the human family, in the past, present, and all future generations of men. The efficacy of his sacrifice reached backward to the fall of man, as well as to the end of time. Christ is the atonement for the sins of the world. Hence John the Baptist calls him "the Lamb of God which taketh away the sin of the world." He is the "Lamb slain from the foundation of the world," Rev. xiii, 8; "Who verily was foreordained—προεγνωϲμενου—foreknown—before the foundation of the world."

Redemption of the race of man through the sacrifice of Christ is antagonistic to slavery. Almighty God delivered the Israelites from bondage, because such a state was incompatible with the true interests of man; and the Hebrews were commanded expressly not to allow slavery among themselves: "For they [the Hebrews] are my servants, which I have brought forth out of the land of Egypt: they shall not be sold as bondsmen," Lev. xxv, 42; and the servitude which God ordained to the Hebrews, whether among themselves or with other nations, was not slavery; for it differed from slavery in all the elements which constitute slavery.

St. Paul, too, declares, that slavery is opposed to redemption: "Ye are bought with a price; be not ye the servants of men," 1 Cor. vii, 23. There are many evils, snares, dangers, and disabilities inseparable from a state of slavery. Civil slavery is utterly unbecoming the freed man of Christ: "For ye are bought with a price; therefore, glorify God in your body and in your spirit, which are God's," 1 Cor. vi, 20. Christians, even in their bodies, are represented as "the temple of God," 1 Cor. iii, 16, 17; and "the temple of the living God," 1 Cor. vi, 16; and "the temple of the Holy Ghost," 1 Cor. vi, 19; plainly showing, that Christians are consecrated to God. They are, therefore, as the redeemed creatures of God, to "glorify God in their body," by temperance, chastity, and purity; and "in their spirit," by faith, hope, and love—humility, resignation, patience—by meekness, gentleness, long-suffering, and universal benevolence. The privileges of redemption elevate men to the high moral station of "kings and priests unto God," Rev. v. 9, 10, with the exercise of which slavery continually interferes.

The same great sacrifice has been made for the slave as for the master; and therefore, the soul of the slave is worth as much as the soul of the master. As a redeemed sinner—an heir of heaven—the slave is equal to his master. He has the same right to forsake his sins, repent, believe, pray, worship God, practice all the duties of religion, enjoy all its privileges—as marriage, government of his children and his house, etc.—as his master has. All this is indisputable, from the privileges of redemption; in consequence of which the slave is entitled to employ his body and soul in God's service, and to enjoy all the means of grace.

But slavery takes no cognizance of its victims as the redeemed creatures of God. It exposes them to sale, robbery, deprivations, and cruel treatment. It forbids them to read or to learn to read. Its code puts their time, conscience, body, and soul into the hands of an oppressor; and all the duties, privileges, and advantages flowing from redemption are neither known, heeded, nor provided for, in the code of American slavery. If some slaveholders treat their slaves differently from this, no thanks to slavery for this.

And how can any Christian, who has himself partaken of the benefits of redemption, hold another *Christian brother* in bondage, regard him as property, sell him to others, break up his domestic relations, or interfere with any of his rights as a husband, father, son, Christian? Where is the *right, authority*, or *warrant*, from the word of God, by which one Christian holds another as *property?* Where is his right to sell him or keep him, to transfer him, by contract or will, to others, to appropriate the avails of his labor to his own use, to regulate exactly his manner of living, to separate him from his wife, and children, and home, and to determine the times and seasons, if any, when he may worship God? There is no warrant for such treatment of a fellow-Christian, or a human being, derived from the word of God.

Indeed, the early Christians very generally deemed it repugnant to Christianity, for any Christian to hold another in slavery, basing their argument on the declaration of Paul: "Ye are bought with a price; be ye not the servants of men." Accordingly, Constantine the Great, in 330, made a decree that no Jew or Pagan should retain a Christian as a slave. (See lib. i, Codicis, tit. *Ne Christianum*, etc.) And the three sons of Constantine confirmed and continued the same law. (Sozomen, lib. iii, c. 17.) Gregory the Great did the same. (Greg. Mag., lib. iii, Epist. 9.) The Council of Toledo enacted similar laws. (Concil. Toletani, iv, c. 64.) Aquinas speaks approvingly of these laws. (Aquinas Sum. Theologiae, 2, 2, q. 10, ar. 10.) (See Cornelius a Lapide on 1 Cor. vii, 22.)

4. Slavery is a usurpation of Divine right. Man is responsible to God for the use of his powers. It is true, we may exercise our powers under such limitations as still leave us at liberty to govern them by a supreme regard to the will of God. A more absolute control than this over us, by any human being, is subversive of the rights of the Divine government. Such is the power of

the slaveholder, by which the will of the slave is subjected, on pain of fearful penalties, to the absolute dictation of his master. "A slave is one who is in the power of a master, to whom he belongs. The master may sell him, dispose of his person, his industry, and his labor; he can do nothing, possess nothing, nor acquire any thing, but what must belong to his master." (Lousiana Civil Code, art. 35.)

The claim of slavery equals the claim of God. It claims the whole man— his soul, body, and strength—all he can possess, all he can acquire. The slave may be legally required to sin against God, by restraining prayer and exhortation, by whipping his parents, by lying, by Sabbath-breaking, by adultery; and, in case of refusal, he may be doomed to excruciating pain. It is that despotic power which can not be exercised without oppression, and which it is sinful to confer on any other; or to hold it, except under protest, with the purpose of getting rid of it as soon as possible. It never can be exercised without sin. And, if conferred by law, it can never be held except so far as to hold it in view of getting rid of it for the benefit of the oppressed. No one can long, if at all, hold this power without exercising it. And the exercise of it interferes with the freedom of conscience and moral agency, by forcibly detaining another in a condition where the duties of parents, children, friends, citizens, Christians, etc., can not be freely and fully discharged. Whatever liberty may be allowed a *slave*, he must suffer restraint in regard to plans of prospective duty, enjoyment, and usefulness. Yet, were the slaveholder's power not employed to involve the slave in the commission of sin or the omission of duty, the possession of such power is usurpation; it is holding Divine power, or it is exercising the prerogative of God. It is placing man in complete dependence on the will of his fellow, and holding him under legal liability to be forced against his conscience and his duty. It is putting one man in the place of God to another, as far as this can be done, than which no sin can be greater. And whenever this fearful power is conferred by law on a person without his knowledge or consent, he can not exercise the power without sin, or even retain it except under protest—that he can not hold it, much less exercise it, except so long as legally to get rid of it.

5. The system of slavery is contrary to the natural equality of mankind.

The Bible teaches this equality. "God hath made of one blood all nations of men to dwell on all the face of the earth," Acts xvii, 26. And Malachi asks, "Have we not all one Father? hath not one God created us? why do we deal treacherously every man against his brother?" Mal. ii, 10. (See, also, Job xxi, 15.) Here is established the unity and sameness of human nature, wherever men are found, and whatever their varieties may be. There are as many *distinct persons* as there are individuals in the human family; but there is only *one nature* in all. Human nature is a unit, and all possess it in common. Hence, all men are born equal, and have equal natural rights. No man, according to God's law, can be born either the lord or the slave of another. The Declaration of Independence, the echo of Scripture in this matter, declares, "All men are created free and equal." Hence, all men are entitled to their natural rights, of personal liberty, personal security, and the right of holding property; although these very rights are withheld from nearly three millions of human beings, who live under the flag of liberty.

This declaration of human equality, borrowed from the Bible, does not mean that all men possess equal wealth or learning; that the parent shall have no right to the services of the child; that the wife shall not be in subjection to her husband. This equality, according to the plain dictates of common sense, means, that all men, in coming into the world and going through it, have an equal opportunity to exercise all their own powers of body and mind for their own happiness; that one parent shall have as good a right to the services of his own children as any other shall have to the services of his children; that every wife shall be in subjection to her own husband, and to no one else; and that no man shall be deprived of his liberty for an alleged crime, "without due process of law."

The natural equality of mankind is one of the fundamental doctrines of Christianity, on which the whole system is based, and which sends its influence into all parts of the system. One of the fundamental doctrines of slavery, that one class of men is superior to another, is at variance with this Scripture doctrine. On this ground Aristotle maintained slavery. And the doctrine of the essential equality of mankind, will prove fatal to slavery: that all men have one common father, that the same blood flows in all human veins, that all are redeemed by the blood of Christ, that all are partakers alike of Christian privileges, that all are bound to perform the same Christian duties, that all are heirs to the same everlasting inheritance—these great truths, flowing from the equality of human nature, are directly subversive of slavery, and at no distant day they will overthrow it.

6. Slavery is contrary to the end or chief good of man, which is to glorify God, and enjoy him forever.

As slavery so places men under the complete dominion of a master, that the slaves are not at liberty to dispose of their time for the service of God or the enjoyment of him, they are prevented from the exercise of reading, meditation, and prayer. God commands all men to seek and exercise religion. But the slave is bound to submit to the master's authority, come what will. The slaveholder's power is exercised over the *private relative duties* of the slave, without being controlled by the laws of government. The usurpation of that power constitutes the sin of slavery. The cruel administration of that power is only an aggravation of that crime. The grand reason why a tyrant should be deposed, is not merely because his administration is cruel, but because he has usurped the power which knows neither bounds nor restraints. Now, this power interferes with or even frustrates the great end of man's being—to glorify God and enjoy him. (Source: Rev. Charles Elliott, *Sinfulness of American Slavery*, edited by B. F. Tefft, Cincinnati: L. Swormstedt and J. H. Power, 1851, vol. 1, pp. 299-309.)

WOMEN MAKE THE CASE FOR EQUALITY

Sarah Grimké

Sarah Grimké wrote her *Letters on the Equality of the Sexes and the Condition of Woman* in reaction to the furor that erupted when she and her sister Angela toured New England as lecturers for the American Anti-Slavery Society in 1837. Stung that the Congregational clergy of Connecticut issued a pastoral letter condemning women who lectured to audiences containing both men and women, the Grimkés concluded that they were useless to the antislavery crusade unless they first established their rights—as women—to full citizenship. Their dream, and that of many other abolitionists, was to establish a society in which blacks and whites, men and women, enjoyed equal rights and equal opportunities. If the Grimkés were not free to speak on behalf of the slave, then the first step toward the social order they hoped to create was to establish their claim to the civil rights commonly accorded white males.

Sarah Grimké began her *Letters on the Equality of the Sexes* by facing head-on the biblical text that undergirded the subordination of women. She denounced traditional hierarchical readings of Genesis 1-3 and articulated an unprecedented defense of the "original equality" of men and women. Her argument that Genesis 1 depicted the divine image as reflected equally in male and female echoed previous egalitarian readings of the text, and her insistence that Eve shared dominion over the creation with Adam strengthened that reading. Knowing that Genesis 3 presented a challenge to her position, she asserted that Eve and Adam fell from innocence in Genesis 3, but not from equality. She attributed man's desire to subordinate woman to the effects of the Fall and concluded—in typical abolitionist fashion—that any man who sought to deprive another person of free moral agency was usurping God's position as moral governor of individuals and was thus guilty of blasphemy. (Source: Sarah Grimké, *Letters on the Equality of the Sexes and the Condition of Woman*, Boston: Isaac Knapp, 1838, pp, 3-13.)

Letters on the Equality of the Sexes and the Condition of Woman (1838 CE)
SARAH GRIMKÉ

Letter I: The Original Equality of Woman

Amesbury, 7th Mo. 11th, 1837
My Dear Friend,
  In attempting to comply with thy request to give my views on the Province of Woman, I feel that I am venturing on nearly untrodden ground, and

that I shall advance arguments in opposition to a corrupt public opinion, and to the perverted interpretation of Holy Writ, which has so universally obtained. But I am in search of truth; and no obstacle shall prevent my prosecuting that search, because I believe the welfare of the world will be materially advanced by every new discovery we make of the designs of Jehovah in the creation of woman. It is impossible that we can answer the purpose of our being, unless we understand that purpose. It is impossible that we should fulfil our duties, unless we comprehend them; or live up to our privileges, unless we know what they are.

In examining this important subject, I shall depend solely on the Bible to designate the sphere of woman, because I believe almost every thing that has been written on this subject, has been the result of a misconception of the simple truths revealed in the Scriptures, in consequence of the false translation of many passages of Holy Writ. My mind is entirely delivered from the superstitious reverence which is attached to the English version of the Bible. King James's translators certainly were not inspired. I therefore claim the original as my standard, *believing that to have been inspired*, and I also claim to judge for myself what is the meaning of the inspired writers, because I believe it to be the solemn duty of every individual to search the Scriptures for themselves, with the aid of the Holy Spirit, and not be governed by the views of any man, or set of men.

We must first view woman at the period of her creation. "And God said, Let us make man in our own image, after our likeness; and let them have dominion over the fish of the sea, and over the fowl of the air, and over the cattle, and over all the earth, and over every creeping thing that creepeth upon the earth. So God created man in his own image, in the image of God created he him, male and female created he them." In all this sublime description of the creation of man, (which is a generic term including man and woman,) there is not one particle of difference intimated as existing between them. They were both made in the image of God; dominion was given to both over every other creature, but not over each other. Created in perfect equality, they were expected to exercise the vicegerence intrusted to them by their Maker, in harmony and love.

Let us pass on now to the recapitulation of the creation of man—"The Lord God formed man of the dust of the ground, and breathed into his nostrils the breath of life; and man became a living soul. And the Lord God said, it is not good that man should be alone, I will make him an help meet for him." All creation swarmed with animated beings capable of natural affection, as we know they still are; it was not, therefore, merely to give man a creature susceptible of loving, obeying, and looking up to him, for all that the animals could do and did do. It was to give him a companion, *in all respects* his equal; one who was like himself *a free agent*, gifted with intellect and endowed with immortality; not a partaker merely of his animal gratifications, but able to enter into all his feelings as a moral and responsible being. If this had not been the case, how could she have been an help meet for him? I understand this as applying not only to the parties entering into the marriage contract, but to all men and women, because I believe God designed woman to be an help meet for man in every good and perfect work. She was a part of himself, as if Jehovah designed to make the oneness and identity of man and woman perfect and complete; and when the glorious work of their creation was finished, "the morning stars sang together, and all the sons of God shouted for joy."

This blissful condition was not long enjoyed by our first parents. Eve, it would seem from the history, was wandering alone amid the bowers of Paradise, when the serpent met with her. From her reply to Satan, it is evident that the command not to eat "of the tree that is in the midst of the garden," was given to both, although the term man was used when the prohibition was issued by God. "And the woman said unto the serpent, WE may eat of the fruit of the trees of the garden, but of the fruit of the tree which is in the midst of the garden, God hath said, YE shall not eat of it, neither shall YE touch it, lest YE die." Here the woman was exposed to temptation from a being with whom she was unacquainted. She had been accustomed to associate with her beloved partner, and to hold communion with God and with angels; but of satanic intelligence, she was in all probability entirely ignorant. Through the subtlety of the serpent, she was beguiled. And "when she saw that the tree was good for food, and that it was pleasant to the eyes, and a tree to be desired to make one wise, she took of the fruit thereof and did eat."

We next find Adam involved in the same sin, not through the instrumentality of a supernatural agent, but through that of his equal, a being whom he must have known was liable to transgress the divine command, because he must have felt that he was himself a free agent, and that he was restrained from disobedience only by the exercise of faith and love towards his Creator. Had Adam tenderly reproved his wife, and endeavored to lead her to repentance instead of sharing in her guilt, I should be much more ready to accord to man that superiority which he claims; but as the facts stand disclosed by the sacred historian, it appears to me that to say the least, there was as much weakness exhibited by Adam as by Eve. They both fell from innocence, and consequently from happiness, *but not from equality.*

Let us next examine the conduct of this fallen pair, when Jehovah interrogated them respecting their fault. They both frankly confessed their guilt. "The man said, the woman whom thou gavest to be with me, she gave me of the tree and I did eat. And the woman said, the serpent beguiled me and I did eat" [Gen. 3:12]. And the Lord God said unto the woman, "Thou wilt be subject unto thy husband, and he will rule over thee" [Gen. 3:16]. That this did not allude to the subjection of woman to man is manifest, because the same mode of expression is used in speaking to Cain of Abel [Gen. 4:10-12]. The truth is that the curse, as it is termed, which was pronounced by Jehovah upon woman, is a simple prophecy. The Hebrew, like the French language, uses the same word to express shall and will. Our translators having been accustomed to exercise lordship over their wives, and seeing only through the medium of a perverted judgment, very naturally, though I think not very learnedly or very kindly, translated it *shall* instead of *will*, and thus converted a prediction to Eve into a command to Adam; for observe, it is addressed to the woman and not to the man. The consequence of the fall was an immediate struggle for dominion, and Jehovah foretold which would gain the ascendency; but as he created them in his image, as that image manifestly was not lost by the fall, because it is urged in Gen. 9:6, as an argument why the life of man should not be taken by his fellow man, there is no reason to suppose that sin produced any distinction between them as moral, intellectual and responsible beings. Man might just as well have endeavored by hard labor to fulfil the prophecy, thorns and thistles will the earth bring forth to thee, as to pretend to accomplish the other, "he will rule over thee," by asserting dominion over his wife.

> Authority usurped from God, not given.
> He gave him only over beast, flesh, fowl,
> Dominion absolute: that right he holds
> By God's donation: but man o'er woman
> He made not Lord, such title to himself
> Reserving, human left from human free.

Here then I plant myself. God created us equal;—he created us free agents;—he is our Lawgiver, our King and our Judge, and to him alone is woman bound to be in subjection, and to him alone is she accountable for the use of those talents with which her Heavenly Father has entrusted her. One is her Master even Christ.

Thine for the oppressed in the bonds of womanhood,

Sarah M. Grimké

Letter II: Woman Subject Only To God

Newburyport, 7th mo. 17, 1837

My Dear Sister,

In my last, I traced the creation and the fall of man and woman from that state of purity and happiness which their beneficent Creator designed them to enjoy. As they were one in transgression, their chastisement was the same. "So God drove out *the man*, and he placed at the East of the garden of Eden a cherubim and a flaming sword, which turned every way to keep the way of the tree of life." We now behold them expelled from Paradise, fallen from their original loveliness, but still bearing on their foreheads the image and super-scription of Jehovah; still invested with high moral responsibilities, intellectual powers, and immortal souls. They had incurred the penalty of sin, they were shorn of their innocence, but they stood on the same platform side by side, acknowledging *no superior* but their God. Notwithstanding what has been urged, woman I am aware stands charged to the present day with having brought sin into the world. I shall not repel the charge by any counter assertions, although, as was before hinted, Adam's ready acquiescence with his wife's proposal, does not savor much of that superiority *in strength of mind*, which is arrogated by man. Even admitting that Eve was the greater sinner, it seems to me man might be satisfied with the dominion he has claimed and exercised for nearly six thousand years, and that more true nobility would be manifested by endeavoring to raise the fallen and invigorate the weak, than by keeping woman in subjection. But I ask no favors for my sex. I surrender not our claim to equality. All I ask of our brethren is, that they will take their feet from off our necks, and permit us to stand upright on that ground which God designed us to occupy. If he has not given us the rights which have, as I conceive, been wrested from us, we shall soon give evidence of our inferiority, and shrink back into that obscurity, which the high souled magnanimity of man has assigned us as our appropriate sphere.

As I am unable to learn from sacred writ when woman was deprived by God of her equality with man, I shall touch upon a few points in the Scriptures, which demonstrate that no supremacy was granted to man. When God had destroyed the world, except Noah and his family, by the deluge, he renewed the grant formerly made to man, and again gave him dominion over every beast of the earth, every fowl of the air, over all that moveth upon the earth, and over all the fishes of the sea; into his hands they were delivered. But was woman, bearing the image of her God, placed under the dominion of her fellow man? Never! Jehovah could not surrender his authority to govern his own immortal creatures into the hands of a being, whom he knew, and whom his whole history proved, to be unworthy of a trust so sacred and important. God could not do it, because it is a direct contravention of his law, "Thou shalt worship the Lord thy God, and *him only* shalt thou serve" [Mt. 4:10]. If Jehovah had appointed man as the guardian, or teacher of woman, he would certainly have given some intimation of this surrender of his own prerogative. But so far from it, we find the commands of God invariably the same to man and woman; and not the slightest intimation is given in a single passage of the Bible, that God designed to point woman to man as her instructor. The tenor of his language always is, "Look unto ME, and be ye saved, all the ends of the earth, for I am God, and there is none else."

The lust of dominion was probably the first effect of the fall; and as there was no other intelligent being over whom to exercise it, woman was the first victim of this unhallowed passion. We afterwards see it exhibited by Cain in the murder of his brother, by Nimrod in his becoming a mighty hunter of men, and setting up a kingdom over which to reign. Here we see the origin of that Upas of slavery, which sprang up immediately after the fall, and has spread its pestilential branches over the whole face of the known world. All history attests that man has subjected woman to his will, used her as a means to promote his selfish gratification, to minister to his sensual pleasures, to be instrumental in promoting his comfort; but never has he desired to elevate her to that rank she was created to fill. He has done all he could to debase and enslave her mind; and now he looks triumphantly on the ruin he has wrought, and says, the being he has thus deeply injured is his inferior.

Woman has been placed by John Quincy Adams, side by side with the slave, whilst he was contending for the right side of petition. I thank him for ranking us with the oppressed; for I shall not find it difficult to show, that in all ages and countries, not even excepting enlightened republican America, woman has more or less been made a *means* to promote the welfare of man, without due regard to her own happiness, and the glory of God as the end of her creation.

During the *patriarchal* ages, we find men and women engaged in the same employments. Abraham and Sarah both assisted in preparing the food which was to be set before the three men, who visited them in the plains of Mamre; but although their occupations were similar, Sarah was not permitted to enjoy the society of the holy visitant; and as we learn from Peter, that she "obeyed Abraham, calling him Lord," we may presume he exercised dominion over her. We shall pass on now to Rebecca. In her history, we find another striking illustration of the low estimation in which woman was held. Eleazur is sent to seek a wife for Isaac. He finds Rebecca going down to the well to fill her pitcher. He accosts her; and she replies with all humility, "Drink, my lord." How does he endeavor to gain her favor and confidence? Does he approach her as a dignified creature, whom he was about to invite to fill an important station in his master's family, as the wife of his only son? No. He offered incense to her vanity, and "he took a golden ear-ring of half a shekel weight, and two bracelets for her hands of ten shekels weight of gold," and gave them to Rebecca.

The cupidity of man soon led him to regard woman as property, and hence we find them sold to those, who wished to marry them, as far as appears, without any regard to those sacred rights which belong to woman, as well as to man in the choice of a companion. That women were a profitable kind of property, we may gather from the description of a virtuous woman in the last chapter of Proverbs. To work willingly with her hands, to open her hands to the poor, to clothe herself with silk and purple, to look well to her household, to make fine linen and sell it, to deliver girdles to the merchant, and not to eat the bread of idleness, seems to have constituted in the view of Solomon, the perfection of a woman's character and achievements. "The spirit of that age was not favorable to intellectual improvement; but as there were wise men who formed exceptions to the general ignorance, and were destined to guide the world into more advanced states, so there was a corresponding proportion of wise women; and among the Jews, as well as other nations, we find a strong tendency to believe that women were in more immediate connection with heaven than men."—L. M. Child's Con. of Woman. If there be any truth in this tradition, I am at a loss to imagine in what the superiority of man consists.

Thine in the bonds of womanhood,

Sarah M. Grimké.

The Woman's Bible

Published in 1895 and 1898, *The Woman's Bible* was a landmark in feminist interpretation of the Bible. Never before had interpreters defined so clearly what it meant to approach a text with what we today would call a "hermeneutic of suspicion." The leader of the *Woman's Bible* project was suffragist Elizabeth Cady Stanton. Stanton was convinced that, if interpreters could strip away centuries of sexist interpretation, as well as distinguish from the biblical text those passages that represented God's inspiration and those which reflected male bias, the message of the Bible would be liberating to women. Stanton recognized, in other words, that both the writers and the readers of the Bible were the products of cultures that subordinated women to men. Her goal was to read the text without sexist presuppositions. She assembled a team of women exegetes and set them to work. Though they never managed to work their way through the entire Bible, they did publish the results of their study of a number of important texts. Among them was Genesis 1-3 as well as New Testament commentary on Genesis 1-3.

Like many interpreters inclined toward an egalitarian reading, Stanton celebrated the first creation account. She saw in Genesis 1 a sign that God, like the humanity God created in the divine image, was both male and female; and she dismissed Genesis 2 as the writer's attempt to convince his wife that God desired her to obey her husband. Stanton was equally dismissive of New Testament passages that cited the story of Adam and Eve as proof of woman's inferiority to man. For her, the inspired message of Scripture proclaimed gender equality. (Source: *The Original Feminist Attack on the Bible* [*The Woman's Bible*], edited by Elizabeth Cady Stanton, New York: Arno Press, 1974, pp. 14-27, 163-64.)

The Woman's Bible (1895, 1898 CE)
ELIZABETH CADY STANTON, EDITOR

The Book of Genesis.

Chapter I.

> *Genesis i: 26, 27, 28.*
>
> 26 And God said, Let us make man in our image, after our likeness: and let them have dominion over the fish of the sea, and over the fowl of the air, and over the cattle, and over all the earth, and over every creeping thing that creepeth upon the earth.
>
> 27 So God created man in his *own* image, in the image of God created he him; male and female created he them.
>
> 28 And God blessed them, and God said unto them, Be fruitful and multiply, and replenish the earth, and subdue it; and have dominion over the fish of the sea, and over the fowl of the air, and over every living thing that moveth upon the earth.

HERE is the sacred historian's first account of the advent of woman; a simultaneous creation of both sexes, in the image of God. It is evident from the language that there was consultation in the Godhead, and that the masculine and feminine elements were equally represented. Scott in his commentaries says, "this consultation of the Gods is the origin of the doctrine of the trinity." But instead of three male personages, as generally represented, a Heavenly Father, Mother, and Son would seem more rational.

The first step in the elevation of woman to her true position, as an equal factor in human progress, is the cultivation of the religious sentiment in regard to her dignity and equality, the recognition by the rising generation of an ideal Heavenly Mother, to whom their prayers should be addressed, as well as to a Father.

If language has any meaning, we have in these texts a plain declaration of the existence of the feminine element in the Godhead, equal in power and glory with the masculine. The Heavenly Mother and Father! "God created man in his *own image, male and female*." Thus Scripture, as well as science and philosophy, declares the eternity and equality of sex—the philosophical fact, without which there could have been no perpetuation of creation, no growth or development in the animal, vegetable, or mineral kingdoms, no awakening nor progressing in the world of thought. The masculine and feminine elements, exactly equal and balancing each other, are as essential to the maintenance of the equilibrium of the universe as positive and negative electricity, the centripetal and centrifugal forces, the laws of attraction which bind together all we know of this planet whereon we dwell and of the system in which we revolve.

In the great work of creation the crowning glory was realized, when man and woman were evolved on the sixth day, the masculine and feminine forces in the image of God, that must have existed eternally, in all forms of matter and mind. All the persons in the Godhead are represented in the Elohim the divine plurality taking counsel in regard to this last and highest form of life. Who were the members of this high council, and whether a duality or a trinity? Verse 27 declares the image of God male and female. How then is it possible to make woman an afterthought? We find in verses 5-16 the pronoun "he" used. Should it not in harmony with verse 26 be "they," a dual pronoun? We may attribute this to the same cause as the use of "his" in verse 11 instead of "it." The fruit tree yielding fruit after "his" kind instead of after "its" kind. The paucity of a language may give rise to many misunderstandings.

The above texts plainly show the simultaneous creation of man and woman, and their equal importance in the development of the race. All those theories based on the assumption that man was prior in the creation, have no foundation in Scripture.

As to woman's subjection, on which both the canon and the civil law delight to dwell, it is important to note that equal dominion is given to woman over every living thing, but not one word is said giving man dominion over woman.

Here is the first title deed to this green earth giving alike to the sons and daughters of God. No lesson of woman's subjection can be fairly drawn from the first chapter of the Old Testament.

E. C. S.

The most important thing for a woman to note, in reading Genesis, is that that portion which is now divided into "the first three chapters" (there was no such division until about five centuries ago), contains two entirely separate, and very contradictory, stories of creation, written by two different, but equally anonymous, authors. No Christian theologian of to-day, with any pretensions to scholarship, claims that Genesis was written by Moses. As was long ago pointed out, the Bible itself declares that all the books the Jews originally possessed were burned in the destruction of Jerusalem, about 588 B.C., at the time the people were taken to Babylonia as slaves to the Assyrians, (see II Esdras, ch. xiv, v. 21, Apocrypha). Not until about 247 B.C. (some theologians say 226 and others 169 B.C.) is there any record of a collection of literature in the re-built Jerusalem, and, then, the anonymous writer of II Maccabees briefly mentions that some Nehemiah "gathered together the acts of the kings and the prophets and those of David" when "founding a library" for use in Jerusalem. But the earliest mention anywhere in the Bible of a book that might have corresponded to Genesis is made by an apocryphal writer, who says that *Ezra* wrote "all that hath been done in the world since the beginning," after the Jews returned from Babylon, under his leadership, about 450 B.C. (see II Esdras, ch. xiv, v. 22, of the Apocrypha).

When it is remembered that the Jewish books were written on rolls of leather, without much attention to vowel points and with no division into verses or chapters, by uncritical copyists, who altered passages greatly, and did not always even pretend to understand what they were copying, then the reader of Genesis begins to put herself in position to understand how it can be contradictory. Great as were the liberties which the Jews took with Genesis, those of the English translators, however, greatly surpassed them.

The first chapter of Genesis, for instance, in Hebrew, tells us, in verses one and two, "As to origin, created the gods (Elohim) these skies (or air or clouds) and this earth. . . . And a wind moved upon the face of the waters." Here we have the opening of a polytheistic fable of creation, but, so strongly convinced were the English translators that the ancient Hebrews must have been originally monotheistic that they rendered the above, as follows: "In the beginning God created the heaven and the earth. . . . And the spirit of God (!) moved upon the face of the waters."

It is now generally conceded that some one (nobody pretends to know who) at some time (nobody pretends to know exactly when), copied two creation myths on the same leather roll, one immediately following the other. About one hundred years ago, it was discovered by Dr. Astruc, of France, that from Genesis ch. i, v. 1 to Genesis ch. ii, v. 4, is given one complete account of creation, by an author who always used the term "the gods" (*Elohim*), in speaking of the fashioning of the universe, mentioning it altogether thirty-four times, while, in Genesis ch. ii, v. 4, to the end of chapter iii, we have a totally different narrative, by an author of unmistakably different style, who uses the term "Iahveh of the gods" twenty times, but "Elohim" only three times. The first author, evidently, attributes creation to a council of gods, acting in concert, and seems never to have heard of Iahveh. The second attributes creation to Iahveh, a tribal god of ancient Israel, but represents Iahveh as one of two or more gods, conferring with them (in Genesis ch. xiii, v. 22) as to the danger of man's acquiring immortality.

Modern theologians have, for convenience sake, entitled these two fables, respectively, the Elohistic and the Iahoistic stories. They differ, not only in the point I have mentioned above, but in the order of the "creative acts;" in regard to the mutual attitude of man and woman, and in regard to human freedom from prohibitions imposed by deity. In order to exhibit their striking contradictions, I will place them in parallel columns:

ELOHISTIC.	IAHOISTIC.
Order of Creation:	Order of Creation:
First—Water.	First—Land.
Second—Land.	Second—Water.
Third—Vegetation.	Third—Male Man, only.
Fourth—Animals.	Fourth—Vegetation.
Fifth—Mankind; male and female.	Fifth—Animals.
	Sixth—Woman.

*   *   *   *   *   *   *   *

In this story male and female man are created simultaneously, both alike, in the image of the gods, *after* all animals have been called into existence.

In this story male man is sculptured out of clay, *before* any animals are created, and *before* female man has been constructed.

*   *   *   *   *   *   *   *

Here, joint dominion over the earth is given to woman and man, without limit or prohibition.

Here, woman is punished with subjection to man for breaking a prohibitory law.

*   *   *   *   *   *   *   *

Everything, without exception, is pronounced "very good."

There is a tree of evil, whose fruit, is said by Iahveh to cause sudden death, but which does not do so, as Adam lived 930 years after eating it.

*   *   *   *   *   *   *   *

Man and woman are told that "every plant bearing seed upon the face of the earth and *every tree* ... "To you it shall be for meat." They are thus given perfect freedom.

Man is told there is *one tree* of which he must not eat, "for in the day thou eatest thereof, thou shalt surely die."

*   *   *   *   *   *   *   *

Man and woman are given special dominion over all the animals— "every creeping thing that creepeth upon the earth."

An animal, a "creeping thing," is given dominion over man and woman, and proves himself more truthful than Iahveh Elohim. (Compare Genesis chapter ii, verse 17, with chapter iii, verses 4 and 22.)

*   *   *   *   *   *   *   *

Now as it is manifest that both of these stories cannot be true; intelligent women, who feel bound to give the preference to either, may decide according to their own judgment of which is more worthy of an intelligent woman's acceptance. Paul's rule is a good one in this dilemma, "Prove all things: hold fast to that which is good." My own opinion is that the second story was manipulated by some Jew, in an endeavor to give "heavenly authority" for requiring a woman to obey the man she married. In a work which I am now completing, I give some facts concerning ancient Israelitish history, which will be of peculiar interest to those who wish to understand the origin of woman's subjection.

E. B. D.

Many orientalists and students of theology have maintained that the consultation of the Gods here described is proof that the Hebrews were in early days polytheists—Scott's supposition that this is the origin of the Trinity has no foundation in fact, as the beginning of that conception is to be found in the earliest of all known religious nature worship. The acknowledgment of the dual principal, masculine and feminine, is much more probably the explanation of the expressions here used.

In the detailed description of creation we find a gradually ascending series. Creeping things, "great sea monsters," (chap. i, v. 21, literal translation). "Every bird of wing," cattle and living things of the earth, the fish of the sea and the "birds of the heavens," then man, and last and crowning glory of the whole, woman.

It cannot be maintained that woman was inferior to man even if, as asserted in chapter ii, she was created after him without at once admitting that man is inferior to the creeping things, because created after them.

L. D. B.

Chapter II.

Genesis ii: 21-25.

21 And the Lord God caused a deep sleep to fall upon Adam, and he slept; and he took one of his ribs, and closed up the flesh thereof.

22 And the rib which the Lord God had taken from man, made he a woman, and brought her unto the man.

23 And Adam said, This *is* now bone of my bone, and flesh of my flesh: she shall be called Woman, because she was taken out of man.

24 Therefore shall a man leave his father and his mother, and shall cleave unto his wife; and they shall be one flesh.

25 And they were both naked, the man and his wife, and were not ashamed.

As the account of the creation in the first chapter is in harmony with science, common sense, and the experience of mankind in natural laws, the inquiry naturally arises, why should there be two contradictory accounts in the same book, of the same event? It is fair to infer that the second version, which is found in some form in the different religions of all nations, is a mere allegory, symbolizing some mysterious conception of a highly imaginative editor.

The first account dignifies woman as an important factor in the creation, equal in power and glory with man. The second makes her a mere afterthought. The world in good running order without her. The only reason for her advent being the solitude of man.

There is something sublime in bringing order out of chaos; light out of darkness; giving each planet its place in the solar system; oceans and lands their limits; wholly inconsistent with a petty surgical operation, to find material for the mother of the race. It is on this allegory that all the enemies of women rest their battering rams, to prove her inferiority. Accepting the view that man was prior in the creation, some Scriptural writers say that as the woman was of the man, therefore, her position should be one of subjection. Grant it, then as the historical fact is reversed in our day, and the man is now of the woman, shall his place be one of subjection?

The equal position declared in the first account must prove more satisfactory to both sexes; created alike in the image of God—The Heavenly Mother and Father.

Thus, the Old Testament, "in the beginning," proclaims the simultaneous creation of man and woman, the eternity and equality of sex; and the New Testament echoes back through the centuries the individual sovereignty of woman growing out of this natural fact. Paul, in speaking of equality as the very soul and essence of Christianity, said, "There is neither Jew nor Greek, there is neither bond nor free, there is neither male nor female; for ye are all one in Christ Jesus." With this recognition of the feminine element in the Godhead in the Old Testament, and this declaration of the equality of the sexes in the New, we may well wonder at the contemptible status woman occupies in the Christian Church of to-day.

All the commentators and publicists writing on woman's position, go through an immense amount of fine-spun metaphysical speculations, to prove her subordination in harmony with the Creator's original design.

It is evident that some wily writer, seeing the perfect equality of man and woman in the first chapter, felt it important for the dignity and dominion of man to effect woman's subordination in some way. To do this a spirit of evil must be introduced, which at once proved itself stronger than the spirit of good, and man's supremacy was based on the downfall of all that had just been pronounced very good. This spirit of evil evidently existed before the supposed fall of man, hence woman was not the origin of sin as so often asserted.

E. C. S.

In v. 23 Adam proclaims the eternal oneness of the happy pair, "This is now bone of my bone and flesh of my flesh;" no hint of her subordination. How could men, admitting these words to be divine revelation, ever have preached the subjection of woman!

Next comes the naming of the mother of the race. "She shall be called Woman," in the ancient form of the word Womb-man. She was man and more than man because of her maternity.

The assertion of the supremacy of the woman in the marriage relation is contained in v. 24: "Therefore shall a man leave his father and his mother and cleave unto his wife." Nothing is said of the headship of man, but he is commanded to make her the head of the household, the home, a rule followed for centuries under the Matriarchate.

L. D. B.

Chapter III.

. . . Adam Clarke, in his commentaries, asks the question, "is this [Gen. 3:1–24] an allegory?" He finds it beset with so many difficulties as an historical fact, that he inclines at first to regard it as a fable, a mere symbol, of some hidden truth. His mind seems more troubled about the serpent than any other personage in the drama. As snakes cannot walk upright, and have never been known to speak, he thinks this beguiling creature must have been an ourang-outang, or some species of ape. However, after expressing all his doubts, he rests in the assumption that it must be taken literally, and that with higher knowledge of the possibilities of all living things, many seeming improbabilities will be fully realized.

A learned professor in Yale College, before a large class of students, expressed serious doubts as to the forbidden fruit being an apple, as none grew in that latitude. He thinks it must have been a quince. If the serpent and the apple are to be withdrawn thus recklessly from the tableaux, it is feared that with advancing civilization the whole drama may fall into discredit. Scientists tells us that "the missing link" between the ape and man, has recently been discovered, so that we can now trace back an unbroken line of ancestors to the dawn of creation.

As out of this allegory grows the doctrines of original sin, the fall of man, and woman the author of all our woes, and the curses on the serpent, the woman, and the man; the Darwinian theory of the gradual growth of the race from a lower to a higher type of animal life, is more hopeful and encouraging. However, as our chief interest is in woman's part in the drama, we are equally pleased with her attitude, whether as a myth in an allegory, or as the heroine of an historical occurrence.

In this prolonged interview, the unprejudiced reader must be impressed with the courage, the dignity, and the lofty ambition of the woman. The tempter evidently had a profound knowledge of human nature, and saw at a glance the high character of the person he met by chance in his walks in the garden. He did not try to tempt her from the path of duty by brilliant jewels, rich dresses, worldly luxuries or pleasures, but with the promise of knowledge, with the wisdom of the Gods. Like Socrates or Plato, his powers of conversation and asking puzzling questions, were no doubt marvellous, and he roused in the woman that intense thirst for knowledge, that the simple pleasures of picking flowers and talking with Adam did not satisfy. Compared with Adam she appears to great advantage through the entire drama.

The curse pronounced on woman is inserted in an unfriendly spirit to justify her degradation and subjection to man. With obedience to the laws of health, diet, dress, and exercise, the period of maternity should be one of added vigor in both body and mind, a perfectly natural operation should not be attended with suffering. By the observance of physical and psychical laws the supposed curse can be easily transformed into a blessing. Some churchmen speak of maternity as a disability, and then chant the Magnificat in all their cathedrals round the globe. Through all life's shifting scenes, the mother of the race has been the greatest factor in civilization.

We hear the opinion often expressed, that woman always has, and always will be in subjection. Neither assertion is true. She enjoyed unlimited individual freedom for many centuries, and the events of the present day all point to her speedy emancipation. Scientists now give 85,000 years for the growth of the race. They assign 60,000 to savagism, 20,000 to barbarism, and 5,000 to civilization. Recent historians tell us that for centuries woman reigned supreme. That period was called the Matriarchate. Then man seized the reins of government, and we are now under the Patriarchate. But we see on all sides new forces gathering, and woman is already abreast with man in art, science, literature, and government. The next dynasty, in which both will reign as equals, will be the Amphiarchate, which is close at hand.

Psychologists tell us of a sixth sense now in process of development, by which we can read each other's mind and communicate without speech. The Tempter might have had that sense, as he evidently read the minds of both the creature and the Creator, if we are to take this account as literally true, as Adam Clarke advises.

E. C. S.

Note the significant fact that we always hear of the "fall of man," not the fall of woman, showing that the consensus of human thought has been more unerring than masculine interpretation. Reading this narrative carefully, it is amazing that any set of men ever claimed that the dogma of the inferiority of woman is here set forth. The conduct of Eve from the beginning to the end is so superior to that of Adam. The command not to eat of the fruit of the tree of Knowledge was given to the man alone before woman was formed. Genesis ii, 17. Therefore the injunction was not brought to Eve with the impressive solemnity of a Divine Voice, but whispered to her by her husband and equal. It was a serpent supernaturally endowed, a seraphim as Scott and other commentators have claimed, who talked with Eve, and whose words might reasonably seem superior to the second-hand story of her companion—nor does the woman yield at once. She quotes the command not to eat of the fruit to which the serpent replies "Dying ye shall not die," v. 4, literal translation. In other words telling her that if the mortal body does perish, the immortal part shall live forever, and offering as the reward of her act the attainment of Knowledge.

Then the woman fearless of death if she can gain wisdom takes of the fruit; and all this time Adam standing beside her interposes no word of objection. "Her husband with her" are the words of v. 6. Had he been the representative of the divinely appointed head in married life, he assuredly would have taken upon himself the burden of the discussion with the serpent, but no, he is silent in this crisis of their fate. Having had the command from God himself he interposes no word of warning or remonstrance, but takes the fruit from the hand of his wife without a protest. It takes six verses to describe the "fall" of woman, the fall of man is contemptuously dismissed in a line and a half.

The subsequent conduct of Adam was to the last degree dastardly. When the awful time of reckoning comes, and the Jehovah God appears to demand why his command has been disobeyed, Adam endeavors to shield himself behind the gentle being he has declared to be so dear. "The woman thou gavest to be with me, she gave me and I did eat," he whines—trying to shield himself at his wife's expense! Again we are amazed that upon such a story men have built up a theory of their superiority!

Then follows what has been called the curse. Is it not rather a prediction? First is the future fate of the serpent described, the enmity of the whole human race—"it shall lie in wait for thee as to the head" (v. 15, literal translation). Next the subjection of the woman is foretold, thy husband "shall rule over thee," v. 16. Lastly the long struggle of man with the forces of nature is portrayed. "In the sweat of thy face thou shalt eat food until thy turning back to the earth" (v. 19, literal translation). With the evolution of humanity an ever increasing number of men have ceased to toil for their bread with their hands, and with the introduction of improved machinery, and the uplifting of the race there will come a time when there shall be no severities of labor, and when women shall be freed from all oppressions.

"And Adam called his wife's name Life for she was the mother of all living" (v. 20, literal translation).

It is a pity that all versions of the Bible do not give this word instead of the Hebrew Eve. She was Life, the eternal mother, the first representative of the more valuable and important half of the human race.

L. D. B.

Epistles to Timothy.

Chapter I.

1 Timothy ii.

9 In like manner, also, that women adorn themselves in modest apparel, with shamefacedness and sobriety: not with braided hair, or gold, or pearls, or costly array:

10 But (which becometh women professing godliness) with good works.

11 Let the woman learn in silence with all subjection.

12 But I suffer not a woman to teach, nor to usurp authority over the man, but to be in silence.

13 For Adam was first formed, then Eve.

14 And Adam was not deceived, but the woman being deceived was in the transgression.

. . . Had the Apostle enjoined upon women to do good works without envy or jealousy, it would have had the weight and the wisdom of a Divine command. But that, from the earliest record of human events, woman should have been condemned and punished for trying to get knowledge, and forbidden to impart what she has learned, is the most unaccountable peculiarity of masculine wisdom. After cherishing and nursing helpless infancy, the most necessary qualification of motherhood is that of teaching. If it is contrary to the perfect operation of human development that woman should teach, the infinite and all wise directing power of the universe has blundered. It cannot be admitted that Paul was inspired by infinite wisdom in this utterance. This was evidently the unilluminated utterance of Paul, the man, biassed by prejudice. But, it may be claimed that this edict referred especially to teaching in religious assemblies. It is strikingly inconsistent that Paul, who had proclaimed the broadest definition of human souls, "There is neither Jew nor Greek, bond nor free, male or female, but ye are one in Christ Jesus," as the Christian idea, should have commanded the subjection of woman, and silence as essential to her proper sphere in the Church.

It is not a decade since a manifesto was issued by a religious convention bewailing the fact that woman is not only seeking to control her property, but claiming the right of the wife to control her person! This seems to be as great an offence to ecclesiasticism in this hour and this land of boasted freedom, as it was to Paul in Judea nineteen centuries ago. But the "new man," as well as the "new woman," is here. He is inspired by the Divine truth that woman is to contribute to the redemption of the race by free and enlightened motherhood. He is proving his fitness to be her companion by achieving the greatest of all victories—victory over himself. The new humanity is to be born of this higher manhood and emancipated womanhood. Then it will be possible for motherhood to "continue in sanctification."

The doctrine of woman the origin of sin, and her subjection in consequence, planted in the early Christian Church by Paul, has been a poisonous stream in Church and in State. It has debased marriage and made both canon and civil law a monstrous oppression to woman. M. Renan sums up concisely a mighty truth in the following words: "The writings of Paul have been a danger and a hidden rock—the causes of the principal defects of Christian theology." His teachings about woman are no longer a hidden rock, however, for, in the light of science, it is disclosed to all truth seeking minds. How much satisfaction it would have been to the mothers adown the centuries, had there been a testimony by Mary and Elizabeth recording their experiences of motherhood. Not a statement by them, nor one about them, except what man wrote.

NEW RELIGIOUS MOVEMENTS
ON GENDER RELATIONS

Shakers

The Shakers were the most successful communitarian group in American history, and Genesis 1:26-27 was a pivotal text for them. Since Genesis 1:27 described the image of God as "male and female," the Shakers used Genesis to support their theory that God was both male and female. Shakers believed that, since God had been incarnate in the man Jesus, God must also become incarnate in female form. They identified their founder, Mother Ann Lee, as the second coming of the Christ spirit.

Though scholars continue to debate exactly how egalitarian the Shakers were, it is clear that Shakers accorded women higher social status than did American society as a whole. Shaker settlements were always jointly ruled by eldresses and elders. Given their belief that God was both Mother and Father, Shaker discussions of the creation were more egalitarian than was typical of nineteenth-century Christianity. Still, elements of hierarchy were not absent; it was not unusual for Shakers to elevate God the Father to a higher status than God the Mother.

The selections that follow reveal several typical Shaker motifs. Writing in 1843, Paulina Bates, a Shaker medium for "Holy Mother Wisdom," described a creation in which "the essence of eternal male and female principles existed in the first source of all existence." Mother Wisdom subordinated the female divine principle, arguing that it was not until God manifested the divine glory by bringing forth the Mother Spirit that the feminine principle was fully expressed. Yet she also noted that God created humanity in the divine image, male and female. She criticized those who assumed that God was only "of the male order." Such belief led people erroneously to assume that woman was not a living soul, "but merely a machine for the use and benefit of man." To round out the cosmic order, Mother Wisdom contended that, as God was male and female, so too the spirit of evil was also male and female. She noted, as well, that the "second Eve" (Ann Lee) was essential to salvation—she was the female principle made perfect through suffering. Because she was at "one with the Lamb," Christ included both male and female. In Christ, then, "dwelt the fullness of Deity, as respected the *Parentage of the new creation.*"

Elder Frederic Evans (1808-1893) reiterated the Shaker claim that God was male and female, arguing from Genesis 1: 26-27 that there is "as truly in existence a Heavenly Divine Mother as there is a Heavenly Divine Father." Evans also asserted that the effects of the Fall could primarily be seen in the relationship of man and woman. In all other animals, he contended, the female governed the work of reproduction; only among human beings did man rule over woman. Evans understood the divine judgments on Adam and Eve articulated in Genesis 3 as the source for this reversal, and declared male domination to be "contrary to nature." Evans interpreted the serpent as a symbol of man's sensuous nature, and argued that the persistence of male domination of woman was not simply a result of the Fall, but comprised the Fall: "The Fall of Man consists in disorderly social relationship." Like Paulina Bates, Evans contended that Christ was both male and female. Jesus, the second Adam, manifested the divine Father Spirit; and Ann Lee revealed the divine Mother Spirit.

Autobiography of a Shaker (1888 CE)
FREDERICK W. EVANS

Love before Logic in Theology

"How can ye believe"—understand—"that seek honour one of another, and not that honour that cometh from God only?"

John was *in the Spirit* when he wrote, in outward language and symbols, what he then saw and heard. Spiritually-interior ideas translated into images, words, and things of earth, with which other ideas are already associated in the minds of all natural men and women, render it *impossible* for them to understand or comprehend the primary ideas of the Vision, until their state becomes changed, and an interior degree in them is opened, corresponding to the heaven whence the ideas originated and proceeded.

In other words: Of all the Apostles, John was the most divine in his love of God *(in esse)*; and in purity of heart he approximated, in his *soul* history, and spiritual ascension, the nearest to Jesus; and, after the crucifixion, was, of all human beings, the most in rapport with him, and with the seventh Resurrection heaven, or sphere.

And it was not until the earth had produced a woman, the true correspondent and counterpart of the man Jesus, that another step of progress in *that direction* could be taken.

The two Orders, of Generation and Resurrection, being both of God and Nature, like the negative and positive poles, have acted and re-acted upon each other, like Jacob and Esau; or, as Dr. Bellows expresses it, they are centripetal and centrifugal forces acting alternately. They alternated through seven Cycles, or Churches—each having its Saviour, each its rise and fall, from Adam the first to Jesus the last. Then they have alternated through seven Cycles, or Churches, each having its origin, rise, and fall, through seven Saviours, from Peter to Ann Lee.

Man is to Woman *her* God, in physical and intellectual power, as representing and revealing the Father in Deity—*Wisdom*. And Woman is to Man *his* God and Saviour in affectional power, and in Divine spiritual intuition, as representing the Mother in Deity—*Love*.

Woman rising out of Man is his superior, in the complexity and variety of her physical functions and powers, as also in the superior refinement of her organisation generally. She is the intuitional and spiritual Preceptor and Educator, and the "glory of the man." While Man is the originator and inventor, in the arts and sciences, and mechanics, and the Revelator of the heavens; and is the "glory of God."

History repeats itself; and therefore as, in a former Cycle, "they ceased in Israel;" so "they ceased in Israel, until that I," Ann Lee, "arose, that I arose a Mother in Israel."

After the "marriage of the Lamb and Bride," (in the Lord) as the respective heads of the Jesus Christ Church in the spirit world—(which, by reason of the eighteen hundred years of travel in the Divine life, was adorned with the gifts and graces of the Gospel testimony),—and of the Gentile Second Appearing Christ Church upon earth, these two Churches began to come gradually into rapport; so that there will be a perfect union effected in the course of the seven Cycles—"seven thunders"—through which the Shaker Gentile Church of Christ's Second Appearing—the second temple—will have to pass before the restitution of all that God has spoken and wrought through Moses, pertaining to this material world, can be fully accomplished; for the earth itself must, by true science, be subdued and redeemed unto God, as a new earth—New Jerusalem.

And as this comes down gradually from God, out of heaven, the tabernacle of God is with men, and He will dwell among them; and they become in truth his people. "And God shall wipe away all tears from their eyes; and there shall be no more death, neither sorrow, nor crying, neither shall there be any more pain; for the former things," as they now exist in Babylon, are, in the Shaker Order, fast passing away. . . .

God Is Male and Female

Your Scriptures say, "In the beginning God created man in his own image, in the image of God created he him, male and female created he them." How could he do that if God himself was not in the order of male and female? How could man and woman, I ask, be in the image of God, if God himself has no element of the feminine in him? There is, you may depend, so far as my testimony can go, and that of my people, as truly in existence a Heavenly Divine

Mother as there is a Heavenly Divine Father unto whom you pray. And indeed, my friends, how could there be a father where there is no mother? Is it not a little out of order to use the term father? Why do you not use the term "it"? Why do you not use a neutral word? Why use a word representing the male element, and which in itself implies the existence of a counterpart? . . .

The Shakers on the Fall of Man

Then, leaving our starting point, what do we have next? What you call the Fall of Man—what was that? Something that brought shame where there was no shame previously. Was it the eating of an apple? Read the account yourself when you have a little leisure, and revise that opinion. It was not an apple, taking the Scriptures themselves; for we have all sinned after the similitude of "Adam and Eve's transgression." Have we sinned eating apples? and if so, are we particularly ashamed when we eat an apple? But something pertaining to the social relation—the social evil—does work shame and confusion. The curse that was pronounced upon Adam, and upon the ground that it should bring forth thorns and briars, and the curse that was pronounced upon the woman—"I will greatly multiply thy sorrows and thy conception"—are they not multiplied? "Thy desire shall be to thy husband, and he shall rule over thee"—contrary to nature; for in all the animal creation the female governs and rules in the work of reproduction, except amongst the human race. Man rules over woman, to her loss and damage, and to his own confusion of face. There is room for improvement. The Fall of Man consists in disorderly social relationship. But there was a promise given; the serpent is mentioned. Adam Clarke says that the serpent, according to the original, was the sensuous nature of man—the passions—that was the serpent. What is it that tempts a man to drink? It is the sensuous nature—it is the serpent. What is it that tempts a person to become a glutton? It is the serpent—the sensuous nature—*nahash*, curious, prying, seeking. It is not a snake any more than the other was an apple. (Source: Frederick W. Evans, *Autobiography of a Shaker and Revelation of the Apocalypse*, New York: American News Company, 1888, pp. 100-102, 199, 200-201.)

Compendium (1867 CE)

FREDERICK W. EVANS

38. The Shakers believe that the distinction of sex is eternal; that it inheres in the soul itself; and that no angels or spirits exist who are not male and female.

39. From the fact that Adam (and Eve) "was the figure of him that was to come," they argue that the "second Adam, the Lord from heaven, a quickening Spirit," was also *dual*, male and female; and that they were the spiritual Father and Mother of Jesus, begetting, watching over, and bearing him in the regeneration, towards the *new birth*, into their own quickening spiritual element.

40. Every thing is begotten, travails, and is born into the elements of its parents. "That which is [begotten and] born of the flesh, is flesh; and that which is [begotten and] born of the Spirit, is spirit."

41. Jesus, being a male, could only reveal and manifest the *Father* in Christ and God. But when the *second* Adam appeared to Ann, and became her spiritual Parents, she, being a female, revealed and manifested the *Mother Spirit* in Christ and in Deity.

42. The affectional nature in man seeks its Source and Parent—the Maternal Spirit in Deity. Ignorance, or a perverted theology, may divert it into wrong channels, as in the worshipers of female gods in the heathen nations, which are known to be more numerous than all others; or the Roman Catholic adoration of the Virgin Mary—"the Mother of God." But nothing can destroy the intuitive reverence of the human soul for a *Heavenly Mother*. It is as innate and universal as is the belief in Deity. (Source: Frederick W. Evans, *Compendium of the Origin, History, Principles, Rules and Regulations, Government, and Doctrine of the United Society of Believers in Christ's Second Appearing*, 4th ed., New Lebanon, N.Y.: 1867, pp. 108-109.)

The Divine Book of Holy and Eternal Wisdom (1849 CE)
PAULINA BATES

Part VI, Chapter I

6. . . . The beginning of all created things was God. God created the celestial foundations of the heavens, and established the arches of the eternal and invisible world, and laid an eternal foundation for his honor and glory; but although the essence of eternal male and female principles existed in the first source of all existence; still his glory, not being as yet brought forth and revealed; therefore He remained alone without a helper meet in her distinct and co-operative order.

7. And God saw that it was not good to be alone, in his manifest order; and that his glory and happiness could never be completed until the Mother Spirit was brought forth, and set in her proper order; which is his glory, and ever will be through the endless ages of eternity. This is agreeable to my testimony under the name of *Wisdom*, recorded in the scriptures, which ye profess to believe. (See Prov. viii. 22 to 25, & 30.) . . .

26. Men are willing to believe in a God of the male order; they are willing to believe that there are myriads of Angels; but all in the male order; willing to believe in Lucifer or Satan, a fallen angel; but in the male order; willing to believe in the Savior of man, but alone in the male order.

27. Hence ariseth the belief in many, that the female is not in possession of a living soul; but merely a machine for the use and benefit of man in this terrestrial state of existence. And this is not to be wondered at, so long as even

those who have hope of eternal life, acknowledge no other agency, either good or evil, except in the line of the male only.

28. But this is altogether a mistaken idea: for the Deity consists of *two*, male and female, and from these twain proceed all goodness, purity and holiness; so also in the power of opposition, stand male and female, the authors of all impurity, unholiness, uncleanness and filthiness of every name and nature. And from these twain come the filthy fruits of lust and all evil. . . .

30. And thus ye may understand that in the beginning, before the earth was created, there existed the two opposite kingdoms of good and evil; the one headed by the Eternal Father and co-worker, Holy and Eternal Mother Wisdom; while the other was headed by the everlasting prince of darkness, and co-worker, the foul and *abominable mother of harlots*. And this I do declare to be the source and origin of lust and vile affections, which is the corrupt seed that engenders vile offspring. . . .

Part VI, Chapter II

6. I say, as the first man and woman, through the subtility of the serpent, failed to show forth the likeness of God upon earth, and as this was his decree, that He would be glorified by the children of men, how could this be accomplished, unless the same sex which first received the bane of destruction to man's innocence and simplicity, should be the first to receive the weapons whereby this base and fallen nature might be effectually slain in herself, and in her faithful children? . . .

Part VI, Chapter VII

9. Christ is the only mediator between God and the souls of the children of men, and the only soul that ever became the inhabitant of a mortal body, without falling under the powers of death in a greater or less degree. But he kept his rectitude, and never fell under the power of a sinful nature, that a door might thereby be opened for all the fallen race to enter in, and travel in the strait and narrow path which he hath marked out.

10. But because the second tabernacle or female vessel, which received the anointing power of Christ, in his second appearing, was not brought forth in the same miraculous manner as the first, many are left to doubt and disbelieve the divine origin of the work of God, in this day, on the ground that the first subject of it was suffered to see corruption, and was called from that fallen state to this important mission.

11. But this was to open the way, whereby Christ might become the Savior of the whole world; which could not be, unless the saving power descended into the depth of that state where all were suffered to see corruption. Thus they may be redeemed therefrom by this power's being made accessible to them.

12. Therefore, in the vision, the Lamb was seen upon Mount Zion, with his redeemed company, a hundred and forty four thousand. (See Rev. xiv.) This pointed out the second appearing of Christ; and these are both male and female. For in Christ was manifested the fullness of the Deity; and the female must find her spiritual order in the work of redemption, and be brought forth by the power which existed in the first begotten of the Eternal Father.

13. As Wisdom dwelt with the Eternal Father, ere she was brought forth and made a distinct Being; and as Eve dwelt with Adam, ere she was brought forth and made a distinct being; so in Christ the blessed Son, dwelt the fullness of the Deity, as respected the *Parentage of the new creation*, until the woman was brought forth, and made perfect through sufferings, by the power which was dispensed through the first-born Son, and therefore became the first, in the female line, who, through deep tribulation, washed her robes white in the blood of the Lamb.

14. Thus she became one with the Lamb, in the work of redemption. These things speak I, Wisdom, lest ye cavil at the propriety of the person of the Bride, being taken from a fallen state, and made ready for the Lamb, and bring this part of the vision to favor your objections; not considering that in Christ, "neither is the man without the woman, nor the woman without the man." (See I. Cor. xi. 11.)

15. But although ye may spurn at the idea of acknowledging this, in your present dark and benighted state; yet remember my words; If ye ever become the sons and daughters of true liberty, by the free Parentage, this will be your greatest joy.

16. Yea, if ye ever become the children of the free woman, this will be your greatest consolation; that God, through his everlasting wisdom and mercy, hath condescended to meet the fallen race, by extending the hand of a loving and tender Mother, who hath tasted of all their griefs, and partook of all their afflictions, and is easily touched with all their infirmities, and is able to apply the soothing hand of charity.

17. And thus, I Wisdom, the Mother of all mercy and tenderness to the fallen race, and in a special manner to the poor degraded females, who have drank deeply of the cup of sorrow, in their conception and bringing forth children; have for this cause ordered, that the Mother of the *new creation* should come in a vessel who had been immersed in this stream of sorrow, that she might be enabled, in her compassion, to reach beneath the depth of all human depravity; that souls, loaded with sin and defilement, might the more readily approach her, and look for consolation at her hand.

18. Her hand, I do proclaim to be ever loaded with balm of consolation, sufficient to heal the wounded soul, which hath been rent and torn with affliction, that is willing to come to the living fountain, and wash in the flowing stream. Yea, they may receive at her hand, and at the hands of her faithful successors, the healing balm of consolation, which shall wipe all tears from their eyes.

19. And who hath the faculty to soothe and caress a poor afflicted child

like a tender, loving mother? And who can stretch forth the hand and wipe the falling tears with that grace that can a tender and loving mother, that is touched with all the sorrows of her little one?

20. And thus hath God purposed to wipe away all sorrow, and comfort those who are willing to become his sons and daughters, by the new birth; by cleansing their souls from all the works of the fall, which came by the transgression of their first and natural parents. (Source: Paulina Bates, *The Divine Book of Holy and Eternal Wisdom, Revealing the Word of God: Out of Whose Mouth Goeth a Sharp Sword*, 2 vols., Canterbury, N.H.: 1849, vol. 1, pp. 502-509, 533-35.)

Oneida Community

The Oneida Community, founded by John Humphrey Noyes (1811-1886), scandalized nineteenth-century Americans by its practice of "free love." Noyes objected to conventional marriage on two grounds. He noted that, in the absence of reliable methods of birth control, marriage reduced woman to the state of a "propagative drudge." He also believed that marriage prevented the development of genuine Christian community because it formed people into exclusivistic pairs. In response Noyes pioneered a dependable method of birth control (male continence) and developed a system of complex marriage. Community members of Oneida were free to be sexually intimate with any member of the opposite gender who was willing, but no one was permitted to be monogamous.

As the following selection indicates, Noyes contended that he discovered the doctrines of male continence and complex marriage in the Bible. He credited Genesis 1-3 for teaching him that sexuality had more than one purpose; not only did it allow the human race to propagate, but it also provided a means by which to express love. Indeed, Noyes asserted, "amativeness" was the more important of the two functions of sexuality. Eve and Adam's love for one another was originally a reflection of the love of the Father for the Son within the Godhead. The Fall, however, disrupted the harmony natural to human relationships, and brought to women and men a set of interconnected miseries.

Noyes interpreted the divine decree in Genesis 3:16 ("I will greatly multiply thy sorrow and thy conception") as an indication that, in the absence of sin, Eve and Adam would have enjoyed sex but only rarely conceived children. Bearing many children endangered women's health, and providing financial support for large families increased men's labor. Such labor also isolated men from their wives, who tended the children while their husbands worked long hours outside the home. In short, for Noyes, the Fall produced the typical American marriage, where women feared sex because it led to pregnancy, and men suffered lonely, unremitting toil as the price for sexual intimacy with their wives.

If the Fall had disrupted the true love between men and women, the goal of the Oneida Community was to recreate it. Noyes believed that his community undid the curses of the Fall by relieving women of the burden of being propagative drudges and by offering men a living environment in which all persons worked together so that no one was condemned to earn bread through unremitting labor. At Oneida, men and women could express themselves sexually without shame or fear of conceiving children. And community labor was a cooperative endeavor, with men and women working side by side for a few short hours a day. As Noyes concluded, "First, we abolish sin; then shame; then the curse on woman of exhausting child-bearing; then the curse on man of exhausting labor; and so we arrive regularly at the tree of life, (as per Gen. 3)." His model of communal mutuality presumed an egalitarian reading of Genesis 1-3. (Source: John Humphrey Noyes, *History of American Socialisms*, Philadelphia: J. B. Lippincott & Co., 1870, pp. 623-36.)

History of American Socialisms (1870 CE)
JOHN HUMPHREY NOYES

Proposition 1.—The Bible predicts the coming of the Kingdom of Heaven on earth. Dan. 2:44. Isa. 25:6-9. . . .

Proposition 5.—In the Kingdom of Heaven, the institution of marriage, which assigns the exclusive possession of one woman to one man, does not exist. Matt. 22:23-30.

6.—In the Kingdom of Heaven the intimate union of life and interest, which in the world is limited to pairs, extends through the whole body of believers; i.e. complex marriage takes the place of simple. John 17:21. Christ prayed that all believers might be one, even as he and the Father are one. His unity with the Father is defined in the words, "All mine are thine, and all thine are mine." Ver. 10. This perfect community of interests, then, will be the condition of all, when his prayer is answered. The universal unity of the members of Christ, is described in the same terms that are used to describe marriage unity. Compare 1 Cor. 12:12-27, with Gen. 2:24. See also 1 Cor. 6:15-17, and Eph. 5:30-32. . . .

Proposition 9 . . . Now egotism is abolished by the gospel relation to Christ. The grand mystery of the gospel is vital union with Christ; the merging of self in his life; the extinguishment of the pronoun *I* at the spiritual center. Thus Paul says, "I live, yet not I, but Christ liveth in me." The grand distinction between the Christian and the unbeliever, between heaven and the world, is, that in one reigns the We-spirit, and in the other the I-spirit. From *I* comes *mine*, and from the I-spirit comes exclusive appropriation of money, women, etc. From *we* comes *ours*, and from the We-spirit comes universal community of interests.

10.—The abolishment of exclusiveness is involved in the love-relation required between all believers by the express injunction of Christ and the apostles, and by the whole tenor of the New Testament. "The new commandment is, that we love one another," and that, not by pairs, as in the world, but *en masse*. We are required to love one another fervently. The fashion of the world forbids a man and woman who are otherwise appropriated, to love one another fervently. But if they obey Christ they must do this; and whoever would allow them to do this, and yet would forbid them (on any other ground than that of present expedience), to express their unity, would "strain at a gnat and swallow a camel;" for unity of hearts is as much more important than any external expression of it, as a camel is larger than a gnat.

11.—The abolishment of social restrictions is involved in the anti-legality of the gospel. It is incompatible with the state of perfected freedom toward which Paul's gospel of "grace without law" leads, that man should be allowed and required to love in all directions, and yet be forbidden to express love except in one direction. In fact Paul says, with direct reference to sexual intercourse—"All things are lawful for me, but all things are not expedient; all things are lawful for me, but I will not be brought under the power of any;" (1 Cor. 6:12;) thus placing the restrictions which were necessary in the transition period on the basis, not of law, but of expediency and the demands of spiritual freedom, and leaving it fairly to be inferred that in the final state, when hostile surroundings and powers of bondage cease, all restrictions also will cease.

12.—The abolishment of the marriage system is involved in Paul's doctrine of the end of ordinances. Marriage is one of the "ordinances of the worldly sanctuary." This is proved by the fact that it has no place in the resurrection. Paul expressly limits it to life in the flesh. Rom. 7:2, 3. The assumption, therefore, that believers are dead to the world by the death of Christ (which authorized the abolishment of Jewish ordinances), legitimately makes an end of marriage. Col. 2:20. . . .

14.—The law of marriage "worketh wrath." 1. It provokes to secret adultery, actual or of the heart. 2. It ties together unmatched natures. 3. It sunders matched natures. 4. It gives to sexual appetite only a scanty and monotonous allowance, and so produces the natural vices of poverty, contraction of taste and stinginess or jealousy. 5. It makes no provision for the sexual appetite at the very time when that appetite is the strongest. By the custom of the world, marriage, in the average of cases, takes place at about the age of twenty-four; whereas puberty commences at the age of fourteen. For ten years, therefore, and that in the very flush of life, the sexual appetite is starved. This law of society bears hardest on females, because they have less opportunity of choosing their time of marriage than men. This discrepancy between the marriage system and nature, is one of the principal sources of the peculiar diseases of women, of prostitution, masturbation, and licentiousness in general. . . .

17.—The restoration of true relations between the sexes is a matter second in importance only to the reconciliation of man to God. The distinction of male and female is that which makes man the image of God, i.e. the image of the Father and Son. Gen. 1:27. The relation of male and female was the first social relation. Gen. 2:22. It is therefore the root of all other social relations. The derangement of this relation was the first result of the original breach with God. Gen. 3:7; comp. 2:25. Adam and Eve were, at the beginning, in open, fearless, spiritual fellowship, first with God, and secondly, with each other. Their transgression produced two corresponding alienations, viz., first, an alienation from God, indicated by their fear of meeting him and their hiding themselves among the trees of the garden; and secondly, an alienation from each other, indicated by their shame at their nakedness and their hiding themselves from each other by clothing. These were the two great manifestations of original sin—the only manifestations presented to notice in the record of the apostacy. The first thing then to be done, in an attempt to redeem man and reorganize society, is to bring about reconciliation with God; and the second thing is to bring about a true union of the sexes. In other words, religion is the first subject of interest, and sexual morality the second, in the great enterprise of establishing the Kingdom of Heaven on earth. . . .

20.—Dividing the sexual relation into two branches, the amative and propagative, the amative or love-relation is first in importance, as it is in the order of nature. God made woman because "he saw it was not good for man to be alone;" (Gen. 2:18); i.e., for social, not primarily for propagative, purposes. Eve was called Adam's "help-meet." In the whole of the specific account of the creation of woman, she is regarded as his companion, and her maternal office is not brought into view. Gen. 2:18-25. Amativeness was necessarily the first social affection developed in the garden of Eden. The second commandment of the eternal law of love, "Thou shalt love thy neighbor as thyself," had amativeness for its first channel; for Eve was at first Adam's only neighbor. Propagation and the affections connected with it, did not commence their operation during the period of innocence. After the fall God said to the woman, "I will greatly multiply thy sorrow and thy conception;" from which it is to be inferred that in the original state, conception would have been comparatively infrequent.

21.—The amative part of the sexual relation, separate from the propagative, is eminently favorable to life. It is not a source of life (as some would make it), but it is the first and best distributive of life. Adam and Eve, in their original state, derived their life from God. Gen. 2:7. As God is a dual being, the Father and the Son, and man was made in his image, a dual life passed from God to man. Adam was the channel specially of the life of the Father, and Eve of the life of the Son. Amativeness was the natural agency of the distribution and mutual action of these two forms of life. In this primitive position of the sexes (which is their normal position in Christ), each reflects upon the other the love of God; each excites and develops the divine action in the other.

22.—The propagative part of the sexual relation is in its nature the expensive department. 1. While amativeness keeps the capital stock of life circulating between two, propagation introduces a third partner. 2. The propagative act is a drain on the life of man, and when habitual, produces disease. 3. The infirmities and vital expenses of woman during the long period of pregnancy, waste her constitution. 4. The awful agonies of child-birth heavily tax the life of woman. 5. The cares of the nursing period bear heavily on woman. 6. The cares of both parents, through the period of the childhood of their offspring, are many and burdensome. 7. The labor of man is greatly increased by the necessity of providing for children. A portion of these expenses would undoubtedly have been curtailed, if human nature had remained in its original integrity, and will be, when it is restored. But it is still self-evident that the birth of children, viewed either as a vital or a mechanical operation, is in its nature expensive; and the fact that multiplied conception was imposed as a curse, indicates that it was so regarded by the Creator.

Proposition 23.—The amative and propagative functions are distinct from each other, and may be separated practically. They are confounded in the world, both in the theories of physiologists and in universal practice. The amative function is regarded merely as a bait to the propagative, and is merged in it. But if amativeness is, as we have seen, the first and noblest of the social affections, and if the propagative part of the sexual relation was originally secondary, and became paramount by the subversion of order in the fall, we are bound to raise the amative office of the sexual organs into a distinct and paramount function. . . .

27.—In vital society labor will become attractive. Loving companionship in labor, and especially the mingling of the sexes, makes labor attractive. The present division of labor between the sexes separates them entirely. The woman keeps house, and the man labors abroad. Instead of this, in vital society men and women will mingle in both of their peculiar departments of work. It will be economically as well as spiritually profitable, to marry them in-doors and out, by day as well as by night. When the partition between the sexes is taken away, and man ceases to make woman a propagative drudge, when love takes the place of shame, and fashion follows nature in dress and business, men and women will be able to mingle in all their employments, as boys and girls mingle in their sports; and then labor will be attractive.

28.—We can now see our way to victory over death. Reconciliation with God opens the way for the reconciliation of the sexes. Reconciliation of the sexes emancipates woman, and opens the way for vital society. Vital society increases strength, diminishes work, and makes labor attractive, thus removing the antecedents of death. First we abolish sin; then shame; then the curse on woman of exhausting child-bearing; then the curse on man of exhausting labor; and so we arrive regularly at the tree of life. (Source: John Humphrey Noyes, *History of American Socialisms*, Philadelphia: J. B. Lippincott & Co., 1870, pp. 623-36.)

Christian Science

The founder of Christian Science, Mary Baker Eddy (1821-1910) issued the first edition of *Science and Health with Key to the Scriptures* in 1875. Her treatment of Genesis 1-3 was radical. She argued that the first creation account depicted an all-powerful God working to achieve a spiritual creation. Eddy asserted that Genesis 1:27—which described humanity, male and female, as being created in the divine image—was an indication that God was both Mother and Father. She suggested that God's highest quality—Love—was more feminine than male. Eddy regarded the second creation account, on the other hand, as an allegory describing the effects of error. She understood Adam to be a symbol of error, or the belief in the material rather than the spiritual.

Favoring Genesis 1 over Genesis 2 was a typical strategy for those inclined toward an egalitarian reading of the story of creation. But no one ever insisted upon a more radical dichotomy between the two accounts than did Eddy. Genesis 1, she insisted, was incompatible with Genesis 2; readers must choose between them. Eddy urged them to choose Truth—and Genesis 1, where humanity was endowed with God's perfection, rather than Genesis 2, where humanity was mutable, mortal, and estranged from the divine. (Source: Mary Baker Eddy, *Science and Health with Key to the Scriptures*, Boston: Trustees under the Will of Mary Baker Eddy, n.d., pp. 516, 521, 522, 527-30.)

Science and Health with Key to the Scriptures (c. 1875 CE)
MARY BAKER EDDY

> *Genesis* i. 12. And the earth brought forth grass, and herb yielding seed after his kind, and the tree yielding fruit, whose seed was in itself, after his kind: and God saw that it was good.

God determines the gender of His own ideas. Gender is mental, not material. The seed within itself is the pure thought emanating from divine Mind. The feminine gender is not yet expressed in the text. *Gender* means simply *kind* or *sort*, and does not necessarily refer either to masculinity or femininity. The word is not confined to sexuality, and grammars always recognize a neuter gender, neither male nor female. The Mind or intelligence of production names the female gender last in the ascending order of creation. The intelligent individual idea, be it male or female, rising from the lesser to the greater, unfolds the infinitude of Love. . . . Man and woman as coexistent and eternal with God forever reflect, in glorified quality, the infinite Father-Mother God.

> *Genesis* i. 27. So God created man in His own image, in the image of God created He him; male and female created He them.

To emphasize this momentous thought, it is repeated that God made man in His own image, to reflect the divine Spirit. It follows that *man* is a generic term. Masculine, feminine, and neuter genders are human concepts. In one of the ancient languages the word for *man* is used also as the synonym of *mind*. This definition has been weakened by anthropomorphism, or a humanization of Deity. The word *anthropomorphic*, in such a phrase as "an anthropomorphic God," is derived from two Greek words, signifying *man* and *form*, and may be defined as a mortally mental attempt to reduce Deity to corporeality. The life-giving quality of Mind is Spirit, not matter. The ideal man corresponds to creation, to intelligence, and to Truth. The ideal woman corresponds to Life and to Love. In divine Science, we have not as much authority for considering God masculine, as we have for considering Him feminine, for Love imparts the clearest idea of Deity. . . .

Here the inspired record closes its narrative of being that is without beginning or end. All that is made is the work of God, and all is good. We leave this brief, glorious history of spiritual creation (as stated in the first chapter of Genesis) in the hands of God, not of man, in the keeping of Spirit, not matter,—joyfully acknowledging now and forever God's supremacy, omnipotence, and omnipresence. . . .

The reader will naturally ask if there is nothing more about creation in the book of Genesis. Indeed there is, but the continued account is mortal and material.

> *Genesis* ii. 6. But there went up a mist from the earth, and watered the whole face of the ground.

The Science and truth of the divine creation have been presented in the verses already considered, and now the opposite error, a material view of creation, is to be set forth. The second chapter of Genesis contains a statement of this material view of God and the universe, a statement which is the exact opposite of scientific truth as before recorded. The history of error or matter, if veritable, would set aside the omnipotence of Spirit; but it is the false history in contradistinction to the true.

The Science of the first record proves the falsity of the second. If one is true, the other is false, for they are antagonistic. The first record assigns all might and government to God, and endows man out of God's perfection and power. The second record chronicles man as mutable and mortal,—as having broken away from Deity and as revolving in an orbit of his own. Existence, separate from divinity, Science explains as impossible. . . .

> *Genesis* ii. 19. And out of the ground the Lord God [Jehovah] formed every beast of the field, and every fowl of the air; and brought them unto Adam to see what he would call them: and whatsoever Adam called every living creature, that was the name thereof.

Here the lie represents God as repeating creation, but doing so materially, not spiritually, and asking a prospective sinner to help Him. Is the Supreme being retrograding, and is man giving up his dignity? Was it requisite for the formation of man that dust should become sentient, when all being is the reflection of the eternal Mind, and the record declares that God has already created man, both male and female? That Adam gave the name and nature of animals, is solely mythological and material. It cannot be true that man was ordered to create man anew in partnership with God; this supposition was a dream, a myth.

> *Genesis* ii. 21, 22. And the Lord God [Jehovah, Yawah] caused a deep sleep to fall upon Adam, and he slept: and He took one of his ribs, and closed up the flesh instead thereof; and the rib, which the Lord God [Jehovah] had taken from man, made He a woman, and brought her unto the man.

Here falsity, error, credits Truth, God, with inducing a sleep or hypnotic state in Adam in order to perform a surgical operation on him and thereby create woman. This is the first record of magnetism. Beginning creation with darkness instead of light,—materially rather than spiritually,—error now simulates the work of Truth, mocking Love and declaring what great things error has done. Beholding the creations of his own dream and calling them real and God-given, Adam—*alias* error—gives them names. Afterwards he is supposed to become the basis of the creation of woman and of his own kind, calling them *mankind*,—that is, a kind of man.

But according to this narrative, surgery was first performed mentally and without instruments; and this may be a useful hint to the medical faculty. Later in human history, when the forbidden fruit was bringing forth fruit of its own kind, there came a suggestion of change in the *modus operandi*,—that man should be born of woman, not woman again taken from man. It came about, also, that instruments were needed to assist the birth of mortals. The first system of suggestive obstetrics has changed. Another change will come as to the nature and origin of man, and this revelation will destroy the *dream* of existence, reinstate reality, usher in Science and the glorious fact of creation, that both man and woman proceed from God and are His eternal children, belonging to no lesser parent. . . .

No one can reasonably doubt that the purpose of this allegory—this second account in Genesis—is to depict the falsity of error and the effects of error. Subsequent Bible revelation is coordinate with the Science of creation recorded in the first chapter of Genesis. Inspired writers interpret the Word spiritually, while the ordinary historian interprets it literally.

CHAPTER EIGHT

Twentieth-Century Readings: The Debates Continue

INTRODUCTION

Debates about the significance of Adam and Eve persist in our own day, as commentators continue to find in the story enduring models for social ordering. In response to modern reconsiderations of traditional roles for women, advocates of the hierarchical model have argued vigorously for the necessity of subordinating women to men, as prescribed by their readings of Genesis 1-3 and the Qur'an. In no previous century has concern for establishing men as the "head" of women been more pronounced.

And never before has the egalitarian reading of Eve and Adam's story received such determined or sophisticated analysis. The emergence of feminist scholarship has sparked unparalleled interest in "depatriarchalizing" scriptural texts for a generation of readers to whom the very notion of gender hierarchy is abhorrent.[1]

Further, many interpreters have called for a rethinking of the Genesis story that reconsiders not only the relationship between men and women, but also the relationship between human persons and the natural world. Both environmentalists and ecofeminists have found in Genesis 1-3 the roots of Western tendencies to abuse the environment, and vegetarians have argued that "the fused oppression of women and animals . . . can be traced to the story of the Fall in Genesis."[2]

Clearly Genesis 1-3 and its counterparts in the Qur'an remain significant—and much disputed—texts. In the pages ahead, we will examine Jewish, Christian, and Muslim authors from both the hierarchalist and the egalitarian positions. We must confess that this chapter created great difficulties for us as editors; we found so many intriguing twentieth-century treatments of Eve and Adam's story that we can offer here only a small sampling.

Hierarchical Interpretations

Protestants have been particularly colorful in devising defenses for the hierarchical model of interpretation. At the turn of the century, Protestants who believed the Bible subordinated women to men found comfort in a movement dubbed "muscular Christianity." Muscular Christianity sought to convince men, in the face of cultural transformations that assaulted traditional gender roles, that Christianity was, above all else, a religion that put men first. As one proponent explained, nothing "emphasizes and exalts manliness, as does Christianity. The purpose, the incarnate idea of Christianity is to make magnificent manhood; to make men like Christ, the manliest of all men."[3]

Many liberal Protestants were attracted to a masculinized Christianity, producing such memorable titles as Harry Emerson Fosdick's *The Manhood of the Master*[4] and Bruce Barton's *The Man Nobody Knows*. The latter depicted Jesus as a well-muscled outdoorsman who was not only "the most popular dinner guest in Jerusalem" but also a magnetic salesman who became "the founder of modern business."[5]

Not to be outdone, fundamentalists composed such books as John R. Rice's *Bobbed Hair, Bossy Wives, and Women Preachers*—a trio that Rice blamed for most of the ills of modern culture. As he put it, "to be a good Christian, it is clear that a citizen must be subject to his rulers, a child subject to his parents, a servant subject to his masters, a Christian subject to his pastor. God gives authority to some over others. . . . Rebellion against authority is the sin of bobbed hair, bossy wives, and women preachers."[6] To emphasize the point, Rice's daughter Elizabeth Rice Handford published *Me? Obey Him?*, arguing that God placed Eve below Adam in the divine "chain of command," and admonishing every wife "to obey her husband as if he were God Himself," for "she can be as certain of God's will when her husband speaks, as if God had spoken audibly from Heaven!"[7]

More recently, liberal Protestants have tended to find egalitarian readings of Genesis 1-3 more congenial to their democratic sensibilities, but the question of just how God intended men and women to relate to one another has stimulated considerable controversy among theologically conservative Protestants. In the past twenty years, as conservatives have debated the ordination of women, they have devoted considerable attention to Genesis 1-3. Writers such as Elisabeth Elliot have argued that God created women to be subordinate to men, noting that "every creature of God has his appointed place, from cherubim, seraphim, archangels, and angels down to the lowliest beast."[8] Others have echoed that sentiment, insisting, with Duane Litfin, "That the universe should be ordered around a series of over/under hierarchical relationships is His [God's] idea, a part of His original design. Far from being extraneous to the Word of God, a kind of excess baggage that can be jettisoned while retaining the essential truth of the Scriptures, these ideas are the essential truths of the Scriptures. To reject them is to reject the Bible."[9]

Hierarchical interpretations of Genesis 1-3 have had far-reaching ramifications in the Southern Baptist Convention, where conservatives have successfully waged a campaign to wrest control of the denomination from more moderate Baptists.[10] The conservatives made a hierarchical reading of Genesis 1-3 the foundation of their "battle for the Bible." In 1984, they persuaded the Convention to adopt a nonbinding resolution claiming that the apostle Paul "excludes women from pastoral leadership to preserve a submission God requires because man was first in creation and the woman was first in the Edenic fall."[11] In 1987, when a Southern Baptist church in Memphis called Nancy Hastings Sehested as its pastor, the local Southern Baptist Association disfellowshipped the congregation for setting a woman in a position of spiritual authority over men.

That action set off debate throughout the denomination. In 1988, the Convention passed a resolution designed to protect the authority of male pastors. Citing Hebrews 13:17 ("Obey your leaders and submit to them, for they are keeping watch over your souls and will give an account," NRSV), the Convention urged Southern Baptists to obey their pastors and reminded them that 1 Timothy 2:12 forbade women to exercise authority over men. Hastings Sehested responded to the conservatives' campaign against women clergy by complaining that her opponents had acted "like a batterer treats a battered wife—they say they love you, but their actions are violent and abusive."[12]

In the readings selected for this chapter, we offer two contemporary examples of Christians arguing that God intends for women to be subordinate to men. First, "The Danvers Statement" is a position paper of the Council on Biblical Manhood and Womanhood. The Council is a parachurch or nondenominational organization; its roster lists pastors, professors, and homemakers as members. Several members drafted the Statement at a 1987 meeting in Danvers, Massachusetts. Second, we have excerpted an essay entitled "The Head of the Woman is the Man," written by Susan T. Foh, a conservative Christian scholar. In this text, Foh argues that God assigned women subordinate roles within marriage and the church, even though God created women and men as essentially equal. In support of her position, she points to other functional subordinations including those of employee to employer and of Christ to God.[13] Practical applications of her position include prohibiting women from exercising several leadership roles in the church, including ordination to pastoral office.

In Judaism, hierarchical readings of Eve's story also continued in the twentieth century. While the Reform movement had previously loosened the traditional ties between women's religious lives and Eve's story, the backlash from American Orthodox and Conservative Jews in the twentieth century revived those connections.[14] Books like Rabbi Alfred J. Kolatch's work *The Jewish Book of Why* (1981) explain the rationale behind Jewish customs like women's Sabbath candle lighting, women's abstinence from the *Havdala* wine, and women's headcovering.[15] In each case, Kolatch reminds his contemporary readers of the traditional associations between Eve's culpability and Jewish women's ritual lives:

> Why do some women wear a *shaytl*?
>
> In biblical and talmudic times women covered their heads with scarves or veils as a sign of chastity and modesty. To expose a woman's hair was considered a humiliation (Isaiah 3:17 and *Berachot* 24a). Some talmudic scholars regarded the wearing of a headcovering as an expression of guilt for the sin of Eve (Genesis 17:8).
>
> Toward the end of the eighteenth century, despite opposition by some Orthodox authorities, the *shaytl* (Yiddish for "wig") was introduced as a headcovering.
>
> Today, only strictly Orthodox married women wear a headcovering at all times, and the reason generally given is so that they should not appear attractive to men. In the synagogue, although it is not mandatory, it has become the practice for women to cover their heads, particularly in Orthodox and Conservative congregations. Among the Reform it is optional.
>
> . . .
>
> Why are women required to light the Sabbath candles?
>
> The primary but not exclusive obligation for lighting Sabbath candles belongs to women. The traditional explanation is found in the Talmud (*Shabbat* 31b), where Rashi comments that since it was woman who was the cause of man's downfall (Eve when tempted by the snake), causing the light of the world to be dimmed, it is woman's obligation to light the candles and bring back light.
>
> . . .
>
> Why are males the only ones who drink the *Havdala* wine?
>
> . . . Another explanation is that Adam's wife caused his downfall when she ate of the Tree of Knowledge. In Jewish folklore, the fruit of that "tree" was grapes. Eve squeezed the grapes to make wine, and because of her sin, the story goes, women do not drink the *Havdala* wine.[16]

Thus the legacy of first millennium midrashic and halakhic interpretations of Eve is passed down to readers today!

We have included two Jewish readings in the "hierarchical" section of this chapter. The first is a section from a 1945 Jewish prayer book reprinted in 1985 and in current use in some U.S. synagogues. The selection is titled "Marriage and the Position of Women in Judaism" and precedes the prayer book's marriage liturgy. It describes marriage's twofold purpose as "posterity" and "companionship" and appeals to Genesis 1-2 to argue that marriage is "part of the scheme of all Creation, intended for all humanity." Historically, a childless Jewish marriage was one "deemed to have failed in one of its main purposes." Companionship in marriage, however, is also important. A woman is man's "helpmate" and he depends on her for physical, social, and spiritual

completion. Accordingly, only "through married life does human personality reach its highest fulfillment." While in the "higher sphere of the soul's
life," woman is man's "ethical and spiritual superior," in the physical, woman
is "weaker" than man (though the text concedes that women and men share
dominion over the creation). The passage insists, however, that domesticity
is woman's highest calling, for "the hallowing of the Jewish homes" is her
work.[17] The text stresses the sacredness of the male and female union and bans
extramarital affairs, polygamy, and divorce. Absent from the discussion is any
mention of same-sex relationships. Not surprisingly, however, the emphasis on
heterosexual marriage as the Jewish norm led others to appeal to Genesis 1-2
in their critique of gay and lesbian relationships.

In his essay "Homosexuality and the Order of Creation," Jewish scholar
Samuel H. Dresner has articulated this position as clearly as anyone.[18] Dresner
argues that in creating humanity as male and female (Genesis 1:27), God proclaimed heterosexuality to be God's design for "the order of creation." By
commanding humanity to "be fruitful and multiply" (1:28), God also indicated, according to Dresner, that "propagation and companionship are the
purposes of heterosexuality."[19] That God paired Adam with Eve was a sign,
Dresner argues, that "human society is meant to be composed of families, of
monogamous families."[20] Thus, Dresner contends, humanity was by nature
heterosexual. Man and woman were meant to form couples in order to find
fulfillment and to produce children. Any other sexual orientation was abnormal "in the same way that the blind and the deaf are abnormal," as well as
destructive to human morality and culture.[21] As Dresner concludes, "Once the
argument from the order of creation and natural law is abandoned and heterosexuality in the marital bond as a norm is dismissed, then how can adultery,
pedophilia, or bestiality be rejected?"[22]

Concerns for the order God established at the time of creation also permeate the selection we have made from the writings by a Muslim author,
Sayyid Abu al-A'la Mawdudi. These excerpts from Mawdudi's Urdu translation and commentary on the Qur'an, titled in English: *Towards Understanding
the Qur'an*, endorse gender hierarchy and other social hierarchies as conform-
ing to God's will.[23]

Through his work as a journalist and social activist in South Asia,
Mawdudi (d. 1979) played a prominent role in the Islamic revivalist movement. As a "revival" movement, this initiative urges a return to the piety and
practices of "authentic" Islam even as it calls for rejecting the ways in which
Western culture has infiltrated and contaminated Islam. With roots in the
nineteenth century, Islamic revivalism spread into the twentieth century, acquiring much attention through the "Islamic revolution" carried out in Iran
in 1978-79.

Debates about women's place and responsibilities play no small part in revivalist discussions about what constitutes a corruption of Islam. Many revivalists correlate the return to authentic Islam with the repudiation of the ways
that women act and dress in the West. These revivalists usually urge the se-

clusion of women in the home, using Qur'anic passages such as God's description of "toil" in Q.20:117 as injunctions that only men should work in public spheres.[24] They also often encourage women to "veil" their hair and/or their faces. For some revivalists, the revitalization of Islam entails a return to polygyny. For others, including the Islamic Republic of Iran, it also involves reviving the practice of "mut'a" or temporary marriage in which a man cohabits with a woman for a contractually specified length of time in exchange for an agreed upon sum of money.[25]

Mawdudi spent the early years of his adult life as a journalist in India. In 1941 he founded the "Jama'at-i Islami," an organization dedicated to constructing society in accord with Islam, particularly by shaping society to reflect the teachings of the Qur'an and the *hadith*. In 1947 he migrated to Pakistan. A prolific writer, his works include *Purdah and the Status of Women in Islam*.[26] Through his writings he influenced thinkers and activists from Indonesia to Morocco. Reactions have been mixed. As Bruce Lawrence notes, "To some he is the preeminent Muslim reformer of South Asia, to others he is [a] fundamentalist with cultural blinders, to still others he is a preacher gone astray, hopelessly compromised in his ideals by the realities of postindependence Pakistani politics."[27]

Our selection contains portions of Mawdudi's commentary on surah 2 and surah 4. At times, such as in his comments on how God created woman, Mawdudi noted the Qur'an's silence on a particular topic and instructed the reader to follow the Qur'an's example and be similarly silent on the topic. At other times he did not hesitate to spell out meanings that God intends through the Qur'an. Thus, for example, he maintained that although menstruation is a "ritual impurity and sickness," men need not refrain from sitting with menstruating women.[28] In several discussions, he appealed to Adam and Eve or God's design for creation as the basis for social practice, including his arguments against birth control and celibacy.[29] The opening passage in our selection shows Mawdudi's endorsement of God-willed social hierarchies even as it reflects his view that governments often violate God's own ordering, necessitating that "employees" imprison the "magistrate."[30]

In his comments on surah 4, Mawdudi explicitly addressed the matter of gender hierarchies.[31] Here he both described men as the "head" of the family and portrayed what their headship involves. Like many hierarchalists in the twentieth century, he is concerned to promote a type of gender equality, contending that men do not have "superior dignity."[32] Yet this equality is not functional. According to Mawdudi, women and men have separate spheres of responsibility. Indeed, in his commentary he attributed "diverting [women] to perform the functions for which men were created" to the promptings of Satan.[33] Further, even though he contended that wives have the responsibility to disobey their husbands in some instances, he also explicates what—in his understanding—the Qur'an and the Prophet allow husbands to do when wives remain obstinate.[34]

Egalitarian Interpretations

The rise of feminism has changed the field of religious studies. Never before have religions been subject to such a sustained gender critique, for never before have interpreters so consistently noted the male bias of sacred texts as well as of the dominant traditions of interpreting those texts. Feminist critiques, however, have not always resulted in depatriarchalizing sacred texts. Many feminists have concluded that passages like Genesis 1-3 are by their nature so permeated by sexism that they can be interpreted in no liberating way. Other feminists have disagreed, arguing that new exegesis, done without a patriarchal bias, can free sacred texts to speak in ways that affirm the full equality of all persons. The readings included in this section represent such reforming efforts. They address two issues: how to interpret the story of Eve and Adam in ways that will affirm the value of women, and how to rethink the ways that religions use that story in order to subordinate women to men.

Our egalitarian selections, through their very number, indicate the dramatic rise of this reading of Eve and Adam's story during the twentieth century. No other chapter in the anthology contains so many egalitarian interpretations. Another unique feature of these selections is the range of genre. This section opens with a poem written by Sun Ai Lee Park, an ordained minister of the Christian Church (Disciples of Christ) who lives in Korea. The section closes with excerpts from a speech by Nancy Datan, a Jewish woman who taught at the University of Wisconsin-Green Bay. Between this opening and closing lie selections that involve myth and autobiography, exegesis and social commentary.

Two pivotal reworkings of traditional readings of Genesis 1-3 occurred in the early 1970s. Invited in 1972 to give a paper to the faculty of Andover Newton Theological Seminary, Phyllis Trible electrified biblical and theological scholars by offering an alternative interpretation to traditional hierarchical readings of Genesis 2-3. Trible's exegesis was not entirely novel; aspects of it echoed interpretations by Sarah Grimké as well as previous rabbinical interpretations.[35] Yet few people who heard her paper or read subsequent published versions of it had ever imagined that such an egalitarian reading of the second creation account was possible. Trible turned centuries of interpretation upside down, arguing that points traditionally understood to indicate man's priority to woman were actually indications of woman's equality—perhaps even superiority—to man.

Trible found, for example, that Genesis's depiction of God creating Eve out of Adam's side at worst established a parallelism between Adam and Eve, since both owed their being to God, who created each out of raw materials. That God created Eve last, after establishing all other things, suggested to Trible not that Eve was the second sex, but that she was the crowning glory of creation. God had saved the best for last. Similarly, Trible found that God's description of Eve as Adam's "helper" (*ezer*) was not, as traditionally assumed, a sign of her inferiority to Adam, but rather proof of her equality with him. The text described animals as "helpers" who were inferior to humanity, God as a "helper" who was superior to humanity, and Eve as a "helper" who was Adam's counterpart.

Trible proceeded to dispute numerous aspects of the text that interpreters had typically understood as subordinating Eve to Adam, arguing among other things that God did not create man before woman, but rather created an androgynous human creature (*ha-'adam*) that became male only when God separated out that which was female to create Eve. Trible ended with the argument that, contrary to the history of interpretation, Genesis 3:16 did not license male superiority but condemned it. Her conclusion could hardly have been clearer:

> Visiting the Garden of Eden in the days of the Women's Movement, we need no longer accept the traditional exegesis of Genesis 2-3. Rather than legitimating the patriarchal culture from which it comes, the myth places the culture under judgment. And thus it functions to liberate, not to enslave. This function we can recover and appropriate.[36]

Not surprisingly, Trible's paper provoked a flurry of reactions. Since then, no responsible biblical scholar, whether explicating an egalitarian or a hierarchical interpretation of the story of Adam and Eve, has done so without an awareness of Trible's exegesis. We are pleased, in this volume, to offer not only the 1973 article that Trible derived from her original paper, but also an entirely new article in which Trible considers the question of how her mind has changed (or stayed the same) since beginning her study of the opening chapters of Genesis. Here she offers a new and more detailed analysis of *ha-'adam*, while proclaiming that her overall conclusions have changed "not a jot, not a tittle."

Another momentous consideration of the story of Adam and Eve also emerged in 1972, from a Jewish scholar named Judith Plaskow.[37] Plaskow wrote at a time when Jewish women were making tremendous strides toward equal rights. In 1971, for example, the *Ezrat Nashim*[38] was founded and one year later distributed a statement to the Rabbinical Assembly Convention calling for the "end to the second-class status of women" in the Conservative movement.[39] In 1972, Sally Priesand became the first female to be ordained a rabbi by a theological faculty (Hebrew Union College-Jewish Institute of Religion). Looking back on that moment, Priesand remarked:

> When I accepted ordination on June 3, 1972, I affirmed my belief in Judaism and publicly committed myself to the survival of Jewish tradition. I did so knowing that Judaism had traditionally discriminated against women; that it had not always been sensitive to the problems of total equality. I know that there has been a tremendous flexibility in our tradition—it enabled our survival. Therefore, I chose to work for change through constructive criticism. The principles and ideals for which our ancestors have lived and died are much too important to be cast aside. Instead we must accept the responsibili-

ties of the covenant upon ourselves, learn as much as possible of our heritage, and make the necessary changes which will grant women total equality within the Jewish community.[40]

For support of her egalitarian model, Priesand suggested turning to Lilith not Eve:

For thousands of years, women have been taught that it is dangerous to be like Lilith. Independence, aggression, self-assertion, and strength are not admirable qualities for women to possess. It is better to be submissive like Eve. As a result, women have suppressed their own desires and obeyed the wishes of their husbands. While men have been leaders, rabbis, scholars, and authorities, women have for the most part been unassuming and modest, living vicariously through the men in their lives. Even today, most girls are taught to be wives and mothers. Isn't it about time that we present Lilith as an acceptable role model, that we encourage our daughters to be bold and daring?[41]

It was three years before Priesand made these comments on Lilith that Plaskow wrote her classic piece, "The Coming of Lilith" (1972).

Plaskow had attempted, along with other women on retreat at Grailville, to produce a communal theology that would express the participants' apprehension of the women's movement as a religious experience. The result was "The Coming of Lilith," published in Rosemary Radford Ruether's 1974 *Religion and Sexism*.[42] Plaskow then added a reflective essay to the original piece. This combination, first published in Church Women United literature and later as an article in a book Plaskow edited with Carol P. Christ (*Womanspirit Rising*), proved formative for generations of students drawn to Women's Studies.[43]

In her article, Plaskow differentiated between the "yes, but" form of traditional theology, which she described as "inherently nondialogical and out of touch with its own basis in experience," and the "yeah, yeah experience" that she had discovered in the women's movement. "Yeah, yeah," she argued, was "the process through which we come to be sisters." It meant committing one's self "to speak and to really hear" in dialogue with others who were likewise involved in the consciousness-raising process. In an attempt to produce constructive theology from this basis, Plaskow wrote a myth describing the experience of women joining together to do theology.

The myth retold the story of Lilith, casting her as a woman so aware of her own value and worth that she refused to become Adam's servant. Lilith preferred banishment from the garden to subordinating herself to Adam; and Adam convinced God to create a more docile partner for him in Eve. Adam then devoted himself to building walls around the garden so Lilith could not meet and corrupt Eve. As males, God and Adam were naturally closer to one another than were God and the women, but eventually God began to worry that Adam devoted too much energy to excluding Lilith from human society. In the end, all of Adam's labor was for naught. Eve climbed the wall Adam had built, determined to exceed the limited life he had prescribed for her. Eve and Lilith met one another and grew close. They then returned to the garden, bursting with plans to rebuild it, as God and Adam, simultaneously expectant and fearful, waited to see what would become of them.

For Plaskow, the moral of the myth was obvious: "The real heroine of our story is sisterhood, and sisterhood is powerful."[44] Many of her readers agreed, finding in "The Coming of Lilith" a spiritual awareness and vitality they had never previously experienced. Plaskow and Christ urged their students to use "The Coming of Lilith" as a model for writing their own myths and rituals to express the religious power of the women's movement. They found the results impressive, noting that students "have loved these assignments and have displayed amazing creativity in doing them."[45] In this volume, we have reprinted the "Coming of Lilith" and have also invited Judith Plaskow to reflect upon the significance of the piece. Her retrospective adds yet another chapter to the ongoing saga of Lilith, the woman who refused to subordinate herself to men, or to allow God to identify too closely with males.

In addition to rethinking the original Genesis account, scholars interested in more egalitarian readings of the text have also turned their attention to the ways that other sacred texts have interpreted Genesis 1-3. New Testament scholars such as Jouette Bassler, whose article on 1 Timothy appears here, have critiqued the exegesis of New Testament authors who appealed to Genesis 1-3 to justify the subordination of women to men. African American women in particular have been anxious to speak to their own churches' interpretations of the New Testament household codes.

The household codes, which advised wives to obey their husbands and slaves to obey their masters, have played a significant role not only as warrants for gender hierarchies but also for racial and economic hierarchies. As noted in chapter 7, such passages were favorite sermon texts for EuroAmerican ministers who preached to African American slaves in the nineteenth century.

Advocates of the egalitarian model have noted the similarities between proslavery exegesis and exegesis defending the subordination of women.[46] Like the proslavery interpreters of the nineteenth century, contemporary hierarchalists insist that the proper model for human society can be found in the household codes and in Genesis 1-3. That model, in this reading, depicts a great chain of being or a divine chain of command. Most importantly, hierarchalists assert that nothing about redemption in Christ can abrogate that hierarchical order. Whether fallen in sin or saved in Christ, men and women belong in the social stations that God designed for them at the beginning, with men as women's head. Like the defenders of slavery, contemporary hierarchalists typically designate Galatians 3:28 as a text that refers to spiritual equality only. Galatians 3:28 should not, they argue, be mistaken as a description of human society.

Such argumentation makes it difficult for contemporary hierarchalists to explain why, given their reliance upon the chain of command dictated in the household codes, they do not regard slavery as a divinely ordained condition of society. A few have conceded that slavery does seem consistent with the divine plan. Susan Foh, for example, has contended that using the household codes to subordinate wives to husbands and children to parents necessarily involves acknowledging the legitimacy of slavery as well. If slavery were wrong, she contends, the New Testament would condemn it, not seek to regulate it. So long as slavery is understood to mean owning the "labor" of others, rather than owning people, "it would be possible for the institution of slavery to exist in accord with the Christian ethic. . . . Many employer/employee relations (consider the army) can be seen as a form of legitimate slavery."[47]

Most hierarchical interpreters, however, argue that slavery, unlike the subordination of women to men, does not reflect God's will for human society. George Knight offers a typical explanation, conceding that "Paul and Peter deal with slaves in close juxtaposition to husbands and wives as part of . . . the section dealing with the relationships within the household." Nevertheless, Knight asserts, "Not once does Paul appeal to either God's creation order or God's moral law as grounds for the institution of slavery. This radically distinguishes the treatment of slavery from that of marriage and the family."[48]

African American Christians have long denied the validity of the household codes' admonitions for slaves to obey their masters. Nevertheless, there is a long history within African American Christianity of using Genesis 1-3 and the household codes as validation for subordinating women to men.

At least as early as Virginia Broughton's 1904 *Women's Work, as Gleaned from the Women of the Bible*, contingents of African American women have argued, in an effort to ameliorate the sexism of the household codes, that Genesis 1-3 affirmed both the likeness of women and men and their joint calling to participate in Christ's work of redemption.[49] More recently, womanist scholars like Clarice Martin have urged African Americans to ask whether it is possible to "redeem" the household codes so that they cease to function as "texts of terror" for those on the bottom of the social ladder.[50] In this volume, Ann Holmes Redding addresses that issue, arguing that there are no reasons (other than sexist ones) for African American Christians to ignore the household codes' admonitions about slavery while enforcing the codes' instructions for wives to submit to husbands.

Other interpreters vitally interested in egalitarian renderings of their own sacred text's explication of the story of Adam and Eve are Muslims. In this chapter, Riffat Hassan represents Muslims who are concerned to identify and demonstrate the ways that the Qur'an and Islam portray women's subordination to men as deviating from God's intention for gender relations.

Hassan stands within a long tradition of contending that Islam is favorable to women's concerns.[51] For some, this tradition is centuries old, reaching back to the founding of Islam. Pointing to the pre-Islamic "days of ignorance," proponents of this assessment stress improvements Islam made in the status of women, including the way the Qur'an calls for revaluing female life by condemning the infanticide of baby girls (Q.16:58-60).[52] For others, this tradition has a shorter duration. Persons holding this view emphasize more recent events in the nineteenth and twentieth centuries, such as the social activism of Muslim women in working for improving their legal rights and their access to education. They also stress the founding of women's organizations in Muslim countries as another indication that a Muslim may reject androcentrism without rejecting Islam.

This tradition offers significant contrasts to the assessment of many persons that a distinctive feature of Islam is that it has an even more negative view of women than either Judaism or Christianity. Leila Ahmed has examined ways that the position of women in Islamic nations has been compared with their status in Western European countries. Noting the influence played by patterns of cultural imperialism established under Western colonialism, she has contended, "The peculiar practices of Islam with respect to women had always formed part of the Western narrative of the quintessential otherness and inferiority of Islam."[53]

Riffat Hassan agrees with persons who see feminism as an indigenous possibility within Islam. A native of Pakistan, she has described herself as a member of a "Sayyid" Muslim family—a family that traces its lineage back to the Prophet Muhammad. Currently she teaches at the University of Louisville, where she chairs the religious studies department. As a committed Muslim, she participates in the second largest of the world's religions. As a native of Pakistan, she represents the ways in which Islam, although often associated with its Arabic heartland, spans the globe, with the majority of Muslims living in Asia and Africa. Its rich diversities in terms of culture, geography, nation, and race could foster wide variations in terms of customs and convictions concerning women.

Yet these variations have not been as great as one might imagine. Instead, early in its history Islam formulated a patriarchal paradigm for women's status and role. Barbara Stowasser has described features of this paradigm and its effect on subsequent Qur'anic interpretation: "After women had been successfully excluded from institutionalized participation in public life and (at least the upper-class ones among them) had been segregated and secluded . . . , this state of affairs continued to underlie the theological-legal interpretation of the Qur'anic teachings on women."[54] During Islam's vast territorial expansion, this paradigm was exported to the newly converted territories. Thus patriarchal practices, beliefs, and institutions formed a significant part of the worldview and customs that provided what Stowasser terms "transregional solidarities."[55]

Hassan recognizes that Islam, as usually practiced, assigns women a position inferior to men. Yet in her assessment, these traditional practices are not the only possibility for Islam. Indeed, she has repeatedly argued that authentic Islam does not endorse patriarchal and hierarchical understandings of gender relations. To discover what is authentic to Islam, Hassan has conjoined her interpretation of the Qur'an with systematic investigation of Islamic theology.

In so doing, she often has come to negative conclusions about the authority of the hadith, noting that they deviate from the Qur'an's own teachings. The selection of Hassan's writings in this chapter shows both her high regard for the Qur'an and the secondary status she has relegated to the hadith.[56]

This selection, like much of Hassan's writings, pays particular attention to examining understandings of gender and creation.[57] In our selection, she has focused on the issue of woman's creation, particularly whether God created woman in a way that was inferior to or derivative from man. Through a close reading of the Qur'an and careful studies of its Arabic terms, she has reached the conclusion that according to the Qur'an "both woman and man were made in the same manner, of the same substance, at the same time." This, in her estimation, forms the essential teaching of Islam on creation and gender. Any deviation from this teaching—whether maintained by classical authorities, such as the highly influential transmitters of hadith, or by twentieth century Muslims, such as Mawdudi (also Maududi)—should be denounced.

Hassan, like other proponents of an egalitarian interpretation of the story of Eve and Adam, has offered a radical challenge to traditional renderings of the relation of the first woman and the first man. These proponents also share an alertness to the ways that the story of Eve and Adam continues to live on as interpretations of it shape the lives of the extended—and extensive—family of their descendants. The challenge of the egalitarians confronts hierarchalist assumptions and calls for their transformation in the hope that God's intention for gender equality shall one day be enjoyed by the daughters and sons of Eve and Adam.

NOTES TO CHAPTER 8, INTRODUCTION

1. Phyllis Trible coined the term "depatriarchalize"; see her article "Depatriarchalizing in Biblical Interpretation," *Journal of the American Academy of Religion* 41 (1973): 30-48. See also Linda S. Schearing's entry "Depatriarchalization" in Letty M. Russell and J. Shannon Clarkson, editors, *Dictionary of Feminist Theologies* (Louisville, Ky.: Westminster John Knox, 1996), p. 64.

2. Carol J. Adams, *The Sexual Politics of Meat: A Feminist-Vegetarian Critical Theory* (New York: Continuum, 1994), p. 74. See also her *Neither Man nor Beast: Feminism and the Defense of Animals* (New York: Continuum, 1994), pp. 171-74. In agreement with Samuel H. Dresner's analysis in *The Jewish Dietary Laws, Their Meaning for Our Time*, revised and expanded edition (New York: Rabbinical Assembly of America, 1982), pp. 21, 26, Adams argues that God created Adam and Eve as vegetarians. Only after their expulsion from Eden did God allow them to eat meat, and then only as a concession to human weakness.

Discussions of the role of Genesis in legitimizing Western exploitation of the environment are far too many to enumerate. Early classics were Lynn White, Jr., "The Historical Roots of Our Ecologic Crisis," *Science*, Appendix No. 7A, 155 (3767) (March 10, 1967): 1203-1207; and Rosemary Radford Ruether, "Mother Earth and the Megamachine," *Christianity and Crisis* (April 12, 1972).

3. Isaac W. Grimes, "Manliness," *Watchman* 88 (2) (January 11, 1906): 15. Quoted in Betty A. DeBerg, *Ungodly Women: Gender and the First Wave of American Fundamentalism* (Minneapolis: Fortress Press, 1990), p. 92; see also pp. 140-43.

4. Harry Emerson Fosdick, *The Manhood of the Master* (New York: Abingdon Press, 1913).

5. Bruce Barton, *The Man Nobody Knows* (Indianapolis: Bobbs-Merrill, 1924), "How It Came To Be Written," n.p., and "The Founder of Modern Business," p. 159.

6. John R. Rice, *Bobbed Hair, Bossy Wives, and Women Preachers* (Wheaton, Ill.: Sword of the Lord Publishers, 1941), pp. 13, 14. Rice's view of women clergy was particularly grim: "I have no doubt that millions will go to Hell because of the unscriptural practice of women preachers" (p. 59).

7. Mrs. Elizabeth Rice Handford, *Me? Obey Him?* (Murfreesboro, Tenn.: Sword of the Lord Publishers, 1972), pp. 13, 28.

8. Elisabeth Elliot, "Why I Oppose the Ordination of Women," *Christianity Today* 19 (18) (June 1975): 12-15.

9. A. Duane Litfin, "Evangelical Feminism: Why Traditionalists Reject It," *Bibliotheca Sacra* 136 (July-September 1979): 267.

10. Frederick W. Schmidt, Jr., examines discussions of women's ordination in the Southern Baptist Convention as well as several other denominations in *A Still Small Voice: Women, Ordination, and the Church*, with a Foreword by the Reverend Betty Bone Schiess, Women and Gender in North American Religion Series (Syracuse: Syracuse University Press, 1996).

11. *Annual of the Southern Baptist Convention 1984*, distributed by Executive Committee, Southern Baptist Convention, Nashville, n.d.

12. Quotation from Hastings Sehested in Penni Crabtree, "Fundamentalists Left Holding Fort," Memphis *Commercial Appeal*, June 15, 1988, section A, pp. 1, 10.

For a fuller account of the call and installation of Hastings Sehested as pastor of Prescott Memorial Baptist Church, see Valarie Ziegler Morris, "Obey Your Leaders: The Disenfranchisement of Women and the Laity in the Southern Baptist Convention," *The Cumberland Seminarian* 27 (1) (Spring 1989): 8-12; and Valarie Ziegler, "Genesis and Gender Roles: The Southern Baptists Debate over Women's Ordination," unpublished paper, Southeastern Conference on Religion, Atlanta, Ga., March 19, 1994.

An informative treatment of the major protagonists in the Southern Baptist struggle to define itself is Bill Moyers's *God and Politics: The Battle for the Bible* (Public Affairs TV), 1987.

13. In addition to the discussions in the selection, see p. 71 of Foh's "The Head of the Woman is the Man" in Bonnidell Clouse and Robert G. Clouse, editors, *Women in Ministry: Four Views* (Downers Grove, Ill.: InterVarsity Press, 1989).

14. The hegemony enjoyed by the Reform tradition in nineteenth-century America eroded in the face of massive immigrations of Eastern European Jews during the years 1880 to 1914. According to American historian Peter Williams, by the end of World War I, religious Jews in America were divided into three groups: Orthodox, Conservative, and Reform. (Later, a fourth group, Reconstructionist, would join these three.) While all shared "a common tradition," they were nevertheless "irreparably split over differences on how to interpret and implement the dictates of that tradition." Peter W. Williams, *America's Religions: Traditions and Cultures* (New York: Macmillan, 1990) p. 361.

15. Alfred J. Kolatch, *The Jewish Book of Why* (Middle Village, N.Y.: Jonathan David Publishers, Inc., 1981).

16. Kolatch, *The Jewish Book of Why*, pp. 120, 169, 180-81.

17. Joseph Hertz., editor, *The Authorized Daily Prayer Book* (New York: Bloch, 1985; revised from 1945), pp. 1006-1008.

18. Samuel H. Dresner, "Homosexuality and the Order of Creation," *Judaism: A*

Quarterly Journal of Jewish Life and Thought 40 (Summer 1981): 309-21; and in the selection in this chapter.

19. Dresner, "Homosexuality and the Order of Creation," p. 309; and in the selection in this chapter.

20. Dresner, "Homosexuality and the Order of Creation," p. 313; and in the selection in this chapter.

21. Dresner, "Homosexuality and the Order of Creation," p. 319; and in the selection in this chapter.

22. Dresner, "Homosexuality and the Order of Creation," p. 320; and in the selection in this chapter.

23. Sayyid Abu al-A'la Mawdudi, *Towards Understanding the Qur'an*, vol. 1, Surahs 1-3, and vol. 2, Surahs 4-6, edited and translated by Zafar Ishaq Ansari (Leicester, United Kingdom: Islamic Foundation, 1988/1408 A.H. and 1989/1409 A.H.).

24. For a discussion of the "city-oriented bias" of this position and its neglect of rural women's work in the fields, see Barbara F. Stowasser's "Women's Issues in Modern Islamic Thought," in Judith E. Tucker, editor, *Arab Women: Old Boundaries, New Frontiers* (Bloomington and Indianapolis: Indiana University Press, 1993), pp. 23-25.

25. For further information, see Shahla Haeri's "The Institution of Mut'a Marriage in Iran: A Formal and Historical Perspective," in Guity Nashat, editor, *Women and Revolution in Iran* (Boulder, Colo.: Westview Press, 1983), pp. 231-51.

26. Mawdudi, *Purdah and the Status of Women*, 12th ed., edited and translated by Al-Ash 'Ari (Lahore, Pakistan: Islamic Publications, 1992). Fadwa El Guindi describes Mawdudi's book as a "widely read source on the subject for believers in the Islamic movement, providing a nonorthodox interpretation of the Qur'an on gender issues." See the bibliography for Guindi's entry "Hijab" in the *Oxford Encyclopedia of the Modern Islamic World*, vol. 2, *Faqi-Leba*, John L. Esposito, editor (New York and Oxford: Oxford University Press, 1995), vol. 2, p. 111.

27. Bruce B. Lawrence, *Defenders of God: The Fundamentalist Revolt against the Modern Age* (San Francisco: Harper & Row, 1989), p. 207. Lawrence's chapter, "Fundamentalists in Pursuit of an Islamic State," offers a helpful discussion of impulses fueling Islamic fundamentalism, including the situations of Muslim women.

28. Mawdudi, *Towards Understanding the Qur'an*, vol. 1, p. 172; and in the selection in this chapter.

29. Mawdudi, *Towards Understanding the Qur'an*, vol. 2, p. 86; and in the selection in this chapter.

30. Mawdudi, *Towards Understanding the Qur'an*, vol. 1, p. 62; and in the selection in this chapter.

31. Mawdudi, *Towards Understanding the Qur'an*, vol. 2, p. 5f.; and in the selection in this chapter.

32. Mawdudi, *Towards Understanding the Qur'an*, vol. 2, p. 35: and in the selection in this chapter.

For helpful discussions of conservative and fundamentalist Muslims on gender equality, see Barbara F. Stowasser's *Women in the Qur'an, Traditions, and Interpretation* (New York and Oxford: Oxford University Press, 1994), especially pp. 37-38. Also see her "Women's Issues in Modern Islamic Thought," in Judith E. Tucker, editor, *Arab Women: Old Boundaries, New Frontiers* (Bloomington and Indianapolis: Indiana University Press, 1993), pp. 3-28.

33. Mawdudi, *Towards Understanding the Qur'an*, vol. 2, p. 86; and in the selection in this chapter.

34. Mawdudi, *Towards Understanding the Qur'an*, vol. 2, p. 36; and in the selection in this chapter.

35. For exegetical parallels between Trible and Sarah Grimké, see Kristen E. Kvam, "The Grimké Sisters on Genesis 1-3: 'The Only Firm Basis of Human

Rights,' " paper presented at the annual meeting of the Southeastern Commission for the Study of Religion, Atlanta, Ga., March 19, 1994.

36. Phyllis Trible, "Eve and Adam: Genesis 2-3 Reread," in Carol P. Christ and Judith Plaskow, *Womanspirit Rising: A Feminist Reader in Religion* (San Francisco: Harper & Row: 1979), pp. 74-76, 80-81.

37. In addition to writings by Plaskow, feminist discussions of Judaism and gender include: Sylvia Barack Fishman, *A Breath of Life: Feminism and the American Jewish Community* (New York: Free Press, and Toronto: Maxwell Macmillan, 1993); Ellen M. Umansky, editor, *Four Centuries of Jewish Women's Spirituality: A Sourcebook* (Boston: Beacon Press, 1992); Lynn Gottlieb, *She Who Dwells Within: A Feminist Vision of a Renewed Judaism* (San Francisco: HarperSanFrancisco, 1995); and Aviva Cantor, *Jewish Women/Jewish Men: The Legacy of Patriarchy in Jewish Life* (San Francisco: HarperSan-Francisco, 1995).

38. *Ezrat Nashim* normally refers to the women's section of the Temple. It became the name of one women's organization that sought equal rights for women in the Jewish community.

39. Rabbi Sally Priesand, *Judaism and the New Woman* (New York: Behrman House, 1975), p. 37.

40. Priesand, *Judaism and the New Woman*, p. xvi.

41. Priesand, *Judaism and the New Woman*, p. 5.

42. See "Epilogue: The Coming of Lilith," in Rosemary Radford Ruether, editor, *Religion and Sexism: Images of Woman in the Jewish and Christian Traditions* (New York: Simon & Schuster, 1974), pp. 341-43.

43. Carol P. Christ and Judith Plaskow, editors, *Womanspirit Rising: A Feminist Reader in Religion* (San Francisco: Harper & Row, 1979).

44. Judith Plaskow, "The Coming of Lilith: Toward a Feminist Theology," in Christ and Plaskow, *Womanspirit Rising*, pp. 200-201, 206-207.

45. Christ and Plaskow, preface to *Womanspirit Rising*, p. xi.

46. As Nancy Hastings Sehested said of those who opposed the ordination of women in the Southern Baptist Convention, "They are using the Bible to support them in this, just like the Bible was used to support slavery" (Memphis, *Commercial Appeal*, November 12, 1987, section B, p. 3).

47. Susan T. Foh, *Women and the Word of God: A Response to Biblical Feminism* (Phillipsburg, N.J.: Presbyterian and Reformed Publishing Co., 1974), pp. 31-35; the quotation is from p. 34. Foh makes a similar point in the selection in this chapter.

48. George W. Knight III, "Male and Female Related He Them," *Christianity Today* 20 (14) (April 19, 1976): 15.

49. Evelyn Brooks Higginbotham, *Righteous Discontent: The Women's Movement in the Black Baptist Church, 1880-1920* (Cambridge and London: Harvard University Press, 1993), pp. 124-29.

50. Clarice Martin, "Womanist Interpretation of the New Testament: The Quest for Holistic and Inclusive Translation and Interpretation," *Journal of Feminist Studies in Religion* 6 (2) (Fall 1990): 60, 61. Alice Walker's definition of "womanist" is found in her book, *In Search of Our Mother's Gardens* (San Diego, New York, and London: Harcourt Brace Jovanovich, 1984), pp. xi-xii. See also Karen Baker-Fletcher's "Womanist Voice" in Letty M. Russell and J. Shannon Clarkson, editors, *Dictionary of Feminist Theologies* (Louisville: Westminster John Knox, 1996), pp. 316-17; and Toinette M. Eugene's "Womanist Theology" in Donald W. Musser and Joseph L. Price, editors, *A New Handbook of Christian Theology* (Nashville: Abingdon: 1992), pp. 510-12.

51. For discussions of Islam and women, see the papers presented to the Muslim Sisters Organization of Nigeria in Rahmatu Abdullahi, editor, *The Muslim Woman: Challenges of the 15th Hijra* (Ilorin, Nigeria: Woye and Sons, Ltd., 1988). Also see Amina Wadud-Muhsin, *Qur'an and Woman* (Kuala Lumpur, Malaysia: Penerbit Fajar Bakti Sdn. Bhd., 1992).

52. For a list of such improvements, see pages 212-13 of Azizah al-Hibri's "A Study of Islamic Herstory: Or How Did We Ever Get into This Mess?" in Azizah al-Hibri, editor, *Women and Islam* (Oxford and New York: Pergamon Press, 1982). For a different evaluation of women's pre-Islamic status, see Leila Ahmed's *Women and Gender in Islam: Historical Roots of a Modern Debate* (New Haven and London: Yale University Press, 1992), especially chapter 3, "Women and the Rise of Islam."

53. Ahmed, *Women and Gender in Islam*, p. 149.

54. Barbara Freyer Stowasser, *Women in the Qur'an, Traditions, and Interpretation* (New York and Oxford: Oxford University Press, 1994), p. 8.

55. Stowasser, *Women in the Qur'an*, p. 7.

56. Riffat Hassan, "The Issue of Woman-Man Equality in the Islamic Tradition," in L. Grob, R. Hassan, and H. Gordon, editors, *Women's and Men's Liberation: Testimonies of Spirit* (New York: Greenwood Press, 1991), pp. 65-82.

57. Other writings by Riffat Hassan include "Equal before Allah? Woman-Man Equality in the Islamic Tradition," *Pakistan Progressive* 9 (Summer 1987): 46-59; "Women in the Context of Change and Confrontation within Muslim Communities," in Virginia Mollenkott, editor, *Women of Faith in Dialogue* (New York: Crossroad, 1987), pp. 96-109; "Muslim Women and Post-Patriarchal Islam," in Paula M. Cooey, William R. Eakin, and Jay B. McDaniel, editors, *After Patriarchy: Feminist Transformations of the World Religions* (Maryknoll, N.Y.: Orbis, 1991), pp. 39-64. The latter discusses understandings of woman and the first sin, as well as of why woman was created.

HIERARCHICAL INTERPRETATIONS

Council on Biblical Manhood and Womanhood

The Council on Biblical Manhood and Womanhood is a parachurch or non-denominational organization of Christians who interpret the Bible as mandating male leadership and female subordination at least in terms of their roles in the home and in the church. This organization's attention to biblical authority and its concern for Christian proclamation situate it within the broad movement known as "evangelicalism."[1] Its membership roster lists Beverly LaHaye, President of Concerned Women for America,[2] as well as several professors from conservative Christian seminaries, including Trinity Evangelical Divinity School, Concordia Seminary (Fort Wayne, Indiana), and Dallas Theological Seminary.[3]

At a 1987 meeting of the Council in Danvers, Massachusetts, several members drafted what has become known as "The Danvers Statement." About a year later, the Council published the statement in its final form, which we have included in this chapter. As a position paper, the Danvers Statement is fairly terse, without the sustained discussion of essays and articles. Its three major sections enumerate specific points. The Statement stresses what it claims to be God's will for the "complementary differences" between women and men. It points out that sin has distorted these differences. It maintains, however, that the Christian form of life involves returning to God's original intention so that in the home and in the church women willingly accept the limitations of their roles and men humbly exercise their headship. (Source:

Council on Biblical Manhood and Womanhood, "The Danvers Statement," in John Piper and Wayne Grudem, editors, *Recovering Biblical Manhood and Womanhood: A Response to Evangelical Feminism*, Wheaton, Ill.: Good News Publishers, Crossway Books, 1991, appendix 2, pp. 469-71.)

"The Danvers Statement" (1987 CE)
COUNCIL ON BIBLICAL MANHOOD AND WOMANHOOD

Rationale

We have been moved in our purpose by the following contemporary developments which we observe with deep concern:

1. The widespread uncertainty and confusion in our culture regarding the complementary differences between masculinity and femininity;

2. the tragic effects of this confusion in unraveling the fabric of marriage woven by God out of the beautiful and diverse strands of manhood and womanhood;

3. the increasing promotion given to feminist egalitarianism with accompanying distortions or neglect of the glad harmony portrayed in Scripture between the loving, humble leadership of redeemed husbands and the intelligent, willing support of that leadership by redeemed wives;

4. the widespread ambivalence regarding the values of motherhood, vocational homemaking, and the many ministries historically performed by women;

5. the growing claims of legitimacy for sexual relationships which have Biblically and historically been considered illicit or perverse, and the increase in pornographic portrayal of human sexuality;

6. the upsurge of physical and emotional abuse in the family;

7. the emergence of roles for men and women in church leadership that do not conform to Biblical teaching but backfire in the crippling of Biblically faithful witness;

8. the increasing prevalence and acceptance of hermeneutical oddities devised to reinterpret apparently plain meanings of Biblical texts;

9. the consequent threat to Biblical authority as the clarity of Scripture is jeopardized and the accessibility of its meaning to ordinary people is withdrawn into the restricted realm of technical ingenuity;

10. and behind all this the apparent accommodation of some within the church to the spirit of the age at the expense of winsome, radical Biblical authenticity which in the power of the Holy Spirit may reform rather than reflect our ailing culture.

Purposes

Recognizing our own abiding sinfulness and fallibility, and acknowledging the genuine evangelical standing of many who do not agree with all of our convictions, nevertheless, moved by the preceding observations and by the hope that the noble Biblical vision of sexual complementarity may yet win the mind and heart of Christ's church, we engage to pursue the following purposes:

1. To study and set forth the Biblical view of the relationship between men and women, especially in the home and in the church.

2. To promote the publication of scholarly and popular materials representing this view.

3. To encourage the confidence of lay people to study and understand for themselves the teaching of Scripture, especially on the issue of relationships between men and women.

4. To encourage the considered and sensitive application of this Biblical view in the appropriate spheres of life.

5. And thereby
— to bring healing to persons and relationships injured by an inadequate grasp of God's will concerning manhood and womanhood,
— to help both men and women realize their full ministry potential through a true understanding and practice of their God-given roles,
— and to promote the spread of the gospel among all peoples by fostering a Biblical wholeness in relationships that will attract a fractured world.

Affirmations

Based on our understanding of Biblical teachings, we affirm the following:

1. Both Adam and Eve were created in God's image, equal before God as persons and distinct in their manhood and womanhood.

2. Distinctions in masculine and feminine roles are ordained by God as part of the created order, and should find an echo in every human heart.

3. Adam's headship in marriage was established by God before the Fall, and was not a result of sin.

4. The Fall introduced distortions into the relationships between men and women.
— In the home, the husband's loving, humble headship tends to be replaced by domination or passivity; the wife's intelligent, willing submission tends to be replaced by usurpation or servility.
— In the church, sin inclines men toward a worldly love of power or an abdication of spiritual responsibility, and inclines women to resist limitations on their roles or to neglect the use of their gifts in appropriate ministries.

5. The Old Testament, as well as the New Testament, manifests the equally high value and dignity which God attached to the roles of both men and women. Both Old and New Testaments also affirm the principle of male headship in the family and in the covenant community.

6. Redemption in Christ aims at removing the distortions introduced by the curse.
— In the family, husbands should forsake harsh or selfish leadership and grow in love and care for their wives; wives should forsake resistance to their husbands' authority and grow in willing, joyful submission to their husbands' leadership.

— In the church, redemption in Christ gives men and women an equal share in the blessings of salvation; nevertheless, some governing and teaching roles within the church are restricted to men.

7. In all of life Christ is the supreme authority and guide for men and women, so that no earthly submission—domestic, religious, or civil—ever implies a mandate to follow a human authority into sin.

8. In both men and women a heartfelt sense of call to ministry should never be used to set aside Biblical criteria for particular ministries. Rather, Biblical teaching should remain the authority for testing our subjective discernment of God's will.

9. With half the world's population outside the reach of indigenous evangelism; with countless other lost people in those societies that have heard the gospel; with the stresses and miseries of sickness, malnutrition, homelessness, illiteracy, ignorance, aging, addiction, crime, incarceration, neuroses, and loneliness, no man or woman who feels a passion from God to make His grace known in word and deed ever live[s] without a fulfilling ministry for the glory of Christ and the good of this fallen world.

10. We are convinced that a denial or neglect of these principles will lead to increasingly destructive consequences in our families, our churches, and the culture at large.

NOTES TO CHAPTER 8, HIERARCHICAL INTERPRETATIONS, COUNCIL ON BIBLICAL MANHOOD AND WOMANHOOD

[1. For a helpful discussion of diversity within the evangelical movement, see Donald G. Bloesh's "Evangelicalism," in Donald W. Musser and Joseph L. Price, editors, *A New Handbook of Christian Theology* (Nashville: Abingdon, 1992), pp. 168-73. For examples of evangelicals who advocate egalitarianism, see the writings of such authors as Nancy Hardesty, Paul Jewett, Alvera Mickelsen, and Virginia Mollenkott.]

[2. Beverly LaHaye is the author of *I Am a Woman by God's Design* (Old Tappan, N.J.: Revell, 1982).]

[3. For more complete listings of the organization's Council Members and Board of Reference, see John Piper and Wayne Grudem, editors, *Recovering Biblical Manhood and Womanhood* (Wheaton, Ill.: Good News Publishers, Crossway Books, 1991), pp. 471-72.]

Susan T. Foh

Susan T. Foh is a Christian who has written frequently on how God's will for male and female relations should be understood. She is the author of *Women and the Word of God: A Response to Biblical Feminism* and has reviewed many books on gender relations and feminism.[1] She has also contributed articles to books and journals, including "What Is the Woman's Desire?" a study on Genesis 3:16 that was published by the *Westminster Theological Journal.*[2]

Our selection comes from *Women in Ministry*, a collection of essays representing a spectrum of positions concerning the way Christians should view the proper roles and responsibilities of women.[3] In this context, Foh seeks to counter both those who deny women any responsibility outside the home and those who advocate women's full equality. She argues that God created women both "ontologically equal" to men and also "functionally subordinate" in marriage and church. She grounds this position by setting out her interpretations of the opening chapters of Genesis and of several passages from the New Testament.[4] In the final sections of the essay, she considers the practical implications of her position. In this context, she denies the propriety of women's ordination to the pastoral ministry even as she contends that the Bible permits women to pray, prophesy, and—on unofficial matters—teach in church. (Source: Susan T. Foh. "The Head of the Woman Is the Man," in Bonnidell Clouse and Robert Clouse, editors, *Women in Ministry: Four Views*, Downers Grove, Ill.: InterVarsity Press, 1989, pp. 69-105.)

"The Head of the Woman Is the Man" (1989 CE)
SUSAN T. FOH

The Basics

The foundational principles for understanding women's roles are found in the first three chapters of Genesis. In Genesis 1 and 2, there are two accounts of the creation of man and woman. Chapter 1 ("So God created man in his own image, in the image of God he created him; male and female he created them," v. 27 NIV) is acclaimed by those who favor the absolute equality of the sexes, whereas the teaching of the woman's inferiority is often attributed to chapter 2. Neither extreme is true; the two creation narratives complement each other to give the complete picture.

On the sixth day, God created humanity in two sexes in his image. There is nothing in the text to suggest any difference between them. Both man and woman are equally in the image of God. Both are blessed by God, told to multiply and subdue the earth, and given stewardship over creation. This joint custody over the rest of creation has implications for women's roles in society or culture; their place in the work arena is no different from men's. Men and women have the same relationship to God (in his image) and to nature (to fill and exercise dominion over). This principle can be termed "ontological equality" or "equality in being."

In Genesis 2, we learn more about the relationship between man and woman. Because it was not good for the man to be alone (an indication of man's dependence on or need for woman, 1 Cor 11:11-12), God created a helper fit for the man, the woman. The words "helper fit for" or "corresponding to" underline the likeness of the woman to man.[5]

Rather than a separate creation from the dust, the woman was created from the rib of the man. Why is the woman created in this surprising way?

(1) It signifies her correspondence to the man. She is bone of his bone and flesh of his flesh; there is no superiority or inferiority in substance. (2) God's creation of humanity is one act that begins with the man and ends with the woman. (3) All of humanity comes from one source, Adam. As the source of humanity, Adam is the head and consequently the representative of all. As 1 Corinthians 15:22 says, "in Adam all die." (4) The woman's creation from the man establishes the basis for the one-flesh principle in marriage. It is the real, biological and historical foundation for the oneness that should exist between husband and wife (Gen 2:24). Reasons (3) and (4) pave the way for the principle of inequality between the man and woman. (5) Though the way the woman was created does not indicate inferiority, it does indicate a difference in function. The woman was created to help her husband; her function is dependent on him. As she followed him in creation, she is to follow his lead as her husband.[6]

How do we know that the man's temporal priority signifies the husband's headship? Though the answer has obviously failed to convince many, it is: "For man was not made from woman, but woman from man. Neither was man created for woman, but woman for man" (1 Cor 11:8-9; see also 1 Tim 2:13). God, through Paul, explains what we otherwise might have missed. It is likely that the Hebrew mind would have understood the connection between Adam's being the source of the woman and his position as head.[7]

But there is another clue that Adam is to be regarded as having authority over the woman. Adam named her. When Adam named the animals, it is clear that he was exercising his God-given rule over them. To name someone is associated with authority over that person. Even the name that Adam gives the woman indicates their relationship: 'ishshah (woman) because she was taken out of 'ish (man). The name stresses their similarity and their difference in function. James Hurley paraphrases Genesis 2:23, "She is indeed my own kind, from my own body. She is, however, derivative and it is my privilege to assign her a name. Let her be called by the name I give, 'woman,' because she was taken out of me."[8]

Is God's arrangement fair? Our objections, whether philosophical or emotional, to this hierarchical system arise because we do not know what a sinless hierarchy is like. We know only the tyranny, willfulness and condescension that even the best boss-underling relationship has. In Eden, none of these perversions existed. The man and woman knew each other as equals, each in God's image and each with a personal relationship with God. Neither doubted the value of the other or of himself or herself. Each was to do the same work, with husband as head and wife as helper. They functioned as one flesh, one body without discord. Does the rib rebel against the head or the head mistreat the rib?

There are three principles in operation before the Fall. (1) Man and woman are equal in being (Gen 1:27). (2) The woman is functionally subordinate to her husband. He was created first to set up his headship; the woman was created after, from and for the sake of the man to help him (Gen 2:21-23;

1 Cor 11:8-9). (3) Husband and wife are one flesh (Gen 2:24). Because of the third principle, the other two can operate harmoniously. The inter-relatedness of man and woman should prevent both from abusing their positions.

In the Fall, these three principles are also involved. Much speculation, usually with a chauvinistic slant, has revolved around the woman's sin. The serpent picked the weaker person; the woman usurped her husband's place by leading him into sin; the woman enticed or seduced Adam into sin. However, the text does not support any of these notions. The serpent's subtlety consists in his method of argumentation, his persuasive half-truths. The woman's sin is directed primarily against God.

She knew God's command; yet she dared discuss whether or not to obey it with a fellow creature. In the end, she believed the serpent rather than God. The woman sinned against her husband by helping him (what she was supposed to do) in the wrong way, into sin ("She also gave some to her husband, and he ate"—Gen 3:6). Adam is judged not because he heeded his wife's advice per se, but because he followed her bad advice to disobey God (Gen 3:17).

Their oneness and parity are shown in the results of sin: "Then the eyes of both were opened, and they knew that they were naked" (Gen 3:7 RSV). It is as if they sinned simultaneously, as if Adam's sin were a reflex action of the woman's (they were perfectly one flesh). Both made aprons for themselves and hid from God in the garden. They were one in their sin, reactions and guilt.

In Genesis 3:9 God addresses the man first because he is the appointed head. Nevertheless, the woman is also questioned; she is responsible for her own actions. . . .

After the Fall the harmonious working of these three principles is destroyed. In God's judgment against the woman, he tells how the corruptions of these principles will develop, though the usual translation obscures this point. The RSV translation, "yet your desire shall be for your husband, and he shall rule over you," suggests that somehow, through the woman's desire for her husband, he will be able to rule her. However, the rule of the husband is in fact not made easier after the Fall. Common experience suggests few husbands rule their homes. In addition, many wives have no desire—sexual, psychological or otherwise—for their husbands.

For a better understanding of Genesis 3:16, compare it to Genesis 4:7. The Hebrew of these two verses is the same, except for changes in pronouns, nouns and gender. The RSV translates the last part of Genesis 4:7 in an entirely different way: "its [sin's] desire is for you [Cain], but you must master it." Sin's desire[9] for Cain was to control or possess. Cain had to struggle; either sin or Cain would be the conqueror. God's words "you must master it" tell Cain what he should do, but they do not determine the victor.

In addition to identical construction, the proximity of the two passages indicates that they would have the same meaning. As in Genesis 4:7, the latter part of Genesis 3:16 describes a struggle between the one with the desire (the woman) and the one who must rule or master (the husband). The battle of the sexes is the result of sin and the judgment on it for the woman. The woman's willing submission is replaced by a desire to control her husband. Consequently, to maintain his headship the husband must fight for it. Sin has ruined the marital dance, the easy, loving lead of the husband and the natural following of the wife. In its place are struggle, tyranny, domination, manipulation and subterfuge.

This understanding of Genesis 3:16 is corroborated by experience. If it is translated "and he shall rule over you" (RSV), the words are not true; not every husband rules his wife. Instead, marriages are filled with strife and discontent. The loss of the wife's willing submission and the husband's loving "rule" each have two opposite aberrations. Wives manipulate and sometimes dominate their husbands; and some wives, losing all sense of their own worth, live only through their husbands or children. Some husbands, abdicating their position, absent themselves from the home through work, sports or alcohol; and some husbands physically or emotionally abuse their wives.

With this understanding of Genesis 3:16 in view, Paul, in Ephesians 5:22-33, focuses on the areas where wives and husbands tend to sin. As a result of sin, wives no longer naturally submit themselves to their husbands, so Paul says, "Wives, submit yourselves to your husbands, as to the Lord" (Eph 5:22 NIV). In their struggle to rule, husbands tend to resort to any means at their disposal, so Paul forestalls these "blows" with "Husbands, love your wives, as Christ loved the church and gave himself up for her" (Eph 5:25 RSV).

These three principles—ontological equality, functional subordination of the woman to her husband, and oneness—account for the seemingly contradictory strands of material in the Bible. . . .

1 Timothy 2:8–15

. . . What is forbidden to the woman in verse 12? One answer is all forms of teaching and exercising authority over men, including any job with authority over men and teaching in a co-ed college. However, the context suggests that Paul is dealing with a church worship situation. It is likely that the public prayer of verse 8 would occur in a worship service. . . .

If worship is the context for these verses, there are still two alternatives: (1) all forms of teaching and authority, and (2) a specific type of activity defined by teaching and exercising authority (that is, the office of elder, including pastor-teacher or minister of the Word). In any case, the teaching forbidden to women does not include praying and prophesying (1 Cor 11:2-16), private instruction of men (Acts 18:26), teaching other women (Tit 2:3-4) and teaching children (2 Tim 1:5; 3:15; Prov 1:8). . . .

The verb "to exercise authority over" appears only here in the New Testament. Connotations of dictatorship, arbitrariness and interference in an inappropriate area have been associated with it. The NEB translates it: "nor must woman domineer over man." Some have therefore concluded that what is forbidden is being bossy or publicly defying husbands. However, Paul does not say that bossy or domineering women should not teach and exercise authority over men but that a woman should not teach or exercise authority over men. George W. Knight III has researched the use of *authentein* in extrabiblical literature. His conclusion is that this verb's meaning is neutral, without negative connotations. The meaning most commonly suggested by translators and lexicographers is "have authority over."[10] What is forbidden to women in 1 Timothy 2:12 is the exercise of authority.

Paul gives two reasons for his prohibition: (1) Adam was created first, and (2) the woman was deceived, not the man. These two historical events cannot be altered or ignored. 1 Corinthians 11:8 also marks the significance of Adam's earlier creation; consequently, he is head of his wife (11:3), and she is to submit herself to him (Eph 5:22-23). The woman's relationship to the man founded at creation and Eve's deception make it inappropriate for women to teach and exercise authority over men in the church. . . .

This passage does not exalt all men above all women by giving men authority in the church. Authority is not given to all men, but only to the few who meet the qualification of 1 Timothy 3:1-7. . . .

1 Corinthians 14:34–35

On first reading, 1 Corinthians 14:34-35 seems more repressive to women than 1 Timothy 2:11-14. The verb used for "silence" in this passage connotes absence of speech. Is the silence demanded of women then absolute? If so, women should not sing, read responsive readings or pray aloud, even the Lord's Prayer. If so, all that comes before involving speaking in tongues, prophesying and sharing verbally in the church is of no concern to the women and should be marked "For Men Only." The "all" in 14:5 would then exclude women. . . .

The context qualifies the meaning of silence first of all by reference to the law (v. 34). What law does Paul have in mind? Some suppose it is a rabbinic law that requires silence as a mark of the woman's subjection.[11] Although Paul uses "law" in different senses, here he cites the law in order to end any objections. It is "the" law. Such an authoritative usage indicates that the Old Testament is intended (compare the usage in 1 Cor 14:21). The reference is not to Genesis 3:16, which is a judgment, not a prescription; it refers to those parts of the Old Testament which teach the woman's subordination to her husband. Paul's reference to the unchanging law of God marks this command as one for all times and places. . . .

Submission, not silence, is what the law commands. The command in verse 34 would be better translated, "but should submit themselves." "Be subordinate" and "be subject" are passive and have a beaten-down ring to them. The Greek verb is reflexive. It is an act one performs on or to oneself. The woman, man's ontological equal, voluntarily submits herself in recognition of her position as a woman (1 Cor 11:3).

Verse 35 may also define the sense of silence or not speaking that Paul has in mind. Speaking would then be understood as asking questions. Dialogue, with questions and answers, was a common form of education in the first century.[12] The women would not be permitted to ask questions in dialogue because it was a form of teaching. (In the synagogue it was the rabbi or official teacher who asked the questions, not the students.) When Paul directs the women to ask at home, he is providing a way for them to learn; Paul does not neglect women's education. It is important that women learn, though they are not to take part in the official teaching of the church.

1 Corinthians 11:2–16

. . . Headship is the determining element in 1 Corinthians 11:2-16. What does it mean? In the Old Testament, "head" meant "the highest" or "front" in addition to "first thing" or "beginning." Because it included the ideas of height, elevation and precedence, "head" was associated with leadership (Ex 18:25; Num 1:16; 25:15). "Head" was used to denote the president of the synagogue. Paul relates authority and headship. In Ephesians 5:21-33 the woman submits herself to her husband precisely because he is her head, as Christ is the head of the church.[13] The idea of "source" is included. The church has its origin in Christ as the woman has hers in the man (1 Cor 11:8). Being "the source of" is the basis for headship, but the connotation of origin does not eliminate the idea of authority from headship. Being the head involves having authority (see also Col 2:10; Eph 1:21-23).

Nonetheless, headship does not automatically imply superiority. In the examples of headship (v. 3), the head of Christ is God. God and Christ are both equally God. Therefore, the man is not head of his wife because he is intrinsically better. Rather, God established and appointed the man head. . . .

A proper understanding of 1 Corinthians 11:2-16 is essential for the participation of both men and women in worship. The situation Paul regulated is that of 1 Corinthians 14, an informal service in which many made contributions. If the man prays or prophesies, he must be uncovered. If the woman prays or prophesies, she must be covered. This passage does not require women to wear coverings in church per se; they [coverings] are necessary only when and if they [women] participate verbally. The converse is true for men. . . .

Galatians 3:28

According to the advocates of complete sexual equality, Galatians 3:28 was a time bomb dropped by Paul in one of his finer moments into the chauvinistic world of his day. The verse would gradually unfold its meaning until the church realized that there should be no distinctions between women and men—that Ephesians 5:22-33; Colossians 3:18; 1 Corinthians 11:2-16; 14:34-35; and 1 Timothy 2:11-15 were just temporary measures or just Paul's inability to give up his patriarchal heritage without a struggle. One problem with this understanding of Galatians 3:28 is its approach to Scripture. It sets Scripture against Scripture; one verse is said (by some) to contradict another.

Another objection to the egalitarian interpretation of Galatians 3:28 is that it misunderstands the text itself. The point of Galatians 3:23-29 is that faith rather than the law is the way of salvation. Paul's message is that regardless of nationality, social status or gender, all are justified by faith (v. 24), all are children of God (v. 26), all have put on Christ (v. 27), all are heirs according to the promise (v. 29). Clearly the emphasis here is spiritual standing.

This assertion is no small thing, and it was especially good news in the first century. All classes and types of people have the same relationship to God through Christ. There are consequences for human relations, but not necessarily those egalitarians seek. Galatians 3:28 teaches oneness in Christ, not equality; the two words do not coincide in meaning.

In 1 Corinthians 12, Paul explains the practical applications of oneness. Jealousies, resentments and hostilities among believers are to end. This does not mean that the immediate causes—such as the headship of the husband or the variety of gifts—are bad and must be removed. Believers are to work together. Oneness means that what benefits one benefits all and what hurts one hurts all. There should be mutual care and help. . . .

Paul does not say that all "will be" one in Christ; rather, he boldly proclaims that all "are" one. Galatians 3:28 was true when Paul wrote it, even though Jews scorned Gentiles, slavery existed, and women, by civil law and custom, may have been at their husband's mercy. The fulfillment of Galatians 3:28 does not depend on the existence or obliteration of any social institution or custom.

The three categories in Galatians 3:28 differ in nature. Because slavery is a social institution created by sinful humans who failed to see the image of God in all persons, it can be eradicated. Since this relationship can be erased, the biblical commands regulating slavery could be considered conditional or temporary. However, insofar as the categories still exist, as in the case of employer and employee, the commands still apply. The Jew-Gentile distinction has not been removed, and the Bible does not mandate its obliteration. Instead, Paul exhorts the two groups to be reconciled (Eph 2:14-16); this command is still valid. The male-female distinction is more fundamental; God established it at creation, and it cannot be removed. Since the categories of husband and wife and male and female remain, the relevant commands apply. Each of the pairs must be understood in its own terms as the Scriptures present them. . . .

In summary, both Old and New Testaments teach the same three principles: (1) Men and women are equally in the image of God and have the same relationship to God through Christ (Gen 1:26-27; Gal 3:26-29; 1 Pet 3:7). (2) Women have a subordinate role in the church and in marriage (1 Cor 11:3; 14:34; 1 Tim 2:11; Eph 5:22-24). (3) In church and marriage, God has established a unity which harmonizes and balances the first two principles. The oneness of believers in Christ and of husband and wife are based on love (1 Cor 12-14; Eph 5:25-31).

The Next Step

. . . There is only one valid argument against women's ordination to the ministry: scriptural prohibition. This prohibition is found in 1 Tim 2:12. It is debatable whether this passage specifically excludes women from the office of elder or not. But even if it has a more general application, it still prohibits women from becoming ministers (elders or pastor-teachers) because the particular duties of the elder are teaching (1 Tim 3:2) and ruling (1 Tim 5:17). . . . The reasons are (1) the man was created first and (2) the man was not deceived but the woman was. Whether or not these reasons make sense to us or meet our standards of justice is immaterial. They are God's reasons, and we either submit ourselves to him or not.

Are God's reasons arbitrary? To ask that question seems to head in a wrong direction. Perhaps the answer is no, of course not, but finite human reason may not be able to comprehend them. The Bible is clear that we are not let in on everything and that our reasoning powers are not to be totally trusted (Prov 3:5-7; 14:12; Is 55:8-9; Rom 9:20). But there are hints as to why God chose to create humanity in two sexes with one as head.

In the Old Testament, God compares his people to a wife and himself to a husband. With this tangible illustration, God teaches his people how they are to submit themselves to him and how he loves them. In the New Testament, after Christ's perfect example and the internal dwelling of the Spirit in believers, the comparison is reversed. Paul tells the wife to model her submission on the church's submission to Christ and the husband to model his love on Christ's self-sacrificing love for the church. The husband-wife authority structure functions as a picture of the relationship of the church to Christ her Lord. Our submission in authority structures reminds us (even those in the position of leader) of our need to submit to God.[14]

God created humanity from one person; Adam's being created first enables him to represent the whole of humanity. He is its head (Rom 5:12-21; 1 Cor 15:45-49). The woman is included in the man in a way that the reverse is not true. This aspect of the male-female relationship may indicate why elders must be male—so that they can represent the whole congregation, men and women. This line of reasoning is not an argument for male elders but rather an attempt to understand why only men may be elders.

The choice of an all-male apostolate results from the principle expressed in 1 Timothy 2:12-14, the subordination ("ordering under") of women in the church. Though biblical examples on their own are not conclusive, they can be mentioned as support, to show that 1 Timothy 2:12-14 is not an isolated prooftext. Biblical history from beginning to end illustrates this principle. In the Old Testament, only men could be priests and elders; men are conspicuous as patriarchs, kings, prophets, judges and authors of Scripture (all known authors were men). Only men were apostles; every evangelist and missionary mentioned in Acts was a man. The commands to women in 1 Corinthians 11:3-16 and 14:34-35 confirm the prohibition in 1 Timothy 2:12-14. Even the commands to wives (Num 30:1-15; Eph 5:22-25; Col 3:18-19; 1 Pet 3:1-6) add support because they agree that the creation order has consequences and that hierarchy is not contrary to God's will. . . .

What May Women Do in the Church?

. . . Some churches, partly in response to the secularly stimulated cries for women's liberation and partly out of confusion about interpreting the difficult passages related to women, "fence" the law. They take the prohibitions at their most comprehensive application; to make sure that no command is disobeyed, they forbid more than Scripture does. Some denominations have no female choir directors, directors of Christian education or Sunday-school superintendents. Some individuals think women may not teach in co-ed colleges or hold any position, ecclesiastical or secular, that puts men under their authority. . . .

The first step in answering the question of what women may do in the church is a proper understanding of 1 Corinthians 11:2-16; 14:34-35; and 1 Timothy 2:11-14. We have concluded that women are to pray and prophesy[15] in the congregation as long as they are covered, that the silence of 1 Corinthians 14:34-35 refers to not asking questions during the period of instruction, and that the intent of 1 Timothy 2:12 is to eliminate women from consideration for the office of elder, the teaching-ruling position of the church. Unfortunately, these exegetical conclusions do not answer all the questions. The New Testament worship service and church structure were quite different from today's. There are positions in today's church that did not exist in the early church—boards of directors, treasurers, Sunday-school superintendents and teachers, denominational officers and committee chairpersons. How do we know which of these positions women may occupy? . . .

The position of Sunday-school teacher requires special attention. Traditionally, women have taught children and other women in Sunday school, but the above understanding of 1 Timothy 2:12 opens the door to all levels of Sunday school, including the mixed adult class. Is this proper? This question is more complex than that of administrative positions because the Sunday-school teacher often appears to be doing exactly what the minister does in his sermon. Often the Sunday school more closely resembles the instruction period of the early church (1 Cor 14:34-35), in which women were told not to ask questions. . . .

The Sunday-school teacher does not enforce his or her teaching with church discipline. It has a more informal, non-official, open-to-discussion character (that resembles the mutual teaching among all believers, Col 3:16) than the official teaching of the minister during the worship service. Even if the minister teaches the Sunday school, his style usually reflects this difference. The work of the Sunday-school teacher and that of the minister are not the same. . . .

May a lay woman do everything a lay man can do? It is tempting to say yes based on 1 Timothy 2:11-14. After all, not all men are authorized to teach and exercise authority; being male is not the sole qualification for being an elder. However, 1 Corinthians 14:34-35 seems to imply that any man could ask questions and that only women are excluded from the discussion. Therefore, the answer to the question is a qualified yes, with the exception of any participation in the instruction period, including asking questions. . . .

In summary what may women do in the church? In the worship service, they may participate in all but the instruction period and the discussion. Women who are covered may lead in prayer and prophesy (including Scripture reading). In regard to church office, women may not be elders (neither pastor-teachers, nor evangelists, nor ministers, as commonly termed), because these offices involve teaching and ruling. They may be deacons or administrators. In general, the church wastes the gifts of its women and its laity as a whole. A greater effort must be made to help members of the body identify their gifts and use them for the growth of the body and the glory of God.

NOTES TO CHAPTER 8, HIERARCHICAL INTERPRETATIONS, SUSAN T. FOH

[1. Susan T. Foh, *Women and the Word of God: A Response to Biblical Feminism* (Phillipsburg, N.J.: Presbyterian and Reformed Publishing Company, 1979).]

[2. Susan T. Foh, "What Is the Woman's Desire?" *Westminster Theological Journal* 37 (1975): 376-83. See also her "Women Preachers—Why Not?" *Fundamentalist Journal* 4 (1) (January 1985).]

[3. *Women in Ministry: Four Views*, edited by Bonnidell Clouse and Robert G. Clouse (Downers Grove, Ill.: InterVarsity Press, 1989). The four views are called: Traditional, Male Leadership, Plural Ministry, and Egalitarian. The book's contributors articulate their own positions and, in shorter essays, respond to the positions of the other contributors.]

[4. See also Foh's discussion of her hermeneutical principles in an earlier section of "The Head of the Woman Is the Man," pp. 69-71.]

5. "Fit for" means "in front of" (as looking into a mirror).

6. Susan T. Foh, *Women and the Word of God: A Response to Biblical Feminism* (Phillipsburg, N.J.: Presbyterian and Reformed Publishing Company, 1979), pp. 60-61. [This note and the following slightly revised.]

7. James B. Hurley, *Man and Woman in Biblical Perspective* (Grand Rapids, Mich.: Zondervan, 1981), p. 210.

8. Hurley, *Man and Woman*, p. 212.

9. The etymology of the word "desire" supports this interpretation. The root is the Arabic *saqa*, which means "to urge," "drive on," or "impel."

10. George W. Knight, III, "*AYΘENTEΩ* in Reference to Women in 1 Timothy 2:12," *New Testament Studies* 30 (1984): 154.

11. Paul K. Jewett, *Man as Male and Female* (Grand Rapids, Mich.: Eerdmans, 1975), p. 114. [Note expanded.]

12. The rabbis, posing questions which other rabbis or their students would answer, used dialogue to teach. The Greeks (Socrates, for example) also used dialogue to instruct. Since the early church modeled its worship on that of the synagogue, it may have also used it. In Acts 20:7-12, Paul, in the teaching part of the Sunday gathering, used dialogues [*sic*]. His talking is also called "the speech" and "to confess" or "declare," the verb from which the word "homily" is derived.

13. Concerning the meaning of "head," Hurley writes, "Christ's rule is for the sake of his body, the church. Here [Eph. 1:20-22; cf. Eph. 5:22-23] the idea of love, unity and rule for the sake of another are introduced. Paul draws the rule of Christ and Christ's love for his church together by means of two meanings of the word "head" (*kephalē*). Hurley, *Man and Woman*, p. 146.

14. Foh, "Women Preachers—Why Not?" p. 18.

15. Whether or not prophecy still exists is beyond the scope of this chapter. An equivalent act is the reading of Scripture, since the Scriptures are God's direct word to the church, as is prophecy.

The Authorized Daily Prayer Book

According to its flyleaf, *The Authorized Daily Prayer Book* contains "the most comprehensive English commentary and introduction ever published" and "is recognized as one of the greatest historical works on Jewish liturgy." Whether or not this is indeed the case, the Prayerbook enjoyed tremendous popularity in the forty years following its publication in 1945. By 1985, it had undergone eighteen printings, and it is still in use in some American synagogues at the end of the twentieth century. The selection below is an excerpt from its discussion about Jewish marriage. It is designed to provide readers with a historical introduction to the role and function of marriage in Jewish thought. Its explanation of gender roles and its emphasis on heterosexuality and procreation as the Jewish norm, draws heavily on the Genesis accounts. (Source: *The Authorized Daily Prayer Book*, edited by Joseph H. Hertz, New York: Bloch Publishing, 1945; revised 1975, pp. 1006-1009.)

The Authorized Daily Prayer Book (1945 CE)
JOSEPH H. HERTZ, EDITOR

Marriage and the Position of Woman in Judaism

Marriage is that relationship between man and woman under whose shadow alone there can be true reverence for the mystery, dignity, and sacredness of life. Scripture represents marriage not merely as a Mosaic ordinance, but as part of the scheme of Creation, intended for all humanity.

They do less than justice to this Divine institution who view it in no other light than as a civil contract. In a contract, the mutual rights and obligations are the result of agreement, and their selection and formulation may flow from the momentary whim of the parties. In the marriage relation, however, such rights and obligations are high above the fluctuating will of both husband and wife; they are determined and imposed by Religion, as well as by the Civil Law. The contract view fails to bring out this higher sphere of duty and conscience, which is of the very essence of marriage.

The purpose of marriage is twofold—(a) posterity, and (b) companionship.

(a) The duty of rearing a family figures in the Rabbinic codes as the first of the 613 *Mitzvoth* (ordinances) of the Torah (Genesis 1, 28, *Be fruitful and multiply*). To this commandment is due the sacredness and centrality of the child in Judaism—something which even the enlightened nations of antiquity could not understand. The Roman historian Tacitus deemed it a contemptible prejudice of the Jews that "it is a crime among them to kill any child". What a lurid flashlight these words throw on Graeco-Roman society! It is in such a society that Judaism proclaimed the Biblical teaching that the child was the highest of human treasures. *O Lord God, what wilt Thou give me, seeing that I go childless?* was Abraham's agonizing cry. Of what value were earthly possessions to him, if he was denied a child who would continue his work after him? This attitude of the Father of the Hebrew people has remained that of his descendants throughout the ages. A childless marriage was deemed to have failed in one of its main purposes. In little children—it was taught—God gives humanity a chance to make good its mistakes. Little children are "the Messiahs of mankind"—the perennial regenerative force in humanity. No wonder that Jewish infant mortality is everywhere lower than the non-Jewish—often only one-half of that among the general population.

(b) Companionship is the other primary end of the marriage institution. Woman is to be the helpmate of man. . . . A wife is a man's other self, all that man's nature demands for its completion physically, socially, and spiritually. In marriage alone can man's need for physical and social companionship be directed to holy ends. It is this idea which is expressed by the term *kiddushin* ("the sanctities") applied to Jewish marriage—a term which, aside from its original sacerdotal meaning, signifies the hallowing of two human beings to life's holiest purposes. In married life, man finds his truest and most lasting happiness; and only through married life does human personality reach its highest fulfillment. *A man shall leave his father and his mother, and shall cleave to his wife*, says Scripture (Genesis 2.24). Note that it is the man who is to cleave to his wife, and not the woman, physically the weaker, who is to cleave to her husband; because, in the higher sphere of the soul's life, woman is the ethical and spiritual superior of man. "Even as the wife is", say the Rabbis, "so the husband is". The celibate life is the unblessed life: Judaism requires its saints show their saintliness *in* the world, and amid the ties and obligations of family life. "He who has no wife abides without good, help, joy, blessing, or atonement. He who has no wife cannot be considered a whole man" (Talmud). All forms of extra-marital companionship outside the sacred estate of matrimony, unhallowed by Religion and unrestrained by its commandments, Judaism considers an abomination. And such extra-marital relations are prohibited just as sternly with non-Jewish women as with Jewish. Thus, Joseph resists the advances of the *heathen* temptress with the words: *How can I do this great wickedness, and sin against God?* (Genesis 39.9); and the Book of Proverbs is clear on the attitude of Judaism to the "strange woman"—married or unmarried. No less emphatically than in Scripture is purity of life and thought demanded by the Rabbis. The founders of the Christian Church adopted in its entirety the Jewish view on extra-marital relations.

The Biblical ideal of marriage is monogamy. The Creation story and all the Prophetical portions of Scripture speak of the union of a man with *one* wife. Whenever a Prophet speaks of marriage, he is thinking of such a union—lifelong, faithful, holy. Polygamy seems to have well-nigh disappeared in Israel after the Babylonian Exile; and early Rabbinic literature presupposes a practically monogamic society. Though the *formal* abolition of polygamy, through Rabbenu Gershom, only took place in the year 1000, monogamy had been the rule in Jewish life long before the rise of Christianity.

For the questions and problems concerning the dissolution of marriage,. . . . the words of the late Dr. Friedländer should be noted. "We acknowledge the principle laid down in the Talmud, "the law of the Country is binding upon us" . . . ; but only in so far as our civil relations are concerned. With regard to religious questions, our own religious Code must be obeyed. Religiously neither civil marriage nor civil divorce can be recognized, unless supplemented by marriage or divorce according to religious forms. Furthermore, marriages allowed by the Civil Law, but prohibited by our Religious Law, cannot be recognized before the tribunal of our Religion".

It is astonishing to note the amount of hostile misrepresentation that exists in regard to woman's position in Jewish life. Yet the teaching of Scripture is quite clear. *God created man in His own image; male and female created He them* (Genesis 1.27)—both man and woman are in their spiritual nature akin to God, and both are invested with the same authority to subdue the earth and have domination over it. The wives of the Patriarchs are the equals of their husbands. Miriam, alongside her brothers, is reckoned as one of the three emancipators from Egypt (Micah 6.4); Deborah is "*Judge*" in Israel, and leader in the war of independence; and to Hannah (1 Samuel 1.8) her husband speaks: "Why weepest thou? am not I better to thee than ten sons?" In later centuries, we find woman among the Prophets—Huldah; and in the days of the Second Temple, on the throne—Queen Salome Alexandra. Nothing can well be nobler praise of woman than Proverbs 31 . . . ; and, as regards the reverence due to her from her children, the mother was placed on a par with the father in the Decalogue, Exodus 20.12; and before the father, in Leviticus 19.3. A Jewish child would not have spoken to his grief-stricken mother as did Telemachus, the hero's son in the Odyssey: "Go to thy chamber, and mind thine own housewiferies. Speech shall be for man, for all, but for me in chief; for mine is the lordship in the house". . . .

A conclusive proof of woman's dominating place in Jewish life is the undeniable fact, that the hallowing of the Jewish home was her work; and that the laws of chastity were observed in that home, both by men and women, with a scrupulousness that has hardly ever been equalled. The Jewish Sages duly recognized her wonderful spiritual influence, and nothing could surpass the delicacy with which respect for her is inculcated: "Love thy wife as thyself, and honour her more than thyself. Be careful not to cause woman to weep, for God counts her tears. Israel was redeemed from Egypt on account of the virtue of its women. He who weds a good woman is as if he had fulfilled all the precepts of the Torah" (Talmud).

Samuel H. Dresner

Samuel H. Dresner is Visiting Professor of Jewish Philosophy at Jewish Theological Seminary, a Conservative Movement seminary in New York City.[1] A rabbi and scholar, he has written many books on Jewish life, including *Can Families Survive in Pagan America?*, *The Jewish Dietary Laws*, and *Judaism: The Way of Sanctification.*[2] His interest in Jewish thought and practice also is represented in his books *Rachel* and *The World of a Hasidic Master* as well as in the editing he has done on writings by Abraham J. Heschel.[3]

Our selection contains excerpts from Dresner's essay "Homosexuality and the Order of Creation." First published in *Judaism: A Journal of Jewish Life and Thought*, this essay contends that the Bible demonstrates that heterosexuality is God's design for human life, or, as Dresner terms it, "the way in which humans were made and intended to behave."[4] As grounds for this position, Dresner appeals first to the creation accounts in the opening chapters of Genesis and then to the narration concerning Noah and the Flood in Genesis 6-8. The former passages, according to Dresner, set out a positive description of God's intentions for heterosexual marriage; the latter he sees as a judgment against deviating from God's design. Dresner also appeals to the Zohar and Jewish practices as well as to Plato and a legend about Oedipus's father Laius in support of his position that "homosexuality is abnormal in the sense that it violates the natural constitution of humans."[5] (Source: Samuel H. Dresner, "Homosexuality and the Order of Creation," *Judaism: A Journal of Jewish Life and Thought* 40 [1991]: 309-21.)

"Homosexuality and the Order of Creation" (1991 CE)
SAMUEL H. DRESNER

"You shall not copy the practices of the land of Egypt or the land of Cannan [*sic*]: Do not have carnal relations with your mother, your daughter, your sister, with a beast, with one of your own sex. It is an abomination. Do not sacrifice your child to Molekh. It is an abomination. Let not the land vomit you forth for defiling it, as it vomited forth the nation that came before you." (Leviticus, chapters 18 and 20.)

Homosexuality is a violation of the order of creation.

In the passage cited above, the Bible forbids homosexuality, and other illicit sexual expressions, because it affirms heterosexuality as the way in which humans were made and intended to behave. This affirmation is laid out in the first chapters of Genesis.

"Male and female He created Them" (1:27). In taking up the emergence of the human species, heterosexuality is at once proclaimed to be the order of creation.

"It is not good for man to be alone" (2:18). Man is in need of a companion. Who will it be? First the animals are considered. Man *names* them, that is, he understands their nature and comprehends why none is a fitting mate for him.

Here we have an implicit rejection of bestiality. Woman is formed and becomes his partner. In her, man finds completion. So the Sages instruct that a woman should not be without a husband; a man should not be without a wife; and both should not be without the Divine Presence.

"Be fruitful and multiply and fill the earth" (1:28). Replenishment of mankind through propagation and companionship are the purposes of heterosexuality.

"Therefore shall a man leave his father and his mother and cleave unto his wife, and they shall become one flesh" (Gen. 1:27-28; 2:18-24). The husband-wife relationship is axiological. It takes precedence even over the elemental parent-child bond.

"Male and female He created them and called their name adam" (5:2). The name "adam," which here means a human person, is given to the man and woman together and not separately. In other words, we are only fully human, fully *adam*, when male and female are met in a social bonding, in marriage. Therefore, it follows that the blessing, "Praised are You, O Lord . . . Creator of *adam*," is not recited at birth, as one might expect, but at the Jewish wedding service, when male and female are joined, and the intention of creation is biologically completed.

The early Biblical narratives can be read as a continuous attack on the widespread sexual deviance which challenged and often seduced the Israelites, whose fallings away Scripture scrupulously records. . . .

What has not been sufficiently noted, however, is that the principal story of this type, one which includes all forms of sexual deviance, including homosexuality, is the flood, a catastrophe which far outreached other stories limited to family or community.[6] What crime was of such magnitude to have evoked a divine regret over the creation of humankind and require the destruction of almost every living creature? According to the most ancient understanding of the Biblical story found in rabbinic sources, it was the violation of the natural order of sexual life. Sexual deviance was so pervasive and so struck at the heart of God's plan for the world, that a reconstitution of that order could only come from a new creation. But how do we know that the cause of the deluge had to do with the corruption of the sexual order, since Scripture only tells us that its justification was *man's wickedness* but not what this "wickedness" was? Let us examine the text:

> When men began to increase on earth and daughters were born to them, the divine beings saw how beautiful the daughters of men were and took wives from among those that pleased them . . . The Lord saw how great was man's wickedness on earth, and how every plan devised by his mind was nothing but evil all the time. And the Lord regretted that He had made man on earth and . . . said, "I will blot out from the earth the men whom I created" . . . (Gen: 6:1-2, 5-7).

. . . This enigmatic tale of *divine beings* has puzzled Biblical scholars, who usually understand it as a remnant of the pagan mythology of the life of the gods, which somehow escaped the eye of the Biblical censor and found its way into the canon. That may very well be, but, whatever its source, it would seem to be used here to explain the origins of the catastrophe of the deluge. It suggests that the immoral life of the gods was aped by humans, the disastrous effect of which was of such measure that it called into question God's plan for creation. . . .

While other crimes are listed among the catalogue of misdemeanors of the generation of the deluge, the rabbinic understanding of the flood story affirms that their *wickedness* was primarily sexual. The key verse is *"All flesh had corrupted their way on the earth"* (Gen. 6:12).

"Flesh" corrupting its "way" is taken in a sexual sense. Examples that are cited are whoredom,[7] incest[8] and sodomy.[9] Reflecting the custom common among the Greeks,

> [t]he men of the generation of the flood used to take two wives, one for procreation and the other for sexual gratification. The former would stay like a widow throughout her life, while the latter was given to drink a potion of roots, so that she should not bear, and then she sat before him like a harlot.[10]

"All" flesh, including the beast. The natural barriers of sexual distinction had broken down, also those separating man from the brute creation, so that all were now on the same level. . . .

A careful analysis of the story of the flood bears out this focus upon sexual order and disorder. Scripture takes pains to tell us that of those who entered the ark each male had a female companion: Noah and his sons are never mentioned entering or exiting from the ark except with their wives (6:18, 7:7, 13, 8:16, 18). This fivefold repetition is emphatic. . . .

This focus upon the sexual order points to the family. . . . Promiscuous sexual relations between man and man, man and woman, human and beast, would inevitably cripple the institution of the human couple and that of the human family. Therefore, when humans are chosen to repopulate the world, it is not simply a group of men and women who are designated, but a family. Not Noah and "others," but Noah with his "wife," and their sons with their "wives"—which is to say, an entire family unit. So firmly is this teaching embedded in the flood story, that *every animal, every creeping thing, and every bird, everything that stirs on earth came out of the ark "by families"* (8:19).

Nor must the monogamous element be overlooked. Noah and his sons each have a single wife. Their children are born from these wives and not from additional wives or maidservants. In this, the pattern of Adam and Eve in the garden of Eden is replicated. The message seems clear: human society is meant to be composed of families, of monogamous families.

Further, and quite remarkably, this concern to restore sexual normality to humans through the pairing of Noah and his children into husbands and wives, was extended even to the animals. They, too, are brought to the ark *male and female* and each according to *its species* (6:20, 7:14), to reconstitute them into their proper groupings, just like the humans. Most curious is the fact that the animals, upon entering the ark, are not simply described as *male and female* according to their *species*, but *each with his wife* (7:20)[11] (the only such usage in Scripture) and, upon exiting, as we have noted, according to their *families*! These last delineations are taken by the Sages to mean that the only animals allowed in the ark to constitute the new society and re-establish sexual order were those who had not violated their "species" in the past, and only those were allowed out who promised not to do so in the future. . . .[12]

What lies behind the drama of the flood . . . is the avowal that sexual misconduct may open the floodgates of destruction. There comes a time when society can no longer abide the violation of the laws which bind it together; a point is reached when constant batterings finally unravel the cords, and everything falls to pieces. For it was because sexually forbidden restraints were abandoned, we are told, that a global convulsion of enormous proportions took place. Scripture spells out the dynamics of that deluge in Leviticus 18 and 20 (which I have cited above), where a cataclysm of smaller proportions transpires. There, the Israelites are warned that just as "the land vomited forth" the Canaanites for their sexual debauchery and child sacrifice, and replaced them with the Israelites, so will it treat the Israelites themselves should they so behave. Note that Scripture takes care to tell us that it is the "land" which becomes defiled through such behavior, and the "land" which has "vomited forth" its inhabitants (and may do so again). Divine compassion accounts for human frailty, but the moral law is so set into the very fabric of creation, that, when the measure of toleration is exceeded, it spews forth sinners, whether pagan or Hebrew. . . .

Despite the havoc wrought by the flood, Scripture sees it as only an interlude in the moral chaos that prevailed in the ten generations that preceded it and the ten that followed, until the advent of Abraham and Sarah. The patriarchs and matriarchs, Abraham and Sarah, Isaac and Rebekah, Jacob and Rachel, reminiscent of Adam and Eve, attempt to replicate within the mortal and fallible portals of history the monogamous model of the Garden of Eden. With the patriarch-matriarch paradigm, the Bible establishes the human couple as the fulfillment of the order of creation and the archetype for all generations. Their mode is refuted neither by the concubines, who are only brought to Abraham and Jacob by the barren matriarchs, that they may raise the children, nor by Leah, whose position is anomalous and incongruous, a foil for monogamy.[13] It is the institution of marriage and the consequent features of the family—home, permanence, fidelity, and mutuality—which become the national treasure of the Jewish people, the bulwark and irreplaceable center of their society, and which Judaism surrounds with all manner of support and protection. The home which housed the Jewish family became both a school of parental instruction and a sanctuary-in-miniature (as the Talmud calls it), where the family rites were enacted. One needs only to compare the two home occasions, the Jewish Sabbath table with its family presence, its traditions and its religious joy, with the common form of the Greek symposium from which the excluded family was replaced by drink, conversation and sexual liaison with prostitutes or young boys.

Both the Greeks and the Jews possess myths which explain love as the reconstitution of two creatures into their pre-existent unity. One is found in Plato's Symposium, the other in the classic work of Jewish mysticism, the Zohar. The contrast between them, however, is conclusive. In the Symposium, Aristophanes cites the celebrated fable of immensely proportioned pre-existent humans with two heads, four arms, etc., whom Zeus severs in two in a moment of anger, pulls their skins together and sets them free in the world. Ever after they are destined to seek their other half: those who were androgynous searching for one of the opposite sex, while those who were of a single sex, whether male or female, searching for a same-sex mate.

The Zohar presents a counter-myth of reunification.[14] According to its account, human creation was of a single person with two faces. "God sawed [it] in two, separating the female from the male and brought them together, so they would be face to face. And when she was gathered in to man, then God blessed them, as at the wedding service." Note the two differences in this version from that of the Greek legend: first, the pre-existent state is only androgynous and never all-male or all-female, thus rejecting the homosexual option; and, second, the reconstitution of the primeval unity is not simply the working of biological tropism, the blind yearning for another body, as the Greek myth would have it, but the solemn union of husband and wife. The Zohar's fable finds its source, of course, in the Biblical story of creation: "Male and female He made them [androgyny]. He blessed them, and called *their* name adam [marriage]" (5:2). It is here argued that only in the male/female relationship are we fully human beings; that only then is adam, the human person, fully created,[15] and that the male/female relationship is sanctified in the institution of marriage. Until marriage, the individual is said to be incomplete, unfulfilled. As the Zohar puts it, "The Divine Presence rests only upon a married man, because an unmarried man is but half a man, and the Divine Presence does not rest upon that which is imperfect."[16] Similarly, the Talmud, "Whoever is not married is without joy, blessing or good, [and some add] without Torah or peace."[17] Indeed, so important was it to establish marriage as the norm, that the Midrash suggests that God Himself performed the first wedding ceremony for Adam and Eve.

Few mizvot are so richly developed in Jewish literature and Jewish life as marriage. . . . The Bible already exempted a male from army service, in the first year of marriage, that he might "rejoice with his wife" (Deut. 24:5). At the circumcision, the prayer is recited, "As he has entered the covenant of Abraham, so may he enter the study of Torah, the marital state and the practice of good deeds." It was considered a parental duty to arrange for an early marriage for children. "One who reaches the age of twenty and has not yet married," warns the Talmud, " . . . spends all his days with sinful thoughts."[18] Indeed, to protect the holiness of Jerusalem from being contaminated by the presence of unmarried men, those between the ages of 20 and 60 were forbidden to reside there, according to an ordinance of 1749.[19] Hesitant young men might be compelled by the Jewish court to marry.[20] Social pressure was exerted in a variety of ways. For example, an unmarried man does not wear a *talit* or a *kittel* in the synagogue, nor does an unmarried woman cover her hair, by which habits their marital status is clearly identified. . . . The most precious of Jewish possessions, the Torah scroll, cannot be sold, except to pay for a wedding. Jewish society was so structured as to encourage, arrange, and maintain marriage, and, in the event of death, remarriage. In the writing of Church Fathers, on the other hand, not only was celibacy preferred to marriage, but once married, if one's spouse died, widowhood was the chosen state.[21]

An unspoken principle in Jewish life emerged quite early: whatever strengthened the family is to be affirmed, whatever hinders it is to be opposed.

What the doctrine of creation was to the Hebrews, "natural law" was to the Greeks. While popular practice, exemplified by Aristophanes' myth of the divided human searching for his other half, be it male or female, reflected the wide acceptance of homosexuality during certain periods, the philosophic-legal opinion was quite different. Aristophanes' myth, after all, was spoken in the give-and-take of dialogue, and need not represent Plato's view, which, following Aristotle, finds that homosexuality is "unnatural."[22] The Greek thinkers understood certain features to be characteristic of man "by nature," while others are not. Recent scholars, some of whom have their own private sexual agendas, have bridled at Plato's terminology, and try to soften it. Thus, in the Republic (571b), Plato speaks of dreams in which one,

> as if freed from every restraint of shame and reason, attempt[s] to have intercourse with his mother or with any other creature, human or divine or animal . . . and in a word to go to any length in madness and shamelessness.

The translation of Plato's terms for such longings, *paranomoi*, clearly means "against *nomos* or law," and not simply "convention," as one recent author would have it.[23] . . . Furthermore, in Plato's *Laws* we find:

> Were one [legislator] to follow the guidance of nature and adopt the law of the old days before Laius—I mean, to pronounce it wrong to have to do carnally with youthful male as with female, and to fetch his evidence from the life of animals, pointing out that male does not touch male in this way because the action is unnatural [not by *physis*], his contention would surely be a telling one, yet it would be quite at variance with the practice of your societies.[24]

The example of animal behavior cited in this passage hardly lends itself to explanation as a violation of "convention," but quite decisively describes homosexuality as unnatural. . . .

. . . [T]he reference above to the time of the early king, Laius, as the watershed of homosexuality in Greece, suggests a more complex attitude to homosexuality there. We are, of course, familiar with the centerpiece of Freud's theory of the parent-child relationship, the Oedipus complex, in which the killing of one's father to marry one's mother is paradigmatic. Oedipus is the famed character in Sophocles' play of the same name, where the story is played out to a horrified audience which witnesses the killing of his father, king

Laius, and the marrying of his mother in ignorance of her true identity. Less well-known is the mythic origin of the story. For, according to a legend, homosexuality was unaccustomed in Greece before the time of king Laius, the father of Oedipus. The tale goes that a boy, whom Laius had abducted for sexual purposes, committed suicide out of shame, whereupon the boy's father placed a curse upon the king: either that he should have no son or that this son would kill his father. The myth adds that Hera, the goddess of marriage, fearing that homosexuality would undermine her dominion, sent the Sphinx to destroy Thebes, the city of Laius. Thus, the story of Oedipus, the classic tale of family tragedy in Greek drama, has its source in the spread of homosexuality, whose introduction into Greek life was understood to have brought on a familial catastrophe, personal and communal, which, though smaller in scale, has its parallel to the flood myth among the Hebrews that some explain as the result of sexual confusion.[25]

Heterosexuality, is, then, for the Greeks—at least, theoretically and legally—a human characteristic "by nature"—as it is for the Hebrews, who would argue the same for the family, which is established and nurtured by marital sexual union. (By marriage is meant a socially recognized and lasting male-female cohabitation.)

The debate over the argument from normality is illustrated by Roger Scruton's amusing parable of the lion without a mane. It seems that a plague struck and had left lions without manes. Soon, two opinions formed. One argued the obvious: that while lions may not have manes for the time being as the result of a plague, the real lion, the normal lion, the one intended by the order of creation or nature, of course, has a mane, while those presently without them are deviants. The other replied with equal aplomb, that today's modern maneless lions are quite happy as they are, delighted to be rid of those mangy manes. And all this talk about plagues, creation, natural law and normality is sheer nonsense, an insidious effort to pull us back into the past.[26]

Nevertheless, homosexuality is abnormal in the sense that it violates the natural constitution of humans. Even if it is no fault of their own, one can say that homosexuals are abnormal in the same way that the blind and the deaf are abnormal. As the existence of such persons does not deny the fact that humans hear and see "by nature," so humans are heterosexual "by nature," though individual persons may be homosexual, whether by constitutional orientation or environmental influence. Whether one views marriage as a part of the divine order of creation or of natural law, one who is unable to enter into such a sexual relationship is abnormal.

Certainly, for the preponderance of homosexuals today, those "by choice," Jaffa's observation applies: "All normal people have within themselves, at one time or another, desires which they know they ought not to gratify. The difference—by and large—between those who live moral and those who live immoral lives, is that the former refuse to indulge their passions merely because they have them. . . . "[27]

"Why" continues Jaffa, "is sodomy against the natural law? . . . All friendship, all society, indeed, all of human existence, arises from the physical difference of male and female human beings. From this physical difference arises the ground and purpose of human life, because it is the ground and purpose of nature. . . . Equally with rape and incest, homosexuality strikes at the authority and dignity of the family. The distinction between a man and woman is . . . the very distinction by which nature itself is constituted. It is the ability of two members of the same species to generate a third, that confirms them as members of the same species. It thereby confirms male and female members of the human species in that equality of rights to which they are entitled as members of that species. . . . "[28]

When the Bible associates homosexuality in Leviticus 18 and 20 with other sexual deviations, it assumes that the heterosexual marital state is the normal condition for sexual relations. Once the argument from the order of creation and natural law is abandoned and heterosexuality within the marital bond as a norm is dismissed, then how can adultery, pedophilia, incest or bestiality be rejected? I have not been able to find a single argument in opposition to, for example, incest, in the literature which advocates homosexuality. The reason for this is the simple fact that "someone who cannot say that sodomy is unnatural cannot say that incest is unnatural."[29] After all, if pleasure is the measure of all things, sexual pleasure the measure of all pleasures, and deferred sexual pleasure the ultimate sin—and unhealthy to boot—then how object to any means to achieve it, including the above itinerary?

To say that bestiality, pedophilia, sado-masochism, fetishism, necrophilia, and homosexuality are perversions, is to posit a norm from which these deviate. But this is precisely what is denied by present-day sexual nihilists. For them there are no norms. Yet none of our contemporary sexual expressions are new to history. Over the centuries, peoples have suffered the full measure of sexual experimentation and have testified against them, sometimes going so far as to mete out the death penalty when social cohesion was in jeopardy. The most fundamental code of even primitive societies included, at the very least, rules about the improper uses of force and sex. When, through civil edict, religious instruction and family sanction, sexual codes developed and were progressively internalized—though regularly violated—it was a sign of advancing culture. That culture, the "funded wisdom of the ages," is grounded in traditional family values, which modern society, in its attempt to turn civilization back to zero, neglects at its peril. . . .

NOTES TO CHAPTER 8, HIERARCHICAL INTERPRETATIONS, SAMUEL H. DRESNER

[1. For more information on Samuel H. Dresner, see the entry on him in Pamela S. Nadell, editor, *Conservative Judaism in America: A Biographical Dictionary and*

Sourcebook (New York: Greenwood Press, 1988), pp. 70-72. For information on the Conservative Movement, see Nadell's introduction, pp. 1-24.]

[2. Samuel H. Dresner, *Can Families Survive in Pagan America?* (Lafayette, La.: Huntington House, 1995). Dresner, *The Jewish Dietary Laws*, revised and expanded edition (New York: Rabbinical Assembly of America, United Synagogue Commission on Jewish Education, 1982). Dresner and Byron L. Sherwin, *Judaism: The Way of Sanctification* (New York: United Synagogue of America, 1978).]

[3. Dresner, *Rachel* (Minneapolis: Fortress Press, 1994). Dresner, *The World of a Hasidic Master: Levi Yitzhak of Berditchev* (Northvale, N.J.: J. Aronson, 1994). Dresner's work with Heschel's writings includes: *The Circle of the Baal Shem Tov: Studies in Hasidism* (Chicago: University of Chicago Press, 1985); *I Asked for Wonder: A Spiritual Anthology* by Heschel, edited and with an introduction by Dresner (New York: Crossroad, 1983).]

[4. Samuel H. Dresner, "Homosexuality and the Order of Creation," *Judaism: A Journal of Jewish Life and Thought* 40 (Summer 1981): 309; and in the selection in this chapter.]

[5. Dresner, "Homosexuality and the Order of Creation," 319; and in the selection in this chapter.]

6. See Jack L. Lewis, *A Study of the Interpretation of Noah and the Flood (in Jewish) and Christian Literature* (Leiden: Brill, 1968) for a survey of Jewish and Christian understandings of the flood.

7. *Leviticus Rabbah* 23:9.

8. *Pirkei de-Rabbi Eliezer.*

9. B. Sanhedrin 108a; *Genesis Rabbah* 27:3.

10. *Genesis Rabbah* 23:2.

11. The *Targum* resolves the difficulty by translating the phrase, "male and female," as in 7:3. Cf. Maimonides, *The Guide for the Perplexed*, III 6.

12. Rashi, ad. loc.

13. Leah was more a foil for monogamy than a case of polygamy. See [Dresner, *Rachel*].

14. Zohar III 4b. This is based on numerous earlier rabbinic passages. See [Louis] Ginzberg, *The Legends of the Jews* (Philadelphia: Jewish Publication Society of America, 1909-1938)], vol. V, pp. 88-9, for sources and comparisons.

15. "A man without a wife is not a man, for it is said, 'male and female He created them. He blessed them and called their name adam' (5:2)." *B. Yevamot* 63a.

16. *Zohar Hadash* 4,50b.

17. *B. Yevamot* 62b, *Genesis Rabbah* 17:2.

18. *B. Kiddushin* 29b, 30b.

19. D. Feldman, *Birth Control in Jewish Law* (New York: New York University Press, 1968), p. 31, n. 53.

20. [Feldman, *Birth Control*], p. 27.

21. D. Bailey, *Sexual Relation in Christian Thought* (New York: Harper and Bros., 1959), pp. 20, 31-2, quoted by Feldman, [*Birth Control*], p. 23.

22. Plato, *Laws*, Bk. 8, 835d-842a, especially 836d, 838b, c. Cf. Jasper Griffin, *New York Review of Books*, March 29, 1990, p. 10.

23. John J. Winkler, *The Constraints of Desire: The Anthropology of Sex and Gender in Ancient Greece* (New York: Routledge, 1989). Cf. Griffin, [*New York Review of Books*], pp. 9-11.

24. Plato's *Laws*, translated by A. E. Taylor (The Everyman Series, Dutton, 1934), p. 223, quoted by Griffin, [*New York Review of Books*], p. 9. See ahead for further explanation of Laius.

25. Griffin, [*New York Review of Books*], p. 10.

26. Roger Scruton, *Sexual Desire: A Moral Philosophy of the Erotic* (New York: Free Press, 1988); Richard Neuhaus, "The Maneless Lions," *National Review* (May 8, 1987): 5.

27. Harry V. Jaffa, *Homosexuality and the Natural Law* (Montclair, Calif.: Claremont Institute), p. 25.

28. Jaffa, [*Homosexuality*], pp. 33-37.

29. Jaffa, [*Homosexuality*], p. 34.

Sayyid Abu al-A'la Mawdudi

Sayyid Abu al-A'la Mawdudi (1903-1979) has been one of the most influential Muslim thinkers of the twentieth century.[1] As a prolific author and a social activist in South Asia, he contributed greatly to the Islamic revivalist movement and its call to reform society by a return to authentic Islamic institutions and practices. Born and raised in India, Mawdudi formed the "Jama'at-i Islami" (Islamic Party) there in 1941. In 1947 he moved to Pakistan, where he was imprisoned several times because of his political activism.

Mawdudi saw the teachings of the Qur'an and the hadith as foundational to the revivalist agenda. In 1942 he began to write an Urdu translation and commentary on the Qur'an; he completed this work in 1972.[2] Our selection contains portions of his commentary on surah 2 and surah 4. Mawdudi's comments appear after the text of the relevant Qur'anic verses; his numberings for his discussions are retained within these verses or "ayat."

In his commentary, Mawdudi often appealed to God's design for creation as the basis for social practice. Like many hierarchalists in the twentieth century, he endorsed a kind of gender equality in maintaining that men do not have "superior dignity." Yet he also insisted that men were created to be the "head" of the family, that women were created to live under the protection of men, and that wives should obey their husbands unless the men command the women to disobey God. Also significant for our theme are Mawdudi's discussions on such topics as sexuality, procreation, and polygamy. (Source: Sayyid Abu al-A'la Mawdudi, *Towards Understanding the Qur'an*, translated and edited by Zafar Ishaq Ansari, vol. 1, Leicester, United Kingdom: Islamic Foundation, 1988/1408 A.H., pp. 62-64, 172-73; vol. 2, Leicester, United Kingdom: Islamic Foundation, 1989/1409 A.H, pp. 5-8, 35-36, 86.)

Towards Understanding the Qur'an (1942–1972 CE)
SAYYID ABU AL-A'LA MAWDUDI

Surah 2:34: And when We ordered the angels: "Prostrate yourselves before Adam", all of them fell prostrate, (45) except Iblis. He refused, and gloried in his arrogance and became one of the defiers.

Surah 2:35: And We said: "O Adam, live in the Garden, you and your wife, and eat abundantly of whatever you wish but do not approach this tree (48) or else you will be counted among the wrongdoers."

(45) This signifies that all the angels whose jurisdiction embraces the earth and that part of the universe in which the earth is situated were ordered to devote themselves to man's service. Since man had been invested with authority on earth the angels were told that whenever man wanted to make use

of the powers with which he had been invested by God, and which God of His own will had allowed him to use, they should co-operate with him and enable him to do whatever he wanted to do, irrespective of right and wrong.

This can be understood with reference to the manner in which government employees are required to work. When a sovereign appoints a governor or a magistrate, all government employees under his jurisdiction are duty-bound to obey him. As long as the sovereign permits the governor or magistrate to exercise authority on his behalf, people are required to obey him, irrespective of whether he exercises this authority judiciously or not. But as soon as the sovereign indicates to those employees that the governor or magistrate should be barred from doing something, the effective authority of the governor or the magistrate comes to an abrupt end. In fact, were the sovereign to issue the order that the governor be dismissed or imprisoned, the same employees who until then had been moving to and fro at his bidding would not feel hesitant in putting hand-cuffs on him and taking him to prison.

God's order to the angels to prostrate themselves before Adam was of a similar nature. It is possible that prostration signifies the fact of their becoming yoked to man's service. At the same time it is also possible that they were ordered to perform the act of prostration itself as a sign of the envisaged relationship between angels and man. In my view the latter seems more plausible. . . .

(48) This indicates that before man was sent to earth—the realm of his vicegerency—Adam and Eve were kept in Paradise in order to test them and their proclivities. A tree was chosen for this test and they were told not to approach it. They were also told that if they did approach it they would be reckoned as wrongdoers in the sight of God. It is unnecessary to delve into a discussion about what that tree was and what was the particular reason underlying the prohibition to approach it. The actual reason for the prohibition was not that any particular evil inhered in the tree which could harm Adam and Eve, but rather to test how far they would follow the instructions of God and overcome the temptations of Satan. Anything that served this purpose was good enough, and this is why God has mentioned neither the name of the tree nor its attributes.

Moreover, for this kind of test Paradise was the best possible place. What God wanted to impress on man was that the only place that befits man's station is Paradise, and that if man turns from the course of obedience to God as a result of Satanic allurements, he will remain deprived of it in the Next Life even as he was deprived of it once before. The only way he can recover his true status and reclaim the lost Paradise is by resisting effectively the enemy who is always trying to drive him off the course of obedience to God. . . .

> Surah 2:222: They ask you about menstruation. Say: "It is a state of impurity; (238) so keep away from them and do not approach them till they are cleansed. (239) And when they are cleansed, then come to them as Allah has commanded you." (240) Truly, Allah loves those who abstain from evil and keep themselves pure.
> Surah 2:223: Your wives are your tilth; go, then, into your tilth as you

wish (241) but take heed of your ultimate future and avoid incurring the wrath of Allah. Know well that one Day you shall face Him. Announce good tidings to the believers.

(238) The Arabic word *adha* denotes both a state of ritual impurity and sickness. Menstruation is not merely an impurity, but also a state in which the woman is closer to sickness than to health.

(239) With regard to matters such as these the Qur'an resorts to metaphors and figurative language. Hence it instructs men not to approach women. This does not mean that people should either abstain from sitting together on the same floor or eating together when a woman has her monthly period making her virtually an untouchable, as has been the custom among the Jews, Hindus and certain other nations. The explanation of this injunction by the Prophet makes it clear that during this period men are only required to abstain from sexual intercourse; no change is postulated in other relationships, and the woman is to be treated in the normal way.

(240) The "command" of God mentioned here is not a formal legal injunction from God, but that inherent urge with which the nature of both men and animals has been imbued and which is apprehended instinctively.[3]

(241) That is, God's purpose in the creation of women is not merely to provide men with recreation. Their mutual relationship is like that between a farmer and his tilth. A farmer approaches his field not just for the sake of pleasure, but to acquire produce. Similarly, man ought to approach the tilth of the human race with the purpose of acquiring produce, that is, offspring. What is of concern to the Law of God is not the particular mode of cultivating one's tilth, but rather that one should go only to one's tilth and not elsewhere, and that one should go there for the purpose of cultivation. . . .

> Surah 4
> In the name of Allah, the Merciful, the Compassionate.
> Surah 4:1: O men! Fear your Lord Who created you from a single being and out of it created its mate; and out of the two spread many men and women. (1) Fear Allah in Whose name you plead for rights, and heed the ties of kinship. Surely, Allah is ever watchful over you.

(1) What are the mutual rights of human beings, what are the principles on which a sound and stable family life can be established, are questions that are discussed a little further on in this surah. As an appropriate introduction to the subject, the surah opens by exhorting the believers to fear God and to avoid courting His displeasure, and by urging them to recognize that all human beings have sprung from the same root and that all of them are, therefore, of one another's flesh and blood.

The expression "Who created you from a single being (*nafs*)" indicates that the creation of the human species began with the creation of one individual. At another place, the Qur'an specifies that the one person from whom the human race spread in the world was Adam.

The details how out of that "being" its mate was created are not known

to us. The explanation which is generally given by the commentators of the
Qur'an and which is also found in the Bible is that Eve was created out of a rib
of Adam. (The Talmud is even more detailed in that it states that Eve was
created out of Adam's thirteenth rib on the left side.) The Qur'an, however, is
silent on the matter and the tradition which is adduced in support of this statement does not mean what it is often thought to be. It is thus better that we
leave the matter in the same state of ambiguity in which it was left by God,
rather than waste our time trying to determine, in detail, the actual process
of the creation of man's mate. . . .

> Surah 4:3: If you fear that you might not treat the orphans justly, then
> marry the women that seem good to you: two, or three, or four. (4) If you
> fear that you will not be able to treat them justly, then marry (only) one, (5)
> or marry from among those whom your right hands possess. This will make
> it more likely that you will avoid injustice.

(4) Commentators have explained this in the following ways:

(i) There is the view of 'A'ishah who says that men tended to marry orphan girls who were under their guardianship out of consideration for either
their property, beauty or because they thought they would be able to treat
them according to their whims, as they had no one to protect them. After
marriage such men sometimes committed excesses against these girls. It is in
this context that the Muslims are told that if they fear they will not be able to
do justice to the orphan girls, then they should marry other girls whom they
like. (This interpretation seems to be supported by verse 127 of this surah.)

(ii) The second view is that of Ibn 'Abbas and his disciple 'Ikrimah who
expressed the opinion that in the *Jahiliyah* period there was no limit on the
number of wives a man could take. The result was that a man sometimes married as many as ten women and, when expenses increased because of a large
family, he encroached on the rights either of his orphan nephews or other relatives. It was in this context that God fixed the limit of four wives and instructed the Muslims that they may marry up to four wives providing they
possessed the capacity to treat them equitably.

(iii) Sa'id b. Jubayr, Qatadah and some other commentators say that while
the Arabs of the *Jahiliyah* period did not approve of subjecting orphans to
wrong, they had no concept of justice and equity with regard to women. They
married as many women as they wanted and then subjected them to injustice
and oppression. It is in this context that people are told that if they fear per-
petrating wrongs on orphans they ought to be equally worried about perpe-
trating them on women. In the first place they should never marry more than
four, and of those four, they should marry only as many as they can treat fairly.

Each of the three interpretations is plausible and all three may possibly be
correct. Moreover, the verse could also mean that if a person does not find
himself able to treat orphans in a fair manner, then he might as well marry the
women who are looking after those orphans.

(5) Muslim jurists are agreed that according to this verse the maximum number of wives has been fixed at four. This conclusion is also supported by traditions. It is reported that when Ghaylan, the chief of Ta'if, embraced Islam he had nine wives. The Prophet (peace be on him) ordered him to keep only four wives and divorce the rest. Another person, Nawfal b. Mu'awiyah, had five wives. The Prophet (peace be on him) ordered him to divorce one of them.

This verse stipulates that marrying more wives than one is permissible on the condition that one treats his wives equitably. A person who avails himself of this permission granted by God to have a plurality of wives, and disregards the condition laid down by God to treat them equitably has not acted in good faith with God. In case there are complaints from wives that they are not being treated equitably, the Islamic state has the right to intervene and redress such grievances.

Some people who have been overwhelmed and overawed by the Christianized outlook of Westerners have tried to prove that the real aim of the Qur'an was to put an end to polygamy (which, in their opinion, is intrinsically evil). Since it was widely practised at that time, however, Islam confined itself to placing restrictions on it. Such arguments only show the mental slavery to which these people have succumbed. That polygamy is an evil *per se* is an unacceptable proposition, for under certain conditions it becomes a moral and social necessity. If polygamy is totally prohibited men who cannot remain satisfied with only one wife will look outside the bounds of matrimonial life and create sexual anarchy and corruption. This is likely to cause much greater harm than polygamy to the moral and social order. For this reason the Qur'an has allowed those who feel the need for it to resort to polygamy. Those who consider it an evil in itself may certainly denounce it in disregard of the Qur'an and may even argue for its abolition. But they have no right to attribute such a view to the Qur'an, for it has expressed its permission of polygamy in quite categorical terms. Indeed, there is not the slightest hint in the Qur'an that could justify the conclusion that it advocates abolition of polygamy. . . .

> Surah 4:34: Men are the protectors and maintainers of women (56) because Allah has made one of them excel over the other, (57) and because they spend out of their possessions (to support them). Thus righteous women are obedient and guard the rights of men in their absence under Allah's protection. (58) As for women of whom you fear rebellion, admonish them, and remain apart from them in beds, and beat them. (59) Then if they obey you, do not seek ways to harm them. Allah is Exalted, Great.

(56) A *qawwam* or *qayyim* is a person responsible for administering and supervising the affairs of either an individual or an organization, for protecting and safeguarding them and taking care of their needs.

(57) The verb used here—a derivative of the root *fdl*—is not used to mean that some people have been invested with superior honour and dignity. Rather

it means that God has endowed one of the sexes (i.e. the male sex) with certain qualities which He has not endowed the other sex with, at least not to an equal extent. Thus it is the male who is qualified to function as head of the family. The female has been so constituted that she should live under his care and protection.

(58) It is reported in a tradition from the Prophet (peace be on him) that he said: "The best wife is she who, if you look at her, will please you; who, if you bid her to do something, will obey; and who will safeguard herself and your property in your absence." This tradition contains the best explanation of the above verse. It should be borne in mind, however, that obedience to God has priority over a woman's duty to obey her husband. If a woman's husband either asks her to disobey God or prevents her from performing a duty imposed upon her by God, she should refuse to carry out his command. Obedience to her husband in this case would be a sin. However, were the husband to prevent his wife from performing either supererogatory Prayer or Fasting—as distinct from the obligatory ones—she should obey him, for such acts would not be accepted by God if performed by a woman in defiance of her husband's wish.

(59) This does not mean that a man should resort to these three measures all at once, but that they may be employed if a wife adopts an attitude of obstinate defiance. So far as the actual application of these measures is concerned, there should, naturally, be some correspondence between the fault and the punishment that is administered. Moreover, it is obvious that wherever a light touch can prove effective one should not resort to sterner measures. Whenever the Prophet (peace be on him) permitted a man to administer corporal punishment to his wife, he did so with reluctance, and continued to express his distaste for it. And even in cases where it is necessary, the Prophet (peace be on him) directed men not to hit across the face, nor to beat severely nor to use anything that might leave marks on the body. . . .

> Surah 4:116: Truly it is only associating others with Allah in His divinity that Allah does not forgive, and forgives anything besides that to whomsoever He wills. Whoever associates others with Allah in His divinity has indeed strayed far away.
> Surah 4:117: Rather than call upon Him, they call upon goddesses, and call upon a rebellious Satan
> Surah 4:118: upon whom Allah has laid His curse. He said (to Allah): "I will take to myself an appointed portion of Your servants
> Surah 4:119: and shall lead them astray, and shall engross them in vain desires, and I shall command them and they will cut off the ears of the cattle, and I shall command them and they will disfigure Allah's creation." (148)

(148) To alter God's creation in some respect does not mean changing its original form. If that was meant, human civilization would have to be considered Satanic in its entirety. For civilization consists essentially of man's put-

ting to use the resources endowed by God. Hence the alteration of God's creation, which is characterized as Satanic, consists in using a thing not for the purpose for which it was created by God. In other words, all acts performed in violation either of one's true nature or of the intrinsic nature of other things are the result of the misleading promptings of Satan. These include, for instance, sodomy, birth control, monasticism, celibacy, sterilization of either men or women, turning males into eunuchs, diverting females from the functions entrusted to them by nature and driving them to perform the functions for which men were created. These and numerous similar measures are enacted by Satan's disciples in this world, which amounts on their part, to saying that the laws of the Creator were faulty and that they would like to "reform" them.

NOTES TO CHAPTER 8, HIERARCHICAL INTERPRETATIONS, SAYYID ABU AL-A'LA MAWDUDI

[1. Seyyed Vali Reza Nasr provides a good description of Mawdudi's life and work in his entry "Mawdudi, Sayyid Abu Al-A'la" in *The Oxford Encyclopedia of the Modern Islamic World* (New York and Oxford: Oxford University Press, 1995), vol. 3, pp. 71-75.]

[2. For additional information about this text, see the "Foreword" by Khurshid Ahmad and the editor's preface by Zafar Ishaq Ansari in *Towards Understanding the Qur'an* (Leicester, United Kingdom: Islamic Foundation, 1988/1408 A.H.), vol. 1, pp. ix-xviii; xix-xxv.]

[3. In relation to Mawdudi's comment, his translator, Zafar Ishaq Ansari, notes "the verse means, therefore, that after the end of the menstrual course people may again engage in sexual intercourse." See his parenthetical remark, *Towards Understanding the Qur'an*, vol. 1, p. 173.]

EGALITARIAN INTERPRETATIONS

Sun Ai Lee Park

Sun Ai Lee Park is ordained in the Christian Church (Disciples of Christ). She lives in Seoul, Korea, where she is the Coordinator of the Asian Women's Resource Centre for Culture and Theology. She became the Asian Coordinator of the Women's Commission of EATWOT (the Ecumenical Association of Third World Theologians) when this Commission was founded in 1982. She has served as editor of *In God's Image*, a journal of theological reflection for Asian women. In addition to poetry, she has written many essays, including "A Short History of Asian Feminist Theology."[1] She also coedited the anthology *We Dare to Dream: Doing Theology as Asian Women*, to which she contributed "A Theological Reflection."[2]

We discovered Sun Ai Lee Park's poem in the book *The Bible through Asian Eyes*.[3] The poem offers an intriguing reading of Eve and Adam's story. Through its imagery and movement, it evokes attention to matters of knowing, particularly to relationships between knowing and power. The poem opens with the temptation scene of Genesis 3. Near its end, the poem touches on the Genesis 1 theme of woman being created in God's image, before concluding by educing concern for the story's "unfolding" into the present time. (Source: Sun Ai Lee Park, untitled poem, in Masao Takenaka and Ron O'Grady, editors, *The Bible through Asian Eyes*, Auckland, New Zealand: Pace Publishing and the Asian Christian Art Association, 1991, p. 24.)

Poem (Untitled) (c. 1991 CE)
SUN AI LEE PARK

Eve found a tree
With beautiful fruits
Legended to give knowledge
Of good and evil
Of God and the Omni-scient

I want to be wise
I want to be a person of myself
Knowing all and being empowered
Nor being ordered neither dependent
Not even on God, the Controlling Almighty

I want to use good sense of mine
And pursue the infinite realm
Of knowing to have access
To the governance
Of life of mine and my people
Expanding our world to the boundless bountiful
And to the horizons of eternity

Eve took the fruits and ate
And she gave some to her husband
Without reasoning Adam ate
And he became knowledgeable
As much as Eve

But ever since it is Adam
Who monopolizes the power of knowing
For his reasoning has become
More radically capacitated than his wife
Who was wiser than he in the beginning

But Eve, even in her forced subjugation
Still holds Godly pride and self-esteem
Fit to be the image of the Creator

And human history
Unfolds into modernity.

NOTES TO CHAPTER 8, EGALITARIAN INTERPRETATIONS,
SUN AI LEE PARK

[1. Sun Ai Lee Park, "A Short History of Asian Feminist Theology," in Ofelia
Ortega, editor, *Women's Visions: Theological Reflection, Celebration, Action* (Geneva, Swit-
zerland: World Council of Churches Publications, 1995), pp. 37-48.]
  [2. Virginia Fabella and Sun Ai Lee Park, editors, *We Dare to Dream: Doing Theology as Asian Women* (Hong Kong: Asian Women's Resource Centre for Culture and
Theology and The EATWOT Women's Commission in Asia, 1989). See pp. 72-82 for
Park's "A Theological Reflection."]
  [3. Masao Takenaka and Ron O'Grady, editors, *The Bible through Asian Eyes* (Auk-
lund, New Zealand: Pace Publishing and the Asian Christian Art Association, 1991),
p. 24.]

Judith Plaskow

Judith Plaskow is a Jewish theologian who has played a prominent role in the
development of feminist theology. She is Professor of Religious Studies at
Manhattan College. She also has held several leadership positions in the
American Academy of Religion (AAR), becoming AAR President in 1997. In
1983, she cofounded the *Journal of Feminist Studies in Religion*, which she
coedited for over a decade. The author of the Jewish feminist theology *Standing Again at Sinai: Judaism from a Feminist Perspective*, she has shaped Jewish
feminism as well as feminist theology in general.[1] She has influenced the
study of religion and gender through her attention to Christian antisemitism.[2]
Her influence also has been conveyed through several anthologies on women
and religion that she has edited.[3]

   This section contains two selections by Judith Plaskow. The first is her
tale about Lilith, along with excerpts from the essay Plaskow wrote to introduce the tale. Plaskow's telling of the tale, which she first articulated in 1972,
has shaped the imaginations of many who have come into contact with it.
The second is a new work, in which Plaskow "revisits" her earlier discussion.
In this retrospective essay, written nearly a quarter-century after the first,
Plaskow provides a critical analysis that depicts the historical context of the
earlier text. She also describes the development of her thought and scholarship
as she assesses strengths and limitations of "The Coming of Lilith." (Sources:

Judith Plaskow, "The Coming of Lilith: Toward a Feminist Theology," in Carol P. Christ and Judith Plaskow, editors, *Womanspirit Rising: A Feminist Reader in Religion*, New York: Harper & Row, 1979, pp. 202-207; "Lilith Revisited" is an essay written for the present volume.)

NOTES TO CHAPTER 8, EGALITARIAN INTERPRETATIONS, JUDITH PLASKOW

[1. Judith Plaskow, *Standing Again at Sinai: Judaism from a Feminist Perspective* (San Francisco: Harper & Row, 1990). See also "Transforming the Nature of Community: Toward a Feminist People of Israel," in Paula M. Cooey, William R. Eakin, and Jay B. McDaniel, editors, *After Patriarchy: Feminist Transformations of the World Religions*, Faith Meets Faith Series (Maryknoll, N.Y.: Orbis Books, 1991), pp. 87-105.]

[2. See, for example, the following articles by Plaskow: "Appropriation, Reciprocity, and Issues of Power," *Journal of Feminist Studies in Religion* 8 (Fall 1992); "Christian Feminism and Anti-Judaism," *Cross Currents* 28 (Fall 1978);"Christian Feminist Anti-Judaism: Some New Considerations," *New Conversations* 9 (3) (Spring 1987); "Anti-Semitism: The Unacknowledged Racism," in Barbara Hilkert Andolsen, Christine E. Gudorf, and Mary D. Pellauer, editors, *Women's Consciousness, Women's Conscience* (Minneapolis, Chicago, and New York: Winston Press, 1985): pp. 75-84. See also the articles by Plaskow and others in the *Journal of Feminist Studies in Religion's* "Special Section on Feminist Anti-Judaism" in vol. 7 (1991).]

[3. See Judith Plaskow and Carol P. Christ, *Weaving the Visions: New Patterns in Feminist Spirituality* (San Francisco: Harper & Row, 1989). See also Plaskow and Christ, *Womanspirit Rising: A Feminist Reader in Religion* (New York: Harper & Row, 1979).]

"The Coming of Lilith: Toward a Feminist Theology" (1979 CE)
JUDITH PLASKOW

The Women's Movement as a Religious Experience

. . . We began our discussion of the women's movement with the "yeah, yeah experience" rather than with sisterhood because we wanted to get more precisely at the experience of coming-to-wholeness that sisterhood presupposes. If our discussion of the "yeah, yeah experience" got at part of this process, our discussion of religious experience dealt with it from another angle. We saw the stages of consciousness raising as analogous to the stages in a religious journey, culminating in the experience of full, related, selfhood.

Again and again we came back to the word *graceful* to describe certain of our experiences with other women. At moments I can never plan or program, I am given to myself in a way I cannot account for by studying the organic progression of my past. Listening to another woman tell her story, I *concentrate* on words spoken and experienced as if our lives depended on them, and indeed they do. And yet I could not say what enables me to be really there, hearing, in a way that makes me feel that I had never really heard before—or been listened to as I am now.[1] Nor could I say why precisely at this moment I became aware of myself as a total person, why I feel myself as whole, integrated, free, fully human. Some of this feeling we hoped to convey through the "yeah, yeah experience." "Yeah, yeah" is my response to an illumination that includes the intellect but is more than intellectual. In this moment in which I transcend it, I feel sharply the limits of the taken-for-granted definition of myself and my capabilities.

This is where the experience of grace can also become the experience of conversion. Seeing myself in a new way, I am called to the transformation of myself. I must become the possibilities I already am in my moment of vision, for I am really not yet those possibilities. The call necessitates a decision, a response. . . .

Theological Process

. . . With reference to our main, constructive task, we found it easier to discuss the women's movement and religious experience than to reflect theologically on either. What is theology? What does it mean to apply a theological process? Is feminist theology the expression of a new religion? How can we relate ourselves to the old without destroying our new experiences through the attempt to understand them in terms of old forms? These were crucial questions we felt we had to, but could not, answer. There were times we found ourselves getting into some rather traditional discussions—the ambiguity of grace that is both fulfilled and "not yet" fulfilled; the question of which comes first, sisterhood or the "yeah, yeah experience," grace or the experience of grace. Many of the things we talked about set off old associations. There is a clear relation, for example, between the true speaking and hearing of the "yeah, yeah experience" and the I-Thou relation in Martin Buber. We considered what it would mean to write a systematic theology that affirmed the experiences we had been discussing—choosing a philosophical framework, our texts, our rabbis, or our saints. But we were worried about the disappearance of the four of us sitting there, our coming together, behind the framework we would create. We clearly needed a form that would grow out of the content and process of our time together.

Our Story: The Coming of Lilith

It was here that we realized that, although we had failed to come up with a single event or symbol that captured all of feminist experience, there had emerged out of our discussion many of the central elements of a myth. We had a journey to go on, an enemy (or enemies) to vanquish, salvation to be achieved both for ourselves and for humanity. If we found ourselves with a myth, moreover, this was particularly appropriate to our experience, for we had come together to do theology by beginning with our stories. It was no coincidence, then, that we arrived back at the story form.

We recognized the difficulties of "inventing" a myth, however, and so we wanted to tell a story that seemed to grow naturally out of our present history. We also felt the need for using older materials that would carry their own reverberations and significance, even if we departed freely from them. We chose therefore, to begin with the story of Lilith, demon of the night, who, according to rabbinic legend was Adam's first wife. Created equal to him, for some unexplained reason she found that she could not live with him, and flew away. Through her story, we could express not only our new image of ourselves, but our relation to certain of the elements of our religious traditions. Since stories are the heart of tradition, we could question and create tradition by telling a new story within the framework of an old one. We took Lilith for our heroine, and yet, most important, not Lilith alone. We try to express through our myth the process of our coming to do theology together. Lilith by herself is in exile and can do nothing. The real heroine of our story is sisterhood, and sisterhood is powerful.

In the beginning, the Lord God formed Adam and Lilith from the dust of the ground and breathed into their nostrils the breath of life. Created from the same source, both having been formed from the ground, they were equal in all ways. Adam, being a man, didn't like this situation, and he looked for ways to change it. He said, "I'll have my figs now, Lilith," ordering her to wait on him, and he tried to leave to her the daily tasks of life in the garden. But Lilith wasn't one to take any nonsense; she picked herself up, uttered God's holy name, and flew away. "Well now, Lord," complained Adam, "that uppity woman you sent me has gone and deserted me." The Lord, inclined to be sympathetic, sent his messengers after Lilith, telling her to shape up and return to Adam or face dire punishment. She, however, preferring anything to living with Adam, decided to stay where she was. And so God, after more careful consideration this time, caused a deep sleep to fall on Adam and out of one of his ribs created for him a second companion, Eve.

For a time, Eve and Adam had a good thing going. Adam was happy now, and Eve, though she occasionally sensed capacities within herself that remained undeveloped, was basically satisfied with the role of Adam's wife and helper. The only thing that really disturbed her was the excluding closeness of the relationship between Adam and God. Adam and God just seemed to have more in common, both being men, and Adam came to identify with God more and more. After a while, that made God a bit uncomfortable too, and he started going over in this mind whether he may not have made a mistake letting Adam talk him into banishing Lilith and creating Eve, seeing the power that gave Adam.

Meanwhile Lilith, all alone, attempted from time to time to rejoin the human community in the garden. After her first fruitless attempt to breach its walls, Adam worked hard to build them stronger, even getting Eve to help him. He told her fearsome stories of the demon Lilith who threatens women in childbirth and steals children from their cradles in the middle of the night. The second time Lilith came, she stormed the garden's main gate, and a great battle ensued between her and Adam in which she was finally defeated. This time, however, before Lilith got away, Eve got a glimpse of her and saw she was a woman like herself.

After this encounter, seeds of curiosity and doubt began to grow in Eve's mind. Was Lilith indeed just another woman? Adam had said she was a demon. Another woman! The very idea attracted Eve. She had never seen another creature like herself before. And how beautiful and strong Lilith looked! How bravely she had fought! Slowly, slowly, Eve began to think about the limits of her own life within the garden.

One day, after many months of strange and disturbing thoughts, Eve, wandering around the edge of the garden, noticed a young apple tree she and Adam had planted, and saw that one of its branches stretched over the garden wall. Spontaneously, she tried to climb it, and struggling to the top, swung herself over the wall.

She did not wander long on the other side before she met the one she had come to find, for Lilith was waiting. At first sight of her, Eve remembered the tales of Adam and was frightened, but Lilith understood and greeted her kindly. "Who are you?" they asked each other, "What is your story?" And they sat and spoke together, of the past and then of the future. They talked for many hours, not once, but many times. They taught each other many things, and told each other stories, and laughed together, and cried, over and over, till the bond of sisterhood grew between them.

Meanwhile, back in the garden, Adam was puzzled by Eve's comings and goings, and disturbed by what he sensed to be her new attitude toward him. He talked to God about it, and God, having his own problems with Adam and a somewhat broader perspective, was able to help out a little—but he was confused, too. Something had failed to go according to plan. As in the days of Abraham, he needed counsel from his children. "I am who I am," thought God, "but I must become who I will become."

And God and Adam were expectant and afraid the day Eve and Lilith returned to the garden, bursting with possibilities, ready to rebuild it together.

NOTE TO CHAPTER 8, EGALITARIAN INTERPRETATIONS, JUDITH PLASKOW, "THE COMING OF LILITH"

1. [Nelle] Morton, ["The Rising Woman Consciousness in a Male Language Structure," *Andover Newton Quarterly* 12 (1972)]: 180.

"Lilith Revisited" (1995 CE)
JUDITH PLASKOW

Writing "The Coming of Lilith" was one of the few experiences I have ever had of serving as a medium for words and images beyond my own conscious powers. I wrote the Lilith story in 1972 at the Grailville conference on Women Exploring Theology. I had spent the week in a morning group with Karen Bloomquist, Margaret Early, and Elizabeth Farians, exploring and analyzing the early feminist consciousness-raising process as a religious experience. As we repeatedly returned to and shared our own most powerful moments of feminist transformation, we struggled to find a theological vocabulary for expressing those experiences. At the end of our time together, we realized that, although we could not formulate a "feminist theology" apart from particular religious frameworks, we did have a tale we wanted to tell. While the rest of the group was happy to discuss the elements of our journey and leave it at that, I sat down after our last session to see whether I could actually write a story. Rather to my surprise, the words came pouring out of me, and "The Coming of Lilith" was born.

As I read the tale at the final large group gathering at Grailville that night, and as I have reheard or reread it many times since, I repeatedly have been struck by two things: the power of the story to capture a very particular moment in the history of feminism, and the complexity of the issues and feelings it raises and evokes. The spontaneous applause at the first reading, the immediate decision of Rosemary Ruether to publish "The Coming of Lilith" as the epilogue to *Religion and Sexism*, the feelings of delighted recognition numerous women have expressed to me over the years testify to the extent to which the story has touched a chord in many readers. It is clear to me that my ability to write a story that has evoked such a response was rooted in my having spent a week in the Grailville group, immersing myself in the process and content of feminist consciousness-raising. "The Coming of Lilith" works because its method and message are the same: it is a tale of sisterhood that came out of a powerful experience of sisterhood.

While the success of the piece was not accidental, then, in the sense that I and the group at Grailville were trying to articulate experiences that we knew were shared by a much larger community of women, many of the issues the story raises, I was not aware of at the time of writing. Thus Rosemary Ruether's discussion of "The Coming of Lilith" in the preface to *Religion and Sexism* quite amazed me when I first read it. She wrote that the "parable turns male misogynist theology upside down, revealing it for what it is, a projection of male insecurity and demand for dominance." She also commented that "the fearsomeness of Lilith in the male imagination preserves a recognition of suppressed power and creativity in women."[1] While I agreed that these things were there in the story, I certainly had not had such profundities in mind when I wrote it! It was only afterward that I came to see Lilith as a classic example of male projection. Lilith is not a demon; rather she is a woman named a demon by a tradition that does not know what to do with strong women. In a somewhat different vein, it was only when I came out as a lesbian more than a decade after writing the story that I first was struck by the potentially sexual nature of the energy between Eve and Lilith. The erotic possibilities in the intensity of their encounter and their care for each other seem so clear to me now that I am astonished I didn't see them earlier.

One of the elements of "The Coming of Lilith" that I often have been challenged on over the years is the maleness of God in the story. Some women have argued that, in making God male, I adopted and reinforced the patriarchal perspective that I was simultaneously criticizing. This was a deliberate decision on my part, and I still completely stand by it. The story is not saying that God in God's reality is actually male. It is playing with our perceptions of God at a particular point in history. The God of the original medieval Lilith midrash is certainly male. He sides with Adam in the struggle with Lilith for reasons that are utterly mysterious. In 1972 also, God was male! Feminists were beginning to raise questions about male images of God but were moving only in the most tentative ways toward alternative concepts and metaphors. It was the process of consciousness-raising and the long, slow experimentation with new images and liturgies that were gradually to make possible a new understanding of the sacred. In this sense, the coming together of Eve and Lilith precipitates a change in (our perceptions of) God. In depicting God Godself as reflecting on that change I was drawing on what has always been one of my favorite aspects of the Jewish tradition: the fact that God is understood as growing through interaction with and challenge from human beings. In alluding to Abraham's argument with God over Sodom and Gomorrah, I was trying to place the feminist challenge in the larger context of fateful divine/human dialogues within Judaism.

I continue to be proud of "The Coming of Lilith," then, and even were I to want to change it, I do not feel it is quite fully mine to do so. I think it still stands as an expression of the original, heady round of consciousness-raising, an expression that perhaps provides a taste of the moment to those who were not part of it. But if the story as story seems to have had a life of its own apart from me, such is not the case with the theoretical and theological context in which it was originally embedded.[2] My understanding of Lilith as a Jewish story is entirely different from what it was twenty-four years ago, and I would write about its theological meaning and import from a completely different perspective.

Today, when I look at the larger framework in which "The Coming of Lilith" was initially presented, I am shocked by the Christianness of the religious language that we/I chose to impose on our feminist experiences, describing them in terms of "conversion," "grace," and "mission." I do not think that my willingness to use this language stemmed simply from the fact that I was working with three Christian women. Especially since the language is heavily Protestant and two of the women were Catholics, I assume these terms were as much a product of my own immersion in Protestant theology in graduate school as of the influence of the group. I was certainly aware at the time of the tension between this vocabulary and my own Jewish identity, but there was as yet no Jewish feminist discussion of theological issues offering an alternative language and conceptual framework.

Were I reflecting today on the religious dimension of feminism, I would try to remain close to the experiences being described rather than impose on them the foreign vocabulary of any particular tradition. When I think back to the larger conference at Grailville, for example, and especially the contributions of a group that was working on images of God, I see that in coming to a new sense of ourselves as agents in the world with power to shape our destinies, many feminists also experienced a sense of connection to larger currents of power and energy in the universe.[3] One can talk about the relationship of such experiences to specific theological concepts, but one does not *need* the concepts to authorize the experiences, and using traditional language may serve to mask the freshness and iconoclasm of the consciousness-raising process.

Were I interested in using traditional language to interpret feminist experience, however, I now see a much closer fit between the shared communal self-understanding of feminism and Judaism than I do between feminism and an individualistic Protestantism. Central both to our group reflections and the Lilith story is the notion that insight and empowerment emerge from the experience of community. Eve and Lilith by themselves are each isolated and powerless. Their ability to transform the garden and God results from their coming together; it is sisterhood that grows them into consciousness and action. This notion that human personhood is fundamentally social, that one stands in relation to God always as a member of a people, is also central to Judaism.[4] Moreover, rather than using the term "mission" to describe the expansive dimension of feminism, I would now talk about Eve and Lilith's transformation of the garden in terms of *tikkun olam* (repair of the world). While mission to me implies a somewhat condescending "I know better than you what is good for you," *tikkun olam* refers to the obligation and project of healing the world from the ontological and social brokenness that has marked it from creation. In contemporary usage, the concept of *tikkun olam* brings together mystical and social understandings of repair within Judaism in a way that fuses spirituality with a commitment to social justice.[5] By creating a more just social order, either through the liberation of women or commitment to other issues, one is also healing the alienation and separation within God. This, of course, is precisely what Eve and Lilith are doing at the end of the story.

What is most striking to me in revisiting Lilith, however, and most glaringly absent in terms of Jewish categories and analysis, is any understanding of the story as midrash. In referring to "The Coming of Lilith" in the framing material, I consistently label it a myth.[6] This points to a rather interesting paradox. On the one hand, for all that I was willing to adopt a Protestant vocabulary, when our group's convoluted theological discussion was over and done, I/we returned to the old Jewish mode of storytelling to capture the truths we had arrived at. On the other hand, in doing so, I had no conscious awareness of standing in a long Jewish tradition of using midrash as a way of expressing religious insight and grappling with religious questions.

Judaism, unlike Christianity, has no continuous history of systematic theological discourse. A tradition in which deed is more central than creed, it deals with theological issues not through the elaboration of doctrine but through engagement with biblical narratives. Midrash is a form of biblical interpretation that often begins from a question, silence, gap, or contradiction in a biblical story and writes the story forward in response to the interpreter's questions. Thus the original Lilith midrash (see p. 204 of this volume) emerged from the contradiction between the creation narratives in Genesis 1 and Genesis 2. Because in Genesis 1, the man and woman are created simultaneously and apparently equally, while in Genesis 2 Eve is created from Adam's rib, the rabbis wondered whether the stories might not describe two different events in the history of creation. Their response was that, indeed, Adam did have a first wife named Lilith, who fled the garden when Adam tried to subordinate her. God sent three angels after her to bring her back, at which point in the midrash Lilith turns into a demon, killing new babies in retaliation for the deaths of her own children.[7] Midrash as a major technique of interpretation is not limited to this particular narrative, of course. Rabbinic midrash on countless biblical characters and texts functions as a vehicle for exploring religious questions in a way that makes room for disagreement, ambiguity, and complexity.

In the last decade or so, Jewish feminists have begun to use midrash as an important way of both reconnecting with and transforming tradition. Just as rabbinic midrash often begins from some gap or silence in the biblical text, Jewish feminists are using midrash to explore and fill in the great silence that surrounds women's history and experience. Just as the rabbis brought their own questions to the Bible and found there answers that supported their religious world view, so Jewish women are asking new questions of biblical narratives and, in the process of responding, recreating tradition. The flexibility and creativity of midrash, its power to reinvent, easily lends itself to feminist use. What was Sarah thinking and feeling when Abraham took the son she had born at the age of ninety and brought him to the top of Mount Moriah as a sacrifice? How did she feel when God told Abraham to get up and journey to a new land, leaving the home that they had made together? What was the reaction of Miriam when God struck her with leprosy for challenging the authority of Moses, but left Aaron unblemished? Lacking responses to these and many other questions, feminists are creating them through midrash, and, in doing so, engaging with Jewish tradition in a vital and open-ended way.

My story, "The Coming of Lilith," both does and does not fit into this recent explosion of feminist midrash. First of all, unlike most examples of the genre, it is a midrash on a midrash, and not on a biblical text. In beginning from the Lilith story in the *Alphabet of Ben Sira* rather than from Genesis, I comment on the biblical creation narrative only indirectly. Second, and more significantly, I did not intend to write an interpretation of the traditional midrash but to capture the experience of consciousness-raising within a religious framework. I cannot remember now how I had even heard of Lilith, but I borrowed her tale because it fit my contemporary need. I did not realize that in retelling her story, I was doing for the traditional midrash what it had already done for the biblical text. And yet, once the story was completed, it *read* as a midrash on a midrash of creation, and to that extent stands in the stream of Jewish feminist midrash that was to follow.

Revisiting Lilith twenty-four years later, then, it feels very apt to me that, in the context of this book, the midrash appears as a selection on Jewish egalitarian interpretation. I find it interesting that, in beginning from consciousness-raising as a religious experience and moving from there into Protestant theological categories, I nonetheless ended up with a story that, in content and form, reflects important aspects of Jewish tradition. Insofar as "The Coming of Lilith" has spoken to a generation of readers about the transformative implications of feminism, it testifies to the power of story and the power of midrash to create and communicate religious meaning.

NOTES TO CHAPTER 8, EGALITARIAN HIERARCHIES, JUDITH PLASKOW, "LILITH REVISITED"

1. Rosemary Radford Ruether, *Religion and Sexism: Images of Women in the Jewish and Christian Traditions* (New York: Simon & Schuster, 1974), p. 12.

2. See my "The Coming of Lilith: Toward a Feminist Theology," in Carol P. Christ and Judith Plaskow, editors, *Womanspirit Rising: A Feminist Reader in Religion*, (New York: Harper & Row, 1979), pp. 198-209.

3. "Singleness/Community Group," *Women Exploring Theology at Grailville*, packet from Church Women United, 1972. See also my discussion in Judith Plaskow, *Standing Again at Sinai: Judaism from a Feminist Perspective* (San Francisco: Harper & Row, 1990), pp. 86, 143f.

4. Plaskow, *Standing Again at Sinai*, pp. 79-81.

5. Plaskow, *Standing Again at Sinai*, pp. 217-20.

6. See "The Coming of Lilith," in *Womanspirit Rising*, p. 205, and the selection in this volume.

7. The version of the story in Louis Ginzberg's *Legends of the Jews* (rpt., Philadelphia: Jewish Publication Society of America, 1968), vol. 1, p. 65, is somewhat different from the one that appears here.

Phyllis Trible

Through her work as teacher, author, and lecturer, Phyllis Trible has contributed greatly to biblical studies and the development of feminist biblical theology. She is Baldwin Professor Emerita of Sacred Literature at Union Theological Seminary in New York City and Professor of Biblical Studies at Wake Forest University Divinity School. She has employed her skills at feminist analysis and rhetorical criticism in numerous articles and books, including *God and the Rhetoric of Sexuality*, *Texts of Terror*, and *Rhetorical Criticism*.[1] Trible has been active in the leadership of the Society of Biblical Literature and became president of that Society in 1994, the second woman to be elected to serve in this capacity.[2]

Early in the 1970s, Trible charted new territory in biblical studies with her call to "depatriarchalize" interpretations of the Bible. She has contributed to an egalitarian reading of the opening chapters of Genesis by paying careful attention to the literary and linguistic features of the text. Here we offer two selections by Trible. The first essay, "Eve and Adam: Genesis 2-3 Reread," began as a paper Trible read to her colleagues when she was on the faculty of Andover Newton Theological School; it became the seedbed for lengthier examinations, including her ground-breaking essay "Depatriarchalizing in Biblical Interpretation."[3] Our second selection is Trible's retrospective analysis of her "Eve and Adam" article. When asked to write an essay on the theme of "how my mind has changed," she responded with an essay whose title characterizes her assessment: "Not a Jot, Not a Tittle: Genesis 2-3 after Twenty Years." (Sources: "Eve and Adam: Genesis 2-3 Reread," *Andover Newton Quarterly* 13 (1972-73): 251-58; "Not a Jot, Not a Tittle: Genesis 2-3 after Twenty Years" is an essay written for the present volume.)

NOTES TO CHAPTER 8, EGALITARIAN INTERPRETATIONS, PHYLLIS TRIBLE

[1. Phyllis Trible, *God and the Rhetoric of Sexuality*, Overtures to Biblical Theology, edited by Walter Brueggemann and John R. Donahue, S.J., no. 2 (Philadelphia: Fortress Press, 1978); *Texts of Terror: Literary-Feminist Readings of Biblical Narratives*, Overtures to Biblical Theology, edited by Walter Brueggemann and John R. Donahue, S.J., no. 13 (Philadelphia: Fortress Press, 1984); *Rhetorical Criticism: Context, Method, and the Book of Jonah* (Minneapolis: Fortress Press, 1994).]

[2. For Trible's Presidential Address, see "Exegesis for Storytellers and Other Strangers," *Journal of Biblical Literature* 114 (1995): 3-19. For a discussion of women's participation in this organization, see Dorothy C. Bass, "Women's Studies and Biblical Studies: An Historical Perspective," *Journal for the Study of the Old Testament* 22 (1982): 6-12.]

[3. Trible, "Depatriarchalizing in Biblical Interpretation," *Journal of the American Academy of Religion* 41 (1973): 30-48. See also her *God and the Rhetoric of Sexuality*, particularly chapter 1 and chapter 4.]

"Eve and Adam: Genesis 2-3 Reread" (1993 CE)
PHYLLIS TRIBLE

On the whole, the Women's Liberation Movement is hostile to the Bible, even as it claims that the Bible is hostile to women. The Yahwist account of creation and fall in Genesis 2-3 provides a strong proof text for that claim. Accepting centuries of (male) exegesis, many feminists interpret this story as legitimating male supremacy and female subordination.[1] They read to reject. My suggestion is that we reread to understand and to appropriate.

Ambiguity characterizes the meaning of *'adham* in Genesis 2-3. On the one hand, man is the first creature formed (2:7). The Lord God puts him in the garden "to till it and keep it," a job identified with the male (cf. 3:17-19). On the other hand, 'adham is a generic term for humankind. In commanding 'adham not to eat of the tree of the knowledge of good and evil, the Deity is speaking to both the man and the woman (2:16-17). Until the differentiation of female and male (2:21-23), 'adham is basically androgynous: one creature incorporating two sexes.

Concern for sexuality, specifically for the creation of woman, comes last in the story, after the making of the garden, the trees, and the animals. Some commentators allege female subordination based on this order of events.[2] They contrast it with Genesis 1-27 where God creates 'adham as male and female in one act.[3] Thereby they infer that whereas the Priests recognized the equality of the sexes, the Yahwist made woman a second, subordinate, inferior sex.[4] But the last may be first, as both the biblical theologian and the literary critic know. Thus the Yahwist account moves to its climax, not its decline, in the creation of woman.[5] She is not an afterthought; she is the culmination. Genesis 1 itself supports this interpretation, for there male and female are indeed the last and truly the crown of all creatures. The last is also first where beginnings and endings are parallel. In Hebrew literature the central concerns of a unit often appear at the beginning and the end as an *inclusio* device.[6] Genesis 2 evinces this structure. The creation of man first and of woman last constitutes a ring composition whereby the two creatures are parallel. In no way does the order disparage woman. Content and context augment this reading.

The context for the advent of woman is a divine judgment, "It is not good that 'adham should be alone; I will make him a helper fit for him" (2:18). The phrase needing explication is "helper fit for him." In the Old Testament the word helper ('ezer) has many usages. It can be a proper name for a male.[7] In our story it describes the animals and the woman. In some passages it characterizes Deity. God is the helper of Israel. As helper Yahweh creates and saves.[8] Thus 'ezer is a relational term; it designates a beneficial relationship; and it pertains to God, people, and animals. By itself the word does not specify positions within relationships; more particularly, it does not imply inferiority. Position results from additional content or from context. Accordingly, what kind of relationship does 'ezer entail in Genesis 2:18, 20? Our answer comes in two ways: 1) The word *neged*, which joins 'ezer, connotes equality: a helper who is a counterpart.[9] 2) The animals are helpers, but they fail to fit 'adham. There is physical, perhaps psychic, rapport between 'adham and the animals, for Yahweh forms (yasar) them both out of the ground ('adhamah). Yet their similarity is not equality. 'Adham names them and thereby exercises power over them. No fit helper is among them. And thus the narrative moves to woman. My translation is this: God is the helper superior to man; the animals are helpers inferior to man; woman is the helper equal to man.

Let us pursue the issue by examining the account of the creation of woman (21-22). This episode concludes the story even as the creation of man commences it. As I have said already, the ring composition suggests an interpretation of woman and man as equals. To establish this meaning, structure and content must mesh. They do. In both episodes Yahweh alone creates. For the last creation the Lord God "caused a deep sleep (*tardemah*) to fall upon the man." Man has no part in making woman; he is out of it. He exercises no control over her existence. He is neither participant nor spectator nor consultant at her birth. Like man, woman owes her life solely to God. For both of them the origin of life is a divine mystery. Another parallel of equality is creation out of raw materials: dust for man and a rib for woman. Yahweh chooses these fragile materials and in both cases processes them before human beings happen. As Yahweh shapes dust and then breathes into it to form man, so Yahweh takes out the rib and then builds it into woman.[10] To call woman "Adam's rib" is to misread the text which states carefully and clearly that the extracted bone required divine labor to become female, a datum scarcely designed to bolster the male ego. Moreover, to claim that the rib means inferiority or subordination is to assign the man qualities over the woman which are not in the narrative itself. Superiority, strength, aggressiveness, dominance, and power do not characterize man in Genesis 2. By contrast he is formed from dirt; his life hangs by a breath which he does not control; and he himself remains silent and passive while the Deity plans and interprets his existence.

The rib means solidarity and equality. *'Adham* recognizes this meaning in a poem:[11]

> This at last is bone of my bones
>   and flesh of my flesh.
> She shall be called *'ishshah* (woman)
>   because she was taken out of *'ish* (man).(2:23)

The pun proclaims both the similarity and the differentiation of female and male. Before this episode the Yahwist has used only the generic term *'adham*. No exclusively male reference has appeared. Only with the specific creation of woman (*'ishshah*) occurs the first specific term for man as male (*'ish*). In other words, sexuality is simultaneous for woman and man. The sexes are interrelated and interdependent. Man as male does not precede woman as female but happens concurrently with her. Hence, the first act in Genesis 2 is the creation of androgyny (2:7) and the last is the creation of sexuality (2:23).[12] Male embodies female and female embodies male. The two are neither dichotomies nor duplicates. The birth of woman corresponds to the birth of man but does not copy it. Only in responding to the female does the man discover himself as male. No longer a passive creature, *'ish* comes alive in meeting *'ishshah*.

Some read in(to) the poem a naming motif. The man names the woman and thereby has power and authority over her.[13] But again I suggest that we re-read. Neither the verb nor the noun *name* is in the poem. We find instead the verb *qara'*, to call: "she shall be called woman." Now in the Yahwist primeval history this verb does not function as a synonym or parallel or substitute for *name*. The typical formula for naming is the verb *to call* plus the explicit object *name*. This formula applies to Deity, people, places, and animals. For example, in Genesis 4 we read:

> Cain built a city and *called* the *name* of the city after the *name* of his son Enoch (v. 17).
> And Adam knew his wife again, and she bore a son and *called* his *name* Seth (v. 25).
> To Seth also a son was born and he *called* his *name* Enoch (v. 26a).
> At that time men began to *call* upon the *name* of the Lord (v. 26b).

Genesis 2:23 has the verb *call* but does not have the object *name*. Its absence signifies the absence of a naming motif in the poem. The presence of both the verb *call* and the noun *name* in the episode of the animals strengthens the point:

> So out of the ground the Lord God formed every beast of the field and every bird of the air and brought them to the man to see what he would *call* them; and whatever the man *called* every living creature, that was its *name*. The man gave *names* to all cattle, and to the birds of the air and to every beast of the field (2:19-20).

In calling the animals by name, *'adham* establishes supremacy over them and fails to find a fit helper. In calling woman, *'adham* does not name her and does find in her a counterpart. Female and male are equal sexes. Neither has authority over the other.[14]

A further observation secures the argument: *Woman* itself is not a name. It is a common noun; it is not a proper noun. It designates gender; it does not specify person. *'Adham* recognizes sexuality by the words *'ishshah* and *'ish*. This recognition is not an act of naming to assert the power of male over female. Quite the contrary. But the true skeptic is already asking: What about Genesis 3:20 where "the man called his wife's name Eve"? We must wait to consider that question. Meanwhile, the words of the ancient poem as well as their context proclaim sexuality originating in the unity of *'adham*. From this one (androgynous) creature come two (female and male). The two return to their original unity as *'ish* and *'ishshah* become one flesh (2:24):[15] another instance of the ring composition.

Next the differences which spell harmony and equality yield to the differences of disobedience and disaster. The serpent speaks to the woman. Why to the woman and not to the man? The simplest answer is that we do not know. The Yahwist does not tell us anymore than he explains why the tree of the knowledge of good and evil was in the garden. But the silence of the text stimulates speculations, many of which only confirm the patriarchal mentality which conceived them. Cassuto identifies serpent and woman, maintaining that the cunning of the serpent is "in reality" the cunning of the woman.[16] He impugns her further by declaring that "for the very reason that a woman's imagination surpasses a man's, it was the woman who was enticed first."

Though more gentle in his assessment, von Rad avers that "in the history of Yahweh-religion it has always been the women who have shown an inclination for obscure astrological cults" (a claim which he does not document).[17] Consequently, he holds that the woman "confronts the obscure allurements and mysteries that beset our limited life more directly than the man does," and then he calls her a "temptress." Paul Ricoeur says that woman "represents the point of weakness," as the entire story "gives evidence of a very masculine resentment."[18] McKenzie links the "moral weakness" of the woman with her "sexual attraction" and holds that the latter ruined both the woman and the man.[19] But the narrative does not say any of these things. It does not sustain the judgment that woman is weaker or more cunning or more sexual than man. Both have the same Creator, who explicitly uses the word "good" to introduce the creation of woman (2:18). Both are equal in birth. There is complete rapport, physical, psychological, sociological, and theological, between them: bone of bone and flesh of flesh. If there be moral frailty in one, it is moral frailty in two. Further, they are equal in responsibility and in judgment, in shame and in guilt, in redemption and in grace. What the narrative says about the nature of woman it also says about the nature of man.

Why does the serpent speak to the woman and not to the man? Let a female speculate. If the serpent is "more subtle" than its fellow creatures, the woman is more appealing than her husband. Throughout the myth she is the more intelligent one, the more aggressive one, and the one with greater sensibilities.[20] Perhaps the woman elevates the animal world by conversing theologically with the serpent. At any rate, she understands the hermeneutical task. In quoting God she interprets the prohibition ("neither shall you touch it"). The woman is both the theologian and translator. She contemplates the tree, taking into account all the possibilities. The tree is good for food; it satisfies the physical drives. It pleases the eyes; it is aesthetically and emotionally desirable. Above all, it is coveted as the source of wisdom (*haskîl*). Thus the woman is fully aware when she acts, her vision encompassing the gamut of life. She takes the fruit and she eats. The initiative and the decision are hers alone. There is no consultation with her husband. She seeks neither his advice [nor] his permission. She acts independently. By contrast the man is a silent, passive, and bland recipient: "She also gave some to her husband and he ate." The narrator makes no attempt to depict the husband as reluctant or hesitating. The man does not theologize; he does not contemplate; he does not envision the full possibilities of the occasion. His one act is belly-oriented, and it is an act of quiescence, not of initiative. The man is not dominant; he is not aggressive; he is not a decision-maker. Even though the prohibition not to eat of the tree appears before the female was specifically created, she knows that it applies to her. She has interpreted it, and now she struggles with the temptation to disobey. But not the man, to whom the prohibition came directly (2:6). He follows his wife without question or comment, thereby denying his own individuality. If the woman be intelligent, sensitive, and ingenious, the man is passive, brutish, and inept. These character portrayals are truly extraordinary in a culture dominated by men. I stress their contrast not to promote female chauvinism but to undercut patriarchal interpretations alien to the text.

The contrast between woman and man fades after their acts of disobedience. They are one in the new knowledge of their nakedness (3:7). They are one in hearing and in hiding. They flee from the sound of the Lord God in the Garden (3:8). First to the man come questions of responsibility (3:9, 11), but the man fails to be responsible: "The woman whom Thou gavest to be with me, she gave me fruit of the tree, and I ate" (3:12). Here the man does not blame the woman; he does not say that the woman seduced him;[21] he blames the Deity. The verb which he uses for both the Deity and the woman is *ntn* (cf. 3:6). So far as I can determine, this verb neither means nor implies seduction in this context or in the lexicon. Again, if the Yahwist intended to make woman the temptress, he missed a choice opportunity. The woman's response supports the point. "The serpent beguiled me and I ate" (3:13). Only here occurs the strong verb *nsh'*, meaning to deceive, to seduce. God accepts this subject-verb combination when, immediately following the woman's accusation, Yahweh says to the serpent, "Because you have done this, cursed are you above all animals" (3:14).

Though the tempter (the serpent) is cursed,[22] the woman and the man are not. But they are judged, and the judgments are commentaries on the disastrous effects of their shared disobedience. They show how terrible human life has become as it stands between creation and grace. We misread if we assume that these judgments are mandates. They describe; they do not prescribe. They protest; they do not condone. Of special concern are the words telling the woman that her husband shall rule over her (3:16). This statement is not license for male supremacy, but rather it is condemnation of that very pattern.[23] Subjugation and supremacy are perversions of creation. Through disobedience the woman has become slave. Her initiative and her freedom vanish. The man is corrupted also, for he has become master, ruling over the one who is his God-given equal. The subordination of female to male signifies their shared sin.[24] This sin vitiates all relationships: between animals and human beings (3:15); mothers and children (3:16); husbands and wives (3:16); man and the soil (3:17, 18); man and his work (3:19). Whereas in creation man and woman know harmony and equality, in sin they know alienation and discord. Grace makes possible a new beginning.

A further observation about these judgments: They are culturally conditioned. Husband and work (childbearing) define the woman; wife and work (farming) define the man. A literal reading of the story limits both creatures and limits the story. To be faithful translators, we must recognize that women as well as men move beyond these culturally defined roles, even as the intentionality and function of the myth move beyond its original setting. Whatever forms stereotyping takes in our own culture, they are judgments upon our common sin and disobedience. The suffering and oppression we women and men know now are marks of our fall, not of our creation.

At this place of sin and judgment "the man calls his wife's name Eve"

(3:20), thereby asserting his rule over her. The naming itself faults the man for corrupting a relationship of mutuality and equality. And so Yahweh evicts the primeval couple from the Garden, yet with signals of grace.[25] Interestingly, the conclusion of the story does not specify the sexes in flight. Instead the narrator resumes use of the generic and androgynous term 'adham with which the story began and thereby completes an overall ring composition (3:22-24).

Visiting the Garden of Eden in the days of the Women's Movement, we need no longer accept the traditional exegesis of Genesis 2-3. Rather than legitimating the patriarchal culture from which it comes, the myth places that culture under judgment. And thus it functions to liberate, not to enslave. This function we can recover and appropriate. The Yahwist narrative tells us who we are (creatures of equality and mutuality); it tells us who we have become (creatures of oppression); and so it opens possibilities for change, for a return to our true liberation under God. In other words, the story calls female and male to repent.

NOTES TO CHAPTER 8, EGALITARIAN INTERPRETATIONS,
PHYLLIS TRIBLE, "EVE AND ADAM"

1. See, *inter alia*, Kate Millett, *Sexual Politics* (New York: Doubleday, 1970), pp. 51-54; Eva Figes, *Patriarchal Attitudes* (Greenwich: Fawcett, 1970), p. 38f.; Mary Daly, "The Courage to See," *Christian Century*, September 22, 1971, p. 1110; Sheila D. Collins, "Toward a Feminist Theology," *Christian Century*, August 2, 1972, p. 798; Lilly Rivlin, "Lilith: "The First Woman," *Ms.* (December 1972): 93, 114.

2. Cf. E. Jacob, *Theology of the Old Testament* (New York: Harper & Row, 1958), p. 172f.; S. H. Hooke, "Genesis," *Peake's Commentary on the Bible* (London: Thomas Nelson, 1962), p. 179.

3. E.g., Elizabeth Cady Stanton observed that Genesis 1:26-28 "dignifies woman as an important factor in the creation, equal in power and glory with man," while Genesis 2 "makes her a mere afterthought" (*The Woman's Bible*, Part I [New York: European Publishing Company, 1895], p. 20). See also Elsie Adams and Mary Louise Briscoe, *Up Against the Wall, Mother* . . . (Beverly Hills: Glencoe Press, 1971), p. 4.

4. Cf. Eugene H. Maly, "Genesis," *The Jerome Biblical Commentary* (Englewood Cliffs, N.J.: Prentice-Hall, 1968), p. 12: "But woman's existence, psychologically and in the social order, is dependent on man."

5. See John L. McKenzie, "The Literary Characteristics of Gen. 2-3," *Theological Studies* 15 (1954): 559; John A. Bailey, "Initiation and the Primal Woman in Gilgamesh and Genesis 2-3," *Journal of Biblical Literature* (June 1970): 143. Bailey writes emphatically of the remarkable importance and position of the woman in Genesis 2-3, "all the more extraordinary when one realizes that this is the only account of the creation of woman as such in ancient Near Eastern literature." He hedges, however, in seeing the themes of helper and naming (Genesis 2:18-23) as indicative of a "certain subordination" of woman to man. These reservations are unnecessary; see below. Cf. also Claus Westermann, *Genesis, Biblischer Kommentar* 1/4 (Neukirchen-Vluyn: Neukirchener Verlag, 1970), p. 312.

6. James Muilenburg, "Form Criticism and Beyond," *Journal of Biblical Literature* (March 1969): 9f.; Mitchell Dahood, *Psalms I*, The Anchor Bible (New York: Doubleday, 1966), *passim* and esp. p. 5.

7. 1 Chronicles 4:4; 12:9; Nehemiah 3:19.

8. Psalms 121:2; 124:8; 146:5; 33:20; 115:9-11; Exodus 18:4; Deuteronomy 33:7, 26, 29.

9. L. Koehler and W. Baumgartner, *Lexicon in Veteris Testamenti Libros* (Leiden: E. J. Brill, 1958), p. 591f.

10. The verb *bnh* (to build) suggests considerable labor. It is used of towns, towers, altars, and fortifications, as well as of the primeval woman (Koehler-Baumgartner, *[Lexicon in Veteris Testamenti Libros]*, p. 134). In Genesis 2:22 it may mean the fashioning of clay around the rib (Ruth Amiran, "Myths of the Creation of Man and the Jericho Statues," *BASOR* No. 167, October 1962, p. 24f.).

11. See Walter Brueggemann, "Of the Same Flesh and Bone (Gen 2, 23a)," *Catholic Biblical Quarterly* (October 1970): 532-42.

12. In proposing as primary an androgynous interpretation of *'adham*, I find virtually no support from (male) biblical scholars. But my view stands as documented from the text, and I take refuge among a remnant of ancient (male) rabbis (see George Foot Moore, *Judaism* [Cambridge: Harvard University Press, 1927], vol. 1, p. 453; also Joseph Campbell, *The Hero with a Thousand Faces* [New York: Meridian Books, World Publishing Company, 1970], pp. 152ff., 279f.).

13. See, e.g., G. von Rad, *Genesis* (Philadelphia: Westminster Press, 1961), pp. 80-82; John H. Marks, "Genesis," *The Interpreter's One-Volume Commentary on the Bible* (New York: Abingdon, 1971), p. 5; Bailey, ["Initiation and the Primal Woman"], p. 143.

14. Cf. Westermann, *Genesis*, pp. 316ff.

15. Verse 24 probably mirrors a matriarchal society (so von Rad, *Genesis*, p. 83). If the myth were designed to support patriarchy, it is difficult to explain how this verse survived without proper alteration. Westermann contends, however, that an emphasis on matriarchy misunderstands the point of the verse, which is the total communion of woman and man (*Genesis*, p. 317).

16. U. Cassuto, *A Commentary on the Book of Genesis*, Part I (Jerusalem: The Magnes Press, n.d.), p. 142f.

17. von Rad, *Genesis*, pp. 87-88.

18. Ricoeur departs from the traditional interpretation of the woman when he writes: "Eve n'est donc pas la femme en tant que 'deuxième sexe'; toute femme et tout homme sont Adam; tout homme et toute femme sont Eve." But the fourth clause of his sentence obscures this complete identity of Adam and Eve: "tout femme peche 'en' Adam, tout homme est seduit 'en' Eve." By switching from an active to a passive verb, Ricoeur makes only the woman directly responsible for both sinning and seducing. (Paul Ricoeur, Finitude et Culpabilité, II, *La Symbolique du Mal* [Aubier, Editions Montaigne, Paris, 1960]. Cf. Ricoeur, *The Symbolism of Evil* [Boston: Beacon Press, 1969], p. 255.)

19. McKenzie, "The Literary Characteristics," p. 570.

20. See Bailey, "Initiation and the Primal Woman," p. 148.

21. See Westermann, *Genesis*, p. 340.

22. For a discussion of the serpent, see Ricoeur, *The Symbolism of Evil*, pp. 255-60.

23. Cf. Edwin M. Good, *Irony in the Old Testament* (Philadelphia: Westminster Press, 1965), p. 84, note 4: "Is it not surprising that, in a culture where the subordination of woman to man was a virtually unquestioned social principle, the etiology of the subordination should be in the context of man's primal sin? Perhaps woman's subordination was not unquestioned in Israel." Cf. also Henricus Renckens, *Israel's Concept of the Beginning* (New York: Herder and Herder, 1964), p. 217f.

24. *Contra* Westermann, *Genesis*, p. 357.

25. Von Rad, *Genesis*, pp. 94, 148.

"Not a Jot, Not a Tittle: Genesis 2–3 after Twenty Years"
(1995 CE)
PHYLLIS TRIBLE

In the early 1970s, feminist interpretation of the Bible was a cloud no bigger than a woman's hand. Knowing that such clouds can become mighty storms, I began to grapple with two certainties in my life: a love for the Bible and a commitment to feminism. Some friends told me that the twain shall never meet, but I sensed that they had already met within me. The challenge was to articulate the encounter.

I began with a favorite text, the story of the Garden in Genesis 2–3. Throughout the ages people have used this text to legitimate patriarchy as the will of God. They maintained that it subordinates woman to man in creation, depicts her as his seducer, curses her, and authorizes man to rule over her. Well acquainted with the traditional reading, I asked myself a question: If, as it certainly appears, this story is so terribly patriarchal, how come I like it? How come I feel no anger in reading it and no embarrassment in claiming it? How come it gives me a sense of well being despite its tragic ending? Feminist (not feminine) intuition told me that the story invites another interpretation. My job was to find it.

Three clues prepared the way. The first was a childhood memory. A missionary on furlough, whose name I do not know, taught Bible stories to a group of little girls of whom I was one. She said, "Everything that God created got better and better. What was the last thing God created?" Thoroughly indoctrinated, we replied in unison and with vigor, "Man!" She countered, "No, woman." Hers is not the exegesis I now espouse, but nonetheless to this day I am grateful for her insight.

The second clue came in a lecture delivered at Union Theological Seminary in the 1950s by Professor Samuel Terrien. Checking my notes years later, I found this statement: "The portrayal of the man in the garden is not the portrayal of a patriarch. Whereas the woman is depicted as alert, intelligent, and sensitive, the man comes off as passive, bland, and belly-oriented." Whether or not these are Professor Terrien's exact words, they confirm my intuition of a nonpatriarchal perspective at work in the story.

The third clue was a footnote in a study of biblical irony by Professor Edwin M. Good. Writing about Genesis 3:16, he asked, "Is it not surprising that, in a culture where the subordination of woman to man was a virtually unquestioned social principle, the etiology of the subordination should be in the context of man's primal sin? Perhaps woman's subordination was not unquestioned in Israel."[1] For me this blessed footnote removed centuries of misguided interpretation.

Fortified by these clues, I sought an alternative to the patriarchal understanding of Genesis 2–3. An invitation in 1972 to read a paper to the faculty of Andover Newton Theological School provided the first forum for testing my ideas.[2] A section of that paper became a short article, published the next year in the *Andover Newton Quarterly*.[3] Other publications reprinted the article,[4] and it appears again in this volume. Meanwhile, in 1978 a lengthy study expanded the short article and changed some of the interpretation.[5]

The most significant change concerned the use and meaning in Genesis 2:7-22a of the word *ha-'adam* (or *'adam*, without the definite article *ha*). In the second paragraph of the short article I tried to hold together three meanings: the male creature (the traditional reading), the generic term for humankind, and the androgynous creature. This effort showed my early struggles with an ambiguous text. By the time I developed the lengthy study, these struggles had led to a fourth meaning that superseded the others. Though later in the story *ha-'adam* specifies the male and still later acquires a generic usage, in Genesis 2:7-22a, the word does not carry a male, generic, or androgynous meaning.[6] Instead, it signifies a sexually undifferentiated creature: neither male (nor female) nor a combination of the two.

To talk about this sexually undifferentiated creature, I offered the translation of *ha-'adam* as "the earth creature." That translation served two purposes: to move away from gender-specific language and to suggest the pun present in the sentence, "Yhwh God formed *ha-'adam* (the earth creature) from the dust of *ha-'adama* (the earth)" (2:7). Another translation has since come along: "Yhwh God formed the human from the dust of the humus." How I arrived at this reading I do not remember, but it captures well in English the Hebrew pun. And it also eschews gender identification.

The idea that *ha-'adam* in Genesis 2:7 connotes a sexually undifferentiated creature has stirred various responses—grammatical, conceptual, and literary. Grammatically the noun *'adam* is masculine gender as are all the pronouns that refer to it. (Hebrew offers only two genders, masculine and feminine; the neuter is unavailable.) Grammarians know well that no exact equation obtains between gender and sexual identity.[7] For example, that the noun *sûs* in Hebrew is masculine does not mean that every Hebrew horse is male; that the noun *alopeks* in Greek is feminine does not mean that every Greek fox is female; that the noun *khatifa* in Arabic is feminine does not mean that there was ever a female caliph; that the noun *nauta* in Latin is feminine does not mean that the Roman sailor was female. Similarly, the masculine gender of *'adam* does not itself specify a male creature.

If one insists, however, upon an equation of gender and sex for the word *'adam* in Genesis 2:7, then one must recognize the comparable significance of the feminine grammatical gender of the word *'adama* (earth or humus). Not only does the feminine *'adama* exist in the story prior to the masculine *'adam*, but also the latter comes out of the former. From this perspective the "female" both precedes the "male" and provides the material from which he is formed. The "male," then, is subordinate to the "female." By such reasoning, the argument for the primacy of the male, based on the gender of the word *'adam*, turns unwittingly against itself. But grammar is not the issue.

To the conceptual observation that a sexually undifferentiated earth creature would not be "a human being,"[8] the proper rejoinder is "most surely." In the story humanity unfolds gradually. The first creature lacks not just sexual identity but also direct speech and social identity. These features appear only when the earth creature becomes two creatures, female and male (2:22b-23). And the two emerge simultaneously, not sequentially. The reality can be no other way; male requires female and female requires male. Each sex depends upon the other for its separate identity. The forming of the "human from the humus" only begins the process that eventuates in full humanity.

Literary objections to an understanding of the first creature as sexually undifferentiated have focused on two observations: the absence of parallels in other biblical texts and the absence of a linguistic marker to designate a shift in the use and meaning of the word 'adam from sexually undifferentiated to male (cf. 2:22b-3:21).[9] The first observation confirms the point it seeks to counter. Genesis 2:7-22a reports on a unique creature for whom, by definition and narrative sequence, there can be no parallels. With the advent of female and male (2:22b-23), the earth creature is no more. The rest of the Bible then assumes the existence of the two sexes.

The second observation, regarding the absence of a linguistic marker to differentiate between the use of 'adam for the sexually undifferentiated creature and for the male, evokes two different responses, one identifying a linguistic marker and the other relativizing the need for such a marker. On the one hand, a marker is present in 2:22 where the word ha-'adam, occurring twice, bears different meanings. In the first part of the verse the word signifies the earth creature: "And the side that Yhwh God took from the earth creature (ha-'adam) he made into woman ('issa). . . . " The appearance of the noun 'issa, indeed the appearance of woman, radically alters the situation. New to the story, 'issa designates the first sexually identified creature and thereby changes the meaning of ha-'adam. Accordingly, in the latter part of the verse ha-'adam acquires the second meaning, man the male: " . . . he made into woman ('issa) and brought her to the man (ha-'adam)." Coming between two occurrences of ha-'adam, the advent of woman changes the meaning of that word. She makes the difference structurally and narratively. Over against the emphases of a patriarchal culture, the story highlights her creation. By contrast, the man's creation emerges from the leftovers. The word 'issa is the linguistic marker that shifts the meaning of ha-'adam.

On the other hand, the demand for a linguistic marker may hoist one on one's own petard. An examination of the use of ha-'adam at the ending of the story exposes the flaw. In 3:21 the term specifies the man as he appears in parallel to the woman: "Yhwh God made for the man (ha-'adam) and for his woman ('issa) garments of skin. . . . " Given this indisputable meaning of ha-'adam as male, what is one to make of the meaning of this same word in the very next verse where the parallel word 'issa does not appear: "Behold, ha-'adam has become like one of us . . . " (3:22)? Does the noun refer only to the man, by analogy with its use in 3:21? If so, then the woman has not "become like one of us" and thus is not subject to punishment by God. Furthermore, what is one to make of the grammatical masculine singular pronouns identifying the one expelled from the garden? "Therefore Yhwh God sent *him* forth from the garden of Eden to till the ground from which *he* was taken" (3:23). Do these pronouns refer exclusively to the man? Again, what is one to make of the second appearance in this section of the noun *ha-'adam* without the accompanying phrase "and his woman"? Yhwh God "drove out *ha-'adam*" (3:24). If *ha-'adam* has (or must have) the single meaning of man the male throughout the story, then at the end only the man, not the woman, is driven out of the garden.[10]

No exegete accepts such a conclusion. To the contrary, commentator after commentator assigns a generic meaning to the masculine singular noun *ha-'adam* at the end of the story (3:22-24) and so declares that the woman is expelled from the garden along with the man.[11] I agree with this interpretation and want to underscore its meaning for the relationship of female and male. One sign of their shared disobedience in eating the forbidden fruit is patriarchy, the rule of the man over the woman (3:16). One component of patriarchy is so-called generic language. In vocabulary and effect it subsumes the woman to the man. It renders him visible (hence, *ha-'adam*) and her invisible (hence, the absence of the phrase "and his *'issa*" in 3:22-24 in contrast to its presence in 3:21).

What evidence is available for the generic interpretation of *ha-'adam* in the ending of the story? Is there a linguistic marker to signal a shift from the exclusively male use of the word in 3:21 and the generic use in 3:22?[12] That is difficult to find. The clauses "Yahweh God made" (3:21) and "Yhwh God said" (3:22) are parallel, indicating continuity between the two verses. Yet differences in discourse follow. In 3:21 narrated discourse uses the phrase "for *'adam* and his woman"; in 3:22 direct discourse has the deity say, "Behold, *ha-'adam* has become. . . . " If the difference in discourse be used to argue for a shift in the meaning of *ha-'adam* from male to generic, that argument gets undercut in 3:24 where narrated discourse picks up on the deity's use of the single term *ha-'adam*: "He drove out *ha-'adam*." In other words, no linguistic marker signals the shift in meaning between these two uses of the noun *ha-'adam*. And yet no scholar (of whom I am aware) disputes the shift.[13]

By analogy, then, the presumed lack of a linguistic marker to indicate a shift in the meaning of *ha-'adam* near the beginning of the story is of no consequence. To require a marker there would expose the flaw in the unquestioned acceptance of two meanings for *ha-'adam* near the end. In neither place, the beginning or the end of the story, does the lack of a literary marker invalidate the proposed interpretations of *ha-'adam*.

If exegetes throughout the ages have discerned two uses of the word *'adam* in the story, male and generic, then why not three? They work structurally and narratively. At the start, before the creation of woman and man, *ha-'adam* designates a single sexually undifferentiated creature (2:7-22a). In the middle, beginning with the creation of woman and man, *'adam* designates only the male creature (2:22b-3:21). At the close, after the shared disobedience of the woman and the man, *'adam* designates the couple (3:22-24). It becomes generic language that highlights the male and hides the female.

These three uses of *'adam* illustrate well the many ambiguities that permeate Genesis 2-3. The more I live with the story the more I appreciate such ambiguities and their power to evoke diverse responses. Though traditional readings tend to neglect ambiguity, it nevertheless endures to challenge those very readings. Patriarchy, then, has no lasting claim on this story. Indeed, in the years since I began to articulate a nonpatriarchal interpretation, the text has never failed me.[14] Despite voices to the contrary, it remains a foundational document for developing a feminist biblical theology.[15]

In inviting me to contribute to this volume, the editors asked whether, after more than twenty years, I had changed my mind in any significant way about my understanding of Genesis 2-3. If they mean my views as set forth in the short article reprinted here, then the answer is yes. The discussion of the word *'adam* explicates an important change. If they mean, however, the lengthy study that followed the short article, the answer is no. Not a jot, not a tittle.

NOTES TO CHAPTER 8, EGALITARIAN INTERPRETATIONS,
PHYLLIS TRIBLE, "NOT A JOT, NOT A TITTLE"

1. Edwin M. Good, *Irony in the Old Testament* (Philadelphia: Westminster Press, 1965), p. 84. Cf. the second edition published in 1981 in Sheffield by the University of Sheffield Press.

2. This paper became Phyllis Trible, "Depatriarchalizing in Biblical Interpretation," *Journal of the American Academy of Religion* 41 (1973): 30-48.

3. Phyllis Trible, "Eve and Adam: Genesis 2-3 Reread," *Andover Newton Quarterly* (March 1973): 251-58.

4. E.g., Phyllis Trible, "Eve and Adam: Genesis 2-3 Reread," in Carol P. Christ and Judith Plaskow, editors, *Womanspirit Rising: A Feminist Reader in Religion* (New York: Harper & Row, 1979), pp. 74-83; cf. the 1992 edition. See also Trible, "Eve and Adam: Genesis 2-3 Reread," in Marcia Stubbs and Sylvan Barnet, editors, *The Little, Brown Reader* (Boston: Scott, Foresman and Company, 1989), pp. 1015-24.

5. Phyllis Trible, *God and the Rhetoric of Sexuality* (Philadelphia: Fortress Press, 1978), pp. 72-143.

6. Cf. note 17 in Trible, *God and the Rhetoric of Sexuality*, p. 141.

7. See Bruce K. Waltke and M. O'Connor, *An Introduction to Biblical Hebrew Syntax* (Winona Lake, Ind.: Eisenbrauns, 1990), pp. 99-101.

8. See Elizabeth Achtemeier, "The Impossible Possibility: Evaluating the Feminist Approach to Bible and Theology," *Interpretation* 42 (1988): 51.

9. See most recently Terence E. Fretheim, "The Book of Genesis," *The New Interpreter's Bible* (Nashville: Abingdon Press, 1994), p. 353.

10. Cf. Jean M. Higgins, "The Myth of Eve: The Temptress," *Journal of the American Academy of Religion* 44 (1976): 645.

11. E.g., Fretheim, "The Book of Genesis," p. 353; Claus Westermann, *Genesis 1-11: A Commentary*, translated by John J. Scullion (Minneapolis: Augsburg Publishing House, 1974), pp. 271-75.

12. To be sure, the very first line of the next story shows that the woman did leave the garden with the man. Adam and Eve mate to produce Cain (4:1). But a resort to

extrinsic evidence changes the rules of the literary game. The point is to find intrinsic evidence for the shift in the meaning and use of *ha-'adam*.

13. Cf. the contradictory stance of Fretheim who first declares that the word *'adam* "should be read with the same [male] meaning throughout" and later declares that "we should note that *'adam* functions generically" in 3:22-24. (Fretheim, "The Book of Genesis," pp. 353, 364.)

14. *Contra*, e.g., Pamela J. Milne, "Eve and Adam: A Feminist Reading," in Harvey Minkoff, editor, *Approaches to the Bible* (Washington, D.C.: Biblical Archaeology Society, 1995), vol. 2, pp. 259-69. Feminists who support the patriarchal reading ironically capitulate to the view they assail.

15. Cf. Phyllis Trible, "Treasures Old and New: Biblical Theology and the Challenge of Feminism," in Francis Watson, editor, *The Open Text* (London: SCM Press Ltd., 1993), pp. 32-56.

Jouette M. Bassler

Jouette Bassler is Professor of New Testament at Perkins School of Theology, Southern Methodist University, Dallas, Texas. While she teaches broadly in the field of New Testament studies, the Pauline and Deutero-Pauline materials provide her current research focus. The author of several articles, she also has written *God and Mammon: Asking for Money in the New Testament* and a commentary on the Pastoral Letters, *1 Timothy, 2 Timothy, Titus*.[1] Currently Bassler is the general editor of the *Journal of Biblical Literature*, one of two journals published by the Society of Biblical Literature. She has also served as the New Testament editor for the *HarperCollins Study Bible*.[2]

In the essay Bassler wrote for this anthology, she examines the ways that the author of 1 Timothy interprets Eve and Adam's story. She assesses relations between the Genesis text and 1 Timothy's injunctions concerning women's silence and submission and its concern about childbearing and heresy. Through descriptions of the text's historical setting—particularly the situation of the author's church—Bassler explores how social context influences the interpretation of Eve that is set forth in 1 Timothy, especially the context generated by debates between the author of 1 Timothy and the author's opponents. Bassler also notes how the interpretation of Eve set forth by this New Testament text is used to explain the nature and faults of Eve's daughters. (Source: Jouette M. Bassler wrote, "Deception in the Garden: 1 Timothy 2:11-15" for this volume.)

"Deception in the Garden: 1 Timothy 2:11–15" (1994 CE)
JOUETTE M. BASSLER

Let a woman learn in silence with full submission. I permit no woman to teach or to have authority over a man; she is to keep silent. For Adam was formed first, then Eve; and Adam was not deceived, but the woman was deceived and became a transgressor. Yet she will be saved through childbearing, provided they continue in faith and love and holiness, with modesty.

Few interpretations of Genesis have had such fateful results as this one from 1 Timothy 2:11-15, for it has traditionally been used to define the appropriate ecclesial role for women (a nonrole).[3] Recently, however, this text has come under intense fire for its androcentrism and misogyny.[4] The commentaries weigh in on both sides of the debate. Barclay, for example, insists that "the passage ends with a note of real truth. Women will be saved in childbearing . . . not in addressing meetings,"[5] and Schlatter suggests that the injunctions in this passage are actually a blessing from God, who *allows* women to be silent and thereby frees them from the onerous tasks of instructing and guiding the church.[6] Hanson, on the other hand, rather grudgingly concedes that though "the modern conventions which govern women's place in society have still to be proved superior to the old ones . . . Christians are under no obligation to accept (this) teaching on women."[7] Johnson states unequivocally that the commands in these verses "are time-conditioned and relative," and laments the fact that they have "become an instrument of terror and suppression in the hands of (their) interpreters."[8]

The passage clearly raises blood pressures as well as a crucial hermeneutical issue. It is time to reassess this application of the story of Adam and Eve, but we will want to explore not only what the text says about the primal pair, but also how this interpretation was shaped by—and how itself shaped—the author's social world. At the conclusion of this study we should have achieved some clarity about the origins and implications of these injunctions to silence and submissiveness and the insistence that Eve, but not Adam, was deceived.

Historical Circumstances

Exegetes of the Pastoral Epistles have long recognized the necessity of viewing this appropriation of the Genesis myth against the background of the historical and social circumstances of the author's time, but not all define the author or his circumstances in the same way. Though some hold to Pauline authorship,[9] many now assume that the author of these three epistles was not the apostle Paul but some second-century church leader who appropriated the apostle's name and authority in order to deal more effectively with a threat to his church from some religious opponents.[10] Though much of the author's argument against these opponents is couched in stock insults and traditional polemics, some distinctive elements of their theology and behavior can be deduced from the letters. Robert Karris has summarized these elements as follows:

> The opponents are Jewish Christians who are teachers of the law (1 Tim 1:7; Tit 3:9; cf. Tit 1:14). They teach Jewish myths (Tit 1:14; cf. 1 Tim 1:4; 4:7; 2 Tim 4:4) and genealogies (1 Tim 1:4; Tit 3:9). They forbid marriage and enjoin abstinence from food (1 Tim 4:3-5). They teach that the resurrection has already occurred (2 Tim 2:18). They may have had significant success among the womanfolk [sic], especially because of their teaching about emancipation (2 Tim 3:6-7; cf. 1 Tim 2:11-15; 5:13; Tit 2:5).[11]

Though Karris indicates some ambivalence about the last point (success among women), and though he does not fully explain the "teaching about emancipation," this point seems to me to be at least as assured as the others and of somewhat greater importance for understanding the implications of our text. Throughout these letters the instructions concerning women seem to be focused on issues raised by the opponents (e.g., teaching roles and celibacy), and the author describes these opponents as "those who make their way into households and captivate silly women, overwhelmed by their sins and swayed by all kinds of desires, who are always being instructed and can never arrive at a knowledge of the truth" (2 Tim. 3:5-7). Though Spicq insists that this derogatory description cannot apply to Christian women, who *have* arrived at a knowledge of truth,[12] the author's pervasive concern to strengthen the women of his congregation against a message of celibacy strongly suggests that these opponents *have* enjoyed success in attracting Christian women to that message.[13]

Why was this so? It will no longer suffice merely to appeal to a general proclivity of women for new religious views.[14] The opponents offered something concrete to the women that made this shift of allegiance attractive. One aspect of this "something" was freedom from the patriarchal structures that characterized the Greco-Roman world and was increasingly characterizing the church.[15]

Insofar as Galatians 3:28 was more than mere baptismal rhetoric, Christianity seems to have begun as a rather egalitarian movement, with equality affecting even the structure of Christian marriages (see 1 Cor. 7:1-16). But Christianity did not long remain egalitarian. Social pressures both within and without soon forced the church to restructure both itself and the families within it according to the hierarchical, patriarchal pattern of contemporary society. This is particularly evident in the Pastoral Epistles, and it is also evident from these epistles that some women sought to escape this pattern to some degree by embracing a celibate lifestyle.[16] At first this was possible within the widows' office of this church, but increasingly it was the opponents, with their blanket renunciation of marriage, who offered the best avenue to freedom. Thus the success of the author's opponents with the "silly women" can be attributed in large measure to the fact that they still offered social benefits once promised by the church. Against this background we can explore the version of the story of Adam and Eve in 1 Timothy 2.

Silence and Submission

1 Timothy 2:8-15 opens with brief instructions for men concerning the proper attitude toward prayer and continues with somewhat more extensive admonitions to women:

> I desire, then, that in every place the men should pray, lifting up holy hands
> without anger or argument; also that the women should dress themselves
> modestly and decently in suitable clothing, not with their hair braided, or

with gold, pearls, or expensive clothes, but with good works, as is proper for women who profess reverence for God. (vv. 8-10)

The meaning of this text is somewhat ambiguous since the instructions to women in verse 9 do not contain a finite verb. Certainly the instructions both to men and to women are governed by the introductory βούλομαι ("I desire"), but are both governed by the reference to prayer as well? Some would have it so, in which case both men and women are instructed to pray, but the two groups are given separately tailored, but quite traditional instructions regarding the proper attitude and attire to accompany this prayer.[17] Yet the more natural reading (reflected in the NRSV quoted above) is to let βούλομαι govern two separate infinitive clauses, one instructing men to pray peacefully (προσεύχεσθαι), the other instructing women to adorn themselves properly (κοσμεῖν). This reading, however, implies a decisive imbalance in liturgical participation.

The subsequent instructions, now addressed solely to women, increase this imbalance: "Let a woman learn in silence with full submission. I permit no woman to teach or to have authority over a man; she is to keep silent." (vv. 11-12).

Again there is some debate over the meaning of these words, resulting in some disagreement over what is demanded by the text. It has been argued, for example, that the word ἡσυχία does not demand silence of the women but an attitude of quiet and repose that will facilitate learning.[18] This seems, however, to overlook the harsh tone of these verses, which require not only ἡσυχία but also subordination (ὑποταγή), which forbid teaching, and which accuse Eve, the prototypical woman, of being deceived (or seduced!) and of falling into sin. Silence is the logical corollary to all of this, not repose. Moreover, the author presents his demands in a chiastic pattern (*abcb'a'*), which places the emphasis on the central element, the prohibition of teaching:

   (a) learn in silence
      (b) with full submission
         (c) [not] to teach
      (b') [not] to have authority
   (a') keep silent.

Throughout the Pastoral Epistles there is a persistent concern for good teaching and orthodox teachers, underscoring the significance of this issue in these instructions. Prohibition of teaching is, however, more directly supported by a demand for silence than by a concern for peace.

Others have tried to mitigate the harshness of the verses by limiting their applicability to the subordination of a married woman to her husband,[19] or to the temporary subordination of particular women to church authorities,[20] or to the prohibition of bossy interruptions of the worship service.[21] Apologetic considerations aside, the wording of the text speaks rather clearly of a comprehensive demand for silence and submission and of a comprehensive denial of any public teaching role for women in the church (see, however, Titus 2:3).

These injunctions, particularly the rejection of women's authority over men, are then grounded by an appeal to two aspects of the Genesis myth:

> For Adam was formed first, then Eve; and Adam was not deceived, but the woman was deceived and became a transgressor. (vv. 13-14).

The author appeals first to the sequence of creation in the Yahwistic account (Gen. 2). "Adam was formed first," and the first-born was universally recognized as having superior status and rightful authority over subsequent siblings (see Gen. 27:27; Deut. 21:15-17; Heb. 1:6). But Adam was not *born* first, he was *formed* first, and Genesis clearly states that God was the one who formed him (Gen. 2:7). The author of the letter recalls this aspect of the story, indicating that the sequence of creation was God's doing and consequently reveals God's will for the relationship of the two sexes. Thus women in roles of authority over men are viewed as flouting not just human conventions but the divine will itself.

To this argument based on God's will as revealed through the creation sequence, a second is added based on human merit as revealed by the fall. At first glance the argument is an astonishing one. The author does not merely argue for Eve's primacy in the fall, but he seems to exculpate Adam altogether: "Adam was not deceived, but the woman was deceived and became a transgressor." In order to find some explanation for this insistence—in spite of the clear biblical testimony to the contrary (see Gen. 3:17-19)—that Eve and *only* Eve was culpable, a number of scholars have suggested that behind it stands an allusion to the legend of Eve's seduction by the serpent.[22] That, at least, would be the one aspect of the fall in which Adam manifestly did not participate. Textual support for this hypothesis is found in the verb ἐξαπατάω in the second half of v. 14, a prefixed form of ἀπατάω which intensifies the concept of deception and can suggest sexual seduction. Thus the text lends some support to this hypothesis, but the point is not emphasized.

Quite apart from the legend of seduction, a literal reading of Genesis 3 could generate the claim we find in 1 Timothy 2, for only the woman admits there to succumbing to deception (ὁ ὄφις ἠπάτησέν με, καὶ ἔφαγον, Gen. 3:13). Adam, on the other hand, admits only to receiving and eating the fruit, not to being deceived (αὕτη μοι ἔδωκεν ἀπὸ τοῦ ξύλου, καὶ ἔφαγον, Gen. 3:12). The primary reason for the author's emphasis on Eve's deception, however, was not exegetical but practical. He stressed the connection between Eve's fall and her deception because he wanted to address the situation of deception that existed in his church, where Eve's daughters, the women of the church, were (in his view) being deceived by his opponents.[23] Because of this "gullibility," it seemed to the author unwise for women to occupy positions of authority or influence within the church. Thus he highlighted the motif of deception in Genesis 3 in order to provide a scriptural warrant for his convictions and his injunctions. Eve, the prototype of all women, was the one in the garden who was deceived, and her daughters, who seem to have inherited this proclivity, must therefore be excluded from positions in which this tendency could further endanger the church.

The key points in this argument are thus: (1) the prior identification of the opponents as deceivers, (2) the conviction that women in the church were far too frequently deceived by these people, and (3) the wording of Genesis 3:12-13, in which the primal woman, but not the primal man, admits to succumbing to deception. It is thus the idea of deception on which the author seeks to build his argument, and any allusion to the legend of Eve's *seduction* is accidental or incidental.

If the idea of deception provided the primary connection with Genesis, two other features of the story of Adam and Eve are echoed in this text. First, according to Genesis 3:16 one aspect of God's punishment of the woman, in addition to the pain of childbirth, was her strict subordination to her husband ("he shall rule over you"). Though the author does not quote this verse, its sentiment matches his pervasive concern to emphasize hierarchical order.[24] Its message is reflected here in his insistence on women's subjugation, whether to men or to the teaching of these men, and in his explicit rejection of any inversion of this rule through women exercising authority over men.

Second, according to Genesis 3:17 God's punishment of Adam was based not only on the fact that he broke the divine commandment and ate from the forbidden tree, but also—and apparently primarily—on the fact that he *listened to Eve's advice*: "Because you have listened to the voice of your wife, and have eaten of the tree . . . , cursed is the ground because of you." It is easy to see these words reflected in the author's insistence on the women's silence. They must not be allowed to exercise this sort of verbal influence again. But do these words also reflect a problem within the author's church? That is, was experience controlling exegesis here too?

"Saying What They Should Not Say"

In 1 Timothy 5 we learn that members of one group of women in this church, the widows, had already been attracted to the opponents (1 Tim. 5:15). Furthermore, these women, while not commanded to silence, were accused of "gadding about from house to house . . . saying what they should not say" (λαλοῦσαι τὰ μὴ δέώρῆϊ, 1 Tim. 5:13). The condemnation of excessive or pretentious speech, especially in women, was quite traditional,[25] but the author does not seem to object here to the *manner* of speaking as much as to the *content*.[26] He does not explicitly spell out this content here, but elsewhere the letters provide a few clues. A similar objection, for example, is raised against the opponents, who teach what they should not teach (διδάσκοντες ἃ μὴ δεῖ, Tit. 1:11), and both the widows and the opponents espoused celibacy (1 Tim. 4:3; 5:11-12). It is thus possible that the conversations of these widows as they went from house to house included this message of celibacy. At any rate, the author probably feared that it did and this brought the women too close to the opponents' camp. They had to be stopped. If this line of speculation reflects with any degree of accuracy the situation in the author's church, the insistence on ἡσυχία in 1 Timothy 2:11-12 should probably be seen as an extension of this concern. It is interesting that the only place in the Pastoral Epistles that encourages women to speak limits the content of that speech to the distinctly anticelibate topics of marital submissiveness and maternal love (Tit. 2:3-5).

After the strict injunctions against women in verses 11 and 12 and the rather harsh description of Eve's actions in the garden in verses 13 and 14, the author concludes this section on a note of mollification as he reassures women of their ultimate salvation: "Yet she will be saved through childbearing, provided they continue in faith and love and holiness, with modesty" (v. 15). The precise nature of this reassurance and its intended relationship to the Genesis story is not at all clear. In the first place, the verbs in verse 15 have no explicit subjects. It is easy to supply γυνή ("the woman") from verse 14 as the subject of σωθήσεται in verse 15 ("she will be saved"), but the next verb (μένειν) shifts rather inexplicably to a plural form ("if *they* continue"). This raises the question of whether the author still had just the woman in mind. In the second place, the idea of salvation achieved through childbirth seems too foreign to Christian thought to be the intended message.

The various solutions proposed for these problems can be divided into two groups.[27] One line of interpretation takes "save" in the sense of physical safekeeping and ignores the shift from a singular to a plural verb. The preposition διά ("through") then designates the circumstances through which the woman is safely brought, and the clause introduced by ἐάν ("if") contains the key thought that the woman is brought safely through these difficult circumstances by exercising the Christian triad of virtues—faith, love, and holiness.[28]

The implication of this interpretation is that the author views the punishment prescribed in Genesis 3:16, the pain of childbirth, as remaining in effect, though now the woman is provided with a palliative. Women must still pass through the dangers of childbirth as retribution for Eve's sin, but they are now assured of *safely* passing through them if they live a true Christian life. Though this interpretation has a certain appeal, it also creates certain difficulties. It demands a secular interpretation of σώζειν ("save"), although everywhere else in the Pastoral Epistles the word is used in a clearly religious sense;[29] and it requires an unusual, though not totally unattested, meaning for διά.[30] Hanson seems to supply the true reason for the popularity of this interpretation: "One is tempted to prefer this translation, *even if only for the sake of the author's reputation as a Christian teacher.*"[31]

The other line of interpretation takes "save" in its usual religious sense and διά in its usual instrumental sense. The theological problem this creates (salvation through childbearing) is then partially mitigated in one of two ways. If one supplies "the children" as the plural subject of the verb "remain," salvation no longer rests merely on childbirth, but also on the nurture of these children in the Christian tradition.[32] The unmarked shift of subject, however, poses a serious difficulty to this interpretation, as does the new implication that a woman's salvation depends upon her offsprings' behavior. Alternatively, some draw on the allusion to seduction in verse 14 to defend the concept of salvation through childbirth as a loose application of the idea of *quo quis peccat, eo salvetur* (one is saved by the same thing through which one has sinned).[33] Since Eve sinned by succumbing to the sexual overtures of the serpent, her descendants can only be saved by a related act, that is, by bearing children. Here the fall of Genesis, interpreted as a seduction, dictates the necessity of childbirth as a means of salvation.

The best framework for understanding this insistence on childbearing is not, however, the legend of seduction but the clear threat of the opponents' message of celibacy. Because of the author's concern to reject the celibate life-style advocated by his opponents, he here counters the suggestion in Genesis that childbirth is a curse, an idea that would play into the hands of his opponents. Indeed, the opponents, who were skilled in manipulating Jewish myths,[34] may have already exploited the potential of this idea. In any case, the author has transformed the Genesis curse into a Christian blessing, which operated on two levels. A woman will be saved *from the opponents' message of celibacy* by bearing children, and because she thus avoids making a shipwreck of her faith, she will also be saved in the eschatological sense of the word, provided, of course, she continues in faith, love, and holiness.

Eve, the Mother of Heresy

In true midrashic fashion, the experiences of the author and his church provided the lens through which he read the Genesis story. The perceived gullibility of women for the opponents' message suggested a line of interpretation that made the story of Adam and Eve a useful support for the rather strict measures the author took to deal with the problem. His goal, of course, was to distance the women from the opponents, yet in his argument he describes Eve, the primal woman, in such a way that she is linked *with* the opponents.

1. Eve was deceived; the author strongly emphasizes this. Yet not only are the opponents labeled "deceivers" (Tit. 1:10), they and those who join them are also called "deceived" (1 Tim. 4:1; 2 Tim. 3:13).
2. Not only was Eve deceived, but according to 1 Tim. 2:14 she *and only she* became a transgressor. This label places the woman in close association with the opponents, who are repeatedly pilloried in these letters as godless sinners who have swerved from the truth.[35]
3. Eve was formed second, after Adam, with the clear implication that she is therefore inferior. Likewise, the opponents are presented as the more recent and therefore inferior arrival on the religious scene, whereas the author's church holds the Adamic position of priority.

The development of this theme is subtle but clear. The antiquity of the author's church is suggested first of all by the pseudonymity of the letters. By claiming Pauline authorship, the author claims that his church stands within the tradition of the first apostle to the gentiles, whose service to God is in direct continuity with that of his ancestors (2 Tim. 1:3). Timothy, too, displays a faith that can be traced back several generations (2 Tim. 1:5). Moreover, the gospel message itself reflects the purpose and promises of God that were established ages ago (Tit. 1:2), so that Paul's own election (and Timothy's as well) is coterminous with the eternal plan of God (2 Tim. 1:9). The opponents, on the other hand, display a faith that is a weak and false copy of the original (2 Tim. 3:8), for their appearance on the stage of history is recent.[36] Indeed, far from having roots of any antiquity, their arrival is presented as a sign of the end (1 Tim. 4:1; 2 Tim. 3:1). Thus the opponents, like Eve, are second in sequence and inferior in quality, holding merely the form and not the reality of religion (2 Tim. 3:1-5).

With these connections in place, the language and mythology of the Pastoral Epistles function to make Eve the archetype not merely of women, but of the opponents, and thus of heresy. Indeed, in one important way the women are treated *like* the opponents: they are silenced in the church and are forbidden to teach. The opponents, too, are silenced (Tit. 1:11) and forbidden to teach their contrary doctrine (1 Tim. 1:3), and many of the evils charged against them are associated with speaking. With regard to the important social and ecclesial functions of speaking and teaching, then, the women and the opponents were treated in much the same way.

That a complete identification had *not* taken place in the author's church is clear.[37] There are admonitions to treat women with consideration (1 Tim. 5:2-3); two were singled out for special approbation (2 Tim. 1:5); women may have retained vestiges of a diaconal office (1 Tim. 3:11);[38] and their teaching skills were not completely rejected but were redirected to a domestic arena where women were expected to counter rather than complement the celibate message of the opponents (Tit. 2:3-5). Yet the story of Adam and Eve as it was developed in these letters is not far from functioning in a purely dualistic way, with Eve not the partner, but the negative counterpoint of Adam, the archetype of all heresy.

NOTES TO CHAPTER 8, EGALITARIAN INTERPRETATIONS, JOUETTE M. BASSLER

[1. Jouette M. Bassler, *God and Mammon: Asking for Money in the New Testament* (Nashville: Abingdon Press, 1991); *1 Timothy, 2 Timothy, Titus*, Abingdon New Testament Commentary series (Nashville: Abingdon Press, 1996). See also her earlier article, "Adam, Eve, and the Pastor," in Gregory Allen Robbins, editor, *Genesis 1-3 in the History of Exegesis: Intrigue in the Garden*, Studies in Women and Religion, 27 (Lewiston, N.Y., and Queenston, Ontario: Edwin Mellen Press, 1988), pp. 43-65.]

[2. *HarperCollins Study Bible: New Revised Standard Version, with Apocryphal/ Deuterocanonical Books*, Wayne Meeks, general editor (New York: HarperCollins, 1993).]

3. See, e.g., Section 20 of the "Declaration on the Question of the Admission of Women to the Ministerial Priesthood," published in 1976 by the Roman Catholic Church. For an earlier example, see *Apostolic Constitutions* 3.6.1-2.

4. See, e.g., Elizabeth Cady Stanton, *The Woman's Bible* (New York: European Publishing Co., 1895; reprint ed., New York: Arno Press, 1972), p. 162; Elisabeth Schüssler Fiorenza, "The Study of Women in Early Christianity: Some Methodological Considerations," in T. J. Ryan, editor, *Critical History and Biblical Faith: New Testament Perspectives* (Villanova, Penn.: College Theology Society, 1979), pp. 30-58; Wayne A. Meeks, "The Image of the Androgyne: Some Uses of a Symbol in Earliest Christianity," *History of Religions* 13 (1974): 165-208, esp. pp. 206-208; Joanna Dewey, "1 Timothy," in C. A. Newsom and S. H. Ringe, editors, *The Women's Bible Commentary* (Louisville: Westminster/John Knox, 1992), pp. 353-56.

5. William Barclay, *The Letters to Timothy, Titus and Philemon* (Philadelphia: Westminster, 1975), p. 68.

6. Adolf Schlatter, *Erläuterungen zum Neuen Testament. Zweiter Band. Die Briefe des Paulus* (Stuttgart: Calwer, 1928), p. 142.

7. Anthony T. Hanson, *The Pastoral Letters* (Cambridge: Cambridge University Press, 1966), pp. 36-38.

8. Luke T. Johnson, *1 Timothy, 2 Timothy, Titus*, Knox Preaching Guides (Atlanta: John Knox, 1987), pp. 73-74.

9. See, e.g., Schlatter; C. Spicq, *Saint Paul: Les Épitres Pastorales*, 4th ed., 2 vols., Études bibliques (Paris: J. Gabalda, 1969); Gordon Fee, *1 and 2 Timothy, Titus* (Peabody, Mass.: Hendrickson, 1984, 1988); and George W. Knight, III, *Commentary on the Pastoral Epistles*, The New International Greek Testament Commentary (Grand Rapids, Mich.: Eerdmans, 1992).

10. Thus, e.g., Hanson; Jürgen Roloff, *Der erste Brief an Timotheus*, Evangelisch-katholischer Kommentar zum Neuen Testament 15 (Neukirchen-Vluyn: Neukirchener Verlag, 1988); Arland J. Hultgren, *I-II Timothy, Titus* (Minneapolis: Augsburg, 1984); Victor Hasler, *Die Briefe an Timotheus und Titus* (Zürich: Theologischer Verlag, 1978); Norbert Brox, *Die Pastoralbriefe*, Regensburger Neues Testament 7.2 (Regensburg: Friedrich Pustet, 1969); Gottfried Holtz, *Die Pastoralbriefe*, Theologischer Handkommentar zum Neuen Testament 13 (Berlin: Evangelischer Verlag, 1965).

11. Robert J. Karris, "The Background and Significance of the Polemic of the Pastoral Epistles," *Journal of Biblical Literature* 92 (1973): 562-63.

12. Spicq, *Saint Paul: Épitres Pastorales*, vol. 2, p. 777.

13. See 1 Timothy 2:11-15; 5:13-15; Titus 2:3-5 (cf. Titus 1:11). The connection between the opponents and the admonitions to and about women is widely recognized, though it is not always adequately developed.

14. See, e.g., Spicq, *Saint Paul: Épitres Pastorales*, vol. 2, p. 778.

15. Though the picture of Early Christianity summarized below is gaining wide recognition, it is perhaps most forcefully argued by Schüssler Fiorenza; see her "Study of Women" and her monograph, *In Memory of Her* (New York: Crossroad, 1983).

16. Celibacy is increasingly being recognized as an avenue to freedom in the early church. See, e.g., Stevan L. Davies, *The Revolt of the Widows: The Social World of the Apocryphal Acts* (Carbondale: Southern Illinois University Press, 1980), and my own article, "The Widows' Tale: A Fresh Look at 1 Tim 5:3-16," *Journal of Biblical Literature* 103 (1984): 23-41, which summarizes this research.

17. See, e.g., Spicq, *Saint Paul: Épitres Pastorales*, vol. 1, pp. 374-75; for a thorough documentation of the traditional quality of these injunctions, see his comments on these verses.

18. See, e.g., 2 Thessalonians 3:12; 1 Timothy 2:2; 1 Peter 3:4. Thus Holtz (*Pastoralbriefe*, p. 69); Margaret D. Gibson (" 'Let the Woman Learn in Silence,' " *Expository Times* 15 [1903-04]: 379-80); Aida D. B. Spencer ("Eve at Ephesus," *Journal of the Evangelical Theological Society* 17 [1974]: 215-22); Alan Padgett ("Wealthy Women at Ephesus: 1 Tim 2:8-15 in Social Context," *Interpretation* 41 [1987]: 24) see this injunction as an improvement over the demand for σιγή in 1 Corinthians 14:34.

19. This argument, which is advocated by N. J. Hommes ("Let Women Be Silent in Church," *Calvin Theological Journal* 4 [1969]: 5-22) and Gibson (" 'Let the Woman Learn in Silence' "), rests on the assumption that the reference to a woman and a man in singular form in verse 12 implies husband and wife (cf. the plurals in vv. 8-10). Yet this reading is not supported by any possessive pronouns (e.g., "*her* husband") and, as G. Engel points out (" 'Let the Woman Learn in Silence,' " *Expository Times* 16 [1904-05]: 189-90), the consequence of such a prohibition would still be that married women would be prevented from teaching in public when their husbands were present.

20. Padgett, "Wealthy Women," pp. 24-25.

21. This argument, advocated by Robert Falconer ("1 Timothy 2.14,15. Interpretative Notes," *Journal of Biblical Literature* 60 [1941]: 375-79) and Martin Dibelius and Hans Conzelmann (*The Pastoral Epistles* [Philadelphia: Fortress, 1972], p. 47), takes αὐθεντεῖν in the limited sense of "to be domineering" and allows this to control the meaning of the verse. Even less recommended is Spicq's retrieval of this verb's etymological roots in the word for murder, which allows him to claim that the first woman was a murderess, because she induced the man to sin and thus to suffer mortality (*Saint Paul: Épitres Pastorales*, vol. 2, p. 380). For an assessment of these arguments, see G. W. Knight, "ΑΥΘΕΝΤΕΩ in Reference to Women in 1 Timothy 2.12," *New Testament Studies* 30 (1984): 143-57.

22. See *b. Yebam.* 103b; *b. 'Abod. Zar.* 22b; *b. Šabb.* 146a; 2 *Enoch* 31:6; and *Prot. Jas.* 13.1.

23. Opponents are frequently labeled "deceivers" in these letters (see 1 Tim. 4:1 [πλάνοι]; 2 Tim. 3:13 [πλανῶντες]; Tit. 1:10 [φρεναπάται]), a label common in contemporary philosophical polemics (see Karris, "Polemic," 552).

24. See, e.g., 1 Timothy 3:4, 12; 5:1-2; 6:1-2; Titus 2:4-5, 9; 3:1.

25. See, e.g., Musonius Rufus, *Or.* 3; Juvenal, *Sat.* 6; see also Karris, "The Background and Significance of the Polemic," p. 553.

26. Isocrates, e.g., uses a very similar phrase, λέγειν πάντα τὰ δέοντα, to refer to the content of a speech (see *Areopagiticus* 10; *On the Peace* 115) and a somewhat different one, τὸ λέγειν ὡς δεῖ, to refer to the manner of speaking (see *Nicocles* 7; *Antidosis* 255; *Panegyricus* 10).

27. One can easily exclude the two other lines of interpretation that occasionally surface. To interpret διὰ τῆς τεκνογονίας as "through the birth of *the* child" (i.e., through the birth of Jesus) may rescue the theology of the passage, but it is an improbable rendering of the Greek. Likewise, to see here a reference to some atoning power connected with the pain of childbirth is pure eisegesis.

28. Thus, e.g., C. K. Barrett, *The Pastoral Epistles* (Oxford: Clarendon, 1963); P. Dornier, *Les Épitres Pastorales*, Sources bibliques (Paris: J. Gabalda, 1969); Hanson, *The Pastoral Letters*; Holtz, *Die Pastoralbriefe*; E. F. Scott, *The Pastoral Epistles*, Moffatt New Testament Commentary (New York: Harper, 1936); Roloff, *Der Erste Brief*.

29. See 1 Timothy 1:15; 2:4; 4:16; 2 Timothy 1:9; 4:18; Titus 3:5.

30. Holtz points to Acts 14:22; 1 Corinthians 3:15; and Revelation 21:24 as examples of similar uses of the preposition (*Die Pastoralbriefe*, 71).

31. Hanson, *The Pastoral Letters*, 38.

32. Anne-Marie Malingrey ("Note sur l'exégèse de 1 Tim. 2.15," in E. A. Living-

stone, editor, *Texte und Untersuchungen zur Geschichte der Altchristlichen Literatur* 115; *Studia Patristica* 12.1 [Berlin: Akademie Verlag, 1975], pp. 334-39) points out the antiquity of this interpretation, which J. Jeremias (*Die Briefe an Timotheus und Titus*, Das Neue Testament Deutsch 9 (Göttingen: Vandenhoeck & Ruprecht, 1975]) and J. L. Houlden (*The Pastoral Epistles: 1 and 2 Timothy, Titus* [New York: Penguin, 1976]) embrace.

33. Thus, e.g., Dibelius and Conzelmann, *The Pastoral Epistles*, p. 48; A. T. Hanson, *Studies in the Pastoral Epistles* (London: SPCK, 1968), p. 73; and Hans-Werner Bartsch, *Die Anfänge Urchristlicher Rechtsbildungen: Studien zu den Pastoralbriefen*, Theologische Forschung 34 (Hamburg: Evangelischer Verlag, 1965), p. 71.

34. See Titus 1:14; see also 1 Timothy 1:4; 4:7; 2 Timothy 4:4.

35. See 1 Timothy 4:7; 6:20; 2 Timothy 2:16-18; 3:2-5; Titus 1:16; 3:11.

36. See also Irenaeus's comparison of the antiquity of the apostolic church with the novelty of the heretics' message (*Adversus Haereses* 3.3.3 and 3.4.3).

37. Dennis R. MacDonald (*The Legend and the Apostle: The Battle for Paul in Story and Canon* [Philadelphia: Westminster, 1983]) argues that this identification *had* essentially taken place, that the women *are* the "heretics" of the Pastoral Epistles, and that the primary purpose of these letters was to silence these women and to correct their portrait of Paul. Though I agree with many points in this fine study, including the association of the women of the author's church with the Thecla traditions, the evidence in the letters seems to point to the existence of a separate group of opponents and the problem with the women, especially those with celibate inclinations, was not that they were the opponents but that they formed a potential bridge to this group.

38. The debate over whether this verse refers to women deacons or to the wives of deacons will probably never be fully resolved.

Ann Holmes Redding

Ann Holmes Redding is a womanist biblical scholar and an ordained Episcopal priest. She is Assistant Professor of New Testament at the Interdenominational Theological Center in Atlanta, Georgia, where she teaches courses in New Testament studies and in womanist and feminist interpretation of scripture. The Pauline and Deutero-Pauline writings form her research specializations. A Ph.D. candidate at Union Theological Seminary in New York City, she is writing a doctoral dissertation that examines issues of unity and hierarchy in the book of Ephesians.

In the essay by Redding in this chapter, she provides the framework for a womanist analysis of the social orderings set out by the so-called "household codes" found in several New Testament letters. Redding opens her discussion by exploring connections between the role relationships promoted by these household codes or *Haustafeln* and the opening chapters of Genesis. She then offers a typology of four ways that African Americans have interpreted the household codes. Her essay concludes by offering several hermeneutical guidelines for interpreting the household codes from a womanist perspective. This essay is based on a paper Redding presented at the 1994 meeting of the Southeastern Commission for the Study of Religion in Atlanta, Georgia. (Source: Ann Holmes Redding wrote "Not Again: Another Look at the Household Codes" for this volume.)

"Not Again: Another Look at the Household Codes"
(1995 CE)
ANN HOLMES REDDING

Whenever I begin to work on a topic that carries such ideological weight as the household codes in the New Testament (NT),[1] I am haunted by the words of a professor of church history from my seminary years. This professor, who was—not incidentally—a white male, said to our class, "Don't trust the work of Black scholars on slavery: they are too subjective." Since then I have often pondered the vast extent of scholarship by white males that would, on these grounds, also be rendered suspect; we all have a stake in the scholarship we do. My own stake in the topic of this article will become clear. My social location as an African American woman and as the great-granddaughter of both en-slaved and free people and my Christian belief contribute to my sense of out-rage at the subordination of women, slaves, and children in the name of the liberating One known in Jesus the Christ.

This very social location—to which I need add academically trained Bib-lical scholar—calls my attention to the household codes because they legis-late social hierarchy under the banner of the gospel. Furthermore, my aware-ness of the appropriation of the codes in some Christian circles even today to support the maintenance of patriarchal structures prompts me to take an-other look at them. What follows are a description of and commentary on four treatments of the household codes in African American biblical interpreta-tion, thereby laying the groundwork for a reassessment of this material from an African American and, more specifically, from a womanist perspective.[2] I will also propose a series of broad guidelines for such a reassessment. How-ever, before we delve into this project, preliminary questions arise. Why dis-cuss the household codes in a volume on Genesis 1-3? What is the connec-tion?

As is probably obvious, because the stories in the opening chapters of Genesis have to do with the creation of humanity as male and female, not fa-thers and children or masters and slaves, where they relate specifically to the household codes is in the injunctions to wives and husbands. The most con-crete manifestation of this relationship is the explicit use of passages from Genesis as sanctions or explanations for the instructions in the codes. The first example is Eph. 5:31, which consists of a quotation of Gen. 2:24, the only direct citation of the Old Testament (OT) in this part of the code: "For this reason a man will leave his father and mother and be joined to his wife." Here the passage from Genesis gives further support to the exhortation to marital unity. In the other occurrence in 1 Tim. 2:13-14 the author directly refers to Adam and Eve and interprets Gen. 2:7, 21-22, and 3:1-6 to undergird the di-rectives in the preceding verses: "Let a woman learn in silence with full sub-mission. I permit no woman to teach or to have authority over a man, she is to keep silent."

Although the two examples above exhaust the direct quotations from Genesis in the *Haustafeln*, the creation stories were widely known and used in early Christian circles and no doubt were considered, if not the source of the household code's rules about marriage, certainly their justification. Furthermore, twentieth-century interpreters across a wide spectrum of opinions also make the connection between the Genesis stories and the *Haustafeln*. Those who uphold the notions of role relationships as presented in the codes see them as "grounded in the Genesis account of creation and the fall."[3] Others attribute the pattern of dominance and submission to the fall alone and its reinforcement in the codes as a provisional measure to protect the church from outside censure "so that the gospel might not be hindered."[4] Sometimes the pathway between codes and Genesis is not so direct. In recent classes at the seminary where I teach, I have often heard natural law invoked as the foundation of the structures of dominance and subjection in the household codes. Natural law is understood as "the way people are made" or "what God intended in creation." Thus, in various ways and in the service of differing aims, these passages over the years have been linked in the minds of biblical readers.

Four African American Treatments of the Household Codes

A vivid example of the first African American treatment of these sets of instructions to the wives and husbands, slaves and masters, and fathers and children of early Christian congregations comes from the work of the African American mystic and theologian, Howard Thurman. He writes about the scriptural canon within the canon of his grandmother, an ex-slave who never learned to read or write. She had Thurman, as a young boy, read carefully chosen selections from the Bible to her several times a week. She was adamant that her grandson never read to her from the letters of Paul. When he was in college he questioned her for the first time about this selectivity:

> With a feeling of great temerity I asked her one day why it was that she would not let me read any of the Pauline letters. . . . "During the days of slavery", she said, "the master's minister would occasionally hold services for the slaves. Old man McGhee was so mean that he would not let a Negro minister preach to his slaves. Always the white minister used as his text something from Paul. At least three or four times a year he used as a text: 'Slaves, be obedient to them that are your masters . . . , as unto Christ.' . . . I promised my Maker that if I ever learned to read and if freedom ever came, I would not read that part of the Bible."[5]

Thurman's grandmother's vantage point was that of an African American woman exercising a freedom which she did not take for granted.

The second African American treatment of these passages is in many ways a distillation of a broader contemporary phenomenon. Much of the driving force behind the contemporary discussions of "family values" comes from ecclesiastical circles. Interpretations of selected material in the household codes have provided theological justification for certain stances taken within these conversations, usually those stances supporting patriarchal authority in the home. Furthermore, these interpretations are lived out in more than a few Christian families. My initial interest in this topic, in fact, can be attributed to my perceptions about the particular significance of the household codes in present-day African American Christian communities. In these communities, the instructions to wives in Ephesians in particular are used perhaps more than any other biblical passage as a warrant for behavior.[6] The hermeneutical freedom that Thurman's grandmother seized is, to some extent, in practice being abandoned.

In the third treatment, Clarice J. Martin points out the contradiction inherent in the development in African American biblical interpretation described above. In a 1991 article on the household codes,[7] Martin shows that the consistent challenge to the authority of passages advocating the submission of slaves has rarely been extended to the parallel passages concerning wives. Such interpretations have fostered the actual subordination of women in African American church circles and, at the least, their ideological subordination in the family and the larger society. Martin sees combating this situation as a priority for African American Christians, in light of which she proposes "three strategies for promoting more equitable, just, and liberative faith communities."[8] Specifically, she advocates dismissing the household codes as "pagan, anti-Gospel."[9] Although they arrive at the same conclusion, Thurman's grandmother and Martin differ in that Martin does not attribute the *Haustafeln* to Paul. In fact, in her view they fall short of the Pauline standard set in Gal. 3:28-29 and indicate the early Church's capitulation "to the Greco-Roman hierarchalist paradigm"[10] for the relationship between men and women.

An experience in the chapel at Union Theological Seminary in New York exemplifies the fourth African American treatment of the household codes. The Black Women's Caucus, of which I was a member, was responsible for the liturgical leadership that day. As a member of the ad hoc choir for the day, I exchanged anxious glances with some of my sister singers as we realized that one of the day's readings was from the household code in 1 Peter, specifically part of the passage directed to household servants. If I am not mistaken, the woman reading used the King James version.

> Servants, be subject to your masters with all fear; not only to the good and gentle, but also to the froward. For this is thankworthy, if a man for conscience toward God endure grief, suffering wrongfully. For what glory is it, if, when ye be buffeted for your faults, ye shall take it patiently? but if, when ye do well, and suffer for it, ye take it patiently, this is acceptable with God. For even hereunto were ye called: because Christ also suffered for us, leaving us an example, that ye should follow his steps. (1 Pet. 2:18-21, KJV)

"Why," we asked, "did *we* pick such a passage? *Did* we pick it? Surely, the preacher will choose another text." She did not. Instead, the student preacher (now the Reverend Patricia Bennett, an Episcopal priest) addressed the issue of the distrust, fragmentation, and factional posturing on campus using her reading of this text as a message from servants to their peers. She drew on the authority gleaned from the actual social location of African American women as domestic servants to call that particular Christian community to relinquish the need always to be right and to suffer one another in order to move through the time of fractiousness. Her message set the tone, if momentarily, for the conversations to continue with some willingness to listen on the part of those involved. It also set in motion my own work on these passages.

A Brief Commentary on the Four Treatments

Although each of the foregoing treatments has its limitations, all offer important leads in the development of a new strategy for reassessing the codes. Some of them also fall into a larger pattern of African American biblical interpretation outlined by Vincent L. Wimbush in, "The Bible and African Americans: An Outline of an Interpretive History."[11] Thurman's grandmother's reading—or, more precisely, her ban on the reading—of the codes is an example of the approach Wimbush labels as "foundational" and "classical,"[12] because all later streams of African American interpretation flow from it, to some degree or another. He places the genesis of this kind of reading in the eighteenth-century mass conversions of slaves to Christianity. However, conversion to Christianity did not mean acquiescence to the tenets of the white interpreters. Says Wimbush:

> This response . . . is at base hermeneutically and socially critical. It reflects the fact that the Bible, understood as the "white folk's" book, was accepted but not interpreted in the way that white Christians and the dominant culture in general interpreted it. So America's biblical culture was accepted by the Africans, but not in the way white Americans accepted it or in the way the whites preferred that others accept it.[13]

Renita J. Weems, in referring to this same episode from Thurman, writes that it shows "how the experience of oppression has influenced African American women's disposition toward reading the Bible."[14] African American women quickly developed a hermeneutics both of suspicion and resistance because they understood that one's reading was dependent to some measure on one's social location and that to survive one had to maintain independence in biblical interpretation.

One problem with this classical African American reading of the household codes is that it does not directly address the issue of the nature and locus of biblical authority. What are the implications for the authority of the text as a whole if sections can be ignored or rejected? What criteria provide the basis for such judgments? Furthermore, although quite critical in the ways mentioned above, this treatment is also necessarily precritical in terms of modern biblical scholarship. The enslaved Blacks in the United States were generally prohibited to learn to read, not to mention to participate in the formal study of scripture (or of anything else, for that matter). Thurman's grandmother, obviously, could not be expected to anticipate the scholarly consensus, for example, that the household codes were not written by Paul himself nor to consider the consequences of that position.

The second treatment of the household codes can be seen in part as a response to the widespread perception of a crisis in American—and particularly in African American—family life. An African American New Testament scholar writes:

> The family and the Bible, once meaningfully yoked in sacred trust, are being invoked like magical incantations to produce instant cures and realignments for complex modern problems. . . . [T]oday we find a yearning to return to pristine biblical teachings and "traditional family values."[15]

Felder goes on to list what he calls "Hypothetical New Testament 'Ten Commandments' on the Family," of which some of the injunctions in the household codes are part. Proponents of this kind of reading believe that if African Americans followed such instructions all problems in family living would magically cease. Within Wimbush's schema of African American biblical interpretation, this treatment would fall in the fundamentalist category, in which independent interpretation based on identification with liberating stories and characters from one's own social location gives way to the adoption of a moralistic approach shared with a significant sector of the dominant culture. Like the approach of Thurman's grandmother, this treatment does not draw extensively on what it deems liberal biblical scholarship; unlike Thurman's grandmother, those who favor this interpretation *choose* not to do so. They embrace the household codes as unquestionably Christian and specifically Pauline in origin and lay claim to biblical authority to support the enforcement of their injunctions. Curiously enough, however, these same interpreters often deny equivalent authority to the instructions to slaves and masters also found in the *Haustafeln*. Furthermore, although there is little question as to their sincere concern for African American families, these readers rarely question whether their uncritical embrace of this material will truly contribute to the health and well-being of African American families and communities.

Martin's reading represents a phenomenon so new that Wimbush does not even have a category for it. In modern formal biblical scholarship, African Americans in general and African American women in particular are still severely underrepresented. In fact, African American women with advanced degrees in biblical studies can be numbered on the fingers of one hand. Martin consciously draws on the critical independence and consideration of social location of the classical reading. She also unapologetically espouses liberation as a goal. She shares with advocates of the second treatment a deep concern for the survival and growth of healthy African American communities. She parts company from them in that she draws on historical critical conclusions in rendering the codes meaningless. Specifically because she concurs with those form critics who see the *Haustafeln* as pagan or, possibly, Jewish imports that have been barely Christianized, they can be discarded.

One problem with this reading is that recent commentators have questioned these very conclusions about the source of the codes. Focusing on the Colossians code as an example, Lars Hartman[16] uses methods from text linguistics to analyze the NT material in comparison with a supposed Greco-Roman model. He points out that, in terms of syntax, semantics, and pragmatic function, a philosophical treatise is strikingly different from an NT epistle. The former is theoretical, expository, and aimed at a general educated audience, while the latter is practical, exhortatory, and written to shape the behavior of concrete Christian communities. Sarah J. Tanzer, a historian writing on the Ephesians code, cautions against blaming the stance seen in the household codes on either the Jews or the pagans.[17] From her vantage point as a Jewish feminist, Tanzer sees such explanations as a failure of some Christians to take responsibility for the codes. Martin's reading also raises questions about criteria used to judge one part of scripture—e.g., the baptismal formula in Galatians 3:28—as having moral authority as "true gospel," while another part is not valid at all—the household codes.[18]

The approach used by Bennett in her Union Seminary sermon has commonalities, in various ways, with all preceding treatments. She certainly seizes interpretive freedom and makes use of social location as a vantage point. In fact, she uses the experience of African American women as domestics as a position from which not only to read independently but to proclaim with specific authority that reading for the edification of a larger Christian body. Bennett's employment of social location calls attention in a new way to the issue of the social location of the original hearers of these passages. Does modern interpretation of the codes depend in some measure upon whether they were, on one hand, instructions from the top down in order to maintain the status quo or, on the other, peer-to-peer admonitions resulting from the participants' understanding of a new kind of social network in Christ? Also, the sermon uses scripture as authoritative, but not in a fundamentalist sense. Part of this view of authority has to do with honoring the text in part because there are correspondences between its social world and that of the interpreters.

Working Guidelines for a New Womanist Interpretation

These guidelines are presented in sketchy form, as works in progress. Furthermore, despite the word "new" in the subtitle, I realize that something like these propositions—in various combinations—has guided many other interpreters.

1. A womanist approach to the household codes sees liberation as a means as well as an end in biblical interpretation; that is, a womanist interpreter freely claims and defines her own interpretive bounds as she intentionally pursues liberation and empowerment of oppressed peoples as a primary goal of her work.

2. Issues of social location as they pertain both to the interpreter and to the biblical text are important in a womanist treatment.

3. A womanist interpreter wants to maintain a dialogue with other African American interpreters concerned about African American survival and thriving. Therefore, she takes the household codes seriously as *Christian* material, in part in order to stay in the conversation.

4. In light of the abiding authority given to the Bible by many African Americans, a womanist reader clearly states her understanding of the locus and nature of scriptural authority.

5. Honoring the centrality of identification with narrative and characters in African American biblical interpretation, when dealing with exhortatory texts, a womanist treatment explores the idea of the "story behind the text." What did the social categories addressed in these passages mean in their context? Within what sorts of situations in the early church did these texts arise? How can we imagine the effects of the instructions on the women, men, and children and on the slaves and masters of early Christian communities?

6. Finally, a womanist reading is a provisional, working reading of the text. It is anti-imperialistic, in that the reader does not intend to impose it upon others. She remains open to the revision of the Spirit mediated through the struggling community as well as her own mind, body, and soul.[19]

These statements, although rudimentary, appear here as part of an ongoing academic discipline. They act as a kind of plumb line, so that I might remain conscious about what I bring to my work and accountable in my commitments. They also are the starting points for looking not only at the household codes specifically, but also at scripture in general from a womanist perspective.

NOTES TO CHAPTER 8, EGALITARIAN INTERPRETATIONS,
ANN HOLMES REDDING

1. The household codes (also known as *Haustafeln* or house tables) in the NT are those passages that contain instructions to the various parties of the household, usually in pairs of reciprocal roles, i.e., wives and husbands, children and fathers, slaves and masters. The three examples that conform most closely to the pattern are Eph. 5:2–6:9, Col. 3:18–4:1, and 1 Pet. 2:18–3:7. In 1 Tim. 2:1–6:1 and Tit. 1:5–9 and 2:1–10, while there are remnants both of the structure and content of the other codes, the concerns of the author clearly have moved beyond the household alone to the larger community of faith. These latter examples are still of interest here because in them the patriarchal household not only continues to be advocated as the Christian norm, it also becomes the model for relationships within the church. See D. C. Verner, *The Household of God: The Social World of the Pastoral Epistles* (Chico, Calif.: Scholars Press, 1983).

2. In this case, a womanist perspective is one that is based on the particular vantage point of an African American woman committed to the eradication of all forms of social oppression, filtered through personal experience of racism and sexism. Womanist Biblical scholars attend to issues of gender, race, and class, using appropriate meth-

odologies to do so. See C. J. Martin, "Womanist Interpretations of the New Testament," *Journal of Feminist Studies in Religion* 6 (1990): 41-59. Martin adds language to the three issues above.

3. C. C. Ryrie, *The Place of Women in the Church* (New York: Macmillan, 1958), p. 79; quoted in W. M. Swartley, *Slavery, Sabbath, War, and Women: Case Issues in Biblical Interpretation* (Scottdale, Penn.: Herald, 1983), p. 154.

4. David Fraser and Elouise Fraser, "A Biblical View of Women: Demythologizing Sexegesis," *Theology, News and Notes* (Fuller Theological Seminary) (June 1975): 18; quoted in Swartley, *Slavery*, p. 268.

5. H. Thurman, *Jesus and the Disinherited* (New York: Abingdon-Cokesbury Press, 1949; repr., Richmond, Ind.: Friends United, 1981), pp. 30-31.

6. Anne Wimberly and Edward P. Wimberly, pastoral theologians and counselors who have done extensive work in African American churches, have asserted that their experience confirms this hypothesis.

7. Clarice J. Martin, "The *Haustafeln* (Household Codes) in African American Biblical Interpretation: 'Free Slaves' and 'Subordinate Women,' " in C. H. Felder, editor, *Stony the Road We Trod: African American Biblical Interpretation* (Minneapolis: Fortress, 1991), pp. 206-31.

8. Martin, "The *Haustafeln*," p. 228.

9. Martin, "The *Haustafeln*," p. 229, citing F. Stagg, "The Gospel, *Haustafel*, and Women: Mark 1:1; Colossians 3:18-4:1," *Faith and Mission* 2 (2) (1985): 63.

10. Martin, "The *Haustafeln*," p. 229.

11. Vincent L. Wimbush, "The Bible and African Americans: An Outline of Interpretive History," in Felder, *Stony the Road We Trod*, pp. 81-97.

12. Wimbush, "The Bible and African Americans," p. 89.

13. Wimbush, "The Bible and African Americans," p. 89.

14. Renita J. Weems, "Reading *Her Way* through the Struggle: African American Women and the Bible," in Felder, *Stony the Road We Trod*, pp. 57-77, especially p. 63.

15. C. H. Felder, *Troubling Biblical Waters: Race, Class, and Family* (Maryknoll, N.Y.: Orbis, 1989), p. 150; and see p. 156.

16. L. Hartman, "Some Unorthodox Thoughts on the 'Household-Code Form,' " in J. Neusner et al., editors, *The Social World of Formative Christianity and Judaism: Essays in Tribute to Howard Clark Kee* (Philadelphia: Fortress, 1988), 219-32.

17. S. J. Tanzer, "Double Jeopardy: The Writing of a Feminist Commentary on Ephesians from a Jewish Perspective," unpublished paper presented at American Academy of Religion/Society of Biblical Literature Annual Meeting, November 1993; see particularly pp. 7-12.

18. I am not denying Martin's right to a canon within a canon; I simply want her—and all of us—to be clear about the criteria on which we base our particular claims about biblical authority.

19. In the devising of these guidelines, I acknowledge my great debt to my co-laborers in the class on womanist and feminist approaches to scriptural interpretation at the Interdenominational Theological Center in the spring semester of 1994.

Riffat Hassan

Riffat Hassan is Professor of Humanities at the University of Louisville in Louisville, Kentucky, where she directs the Religious Studies Program. Born and raised in Lahore, Pakistan, she is a member of a Sayyid Muslim family (a family that traces its lineage back to the Prophet Muhammad).[1] As a committed Muslim who is concerned about theological understandings of gender, she has forged new ground in developing a feminist theology indigenous to Islam. She has written numerous articles on women and Islam in which she systematically investigates Islamic theology and its primary sources in the Qur'an and the *hadith*.[2] She also is the author of two books on the Muslim poet and thinker Allama Muhammad Iqbal.[3]

In the selection in this chapter, Hassan focuses on Islamic views on woman's creation. She notes that most Muslims believe Eve was created as Adam's subordinate. She argues, however, that Islam—when it is true to its scripture—promotes equality between women and men. Hassan examines the Qur'an in order to demonstrate its lack of support for notions of woman's original inferiority to man. Following this exegetical analysis, she assesses the interpretive positions set forth by several Muslim exegetes. In this assessment, she evaluates several passages from *hadith* literature, noting their conflicts with the Qur'an's depictions of gender. She also quotes a passage from Sayyid Abu al-A'la Mawdudi's commentary on the Qur'an and offers an interesting assessment of the position taken by Mawdudi.[4] (Source: Riffat Hassan, "The Issue of Woman-Man Equality in the Islamic Tradition," in Leonard Grob, Riffat Hassan, and Haim Gordin, editors, *Women's and Men's Liberation: Testimonies of Spirit*, New York: Greenwood Press, 1991, pp. 68-82.)

"The Issue of Woman-Man Equality in the Islamic Tradition" (1993 CE)
RIFFAT HASSAN

. . . I remember how stricken I felt when I first began to see the glaring discrepancy between Islamic ideals and Muslim practice insofar as women are concerned. Convinced of the importance of underscoring this discrepancy and believing that most Muslim women (even those who were all too well aware of the reality of their own life-situation) were largely unaware of it, I set out to articulate what I considered to be the normative Islamic view of women. This view is rooted largely in what all Muslims accept as *the* primary source, or highest authority, in Islam—the Qur'an, which Muslims believe to be the Word of Allah conveyed through the agency of the angel Gabriel to the Prophet Muhammad, who transmitted it without change or error to those who heard him.

In 1979, while I participated in an ongoing "trialogue" of Jewish, Christian, and Muslim scholars (under the sponsorship of the Kennedy Institute of Ethics in Washington, D.C.) who were exploring women-related issues in the three "Abrahamic" faith-traditions, I wrote the draft of a monograph entitled *Women in the Qur'an*. In this study I gave a detailed exposition of those passages of the Qur'an that related to women in various contexts. . . . In particular, I focused attention upon those passages that were regarded as definitive in the context of woman-man relationships and upon which the alleged superiority of men to women largely rested. It was this study that I hoped to finalize when in the spring of 1983 I went to Pakistan and spent almost two years there, doing research but also watching, with increasing anxiety, the enactment of anti-women laws in the name of Islam and the deluge of anti-women actions and literature that swept across the country in the wake of the "Islamization" of Pakistani society and its legal system.

As I reflected upon the scene I witnessed, and asked myself how it was possible for laws that were archaic if not absurd to be implemented in a society that professed a passionate commitment to modernity, the importance of something that I had always known dawned on me with stunning clarity. Pakistani society (or any other Muslim society for that matter) could enact or accept laws that specified that women were less than men in fundamental ways because Muslims, in general, consider it a self-evident truth that women are not equal to men. Anyone who states that in the present-day world it is accepted in many religious as well as secular communities that men and women are equal, or that evidence can be found in the Qur'an and the Islamic tradition for affirming man-woman equality, is likely to be confronted, immediately and with force, by a mass of what is described as "irrefutable evidence" taken from the Qur'an, Hadith, and Sunnah to "prove" that men are "above" women.[5] Among the arguments used to overwhelm any proponent of man-woman equality, the following are perhaps the most popular: according to the Qur'an, men are *qawwamun* (generally translated as "rulers," or "managers") in relation to women;[6] according to the Qur'an, a man's share in inheritance is twice that of a woman;[7] according to the Qur'an, the witness of one man is equal to that of two women;[8] according to the Prophet, women are deficient both in prayer (due to menstruation) and in intellect (due to their witness counting for less than a man's).[9]

Since I was (in all probability) the only Muslim woman in the country who was attempting to interpret the Qur'an systematically from a nonpatriarchal perspective, I was approached numerous times by women leaders (including the members of the Pakistan Commission on the Status of Women, before whom I gave my testimony in May 1984) to state what my findings were and if they could be used to improve the situation of women in Pakistani society. I was urged by those spirited women who were mobilizing and leading women's protests in the streets to help them refute the arguments that were being used to make them less than fully human on a case-by-case or point-by-point basis. I must admit that I was tempted to join the fray in support of my beleaguered sisters who were being deprived of their human rights in the name of Islam. But I knew through my long and continuing struggle with the forces of Muslim traditionalism (which were now being gravely threatened by what they described as "the onslaught of Westernization under the guise of modernization") that the arguments that were being broadcast to "keep women in their place" of subordination and submissiveness were only the front line of attack. Behind and below these arguments were others, and no sooner would one line of attack be eliminated than another one would be set up in its place. What had to be done, first and foremost, in my opinion, was to examine the theological ground in which all the anti-women arguments were rooted to see if, indeed, a case could be made for asserting that from the point of view of normative Islam, men and women were *essentially* equal, despite biological and other differences.

My inquiry into the theological roots of the problem of man-woman inequality in the Islamic tradition led to the expansion of my field of study in at least two significant areas. First, realizing the profound impact upon Muslim consciousness of Hadith literature, particularly the two collections *Sahih al-Bukhari* and *Sahih Muslim* (collectively known as the *Sahihan*, which the Sunni Muslims regard as the most authoritative books in Islam next to the Qur'an), I examined with care the women-related ahadith in these collections. Second, I studied several important writings by Jewish and Christian feminist theologians who were attempting to trace the theological origins of the anti-feminist ideas and attitudes found in their respective traditions.

As a result of my study and deliberation I came to perceive that not only in the Islamic, but also in the Jewish and Christian traditions, there are three theological assumptions on which the superstructure of men's alleged superiority to women (which implies the inequality of women and man) has been erected. These three assumptions are: (1) that God's primary creation is man, not woman, since woman is believed to have been created from man's rib, hence is derivative and secondary ontologically; (2) that woman, not man, was the primary agent of what is customarily described as the "Fall," or man's expulsion from the Garden of Eden, hence all "daughters of Eve" are to be regarded with hatred, suspicion, and contempt; and (3) that woman was created not only *from* man but also *for* man, which makes her existence merely instrumental and not of fundamental importance. The three theological questions to which the above assumptions may appropriately be regarded as answers, are: How was woman created? Was woman responsible for the "Fall" of man? Why was woman created?

Given the profound significance—both theoretical and practical—of these three questions in the history of ideas and attitudes pertaining to women in the Islamic (as well as the Jewish and Christian) tradition, I hope to write a full-scale book in response to each. However, at this time I would like to focus on the first question, which deals with the issue of woman's creation. I consider this issue to be more basic and important, philosophically and theologically, than any other in the context of woman-man equality, because if man and woman have been created equal by Allah who is the ultimate arbiter of value, then they cannot become unequal, essentially, at a subsequent time. On the other hand, if man and woman have been created unequal by Allah, then they cannot become equal, essentially, at a subsequent time.

Made from Adam's Rib? The Issue of Woman's Creation

The ordinary Muslim believes, as seriously as the ordinary Jew or Christian, that Adam was God's primary creation and that Eve was made from Adam's rib. If confronted with the fact that this firmly entrenched belief is derived mainly from the Bible and is not only extra-Qur'anic but also in contradiction to the Qur'an, this Muslim is almost certain to be shocked. The rather curious and tragic truth is that even Western-educated Muslims seldom have any notion of the extent to which the Muslim psyche bears the imprint of the collective body of Jewish and Christian ideas and attitudes pertaining to women. . . .

While in Genesis specific reference is made to the creation of Adam and Eve, there is no corresponding reference in the Qur'an. In fact, there is no mention of Eve (*Hawwa'*) at all in the Qur'an. The term "Adam" occurs twenty-five times in the Qur'an, but there is only one verse (Surah 3:59) that refers to the creation of Adam: "Certainly with Allah the likeness of 'Isa [Jesus] is as the likeness of Adam. Allah created him from the earth, then said to him, 'Be,' and he was." Here it needs to be mentioned that the term "Adam" is not an Arabic term but a Hebrew term, and the description of Adam as a creature of earth in the verse cited above is no more than an explication of the meaning of the term. There are three other verses (Surah 3:35; Surah 19:58; Surah 5:30) in which the term "Adam" is used as a proper name for an individual who was probably a prophet. Since Arabic has no capital letters, it is often not possible to tell whether a term is used as a proper name or as a common noun without looking at the context in which it occurs. However, there is no categorical statement in the Qur'an to the effect that Adam was the first human being created by Allah. The term is used most frequently in reference to more than one or two human beings. That the term "Adam" functions as a collective noun and stands for humankind is substantiated by an analysis of several verses in which this term occurs. It is also corroborated by the fact that all human beings are assimilatively addressed as "Children of Adam (*Bani Adam*) in Surah 7:26, 27, 31, 35, 172, Surah 17:70, and Surah 36:60, and also by the fact that the Qur'an sometimes replaces the term "Adam" by *al-insan* or *bashar*, which are both generic terms for humanity. Here it is important to note that though the term "Adam" mostly does not refer to a particular human being, it does refer to human beings in a particular way. As pointed out by Muhammad Iqbal:

> Indeed, in the verses which deal with the origin of man as a living being, the Qur'an uses the word "Bashar" or "Insan," not "Adam," which it reserves for man in his capacity of God's vicegerent on earth. The purpose of the Qur'an is further secured by the omission of proper names mentioned in the Biblical narration—Adam and Eve. The word "Adam" is retained and used more as a concept than as the name of a concrete human individual. This use of the word is not without authority in the Qur'an itself.[10]

It is noteworthy that the Qur'an uses the terms *bashar*, *al-insan*, and *an-nas* while describing the process of the physical creation of human beings. It uses the term "Adam" more selectively to refer to human beings only when they become representative of a self-conscious, knowledgeable, and morally autonomous humanity.

Instead of "Adam and *Hawwa'*," the Qur'an speaks of "Adam and *zauj*" in

Surah 2:35, Surah 7:19, and Surah 20:117. Muslims, almost without exception, assume that "Adam" was the first human being created by Allah and that he was a man. If "Adam" was a man, it follows that "Adam's *zauj*" would be a woman. Hence the *zauj* mentioned in the Qur'an becomes equated with *Hawwa'*. Neither the initial assumption nor the inferences drawn from it are, however, supported in a clear or conclusive way by the Qur'anic text. The Qur'an states neither that Adam was the first human being nor that he was a man. The term "Adam" is a masculine noun, but linguistic gender is not sex. If "Adam" is not necessarily a man, then "Adam's *zauj*" is not necessarily a woman. In fact, the term *zauj* is also a masculine noun and, unlike the term "Adam," has a feminine counterpart, *zaujatun*. (Here, it may be noted that the most accurate English equivalent of *zauj* is not "wife" or "husband," or even "spouse," but the term "mate." The Qur'an uses the term *zauj* with reference not only to human beings but to every kind of creation, including animals, plants, and fruits.) However, neither the term *zaujatun* nor the plural form *zaujatun* is used anywhere in the Qur'an, which consistently uses the masculine forms *zauj* and *azwaj*. It has been pointed out by the authoritative Arabic lexicon *Taj al-'Arus* that only the people of Al-Hijaz (Hejaz) used the term *zauj* in reference to women, and elsewhere the usage was *zaujatun*. Also, Arabic legal terminology always uses the term *zaujatun* in reference to women. Why, then, does the Qur'an, which surely was not addressed only to the people of Al-Hijaz, use the term *zauj* and not *zaujatun* if the reference is indeed to woman? In my opinion, the reason the Qur'an leaves the terms "Adam" and *zauj* deliberately unclear, not only as regards sex but also as regards number, is because its purpose is not to narrate certain events in the life of a man and a woman (i.e., the Adam and Eve of popular imagination), but to refer to some life experiences of all human beings, men and women together.

The Qur'an describes human creation in thirty or so passages that are found in various chapters. Generally speaking, it refers to the creation of humanity (and nature) in two ways: as an evolutionary process whose diverse stages or phases are mentioned sometimes together and sometimes separately, and as an accomplished fact or in its totality. In the passages in which human creation is described "concretely" or "analytically," we find that no mention is made of the separate or distinct creation of either man or woman, as may be seen, for instance, from the following: Surah 15:26, 28, 29; Surah 16:4; Surah 22:5; Surah 23:12-14; Surah 25:54; Surah 32:7-9; Surah 36:77; Surah 38:71-72; Surah 39:6; Surah 40:67; Surah 55:3, 4, 14; Surah 71:14, 17; Surah 76:2; Surah 77:20-22; Surah 82:6-8; Surah 86:5-7; Surah 95:4; and Surah 96:1-2. In some passages (e.g., Surah 49:13; Surah 53:45; Surah 78:8), though reference is made to Allah's creation of human beings as sexually differentiated "mates," no priority or superiority is accorded to either man or woman.

There are, however, some verses in the Qur'an that are understood in such a way that they appear to endorse a version of the Genesis 2 story of woman's creation from man. These verses can be grouped into two categories. The most important verses in the first group are: Surah 16:72; Surah 30:20-21;

and Surah 35:11. Muslim arguments that women were created from and for men are supported as follows: (1) Surah 30:21 uses the term *ilaiha* to refer to "mates" created from, and for, the original creation. Since *ha* is a feminine attached pronoun, the "mates" it refers to must be female (thus making the original creation male); (2) all three verses cited use *kum* as a form of address. Hence these verses are addressed not to humanity collectively, but only to men, since the term used is a masculine attached pronoun (second person plural). Men are, therefore, the primary creation from and for whom the "mates" were created. Regarding (1), *ilaiha* literally means "in her" and not "in them" and refers not to women (who are not mentioned here) but to *azwaj* (masculine plural used in the Qur'an for both men and women). If the "mates" were clearly designated as women, the term used would be *hunna*, not *ha*. The use of *ha* here is consistent with the Arabic grammatical rule that permits the use of feminine singular terms for a class or collectivity. The fact that the creatures to whom the passage is addressed are referred to as *bashar* further supports the argument that the "mates" created by Allah are not only women (for men), since *bashar* obviously has a bisexual reference. Regarding (2), Arabic usage permits the use of *kum* in reference to men and women together. When women alone are concerned, *"kunna"* is used. Here it is of interest to note that in his book *Haquq-e-Niswan* (The Rights of Women, 1898), Mumtaz 'Ali pointed out that the Qur'an uses the masculine form of address to prescribe fundamental duties (e.g., *salat*, *zakat*, fasting) to Muslim men and women. If masculine terms of address are understood by the entire Muslim *ummah* to apply to both men and women in highly significant contexts, such as the prescription of basic religious duties, then it cannot consistently be argued that these terms apply to men invariably and exclusively.

Regarding the second group of verses that are cited to prove man's ontological priority and superiority to woman, the following are of exceptional importance: Surah 4:1; Surah 7:189; and Surah 39:6. In these verses (as also in Surah 6:98 and Surah 31:28) reference is made to the creation from one source or being (*nafsin wahidatin*) of all human beings. Muslims, with hardly any exceptions, believe that the one original source or being referred to in these verses is a man named Adam. This belief has led many translators of the Qur'an to obviously incorrect translations of simple Qur'anic passages. For instance, Surah 4:1, if correctly translated, reads as follows: "O *an-nas* be circumspect in keeping your duty to your Sustainer who created you [plural] from one being [*nafsin wahidatin*] and spread from her [*minha*] her mate a [*zaujaha*] and spread from these two beings many men and women." However, most translators (e.g., Hashim Amir-'Ali, Muhammad Ali, A. J. Arberry, A. K. Azad, A. M. Daryabadi, N.J. Dawood, S. A. Latif, A. A. Maududi, M. M. Pickthall, George Sale, and M. Y Zayid) translate the feminine attached pronoun *ha* in *minha* and *zaujaha* as "his" instead of "her." How is such a mistake possible? Could it be the case that given their preconceptions and psychological orientation, these interpreters of the Qur'an (who all happen to be men) are totally unable to imagine that the first creation could have been other than male? Or are they afraid that a correct translation of *ha* might suggest the idea—even for an instant—that woman, not man, was the prior creation (and therefore superior if priority connotes superiority) and that man was created from woman and not the other way around (which, in a reversal of the Eve from Adam's rib story would give Eve the primacy traditionally accorded to Adam)? Certainly no Qur'anic exegete to date has suggested the possibility that *nafsin wahidatin* might refer to woman rather than man.

Summing up the Qur'anic descriptions of human creation, it needs to be emphasized that the Qur'an evenhandedly used both feminine and masculine terms and imagery to describe the creation of humanity from a single source. That Allah's original creation was undifferentiated humanity and not either man or woman (who appeared simultaneously at a subsequent time) is implicit in a number of Qur'anic passages, in particular Surah 75:36-39, which reads:

> Does *al-insan* think that he will be left aimless? Was he not a drop of semen emitted then he became something which clings; Then He [Allah] created and shaped and made of him [*minhu*] two mates [*zaujain*] the male and the female.

If the Qur'an makes no distinction between the creation of man and woman, as it clearly does not, why do Muslims believe that Hawwa' was created from the rib of Adam? Although the Genesis 2 account of woman's creation is accepted by virtually all Muslims, it is difficult to believe that it entered the Islamic tradition directly, for very few Muslims ever read the Bible. It is much more likely that it became a part of Muslim heritage through its assimilation in Hadith literature, which has been, in many ways, the lens through which the Qur'an has been seen since the early centuries of Islam.

Hadith literature, which modernist Muslims tend to regard with a certain skepticism, is surrounded by controversies, centering particularly around the question of the authenticity of individual ahadith as well as the body of the literature as a whole. These controversies have occupied the attention of many Muslim scholars since the time of Ash-Shafi'i (d. A.H. 204/A.D. 809). . . . That the story of Eve's creation from Adam's rib had become part of the Hadith literature is evident from the following Hadith related from Ibn 'Abbas and Ibn Mas'ud, which is referred to by authoritative commentators on the Qur'an, . . . :

> When God sent Iblis out of the Garden and placed Adam in it, he dwelt in it alone and had no one to socialize with. God sent sleep on him and then He took a rib from his left side and placed flesh in its place and created Hawwa' from it. When he awoke he found a woman seated near his head. He asked her, "Who are you?" She answered, "Woman." He said, "Why were you created?" She said, "That you might find rest in me." The angels said, "What is her name?" and he said, "Hawwa'." The said, "Why was she called Hawwa'?" He said, "Because she was created from a living thing."[11]

Another Hadith, related from Ibn 'Abbas and cited by Ibn Kathir in his *Tafsir*, which also refers to the creation of Hawwa' from Adam's rib, reads as follows:

After Iblis had been chastised and Adam's knowledge had been exhibited, Adam was put to sleep and Hawwa' was created from his left rib. When Adam awoke he saw her and felt affection and love for her since she was made from his flesh and blood. Then Allah gave Hawwa' in wedlock to Adam and told them to live in al-jannah.[12]

Both of the above ahadith clash sharply with the Qur'anic accounts of human creation, while they have an obvious correspondence to Genesis 2:18-33 and Genesis 3:20. Some changes, however, are to be noted in the story of woman's creation as it is retold in the above ahadith. Both mention "the left rib" as the source of woman. In Arab culture great significance is attached to "right" and "left," the former being associated with everything auspicious and the latter with the opposite. In Genesis, woman is named "Eve" after the Fall, but in the above ahadith she is called Hawwa' from the time of her creation. In Genesis, woman is named Eve because "she is the mother of all who live" (thus a primary source of life), but in the first of the aforementioned ahadith, she is named Hawwa' because "she was created from a living thing" (hence a derivative creature). These variations are not to be ignored. Biblical and other materials are seldom incorporated without alteration into ahadith. The above examples illustrate how in respect of woman, Arab biases were added to the adopted text.

The citing of the above ahadith by significant Muslim exegetes and historians shows the extent to which authoritative works both of Qur'anic exegesis and Islamic history had become colored by the Hadith literature. In course of time, many ahadith became "invisible," the later commentators referring not to them but to the authority of earlier commentators who had cited them, to support their views. This made it very hard to curtail their influence since they became diffused throughout the body of Muslim culture. A typical example of how the Qur'anic account of human creation is distorted by means of inauthentic ahadith (which identify *nafsin wahidatin*, from which all human beings, including Hawwa', originated, with Adam the man), even when these ahadith are not mentioned or affirmed directly, is provided by A. A. Maududi, author of a well-known modern commentary on the Qur'an[13] and one of contemporary Islam's most influential scholars. In commenting on Surah 4:1, Maududi observes:

> "He created you of a single soul." At first one human being was created and then from him the human race spread over the earth. . . . We learn from another part of the Qur'an that Adam was that "single soul." *He was the first man from whom the whole of mankind sprang up* and spread over the earth. "And of the same created his mate": we have no definite detailed knowledge of how his mate was created of him. *The Commentators generally say that Eve was created from the rib of Adam and the Bible also contains the same story. The Talmud adds to it that she was created from the thirteenth rib of Adam. But the Qur'an is silent about it, and the Tradition of the Holy Prophet that is cited in support of this has a different meaning from what had been understood.* The best thing, therefore, is to leave it undefined as it has been left in the Qur'an, and not to waste time in determining its details.[14]

In the above passage, Maududi has no difficulty in affirming what has traditionally been made the basis of asserting woman's inferiority and subordination to man, namely that woman was created from man. Having made the deadly affirmation, however, he is reluctant to explicate it further, nor does he reveal what he considers to be the "true" meaning of the Hadith pertaining to Eve's creation from Adam's rib. His justification for not discussing the issue of woman's creation is that the Qur'an has deliberately left it undefined. But this is simply not the case. The creation of woman is as clearly defined in the Qur'an as the creation of man, and the Qur'anic statements about human creation, diverse as they are, leave no doubt as to one point: both man and woman were made in the same manner, of the same substance, at the same time. Maududi (like the majority of Muslim exegetes, who happen to be all men) does not want to face this fact, so he declares that the discussion of the issue of woman's creation is a waste of time. If the issue in question was not worthy of serious theological reflection, or one that had no significant effect on the lives of human beings, particularly of women, one would, perhaps, be less critical of this scholar, who has had massive impact on the minds of the Muslim masses, for dereliction of scholarly duty. But theologically the issue of [the] creation of woman is of such import that it cannot be allowed to be dismissed in the manner in which Maududi has done.

Perhaps no better proof can be given of how totally ahadith such as the ones cited above have penetrated Muslim culture than the fact that the myth of the creation of Hawwa' from Adam's rib was accepted uncritically even by Qasim Amin (1863-1906), the Egyptian judge and feminist whose books *Tahrir al-Mara'* (The Emancipation of Women, 1899) and *Al-Mara' al-Jadida* (The Modern Woman, 1900) were epoch-making in the history of Muslim feminism. Amin's romantic interpretation of the myth, reminiscent of Milton's, shows that he did not realize how fundamentally the issue that concerned him most deeply, namely, woman's social equality with man in a strongly male-centered and male-dominated Muslim society, hinged upon the acceptance or rejection of a creation story that asserted woman's derivative status and had been interpreted traditionally to affirm her inferiority and subordination to man. It is unfortunate that many present-day Muslim advocates of women's rights also do not realize the profound implications of this myth that undergirds the anti-women attitudes and structures they seek to change.

Anti-women ahadith are found not only in the significant secondary sources of Islam but also in *Sahih al-Bukhari* (compiled by Muhammad ibn Isma'il al-Bukhari, A.H. 194-256/A.D. 810-870) and *Sahih Muslim* (compiled by Muslim bin al-Hajjaj, A.H. 202 or 206-261/A.D. 817 or 821-875), the two most influential Hadith collections in Sunni Islam. Cited below are [two] ahadith, the first . . . from *Sahih al-Bukhari* and the last . . . from *Sahih Muslim*, that have had a formative influence upon the Muslim mind:

> 1. Abu Karaith and Musa bin Hazam related to us: Husain bin 'Ali told us that he was reporting on the authority of Zai'dah who was reporting on the

authority of Maisarah al-Ashja'i who was reporting on the authority of Abu Hazim who was reporting on the authority [of] Abu Hurairah (with whom may Allah be pleased) who said: Allah's Rasul[15] (may peace be upon him) said:

> Treat women nicely, for a woman is created from a rib, and the most curved portion of the rib is its upper portion, so if you should try to straighten it, it will break, but if you leave it as it is, it will remain crooked. So treat woman nicely.[16]

. . . .

[4.] Harmalah bin Yahya related to me: Ibn Wahb informed us: Yunus informed me that he was reporting on the authority of Ibn Shihab who said: Ibn al-Musayyab told me that he was reporting on the authority of Abu Hurairah (with whom may Allah be pleased) who said: Allah's Rasul (may peace be upon him) said:[17]

> Woman is like a rib. When you attempt to straighten it, you would break it. And if you leave her alone you would benefit by her, and crookedness will remain in her.[18]

. . . While it is not possible, within the scope of this chapter, to give a detailed analysis of either the *isnad* (list of transmitters) or *matn* (content) of the above ahadith, a few comments on both may be useful. With regards to the *isnad* the following points may be noted: (1) All these ahadith are cited on the authority of Abu Hurairah, a Companion who was regarded as controversial by many early Muslim scholars, including Imam Abu Hanifah (A.D. 700-767), founder of the largest Sunni school of law. Here it is pertinent to point out that though a more critical attitude toward Hadith and Hadith-transmitters prevailed during the earliest phase of Islam, later, as stated by Goldziher,[19] it became "a capital crime" to be critical of any Companion; (2) . . . The above ahadith are *gharib* (the lowest grade of Hadith classification) because they contain a number of transmitters who were single reporters. (Al-Hakim Abu 'Abd Allah al-Naysaburi and Ibn Hajar al-'Asqalani, who were eminent scholars of Hadith, defined a *sahih* or sound Hadith as one that is related in the first place by a well-known Companion, in the second place by at least two Followers, and thereafter by many narrators.);[20] (3) All of the above ahadith are *da'if* (weak) because they have a number of unreliable transmitters (e.g., Maisarah al-Ashja'i, Harmalah bin Yahya, Zaidah, and Abu Zinad).[21]

Analysis of the *matn* of the above ahadith leads to the following statements: (1) Woman is created from a rib or is like a rib; (2) The most curved and crooked part of the rib is its top; (3) The crookedness of the rib (and of the woman) is irremediable—any effort to remove it will result in breakage; and (4) In view of the above, an attitude of kindness is recommended and those who wish to benefit from women are advised to do so "while crookedness remains in her." Concerning these statements the following observations are made: (a) The rib story obviously originates in Genesis 2, but no mention is made of any of these ahadith of Adam. This eliminates the Yahwist's androcentrism but also depersonalizes the source of woman's creation (i.e., the "rib" could, theoretically, be nonhuman); (b) The misogynist elements of the ahadith, absent from Genesis, clash with the teachings of the Qur'an which describes all human beings as having been created *fi ahsan-i taqwim* (most justly proportioned and with the highest capabilities); (c) I cannot understand the relevance of making the statement that the most crooked part of the rib is at the top; (d) The exhortation to be kind to women would make sense if women were, in fact, born with a natural handicap and needed compassion. Is "irremediable crookedness" such a handicap? (e) The advice to benefit from women without making any effort to help women deal with their "crookedness" (in case it is a natural handicap) smacks of hedonism or opportunism and is hard to appreciate even if women were indeed "irremediably crooked."

The theology of woman implicit in the above ahadith is based upon generalizations about her ontology, biology, and psychology that are contrary to the letter and spirit of the Qur'an. These ahadith ought to be rejected on the basis of their content alone. However, "*matn*-analysis" (which was strongly urged by Ibn Khaldun, A.D. 1332-1406)[22] has received scant attention in the work of many Muslim scholars, who insist that a Hadith is to be judged primarily on the basis of its *isnad*. It is not difficult to see why *isnad*-criticism— particularly if it excludes a scholarly scrutiny of initial reports of a Hadith—is not a sufficient methodological tool for establishing the reliability of a Hadith. Not all initial reporters of ahadith were the Prophet's close Companions whose word would be difficult to question. (The word "Companion" has come to be applied rather loosely to a variety of persons, some of whom spent only a limited amount of time with the Prophet and cannot necessarily be presumed to have known him well.) Furthermore, it is not always possible to say in the case of a Hadith whether its *isnad* (including the name of the Companion initially narrating the Hadith) is authentic and not fabricated. In such cases references to the *matn* of other ahadith ascribed to the same initial narrator, or to other ahadith with similar content, become critically important in determining the degree of reliability of both the narrator and the Hadith in question.

Conclusion

To sum up the foregoing discussion on the issue of woman's creation, I would like to reiterate that according to the Qur'an, Allah created woman and man equal. They were created simultaneously, of like substance, and in like manner. The fact that almost all Muslims believe that the first woman (Hawwa') was created from Adam's rib shows that, in practice, the Hadith literature has displaced the teaching of the Qur'an at least insofar as the issue of woman's creation is concerned.

While all Muslims agree that whenever a Hadith attributed to the Prophet conflicts with the Qur'an it must be rejected, the ahadith discussed in this chapter have not only not been rejected, they have in fact remained overwhelmingly popular with Muslims through the ages, in spite of being clearly contradictory to the Qur'anic statements pertaining to human creation. While being included in the *Sahihan* gives the ahadith in question much weight among Muslims who know about the science of Hadith, their continuing popularity among Muslims in general indicates that they articulate something deeply embedded in Muslim culture—namely, the belief that women are derivative creatures who can never be considered equal to men.

Even the courageous Muslim women presently leading women's movements in oppressively conservative Muslim societies, which in the name of "Islamization" are systematically legitimizing the reduction of women to a less than fully human status, are not aware of the far-reaching implications of the ahadith that make them derivative or devious creatures. It is imperatiave for the Muslim daughters of Hawwa' to realize that the history of their subjection and humiliation at the hands of sons of Adam began with the story of Hawwa's creation, and that their future will be no different than their past unless they return to the point of origin and challenge the authenticity of ahadith that make them ontologically inferior, subordinate, and crooked. While it is not a little discouraging to know that these ahadith (like many other anti-woman ones) represent not only the ideas and attitudes regarding women of the early generations of Muslims (whose views were reflected in the Hadith literature), but also of successive generations of Muslims until today, it is gratifying to know that they cannot be the words of the Prophet of Islam, who upheld the rights of women (as of other disadvantaged persons) throughout his life. Furthermore, regardless of how many Muslim men project their own androcentrism and misogyny upon the Prophet of Islam, it is valid to question how, being the recipient of the Qur'an, which states that all human beings were made from a single source (i.e., *al-insan*, *bashar*, or *nafsin wahidatin*), the Prophet of Allah could say that woman was created from a crooked rib or from Adam's rib.

NOTES TO CHAPTER 8, EGALITARIAN INTERPRETATIONS,
RIFFAT HASSAN

[1. For additional biographical information about Hassan, see earlier sections of the essay excerpted here, "The Issue of Woman-Man Equality in the Islamic Tradition," in Leonard Grob, Riffat Hassan, and Haim Gordon, editors, *Women's and Men's Liberation: Testimonies of Spirit* (New York: Greenwood Press, 1991), especially pp. 65-68. See also her " 'Jihad fi Sabil Allah': A Muslim Woman's Faith Journey from Struggle to Struggle to Struggle," in Grob, Hassan, and Gordon, *Women's and Men's Liberation*, p. 11-30.]

[2. In addition to the essays cited in the introduction to this chapter, see: "The Issue of Gender Equality in the Context of Creation in Islam," *Chicago Theological Seminary Register* 83 (1993): 3-15; "Muslim Women and Post-Patriarchal Islam," in Paula M. Cooey, William R. Eakin, and Jay B. McDaniel, editors, *After Patriarchy: Feminist Transformations of the World Religions*, Faith Meets Faith Series, edited by Paul F. Knitter (Maryknoll, N.Y.: Orbis, 1991), pp. 39-64; "The Burgeoning of Islamic Fundamentalism: Toward an Understanding of the Phenomenon," in N. Cohen, editor, *The Fundamentalist Phenomenon: A View from Within, a Response from Without*, (Grand Rapids, Mich.: W. B. Eerdmans, 1990), pp. 151-71; "An Islamic Perspective," in Jeanne Becher, editor, *Women, Religion, and Sexuality*, Studies on the Impact of Religious Teachings on Women, Papers sponsored by the World Council of Churches, Sub-unit on Women in Church and Society (Philadelphia: Trinity Press International, 1990), pp. 93-128.]

[3. Riffat Hassan, *An Iqbal Primer: An Introduction to Iqbal's Philosophy* (Lahore, Pakistan: Aziz, 1979); *The Sword and the Sceptre: A Collection of Writings on Iqbal* (Lahore, Pakistan: Iqbal Academy, 1977).]

[4. This chapter's section on hierarchical interpretations also includes this passage from Mawdudi's commentary.]

[5. In endnotes to earlier sections, Hassan defined *hadith* and its plural *ahadith* as "oral traditions attributed to the Prophet Muhammad" and *Sunnah* as "practical traditions attributed to the Prophet Muhammad." See notes 3 and 4, page 81.]

6. Surah 4: An-Nisa': 34.

7. Surah 4: An-Nisa': 11.

8. Surah 2: Al-Baqarah: 282.

9. Reference here is to ahadith from *Sahih al-Bukhari*.

10. Muhammad Iqbal, *The Reconstruction of Religious Thought in Islam* (Lahore: Shaikh Muhammad Ashraf, 1962), p. 83.

11. Hadith quoted in Jane I. Smith and Yvonne Y. Haddad, "Eve: Islamic Image of Woman," *Women's Studies International Forum* 5 (2) (1982): 136-37.

12. I. B. U. Ibn Kathir, *Tafsir Ibn Kathir* (Karachi: Nur Muhammad Karkhana Tijarat-e-Kutub, n.d.) vol. 1, p. 101.

13. A. A. Maududi, *The Meaning of the Qur'an* and *Tafhim ul-Qur'an*, 6 vols. (Lahore: Maktaba-e-Ta'mir-e-Insaniyyat, 1974).

14. Maududi, *The Meaning of the Qur'an*, vol. 2, p. 298, footnote 1 (emphasis mine).

15. Rasul: a Prophet of God with a book. Reference here is to the Prophet Muhammad. [This note has been slightly revised.]

16. M. M. Khan, translation with notes of *Sahih al-Bukhari* (Lahore: Kazi Publications, 1971), vol. 4, "Book of Prophets," chap. 1, Hadith 548, p. 346.

17. Muslim bin al-Hajjaj, *Sahih Muslim*, 2 vols. (Cairo: 'Isa al-Babi al-Halbi, n.d.), vol. 1, p. 625.

18. A. H. Siddiqui, translation with notes of *Sahih Muslim* (Lahore: Shaikh Muhammad Ashraf), vol. 2, "Book of Wedlock," chap. 576, Hadith 3466, p. 752.

19. Ignaz Goldziher, *Muslim Studies*, translated by C. R. Barber and S. M. Stern, edited by S. M. Stern (Chicago: Aldine Publishing Company, 1971), vol. 2, p. 163.

20. See Muhammad bin 'Abd Allah al-Hakim, *Ma'rifat 'Ulum al-Hadith*, edited by Mu'azzam Hussain (Cairo, 1937), p. 62; and Ibn Hajar al-'Asqalani, *Sharh Nukhbat ul-Fikr fi Mustaleh Ahl al-Athar* (Cairo, 1934), 5.

21. See, for example, Shams ad-Din Adh-Dhahabi, *Mizan l'tidal fi Naqd ar-Rijal*, 4 vols. (Cairo: 'Isa al-Babi al-Halbi, n.d.). This is a highly authoritative work investigating the credentials of Hadith-transmitters by a renowned Hadith critic (A.D. 1274-1348).

22. [Marshall G. S.] Hodgson, *The Venture of Islam: Conscience and History in a World Civilization* (Chicago: University of Chicago Press, 1975), vol. 2, p. 480.

Nancy Datan

Nancy Datan (1941-1987) was Professor of Human Development and Chair of Women's Studies at the University of Wisconsin-Green Bay at the time of her death in 1987. She also had taught in Israel and at West Virginia University. She wrote over eighty articles and edited four books.[1] She was coauthor of *A Time to Reap: The Middle Age of Women in Five Israeli Sub-Cultures* (Baltimore: Johns Hopkins University Press, 1981), which was nominated for the National Jewish Book Award in 1982.

Our selection contains excerpts from an essay in which Datan explored the interpretations of Eve in several traditions, including her own Jewish heritage as well as some traditions lodged in popular culture in the United States of America. She observes that a common strand of these interpretations is that none of them has been forged by a Jewish woman. She then points to alternate ways her daughters viewed Eve when they were studying Genesis in public schools in Israel. The selection opens by drawing a comparison between Jewish identity in the United States and Eve's identity. It closes with a poignant question. This essay is based on an address Datan gave in August of 1985 at the 93rd Annual Convention of Division 36 of the American Psychological Association. (Source: Nancy Datan, "Forbidden Fruits and Sorrow: Eve and the Sociology of Knowledge," *Journal of Pastoral Counseling* 21 (1986): 108-11.)

"Forbidden Fruits and Sorrow" (1986 CE)
NANCY DATAN

. . . Paradoxically, although "the Jew" may be visible as a symbol, the symbol was not created by the Jews themselves, and the Jews, as a people and as a tradition, remain invisible and unknown.

This paradox leads us to Eve. In the evolution of Western religion, Eve stands midway between Ashtoret, goddess of fertility, and Mary, virgin and mother.[2] Ashtoret, earliest of the three, represents pre-Mosaic fertility goddesses throughout the fertile crescent. Without a doubt, Ashtoret is the most autonomous of these three women, powerful and fecund, savior of her young lover Tammuz in an annual cycle of death and rebirth, abstinence and orgy. Eve does not fare well by comparison: created by God to be the helpmate of Adam, taken from his side, created second. Fertility is a blessing bestowed by Ashtoret, but a curse laid upon Eve. Nor does Eve fare well by comparison to Mary; Eve is told that she will bear children in sorrow as she is expelled from Eden, while Mary ascends through virgin motherhood to heaven. Thus childbirth is a curse laid upon Eve, but a blessing for Mary.

Consider also the lessons we learn, not in religious classrooms, but in the secular setting: Mary might be encountered in an art history class, through a study of "The Assumption of the Virgin." Eve is everywhere. She has taken the first bite from the rainbow-colored apple which, standing alone with no other message at all on a billboard, conveys all the following messages: knowledge-power-seduction-temptation-enticement. Lose your innocence with an Apple computer—Eve's apple, only one bite missing. Come on, Adam. And after Adam gives in and buys, and spends a hard day at the computer, he can take pleasure of another sort at night with that other Eve, the sexual Eve, female and polluted, who might seek partial redemption by trying to clean herself up with a douche which promises to restore her original purity under the brand name "Summer's Eve."

I grew up with this all-American Eve, a transitional figure in religious history, a perennial hot item on Madison Avenue. Judaism differs from Christianity in a number of ways which bear directly on the interpretation of the story of Creation and the Garden of Eden in Judaism: sexuality is a blessing; sexual pleasure in marriage a *mitzvah*, a divine commandment; there is no notion of children born into original sin. Nevertheless, growing up in America colored my phenomenological awareness of Eve and Eden: today, when my Christian women's studies students recall their sense of shame and personal guilt from Sunday School lessons in which they were taught that they shared responsibility for mankind's fall from grace with Eve their sinful mother, I recognize their guilt through my early memory of this phenomenology, even as I reject it with a more recently acquired Talmudic logic.

In my theological view, Eve is a fiction. The question is: who is the author? I suggest that the marriage of Adam and Eve as we know it represents an archetypal male crisis of intimacy in which the woman functions as a projective screen for the needs of the man. We know the story of the Garden of Eden through the telling and retelling and interpretation and reinterpretation of men. Some are male Jewish scholars. Others are male Christian scholars, for whom Eve serves as a dramatic prop: the vehicle of the Fall, prelude to the Redemption. And finally we have recent feminist scholarship, which recognizes that Scripture has been used as a tool for the oppression of women. Nearly a century ago, Elizabeth Cady Stanton's *The Woman's Bible* had this to say about the two accounts of creation in Genesis: "My own opinion is that the second story was manipulated by some Jew, in an endeavor to give 'heavenly authority' for requiring a woman to obey the man she married."[3] This is one more unhappy expression of the antisemitic view that "the Jew" controls the media;[4] I wonder how many contemporary feminist scholars, who rejoice in Stanton's courageous challenge to Scriptural tradition, absorb this comment without flinching. I can't.

Thus Eve is a cumulative fiction with multiple authorship, a narrative written over the centuries by countless authors with little in common. However, one identity is *not* theirs: the creators of this Eve are not Jewish women. Yet cultural legacies are never simple: I am indebted in this invited address to a long line of stiff-necked Jewish men who kept the traditions of the tiny minority to which I belong, and to the tradition of Christian scholasticism which has contributed so much . . . , and to the battles fought by Elizabeth Cady Stanton and her sisters, through which a political platform for women's voices was achieved. . . . It is by means of this complex and ambivalent indebtedness that I am granted a voice to speak for those silent Jewish daughters. Thus, I began with my gratitude to the traditions of religious sanctuary and feminist sisterhood; but it is clear that my gratitude is mixed with other feelings. And, since Freud tells us that every significant relationship is marked by conflict, I am certain that this feeling is mutual: of those who contributed over the centuries to the religious and feminist traditions which give me this forum, not everyone would rejoice to hear me. But this very ambivalence is integral to my belief that Eve and Adam stand for Everywoman and Everyman. For if our cultural imagery shapes our images of ourselves, female and male and the sexual relationship, the imagery is not simple but complex, and the heart of its complexity is ambivalence.

We know the story of the Garden of Eden through men's eyes, minds, and voices. Even recent feminist criticisms and alternative interpretations have found expression in the broader context of a long tradition of patriarchal scholarship; a woman who sits down to write a piece of scriptural interpretation must begin by saying, *"Yes, but,"* exactly as I have been doing.

Virginia Woolf has said that a woman in writing looks back through her mothers:[5] thus she reminds us that contemporary women writers have a slender, fragile heritage of women who have gone before them, recording women's experiences. By contrast, a man who explores the world of men can look to ancient, medieval, and contemporary poets, philosophers, historians, playwrights, novelists, and of course, religious scholars. No such wealth of prior experience, recorded, interpreted, or imagined, is available to women. Perhaps that is why my own remarks have such an unusual point of departure: I do not begin by looking backward to my mothers, but rather forward, to my daughters.

I have spoken at length about the several traditions which bring me here today. But my own first steps on this path have quite a different beginning. My thesis, I claim, is simple: that the marriage of Adam and Eve as we know it is an achetypal male crisis of intimacy, and Eve a mirror for the needs of Adam and all men after him. If so, those needs will be complex and Eve herself, even as Adam sees her, more than a passive helpmate. I must admit, however, that my firm conviction on this point is not based on years of scholarship; on the contrary, things happened just the other way round. First I developed the conviction, and then it proved easy to find support through scholarship. And the conviction was born on the day when I saw Eve through my daughters' eyes.

I grew up in Chicago and read the Bible in English; my daughters grew up in Jerusalem and learned Torah in Hebrew. Tamar was five years old when she came home from kindergarten and asked, in the special voice a young child reserves for proof positive of an elemental truth, . . . [Haisha pitatah et ba'alah, nachon, Ima?]—"The woman seduced her husband, isn't that so, Ima?" And when I told her yes, that was true, she declared with triumph, "Then she was the *first* to eat the fruit of the tree of knowledge of good and evil!"

Her older sister Merav came home in that same week from the study of Genesis in first grade and declared: "I want to eat from the fruit of the tree of knowledge of good and evil." To her I answered, "Don't you think that's what it means to be going to school?" And Merav replied to me, in the special voice a child reserves for a parent who doesn't know any better, "But I want *my* eyes to be opened *all* the way."

I grew up with an Eve who was acquitted for lack of evidence. My concept of original sin was diluted, secondhand knowledge: God the all powerful, it seemed to me, had to take responsibility for everything; Adam had to answer for his own actions; Eve, at worst a co-defendant, could not be proven guilty, and surely was not to blame for the state of the world. Her case could be dismissed.

My daughters' Eve was altogether different: like the Eve of the Christians, of whom I knew a little, she was the Prime Mover in Eden. But unlike the Eve of anyone I had met before, she was the heroine, not the villain. Elizabeth Cady Stanton, defending Eve in 1895, wrote: "the unprejudiced reader must be impressed with the courage, the dignity, and the lofty ambition of the woman."[6] But where in the world, asks Stanton, can we expect to find an unprejudiced reader? Quite by accident I produced a couple of them and nurtured them in a friendly climate, where, when these views of Eve were voiced—certainly not for the first time in the history of the world—they were not silenced by competing cultural messages. The establishment of the State of Israel gave them a homeland with a native tongue which was that of Genesis; they grew up completely untouched by the notion of Original Sin; the reform movement in nineteenth-century Judaism had given their mother a tradition which unlike Orthodox Judaism did not divide women from men, nor set women apart as unclean; the feminist movements of nineteenth-century Europe and twentieth-century America, in which Jewish women had played so large a part,[7] had given their mother the bare beginning of a critical sensibility, just enough to be astonished by the clarity and simplicity of the vision of two little girls, five and six years old, for whom Eve was a heroine and the fruit of the tree of knowledge of good and evil a heroine's prize. To paraphrase Hillel, that is all I have to say; the rest is commentary: why didn't anyone else see Eden through my daughters' eyes? . . .

NOTES TO CHAPTER 8, EGALITARIAN INTERPRETATIONS, NANCY DATAN

[1. Articles written by Nancy Datan include "Midas and Other Midlife Crises," in W. H. Norman and T. J. Scaamella, editors, *Mid-life: Development and Clinical Issues* (New York: Brunner/Mazel, 1980), and "Oedipal Conflict, Platonic Love: Centripetal Forces in Intergenerational Relations," in N. Datan, A. Greene, and H. W. Reese, editors, *Life-span Developmental Psychology: Intergenerational Relations* (Hillsdale, N.J.: Lawrence Erlbaum Associates, 1986).]

[2. (Notes 2 through 7 incorporate referencs from the source text.) Nancy Datan, "Ashtoret, Moses, and Mary: Perspectives on the Sexual Dialectic in Canaanite, Judaic, and Christian Traditions," in K. F. Riegel and J. F. Meacham, editors, *The Developing Individual in a Changing World* (Chicago: Aldine, 1976).]

[3. Elizabeth Cady Stanton, editor, *The Woman's Bible* (New York: European Publishing Company, 1895), Dietrick, p. 18. (Ellen Battelle Dietrick was one of the writers for *The Woman's Bible*. A member of the project's Revising Committee, she died before the second volume was published.)]

[4. R. Hilberg, *The Destruction of the European Jews* (New York: Harper & Row, 1979).]

[5. Virginia Woolf, *A Room of One's Own* (New York: Harcourt Brace Jovanovich, 1957).]

[6. Stanton, *The Woman's Bible*, p. 24.]

[7. Nancy Datan, Aaron Antonovsky, and Benjamin Maoz, *A Time to Reap: The Middle Age of Women in Five Israeli Subcultures* (Baltimore: Johns Hopkins University Press, 1981).]

APPENDIX

The Preadamite Theory and the Christian Identity Movement: Race, Hierarchy, and Genesis 1–3 at the Turn of the Millennium

INTRODUCTION

In chapter 7 of this volume we examined the use of Genesis 1-3 in discussions for and against American slavery. There we saw how arguments dependent upon Genesis 1-3 used a hierarchical reading of Adam and Eve's story. We did not mention, however, the argument that Adam and Eve (understood as progenitors of the Caucasian race) were racially superior to the man and woman of Genesis 1 (progenitors of the "other" races). This idea, called the "preadamite theory," was not widely accepted in the nineteenth century. It has, however, achieved notoriety in our own decade through the media's focus on the racial and antisemitic beliefs of groups like the Aryan Nations.

We begin our selections in this appendix with a quick look at two nineteenth-century writings that establish for us a continuity of thought between nineteenth-century preadamite theories and twentieth-century white supremacy beliefs. Our first two readings are from the period immediately following the Civil War. They are favorable responses to an 1867 article entitled "The Negro: What Is His Ethnological Status?"[1] In the article, Buckner H. Payne (a Tennessee clergyman writing under the pseudonym "Ariel") questioned whether African slaves could truly be called "human." The question was not simply rhetorical nor did it arise out of an intellectual vacuum. Nineteenth-century ethnologists raised similar queries: Did all races represent one species? Or were the races separated by genus as well as appearance? The question raised and answered by "Ariel" explored biblical as well as "scientific" insights concerning the origin and nature of the races.

Of those nineteenth-century Christians who thought that slavery was scriptural, many believed that the scriptural origin of the African race (and of the institution of slavery) could be traced to the Noah and Ham story in Genesis 9. Others went to the Cain and Abel story of Genesis 4, interpreting the "mark of Cain" as a change of skin color. Both positions assumed, of course, that Adam and Eve were the father and mother of all races. Through some sin (Cain's killing of Abel, or Ham's actions toward his father Noah), a portion of humankind was divinely consigned to slavery. The preadamite theory challenged both of these assumptions by suggesting that Adam and Eve were the ancestors of only one race (the Caucasian) and that by virtue of their creation (not some divine punishment) all other races were innately inferior, even "sub" human.

While the preadamite theory challenged existing monogenetic theories (one creation/one human species) by advocating a polygenetic one (two creations/diverse species), it also reread other parts of Genesis in ways that further strengthened white supremacist interpretations. Earlier rabbinical midrash (see chapter 3 of this volume) suggested that Eve and the serpent conversed at length and with great intimacy. The medieval Jewish works we read in chapter 5 extended this notion to suggest that Cain was not Adam's offspring but the serpent's. Variants of the preadamite theory contributed to this trajectory of interpretation by adding that the "serpent" was a preadamite man—a "negro." Understood in this manner, Eve's disobedience became "race-mixing." The condemnation of race mixing was also found in the story of the commingling of the "sons of God" (adamite men) and the "daughters of men" (preadamite women) in Genesis 6:1-4. Thus miscegenation became the immediate cause of the Flood of Genesis 6-9. Even the Tower of Babel story in Genesis 11:1-9 was read as an affirmation of racial diversity (v. 9) over racial unity (v. 1).

We conclude our appendix with three readings from the latter half of the twentieth century. During this time, preadamite theories emerged in the writings of white supremacists such as Wesley A. Swift (founder of the Church of Jesus Christ Christian) and his student Richard G. Butler (founder of the Aryan Nations). Shortly after Swift's death, Butler moved to Hayden Lake, Idaho, where he established a compound and training facility for his followers. Our selections include excerpts from Swift's "God, Man, Nations & the Races" and excerpts from two of Butler's publications: "The Aryan Warrior" and "Who, What, Why, When, Where: Aryan Nations."

One significant difference between Butler's theopolitical worldview and that of nineteenth-century preadamite theorists lies in Butler's identification of Cain as the progenitor of the Jewish nation. Both Swift and Butler view Cain as the offspring of Satan and Eve, and the forefather of the Jews. For them, the conspiracies behind America's religious, social, and political problems can often be traced to the "children of Satan"—the Jews. Current white supremacist slang for the federal government—ZOG (Zionist Occupation Government)—underscores such scapegoating.

For Swift and Butler, Christians are not simply the "new Israel" (a title long appropriated by Christians). Christians are, and always have been, the *only* Israel. In this, we should mention, Swift and Butler are heirs to another stream of nineteenth-century thought—British Israelism. According to Swift and Butler, most Christians have lost sight of their true identity as God's chosen people—the Israelites. A full-page newspaper ad by the Aryan Nations in 1984 graphically sought to remind the Christians of Spokane, Washington, "Yesterday the Tribes of Israel, Today the Aryan Nations."[2]

The readings in this appendix—two from the 1860s and three from the later half of the twentieth century—explore how the first chapters of Genesis continue to be read as subordinating one group of people to another. Like nineteenth-century arguments for slavery, such readings of the Adam and Eve story have devastating results for women of color. Moreover, the antisemitic sentiments of some white supremacists drive a wedge between Jewish and Christian women, thereby dividing women along lines of faith as well as race. Thus, at the turn of the millennium, after decades of ecumenical and civil rights activities, Americans find themselves confronted with old hatreds in new clothing.

Swift and Butler's reading of Adam and Eve's story elevates a white Eve to heights of racial superiority while it denigrates women of color and Jewish women. Eve becomes mother to the forces of good (the white race), but she also gives birth to the minions of evil (the Jews). Although subordinate to Aryan men, the Aryan woman is herself the head of other women. Thus Aryan readings of Genesis 1–3 place all women on a hierarchical grid—each according to her own race and faith. The Aryan woman leads other women and is subordinate only (but ultimately) to the Aryan man. It is a costly leadership, however, and one that abolishes forever the chance of female unity.

NOTES TO APPENDIX, INTRODUCTION

1. Ariel [Buckner H. Payne], "The Negro: What Is His Ethnological Status? Is He the Progeny of Ham? Is He a Descendant of Adam and Eve? Has He a Soul? Or Is He a Beast in God's Nomenclature? What Is His Status as Fixed by God in Creation? What Is His Relation to the White Race?" (Cincinnati, 1867), pp. 1–48.

2. An Aryan Nations' ad in the Spokane, Washington, *Spokesmen-Review* September 2, 1984, p. B8.

NINETEENTH-CENTURY
PREADAMITE APPROACHES

Written against the backdrop of the 1867 pamphlet entitled "The Negro: What Is His Ethnological Status?" by "Ariel" (the pseudonym of Buckner H.

Payne), the two selections below support Ariel's thesis that blacks were not descendants of Adam and Eve. (While Payne was not the first writer to suggest this thesis—it appears in antebellum proslavery writings as well—he was one of the most notorious in defense of it after the outlawing of slavery in the U.S. postwar period.) While Payne ultimately questioned the humanity of blacks, "Prospero" (whose true identity is unknown) relegated them to a subhuman status. Another writer, "a minister" (the pseudonym of D. G. Phillips of Louisville, Ga.) emphasized the divinely ordained hierarchy of Genesis 1-2 and the preadamite identity of the serpent (in Hebrew, *nachesh*) in Genesis 3. All three arguments viewed Genesis 1-3 as an explanation of the origin and nature of the various races by suggesting that blacks were created before Adam and Eve and thus inferior to them. (Sources: A Minister, "Nachesh: What Is It? Or an Answer to the Question, 'Who and What Is the Negro?' Drawn from Revelation" (Augusta, Ga.: Jas. L. Gow, 1896), pp. 1-46, in *The Biblical and "Scientific" Defense of Slavery: Religion and "The Negro Problem,"* Part 2, vol. 6, John David Smith, editor (New York: Garland, 1993), pp. 1-46; Prospero, *"Caliban. A Sequel to "Ariel"* (New York, 1868), pp. 1-32, in *The "Ariel" Controversy: Religion and "The Negro Problem,"* Part 1, vol. 5, John David Smith, editor (New York: Garland, 1993), pp. 191-222.)

"Nachesh: What Is It? or An Answer to the Question, 'Who and What Is the Negro?' Drawn from Revelation" (1868 CE)
A MINISTER [D. G. PHILLIPS]

Bible Account of the Negro

I think the Bible teaches very clearly that the negro is a distinct race from man, created before Adam—that he is in an inferior degree rational and accountable, and therefore a subject of law—that he was at Adam's creation subordinated to him, not as a slave or *menial*, but as all other things were subordinated to him as the head of this world—that he was bound by law both to Adam and to God, which law was written on his heart, as the law given to Adam was at first written on his—that he was first in the transgression in Eden, and that for his offence he was doomed to a condition of perpetual menial slavery to man, which was to be a source of fretful annoyance and disquiet to both parties, and that if he be civilized and saved at all, it can only be in and through his connection with man as a slave—not necessarily a *chattle* slave—but at least a menial slave.

Christian reader, do not shudder at this outline; I am not going to pour forth a flood of infidel ravings, nor ridicule revelation or commonly received opinions of it. You can have no higher regard for revelation than I have—no firmer belief that it is God's word—and is true though every man be a liar. The question is not "is it true and worthy of confidence?" But the only question with *me* is, "what does it teach?" Come, let us lay aside all former notions and preconceived ideas, and set humbly down at its feet and ask it to teach us God's truth about the negro—it will do so. Its first writer when he commenced to write, had either to plunge at once "*in medias res*," without any intimation of the subject on which he was going to write, or he had to give an introduction or kind of summary outline of his subject. He seems to have adopted the latter plan. Hence the first chapters contain a very sweeping and summary description of the creation and origin of all things—so very summary that a thousand and one very interesting and important questions which he could have answered, are left unanswered. But if he had stopped to answer them all, the world itself would not have contained the books which would have been written. So summary are his first chapters that good and learned men are now debating the question whether the creation he describes was performed in six common days as at present measured, or six days indefinitely long. The question is not yet settled; and if the description of creation is so sweeping as to leave that a debatable question, we should expect to find it less explicit in matters of detail. So it is; the facts which it is essential for man to know, are clearly stated. Unessential things are only referred to, hinted at, suggested, inferred and implied, so far as was necessary to gain the prime end aimed at, which was to teach man his origin, nature and condition, and the cause and cure of that condition. The Bible is not a work on art, science, commerce, history, or *the negro*, but is given to man as a sinner to fit him for Heaven. And it only refers to, or hints at these collateral subjects so far as is necessary, in order to reach its prime object. And yet it makes the negro, which is not of Adam's race, so prominent and conspicuous, both by plain statements and necessary implication, as to leave no room for doubt that he occupies a prominent place in the foreground of the picture. "Order is Heaven's first law." No intelligent Bible reader has failed to notice that a systematic progression characterized the creation of God; so reason teaches; so science teaches; so Moses teaches. Beginning from the lowest, each *order*, by whatever name you choose to call it, is seen to rise above its fellow order, and each by an almost imperceptible link like that uniting the colors in the solar spectrum, is seen to hitch itself to that one next above it. There is no where an intervening space; "nature abhors a vacuum." . . .

The brief history of man's creation is, "so God created man in his own image, in the image of God created he him; male and female created he them," (Gen. 1st, 27th). This is plainly the execution of a design or intention expressed in the preceding verse—"let us make man in our image after our likeness," (26). This is the first time the word man or Adam is used by Moses; this is the only creation of *mankind* mentioned in the Bible. It includes all the race. If the negro is of the human race, he is included here; for God has made of one blood all nations of *men* for to dwell on all the earth; and if he is not included here, he is not of the genus "*homo*." And of this brief passage, so rich as it must be in its vast comprehension of facts, we observe—It is strange the word *Adam* which is here rendered *man*, means *red*—(what we now call *white* as applied to the color of the human countenance or skin). The material of which this last creature was formed, was "red earth." Can all the logic and science of the universe ever evade the silent lesson contained in the color of the material of which man was made, or the trumpet tongued announcement that the material used was different from what had been used before, and that the difference was in color? As the cloud seen by the Prophet no larger than his hand grew into the drenching shower, so this little word in the very connection and circumstances in which it occurs was intended to swell into a broad history, and stand the mark of that Heaven wide distinction which God made between two different races at their creation. When God once makes his mark, man may lamely imitate, but never efface or counterfeit it; but it stands a witness to plead the presence there *once* of the great Jehovah; and it will so plead *in seculum seculorum*. After the creation of the world from nothing by the fiat of the Creator, we are told repeatedly, and in many varied forms, that all things in the world or on the earth were made of the earth as the material used. But there is no intimation any where given of the color of that material—no mention made of color—no reference to color, no hint at color—no importance seems to have attached to color in any thing up to the time *man* was to be made. But just then, as if a new idea (if it were possible) had entered the Divine mind, he says "let us make a *red* man." Now, why does the historian, in a description so very summary as this is universally admitted to be, where the writer seems parsimonious of words, and is trying to express the largest amount of thought possible in the smallest number of words—where, in order to be brief, he leaves untold a thousand facts of both interest and importance to man—where he makes every word count and contain an idea or great class of ideas—why should he stop just here and deviate from his method, and seemingly turn out of his way and drag in a new word containing a useless particularity, and tell us, after having stated distinctly that all creatures were made of earth, that this last one was made of *red earth*, and was therefore *red* in color? It will not do to say "it is a merely accidental circumstance." The Spirit dictated this word. "All scripture is given by inspiration of God." It will not do to say "it means nothing," for God never utters unmeaning words, however much we may misunderstand his word. Unless we are going to wrest or ignore revelation, we must admit that there was a fixed design in the use of this word—some worthy end in view—some great lesson to be taught; and may not—must not candor admit, until some better reason can be assigned, which never can be done, that the intention was to point out the forever visible distinction between the being now formed, wearing the image of God in a high order of intellectual and moral constitution, and some other being somewhat like him in several respects, though of a different color? Does it not look like the historian, consulting that brevity which is everywhere manifest on the face of this narrative, wished to intimate clearly in a new way which could not be misunderstood, yet without stopping to state fully a collateral and unessential fact, that when God made *man*—the *red* man—what we now call *white* man (and there is no other being dignified with the appellation *man* in the Bible; for the name carries the color in and with it) that there was already in existence as a part of the fifth day's work, a being *which*, from his size, shape, and partial conformation to the image of man, and especially from the fact that he possessed the power of speech and a subordinate degree of reason, might some day be confounded with man, and be taken as a specific, or in some way changed and modified part of this last creation—this master piece—this work of the sixth day? And to avoid all such confusion, without stopping to give a set lesson on this extraneous subject, he pointed out the forever un-varying distinction between the two races—the deep stamp of *manhood*—the seal of Almighty God—a word which should sound in the lessons of science and the voice of facts for thousands of generations, and loom up in all history and say, "the creature of the fifth day was not red but some other color—*black* if you choose it, but the creature of the sixth day was *man*—was *red*—was in the image of God—was Anthropos." Now in view of the unquestioned fact that there are many differences between man and the negro, and among them this difference of color—a fact which science has grappled for many centuries, and yet of which she admits today, that she can give no good satisfactory ac-count, on the assumption that the negro is a man—in view of the facts of negro history which have been stated, and which can not be questioned—in view of the stubborn fact that man has always and in every place and social condition naturally, instinctively looked on the negro as an inferior, and stood aloof from social equality with him chiefly on account of his color—in view of the fact which we hope to be able to prove abundantly that there was an inferior rational speaking creature in existence before Adam—in view of the scripture which we have noticed, and shall notice—and especially in view of the fact that man's color is a natural fixture unsusceptible of change by art, it may be sullied and smirched by natural causes, but remove it from under the influence of those causes "it will rise and be itself again" in his descendants, and thus show its nature and origin, and the same is true of the negro, we think it fair to draw the conclusion from the above text that the Bible does teach that the word man (Adam) does carry with it, not the idea of a black, but of a red color, and that it requires that color to be natural to a being before he can in truth and justice be called a *man*. God has placed a mark upon the negro which he can not remove—it is natural. He may scotch, but he can not kill it; the same is true of man. And Moses tells us the origin of this color when he says "the Lord God made *man*," which means a red man, or as we now use the color—a *white man*.

Here, and not in any fancied "curse on Ham" is found the true reason of a difference of color between man and the negro, a difference which has given more perplexity to both scientific men and Bible readers than all other differ-ences. It is chiefly on account of his color that the negro falls in the estimation of men. They always did, do, and always will look down on him as an inferior, on account of his color. "They find him guilty of a skin not colored like their own, and for that worthy cause" they stand aloof from him, or seize upon and enslave him, as marked for that purpose by Almighty God. And whether it be right or wrong in its manner, as it may, in its nature, it is not the result of native cupidity, rapacity, or disregard of law, but is simply like any other outcropping of nature and conscience, within which is a part at least of the oracle of God.

Just here it must be observed that there was given to Adam at his creation, a kind of headship over, or proprietary right in all other creatures. They were distinctly given to him, and placed under him whilst he was placed over them, (Gen. 1, 26). If the negro, therefore, existed before, as he did, he too was subordinated to Adam. This, however, did not and could not imply his slavery in any of its forms, but only that orderly subordination of inferior to superior, which must exist in every system where variety exists in unity, and where "some must and will be greater than the rest." Adam was first in intelligence and exaltation, God had made him so; he possessed an elastic, originating, self-directing, constructive mind, and was in immediate intercourse with his Author. It was meet that he "have dominion;" and his duty and highest happiness consisted in his observing all the laws and amenities of his position; and every sentient being below him was to find its highest happiness in observing all the laws of its subordinate position. And this had to be so unless God had established a dead equality destitute alike of variety and capacity of expansion. There was no degradation or slavery implied in the fact that the Sloth was made inferior to the Lion, or the Vulture inferior to the Eagle, and Adam placed over each; so there was neither slavery or degradation implied in the fact that the negro was made inferior to Adam and placed under him; it was for their mutual good and happiness as parts "of that stupendous whole, whose body nature is and God the soul." Slavery never inhered in any way in the original order of things—subordination did. The one manifests the wisdom and goodness of God, and is manifest in all his works, the other displays the punitive justice of God, and is seen only where his law has been violated and as penalty for sin. If the ox or ass be made to serve with rigor, it is not because of their inferiority and subordination, but because their master is a sinner, and they and all parts of nature over which he was placed, sympathize with him in the penalty which he pays; and if there be, as there certainly is, any thing unpleasant to both parties in the slavery of the negro to man, it is not because the former was at the first made inferior and subordinate to the latter, but because both have violated law, and pay the penalty which attaches to such violation. The negro was a sinner before he was a slave, but he was subordinate to Adam before he was a sinner; of which Moses gives us as clear an intimation as he did that the negro existed, and was of a different color from man before the creation of man.

. . . Now in our attempt to find out from the Bible itself, what kind of creature the serpent, was we never question the actual presence of the Devil as prime mover. We only enquire after the agent he used, or the visible form he put on. We are to see that it was not and could not have been the creature now called serpent; and as there is nothing in or about the Hebrew word which is here translated *serpent*, and nothing in the whole connection to favor or suggest such an idea, but the fact that this creature was doomed to crouch or crawl, and the serpent crawls, it seems quite probable that the English translators were governed by the Septuagint, rather than the Hebrew.

. . . We offer some of the evidence found in the Bible that it was not a serpent, but a negro.

. . . The civilization of America for the next century, possibly forever, must depend to a good degree upon the practical answer which *the people* adopt to the question, "who and what is the negro?" A multitude of answers "of all sorts, shapes and sizes," good, bad and indifferent are flying round.

"I have pointed out over a hundred specific differences between the bonal and the nervous systems of the white man and the negro. Indeed their frames are alike in no particular. There is not a bone in the negro's body which is relatively the same shape, size, articulation or chemically of the same composition as that of the white man, the whole physical organism of the negro differs quite as much from the white man's as it does from that of the Chimpanzee, that is, in his bones, muscles and fibers. The Chimpanzee has not much farther to progress to become a negro, than a negro to become a white man. *This fact, science inexorably demonstrates.* Climate has no more to do with the difference between the white man and the negro, than it has with that of the negro and the Chimpanzee, or than it has between the horse and ass, the eagle and the owl. *Each is a separate and distinct creation.* The negro is no more a negro by *accident* or *misfortune* than an owl is the sister of the eagle, or the ass is the brother of the horse. How stupendous, and yet how simple is the doctrine of the Almighty maker of the universe, who has created different species of the lower animals to fill the different places and offices in the grand scenery of nature!"

"Caliban: A Sequel to 'Ariel' " (1868 CE)
PROSPERO

The Bible is an inspired book, and every word of it is true. This proposition would never have been disputed, if the Bible had been properly understood. But theologians have put into Scripture what was not to be found there, and brought revelation into conflict with history and science. Thus, when divines asserted that, according to Genesis, the earth was created some six or seven thousand years ago, that it is the centre of the universe, and the heavens revolve around it, geology and astronomy contradicted the assertion, and seemed to set science at war with revelation, until a more correct interpretation of Scripture brought them into harmony.

It has been supposed that the different races of mankind sprang from the same stock; whereas history and science prove the existence of races which could not have had a common origin. If, therefore, the Bible taught the unity of the race, it would contradict an established fact. But does the Bible teach this? So far from doing so, it records, at least, two distinct creations of human beings. *There were men upon the earth before Adam.* For proof of this proposition, consult the book of Genesis, the only historical authority.

The creation of the Caucasian, or white race, is recorded in *Gen.* 2:7-25.

Up to this period, the earth, moistened by mists, yielded its spontaneous fruits for the support of the nomadic hunters; but no rain had fallen upon the soil, and "there was not a man to till the ground." Deity resolved to create a new race, a race of tillers of the ground, and settle them in a definite locality furnished with all the natural facilities for successful agriculture. The Adamic race began its career with agriculture, domestic life and social organization. The goal of the preadamite is the starting-point of the Caucasian.

There are certain marked peculiarities in the origin and destination of the superior race.

1. JEHOVAH "formed the man of the dust of the ground and breathed into his nostrils the breath of life." He did not spring out of the earth, but was fashioned by the plastic hands of the Creator, shaping the material into human form; and then the breath of Deity, the divine *afflatus*, was infused into him. In this way, not by the mere fiat of his Maker, he "became a living soul." The Creator intended the Caucasian to be a workman, a builder, an artist; and hence he performed the part of a divine artist in creating him.

2. The Caucasian was to be engaged in agriculture, and to be blessed with the elevating influences of that noblest of occupations. Hence, his Maker did not command the earth to bring forth grass, etc., as at the first creation, but "*planted* a garden, eastward—on the east of the preadamites—in Eden, and there he put the man whom he had formed. And out of the ground, thus planted, made JEHOVAH to grow every tree," etc.

3. The Caucasian was endowed with a high aesthetic faculty, the love of the beautiful. He was to create and foster the fine arts. Hence, his primitive abode contained trees "pleasant to the sight," as well as "good for food." The savage is insensible to the charms of nature and art. The loveliness of Eden would have been wasted on the preadamites. The negro, in his native wilds, never constructs a house nor plants a rose. The Chinaman knows nothing of perspective or the effect of light and shadow in painting.

4. The Caucasian, as a tiller of the ground, was provided with the means of artificial irrigation, in showers of rain, which, collecting into lakes, or flowing in streams, could be diverted to his fields.

5. The ornaments of civilization were placed within his reach. Eden contained gold and precious stones; both of them to decorate his fair daughters, whilst gold would serve as a standard of value and a medium of exchange in the commerce which flows from agriculture. Savages only barter; the civilized man is a merchant.

6. He was to advance the sciences. Hence, the Great Teacher gave him the first lesson, by bringing to him the inferior animals—the Fauna of Eden—"to

see what he would call them." This was the first classification and nomenclature in natural history. From that day to this, science has been the exclusive possession of his descendants.

7. But the loftiest distinction of the Caucasian consisted in his being made the head and representative of universal humanity. He was placed on trial for all mankind. It may be objected that Adam could not have represented the preadamites, who lived before him and knew nothing of him. But it may be objected, with equal propriety, that he could not have represented their descendants now living; whilst all orthodox divines hold that he did represent them. The fall was retrospective as well as prospective. This doctrine, however, is the Gordian knot of theology, which human wisdom is incompetent to untie. This much may be said, in vindication of Divine Providence, that if the Caucasian has no right to complain, much less have the Mongol and the Negro; for they were represented by one much better qualified to stand the test than any of their progenitors. Besides, Christianity, the remedy of the fall, is designed for all races. This is affirmed by the Apostle of the Gentiles, in a part of his writings, which has greatly puzzled his interpreters. Col. 3:11. His words are, *Greek, Jew, Barbarian, Scythian*. According to his interpreters, the last term is superfluous; for were not these Scythians barbarians? They certainly were the wildest of the Caucasian race; and this circumstance ought to have opened their eyes to St. Paul's meaning, which undoubtedly is, that the gospel is to be preached not only to Jew, Greek and Scythian—the most untutored of the children of Adam—but also to the progeny of the preadamite barbarians.

8. The Caucasian is, in form, color, and mental and moral qualities, unlike the Mongolian, and the very antithesis of the Negro, who is

"as disproportioned in his manners
As in his shape,"

and no more resembles the white man than Caliban resembled Ferdinand, or the old hag Sycorax the beautiful Miranda. He is a being,

"On whose nature
Nurture can never stick—
And as with age, his body uglier grows,
So his mind cankers."

Adam, in the garden, needed only one thing to complete his happiness—a wife. But among the races already in existence, "there was not found a help-*meet* for him." The Hebrew is *chenegdo, according to his front presence,* i. e., resembling him as one of the same race. As JEHOVAH had shaped Adam from the dust, he formed a suitable help for him, by building a rib taken from his side into a woman. She did not spring out of the earth, but was part of himself transformed and sublimated, "The precious porcelain of human clay." Our first father, enraptured at the spectacle of feminine loveliness, exclaimed,

"The very thing! capital! Bone out of my bones, and flesh out of my flesh; this shall be called *ishah*, woman, for she was taken out of *ish*, man." Thus, the planter became a husband, and the family organization took the place of the capricious concubinage of the other races. Happy had it been for him and our fair, sweet mother, had they retained their innocence and bliss.

The narrative of the Fall is given in the third chapter of Genesis. The tempter was the serpent, who is said to have been "more subtle than any beast of the field which JEHOVAH ELOHIM had made." Here the comparative degree is used, as is also the case in the Targum of Onkelos, the earliest and best Chaldee translation of the passage. (Riggs' Chaldee Manual, p. 93.) The tempter was more cunning than any beast of the second creation, that by JEHOVAH, these being superior in organization to those of the first creation. He surpassed all brutes in intelligence; and, therefore, was not himself a brute. What was he? Unquestionably, one of the preadamites, the only human beings prior to Adam. True, he is called a serpent; and this has puzzled the commentators. Dr. Adam Clarke, pressed by the difficulties of the case, is driven to the supposition that he was an ape or ourang-outang, in which he came very near the truth. The tempter was a preadamite, perhaps a negro; and he is denominated a serpent, by a common figure of speech, just as a vile man is called a reptile, brute, a dog, etc. The Hebrew verb, from which the appellation is derived, signifies, according to Gesenius, "to utter a low, hissing sound, to whisper, especially of the whispering or muttering of sorcerers." It presents a vivid picture of an African medicine-man, or conjurer, with his "grey dissimulation," whispering his diabolical temptation into the ear of unsuspecting Eve. That the tempter was a preadamite is evident from his name for Deity, "Yea, hath ELOHIM said." He knew nothing of JEHOVAH. The first false step taken by Eve was her recognition and repetition of his title of Deity. "ELOHIM hath said." In this, she virtually renounced JEHOVAH and forfeited his protection. She fell, and became the occasion of her husband's fall. But, although fallen, they were not utterly degraded. "They knew that they were naked," and, with the modesty of their race, "they sewed fig-leaves together, and made themselves aprons." Whilst the preadamites have always been shameless in their nudity, the Caucasian covers his person. It is the unanimous testimony of travelers that the negro, even the female, appears perfectly naked, without any sense of indecorum.

. . . It is unnecessary to pursue the Biblical argument further. In it, Heaven's protest against admixture of race, the contamination of Caucasian by inferior blood, is as plain as if traced in letters of fire, like the "handwriting on the wall." Our own country affords the most recent illustration of the primitive and unrepealed law. It has been said that the institution of slavery was wrong, and God punished the people of the South for sustaining it. This is rank fanaticism and falsehood. Nothing can be clearer than that slavery was not only tolerated, but sanctioned, by Abraham, Moses, our Saviour and his Apostles, and by the whole Christian Church, down to a very recent period.

This was proved, some years ago, by that learned prelate, Dr. England, Roman Catholic Bishop of Charleston, S.C., in his LETTERS TO THE HON. JOHN FORSYTH, and, more recently, by the late revered Bishop Hopkins, of Vermont. Southern slavery involved no violation of any law, human or divine; and it was the best condition for the negro. He can live with the white man, only as his slave. The South sinned; and the South has suffered, in consequence; but her crime was not slavery, but amalgamation. Boston, New York and Philadelphia were, and are yet, more licentious than Charleston, Mobile and New Orleans; but, in the former cities, illicit intercourse was confined to the same race; whilst the sexual commerce of the latter was debased by miscegenation. The men of the South are, in many respects, a noble race; but they tolerated among them a crime which Divine Justice never passes by. They contaminated their blood by admixture with the lowest type of humanity. For this, they have been punished—most significantly—by subjection to the accomplices of their crime. God has permitted unprincipled politicians, vile and wicked men, the basest that the world has ever seen, to inflict this penalty upon them. So, He permitted the Pharisees to murder our Saviour; but took vengeance on them for the crime.

. . . The vengeance of JEHOVAH, the guardian of our race, will pursue those miscreants, and will vouchsafe neither peace nor union to our unhappy country, until they are hurled from office, stript of the power they have abused, and trampled in the dust by the people, whose confidence they have betrayed, whose honor they have stained. This fair land of ours is the heritage of the Caucasian, the Western home of the German, the Briton, the Irishman; in short, of all in whose veins beat the proud pulsations of "earth's best blood." It is a WHITE MAN's country. The Caucasian, after occupying and embellishing the fairest seats of the Old World, has reared a mighty Republic on this continent, from whose western shore, he looks over the Pacific, to the primitive cradle of his race. This is his possession. The negro is an intruder here, an alien and a foreigner, a vagabond, as all his fathers were—and this great Commonwealth will never achieve its destiny, so long as the negro is allowed to vote, or to exercise any political right or privilege whatever.

To subject the Caucasian to the Negro is a higher crime against nature than to place the negro under the ape or the baboon; and nothing can equal its atrocity. It is "the sum of all villanies, a league with death and a covenant with hell." The doom of the felons, who have perpetrated this foul iniquity, this *crimen loesce majestatis* against the noblest type of humanity, has already been pronounced by the American People. Outraged justice and insulted virtue cry out against them,

> Never pray more, abandon all remorse,
> On horror's head horrors accumulate,
> Do deeds to make heaven weep, all earth amazed;
> *For nothing cans't thou to damnation add*
> GREATER THAN THAT.

GENESIS AND WHITE SUPREMACY
IN THE TWENTIETH CENTURY

Wesley A. Swift

Dr. Wesley A. Swift (died 1970), son of a Methodist minister, was an avid anticommunist crusader who at one time served as Ku Klux Klan Kleagle. As founder of the "Church of Jesus Christ Christian," Swift became the mentor of numerous leaders of later Christian/Israel Identity groups. One such leader is Richard Butler, founder of the Aryan Nations. Introduced to Smith in the early 1960s, Butler confesses that "He [Smith] was the total turning point in my life." According to Butler, Swift "had the answers" that Butler was trying to find.[1]

Swift's writings gave white supremacy and anticommunist movements a scriptural foundation on which to base their bigotry. The selections below are excerpts from a sermon delivered by Smith to his California congregation. In these selections, Swift explains his interpretation of Genesis 1-3: that Caucasian men and women are God's people and a white America, by implication, is God's Kingdom. (Source: Wesley A. Swift, "God, Man, Nations & the Races," reprint; Hayden Lake, Idaho: Aryan Nations, no date, pp. 5, 6, 28-31, 42.)

NOTE TO APPENDIX, WESLEY A. SWIFT

1. As cited in James A. Aho, *The Politics of Righteousness: Idaho Christian Patriotism* (Seattle: University of Washington Press, 1990), p. 55.

"God, Man, Nations & the Races" (no date)
WESLEY A. SWIFT

We point out that truth sets men free. When men know the truth, they can't be taken in by the pattern of propaganda. This also involves very important statements concerning God, concerning the time element as it relates to earth. It has a lot to do with man, and how long people or beings who walk upright, who are in the same general image as you and I, who are called men and belong to the general homo sapiens, how long have they been on the earth? Let us go a little further back, and it relates to nations. Did nations have a common origin, or did nations, emerging out of men, all have a common background, or races have a common pattern of origin? Theology also makes a statement, that some period back (which in the chronology of some is about 2348 B.C., or 3145 to 4600 B.C. in other chronologies), that "a flood" drowned everybody on the face of the earth, that all people who today survive are the descendants of the three sons of Noah and his wife. So Noah and his wife and his sons, Ham, Shem and Japheth, they tell us, have begotten all the people that are upon the face of the earth. That means, therefore, that they would be common parents, within a period of some 2,400 years before Christ, of all the Asiatics, all the Negroids and all the White men on the face of the earth. In fact, by this declaration they would have had three sons, and each one of these sons would have had to father a different race. This may fall into the theology of some people, but it is biologically unsound, unscientific, it is not genetic, and there isn't any truth in it.

Now don't go out of here and say we said there wasn't any flood, there wasn't any ark, and there were no sons of Noah. There were. But they did not represent all the people on the face of the earth. They represented the land wherein this happened, and the Hebrew word for the earth, there, is "erets," meaning that place, that country, that land; and all the catastrophe happened in that land, in that place. We can establish, as we will, that each race had a distinct and different origin upon the face of the earth, as to time and as to the experiences by which they came into being, came into existence, all of them a part of Divine creation.

. . . I want to point out to you, that in the record of man and of time, we are told here in the first chapter of the Book of Genesis concerning the patterns of creation, that in the sixth era, having already created everything that was upon the earth, including the various things in the fields of necessary botany, all the necessary growing herbs and necessary trees, He then put on the earth the necessary animal life that has to live on the plants.

On the sixth day, the sixth cycle of time, God created man, male and female created He them. (This is the first chapter of the Book of Genesis, the twenty-seventh verse.) God blessed them and said, "Be fruitful and multiply and repopulate the earth." Now listen to this: The Scripture says, "Be fruitful, multiply, and re-populate (replenish) the earth." So therefore it had been populated at one time, had been decimated, and was now being repopulated. He didn't make two or three kinds of men, He made one kind. And when He made him, He also made a woman. And these were male and female. They multiplied and extended their dominion over the earth in that era. They succumbed to the Luciferian fallen arch-angel's dominion in that era. And it was in that era that the ancient patterns of revealed truth, even interwoven through all the New Testament, came to pass, for God turned to His Own household, His Elohim, which is plural for God; God turned to the Elohim, and this is the word used in the eighty-second chapter of the Psalms, where it says "Yahweh said to the Elohim, 'Ye are Gods and all of you are the children of God.' " So in the Book of the Psalms, David says that

God said, "You are Gods and all of you are the children of God." It says, "Ye are Elohim and all of you are the children of Yahweh." The Eternal speaks out. He has finished the heavens and the earth, He has finished His creation.

And in the second chapter it says that on the seventh day, or in the seventh era, God rested from the works He had previously made. He viewed them and He contemplated them and He said, "I have made the earth, and I have made all the things you see. I have made all of the creatures. I have put upon it all kinds of animal life." He didn't have to bother to produce a second time the life that was in the sea, because the water on the earth didn't drown them at all; they lived through the catastrophe. Of those He had said, "Let the waters bring forth abundantly," and they did.

But when He comes to the seventh day, He talks about all the things that He had made, and He blessed them on the seventh day, and He set it apart, and then He rested from His work. And then God looks out over it and He said, Of every plant of the field, before it was in the earth, and every herb in the field before it grew, Yahweh had not caused it to rain—as we know rain. It was watered with the mist of the earth. And behold, there wasn't any man to till the ground. (Genesis 2:5.)

Now listen. We have passed from the first chapter of Genesis over to the second. We are in the great speculation of God's creative work. We have now moved over to God's saying, "Behold, I put all these plants and all these things here, but there is no Adamite." The word here now is "Adam." Behold, there isn't any Adam to till the ground. We have nomads, we have warriors, we have old races that have hinged on their nomadic existence like the Tungus, but we don't have anybody to till the ground. My household is not here, and their knowledge and their adaptability to make the earth produce its food, the agricultural experts, the Adamic race are not here.

So in this seventh day God plants a garden eastward in Eden, and He puts into that garden all of the finest of the fruits which are pleasant for sight, every tree that is good for food. He plants it all in the garden. Also in that garden is the tree of life. Now, we are told that after He planted the garden, God took and put Adam in the garden. And when He put Adam in the garden He said, I command that thou mayest eat of the garden of all that you truly see here, you may freely eat. Every tree which is for herbs and for food you may eat of it. There is only one tree that you can't touch, that is the tree that has knowledge of good and evil. This is a racial tree. This is a tree with intellect of right and wrong. It is made up of peoples and races. You can't touch that one. You are not to mongrelize. You are to maintain a holy seed.

What about this Adam, anyhow? You have to go into the record to find out about Adam. For you will discover that when it talks about the pattern of Adam, it says that God had brought forth Adam, and the old word is "bara"— He brought forth issue, and the offspring was Adam. And then He caused a deep sleep to fall on Adam, and, the original Hebrew says, He separated out of

Adam the female portion. There is nothing that says anything about a rib in the old text. Then out of this female portion God made Eve, and He said, "I have taken woman out of Adam. Now, this hasn't anything to do with that sixth day creation when He just made man and woman. This one was a separate act. This was a work of surgery. He put Adam to sleep, He removed a part, and He produced woman that they might be one flesh, His household in the earth. This is the beginning of the Adamic race.

All of this is important because we, today, are the United States of America. We, who make up a part of the great White race of the Western nations, are the Kingdom of God. We are a race that was begotten of God, the last race God placed in the earth. Our destiny is to keep our race intact, to repudiate all policies of integration and mongrelization, to retain the supremacy and leadership in this our country, and to carry out our destiny for the building of God's Kingdom. It requires that we have an answer and that we have the knowledge and that we know. You shall know the truth, and the truth will make you free.

Richard G. Butler

Richard Butler, once an engineer at Lockheed Aircraft Company (Palmdale, Calif.), is the founder of Aryan Nations, a radical white supremacist organization currently headquartered in Hayden Lake, Idaho. Butler studied with Wesley Swift from 1961 until Swift's death in 1970. In the mid-1970s, Butler moved from northern California to Idaho, where he established Aryan Nations as a political arm to the Church of Jesus Christ Christian. In the years that followed he worked to establish lines of communication between his group and other neo-Nazi, Christian Identity, and Ku Klux Klan groups around the nation. Central to Butler's vision is the establishment of a white homeland free from the presence of minorities and "race mixers." Butler's message, couched in violent, holy war rhetoric, found a ready audience with the radical right. By the mid-1980s, Butler had emerged as a leader of white supremacist groups in America.[1]

According to Butler, Christians have been misled as to their true identity. White Anglo Saxons are the true Israel, not the Jews. As the chosen race, Aryans have a duty to their race to maintain its purity. In the first selection below, Butler offers a statement of Aryan beliefs that exemplifies the theology of the Aryan Nations. In the second selection he summarizes Aryan duties toward race and country and describes the treatment of, roles, and duties of Aryan women. (Sources: Richard G. Butler, "Who, What, Why, When, Where: Aryan Nations," Hayden Lake, Idaho: Aryan Nations, no date, pamphlet; and "The Aryan Warrior," Hayden Lake, Idaho: Aryan Nations, no date, pp. 9, 11.)

NOTE TO APPENDIX, RICHARD G. BUTLER

1. Robert Crawford et al., "The Northwest Imperative: Documenting a Decade of Hate" (Portland, Ore.: Paragon, 1994), pp. 1.3-1.37.

"Who, What, Why, When, Where: Aryan Nations"
(no date)

RICHARD G. BUTLER

WE BELIEVE the Bible is the true Word of God written for and about a specific people. The Bible is the family history of the White Race, the children of Yahweh placed here through the seedline of Adam.

WE BELIEVE that Adam-man of Genesis was the placing of the White Race upon this earth. All races did not descend from Adam. Adam is the father of the White Race only. (Adam in the original Hebrew is translated, "to show blood; flesh; turn rosy.")

WE BELIEVE that the true, literal children of the Bible are the 12 tribes of Israel which are now scattered throughout the world and are now known as the Anglo-Saxon, Celtic, Scandanavian [*sic*], Teutonic people of this earth. We know that the Bible is written to the family of Abraham, descending from Shem, back to the man, Adam. God blessed Abraham and promised that he would be the "Father of Nations." This same promise continued through the seedline of Abraham's son, Isaac, and again to Isaac's son, Jacob, the Patriarch of the 12 tribes, whose name God changed to Israel (meaning "he will rule as God.")

WE BELIEVE that there are literal children of Satan in the world today. These children are the descendents of Cain, who was a result of Eve's original sin, her physical seduction by Satan. We know that because of this sin, there is a battle and a natural enmity between the children of Satan and the Children of The Most High God.

WE BELIEVE the Jew is the adversary of our race and God, as is attested to by all secular history as well as the word of God in scripture; that he will always do what he was born to do, that is, be the 'cancer' invading the Aryan body politic to break down and destroy the dross from Aryan culture and racial purity; that those who are able to resist this satanic 'disease' are the "called chosen and faithful."

WE BELIEVE there is a battle being fought this day between the children of darkness (today known as Jews) and the children of light (God), the Aryan race, the true Israel of the Bible.

WE BELIEVE that God created pure seed lines, races, and that each have a specific place in His order on this earth under the administration of His Life Law. We know that man (Adam) was given the command to have dominion over the earth and subdue it, but that, in great part, our race has been deceived into rejecting this divine order. They have forgotten the words of Yahweh to Abraham, "In thee shall all the families of the earth be blessed." (Genesis 13:3) There is no race hatred in this statement. It was and is the plan of Yahweh to bless all, through the seed of Abraham.

WE BELIEVE in the preservation of our race individually and collectively as a people as demanded and directed by God. We believe a racial nation has a right and is under obligation to preserve itself and its members.

WE BELIEVE that the present world problems are a result of our disobedience to God's laws. God's intended purpose was that His racial kinsmen were to be in charge of this earth. Our race, within itself, holds divine power; and when we abrogate and violate divine law, we give power to our God's enemies. Evil is the result to all.

WE BELIEVE that the redemptive work of Jesus was finished on the cross. As His divine race, we have been commissioned to fulfill His divine purpose and plans—the restitution of all things.

WE BELIEVE that there is a day of reckoning. The usurper will be thrown out by the terrible might of Yahweh's people as they return to their roots and their special destiny. We know there is soon to be a day of judgment and a day when Christ's Kingdom (Government) will be established on earth as it is in heaven. "And in the days of these kings shall the God of heaven set up a kingdom which shall never be destroyed; and the kingdom shall not be left to other people, but it shall break in pieces and consume all these kingdoms and it shall stand forever. But the saints of the Most High shall take the kingdom and possess the kingdom forever, even for ever and ever. And the kingdom and dominion and greatness of the kingdom under the whole heaven shall be given to the people of the saints of the Most High, whose kingdom is an everlasting kingdom, and all dominions shall serve and obey Him." (Daniel 2:44; 7:18; 7:27.)

"The Aryan Warrior" (no date)
RICHARD G. BUTLER

Population and Race

The Aryan world idea is accepted by Aryans universally both as revealed Christianity and legislative law. It is an Idea comprising both the spiritual and the material, a Guide to nation-builders and to the individual in his search for the truth.

The very foundation of faith and worship is Racial Truth, for with the Aryan, Christianity and Race are one. On this foundation arises the will to power and world leadership inherent in the soul of the seed of Adam. Through racial purity and an unfettered instinct in procreation the Aryan goes forward to the repeopling of his world.

The Aryan does not have sexual union outside his own race, but seeks always the improvement of his own species.

Perfection in type is the union between men and women who are fair with comely eyes and an open countenance. These traits constitute the Adamic ideal, in whom the Aryans acknowledge their heritage as the Israel of God.

The Aryan honors the science of eugenics, founded by the English biologist, Sir Francis Galton in the 19th century, which science continues today through those such as Dr. Shockley and Dr. E. O. Wilson.

Women

Every child that an Aryan mother brings into the world is a battle waged for the existence of her people.

The program on the National Aryan Women's Movement has truly a single point—the child.

The sphere and tasks of man and woman in life are separate but complementary. Mutual respect lies in the fact that both man and woman know that each is doing everything which is necessary to maintain the whole National community.

The Aryan way of life is determined not by material considerations but by the soul of a nation. Aryan woman gives herself in conscious idealism to the concept of the national interest before private interest.

The thoughts of Aryan woman are dominated by the desire to enter family life.

A creed of the Aryan woman is this: "We serve the life of our people. We regard our household tasks as a means for achieving and maintaining the physical and spiritual health of the nation."

Aryan woman brings true love and affection and a happy, well-run home to refresh and inspire her man.

Aryan woman is treated with chivalry and respect by Aryan man. The morality of the Aryan girl is very important. As girls, you must learn to play your part in the national community and you have to school yourselves for the day when you shall become the wives of our men and the mothers of the new generation. For, the men who are to shape the future of our race need women of your kind, women who, in profound faith and in brave spirit, are prepared to share with their menfolk every hardship and sacrifice. This is a high aim for every girl for the attainment of which is very worthwhile to devote years to making oneself pure with a view to being able—in all honesty to fulfill this mission.

INDEX

KRISTEN E. KVAM is Associate Professor of Theology at Saint Paul School of Theology in Kansas City, Missouri. Since 1994 she has served on the Lutheran–Roman Catholic Commission on Unity. She is a contributor to the *Dictionary of Feminist Theologies* and she has written about scriptural interpretation, the relationships between theological anthropology and ecclesiology, and about Martin Luther's theology.

LINDA S. SCHEARING is Associate Professor of Religious Studies at Gonzaga University in Spokane, Washington. She has written numerous articles for the *Anchor Bible Dictionary*, for *Eerdman's Dictionary of the Bible*, and for *Women in Scripture: A Dictionary of Named and Unnamed Women in the Hebrew Bible*. With Steve McKenzie, she is currently coediting *Those Elusive Deuteronomists: Pandeuteronomism in the Hebrew Scriptures*.

VALARIE H. ZIEGLER is Professor of Religious Studies at DePauw University in Greencastle, Indiana. She is author of *The Advocates of Peace in Antebellum America*, and she is currently working on a biography of Julia Ward Howe.